TROLLOPE: THE CRITICAL HERITAGE

THE CRITICAL HERITAGE SERIES

GENERAL EDITOR: B. C. SOUTHAM, M.A., B.LITT.(OXON.)
Formerly Department of English, Westfield College, University of London

---

Volumes in the series include

TROLLOPE

THE CRITICAL HERITAGE

Edited by

DONALD SMALLEY

Professor of English Literature
University of Illinois

LONDON: ROUTLEDGE & KEGAN PAUL

NEW YORK: BARNES & NOBLE INC

Published 1969
in Great Britain
by Routledge & Kegan Paul Limited
and in the United States of America
by Barnes & Noble Inc
SBN 7100 6153 6

Printed in Great Britain
by W & J Mackay & Co Ltd, Chatham

General Editor's Preface

The reception given to a writer by his contemporaries and near-contemporaries is evidence of considerable value to the student of literature. On one side we learn a great deal about the state of criticism at large and in particular about the development of critical attitudes towards a single writer; at the same time, through private comments in letters, journals or marginalia, we gain an insight upon the tastes and literary thought of individual readers of the period. Evidence of this kind helps us to understand the writer's historical situation, the nature of his immediate reading-public, and his response to these pressures.

The separate volumes in the *Critical Heritage Series* present a record of this early criticism. Clearly for many of the highly-productive and lengthily-reviewed nineteenth- and twentieth-century writers, there exists an enormous body of material; and in these cases the volume editors have made a selection of the most important views, significant for their intrinsic critical worth or for their representative quality—perhaps even registering incomprehension!

For earlier writers, notably pre-eighteenth century, the materials are much scarcer and the historical period has been extended, sometimes far beyond the writer's lifetime, in order to show the inception and growth of critical views which were initially slow to appear.

In each volume the documents are headed by an Introduction, discussing the material assembled and relating the early stages of the author's reception to what we have come to identify as the critical tradition. The volumes will make available much material which would otherwise be difficult of access and it is hoped that the modern reader will be thereby helped towards an informed understanding of the ways in which literature has been read and judged.

B.C.S.

Note on the Text

The materials printed in this volume follow the original texts in all important respects. Lengthy extracts from the novels of Anthony Trollope have been omitted whenever they are quoted merely to illustrate the work in question. These omissions have been indicated in the text. Typographical errors in the originals have been silently corrected, but contemporary spelling and the original forms of titles have been allowed to stand.

Contents

CONTENTS

CONTENTS

Orley Farm (1862)

Rachel Ray (1863)

The Small House at Allington (1864)

Miss Mackenzie (1865)

CONTENTS

CONTENTS

CONTENTS

The Duke's Children (1880)

Dr. Wortle's School (1881)

Ayala's Angel (1881)

The Fixed Period (1882)

Marion Fay (1882)

Kept in the Dark (1882)

CONTENTS

CONTENTS

The Kellys and the O'Kellys (1848)

La Vendée (1850)

Preface

This book contains material that should be of interest to readers of at least three varieties. For the student of Victorian life and literature it offers a profile in some depth of the career of one of the most prolific and most popular of novelists during the second half of the nineteenth century, in himself a phenomenon of more than passing significance. Trollope's particular subject was the interaction of character with the pressures of the social life and social values of his time. Contemporary critics of his novels were in the habit of dealing with Trollope's characters as if they were part of the present scene, and there is in consequence much social commentary, both conscious and inadvertent, in the reviews.

Trollopians—those who read the novels mainly for the special pleasure to be derived from excursions into the world of Anthony Trollope—will find here an account of each of the forty-seven successive novels. Few even among the most devoted Trollopians have read all forty-seven, and there should be reward in seeing the familiar stories placed in the context of this novelist's total career. The reviews may, it is hoped, lead readers to fresh discoveries among the volumes that are now seldom read. There is also, of course, an interest in seeing what enlightened judges in the author's own time made of Archdeacon Grantly, Signora Neroni, Sir Roger Scatcherd, Messrs. Kantwise and Moulder, Adolphus Crosbie, Dolly Longestaffe, Dr. Wortle, Mr. Neefit, and far too many other personages brought to life by Trollope to venture here on even a representative list.

For the student of the history of criticism, this book may be of service partly as a convenient quarry for bad examples—illustrations of false values among the Victorians. But he is urged to read selectively and is promised rewards for doing so. He should find special interest in such entries as Nos. 10, 26, 28, 38, 39, 55, 60, 63, 72, 86, 92, 93, 110, 116, 127, 155, 157, 163, 164, and 185. He will find, at least, that though the better critics for the magazines of Trollope's day had not worked out a really adequate vocabulary, they knew rather clearly what they wanted and what they did not want to find in a novel. Then Trollope's self-criticism, in his running commentary on his works through 1876 (made in

PREFACE

passages of the *Autobiography* and quoted here at some length in the headnotes for the successive novels), should suggest much, often indirectly, of what Trollope himself thought about the possibilities and limitations in the art of fiction.

In any event, the attempt has been to present faithfully the contemporary reaction to Trollope both as a literary artist and as the portrayer of the life of his age. Usually with Trollope, as will be seen, the best critiques serve both purposes.

It is a pleasure to acknowledge my various indebtednesses—first and specially to Mrs. Annette Constantine for her good work as my research assistant in preparing this edition, and to the University of Illinois Research Board for its generosity in granting funds to support this project. To the librarians of the University of Illinois I owe much gratitude for their many kindnesses in making fully available the remarkable resources of the Library in Victorian periodicals and in all other aids for research in the Victorian novel, with particular mention of the reference librarians for all their patience and skill in procuring additional materials through interlibrary loan services. For various favours in the course of preparing this edition I give thanks to Professor Bradford Allen Booth, Dr. Norris L. Brookens, Professor Leon Edel, and Professor Dale Kramer.

Grateful acknowledgement is due to the proprietors and editors of the following magazines and newspapers for permission to publish reviews from their files: *The New Statesman* (for notices from *The Athenaeum*); *Blackwood's Magazine*; *The Cornhill Magazine* (John Murray, Ltd.); *The Dublin Review*; *The London Quarterly Review* (the Epworth Press); *Harper's Magazine*; *The Month*; *The Nation* (New York); *The Spectator*; and *The Times*. I also acknowledge with gratitude the permission of the University of California Press to quote at length from Trollope's *An Autobiography* in the edition of Bradford Allen Booth (1947).

DONALD SMALLEY

xviii

Introduction

I

TROLLOPE'S FORTY-SEVEN NOVELS AND THE PROBLEM OF SELECTION

For more than a quarter-century Anthony Trollope regularly drew attention as one of the most popular and most accomplished of English novelists. Even in the early part of his career, still within the late eighteen-fifties, thoughtful readers and critics were taken aback by the number of books Trollope was producing. But this intrepid and industrious writer, despite a full-time appointment in the postal service, went on averaging well over a novel a year, and both the great public of the circulating libraries and a sizeable audience of educated and demanding persons went on reading him. Critics continued to review him, often with a mixture of disapproval for his unevenness and his sheer fecundity, and pleasure in the lifelike quality of his best scenes and characters. Usually they placed him well below the great names, Dickens and Thackeray and George Eliot and sometimes Charlotte Brontë; but they judged him nevertheless worthy of regular and extensive discussion, a writer many cuts above the run of merely popular novelists. In all, Trollope published forty-seven novels as well as an additional shelf-ful of widely read books of travel, short stories (regularly collected into volumes), and occasional disquisitions at book length upon such varied topics as the Anglican clergy, hunting, Caesar's *Commentaries*, Lord Palmerston, and the life and writings of Thackeray.

The problem in editing a collection drawn from criticism written in or near Trollope's own lifetime is coping with a disconcerting amount of riches. One can cheerfully dismiss the merely perfunctory brief notices of the novels and surrender with reluctance nearly all reviews of the incidental books. Even then there is far more left than it is practicable to use. From well over a million words of material possessing interest and value, it has been necessary to choose with much thought and astringency.

Clearly the most rewarding of the general critiques dealing with Trollope's special subjects, his attitudes, his manner of working, need to be included with relatively slight abridgement—such astute early views, for example, as appeared from time to time in the *Saturday Review*, the *Spectator*, and *The Times*. The *National Review* essay of January 1863, though it runs to well over five thousand words even after excision of the lengthy quotations from the novels, is obviously an essay worth including. So are a number of later pieces of some length, the last and probably the best of which is Henry James's ambitious overview of Trollope's career written for the New York *Century* in 1883, an essay that shows to what extent James at forty, by now the author of *The American* and *The Portrait of a Lady*, had modified his early opinions—how much more clearly James now saw the qualities of Trollope's art than he had managed as a neophyte of twenty-two when writing his three critiques, harsh but full of point, for the New York *Nation*. Beyond such imperative choices, however, it has seemed desirable to place the emphasis in this book upon reviews that appeared within a few months of the publication of a single one of the long succession of Trollope's novels and that concentrate upon the problems and the characters of a particular novel. Each of the novels, even the last of them, received an amount of attention in the periodicals of the time, and there is material for each that seems worth presenting as an enlightening view of contemporary reaction. The best of the reviews offer an opportunity for seeing the characters and their dilemmas as they appeared to contemporaries—a fresh and rewarding perspective upon the world of Trollope's novels.

II
TROLLOPE'S APPRENTICESHIP

Trollope's life as it is recorded in his *Autobiography* had strong elements of the Cinderella story, though in Trollope's instance the period of trial was long. 'It's dogged as does it', the phrase that helps the Reverend Josiah Crawley in *The Last Chronicle of Barset*, could well have been Trollope's own motto. Born in 1815, the fourth son of Frances Trollope (who was herself to become in middle age an author of some celebrity) and Thomas Anthony Trollope, a barrister of unequable temperament and declining fortunes, Anthony passed an unhappy childhood during which, as he remembered it, he was the ugliest, the poorest, and the most miserable of students at two public schools. His unhappiness and isolation continued through years as a hobbledehoy postal clerk who fell by small debts into the hands of moneylenders, blundered innocently into an affair that threatened an enforced marriage, and suffered an extended illness that brought him close to death. At twenty-five he was a depressed young man who hated his work and despised himself for his own habits of idleness (though, to be sure, he read widely and kept a journal). He had early resolved that he would write a novel. Nearly every member of his remarkable family wrote; and his mother, after the success of her *Domestic Manners of the Americans* (1832), based chiefly upon her experiences attempting to start a bazaar or department store in Cincinnati, Ohio, had by the eighteen-forties become a prolific and popular writer of novels and travel books. But year after year went by without Anthony's doing more than reproach himself with his sloth and his indecision.

It was not until after his removal to Ireland, where he found more congenial work in the postal service, a wife, and a happier way of living, that he at last settled to the writing of his first novel, *The Macdermots of Ballycloran*. Another two years went by before this work, in 1847, reached print. Anthony did not expect success, he tells us, with this first venture. 'I was sure the book would fail, and it did fail most absolutely.'[1] There were reviews of *The Macdermots* in the English periodicals, but Trollope made no effort to seek them out. 'If there was any notice taken . . . by any critic of the day, I did not see it. I never asked any question about it, or wrote a single letter on the subject to the publisher.' The notices were, most of them, distinctly favourable; but it may have been as well that Trollope, now in his thirty-second year, was not aware of the judgment passed upon him by an anonymous writer in *The Critic*, who suspected and even dared hope that Trollope was still a boy. 'But if he have already reached maturity of years, his case is hopeless.'[2] Trollope was to maintain his policy of ignoring the critics through two more novels and eight more years. He saw but one review in all that time, he tells us in the *Autobiography*, and that one, a short and supercilious notice in *The Times*,[3] was not of a sort to give him a favourable opinion either of himself or of his critic.

A second novel, entitled *The Kellys and the O'Kellys*, again a tale of Irish life but in a much lighter vein, was published in 1848. It did no better than *The Macdermots* had done. 'I changed my publisher,' Anthony tells us in the *Autobiography*, 'but did not change my fortune.' Nor did his third try with *La Vendée* (1850), a historical novel in form with the French Revolution as its setting, but a book much given to political argument and dreary factual detail, meet with the slightest success. Nevertheless, two years later Trollope began his fourth novel, *The Warden*, and in 1855 saw it published. After more than ten years of trying without success to reach a public, he was beginning to feel that 'if any success was to be achieved, the time surely had come. I had not been impatient; but, if there was to be a time, surely it had come.'

III
THE YEARS OF POPULARITY

Critics found in *The Warden* a new voice among novelists; the book was acclaimed as clever, spirited, and promising much for the author's future as a writer of significance. Trollope learned with pleasure that 'there were notices . . . in the press, and I could discover that people around me knew that I had written a book'. Longman, the publisher, was complimentary. Though *The Warden* was a critical success, however, the financial rewards were small. At the end of 1855 Anthony had received approximately ten pounds, and after another year an additional ten. So far as remuneration was concerned, as he wryly remarks in the *Autobiography*, stone-breaking would have done better. Nevertheless, Trollope's luck had turned. As novel followed novel with a rapidity that pleased the public but disconcerted some reviewers, Trollope found publishers and editors increasingly generous. Thackeray, who had read *The Three Clerks* (1858) with much enthusiasm, gave Trollope's fortunes fresh acceleration by making *Framley Parsonage* a feature of the *Cornhill Magazine*, which began publication under Thackeray's editorship in January 1860, ushered in with much advance publicity and a first monthly issue of over a hundred thousand copies.[4] By 1863 the *National Review* averred that Trollope had become 'almost a national institution'. Even if we discount the statistics of the *National* (a sober and usually responsible Unitarian review, edited by Walter Bagehot and Richard Holt Hutton), the tribute to Trollope's popularity is impressive:

The *Cornhill* counts its readers by millions, and it is to [Trollope's] contributions, in ninety-nine cases out of a hundred, that the reader first betakes himself. So great is his popularity, so familiar are his chief characters to his countrymen, so wide-spread is the interest felt about his tales, that they necessarily form part of the common stock-in-trade with which the social commerce of the day is carried on. . . . [There are] imaginary personages on Mr. Trollope's canvas with whom every well-informed member of the community is expected to have at least a speaking acquaintance. The disappointment of Sir Peregrine,[5] the boyish love of his grandson . . . have probably been discussed at half the dinner-tables in London, as often and with as much earnestness as Royal Academies, International Exhibitions . . . or any other of the standing conversational topics. . . . The characters are public property. . . .[6]

Nearly four years earlier *The Times* critic had declared that already

Trollope was 'the most fertile, the most popular, the most successful author' among the vast public of the circulating libraries.[7] Though neither *The Times* critic nor the *National Review* critic is willing to grant Trollope a place with Dickens or with Thackeray in the highest art of the novel, he is for both of them a writer of unusual significance. 'He is always clever,' writes *The Times* critic, 'often amusing, sometimes even great, or very near being great. . . .' The writer in the *National* maintains as the thesis of his fourteen-page essay that Trollope's great popularity is enough in itself to refute the insinuations of M. Forgues[8] and other French critics. English fiction and the English public continue, despite small indications to the contrary, in a state of 'purity, innocence, and cheerfulness'. So long as an author so sane, so solidly English in his values, flourishes in the public literature, there is little cause for worry about the moral health of England.

Evidences of Trollope's popularity and the high value placed upon his novels appear throughout his long career from the late eighteen-fifties onward. By the early eighteen-sixties, Trollope could feel he had reached the sort of success that in his lonely boyhood he had dreamed of one day achieving. 'I had created for myself a position among literary men,' he writes in the *Autobiography* (p. 141), 'and had secured to myself an income on which I might live in ease and comfort. . . . From this time [1862] for a period of twelve years my income averaged £4500 a year.' In the eighteen-sixties and eighteen-seventies this was indeed an impressive income. It represented, if not the million readers estimated by the *National Review*, at least a very large audience. Even in the last years of his career, Trollope continued to be a widely read and highly valued author, whose successive novels brought large sums from the publishers and commanded much attention in the Press. In the United States, from *Doctor Thorne* in late 1858 or early 1859 through the last of the posthumously issued novels over two decades later, nearly all of Trollope's works of fiction were published by Harper and often by other companies.[9] American periodicals reviewed Trollope's successive novels. In France, the *Revue des deux mondes* critics found Trollope's early novels phenomena worthy of extended reviews mainly devoted to long synopses of his narratives.[10] His later novels received more perfunctory attention, but a demand for Tauchnitz editions of Trollope seems to have continued. Tauchnitz issued *Doctor Thorne* in 1858 and followed it in 1859 with publication of *The Warden*, *Barchester Towers*, and *The Bertrams*. From that time on Tauchnitz editions appeared for nearly every successive novel to the end of Trollope's career.

IV

TROLLOPE AS SELF-CRITIC: *An Autobiography* (1883)

Trollope in the last years before his death in 1882 continued to hold a considerable part of the public and to receive generous sums from the publishers. In the two decades following his death, however, the demand for his books suffered a precipitous drop to something approaching nullity. This abrupt decline has often been attributed to the damaging effect upon his reputation of the publishing of his *An Autobiography* in 1883. Written in 1875–6, but expressly designed for posthumous publication, this work is famous in its own right as one of the notable exemplars of autobiography in an age that excelled in this literary form. Passages in Trollope's memorable self-portrait did indeed encourage readers and critics to dismiss him at his own professed evaluation as a simple craftsman who could not lay serious claim to a place among the literary artists of his time. It is easy, on the other hand, to lay too much stress on the part the *Autobiography* played in the neglect of Trollope by the public until the turn of the century, and the generally low estimate of Trollope among the critics during this time and well into the twentieth century. With a few notable exceptions, the critics had never shown much inclination to grant Trollope a place among the great names in the art of the novel. Their emphasis even at the height of his celebrity went to the entertainment to be derived from his works. He produced characters that came alive for his audience; he was exceedingly clever, and he was far and away above the average of the novelists of the time. But he did not, it was the custom to observe, penetrate to the deeper levels of moral and spiritual experience. He worked like a craftsman, producing a solid product, but a product that showed neither the intensity of conception nor the care in execution that one expected from the true artist. He wrote too fast, and he wrote too much. Largely the *Autobiography* put into succinct statements from the mouth of the author himself derogations that the critics (mingling them with much praise) had been making for years. It is likely that Trollope would have suffered neglect from the reading public and from the critics for a period even if the *Autobiography* had never been published. A new generation with new predilections found the scenes and characters of Trollope too remote for the impact of immediacy and too near for possessing the charm of the remote. Nevertheless, Trollope's self-revelations in the *Autobiography* coloured nearly all subsequent evaluations of his work in some degree, and it may be well to consider them in some detail at this point as a significant aspect of his reputation with the critics.

6

Though Trollope in the *Autobiography* struggled hard to portray himself with simple candour, he produced a book that often—where his practice as a novelist is described—becomes deceptive in the author's very struggles for complete honesty. Thus Trollope informs us that when he begins a new story he is relatively careless about the course that his narrative will take. 'When I sit down to write a novel I do not at all know, and I do not very much care, how it is to end' (p. 214). It is easier to work that way, Trollope assures his reader later in the book, because the author then has only the simple task of making 'everything as it comes fit in with what has gone before' (p. 286). Apparently Trollope was not aware that he was describing a way of making things easy that few writers—probably only those endowed with what would have to be called genius—could find anything but disastrous. Then there is the famous passage regarding Trollope's daily schedule—his three hours every morning, on ship or on shore, on foreign trains or in foreign hotels, totting up his 250 words every quarter-hour, with his watch before him. 'I have found that the 250 words have been forthcoming as regularly as my watch went' (pp. 227–8). Small wonder that when it appeared in the year following Trollope's death the *Autobiography* was viewed with aversion by young critics versed in Walter Pater's dicta on high art. Some of them had already found Trollope's novels convenient objects of attack.[11] The sentences immediately following the famous self-incriminating passage just quoted have been generally passed over without comment: 'I always began my task by reading the work of the day before, an operation which would take me half an hour, and which consisted chiefly in weighing with my ear the sound of the words and phrases . . . by reading what he has last written, just before he recommences his task, the writer will catch the tone and spirit of what he is then saying, and will avoid the fault of seeming to be unlike himself.' At first glance the words add up to nothing more than further detail in Trollope's portrait of himself as a plodding craftsman. When, however, one recalls the wise nuances, the rich (though, indeed, sometimes ponderous) ironies, the great relish for almost every variety of comedy in the human scene in Trollope's novels from *The Warden* onward, they suggest something more. The prominence of the narrator's own voice was assumed by many critics of Trollope's own day as among the prime enjoyments of his novels. In relatively recent years it seems in process of being rediscovered on a profounder level as one of the real keys to Trollope's special art.[12]

If Trollope could not tell where his characters would lead him, the reason was not their vagueness in his thinking but the fact that they had already taken on for him something like a life of their own. In periods of concentration Trollope was able to give himself almost entirely to the world of his fiction: 'At such times I have been able to imbue myself thoroughly with the characters I have had in hand. I have wandered alone among the rocks and woods, crying at their grief, laughing at their absurdities, and thoroughly enjoying their joy. I have been impregnated with my own creations till it has been my only excitement to sit with the pen in my hand, and drive my team before me at as quick a pace as I could make them travel' (pp. 147–8). For Trollope, indeed, his characters were the novel. For the reader, there is present another element—the unifying play of the author's voice, the sense of a mind that experienced all this life and brought it all under the narrator's control, with a special quality of ironic self-effacement that is sometimes taken for simple maladroitness.

It is so that I have lived with my characters, and thence has come whatever success I have obtained. There is a gallery of them, and of all in that gallery I may say that I know the tone of the voice, and the colour of the hair, every flame of the eye, and the very clothes they wear. Of each man I could assert whether he would have said these or the other words; of every woman, whether she would then have smiled or so have frowned. When I shall feel that this intimacy ceases, then I shall know that the old horse should be turned out to grass. That I shall feel it when I ought to feel it, I will by no means say . . . but I do know that the power indicated is one without which the teller of tales cannot tell them to any good effect (p. 195).

Nearly ten years after Trollope had recorded Mrs. Proudie's demise in *The Last Chronicle of Barset*, Mrs. Proudie still stayed alive in his private world: '. . . I have never disseveured myself from Mrs. Proudie, and still live much in company with her ghost' (p. 231). This power for 'living' with one's characters Trollope considered the prime test for creative vitality in other authors. Thackeray, the greatest of novelists, had in his best days lived fully with Pendennis and Becky Sharp and Esmond. Dickens in his best years had lived thus with Mrs. Gamp and Pickwick, but had lost a part of his power in the time of the Boffins and the Veneerings. George Eliot, whom Trollope placed second only to Thackeray among the novelists of his age, was also a philosopher and was increasingly in her later years prone to dissect the characters that her imagination brought so graphically before her. 'Everything that comes before her is pulled to pieces so that the inside of it shall be seen, and be seen if possible by her readers as clearly as by herself.' Mrs. Poyser and Maggie and, more than any other, Tito Melema showed her great powers as a novelist. Trollope wrote the *Autobiography* while *Daniel Deronda* was still appearing in monthly parts.[13] There was no sign in this work of any loss of creative vitality, Trollope felt, but of a shift in purpose. 'It is not from decadence that we do not have another Mrs. Poyser, but because the author soars to things which seem to her to be higher than Mrs. Poyser.' Trollope felt a lack of ease in Eliot's recent work, but modestly disclaimed power of judging, or of fully understanding, her achievement. Here as elsewhere in the *Autobiography*, Trollope not only allows but positively encourages the reader to dispense with any search for subtleties in his own art. George Eliot was among his 'dearest and most intimate friends', but he professes himself so far beneath her in his own less-complicated way of living with his creations that there is much in *Daniel Deronda* he will not pretend to have plumbed to its depths. It is unfortunate that young people find the later works of Eliot too hard for them. 'I know that they are very difficult to many that are not young' (p. 205). For his own novels (in which, Trollope implies, the young will encounter little that escapes them), he has no great hope of immortality. He had turned them out so prolifically, year after year, that he claimed 'no right to expect that above a few of them shall endure even to the second year beyond publication' (p. 165). Even the best of them might well go into oblivion before the turn of the century, though he had some hope that a few of his creations might survive: 'I do not think it probable that my name will remain among those who in the next century will be known as the writers of English prose fiction;—but if it does, that permanence of success will probably rest on the character of Plantagenet Palliser, Lady Glencora, and the Rev. Mr. Crawley' (p. 300). For Plantagenet Palliser and his wife, Lady Glencora, the preceding paragraph makes a suggestion that is rare for the *Autobiography*: a few of the novels would reward a closer reading than they are likely to get—closer than critics have been inclined to award them.

That the man's character should be understood as I understand it—or that of his wife's, the delineation of which has also been a matter of much happy care to me—I have no right to expect, seeing that the operation of describing has not been confined to one novel, which might perhaps be read through by the majority of those who commenced it. It has been carried on through three or four, each of which will be forgotten even by the most zealous reader almost as soon as read. In *The Prime Minister*, my Prime Minister will not allow his wife to take office among, or even over, those ladies who are attached by office to the Queen's court. 'I should not choose,' he says to her, 'that my wife should have any duties unconnected with our joint family and home.' Who will remember in reading those words that, in a former story, published some years before, he tells his wife, when she has twitted him with his willingness to clean the Premier's shoes, that he would even allow her to clean them if it were for the good of the country? And yet it is by such details as these that I have, for many years past, been manufacturing within my own mind the characters of the man and his wife.

V

THE PERSPECTIVE OF ANOTHER CENTURY

Nearly a century later it is quite clear that Trollope wrote with greater subtlety and with greater power than he generally professed to think. Critics and readers from the beginning of his career to the present have granted him his remarkable gift for creating characters that come to life in the imagination. Though the number of them he could call up is perhaps exceptional, Charles Reynolds Brown in the nineteen-thirties was merely proving himself one of myriads of Trollopians when on a train trip he entertained himself by counting the characters from Trollope's novels that lived as separate entities in this reader's imagination. There were seventy-eight, Brown discovered, that stood out 'as definitely as if they had been sitting in the seats around me'.[14] Nathaniel Hawthorne had in 1860 testified to the sense of life he had found in Trollope's novels, which were 'just as real as if some giant had hewn a great lump out of the earth and put it under a glass case, with all its inhabitants going about their daily business, and not suspecting that they were being made a show of'.[15] Edward FitzGerald, who was fond of having Trollope's novels read aloud to him, found himself treating Trollope's men and women as if they were living people; he was 'constantly breaking out into Argument with the Reader (who never replies) about what is said and done by the People in the several Novels. I say, "No, no! She must have known she was lying! etc." '[16] Robert Browning found *The Belton Estate* 'very unpretending, but surely *real*, and so far a gain'.[17] This special gift of Trollope's for endowing his characters with the effect of reality was so often praised by the critics of his own time that it runs as a refrain through the critiques (I have excised a great many such remarks in cutting this edition to size, but have left many more). 'It was impossible', wrote a reviewer of *The Small House at Allington* (1864), 'to avoid speaking of [Trollope's] personages as of real men and women.' For the last year Adolphus Crosbie had been 'as much a public character as Lord Palmerston'.[18] An especially discerning tribute to Trollope's power is the review of *Ralph the*

Heir in the *Spectator* (15 April 1871), probably the work of Richard Holt Hutton, a critique that recognizes a depth to Trollope's portrayals that critics often felt they lacked:

Which of us can say that we know even our own circle of friends, political and social, half as well as we have learned within the last twelvemonth to know Sir Thomas Underwood and his daughters and niece, his ward Ralph, and his ward's cousins; the old squire, Gregory Newton; the Eardham girls, and their scheming mama . . . or that we know the heart of any person at all resembling the breeches-maker of Conduit Street, nearly as completely as we know that Mr. Neefit, with the pertinacious and half-pathetic workings of whose vulgar but tough little ambition we have been becoming more and more intimate every month for the last year?[19] To the mass of men, such a novel as *Ralph the Heir* brings not only a very large increase in their experience of men, but a very much larger increase than their own personal contact with the prototypes, if prototypes there be, of these personages, would ever have afforded them.

To many of the reviewers, Trollope's achievement seemed only a sort of photography. It produced faithful likenesses of living people, but gave little idea of what went on inside them. Trollope's verisimilitude was at once his highest gift and the quality that marked him for a craftsman rather than an artist. He could make faithful copies from life because he was not a man of 'poetic genius, or of a very original cast of thought'. A genius inevitably tinted his work with his 'own peculiar humour', but Trollope's mind was not burdened by any such 'troublesome imaginative power'.[20] Trollope would lose his audience once the people that he depicted were no longer living to admire their reflections. 'No amount of skill', a critic declared in 1869, 'can make commonplace men and common-place incidents and common-place feelings fit subjects of high or true literary art. . . . Why should they live?'[21] In the two decades following Trollope's death the prophecy seemed well on its way to fulfilment. Herbert Paul in 1897 noted that whereas twenty years earlier it would hardly have been too much to say that half the novels in the railway bookstalls were by Trollope, his works were now never seen there 'and seldom seen anywhere else'.[22]

With the turn of the century, however, signs appeared of a new interest in Trollope on the part of both the critics and the public. In 1901 Walter Frewen Lord granted that in the period since Trollope's death his novels had been 'going steadily out of fashion', but Lord could at the same time insist that if Trollope's art was a sort of photography, it was photography that 'was consummate' and might ultimately entitle Trollope to a 'very high place' among novelists.[23] Harry Thurston

Peck in the same year insisted on the enduring excellence of Trollope's work despite his temporary decline in a period that preferred the morbid French brand of realism.[24] Peck's essay, a note informs us, was designed to serve as introduction to a new American edition of a large number of Trollope's novels. That a new audience for Trollope was developing in the first decade of the twentieth century seems quite clear. In this ten years English and American publishers made not less than twenty of Trollope's forty-seven novels available to the public. A resourceful book-dealer could in 1910 procure for his customer all or nearly all of the following (all of them were published in England or the United States or both in the years 1901–10): *Barchester Towers, The Bertrams, Can You Forgive Her? Castle Richmond, Doctor Thorne, The Duke's Children, The Eustace Diamonds, Framley Parsonage, Is He Popenjoy?, The Last Chronicle of Barset, The Macdermots of Ballycloran, Orley Farm, Phineas Finn, Phineas Redux, The Prime Minister, Rachel Ray, The Small House at Allington, The Three Clerks, The Vicar of Bullhampton, The Warden.*[25] When Ernest Baker in 1913 published his *A Guide to the Best Fiction* he included seventeen of Trollope's novels in his listings. There are many evidences of continued interest in Trollope on the part of a sizeable audience through the next two decades. By the late nineteen-twenties many of Trollope's novels had been made available in good editions. Michael Sadleir in 1928, partly on the basis of the growing demand for first editions of Trollope, was emboldened to say that this author, 'who in a literary sense was for decades absurdly under-rated', had at last 'with a rush . . . come into his own'.[26] If critical esteem for Trollope did indeed take an abrupt rise in the late nineteen-twenties and the nineteen-thirties, it is likely that Sadleir's own *Trollope: A Commentary* (1927) was a major factor. But there is no really impressive evidence in these years of a general movement among critics and scholars to grant Trollope a place among the chief novelists of the nineteenth century. David Cecil in his *Early Victorian Novelists* (1935) praises Trollope's quality of humour and his gift for evoking the Victorian scene; but the ultimate impression left by Cecil's essay is that Trollope belongs among the minor novelists of his period. Ernest Baker, in his monumental *History of the English Novel* (VIII, 1937), seems to have lost some of his earlier esteem for Trollope: A superlative craftsman, Trollope is, Baker concludes, worth reading for his faithfully mirroring the life of his day; but the vision essential to great creative art was beyond him.

By 1945 it is clear that Trollope is not only being widely read but viewed seriously as a literary-artist. Important evidences are the establishment of *The Trollopian* in that year, a critical and scholarly journal devoted to studies of nineteenth-century fiction in general, but with the emphasis implied by its title,[27] and the publication of Lucy and Richard Poate Stebbins, *The Trollopes: The Chronicle of a Writing Family*, also in 1945. From that time to the present the number of serious studies of Trollope's art has gone on multiplying. Elizabeth Bowen's sensitive *Anthony Trollope: A New Judgment*, first presented as a radio broadcast, was published as a booklet in 1946, and her extended essay on Trollope was published as an introduction to *Doctor Thorne* in 1959. This excellent critique, in line with much critical opinion of recent years, finds in Trollope a degree of artistic achievement greater than any Trollope ever claimed for himself. Bradford Booth's edition of *The Letters of Anthony Trollope* was published in 1951. Book-length studies of Trollope's art in the nineteen-fifties include Beatrice Curtis Brown's *Anthony Trollope* (1950), A. O. J. Cockshut's *Anthony Trollope: A Critical Study* (1955), and Bradford Booth's informative and valuable *Anthony Trollope: Aspects of His Life and Art* (1958). In 1958 there also appeared Arthur Mizener's brilliant essay, 'Anthony Trollope: the Palliser Novels',[28] a penetrating study of Trollope's particular achievement in the art of fiction. The number and range of essays and studies devoted to Trollope in the last twenty years show that Trollope has been viewed increasingly as a novelist of significance, with complexities in his art and in his view of society that challenge the critics' resources.[29] The analogy of Trollope's fiction with photography, so often employed even in the earlier years of this century, is clearly an unfortunate one. Trollope's world is, as Hawthorne observed in 1860, very much in motion, with its inhabitants absorbed in pursuing their daily business. Moreover, Trollope sees a great deal that the finest camera lens could not register. Though his novels, even the best of them, fail of the finish and proportion that less prolific writers can effect, and do not often penetrate to a depth of experience plumbed by George Eliot or Henry James, they go well beneath the surface of life. They work subtly, not with character in isolation, but with the delicacies of interaction among characters, with the many pressures of personality upon personality, with the demands of custom or propriety at war with the demands of the heart—with what an astute critic of *Miss Mackenzie* for the *Spectator* (it was probably Richard Holt Hutton) called 'the small manœuvres and petty tactics of social life . . . the mutual influence exerted by men and women over each other', where the difference of a hair may sometimes 'turn the scale between temporary failure or temporary success . . . '. Trollope's special art, this early critic notes, is intimately concerned with a 'great characteristic of his,—that his mind as an artist is engaged much more upon elaborating the infinitely varying social occasions for reflecting character than on creating character itself . . . '.[30] The reviewer is here getting close to the quality that recent critics have been discovering in Trollope, a quality that induces some of them to speak unabashedly not only of his 'richness and complexity' but of his 'great art'.[31] Without resort to melodrama, by means of incidents having mainly to do with normal daily living, Trollope can weave a pattern of interaction among his personages that reveals them 'interlocked in a hundred ways'.[32] Critics of Trollope's own time were unwilling to value his gift so highly, though they could speak with delight of Trollope's ability to portray 'all those infinite shades of character which make society . . . amusing and interesting'.[33]

It seems significant that in evaluating Trollope's work critics of his time so often compared it to the work of Jane Austen. Both Trollope and Austen could, it was felt, present the surface of society with remarkable deftness; but both stopped short of the depth of vision or the high seriousness that were essential to art of a more elevated sort. Both were, however, wonderfully amusing. The *Dublin Review* in summing up Trollope's career in 1883 linked the two writers as unexcelled in the offering of sheer entertainment. Like Jane Austen, Trollope, it observed, rarely portrayed the 'deeper feelings' of his creations. 'We see no further into most of his characters', the anonymous critic complained, 'than we see into our intimate friends'.[34] From the vantage-point of another century this seems a curious judgment that dismisses the comedy of manners and a good deal else at too low an estimate. Such reviews go into the dilemmas of Trollope's characters, their motivations and the faults and virtues of their moral natures, as though the persons of the novel were indeed scarcely products of art at all. Trollope had followed the advice of Horace only too well. He had hidden his art to the point where it had ceased to exist—not only for the majority of his critics but, apparently, in large part for himself as well.

VI
TROLLOPE'S VIEW OF HIS CRITICS

'As an author, I have paid careful attention to the reviews,' Trollope wrote in the *Autobiography*, '. . . and I think that now I well know where I may look for a little instruction, where I may expect only greasy adulation, where I shall be cut up into mince-meat for the delight

of those who love sharp invective, and where I shall find an equal mixture of praise and censure so adjusted, without much judgment, as to
exhibit the impartiality of the newspaper and its staff.' He had learned,
he felt, to recognize the worthless chaff and throw it to the winds
whether it offered hollow praise or inept stricture, 'but I have also found
some corn, on which I have fed and nourished myself, and for which
I have been thankful' (p. 225). Yet even after a lapse of nearly twenty
years Trollope could feel it necessary to defend himself in the *Autobiography* against the imputation of *The Times* reviewer that he had
indulged his readers' 'morbid tendencies' by caricaturing a certain
writer for that newspaper as Tom Towers of the *Jupiter*. Trollope denied
any knowledge of *The Times*'s contributors of that period: 'As I created
an archdeacon, so had I created a journalist, and the one creation was
no more personal or indicative of morbid tendencies than the other'
(p. 84). Trollope was, more than the average of authors, eager for public
approbation. When toward the end of his life a young relative wrote
him of a recent article praising *Barchester Towers*, the letter assumed that
Trollope had long ago forgotten specific episodes of the book. Trollope
replied that he remembered every passage, though he sometimes found
it due to modesty to appear to have forgotten. 'And when after 30
years [the author] is told by some one that he has been pathetic, or
witty, or even funny, he always feels like lending a five-pound note to
that fellow.'[35]

Perhaps because he valued so highly praise that he felt was duly
earned, however, Trollope kept himself fiercely aloof from his critics.
It was probably E. S. Dallas who received something approaching
rudeness rather than complaisance when he showed Trollope a manuscript presented to him in appreciation of a review that had pleased the
author:

Some years since a critic of the day, a gentleman well known then in literary
circles, showed me the manuscript of a book recently published,—the work of a
popular author. It was handsomely bound, and was a valuable and desirable
possession. It had just been given to him by the author as an acknowledgment
for a laudatory review in one of the leading journals of the day. As I was
expressly asked whether I did not regard such a token as a sign of grace both in
the giver and in the receiver, I said that I thought it should neither have been
given nor have been taken. . . . This man was a professional critic, bound by
his contract with certain employers to review such books as were sent to him.
How could he, when he had received a valuable present for praising one book,
censure another by the same author? (pp. 220–1)

Dallas was a powerful critic for *The Times*; Dickens had given him the manuscript of *Our Mutual Friend* under similar circumstances.[3] Trollope, with a forthrightness and a vehemence typical of him, was running the risk of affronting two formidable opponents in speaking out as he did on a subject that meant much to him. Trollope devotes a chapter of the *Autobiography* to his deeply felt conviction: 'The critic as critic, should not know his author, nor the author, as author, his critic. As censure should beget no anger, so should praise beget no gratitude' (p. 222).

When, in 1873, Trollope came to write *The Way We Live Now*, his bitterest satire upon the evils of his age, he described in some detail Lady Carbury's stratagems for wheedling favourable notices for her worthless books. Her devices ranged from flattery and mild flirtation to a tacit exchange of puffing critiques:

. . . both Mr. Broune of the 'Breakfast Table,' and Mr. Booker of the 'Literary Chronicle,' had been true to her interests. Lady Carbury had, as she promised, 'done' Mr. Booker's 'New Tale of a Tub' in the 'Breakfast Table.' That is, she had been allowed, as a reward for looking into Mr. Broune's eyes and laying her soft hand on Mr. Broune's sleeve, and suggesting to Mr. Broune that no one understood her so well as he did, to bedaub Mr. Booker's very thoughtful book in a very thoughtless fashion,—and to be paid for her work. What had been said about his work in the 'Breakfast Table' had been very distasteful to poor Mr. Booker. It grieved his inner contemplative intelligence that such rubbish should be thrown upon him; but in his outside experience of life he knew that even the rubbish was valuable, and that he must pay for it in the manner to which he had unfortunately become accustomed. So Mr. Booker himself wrote the article on the 'Criminal Queens' in the 'Literary Chronicle,' knowing that what he wrote would also be rubbish. 'Remarkable vivacity.' 'Power of delineating character.' 'Excellent choice of subject.' 'Considerable intimacy with the historical details of various periods.' 'The Literary world would be sure to hear of Lady Carbury again.' The composition of the review together with the reading of the book, consumed altogether perhaps an hour of Mr. Booker's time. He made no attempt to cut the pages, but here and there read those that were open. He had done this kind of thing so often, that he knew well what he was about. He could have reviewed such a book when he was three parts asleep. When the work was done he threw down his pen and uttered a deep sigh. He felt it to be hard upon him that he should be compelled, by the exigencies of his position, to descend so low in literature; but it did not occur to him that in fact he was not compelled, and that he was quite at liberty to break stones, or to starve honestly, if no other honest mode of carrying on his career was open to him. 'If I didn't, somebody else would,' he said to himself

But the review in the 'Morning Breakfast Table' was the making of Lady Carbury's book, as far as it ever was made. . . . There had been no hesitation in the laying on of the paint (Ch. XI).

If the name 'Alfred Shand' placed beside the entry for Mr. Booker in Trollope's work plan for *The Way We Live Now* is meant for A. Innes Shand in line with Trollope's practice of sometimes naming in his work plans actual persons who were to serve him as originals for his characters,[37] it is as well that Shand did not identify himself with the part when he read the novel. Two years after the publication of *The Way We Live Now* in 1875, Trollope was 'very anxious' to see the extended essay upon his novels which he understood had appeared in the *Edinburgh Review*. He thought it was likely that Henry Reeve, the editor, had written the essay; but the actual writer of a warmly appreciative survey of Trollope's work, extending to over thirty pages, was the man he had probably had in mind when he created Mr. Booker.[38] There is much more satire upon the critics in Chapter XI of *The Way We Live Now*. Most of it is more savage in tone and directed at the ruthless commercialism of the professional reviewers, who write in praise or blame, to sell a book or to snuff it out, at the dictation of their employers, without concern for the value of the work itself. The 'crushing review' is most popular because it reads well. When circulation is down 'proprietors should, as a matter of course, admonish their Alf to add a little power to the crushing department'.

That adverse criticism could sorely wound Trollope seems evident in various passages of the *Autobiography* and elsewhere. Trollope in a note to his account of *The Prime Minister* in the *Autobiography* states that he was 'specially hurt' by a criticism of this novel in the *Spectator*: 'The critic who wrote the article I know to be a good critic, inclined to be more than fair to me; but in this case I could not agree with him . . .' (p. 299n). Adverse criticism of *The Prime Minister* apparently disturbed Trollope so much that he began to doubt his own powers. It 'seemed to tell me that my work as a novelist should be brought to a close' (p. 301n). Fortunately, Trollope persisted and felt that his next two novels met with 'fair success' (ibid.). In referring to the *Spectator* critic of *The Prime Minister*, Trollope is in all likelihood referring to Richard Holt Hutton, whom he calls in another passage of the *Autobiography* 'the most observant, and generally the most eulogistic' of his critics (p. 171). He would have felt less dismayed by the adverse critique of the *Spectator* if he could have known that the review in question was actually written not by Hutton but by his co-editor, Meredith White Townsend, as were at least two other of the *Spectator* reviews of Trollope's novels in the eighteen-seventies, including the disparaging notice of *The Way We Live Now*.[39] The fact is, however, that Trollope had much less to complain of at the hands of the reviewers than the majority of novelists. He was generally treated with respect, often praised (though rarely in the highest terms), scarcely ever subjected to anything mildly approaching the 'rabid malignity' that poor Lady Carbury suffered at the hands of a Mr. Jones. In the main Trollope's vehemence against the misuse of criticism in the periodicals seems to have been a disinterested concern for the plight of young authors and for the threat such malpractice posed to the cause of literature. It was at the height of his own fame that Trollope carried out what was surely one of the most curious experiments that an established author could attempt. Trollope in the *Autobiography* offers a rationale for his project, but it is doubtful that he himself understood more than a part of his motives.

From the commencement of my success as a writer, which I date from the beginning of the *Cornhill Magazine*, I had always felt an injustice in literary affairs which had never afflicted me or even suggested itself to me while I was unsuccessful. It seemed to me that a name once earned carried with it too much favour. I indeed had never reached a height to which praise was awarded as a matter of course; but there were others who sat on higher seats to whom the critics brought unmeasured incense and adulation, even when they wrote, as they sometimes did write, trash which from a beginner would not have been thought worthy of the slightest notice. I hope no one will think that in saying this I am actuated by jealousy of others. Though I never reached that height, still I had so far progressed that that which I wrote was received with too much favour. The injustice which struck me did not consist in that which was withheld from me, but in that which was given to me. I felt that aspirants coming up below me might do work as good as mine, and probably much better work, and yet fail to have it appreciated. In order to test this, I determined to be such an aspirant myself, and to begin a course of novels anonymously, in order that I might see whether I could obtain a second identity,—whether as I had made one mark by such literary ability as I possessed, I might succeed in doing so again (p. 170).

Accordingly Trollope sold *Nina Balatka*, a short novel with Prague as its setting, to Blackwood in 1865 on the proviso that the tale was to be published anonymously, both in his magazine and in book form. He thus surrendered his story for a portion of the sum he could have commanded if it had come out under his name. A year later he turned over

Linda Tressel, another short novel, to Blackwood on the same understanding.

The two anonymous novels 'had no real success' and were not widely reviewed. However, critics who dealt with the books at all rendered them the sort of praise that they merited. The *Athenaeum* (2 March 1867) recommended *Nina Balatka* to 'every thoughtful, not vacant, reader of novels', and especially to those who valued the revelation of character more than the excitement of a clever plot. The *London Review* notice, which appeared on the same day, gave two full columns to this short anonymous novel and hailed it as 'one of the most charming stories that has appeared for a long time', a tale that excelled in insight into the human heart. The *Examiner* (11 May 1867) also gave the book praise. The experiment took a turn the author thought he had provided against when the *Spectator* review appeared (23 March 1867). It was in all likelihood Richard Holt Hutton, as Trollope surmised (*Autobiography*, p. 170), who recognized tricks of Trollope's phrasing and declared the book's origin despite the author's choice of foreign setting and characters and a modulation of style: 'If criticism be not a delusion from the very bottom,' the critic declared, 'this pleasant little story is by Mr. Anthony Trollope. We have no external evidence for saying so, and there is the presumption against it that Mr. Trollope's name is worth a great deal in mere money value to the sale of any book. Still, no one who knows his style at all can read three pages of this tale without detecting him as plainly as if he were present in the flesh.' Since the novel was little known, however, the *Spectator*'s declaration made no great stir. Once or twice Trollope 'heard the story mentioned by readers who did not know me to be the author, and always with praise'; but the novel, in spite of its considerable merits, attracted relatively little attention and did not take on with the public.

Linda Tressel, a tale of life in Nuremburg published a year later, received less notice than *Nina Balatka*, though the *British Quarterly Review* (July 1868) found in it 'great cleverness and power' and the *Spectator* (9 May 1868) praised it at length, again intimating that the book was from the hand of the actual writer. That Trollope's authorship of the two novels was not widely accepted is suggested by a curious notice in the *London Review* (30 May 1868), which flatly rejects the idea that Trollope could have written either of the two anonymous tales—apparently on the ground that he could not have achieved anything like the lyrical quality that distinguished them: 'The authorship was attributed to one or two gentlemen who—with all respect be it said—might as appropriately have been suspected of writing Browning's "Evelyn Hope," or Tennyson's "St. Agnes' Eve." We are not aware that "Nina Balatka" was ever said to be the writing of a woman . . . but the appearance of "Linda Tressel" almost settles the point. The heroic fortitude, the simple frankness, and maidenly honour of Nina Balatka were the attributes of a creation which might have arisen in the mind of a male artist; but Linda Tressel seems to us to be altogether a woman's woman.' Whoever the real author might be, the reviewer concludes, *Linda Tressel* is 'one of the tenderest and truest pictures of life and character' of recent years and proof in itself that English fiction still flourishes. Such notices should have encouraged Trollope to think better of the powers of some among the critics for evaluating works on their merits rather than on the name of the author. The public, however, refused to follow suit. Trollope had intended *The Golden Lion of Granpère* for a third experiment in anonymity, but after Blackwood declined it he was convinced that it should appear with his name upon the title-page.[40]

Though he may not have known it, one of Trollope's motives for attempting 'a second identity' may well have been to break free for a time from the identity he had established for himself almost too successfully. By 1867 many critics had begun to find him reliable but unexciting: he was for them the regular, often satisfying, but sometimes monotonous purveyor of realistic pictures of English society and English character. He must have found a wry enjoyment in a review that conceded the author of *Nina Balatka* and *Linda Tressel* not only a fresh charm and novelty but a lyrical gift that proved, contrary to current rumour, that Anthony Trollope could not be the author.

Some years later Trollope was to make plans for still another experiment in fooling the critics. In the *Autobiography*, completed in 1876, but expressly designed for posthumous publication, Trollope announced that he had by him the manuscript of a novel which he had written six years earlier. It had not been exposed to daylight since it had first been bound up in the wrapper that still contained it. Trollope looked forward 'with some grim pleasantry to its publication after another period of six years, and to the declaration of the critics that it has been the work of a period of life at which the power of writing novels has passed from me' (pp. 228-9).[41] Thus nearly ten years after *Nina Balatka* and *Linda Tressel* Trollope could view his critics with what might pass for amused irony—except for the strange elaborateness of his plan for proving to himself that the critics were wrong.

VII
THE WEIGHT OF THE *Spectator*, THE *Saturday Review*, AND *The Times*

In commenting upon the power that critics wielded over authors, Trollope in the *Autobiography* singled out for mention 'all the weight of *The Times, The Spectator*, or *The Saturday* [*Review*]'.[42] The three undoubtedly exerted great influence upon the educated public, and all three gave much attention to Anthony Trollope's novels, even from an early point in his career. Indeed, Trollope is so extensively reviewed in the columns of these three that critiques from these sources alone, if unabridged, would more than fill this volume. The *Spectator* reviews of the early novels from *The Warden* up to *Framley Parsonage* (which it seems to have ignored) are relatively undistinguished. It was only after Richard Holt Hutton became joint editor of the magazine in 1861 that the *Spectator* reviews began to show unusual qualities of insight into Trollope's novels. The first of these was the splendid notice of *Orley Farm* (11 October 1862), one of the most penetrating critiques of a single novel of Trollope's to appear within the century since its publication. Whether this review is by Hutton himself, it is impossible to say with absolute confidence. It bears earmarks of his distinctive style (the intricate sentence structures, the unusual trick of beginning paragraphs abruptly, often with co-ordinate conjunctions, the employment of novel analogies), but no marked file, so far as I have found, identifies reviews for the *Spectator* during this period, and internal evidence can sometimes be misleading. A periodical (or its dominant editor) to a degree established a style and tone to which individual reviewers tended to subordinate their personal styles and points of view—so much so that J. D. Jump feels, on the basis of much familiarity in the field, that he is justified in speaking of the opinion of one of the leading journals and 'not merely of that of some individual contributor to one of these'.[43] Leslie Stephen, who had reviewed uncounted numbers of books for the *Saturday Review*, found on going through the files some years later that he could not often distinguish his own writings from the mass of other materials. 'I had', he writes, 'unconsciously adopted the tone of my colleagues, and, like some inferior organisms, taken the colouring of my "environment".'[44] A few of the later reviews in the *Spectator* can be identified positively as Hutton's by means of fragmentary records.[45] Trollope himself, as we have seen, could mistakenly attribute the disparaging review of his *Prime Minister* to Hutton. The records do make it clear that two among the most notable critiques of Trollope in the

Spectator, written shortly after Trollope's death—'Mr. Anthony Trollope' (9 December 1882) and 'From Miss Austen to Mr. Trollope' (16 December 1882)—came from Hutton's hand. It is probable that a good many of the remarkably discerning reviews of Trollope's novels that appear in the *Spectator* from time to time during twenty years beginning in 1862 were, as Trollope surmised, the work of Hutton. William Beach Thomas's account of contributors to the *Spectator* shows that there were many who in other places wrote ably on the novels of Trollope and might have done so in the *Spectator*. These include Leslie Stephen, George Saintsbury, John Morley, H. D. Traill, and Margaret Oliphant,[46] the last of whom was an especially generous and knowledgeable admirer of Trollope, though scarcely, one would judge, a writer capable of the insight into Trollope's special style and substance that is shown in the best of the *Spectator* reviews. Both Stephen and Saintsbury were enthusiastic devotees of Trollope for a period of years; both recanted at the turn of the century; and Saintsbury still later rejected his recantation.[47] Neither seems, judging from the later signed analyses, likely to have been the author of the remarkable critiques that signalize the *Spectator* as the most valuable of all sources for contemporary criticism of Trollope's novels. It seems nearly certain that Trollope in the *Autobiography* was right in calling Richard Holt Hutton the 'most observant' of all his critics (p. 171).

For the early novels up to *Framley Parsonage* (1861), however, many of the most cordial and discerning critiques of Trollope's novels appeared not in the *Spectator* but in the *Saturday Review*. If Trollope later looked to the *Spectator* for the most appreciative reviews of his novels, there is evidence that at least up to *Doctor Thorne* (1858) he read most attentively, and reacted most strongly to, the opinions of the *Saturday*. This journal devoted two full columns to *Barchester Towers* (30 May 1857) as a 'very clever book' whose main fault was being too clever. The novel added up to 'a series of brilliant but disjointed sketches' and resembled a pudding that was all plums. The reviewer retells the story at considerable length and with obvious relish. Six months later (5 December 1857) the *Saturday* critic finds *The Three Clerks* a novel 'rich in promise', though fuller of faults than might be easily passed over coming from a writer who 'must be conscious that he has a real reputation within his grasp', a novelist who showed a power to delineate character that might, granted time and practice, place him close to the genius of Thackeray. Part of the faults of *The Three Clerks* stemmed from Trollope's inadequate knowledge of the law. The critic specifies such errors in a detail that strongly suggests that he himself is a member of the profession. Trollope would do well, he maintained, and other novelists also, to get expert opinion: 'Why do not novelists consult some legal friend before they write about the law? Is it impossible to find a barrister who has a hobby for criminal law, and also a hobby for criticizing novels, and who would bring his skill in both lines to bear upon the correction of a layman's mistakes? We think that such a man might be found, and he would be invaluable to all fiction writers who evolve descriptions of English trials out of the depth of their consciousness, and square them to meet the principles of eternal justice.'

In *Doctor Thorne*, his next novel, Trollope broke through the narrative of a chapter turning on legal problems to reply to the *Saturday* critic: 'It has been suggested that the modern English writers of fiction should among them keep a barrister, in order that they may be set right on such legal points as will arise in their narratives. . . .' Trollope professed himself willing to pay what modest part of the cost might fall to him. 'But as the suggestion has not yet been carried out, and as there is at present no learned gentleman whose duty would induce him to set me right, I can only plead for mercy if I be wrong in allotting all Sir Roger's vast possessions in perpetuity to Miss Thorne, alleging also, in excuse, that the course of my narrative absolutely demands that she shall be ultimately recognized as Sir Roger's undoubted heiress' (Ch. 35). And Trollope returns to the subject briefly in his next chapter, addressing his critic this time directly: 'I know I am wrong, my much and truly-honoured critic, about these title-deeds and documents. But when we've got that barrister in hand, then if I go wrong after that, let the blame be on my own shoulders—or on his.'

The effect of the author's stepping thus before his characters to reply to the critic of his last novel can hardly be defended. It is a glaring instance of what Henry James later called Trollope's 'suicidal satisfaction' in reminding the reader at times that his story is only make-believe.[48] Arthur Mizener has shown that Trollope could employ authorial intrusions with consummate skill and a delightful play of irony, but intrusions of the sort just presented are not among those that can be admired. Moreover, one must agree with the reviewer for the *Saturday* when he came in turn to review *Doctor Thorne* (12 June 1858) that apologizing in advance for a piece of carelessness does not condone the act. The outcome of Trollope's novel hinged upon the particular character of Sir Roger Scatcherd's will.

Mr. Trollope states as a fact that it *had* the effect which he attributes to it, and that if it had not, the point has been misstated. He adds that he wishes that, in order to avoid the responsibility of legal mistakes, novelists could adopt a suggestion which we offered in our review of his last novel, that they should have their books settled by counsel. We are flattered by his readiness to take advice, and in return we will not discuss the question whether Sir Roger Scatcherd's will was not altered just before his death (though we rather think it was), but we must observe that Mr. Trollope does not meet our point. The contract of the writer with the reader is to create and maintain a reasonably perfect illusion as to the reality of the events which he relates, and he breaks that contract if he wantonly points out the difficulties of his task, and says that there is a way out of them, but that he does not choose to take the trouble to find it.

Reviews in the *Saturday* of the novels that immediately follow *Doctor Thorne* do not carry on the debate; but the reviewer of *Orley Farm* (11 October 1862) devotes half of a long critique to prejudices against barristers that Trollope manifests in that work. The tone, however, is not unduly sharp, and the novel is praised as one of Trollope's best.

It is likely that this cordial reviewer of Trollope's early novels for the *Saturday* was Sir Henry Maine (1822–88), jurist and author, who wrote regularly for the *Saturday Review* from its beginning until early 1861 and occasionally thereafter.[49] Frederic Harrison, who was a pupil in chambers of Maine's at the time, later recalled the pleasure of his master, 'then a famous critic of the "Saturday Review"', when *The Warden* was first published. 'I well remember his interest and delight in welcoming a new writer, from whom he thought so much might be effected.'[50]

The *Saturday Review* may also have encouraged Trollope to adopt his characteristic defiant analogy for himself as an industrious craftsman, a man who wrote by schedule and not by inspiration. 'Sticking to one's last' is scarcely a phrase or a figure of speech that an author would need help in searching for; but Trollope's application has a particular bent and detail. The reviewer of the *Saturday* had commented in his notice of *Castle Richmond* (19 May 1860) that Trollope had sacrificed some of his earlier freshness and enthusiasm in the process of turning out one novel after another with a minimum of waste motion. Trollope had arrived at the point where he went about putting together a novel 'just as he might make a pair of shoes, with a certain workmanlike satisfaction in turning out a good article'. The product was more than acceptable, but Trollope's early work had promised still better. In the autumn of 1861 during his visit to Boston, Trollope told James Russell Lowell that he went to work 'just like a shoemaker on a shoe, only taking care to make honest stitches'.[51] Trollope was still using the analogy in the same way when he wrote his *Autobiography*. He was, he wrote, 'a professional writer of books' and could no more pause in his work to rest on his laurels than a shoemaker could sit idly contemplating his last pair of shoes. 'The shoemaker who so indulged himself would be without wages half the time.' The image had become part of Trollope's reflex of defensive self-deprecation. 'Having thought much of all this, and having made up my mind that I could be really happy only when I was at work, I had now [by 1868] quite accustomed myself to begin a second pair as soon as the first was out of my hands' (p. 268).

For the length of his full career Trollope received much space in the *Saturday Review* and on the whole enjoyed a favourable and intelligent reading. Critics for the *Saturday* who wrote upon Trollope's works in other journals and may well have written critiques of his novels in the *Saturday* as well include James Bryce, E. S. Dallas, Leslie Stephen, John Morley, Edward Augustus Freeman, and Amelia Edwards. The strong feminist note in a few of the reviews suggests the hand of Eliza Lynn Linton, novelist and propagandist and a frequent contributor to the *Saturday*.[52]

In *The Times*, as was mentioned earlier, Trollope read the first review he saw of any of his novels. Nearly thirty years later Trollope could quote from memory a considerable part of this brief and disparaging notice of *The Kellys and the O'Kellys*.[53] In later reviews he was to fare much better. Despite its protest over Trollope's depiction of Tom Towers of 'The Jupiter', an obvious burlesque of a *Times* political writer, the review of *The Warden* and *Barchester Towers* (13 August 1857) was distinctly favourable. Trollope in the *Autobiography* remembered it as dealing with his two novels in 'terms which were very pleasant to the author' (p. 83). This cordial notice and the extended essay on Trollope's novels appearing in *The Times* for the 23 May 1859 must have meant a great deal to Trollope in the early stages of his career. The *Times* review, indeed, treated Trollope as an author who had already arrived. He is the star of the circulating libraries; and if he is a little lower than Thackeray and Dickens, the greatest artists of the novel, he is 'one of the most amusing of authors'. He is recommended not only to the patrons of Mudie's but to thoughtful men who seldom deem novels worthy of their attention, who generally prefer blue books and statistics and the annals of Parliament. From the supercilious critic of *The Times* this was, as Trollope fully realized, praise of a high order. The reviewer for Trollope's novels during the early years of his career, from 1857 up to the critique of *Orley Farm* in December 1862 and possibly for some of the reviews that followed up to about 1867, was the eminent journalist and author E. S. Dallas (1828–79).[54] Beyond *Orley Farm* reviews of Trollope in *The Times* often seem to have gone to less talented hands and are frequently given largely to retelling the narratives of the novels. One of the notable exceptions is the review of *The Way We Live Now* (24 August 1875), an approving voice (though with more than a hint of subtle mockery—not against Trollope but against his attackers) amid the almost universal condemnation of that novel as irresponsible caricature. The *Times* reviewer insisted that Trollope's fierce satire was 'only too faithful a portraiture of the manners and customs of the English at the latter part of this 19th century'. *The Times* itself had had a good deal to say in recent months, both editorially and otherwise, about the decline in English values and in English manners. It was quite willing to pronounce Trollope's work 'a likeness of the face which society wears today' and, contrary to the general verdict, one of the best of Trollope's novels.

Though the *Spectator*, the *Saturday*, and *The Times* figure strongly in the pages that make up the body of this volume, a great variety of other periodicals, English and American, are represented in it, both for the intrinsic merit of their reviews and for their significance as points in the profile of reaction to Trollope's successive novels. The best general pronouncements of the time on Trollope's art in the great vehicles and in the small have not, it is hoped, been neglected. Much space, however, has been given in this book to reviews or, more often, sections of reviews, that do not have much to do with formal criticism. Victorian critics were on the whole reluctant to use the word *genius* in speaking of Trollope, and few of them thought him at all likely to take a place with the immortals. On the other hand, a great many of them considered him a popular novelist delightful to read and possessed of much more than common ability. Their reviews, especially from the 1860s onward, often convey surprisingly graphic insights into how Trollope's characters and their dilemmas struck their contemporaries. It is probably the better for us that a good many of the pieces that appear in this book were written by critics who were convinced they saw less of art than of life itself in the men and women that crowd Trollope's vast human comedy.

NOTES

1 *An Autobiography*, ed. Bradford Allen Booth (University of California Press, 1947), pp. 62–3. This edition is quoted throughout and referred to hereafter by page numbers in parentheses. Trollope's account of his experiences with his first four novels is contained in pages 62–84.

2 1 May 1847, v. 344.

3 Reviews of *The Macdermots*, *The Kellys and the O'Kellys*, and *La Vendée* are given in an appendix to this book.

4 The *Cornhill Magazine* is said to have begun publication in 1860 with an initial issue of no less than 120,000 copies. It averaged 84,000 copies per monthly issue for its first two years.—George M. Smith, 'Our Birth and Parentage', *Cornhill Magazine* (1901), n.s. x. 9.

5 Sir Peregrine Orme of *Orley Farm*. The writer is mistaken, however, in assuming that this novel had appeared in the *Cornhill*. Instead, it was issued in twenty one-shilling parts appearing monthly from March 1861 through October 1862.

6 January 1863, xvi. 28–29.

7 23 May 1859, p. 12.

8 E. D. Forgues, 'Dégénerescence du roman', *Revue des deux mondes* (August 1862), xl. 688–706.

9 Data for American and Tauchnitz editions mentioned in this paragraph are given in detail in Michael Sadleir, *Trollope: A Bibliography* (1928).

10 See, for example, Émile Montégut, 'Le roman réligieux [*The Warden*]' (August 1855), liv. 689–728 (this deals also with Charlotte Yonge); 'Le roman des mœurs [*Barchester Towers* and *Doctor Thorne*]' (October 1858), n.s. xvii. 756–88; E. D. Forgues, 'Une thèse sur le mariage en deux romans [*The Bertrams* and *Castle Richmond*]' (September 1860), xxix. 369–98.

11 See, for example, the unsigned article 'Polar Opposites in Fiction', *The Dublin University Magazine* (October 1879), iv. 436–42. The critic contrasts Trollope and his earthenware with Hawthorne, a 'true artist'. The essay is given in abridged form as No. 185 in this book.

12 See especially the critiques of Joseph Baker, Arthur Mizener, and Elizabeth Bowen discussed in Section V of this Introduction.

13 *Daniel Deronda* was first published in eight monthly parts, February to September 1876.

14 *They Were Giants* (1934), pp. 66–7.

15 See No. 39 in this book.

16 See No. 144.

17 *Letters of Robert Browning Collected by Thomas J. Wise*, ed. Thurman L. Hood (1933), p. 91.

18 Unsigned notice, *Reader* (2 April 1864), iii. 418–19.

19 *Ralph the Heir* first appeared in nineteen sixpenny parts published monthly from January 1870 to July 1871.

20 See note 18.

21 J. Herbert Stack, 'Mr. Anthony Trollope's Novels', *Fortnightly Review* (February 1869), xi. 196.

22 'The Apotheosis of the Novel', *The Nineteenth Century* (May 1897), xli. 782.

23 'The Novels of Anthony Trollope', *The Nineteenth Century* (May 1901), xlix. 805–16.

24 'Anthony Trollope', *The Bookman* (N.Y.) (April 1901), xiii. 114–25.

25 Data drawn from the *British Museum Catalogue*; the *Library of Congress Catalog of Printed Cards*; the *British National Bibliography*; the *National Union Catalog Authors' List*.

John Lane Company brought out *The Macdermots of Ballycloran* and *The Kellys and the O'Kellys* in both New York and London (1906).

26 *Trollope: A Bibliography*, p. 258. A first edition of *The Kellys and the O'Kellys* had sold in 1927 for £60 and a *Linda Tressel* in 1928 for £58.

27 The journal was to be renamed *Nineteenth-century Fiction* after a few numbers; but it continues a major vehicle for studies of Trollope's novels. Bradford Booth, the eminent Trollope scholar, remained chief editor of the journal from its beginning up to the mid-nineteen-sixties.

28 In *From Jane Austen to Joseph Conrad*, ed. Robert C. Rathburn and Martin Steinmann, Jr. (1958), pp. 160–76. The essay reappears in slightly altered form as 'The Realistic Novel in the Nineteenth Century: Trollope's Palliser Novels', Chapter II in Mizener's *The Sense of Life in the Modern Novel* (1964), pp. 25–54.

29 A more ambitious survey of studies of Trollope up to 1962 is given in Donald Smalley, 'Anthony Trollope', *Victorian Fiction: A Guide to Research*, ed. Lionel Stevenson (1964), pp. 188–213.

30 4 March 1865, xxxviii. 244.

31 Joseph Baker, 'Trollope's Third Dimension', *College English* (1954), xvi. 222–32.

32 Mizener, p. 163.

33 [Margaret Oliphant], 'Novels', *Blackwood's Edinburgh Magazine* (September 1867), cii. 277.

34 Unsigned notice, 'The Novels of Anthony Trollope' (April 1883), xcii. 318. For an excellent essay making distinctions much needed at the time, see Richard Holt Hutton's 'From Miss Austen to Mr. Trollope', *Spectator* (16 December 1882), No. 227 in this book.

35 *The Letters of Anthony Trollope*, ed. Bradford Allen Booth (1951), p. 465 (5 December 1881, to Arthur Tilley).

36 See K. J. Fielding, *Charles Dickens: A Critical Introduction* (1964), pp. 228–9. The review, however, was not by any means purely laudatory, and Dickens seems to have been as grateful for the critic's advice as for the more flattering parts of the critique.

37 The work plan is reproduced in an appendix to Michael Sadleir, *Trollope: A Commentary* (1947), p. 427. No Alfred Shand is listed in any of the likely places, and it seems reasonably safe to assume that Trollope had A. Innes Shand (though *A* stands for Alexander) in mind. Shand was, like Mr. Booker, both author of books and a professional reviewer.

38 See *Letters*, ed. Booth, p. 386 (19 November 1877, from Cape Town, to Henry Merivale Trollope).

39 Robert H. Tener, 'The *Spectator* Records, 1874–1897', *Victorian Newsletter* (Spring 1960), No. 17, p. 34. The records are far from complete, but they make many valuable identifications of *Spectator* authors in the years specified.

40 *Autobiography*, p. 171; Sadleir, *Trollope: A Commentary*, pp. 271–2.

41 What novel Trollope had in mind, and whether he, in fact, waited another six years to publish the manuscript he refers to, is not at all clear. A likely candidate would be *An Old Man's Love* (1884); but so far as I have found, no one has attempted to find a way around the difficulties that stand in the way of assigning this novel or another to the packet Trollope had in his possession at the time of writing the passage.

42 pp. 160–1. See also p. 225. Indications of the great power of the three vehicles for reviews are abundant. See, for example, the studies of the three cited in the notes that follow. See also E. E. Kellett, 'The Press', in *Early Victorian England, 1830–1865*, ed. G. M. Young (1934), II. 3–97; J. D. Jump, 'Weekly Reviewing in the Eighteen-fifties', *Review of English Studies* (1948), xxiv. 42–57.

43 J. D. Jump, 'Weekly Reviewing in the Eighteen-sixties', *Review of English Studies* (1952), n.s. iii. 245. See also p. 261.

44 *Some Early Impressions* (1924), p. 130.

45 See note 39.

46 *The Story of the 'Spectator' 1828–1928* (1928), *passim*.

[47] Leslie Stephen, 'Anthony Trollope', *National Review* (1901), xxxviii. 69–84; George Saintsbury, *Corrected Impressions* (1895), pp. 172–7; 'Trollope Revisited', *Essays and Studies by Members of the English Association* (1920), VI. 41–66.

[48] 'Anthony Trollope', *Century Magazine* (N.Y.) (July 1883), n.s. iv. 390. The essay is given in full in this book as No. 239.

[49] Merle Mowbray Bevington, *Saturday Review 1855–1868* (1941), p. 358, and *DNB*.

[50] 'Anthony Trollope's Place in Literature', *The Forum* (N.Y.) (May 1895), xix. 334.

[51] Introduction to Trollope's *North America*, ed. Donald Smalley and Bradford Allen Booth (1951), p. xvii.

[52] Bevington, *passim*.

[53] *Autobiography*, pp. 64–5. The full review is given as No. 251 (b) in an appendix to this book, with Trollope's version preceding it as No. 251 (a).

[54] [Anonymous], *The History of 'The Times'* (1939), II. 484–8; *DNB*. It has been suggested in Section VI of this Introduction that Dallas is the reviewer who showed Trollope a bound manuscript that he had received from a grateful popular author (Charles Dickens). The incident could not have occurred in that event before 1865, the year *Our Mutual Friend* was published.

THE WARDEN

1855

Anthony Trollope's career began with *The Warden*, his fourth novel and his first critical success. He was to wait still longer for material rewards (see Introduction, III). Trollope's experiences with his first three novels are recounted in Introduction, II, and the reviews of these works (reviews that Trollope with but one exception did not read, probably avoiding them on principle) are reproduced in the Appendix. Though *The Warden* received friendly treatment at some length in the *Athenaeum*, the *Examiner*, and the *Spectator*—and these notices must have meant much to Trollope at the time—additional praise in important places came some two or three years later, when *The Warden* could be paired with *Barchester Towers*, which some critics viewed as a longer, more polished sequel and a stronger promise that a new talent had arrived among English novelists (see Nos. 6, 8, 12, and 13, below).

1. Unsigned notice, *Examiner*

6 January 1855, p. 5

This cordial review may well have been written by John Forster (1812–76), influential critic and friend of Browning, Dickens, and other authors, in his last year as editor of the *Examiner*. A second notice of a sort appeared in the next issue (13 January 1855), pp. 21–2, chiefly a long quotation from 'this very clever though unsatisfactory book' to illustrate the 'smart and observing way in which it is written'.

The Warden is a clever novel, though we are not quite content with it. There is good matter for a novel in a topic of this kind, and Mr. Trollope has done well to paint his warden as a worthy old gentleman, a player of the violoncello, a believer in all goodness; generous, gentle, sensitive; accepting his position without sense of wrong, where nobody had ever hinted that wrong was; stung to the quick as soon as his eyes were opened to the unworthy character of his position; throwing his office up at last when none required that he should do so, and retiring into noble poverty. Mr. Trollope has done well in this, and he has painted the warden's character with not a little skill. It is well, also, to have shown how the old men of the charity suffered from the vigour of the efforts made in their behalf. But at the same time there is a half-mocking spirit put into the account of John Bold's proceedings—a half-sneering at his 'Roman virtue'—which will tend to confuse some readers as to Mr. Trollope's real meaning. The vigorous sketch of the Archdeacon, the pillar of all clerical abuse—harsh, overbearing, worldly—will indeed keep the reader's mind from wandering too far astray as to the actual intention, but it is not, on the whole, so clearly put as it should be, if the book be meant for a didactic novel.

There are a good many touches of satire pointed at contemporaries scattered about the book. The addition to the household of the Archdeacon, of three sons, Charles James, Henry, and Samuel, whose characters are taken from three bishops frequently before the public, has an effect now and then amusing. But the introduction of the *Times* newspaper into the novel is not managed in good taste, and the imitations of *Times* leaders are far from clever. The caricatures and burlesques of living writers are also in very bad taste, anything but successful, and not calculated to raise Mr. Trollope in the estimation of the public. We have glanced at enough defect to justify more than the amount of discontent we have expressed at a novel in which we find much to praise. As to its main scheme it is well invented, and much of it is well written, though the invention of the scenes is often better than the composition of them. The vice of the whole is that its matter is not at all times well felt, and that it shows the author's need of a much stricter education of his taste. It sometimes serves him admirably, for it does not lack acuteness, but for lack of proper training it is apt to go astray.

2. Unsigned notice, *Spectator*

6 January 1855, xxviii. 27–8

In the omitted sections, the reviewer puzzles over the exact point of Trollope's satire: 'The object of the writer is not clear, nor would it seem that he has reached any definite conclusion himself.' The reviewer also quotes at length satirical passages concerned with the law and with Tom Towers.

Keen observation of public affairs, a pungent closeness of style, and great cleverness in the author, are the distinguishing features of *The War-den*. . . . Resolved into its merest elements, the story of *The Warden* is a lawsuit, begun—against the wrong persons, as it happens—to give effect to the will of John Hiram; and the incidents as well as the persons mostly revolve round these legal proceedings. Besides the Warden, Bold, Eleanor Harding, and the bedesmen, there are the Bishop—an amiable old man, a friend of Mr. Harding; Dr. Grantley, the Bishop's son and Archdeacon—a portly man, of great physical powers, strong nerve, and High Church opinions, respectable, honourable, yet of the world worldly, and looking at the case like a man of the world and a champion of the Church. He is also the son-in-law of Mr. Harding; and by dint of his activity and firmness, manages both father and father-in-law. Then the lawsuit brings several legal men into the story, including the great Sir Abraham Haphazard, and enables the author to give some sharp blows at the principles of legal advocacy. The lawsuit also carries Mr. Bold to town; where he falls in with an old friend of his student days, then a briefless barrister, now Tom Towers, who contributes thunder to 'the Jupiter.' Then there is Dr. Anti-Cant, (Thomas Carlyle,) who attacks among others the Barchester abuse, but over-writes the matter; and Mr. Popular Sentiment, a gentleman who reforms society by means of novels published in numbers, and who brings out the first part of 'The Almshouses,' glaringly coloured up to the taste of the million. These and similar things furnish opportunity for the discharge of many sharply-pointed arrows at existing abuses or humbugs. There are also some pleasant sketches of clerical family life, and of society in a cathedral town, mixed up with the more humorous pictures.

3. Unsigned notice, *Athenaeum*

27 January 1855, pp. 107–8

Probably by H. F. Chorley (see Leslie A. Marchand, *The Athenaeum: A Victorian Mirror of Culture* [1941], p. 192). Much of the review, which takes up nearly three columns, is devoted to a retelling of the story and a long quotation from Chapter 2 presenting Archdeacon Grantly and his wife in their bed-curtain colloquy.

'The Warden' is a clever, spirited, sketchy story, upon the difficulties which surround that vexed question, the administration of the charitable trusts in England. . . . The whole story is well and smartly told, but with too much indifference as to the rights of the case. The conclusion is inconclusive enough, inasmuch as it is left for the reader to infer that nobody has any right to the charity, which is left to fall into abeyance; and even the little modicum of good which was enjoyed by the twelve old men is lost; and the moral, if one there be, is, that it would have been far better if John Bold had never meddled in the matter at all,— seeing that the only result of his labours is to bring much trouble and inconvenience upon everybody connected with the charity, and to leave things far worse than he found them,—a warning to all ardent reformers how they lightly question a vested grievance! . . . With this grave drawback, the book is, as we have said, an extremely clever and amusing one: all the characters are well and vigorously sketched. The twelve old men in the almshouses, the mild, simple-minded, conscientious Warden, who has received his income without doubt or misgiving till the day his conscience is rudely awakened by the voice of the 'Jupiter,' and his childlike anxiety to do right at whatever cost to himself; the pompous, wordly high Churchmen,—the archdeacon, who bullies his father the bishop, and tyrannizes over his father-in-law the warden,—Tom Towers, the oracle of the 'Jupiter;' the sketch of the 'Jupiter' itself, are one and all excellent, and do all that is possible towards blinding the reader to the *laisser faire, laisser aller* spirit that pervades the book—or if he sees it of inducing him to pardon it. We had marked many passages for extract as we went along, and we are divided in our choice amongst them, but on the whole we will resist the description of Tom Towers and the 'Jupiter,' and give instead a scene between the archdeacon and his inestimable wife. . . . Some of the characters in the story are drawn from the life,—and no reader of newspapers will mistake the original of the 'Jupiter.'

4. Unsigned notice, *Leader*

17 February 1855, pp. 164–5

In these days, when people sit down to compose fictions, having nothing in the world to write about, a novel with a subject claims honour as a work of unusual merit. *The Warden* has the first great recommendation of being a story based on a good and solid foundation. Mr. Trollope has a subject which it is worth while to describe, if we can do so briefly without damaging the legitimate interests of his plot. He starts with the very recognizable fact of a public charity, in a cathedral town, which has been fairly and admirably founded in bygone times, and which is very dishonestly managed at the (modern) period of the story. The 'Warden,' or principal local manager of the charity, is a quiet, honourable, kind-hearted clergyman, who, in perfect ignorance of business matters, has accepted his trust without inquiring at all peremptorily into the conditions on which he holds his preferment, and who honestly believes that he is performing all the duties of his station if he bestows the most watchful kindness and attention on the fixed number of destitute old men whom the rules of the charity place under his charge. From this pleasant and innocent delusion he is rudely enough awakened by one ardent gentleman of liberal principles, who discovers that the funds of the charity are shamefully diverted from their proper use, and who—although he is the accepted lover of the good Warden's youngest daughter—does not hesitate to expose the abuse publicly. The various incidents built up on this foundation (incidents at which we will not look too closely here, for fear of spoiling the interest of the story) resolve into the conscientious resignation of his place by the Warden, and into the marriage of the active local reformer to the good clergyman's daughter: said reformer, be it understood by the ladies, having most uxoriously and properly abandoned all assaults against the administration of the charity, so far as he was personally concerned, at the request of his bride elect. Here, assuredly, is a new and an excellent subject for a novel—a subject which Mr. Trollope has, in some respects, treated very cleverly. The character of the Warden is delightfully drawn, with a delicacy and truth to nature which deserves the highest praise. Equally good in their way are the feeble old Bishop, his trucu-

36

lent and intensely clerical son, who has married the Warden's eldest daughter, and the old men who live on the mismanaged funds of the charity. The defective part of the book is the conclusion, which seems to us careless and unsatisfactory—as if the author had got tired of his subject before he had done with it. The passing introduction too of living authors, under farcically fictitious names, for the sake of criticizing their books is a mistake—Mr. Trollope is far too clever a man, and has far too acute and discriminating an eye for character to descend success-fully to such low literary work as that. We will support our better opinion of him by giving the reader a specimen of his powers, drawn from one of the best passages in his book. We quote the scene in which the truculent son-in-law of the amiable Warden tries to weaken the effect of the local Reformer's exposures, by making a highly conserva-tive speech to the Bedesmen of the mismanaged charity. . . .

This certainly promises well for the author's future, if he gives us more books. Assuming and hoping that he has not written his last novel yet, we will venture to point out to his notice two defects in his manner as a writer which he may easily remedy, and which, he may take our word for it, are felt as serious faults, not by critics only, but by the general public as well. The first of the defects is, that Mr. Trollope speaks far too much in his own person in the course of his narrative. It is always the reader's business, never the author's, to apostrophize characters. The 'illusion of the scene' is invariably perilled, or lost altogether, when the writer harangues in his own person on the behavi-our of his characters, or gives us, with an intrusive 'I', his own experi-ences of the houses in which he describes those characters as living. This is a fault in Art; and, if Mr. Trollope should doubt it, we refer him to the stage as an illustration. Did he ever see a great comedian talk to the audience over the footlights—except perhaps when a writer of bur-lesques forced him to forget what was due to his Art? On the other hand, does not a Clown in a pantomime—who has nothing whatever to do with Art, in any high sense of the word—always talk to the audience? This is a rough illustration; but it will do to express what we mean.

The second defect of manner which we have noticed in Mr. Trollope is a want of thorough earnestness in the treatment of the more serious passages of his story. The mocking tone is well enough where the clerical aristocracy, and the abuses on which they live, form the subject for treatment. But where the main interest touches on the domain of real feeling—as in the chapter which illustrates the filial affection of the Warden's daughter, and the struggle between love and duty in the heart of her reforming lover—it is vitally important to the true effect of the scene on the reader, that the author should at least appear to feel sincerely with his characters. This Mr. Trollope, in the case of the young lady especially, seems to avoid. He exposes the womanly weakness of some of her motives with an easy satirical pleasantry which convinces us that he was himself not in the least affected by his love scene while he was writing it. There are certain maxims in Horace's *Art of Poetry* (to refer to a classical example, this time) which will remain great critical truths to the end of the world. Mr. Trollope must know the maxims to which we refer very well, and he cannot do better than apply them to himself the next time he gives us a novel. *The Warden* abundantly shows that he has powers far above the average as a writer of fiction.

5. Unsigned notice, *Eclectic Review*

March 1855, n.s. ix. 359–61

There is considerable talent displayed in this volume. It is visible in the delineation of character rather than in the construction of the plot. The latter is meagre and unsatisfactory, wanting a moral, and failing to satisfy reasonable expectation; but the former is spirited and clever, frequently effecting by a few bold touches what a mere elaborate description might fail to accomplish. . . . We shall not detail the incidents of the narrative. Those who wish to learn them will consult the volume itself. It is enough to say that in the sketch of the Bishop of Barchester and of his son, Dr. Grantly, as also in that of the feeble-minded but conscientious warden, much descriptive power is evinced. There is, however, one defect in the volume, which, in our judgment, mars the whole. A *moral* is wanting. To say nothing of the fact—in itself significant—that the views of the author on the subject of ecclesiastical revenue are not apparent, there is no fitting end attained by all which is done. The only result of the measures adopted by John Bold is to unsettle everything, and to make all parties miserable. The bishop, the dean, the warden, the bedesmen, John Bold himself, and the queen of his idolatry, are all perplexed and rendered wretched. The impression left, so far as it assumes any definite form, is that of regret at the affairs of the hospital having been brought into question. The facts of the case are sufficiently indicative of the inequitable arrangement maintained. But there is no indication of the better things that might have been done with the property bequeathed. Everything is left in disorder and ruin, as though the design of the writer was to teach the folly of attempting to rectify abuses which have grown up under our charitable trusts. It would have been a better, a wiser, and certainly a more useful course, to have shown how such funds might have administered to the comfort and well-being of a much larger number of aged men.

BARCHESTER TOWERS

1857

Trollope received his first adverse critique of this novel from the publisher's reader, but he wisely refused to follow many of this critic's suggestions:

> In the writing of *Barchester Towers* I took great delight. The bishop and Mrs. Proudie were very real to me, as were also the troubles of the archdeacon and the loves of Mr. Slope. When it was done, Mr. W. Longman required that it should be subjected to his reader; and he returned the MS. to me, with a most laborious and voluminous criticism,—coming from whom I never knew. This was accompanied by an offer to print the novel on the half-profit system, with a payment of £100 in advance out of my half-profits,—on condition that I would comply with the suggestions made by his critic. One of these suggestions required that I should cut the novel down to two volumes. In my reply, I went through the criticisms, rejecting one and accepting another, almost alternately, but declaring at last that no consideration should induce me to put out a third of my work. I am at a loss to know how such a task could be performed. I could burn the MS., no doubt, and write another book on the same story; but how two words out of six are to be withdrawn from a written novel, I cannot conceive. I believe such tasks have been attempted—perhaps performed; but I refused to make even the attempt. Mr. Longman was too gracious to insist on his critic's terms; and the book was published, certainly none the worse, and I do not think much the better, for the care that had been taken with it.
>
> The work succeeded just as *The Warden* had succeeded. It achieved no great reputation, but it was one of the novels which novel readers were called upon to read. Perhaps I may be assuming upon myself more than I have a right to do in saying now that *Barchester Towers* has become one of those novels which do not die quite at once, which live and are read for perhaps a quarter of a century; but if that be so, its life has been so far prolonged by the vitality of some of its younger brothers. *Barchester Towers* would hardly be so well known as it is had there been no *Framley Parsonage* and no *Last Chronicle of Barset* (*Autobiography*, pp. 87–8).

6. Unsigned notice, *Examiner*

16 May 1857, p. 308

Mr. Anthony Trollope has found more to tell of his friend, the gentle Warden of Hiram's Hospital at Barchester, and of the various members of the Warden's family. . . . The new story is so far complete in itself, that acquaintance with or recollection of its predecessor, though desirable, is not at all essential. The former tale was good, but this is better. In *The Warden* there were certain characters developed carefully, and their creator, by the time the book was ended, had made the best of them real to his own mind. In *Barchester Towers* we begin with them as real. They speak for themselves, and make themselves known promptly to the stranger without need of formal introduction. The story, however, is quite new, and most of the characters are new, beginning with the new Bishop of Barchester, whose palace is the centre of the plot. . . .

We have thus indicated what is the subject of Mr. Trollope's novel of *Barchester Towers*, but we should add that it does not depend only on story for its interest; the careful writing, the good humour with a tendency often to be Shandean in its expression, and the sense and right feeling with which the way is threaded among questions of high church and low church, are very noticeable, and secure for it unquestionable rank among the few really well-written tales that every season furnishes.

7. Unsigned review, *Spectator*

16 May 1857, xxx. 525–6

Much of the review is taken up by a long quotation from the scene in which Obadiah Slope proposes to Eleanor Bold.

Mr. Trollope's new fiction of *Barchester Towers* is a species of continuation of 'The Warden,' with greater variety of persons and interests, and a little more of novel story. That, however, is not much, and mainly consists in the marriage of Eleanor Bold née Harding, now a widow. The larger part, and perhaps the greater interest of the book, turns upon clerical characters and clerical ideas and doings, respecting which Low Church comes in for some hard hits; for as the romantic action consists in the marriage of Eleanor, so the religious action involves the struggles, exposure, and defeat of the new Bishop of Barchester's Low Church chaplain, the Reverend Mr. Slope. This worthy is not exactly painted with anger, for indignation is not Mr. Trollope's satiric vein; but the pen that delineates him is ever dipped in gall. . . .

In a technical sense, there is greater variety in *Barchester Towers* than in 'The Warden,' and consequently more of the novel. From this very extension and complexity it is scarcely so complete or satisfactory a book. The first work was obviously a satire, in which caricature is allowable provided the features of the person or the points of the case are markedly presented. This licence does not extend to the more regular novel, and Mr. Trollope has a peculiarity that lessens his power in this direction. His characters are frequently rather abstractions of qualities than actual persons. They are rather the *made* results of skill and thought than the spontaneous productions of genius operating instinctively. There is some exaggeration, too, in other directions than mere satire. All religious parties are represented—High Church, Low Church, and their varieties; there is also an easy-going divine without any religion, with two daughters—one only bad in the usual worldly way of selfishness, but the other, Signora Neroni, separated from a bad Italian husband, is daringly philosophical and desperately wicked. Poor Slope is drawn by her arts into equivocal positions even while pursuing Mrs. Bold and her thousand a year. Here is the beginning and end of his proposal in that quarter. . . .

8. Unsigned review, *Leader*

23 May 1857, p. 497

The Warden was a remarkable book; *Barchester Towers* is still more remarkable. The one, indeed, is a development of the other. In the former, the interest was in connexion with a charitable trust, the warden of which enjoyed his comparative sinecure in peace of conscience until an article in the *Jupiter* almost persuaded him that he had been for years engaged in robbing the poor; in the latter, the texture is not so simple. There is more story, more action, less concentration; the characters are more abstract, the incidents more diversified. First in bad eminence is Mr. Slope, the Low Church chaplain of Bishop Proudie. He is a large-handed, large-footed, broad-chested, wide-shouldered Evangelical; his hair is red and lank; his complexion is that of questionable beef; his forehead shines unpleasantly; from his immense mouth, between his thin, bloodless lips, and under his spongy, porous nose, he pours forth divine anger against high-pitched roofs, full-breasted black silk waistcoats, prayer-books printed in red letters, and other Puseyisms. This pillar of the Low Church stands confronted by Dr. Grantly, son of that mild-eyed bishop whom we knew in *The Warden*; but he has [for] long an ally in Mrs. Proudie, wife of a wretched bishop, who at the last, however, is the mortal enemy of Slope. Slope's projects fill a large part of the novel, and it may appear surprising that, out of materials so unpromising, Mr. Trollope should have elicited so much that is interesting. But the book is not so pleasing as it is powerful; we may object to the unequal and prejudiced distribution of satire, yet the astonishing energy with which the author writes, the sharpness and concision of his style, the light, unlaboured scatterings of allusion, the points that strike in all directions against the farces and follies of our ecclesiastical civilization, more than atone for all that is unfair, and the little that is repulsive, in the three volumes. In contrast with the red-headed chaplain, bony, florid, redundant in joint and sinew, attitudines [*sic*] Madeline Vesey Neroni, daughter of Dr. Stanhope, but wife of an infamous Italian, by whom she had been deserted. This beauty, crippled by violence, but retaining a perfect nose, mouth, chin, and bust, resolves never more to be seen, except upon a couch, and is carried like a goddess from saloon

43

to saloon. She stamps her name under a gold coronet on a gilt bordered card, and, crowned with some mystery and endless grace, is enthroned upon a sofa in the episcopal palace while a reception is at its height. A white velvet robe, white lace worked with pearls across her bosom and round the armlets, a band of red velvet across her brow, a crimson silk mantle flowing from her waist downwards, form the attire of this half-northern, half-southern Juno, by whom Obadiah Slope is entangled in an impure passion. The contrasts between them are excellently drawn: 'Her hand in his looked like a rose among carrots, and when he kissed it he looked as a cow might do on finding such a flower among her food.' Madeline Neroni, however, is not the only idol of Obadiah, who worships also Eleanor Bold, daughter of the ex-warden, whom he approaches less reverentially, and who replies to him not with the language of Roman eyes, but with the palm of a matronly English hand. Without going further, or sketching the outline of Mr. Trollope's story, we cannot but describe it as uncommonly graphic and clever; it is a book to rouse the reader, and, if it does not charm him, he will, at all events, be cordially amused.

9. Unsigned notice, *Athenaeum*

30 May 1857, pp. 689–90

Probably by H. F. Chorley (see headnote to No. 3). A four-column review, over half of which is occupied by an extended quotation from 'the passionate interview between Mr. Slope and Signora Neroni'.

Entering the episcopal palace of Barchester we find, at once, that 'The Warden' was an uncompleted story. Mr. Harding is again upon the stage, with Eleanor, Tom Towers, and the *Jupiter*. There is, however, a new bishop of the diocese, Dr. Proudie, successor of Dr. Grantly, with Mrs. Proudie, of evangelical ambition, supplemented by a loose-jointed Low-church chaplain, Obadiah Slope. But we again make acquaintance with the loud, clear-voiced, overbearing Archdeacon, the tyrant of his father and father-in-law, who has a theory about oblong dining-tables, and sets down any obnoxious brother as a 'beast.' Thus, Mr. Trollope has not to contend against the difficulty of interesting us, at the outset, in his personages or in his narrative; we are by no means strangers in Barchester; but he has, perhaps, to meet a worse difficulty,—that of prolonging successfully the interest of a tale which seemed some time ago to have been brought to a natural conclusion. Yet we doubt whether 'Barchester Towers' is not a more satisfactory book than 'The Warden': it is certainly more dramatic in its construction; the characters are more varied; an infusion of romance gives lightness and brightness to the ecclesiastical picture. It may still be said, indeed, that Mr. Trollope has a happier art of drawing sketches from life, and striking off pungent sayings hot and vivid upon the page, than of elaborating the action of a novel: nevertheless, the incidents that lead up to the marriage of Eleanor, if to some extent conventional, are yet contrived with skill, and will engage the sympathies of other readers than those who appreciate the excitement kindled in a cloistered city whenever a bishopric or deanery is vacant. Parallel with the many wooings and one love of the youthful widow moves the tearful tragedy of Obadiah Slope,—tragic in all but its consummation, for the oily Obadiah—beaten, thwarted, slapped in the face, confuted, confounded, detected in the act of kissing a married lady's white hands, discarded by his querulous patroness, and driven with shame from the Eden of virtual episcopacy—is comforted at last, contracts an offensive and defensive alliance, till death them do part, with the opulent relic of a sugar-refiner, (including a house in Baker Street,) mounts a metropolitan pulpit, and ripens in the golden warmth of patronage until the soul of sweetness, enriched within him, suffuses his plump rotundity, and he ages, and mellows, and excites the envy of the irreligious and the poor. This reverend Slope is the Low Church personified, and it is Mr. Trollope's pleasure to mock his red hair, large hands, weazel eye, and sardonic intonations. Perhaps some of this sarcastic finish is unfairly applied; but we are to take 'Barchester Towers' for what it is—a satire on men and opinions in a certain corner of the *ecclesia*; and if Mr. Trollope makes Low Church ridiculous he does not make High Church sublime. . . .

By far the larger proportions of 'Barchester Towers' is ecclesiastical in its interest; but we have quoted that which will show that Mr. Trollope is not occupied only with the dialogues and dealings of Church men or Church matters. It should be added that Tom Towers, oracle of the *Jupiter*, is an ally of Obadiah Slope, and thunders in his behalf in vain.

10. Unsigned notice, *Saturday Review*

30 May 1857, iii. 503–4

Much of this long review is taken up with a perfunctory retelling of the story, interspersed with quotations of some length, in all of which Obadiah Slope figures.

Barchester Towers is a very clever book. Indeed it is, if anything, too clever, and the whole story is rather too much a series of brilliant but disjointed sketches. It is a continuation of Mr. Trollope's former story, the *Warden*, and is written in the same vein, but with more power and finish. The interest chiefly turns on the fortunes of a chaplain who is in attendance on a new bishop appointed to preside over Barchester. He is of the oily school, and governs through the devotion of female admirers, and by his own consummate impudence. Naturally he stirs the wrath of the archdeacon, whom readers of the *Warden* will remember to have played so conspicuous a part in that tale. The archdeacon is furious at this interloper, and wages deadly war against him. To oppose him, he brings down from Oxford a noted adherent of the tenets most directly conflicting with those of his Exeter Hall enemy. Then comes the tug of war; for not only are the combatants at the opposite poles of English theology, but they are rivals in love, and excellently is the war described. Every chapter is full of fresh amusement; and although we know that poetical justice is sure ultimately to fall heavily on the chaplain, for a long time he has it all his own way, and treads on the necks of his foes. Such a conflict is a hard matter to describe. It is necessary to make it lively, and yet real—to give characteristic touches, and yet escape vulgarity—to handle theological disputes without bitterness, injustice, or profanity. Considering the dangers he runs, Mr. Trollope's success is wonderfully great. The theologians, unlike most theologians in novels, are thoroughly human, and retain the mixed nature of ordinary men; and, what is more, they are described impartially. The author is not a party writer, trying to run down the wrong party by painting it all black and the right party all white. He sees and paints the follies of

47

either extreme. Then, again, he has the merit of avoiding the excess of exaggeration. He possesses an especial talent for drawing what may be called the second-class of good people—characters not noble, superior or perfect, after the standard of human perfection, but still good and honest, with a fundamental basis of sincerity, kindliness, and religious principle, yet with a considerable proneness to temptation, and a strong consciousness that they live, and like to live, in a struggling, party-giving, comfort-seeking world. Such people are so common, and form so very large a proportion of the betterish and more respectable classes that it requires a keen perception of the ludicrous, and some power of satire, to give distinctness to the types taken from their ranks by the novelist. Mr. Trollope manages to do this admirably; and though his pudding may have the fault of being all plums, yet we cannot deny it is excellent eating.

11. Unsigned notice, *Eclectic Review*

July 1857, n.s. ii. 54–9

The critic in this strenuously Nonconformist organ devotes half
his review to Trollope's description of the experiments in religion
and dalliance of Bertie Stanhope, finding much significance,
obviously, in the fact that Bertie is the son of an Anglican clergyman.

Surely such a book never came before into the hands of a Nonconformist reviewer, uninitiated into the mysteries of bishop's palace and
cathedral close. The Book is full of clergymen. . . . The first chapter
is about the mortal illness of a bishop. The archdeacon watches anxiously by his bed-side, with hope in his heart of winning the mitre, but
wondering whether death will come before a friendly ministry resigns,
and hostile politicians, from whom he can hope nothing, inherit their
patronage and power. The good old man should have died a few hours
sooner, and the hopes which ended in bitter disappointment might have
been realized. But alas! instead of the gentlemanly aristocratic archdeacon, there succeeds to the vacant see a man well known by his semi-
political, semi-ecclesiastical labours on sundry commissions appointed
to inquire into the revenues of cathedral chapters, into the working of
the Irish education scheme; into the *regium donum* and Maynooth; a
clergyman who served the Whigs when in opposition; and, wonderful
to say, was not forgotten by them when they came into office; with no
faith in the High Church principles which reigned supreme at Barchester; and with a wife who petted and patronized a sleek, vulgar,
ambitious, evangelical preacher. . . . The story is told with a flowing
ease which is very captivating. The characters are vigorously conceived,
and artistically grouped. Mr. Trollope has achieved a decided success.
But we would fain hope that the book, clever as it is, fails to do justice
to the dignitaries and clergy of the Establishment.

12. Unsigned notice, *The Times*

13 August 1857, p. 5

Trollope in his *Autobiography* (pp. 83–4) remembered this review across nearly twenty years as having dealt with his two novels 'in terms very pleasant to the author'. He defended himself, however, against the reviewer's intimation that he had trafficked morbidly in personalities. He had, he said, created a journalist as he had also created an archdeacon. Living in Ireland at that time, he had 'not even heard the name of any gentleman connected with *The Times* newspaper, and could not have intended to represent any individual by Tom Towers'.

To be compared to G. W. Reynolds (as Trollope is at the close of the notice) was, indeed, not flattering. Reynolds's *Mysteries of the Court of London* was a sensation novel published in penny numbers over a span of seven years ending in December 1855. There was by then enough to fill eight royal octavo volumes. Reynolds specialized in 'the vulgar sensational and exciting topics of love, seduction, persecution, and moral guilt'.—'Mischievous Literature', *The Bookseller* (July 1868), xi. 447–8.

As the first sentences intimate, *The Times* review deals as well with another novel and novelist—Mrs. Catherine Gore's *The Two Aristocracies* (1857).

From the innumerable novels which annually invade our English litera ture as the swallows pervade our English summer, to catch at folly as i flies, we select two, which are remarkable not only for the exhibition o much power, but also for the utter absence of pretension. It is the vice o an immense number of fictions that they are novels only in form; i spirit they are sermons, they are political pamphlets, they are philoso phical inquiries, they are books of elegant extracts, they are guides t French conversation, they are complete letter-writers—anything bu novels. . . . It is a pleasure to meet with storytellers who write becaus they have something to say and because they are anxious to tell it, wh take our ordinary English life such as they find it, and pour out pleasant gossip abounding in incident and not in mere dialogue. . . . In Mr. Trollope's novel we are presented with a most amusing picture of clerical life in a cathedral town,—a life that is as distinct from our ordinary existence as the life of a strict Jew is in the midst of our London riot.

In the present novel, which, although complete in itself, is a continuation of a previous fiction, entitled *The Warden*, there is scarcely an individual who is not either a parson or a parson's wife; all the ideas are ecclesiastical, the dresses are canonical, and the conversations have a rubrical tinge. Yet the subject is so fresh and the representation so vivid, that the contracted limits of the story are forgotten, and we are left to wonder that more has not long ago been made of such promising materials. The story itself is a mere nothing. The Bishop of Barchester dies, and a successor is appointed in the person of Dr. Proudie; the dean also dies shortly afterwards, and the question is who shall be the new dean. The new bishop is a mild Whig, with very moderate opinions, who would work well with almost any man, but unfortunately he is not his own master, and has not a word to say in the regulation of his own diocess. He is governed by his wife; his wife is governed by the bishop's chaplain, Mr. Slope, a very Low Churchman; and Mr. Slope is governed by his ambition. Through the interference of these good people arise all the complication of the story and all the developments of character. Perhaps the scenes between the bishop and Mrs. Proudie are a little overdrawn, but, although highly coloured, they are not the less amusing delineations of human misery, as experienced by a man who permits himself not only to be henpecked in his private relations, but also to be in his public capacity under female domination. The poor bishop is not only assailed by his wife in the privacy of his dressing-room, he cannot receive a visitor without her permission. When he is asked a question she replies for him; he cannot make an appointment in his diocess without her consent, and it is a fearful act of rebellion when he goes to visit the Archbishop of Canterbury unaccompanied by her. Mr. Slope is a still greater tyrant, and so exercises his authority that he not only arouses the opposition of the whole chapterhouse, but ultimately provokes the jealousy of Mrs. Proudie, who drives him from the diocess in disgrace, after he has made himself ridiculous to everybody by his daring attempts to perpetrate a wealthy marriage. One of the most amusing scenes in these volumes is that in which he appears making love to a young widow . . . [The scene is quoted at length.]

As Mrs. Proudie and Mr. Slope furnish the comedy of the novel, Dr. Grantley, the Archdeacon, and his friends furnish the clerical ideal, good sober people, well-educated, moderate in opinion, and exceedingly correct in all social observances. Fortune favours them in the end; Mrs. Proudie is resisted, Mr. Slope is discomfited, a brother-in-law of the Archdeacon's is appointed dean, and after a few months of turmoil the sedate opinions and time-honoured usages that prevailed in the days of the old bishop regain their influence under the benignant sway of the new one. The whole life thus revealed is curious and interesting, in spite of a tediousness of explanation which seems to be natural to the author as well as to his theme; and it may be regarded as not unreal, in spite of a tendency to caricature which Mr. Trollope continually displays, and especially when he has to deal with subjects out of the clerical sphere. The remarks which in this vein he has made on the influence exerted by the conductors of the newspaper press on public appointments are too insignificant to be seriously criticized; yet, as this is the second clerical novel published within a very short period (the other is the *Perversion* of the Rev. W. Conybeare) in which an account of newspaper management is given by persons who know absolutely nothing about it, we beg to suggest that if any one hereafter chooses to write on the subject he will first of all study it and have the charity to admit that among the conductors and the writers of the public press it is possible to find men who are not only men of talent, but also men of honour and of conscience. Mr. Conybeare has given some account of a widely circulated daily paper which he calls 'The Vane,' and Mr. Trollope has made some reference to a similar paper which he calls 'The Jupiter.' We regret to say of novelists who are not without ability, and who lay claim to an extraordinary amount of good sense and good taste, that these sketches for their value, for their accuracy, and for the motive which led to their being executed (viz., a desire of pandering to a very morbid curiosity) deserve to be placed on a level with Mr. G. W. Reynolds's description of the *Mysteries of the Court of London.*

13. Unsigned notice, *Westminster Review*

October 1857, lxviii. 594–6

A quarterly reviewer of novels has frequently to address his readers when the works under consideration have been perused and their contents distributed to the winds in newspaper extracts. It is seldom his part to introduce the characters and unravel the plot. A novel like 'Barchester Towers,' for instance, is pretty sure to have gone the round of the circulating library before anything we may have to say touching its merits will be heard; and we can hardly expect to assist in extending its circulation in its present form, when we state our opinion of it as decidedly the cleverest novel of the season, and one of the most masculine delineations of modern life in a special class of society that we have seen for many a day. Those who have read its dashing predecessor, 'The Warden,' will be quite up to the style and the story, which are both continued vigorously in 'Barchester Towers,' and with renewed interest. We recommend novel readers, who have not yet made acquaintance with Mr. Trollope, to get the two books immediately. As they are likely to be few, and it is our duty to occupy ourselves with the majority, we shall speak of 'Barchester Towers' as a work well known. Mr. Trollope has satisfactorily solved a problem in this production. He has, without resorting to politics, or setting out as a social reformer, given us a novel that men can enjoy, and a satire so cleverly interwoven with the story, that every incident and development renders it more pointed and telling. In general our modern prose satirists spread their canvas for a common tale, out of which they start when the occasion suits, to harangue, exhort, and scold the world in person. Mr. Trollope entrusts all this to the individuals of his story. The plot is as simple as the siege of Troy. We are sure that Mr. Slope cannot succeed, or that if he is allowed to, another three volumes will confound him. We are equally convinced that the Widow Bold will never surrender to him, or that if she should, he will have to repent it equally. Nevertheless, our appetite for the closing chapters does not languish. We are anxious for the widow, and long to get her havened out of her perilous widowhood in fast wedlock: man's great ambition to become a Bishop, and woman's wonderful art in ruling one, cannot fail to interest us exceedingly, and we hurry on without a halt to the overthrow of Slope and the rare act of self-immolation whereby the Rev. Mr. Harding refuses a deanery, value a considerable sum per annum, and bestows it on his son-in-law. The story is original in books, but common in the land: so is the villain. Mr. Slope is possessed of extraordinary powers. He cannot move without inspiring nausea even in the female bosom (for it is notorious how much the sex can bear); yet he contrives to make men jealous of him. We have all of us met somebody like Mr. Slope, and wished that, if he indeed could lay claim to the odour of sanctity, it were pleasanter to the poor human sense of smell. . . .

Mr. Trollope seems wanting in certain of the higher elements that make a great novelist. He does not exhibit much sway over the emotional part of our nature: though fairer readers may think that the pretty passages between Eleanor and her baby-boy show a capacity for melting woman's heart, at least. He is also a little too sketchy; the scenes are deficient in repose and richness: but let us cut short our complaints, thankful that we have a caustic and vigorous writer, who can draw men and women, and tell a story that men and women can read.

THE THREE CLERKS

1858

Trollope believed *The Three Clerks* was 'certainly the best novel I had as yet written'. The *Autobiography* (pp. 93–4) continues:

> The plot is not so good as that of the *Macdermots*; nor are there any characters in the book equal to those of Mrs. Proudie and the Warden; but the work has a more continued interest, and contains the first well-described love-scene that I ever wrote. The passage in which Kate Woodward, thinking that she will die, tries to take leave of the lad she loves, still brings tears to my eyes when I read it. I had not the heart to kill her. I never could do that. And I do not doubt but that they are living happily together to this day.
>
> The lawyer Chaffanbrass made his first appearance in this novel, and I do not think that I have cause to be ashamed of him.

Though the title-page gives 1858 as the date of publication, the novel appeared late in 1857, and the bulk of the reviews came before the end of that year. One of the most notable critiques of *The Three Clerks*, however, is contained in a general discussion of Trollope's novels in *The Times* for 23 May 1859—No. 38, below.

14. Unsigned notice, *Saturday Review*

5 December 1857, iv. 517–18

Trollope in his next novel was to break narrative to reply banteringly to this critic's complaints at his mishandling of legal matters (see Introduction, VII).

A year ago, those persons who knew that Mr. Trollope was the author of the *Warden* could have been sure of nothing more than that he had a considerable gift for smart writing, and some facility in imitating salient peculiarities of style. In the spring of this year, Mr. Trollope published *Barchester Towers*, and this work at once raised him into a very considerable position among the novelists of the present day. The writing was smart, but it was more than smart. It was full of the fruits of keen observation, and showed an appreciation of the more subtle as well as the coarser characteristics of certain classes of persons. And it also disclosed that Mr. Trollope had powers of a different kind from those which make writing smart and descriptions lively. It evinced a remarkable insight into the workings of minds of an order neither very high nor very low, and especially of the minds of women. The Signora and Eleanor were both very masterly sketches, and their conduct was natural and yet not obvious. Mr. Trollope has followed up his success with a new novel called *The Three Clerks*, which bears many marks of haste, and is fuller of faults than might have been expected from a writer who must be conscious that he has a real reputation within his grasp. With all its faults, however, it is a work rich in promise. It contains plenty of smart writing, but it also contains scenes from family life more true, more pathetic, and more skilfully sustained than any which can be found except in the writings of novelists whose fame is no longer doubtful. There is nothing equal to Colonel Newcome in the book, but there are passages which promise that, if Mr. Trollope will but do himself justice, he may delineate characters that will almost rival that delicate and touching creation of Mr. Thackeray's genius.

The field for liveliness, pleasantry, and ridicule which Mr. Trollope has twice found in the peculiarities of ecclesiastical circles is now furnished by the system of the Civil Service. Of the Three Clerks, two are in the 'Weights and Measures,' and one in the 'Internal Navigation' office. Mr. Trollope evidently knows the service well, and he has collected sufficient of the traits of officials and official life into his picture to make the effect striking. . . .

But it is on the family, not the official, pictures that the reputation of the novel will be chiefly founded. The Three Clerks are provided with centres of their affections by the happy circumstance of a most charming Mrs. Woodward, of Hampton Court, having three charming daughters. These girls are like real girls. They have the strong and the weak points of young women in real life. They love their lovers, and hate their lovers' enemies, and stick by the lovers themselves, both before and after marriage, with a constancy which neither pique, nor poverty, nor disgrace can shake. The eldest and the youngest especially are capital—neither too good nor too bad, and with more freshness and life about them than is to be seen in the heroines of one novel out of a

undred. It is because the Miss Woodwards adorn its pages that we
hink *The Three Clerks* a step in advance of Mr. Trollope's earlier works.
These young ladies give ground for the hope that when experience and
ncreasing good taste shall have toned down the sharpness of the author's
marter style, he will unite the qualities which lie at the bottom of his
atirical power with a matured knowledge of the beauties of character,
nd a skill in tracing the finer webs of human action. No one who could
ave conceived the very touching history of the love of Katie, the
youngest Miss Woodward, and who at the same time has the rougher
aculties which shine through the sketches of the Civil Service, need
lespair of the highest kind of success in fiction.

But *The Three Clerks* is full of faults. All smart story-telling, where
he continuity of the narrative is broken by the insertion of a series of
unconnected pictures of men and women more or less ridiculous, must
necessarily be imperfect. But this book has faults more peculiarly its
own. Subjects are introduced into it which should find no place in a
novel. One whole long chapter is a mere pamphlet on the merits and
demerits of the Civil Service, in which the author advocates the claims
of a class of persons who have been, he thinks, very hardly used, and
who, he insists, ought to have a better opening to fame and wealth
provided for them than they have at present. This may be a right or
wrong view of a political question, but it certainly is not in its right
place when introduced into a story. . . .

In many points the book bears traces of rapid writing, which must
go greatly against it. There is a legal portion of the story, and law is a
pitfall from which few novelists can escape uninjured. The most successful, clever, and gifted of the Three Clerks is made trustee to a young
ady on her marriage. He sells a portion of the fund settled on her, and
uses it to gamble in the share-market. He is rather alarmed, however,
by hearing of the Fraudulent Trustee Act of last session, which was
brought forward about the time of his misconduct. And well he might
be; for his villany was detected, and so swift is the Nemesis of guilt in
omances, that he was tried, convicted, and sentenced in a most edifying
peech from Lord Campbell, all before the Act received the Royal
ssent. On the trial it came out that he had committed the fraud at the
nstigation of a still deeper villain, who was subpœnaed as a witness for
he defence. This witness naturally hesitated when he found that the
object of the prisoner's counsel was to fasten the guilt on him, and gave
his answers with great reluctance. Whereupon the prisoner's counsel
hreatened that if he did not speak out, he should at once be placed in

the dock, and the prisoner would mount into the witness-box, and then and there get him convicted, as an episode in the prisoner's own trial. Why do not novelists consult some legal friend before they write about law? Is it impossible to find a barrister who has a hobby for criminal law, and also a hobby for criticizing novels, and who would bring his skill in both lines to bear upon the correction of a layman mistakes? We think that such a man might be found, and he would be invaluable to all fiction writers who evolve descriptions of English trials out of the depths of their consciousness, and square them to meet the principles of eternal justice. The story then goes on to say, with wild disregard of dates, that the clerk was sentenced to six month imprisonment, which were over next February, and that he then went to Australia, whence, in 1860, his wife wrote a letter describing how their boy—who could not even then have been more than four years old—was a noble fellow, and ran with his satchel on his back to a day-school These are small errors, but Mr. Trollope ought to think too highly of his capabilities to permit himself to fall into them. If he will but wait write seldom and slowly, and curb his tendency to work up isolate sketches at the expense of the main story, he has the path clear before him—he can make himself such a name as will not easily be forgotten

15. Unsigned review, *Spectator*

12 December 1857, xxx. 1300–1

In his new novel of *The Three Clerks*, Mr. Trollope exhibits his wonted skill in seizing upon prominent features of the passing time that admit of pointed satirical embodiment. Reform in the Civil Service—the inferior character and social goings-on of many Public Office clerks—the late exposures of fraudulent speculators and jobbing Members of Parliament —the fatal effects of ill-regulated ambition aiming at lofty positions without duly considering the means—are all pressed into the writer's service. . . .

As a novel, *The Three Clerks* is an improvement upon the Barchester doings narrated in Mr. Trollope's two former publications. There is more of story, with stronger individual interest, as well as greater depth. The Three Clerks are connected with a widow lady and her three daughters; and the lovers are crossed in various ways. The great moral of the book, and indeed its attraction, turns upon Alaric Tudor, one of the three clerks. He is the type of the successful man of the world, with strong will, animal spirits, not over-conscientious when tempted by advantages, and, though agreeable, seemingly honourable, and more than goodnatured, yet thoroughly selfish at bottom. He marries Gertrude Woodward, knowing that his friend Norman was deeply attached to her, and that he had himself excited an affection in her sister Linda. By his energy and worldly tact he passes his friend Norman in his official career; and, as already intimated, lives beyond his income, in order to impose upon the world and forward his own advancement by that imposition. He engages in stockjobbing affairs, and permits his friend Scott to induce him to invest the trust-money in speculations, Undy's object being to get a part. Notwithstanding all this and other traits of selfishness, the more superficial and in a worldly sense attractive qualities are presented to the reader so fully as to cover the essential evil of his disposition. Mr. Trollope may say that in this he is true to nature; that were not this the case in reality, such men could never impose upon mankind as they do. But on this point arises a question, whether the reader is not to see a character from the beginning more completely than the dramatis personae. The terrible nature of his punishment, however, is well brought out, from the first moment of his awaking to the sense of his position, till dishonoured by exposure and sentence, he departs for Australia after his release from prison. . . .

We have dwelt upon the darker portion of the story; but there are many lighter scenes—sketches of the higher 'Civil Service' mind; 'fast' doings of the lower class; and glimpses of the cheap press in the *Daylight*. There is also Captain Cuttwater, a retired naval officer of the old school, who has countless grievances against the Admiralty,—a very capital character. The graver portion of the book, however, forms the substance of the story, though it may not be the most entertaining to many. Probably it may be the most popular, for to appreciate Mr. Trollope requires an observation of public events and characters, which every one may not have given: possibly, too, the satire, though its subjects may be better known, is not so finished as in *The Warden*.

16. Unsigned review, *Examiner*

19 December 1857, pp. 803-4

Mr Anthony Trollope's *Three Clerks* is the best of the new novels. The author has left Barchester Cloisters, and now finds his way into the civil service, upon which he has ideas as strong as those he has expressed about ecclesiastical endowments. He does not contrive to get as picturesque material off the stools of the government offices, as he obtained from the precincts of the cathedral, but in his new novel the story told—apart from the social proposition treated—is unusually good, and the character-painting, which is excellent, has a more intimate relation to the tale than to the problem.

Mr. Anthony Trollope has had three genuine successes as a novelist.
The third, we think, is the most remarkable. In this new work the scene
of action is wider, the interest is more varied, the characters are drawn
from more general classes. The three clerks, whose histories are narrated,
belong to two government offices, and in a quiet family at Hampton
Court they find their counterparts—three graceful girls, of whom one
is proud in her passion, another capricious, another wild. Perhaps the
differences of their natures are more strongly marked than Mr. Trollope
intended. However, he now presents himself with a romance of modern
love, and subtly and delicately has he developed it, but without hanging
before his groups a gauze of theatrical unreality, pallidly glimmering
with moonshine. The spirit of the book is healthy, natural, vigorous.
Mr. Trollope has studied the world, and without being wholly artist or
philosopher, or poet, infuses philosophy into his art and imagination
into his philosophy, so as to render the novel what a novel should be.
Neither *The Warden* nor *Barchester Towers* had prepared us for so much
that is tragic and touching as we find in *The Three Clerks*, contrasted
with many variations of humour, satire, and social criticism. All the
incidents belong to the present day; the terrors are those of Milbank,
not of Otranto; the agony of separation is that of a young wife whose
husband is about to start for the Old Bailey in a cab, and surrender upon
recognizances to take his trial for a breach of trust. All this part of the
novel is strangely true to life, and very much do we admire Mr.
Trollope's treatment of these conspicuous aspects of our times. Without
disclosing too much of the plot, we will add that the conclusion of the
story is adroit and satisfactory, the 'everlasting fitness of things' being
held in view, without the introduction of any repulsive catastrophe.
Yet by many readers the principal charm of these volumes will be
attributed to their rapid and sparkling flow of ironical portraiture—
toned down, as the finest irony invariably is, by interludes of wise and
wholesome seriousness. The Civil Service, we should say, will allow
little rest to the circulating librarians until its clerks of all grades have
glanced into the mirror set in a paper frame by Mr. Anthony Trollope.
The Three Clerks is a novel of uncommon and peculiar merit.

18. Unsigned review, *Athenaeum*

26 December 1857, p. 1621

The story of 'The Three Clerks' has nothing like a consecutive plot; it is as rambling and straggling in its construction as a story well can be, and there is no little of what actors call 'gag' to fill up the required space. Still the book is alive, and the reader will go through with it, digressions, irrelevancies and all. Of the three clerks whose lives and errors are here set forth, poor Charley is our favourite. Alaric, the defaulter, has too many prototypes in every day's newspaper; the gradual process by which the germs of worldliness and ambition choke his better nature, and the self-deception that leads him on from step to step till ruin overtakes him, is extremely well developed. Some of the scenes are very powerful: the one betwixt Alaric and his wife on the morning of the trial, and the interview betwixt Katie and Charlie during her illness, are as touching as any we ever read. Mr. Trollope does not succeed so well in long three-volume novels, where there is a larger space of canvas to be covered, as he does in shorter stories. Readers will, however, be more inclined to take the 'Three Clerks,' and be thankful for what they receive, than to be querulous about what is *not* provided for them.

19. Elizabeth Barrett Browning, letter

c. 1859

From Thomas Adolphus Trollope, *What I Remember* (1887), II. 188–9. A letter addressed to his wife from Elizabeth Barrett Browning 'written very shortly after the publication of my brother's novel called *The Three Clerks*'.

I return *The Three Clerks* with our true thanks and appreciation. W both quite agree with you in considering it the best of the three cleve novels before the public. My husband, who can seldom get a novel t hold him, has been held by all three, and by this the strongest. Also i has qualities which the others gave no sign of. For instance, I wa wrung to tears by the third volume. What a thoroughly *man's* book i is! I much admire it, only wishing away, with a vehemence whic proves the veracity of my general admiration, the contributions to th *Daily Delight*—may I dare to say it?

20. Thackeray, letter

28 October 1859

Letter to Trollope, quoted in Trollope's *Autobiography*, p. 117.

There was quite an excitement in my family one evening when Pater-familias, (who goes to sleep on a novel almost always when he tries it after dinner) came up-stairs into the drawing-room wide awake and calling for the second volume of *The Three Clerks*. I hope the *Cornhill Magazine* will have as pleasant a story. And the Chapmans, if they are the honest men I take them to be, I've no doubt have told you with what sincere liking your works have been read by yours very faithfully,

W. M. Thackeray.

21. Unsigned notice, *American Theological Review*

August 1860, ii. 553-4

We think this the best of this popular author's many works. It contain
a forcible illustration of the difference between good and evil principle
as the basis of character and life—virtue, respectability and final succes
the reward of the former, and short-lived prosperity and ultimate sham
and ruin the wages of the latter. The lessons it teaches are most timely
and we wish they were read and pondered by all our young men
'Alaric Tudor' is not a rare character in these days. The book is marred
however, by abundant profanity, for which there is no excuse. It is a
offensive to true taste as it is to morals. 'Captain Cuttwater' seem
introduced only to soil the pages with his oaths. A story that needs a
oath to spice or point it, had better not be told. The offence is s
serious a one, in our judgment, as to damage the book greatly.

DOCTOR THORNE

1858

Trollope, looking back on his career in the *Autobiography* (pp. 106–7), felt that *Doctor Thorne* had marked a decided falling-off from the quality of *The Three Clerks*, and placed it on a level with *The Bertrams*, the novel that was to follow it in another ten months. For many modern critics, *Doctor Thorne* is Trollope at his best and the other two are among his lesser works. The reviewers of Trollope's own time, as will be seen, saw no such sharp discrepancies among the three, though the public soon made *Doctor Thorne* its favourite.

'*Doctor Thorne* has, I believe, been the most popular book that I have written,—if I may take the sale as a proof of comparative popularity. *The Bertrams* has had quite an opposite fortune. I do not know that I have ever heard it well spoken of even by my friends, and I cannot remember that there is any character in it that has dwelt in the minds of novel-readers. I myself think that they are of about equal merit, but that neither of them is good. They fall away very much from *The Three Clerks*, both in pathos and humour. There is no personage in either of them comparable to Chaffanbrass the lawyer. The plot of *Doctor Thorne* is good, and I am led therefore to suppose that a good plot, —which, to my own feeling, is the most insignificant part of a tale,— is that which will most raise it or most condemn it in the public judgment. . . . You must provide a vehicle of some sort. That of *The Bertrams* was more than ordinarily bad; and as the book was relieved by no special character, it failed. Its failure never surprised me; but I have been surprised by the success of *Doctor Thorne*.'

22. Unsigned notice, *Examiner*

29 May 1858, p. 340

Mr. Trollope in his new story quits his old cathedral town only to pass into its county, and to make acquaintance with some of the county families. He invites us, not to Barchester, but into Barsetshire. Perhaps the county families are over-hardly dealt with, but there is a good deal of shrewd and pleasant malice in the great debates on questions of blood and treasure. The scenes of rivalry among country practitioners of medicine are certainly not overcharged, though the particular turns sometimes given to them are not exactly true to nature. There is more exaggeration also in the picture of the brandy-drinking man of the day, Roger Scatcherd, than belongs fairly to one of the main characters in the story, and his gin-drinking clerk is an extravagant abortion. These objections we suggest to a novelist who has taken already a high position in his art, and who is able to confirm a very genuine success. The quiet touches of satire blended with the careful character-painting in the *Warden* and *Barchester Towers* gave promise of a success more permanent than can be achieved by the more showy strokes of carica-ture, for which we hope that Mr. Trollope has not been emboldened to exchange them. There is plenty of the old grace and of the old sterling quality in *Doctor Thorne*; it is a novel that no sensible reader will con-found with the mass of manufactured fiction that is only meant to last a day. There is sense in it, humour in it, now and then a touch of pathos; it is interesting, and is written in good English. But at the same time there is sign in it of the beginning of an evil that some day will eat away all that is soundest in the author's credit if it be not promptly checked. We speak of Mr. Trollope as of one from whom the public has it knows not what—but surely much—to hope.

23. Unsigned review, *Leader*

29 May 1858, pp. 519–20

For Messieurs E. D. Forgues and Émile Montégut, mentioned at
the end of the review, see Introduction, notes 8 and 10.

We are heartily disposed to place the author of *Doctor Thorne* among
the extremely select few who shine out like a constellation among the
unnumbered lesser luminaries of the 'circulating' firmament. Indeed, we
are prepared to name him among the illustrious living writers of fiction
whom we are able to count off upon our fingers. Each of the works
that he has yet produced has been stamped with its own independent
and original characteristics; each has gained in strength on the preceding; each has been an advance towards a higher and more assured
excellence. In *The Warden*, in *Barchester Towers*, in *The Three Clerks*, he
has manifested a real inventive faculty and a real constructive ingenuity;
above all, a real insight into human character and into the complexities
of human motives. . . . Mr. Anthony Trollope's style is decidedly
improved; it was always masculine, vigorous, and free from any minc-
ing affectations and foreign fripperies, but it was often inelegant and
incorrect: in *Doctor Thorne* it has lost none of its vigour and clearness,
and it is less often marred by wilful negligence or coarseness. In
character-painting, however, the author of *The Warden* has more un-
equivocally gained strength. There is much less propensity to caricature
in *Doctor Thorne*: the handling is broad and powerful, but sure, and
under strong restraint; every touch tells, because every touch is the
result of thought and feeling subdued with rare technical skill. . . .
 Several of the constituents of modern English society are represented
with striking force and fidelity; the factitious aristocracy of birth and
wealth, the self-made aristocracy of brain and will, and the true aristocracy of simple faith and honest worth are contrasted in no forced,
conventional manner, and in no grudging or envious spirit. We are
not quite sure that in making Scatcherd (the type of the 'contractor'
class, a stonemason and self-made millionnaire) die of *delirium tremens*,

69

a confirmed drunkard, Mr. Trollope has not (for an excellent purpose, no doubt, and without malice prepense) traduced the noble and energetic pioneers of the rising democracy of labour in our age of steam. Perhaps he has not only desired to point the moral of intellect without culture, and of wealth without taste and leisure, but he has sentimentally avenged the hereditary mortgagers of old estates now fallen a prey to the new nobility of 'navvies.' Yet, why should the self-made millionnaire baronet's son, educated at Eton and Cambridge, die of *del. trem.* also? If his early death were not indispensable to the denouement, we should complain of this abuse of the bottle in fiction, and we hold the theory according to which Scatcherd is made to baptize his son *Louis Philippe* a satire in the wrong place. But old 'Lady Scatcherd' fully atones for husband and son: she is admirably sketched, and excites our love and compassion, as only truth and nature can. . . . By-the-by, we may here take the liberty to recommend M. E. Forgues, or M. E. Montégut, to take in hand the novels of this sturdy and healthy 'realist,' Mr. Anthony Trollope; they will find English society faithfully and powerfully pictured in his pages, and will be at no loss to extract the purpose which he has, unconsciously perhaps, but inevitably, impressed upon his creations.

24. Unsigned review, *Athenaeum*

5 June 1858, p. 719

There is genuine humour in 'Doctor Thorne,' not strained or am-
bitiously displayed, but arising from the natural play of the characters.
The characters are real creatures of human nature, flesh and blood,
vigorously and broadly drawn, but not caricatured,—they would be
likenesses if they were not types. The grand family at De Courcy
Castle, with their social motto, 'Rank has its drawbacks'—the grand
Countess, the goddess and presiding genius of the family—the minor
deities, Lady Amelia, Lady Margarhetta, and Lady Arabella, who had
been spared to preside over the Greshams—they are all excellent, and
their high mightiness, which somehow always bends to convenience,
is a vein of genuine comedy; they are shown bare to the very heart of
their small natures—their heartlessness, their meanness, their worldliness
are brought into daylight; it is not done contemptuously, but with a
shrewd good-nature that keeps the reader from being pained. It is this
genial quality which marks the ripeness of Mr. Trollope's faculties;
there is nothing acrid in the flavour of his pleasantry; with the touch of
nature which 'makes the whole world kin,' he makes us feel that even
De Courcy Castle is not cut off from our sympathies—we do not disown
the family, and that makes the secret of Mr. Trollope's excellence. Miss
Dunstable, the heiress of the 'ointment of Lebanon,' is charming, and
the letter she writes in reply to the proposal of the Honourable John is
delightful—and the reader feels good naturedly revenged for all the
impertinence and small maliciousness of the Castle. Mr. Moffat and
his wooing, and the fate that befell him, will not the reader find it all
written in the second volume of the chronicle?—and so we shall not
say more. Sir Roger Scatcherd, the railway baronet, is a study, and as
true to the life as the other characters, but he takes a deeper hold on
our sympathies; there is a pathetic, tragic interest about him which
moves to a pity deeper than tears. The interest is not worked up in
scenes, it pervades the whole history of the man. The death-bed, however, is equal in its way to any of the three death-beds in 'Clarissa
Harlowe.' Dr. Thorne is the good genius of everybody in the book,
and is repaid by being indispensable—whether loved or hated, nobody

71

can do without him. The reader, however, perhaps cares less for him than for some of the other characters. Frank Gresham, the lover of the heroine, might, we are quite willing to believe, have been a fine young fellow,—but to speak candidly, and 'not to put too fine a point on it,' we have known heroes much better worth being miserable about. A man worth all the tears he cost would have set about to earn his living earlier,—and if Miss Mary Thorne had seen him with *our* eyes she would have looked at some one else; but everybody knows that those things go by favour, and not by merit. The fault of 'Doctor Thorne' is, that it is too long. The love affairs of Frank and Mary drag,—the difficulties and objections which beset them are said and re-said till they become wearisome. Two volumes would have afforded 'ample room and verge enough' to detail, unravel, and defeat all the machinations of the adverse party. Few tales are strong enough to hold out for three volumes without showing symptoms of distress. Nevertheless, 'Doctor Thorne' is an excellent novel, and as such we commend it to our readers.

25. Unsigned review, *Spectator*

29 May 1858, xxxi. 577–8

A long but undistinguished review, much of it given to quoting the scene between Lady Scatcherd and Dr. Fillgrave.

n Mr. Trollope's first novel of 'The Warden' his satire took a wider yet a closer range than he has since attempted, embracing the law, the church, the press, especially the 'Thunderer' under the title of the Jupiter,' and several of what the author deemed the Reforming cants of the day. His story, however, was bald and purposeless, and constructed without regard to the commonest requirements of art, if, indeed, it could be said to have a structure. In 'Barchester Towers,' his satire was more limited, being mainly confined to Tractarianism, and High and Low Church; the Evangelicals, in their representative Mr. Slope, receiving no mercy at his hands. In 'The Three Clerks' the civil service and competitive examinations were the aim of the satire, while the late misappropriations of other people's money through ill-regulated ambition, or a mere wish to shine beyond one's sphere, were also exhibited. Upon the whole, however, contemporary weaknesses and passing events were scarcely handled with so much pith and pungency as in the two earlier fictions; but there was a completer story, and a greater novel-interest. In the book before us, *Dr. Thorne*, the satire or the hits at passing events are not perhaps so fully obvious, as in 'The Three Clerks'; though some may think they recognize traits in the great Whig noble the Duke of Omnium, and the great heiress Miss Dunstable; there is also the old subject of a contested election very well done, especially in the dinners and gatherings. The satire, however, is mainly directed against a rather worn matter—the formalities and jealousies of the medical profession; and one main source of the trouble consists in the pecuniary embarrassments of a country squire, caused by elections, hounds, and the expenses of a high-bred wife. There *is* a story, however, with characters not merely serving as vehicles for the author's fun or comments, but really interested in the events, and what

73

is more to the purpose, interesting the reader. It may be true that the object of the author as it appears in his work is of a questionable kind and that the main elements of the tale—family trouble arising from pecuniary embarrassment, love crossed by social ambition, and, as Mr. Trollope would say, social prejudice—have been exhibited before The elements, however, are well put together, and the story is narrated with that close observation of human manners, and of human nature as modified by human manners in this middle of the nineteenth century which form the author's distinguishing characteristic; while the writing has the smartness, point, and pungency that always impart an interest to Mr. Trollope's pages, not by mere style, but by the matter which that style displays.

26. Unsigned notice, *Saturday Review*

12 June 1858, v. 618–19

The author of this critique, as of the notice for *The Three Clerks*, was probably Sir Henry Maine. For this identification and for Trollope's bantering reply in *Doctor Thorne* to the *Saturday*'s advice regarding his faulty command of legal questions (a reply that receives attention in turn in the present notice), see Introduction, VII.

In one sense it is good news to the readers of novels that Mr. Trollope has given another proof of his fecundity. What he writes is sure to be very much above the average of the nourishment to which they are accustomed; but those who care for the interests of literature, and wish to see Mr. Trollope take the position to which he is unquestionably capable of rising, cannot but feel a considerable degree of uneasiness at the rapid multiplication of his progeny. A man must have a very long purse, and an extraordinary fund of philoprogenitiveness who would not feel a little cross if his fruitful vine were to plant three olive branches round about his table in the course of a single year. Nature prevents the material nursery from being stocked quite so fast as that; but Mr. Trollope's brain is so prolific that he will soon be the father of as many Minervas as would relieve the Muses and the Graces, too, from their functions. *Barchester Towers* soothed us in the dog-days of 1857; the law of the *Three Clerks* was criticized by at least one of the judges on the last winter circuit; and Dr. Thorne's eventful history filled its appointed three volumes before the end of May, 1858. We are very sorry to say that the results which might have been predicted are obviously following. Mr. Trollope is acquiring great mechanical skill in those parts of his art in which such skill can be acquired, but he is losing what constituted the value and the promise of his style. Here and there he is very clever indeed, and the story is better than most other novels, but it shows a diminution in the life and point which belonged to its author's first tales; and though it must certainly be rated above the *Three Clerks*

75

as a whole, the striking pieces are less striking. There is nothing in *Dr. Thorne* so tiresome as the history of Charley Tudor's first novel; but, on the other hand, there is nothing so good as the cross-examination of Undy Scott (highly irregular as it was in point of law), and nothing that can be for a moment compared to Mr. Slope and Archdeacon Grantley. . . .

The plot is obviously as slight as anything can be; but it affords opportunities for a great deal of description which no one but Mr. Trollope could have written, but which he with proper pains might have written much better. The two young ladies, Mary Thorne and Beatrice Gresham, are, we think, better drawn than any of his former female characters. There is nothing vulgar about them. Instead of boxing the ears of mercenary or heartless admirers in their proper persons, they leave that task to their brother and to the cook. The former flogs a sneaking fellow who wants to get off his engagement, and the latter breaks the nose of a too impetuous lover with the rolling-pin in a very effective manner. The loves of Augusta Gresham, who considers it matter of conscience to marry for money, are exceedingly amusing. The best passage in the book is a letter in which she asks leave of her haughty cousin, Lady Amelia de Courcy, to marry an attorney whom she really likes, and whom she instantly resigns when Lady Amelia tells her that she owes it to her family to do so. The humour of the letters is dexterously heightened by the device of making Lady Amelia marry the rejected suitor herself. Mr. Oriel, the High Church clergyman who marries Beatrice Gresham, and his admirer, Miss Gushing—'a young thing,' who does not perceive that she bores him dreadfully by going to his daily services after he had got sick of them—and almost every character who is only incidentally brought on the stage, especially Lady Scatcherd, are excellently sketched. We cannot say as much for the more prominent characters. Frank Gresham is a mere walking gentleman; and Doctor Thorne does nothing very remarkable, though Mr. Trollope, in one of his asides to his readers, justifies at length his own preference for him over the other characters. There is, however, considerable humour in his passages of arms with Lady Arabella Gresham, who is always trying to patronize and to forgive him, and always finds herself snubbed and forgiven.

The fault of the book throughout is its carelessness. The story is languid. Whenever a difficulty arises, Mr. Trollope tries to cut it instead of solving it. He turns to his reader, points out the difficulty, and coolly passes it over. In the second chapter of the first volume, which makes two separate starts, each dating twenty years before the main story, Mr. Trollope observes—'I quite feel that an apology is due for beginning a novel with two long dull chapters full of description . . . but twist it as I will, I cannot do otherwise.' It was his business to do otherwise, and not to publish the book till he had succeeded. Mr. Trollope must know that nothing in this world is more provoking than a breach of duty urged by way of apology for another breach of duty. Who would not prefer a simple admission that his coat had not been brushed, to a justification on the ground that his servant had over-slept himself? A somewhat similar piece of carelessness occurs about the will on which the catastrophe depends. Mr. Trollope states as a fact that it *had* the effect which he attributes to it, and that if it had not, the point has been misstated. He adds that he wishes that, in order to avoid the responsibility of legal mistakes, novelists could adopt a suggestion which we offered in our review of his last novel, that they should have their books settled by counsel. We are flattered by his readiness to take advice, and in return we will not discuss the question whether Sir Roger Scatcherd's will was not altered just before his death (though we rather think it was), but we must observe that Mr. Trollope does not meet our point. The contract of the writer with the reader is to create and maintain a reasonably perfect illusion as to the reality of the events which he relates, and he breaks that contract if he wantonly points out the difficulties of his task, and says that there is a way out of them, but that he does not choose to take the trouble to find it.

Mr. Trollope has too much sense to write with any very definite moral, but he does the next worst thing that is to be done. He invests his books—and has invested this one in particular—with a sort of atmosphere which is not incapable of being condensed into the moral that people ought to marry for love and not for money, and that wealth and station are in themselves somewhat contemptible. Doctor Thorne, the village doctor, is by mere force of personal character far superior to Mr. Gresham and Lady Arabella his wife; and Frank Gresham is much applauded for his heroism in determining to marry Mary Thorne, a lady by nature and education, though a bastard by birth, at the expense, as he supposes, of forfeiting for ever the family estate. We will not dwell upon the trifling inconsistency of praising a man for being disinterested in the first place, and paying him 300,000*l*. for his disinterested conduct immediately afterwards. No one has a right to object to a novel that it is a novel and not a history, but we will put before Mr. Trollope and other writers of his school a case for their opinion. Mr.

Frank Gresham we leave as he is—the heir of a large but encumbered estate, to which his father, his mother, and his sisters attach perhaps an exaggerated value because for centuries it has been the family seat. Suppose, however, Mary Thorne's mother and her husband to have lived not in America but at Barchester. Let the man be a drunken hypocrite, on the highway to the hulks or the gallows—the woman a disreputable vixen, the mother of a large family of sons and daughters each more profligate, vicious, mean, and idle than the other. Let Miss Patience Oriel be another young lady with good birth, pleasant connexions, plenty of money, and personal qualifications inferior to those of Mary Thorne, though considerable in themselves. Mr. Gresham falls violently in love with Miss Thorne, and she with him. He knows the fact. He also knows that his friends wish him to marry Miss Oriel, and he has himself a very deep regard and esteem for her, almost amounting to the sort of passion which he feels for Mary Thorne. Is Mr. Trollope prepared to say that in this case the principle of marrying the woman you love ought to hold good? If so, he ought to write a fourth volume, depicting the condition of Mr. and Mrs. Gresham ten years after marriage, when two large families instead of one had to live on Greshamsbury—when, Mr. Gresham's father-in-law having been transported, his mother-in-law had introduced to him and his wife a whole brood of dirty sisters and prowling blackguard brothers-in-law, to poach and whine and cringe and bully. If he could prove to the world that, under these circumstances, Mr. Gresham naturally and simply, and not merely as a point of honour, looked on his marriage with satisfaction, and was a better and more useful member of society in consequence of it than he would have been if he had married Miss Oriel and overcome his passion for Miss Thorne, he would have proved a good deal. But neither he nor any other novelist ever has the courage to teach such a lesson. Their heroes make desperate efforts to marry beggary and infamy; but when they try to do so, the desert blossoms as the rose. The fact is, that in his heart every man knows and feels that society has real claims which no man has a right to deny. Of course it is infinitely mean to marry for money a person who is the object of dislike or contempt; but it does not follow that no marriage can be wise or happy unless those who contract it feel for each other an overwhelming passion. The mass of marriages are, no doubt, determined chiefly by feeling, but by feeling of a much more manageable kind than that which novelists describe.

27. Unsigned review, *Harper's Magazine*

September 1858, xvii. 693

In the first sentence the reviewer is alluding to *Domestic Manners of the Americans*, published by Anthony's mother in 1832, a book bitterly resented by the American Press for many years.

The vein of caustic satire which has given a certain bad eminence to the name which this author inherits has become mollified in his case into a sub-acid, piquant humor, which he brings to bear effectually on the weak and ludicrous points of English society. The novel before us is somewhat softened down from the audacious sarcasm of 'Barham Towers,' [*sic*] but it is by no means wanting in vigor and vivacity, nor in occasional touches of the accustomed sharpness. If the author does not indulge in the use of vitriol, he does not place milk and water in its stead. . . . After all, the whole impression of the novel is far from disagreeable. Mr. Trollope well knows how to help his characters out of ugly situations at the right time. With all his love of depicting the foibles and absurdities of weak and absurd people, he is not without a sense of the brighter sides of life, and his keen observation of character lends a life-like interest to his descriptions, which often have the air of personal sketches rather than of fictitious creations. In the present comparative dearth of amusing reading, *Doctor Thorne* is a timely windfall, and will be eagerly seized by the lovers of good novels.

28. 'Mr. Trollope's Novels', *National Review*

October 1858, vii. 416–35

Within the month Trollope wrote his publisher from Dublin expressly for a copy of this ambitious essay, which runs, unabridged, to over eight thousand words. He had heard of it and must know how he was dealt with in it—'whether for good or for bad' (*Letters*, ed. Booth, p. 43). The *National Review* (1855–64) was a Unitarian journal edited by Walter Bagehot and Richard Holt Hutton, later to be Trollope's favourite reviewer (Introduction, VII), who may or may not have written this discerning early critique of Trollope as a significant novelist.

Among the best living writers of the former class [novelists dealing in 'good-humoured satire' and domestic comedy] we are inclined to rank one of the most recent accessions to their number. Mr. Anthony Trollope, the author of *The Warden*, has achieved in a very short time a very considerable success. The tale was brief, perhaps a little incomplete, and somewhat loosely put together. The single incident on which the whole weight of the narrative rested seemed very slight to support its burden; and there was somewhat too much made perhaps of trifles, as is not unfrequently the case where a writer has adopted a framework so simple and apparently insignificant that the whole merit of his story depends upon his way of telling it. . . . Except the most estimable clergyman who gives his title to the first volume, none of the characters in *The Warden* or *Barchester Towers* are such as to inspire any warm interest, and most of them are either depicted as disagreeable and contemptible, or rendered ludicrous either by disposition and conduct of their own, or by the situations in which they are frequently placed. The same holds true, though in a less marked manner, of the *Three Clerks*, their friends, and the young ladies to whom they are devoted.

Yet, despite all these defects, no one need wonder at the general popularity of Mr. Trollope's works, or at the favour which he himself

annot but extend to them, even though he might find it difficult to
justify his partiality on any acknowledged principles of criticism. The
charm of good temper, relieved from insipidity by a dash of sarcasm,
and a keen appreciation of all that is amusing—not merely of all that is
ridiculous—in the varying scenes of human existence, is almost as great
a literature as in life. This charm Mr. Trollope possesses in a very
liberal measure; and this makes even his somewhat objectionable digressions less objectionable than they would be in the pages of a graver
writer. . . . He has more than a lawyer's reverence for prescription;
and his first tale depicts the hardship inflicted by the popular cry for an
investigation of the state of charitable trusts and corporations, and a
return towards the original intentions of the founders. His sympathies
are all on the side of the guardians and rulers who have been for generations receiving more than their share of the founder's benevolent legacy,
not with the poor who, though they have had more than was bequeathed to them, have nevertheless received little indeed of the vast
accession of wealth which time has brought to the institutions founded
for their benefit. And he is evidently encouraged in this feeling by the
knowledge that the popular view is against him. Every one of his three
first works is animated, if it was not originally suggested, by this spirit
of opposition.

. . . the first chapter of *Barchester Towers* closes with the death of
Bishop Grantley only a few hours after the fall of the ministry which
had promised the succession to his son. This misfortune is the root from
which grows the story that fills the rest of the three volumes. The new
ministers belong to the sacrilegious party, which has not only appointed
men who, in the eyes of Barchester, are little better than dissenters to
high places in the Church, but has also laid its impious hands on the
sacred seats of heathen learning and ecclesiastical antiquity, which has
already overthrown the Hebdomadal Board that ruled over Oxford,
and has menaced Cambridge with innovations. . . . And now com-
mences a conflict between High and Low Church for the command of
the diocese. Involved in the result of this contest are two minor issues—
the one, whether the Bishop's wife, or the Bishop's chaplain, shall bear
rule in the Bishop's name; and the other, to which party shall belong
the hand and the fortune of the younger daughter of 'the Warden'—
Warden now no more. For true-hearted, rough, meddlesome John
Bold has departed the world wherein the loaves and fishes are the prizes
of spiritual warfare, and his young widow is left with one child, still a
baby, at the period when the tale opens. Her persecutor, on behalf of

the episcopal faction, is no less a person than the masculine leader of tha
party. We do not mean the Bishop, who is far from aspiring to lead an
one, and is led alternately by his wife, and by the Rev. Obadiah Slope
whom Mrs. Proudie has promoted to the chaplaincy. This gentleman i
the demon of the tale, and the sacrilegious assailant of musical service
and Sunday travelling. He is put forward from the beginning as a typ
of every thing that is disagreeable in the religious innovator. He is sai
to possess the virtue of religious sincerity, but as the author has, wit
great tact, kept all religious questions entirely out of sight, Mr. Slop
is never allowed to manifest any good quality, except perhaps that of
courage which sometimes does more than border on impudence. Th
colours are possibly laid on a little too freely, and the result is a portra
of unrivalled coarseness and vulgarity, which could hardly have suc
ceeded with any lady accustomed to the society of gentlemen even s
far as it is represented to have done with Eleanor Bold, *née* Harding
Bishop Proudie, again, is hardly well drawn. He is made too weak an
helpless before his wife and chaplain for a man who has risen to a goo
position by his labours as a preacher, and has been chosen to take
prominent part in commissions of ecclesiastical reform. Mrs. Proudi
is more lifelike. As a satirical, and consequently an exaggerated figure
the portrait of this episcopal lady must be admitted to be clever an
telling. Her iron rule over her husband, her impertinence to his clergy
her vulgar pride of station, her lectures to Mr. Harding and Archdeaco
Grantly on Sabbath schools and railway Sabbath-breaking, are a
perfectly in character. The family of Dr. Vesey Stanhope, an absente
canon on a rather prolonged visit to Barchester, are apparently intro
duced for no other purpose than that of complicating the story an
prolonging the action. Their acts and characters are nevertheless ski
fully interwoven with the main thread of the book, though not s
skilfully portrayed. The selfish, disappointed old man, whose life ha
been wasted without scruple, and is drawing to a close without honou
and without satisfaction, is a true and a melancholy picture. The light
hearted, frank, hopeless scapegrace Bertie, insensible to shame or re
morse, but not devoid of generous impulses, is a possible, though hardl
a probable child of such birth and such a training as he had received. Th
cold, useful eldest daughter, with no good point in her character bu
that of family affection and household industry, is the best of the num
ber. Her sister, separated from the Italian scoundrel who has wasted he
fortune and crippled her limbs, still intent on conquests to be made b
her wit and beauty, and utterly lost to all sense of shame in the pursui

seems to us absolutely unnatural. She is an intrusion upon the stage, utterly out of harmony with the scenes and persons round her, and we cannot but think with the nature of her sex. It is a pity that such a person should have been allowed to force herself on the reader's acquaintance, or the eminently respectable society of the cathedral city. . . . In point of lively writing and well-restrained humour, this is perhaps the best of Mr. Trollope's novels; and it might have been better, if he would have refrained from frequently and somewhat offensively coming forward as author to remind us that we are reading a fiction. Such intrusions are as objectionable in a novel as on the stage: the actor who indulges in extempore and extra-professional hints and winks to the audience, and the author who interrupts his characters to introduce himself to our notice, are alike guilty of a violation of good taste. Despite this blemish, however, with all the defects of the plot, *Barchester Towers* is undeniably one of the cleverest and best-written novels which has been published of late years. The graver and less brilliant chapters which wind up the story have merits of their own which are not inferior to those of the humorous sketches that form the peculiar characteristic of the book; and there are graceful and touching passages which vindicate Mr. Trollope's claim to rank as something more than a humorist. Both touching and pleasant is the concluding picture, which represents the good gentle old Warden introducing his successor to the home he had loved so well. It is the completion of a character as amiable as novelist ever drew—the finishing touch to a portrait of which the artist has a right to be proud.

The tale of *The Three Clerks* appears to have been suggested by the public attention directed to the abuses and reforms of the Civil Service. It evinces a considerable knowledge of the subject, and an acquaintance with the habits of thought and speech prevalent among officials of the younger generation which any man may possess who has met at his club the junior clerks of government offices, and observed with studious interest the characteristic traits of manner and demeanour which distinguish the various classes of men. The habit of observation Mr. Trollope undoubtedly possesses, and with it an appreciation of minutiæ which enables him always to assign to his characters of every class their fitting costume, language, and mode of mind. His clergymen are always strictly clerical, wearing the mental garb of their order as naturally and invariably as the black vest and white neckcloth which especially distinguish them to the outward eye. So his civil servants carry about them the air and manner of their position in life, and their rank in their respective offices. It may be that Norman is a little too like one of the High-Church curates, with whom Mr. Trollope's career of authorship had hitherto been most familiar. But this is skilfully accounted for by the tendency towards Puseyism which is attributed to him, and which well befits the rigid propriety, the grave demeanour, and the conscientious industry of the Weights and Measures. Sir Gregory Hardlines, the man who through the Civil Service has risen to eminence and 2000*l.* a-year, and who regards the service with profound love and veneration, watching over its interests as his own, and by no means disposed to sacrifice them to any weak indulgence or private partiality towards incapable men, is well though somewhat too harshly drawn, the author having a tendency to make virtue seem unpleasant. But the main interest of the book lies in the history of a man too anxious to succeed to be duly scrupulous as to the means, and the misery which his sin and consequent fall brought on every one around him. Alaric Tudor is the friend and companion of Norman, and the favourite of Mr. Hardlines, the stern chief secretary of the Weights and Measures. His object in life is to rise; and though we find him at first unstained by serious error, it is not long before the first opportunity of rising is made the first step to his ruin. Sent down by the interest of Sir Gregory, now promoted to the supervision of the service generally, to report concerning a mine in which some government rights were involved, he is beguiled by the demon of the story into purchasing shares in the mine he was sent to inspect. From that day he rises in wealth and position, and falls lower and lower in character. He wins by competitive examination the place which his friend Norman should have had, and is proposed at a political club by his tempter Undy Scott. This man, the son of an impoverished Scotch peer, and a late M.P., who afterwards resumes his seat, is about as cold-blooded and detestable a villain as any author ever drew, though far more probable and natural than the monsters who ordinarily figure in the same capacity. Mr. Trollope has too much tact and skill to deform his pages with villains of the ancient conventional type, nor would they at all accord with the general style and plan of his works. But Undecimus Scott is perhaps more revolting than the melodramatic demons of ordinary novelists. Alaric Tudor falls completely into his snares and is undermined in moral character, in peace of mind, and finally in the worldly prosperity to which he had risen with almost unexampled rapidity. He is made trustee to a niece of his tempter, is seduced into speculating with her property, repents too late, and finds himself irreparably disgraced, subjected to a public trial as a swindler and sentenced to imprisonment, and finally driven to seek shelter in exile with his wife and children. He has lost his hold upon the sympathies of the reader less by his dishonesty in pecuniary affairs than by his treachery to those who had loved and trusted him. He and Harry Norman had been intimate with an amiable family living near London, whose home had been always open to them. Alaric first makes love to a younger daughter of Mrs. Woodward, because the elder is understood to be half-engaged to Norman; and then, when Gertrude rejects his friend, he abandons her sister and is accepted by her. He is by this conduct totally estranged from the rejected lover, who afterwards marries the forsaken Linda; and this estrangement aids in delivering him over to the evil spirit that besets him. The two sisters are admirably sketched, though slightly; Gertrude's strong, somewhat unamiable nature being justly adapted to bear and be improved by the terrible sorrows which are brought upon her by her husband's sin and shame; and the gentle Linda is just such a wife as any man who loves a peaceful and cheerful home would wish to secure—a wife worthy of a man so wise and honourable as Harry Norman. Their mother, the good but somewhat worldly Mrs. Woodward, is a truthful though not quite a pleasing figure; it being a defect of which the author appears wholly unconscious, that hardly any of his personages are without some repulsive trait of character which prevents the reader from taking a cordial interest in their fate. Perhaps, however, with the exception of Mr. Harding the warden, the heroes of this later work are more calculated to win the regard of unsophisticated novel-readers than those of its predecessors. The rise of Alaric's fortunes, and their sudden and total ruin, afford an opportunity for displaying whatever power of exciting the sympathy of his readers Mr. Trollope possesses; while the seriousness of the catastrophe restrains and chastens the humour which throughout *The Warden* and *Barchester Towers* repels interest, though affording no small amount of pleasure and entertainment. And the youngest pair of lovers in the story, Alaric Tudor's cousin Charley and the gentle lively Katie Woodward, entitle themselves to nearly as much sympathy as such personages in fiction usually do. Yet, on the whole, even *The Three Clerks* will be read, like Mr. Trollope's other novels, rather for the charm of the author's humour and cleverness than for any graver merits; and judged in this view, it can hardly fail to disappoint his admirers. It is deficient in the elaborate elegance and the light gracefulness of style which were so remarkable in its predecessors, probably because it has been written with much more of haste and with that diminished care which is not unnatural to an author who considers his reputation made. It is rather too much for the patience of a critic or the gravity of a reader when he finds some score of pages filled with the story contributed by Charley Tudor to the columns of the *Daily Delight*; and we are inclined to wonder how the publisher could tolerate such an imposition, and how the author could commit himself to such a solecism as the introduction of this weak and pointless burlesque. But a writer so prolific as Mr. Trollope must write in a hurry; and so doing, it is not strange if he finds a difficulty in expanding his materials to the exact measure of the three volumes which he must fill, and failing in so doing by more legitimate means, he has recourse to interpolations which are little better than a fraud upon the prospective purchasers of his book. However, it is only in this one work that Mr. Trollope has been so glaring a sinner; and we may hope that for the future he will be able to find a better method of apportioning his matter to the space which it has to fill. Such blemishes in such a writer can only be attributed to haste, and the carelessness thereon attendant; errors of which there are other indications in these volumes. But despite the want of equal labour and preparation, which renders *The Three Clerks* very far inferior as a whole to *Barchester Towers*, there are, in the former, scenes and sketches which are fully as good in their way as any thing in its predecessor. Among these we may mention the caricature of 'Uncle Bat,' the old, hard-drinking, unpolished sailor-relative of the Woodwards; the portrait of Mr. Chaffanbrass, the Old-Bailey lawyer; the trial of Alaric Tudor; and above all, the examination of the Hon. Undecimus Scott by the terrible barrister who 'led for Mr. Tudor.' These things do not bear reading and re-reading as well as do the more carefully-written pages of *The Warden* and its sequel; but on a first acquaintance they are full of entertainment, seasoned with sense and truth sufficient to prevent the exaggeration which seems essential to the author's humour from becoming too palpable, and so spoiling our amusement by over-taxing our credulity.

There is, however, one piece of bad taste, which was perceptible in some few instances in *The Warden* and *Barchester Towers*, but which reaches a climax in *The Three Clerks*; a fault analogous to that breach of heraldic decorum known as 'canting heraldry,' which assigns to different families arms or mottoes conveying a pun on the surname of the bearer. We allude to the extraordinary names imposed by Mr. Trollope upon all except the most favoured heroes of the tale,—names which of themselves destroy much of the merit of some passages, by reminding us at every moment that we are reading a purely fictitious story. Who can take interest in the ill-usage of Captain Cuttwater? or who can for a moment believe in the personal existence of Mr. Chaffanbrass, or M. Jaquetanâpe? Why must we be told beforehand by the titles assigned to each, of the respective parts to be played by Mr. Hardlines and Mr. Oldeschole? What wit is there in the threadbare jest which furnishes the name of Dr. Fillgrave? or what reality can be assigned to Messrs. Scatterall, Corkscrew, Uppinall, and Minusex? True, something is saved to the author in the way of description by such a nomenclature, the name given to a minor personage not unfrequently being a sufficient expression of the personality attached to it; as when an official is denominated Alphabet Precis, or an attorney bears the euphonious surname of Gitemthruet. Nearly the whole that we learn about the character of a pair who are instrumental in Alaric's catastrophe is contained in the name of Jaquetanâpe and Golightly. In this species of nicknaming there is neither grace nor sense nor cleverness; and we are glad to find very little of it in *Doctor Thorne*. We hope that Mr. Trollope has become ashamed of it, as of a trick which belongs of right to the lowest order of farcical absurdities.

This is by no means the only respect in which peculiarities strongly marked in the first three of these novels, are softened, or vanish altogether, in the fourth. This could hardly have been expected, as the publication of the last followed within a very few months that of *The Three Clerks*. In the latter, indeed, there is less of the humour and vivacity which scintillated in *Barchester Towers*, and more endeavour to be earnest and interesting. In *Doctor Thorne* this is still more evidently the case. There is more care bestowed on the original conception of the story, and less on the elaboration of details. The characters want the perfect finish which was so conscientiously given to the sketches of the Chapter of Barchester and their connections. Even the godfather—we cannot call him the hero—of the book is by no means as familiar to us when we close the third volume as were the minor personages of *The Warden*. Far less labour, far less loving interest, has the author devoted to his fourth literary bantling than he gave to his first; and consequently, though with a more vigorous frame, it is far less elegant and graceful than its elder brethren. Though it will perhaps be as great a favourite with most ordinary novel-readers, it is far inferior to its predecessors as a work of art. Nor can we wonder at this, when we remember that though this is but October, two novels in three volumes have been given to the world since January bearing the signature of Anthony

Trollope. There is not time to give due polish and completion to works which succeed one another at intervals so short; and we can only regret that the author of *Barchester Towers* should be guilty of the bad taste of counting quantity before quality. The management of his plots sufficiently indicates his increased mastery over his work; and if he were now to bestow equal pains thereon, his next effort would no doubt be greatly superior to any thing he has yet achieved. As it is, there are but a very few living novelists of whom *Doctor Thorne* would be unworthy; but among those we are inclined to rank its author.

The main purpose of Mr. Trollope's last novel is to ridicule the maxims which are supposed to prevail among a certain portion of the aristocracy of this country on the subject of birth and ancient blood. The author is far too good a Tory not to sympathize with the genuine pride of an old English family, whose pedigree dates back to the ages of chivalry, unstained by a single *mésalliance* for some thirty generations. . . . But nothing can exceed his bitter contempt for those who, while pluming themselves on purity of blood and illustrious lineage, consider that money can wipe out any taint; and that he who marries the daughter of a country apothecary commits a mortal sin, while he who allies himself with the heiress of a successful tradesman, so his success have enabled her to count her fortune by hundreds of thousands, merits the thanks of his family and the admiration of high-born neighbours. The heroine of his tale is the illegitimate child of the doctor's brother, who has seduced a poor and pretty girl in the neighbourhood. The victim's brother very righteously sets forth to chastise the villain; but his heavy stick does its work more effectually than perhaps he intended, and the avenger is found guilty of manslaughter and sent to prison for half a year. The child is born; and the mother disappears from the scene. The illegitimate girl is allowed, improbably enough, to become the playfellow of the squire's children, and eventually the beloved of his heir. Meantime her mother's brother, whose wife had nursed the 'young Squire Gresham,' rises in the world by dint of industry and genius, and is presented to us as the wealthy baronet Sir Roger Scatcherd. He and his wife are perhaps the most striking characters in the tale; and his terrible end, when he falls a victim to the intemperance of a lifetime, is powerfully conceived. The niece of Dr. Thorne, the child of Mary Scatcherd, becomes heiress to the wealth left by this great railway-contractor and former stonemason, when his son follows his father's fatal example, and drinks himself to death. Then the family who had scornfully repudiated her engagement to their heir are only too glad to

ccept what they can no longer resist, and the lovers are made happy.
There are similar tales of sordidness and inconsistency interwoven with
his, all illustrating the meanness which can so value money as to let it
over all defects of birth or character, and so despise love, and faith,
nd purity, as to hold them of no account when weighed against gold.
The great Whig family of the county are, with pardonable party-spirit,
nade to furnish all the instances of this paltry huckstering tone which
re presented to us; and a gentle hint is insinuated that the rival faction
ave at once more true reverence for birth and more respect for
lebeian talent.

The low-born persons of the tale are very fairly treated. Mary
Thorne is as perfect as other novel-heroines; Sir Roger Scatcherd is an
onest, clever, really generous-hearted man; his son Louis, and the
ailor-descended Moffat, are as mean, pitiful, insignificant creatures as
hey well could be. Lady Scatcherd, again, once the wet-nurse of Frank
Gresham, is a vulgar, honest, affectionate, womanly woman. Indeed,
he and her husband inspire us with as much interest as any other person-
ge in the tale. There is much truth and pathos in the picture of her
lesolate solitude of spirit, when left absolutely alone to bear 'the burden
f an honour whereunto she was not born.' . . .

And here, for the present, we take our leave of Mr. Trollope. He has
owers which, if used with due painstaking conscientiousness, may
nake him one of the most successful novelists of the day, as they always
ender him readable and entertaining. But above all, he has the gift of
inishing his work to the most minute detail without becoming for an
nstant tedious or trivial; and this is a gift so rare that it should never be
eglected. The author of *Barchester Towers* should never write so as to
empt his readers to 'skip'; and though few do so less often, yet there
re symptoms in some passages of his later works of a somnolency,
vhich we trust will not be allowed to grow upon him. The popularity
vhich he has already earned should be a sufficient stimulus to induce
im steadily and perseveringly to deserve it.

THE BERTRAMS
1859

For the larger part of Trollope's comment on *The Bertrams*, see the headnote to *Doctor Thorne* on p. 67. Trollope (*Autobiography*, p. 108) attributes the poor quality of the love scenes in *The Bertrams* to his having written them during a period of fatigue while coping with problems of the Post Office in Glasgow. 'The men would grumble, and then I would think how it would be with them if they had to go home afterwards and write a love-scene. But the love-scenes written in Glasgow, all belonging to *The Bertrams*, are not good.'

29. Unsigned notice, *Spectator*
19 March 1859, xxxii. 328–9

Mr. Trollope's new fiction of *The Bertrams* is more remarkable for the literary and satirical powers of the author, and his passing sketches of the weaknesses of social life, than for the features requisite to constitute a complete novel. In fact, the present work, like 'The Three Clerks,' and 'Doctor Thorne,' rather neglects the failings and vices of the age, the exposition of which is Mr. Trollope's forte, for a tale of passion, in which it is not clear to us that he is qualified to excel. If he has the constructive gift to form a probable and well-sustained story, and the dramatic genius requisite to create persons of real flesh and blood (which may be doubted), his natural tendency to satire and smart remark interferes with the exercise of the first-named faculties, and introduces elements of suspension, if not of confusion into the narrative. . . .

In carrying out the story there are sketches of society abroad and at home, and many persons are introduced in passing who illustrate in themselves and their discourse some characteristics of the age. The

NOTICE IN *Spectator* MARCH 1859

Bertrams is far beyond the general run of novels, for keen observation, satirical powers, and knowledge of life. It is not, however, worthy of Mr. Trollope's abilities and cannot be said to add to his well-deserved reputation. The fact is he writes too fast. An average six or eight months is too short a time for the gestation and production of a first-class novel.

30. Unsigned notice, *Athenaeum*

26 March 1859, p. 420

A new novel from the author of 'Barchester Towers' is sure of a hearty welcome, and a brisk movement of hopeful expectation from the 'reading public,' including those who do not generally give way to novel reading. 'The Bertrams' will keep up the author's reputation; it has clever, vigorous, boldly-drawn sketches of character. The plot of the story is the least part of the business—it is merely the support over which the vine is trained; but the reader is interested in the individuals brought under his notice: they have a real flesh-and-blood vitality; and he desires to know all that befalls them. As a mere story, the novel drags. The inexorable destiny that presides over the three-volume novel is not to be appeased under the regulation exigence of three hundred pages odd to a volume; and what can a mortal author do but become diffuse and long-winded occasionally? It is laid on him as a necessity to use more words than are needful, and to insert many things that, to say the least, are superfluities. Mr. Trollope, however, writes always with a plain, photograph-like reality, which makes his words convey the emotion to the reader, which the thought has had to himself. The style is rough, and there is an occasional coarseness in 'The Bertrams' stronger than we have remarked in the author's former works: he will do well to guard against it. Delicacy of workmanship does not diminish strength and vigour. . . .

There is a great deal too much about Oriental scenes. Mr. Trollope uses his traveller's journal too lavishly; it disturbs the reader's enjoyment of the story; it is fatiguing to be obliged to travel when one wants to remain at home, and a reader generally turns sulky if he is called upon to go further than Paris, or Brussels at the utmost,—to be taken to the East twice in one novel, passes permission with the most patient reader, a mythic personage rarely met with now. We recommend 'The Bertrams' to our readers; they will appreciate our delicacy in not forestalling their interest by giving them any hint of the story that awaits them, and which, they may accept our word for it, they will find deeply interesting.

31. Unsigned review, *Illustrated London News*

26 March 1859, xxxiv. 308

Scene principally in London, sometimes at Littlebath and other parts of England, occasionally in Jerusalem, Egypt, and other foreign parts; time, circa 1845–50; costume, of the period. Such, in the main, would be the stage directions prefaced to this little drama of modern domestic life, which, upon the whole, is well conceived and powerfully told. The interest is divided between two pair of lovers, whose story is intended to illustrate the oft-repeated maxim that 'the course of true love never did run smooth;' though, to speak honestly of them, the rough handling they meet with is entirely owing to their own stupidity and folly; and in the end they get off much better than they deserve, insomuch that, losing all temper with them in their early and long-protracted blunders, we lose all interest in them before the crisis arrives, and wish that their ultimate destiny had been in the Camden-town burial-ground, or rather in the London Necropolis, where, as we read, the 'sanctity of the grave' is 'combined with economy of charge,' instead of;—but we must not anticipate the story, which we doubt not will engage the reader's attention from end to end, as it did ours, by its very perversity; and, if it do not leave a pleasing impression of human nature upon the mind, will, at any rate, awaken reflections worthy of encouraging as to the secret springs of action which move all us poor mortals in every-day life. Provoking, sad, often humiliating as the adventures here recorded undoubtedly are, we fear that of the numerous readers who will take up these three volumes as part of their light reading not a few will put them down again with a heavy heart, and admit that there are many such histories still playing out in the world, even amongst their own acquaintance—perhaps even amongst themselves; the whole fraternity of neighbours and friends not knowing nor caring anything about it, and all on the surface being as smooth and smiling as if all within were calm and content.

But to our two pair of lovers. Of course, to point a moral and adorn a tale there is nothing so efficacious as strong contrast, and we have it unmistakably in 'The Bertrams.' George Bertram, the hero No. 1, who takes double class at Oxford, and has splendid prospects from his own

talents, to say nothing of the hoarded wealth of an old uncle, fall
hastily in love with Caroline Waddington, a Juno-like heroine, radiant
in beauty, grand in presence, but ambitious in purpose; and is put off for
a couple of years till he shall be *en route* for fortune at the Bar. In reply
to Bertram's impetuous instances she always, in very proper language
intimates that she could never be happy as a poor man's wife; and a
length the former is so disgusted at her apparent coldness that he absolve
her from her promise and goes abroad to travel. Broken-hearted
dejected is Caroline for a few weeks or months; but, cut to the heart by
the continued obstinate silence of him she intensely loves, she in a way
ward moment accepts the hand of the rising barrister, Sir Henry
Harcourt (Solicitor-General in the then existing Ministry), by whom
she is promoted to great show of splendour, with an extensive circle of
visitors, in Eaton-square. The rest follows as a matter of course. Harcour
has been a college friend of Bertram, and has insidiously taken advantage of the little differences between him and his intended to supplan
him in her good graces. Harcourt is a mere man of the world, an
unscrupulous place-hunter, a low-minded money-hunter, fond of
display, fonder of himself, and avowing candidly that he married his
handsome wife partly as an ornament to his establishment, and partly
for the fortune she might be expected one day to inherit. Is it to be
wondered at that Caroline, who loved the intellectual Bertram, which
love her proud spirit would never allow her to admit, should hate the
time-serving Harcourt, and that when thrown together with the former
in society the whole truth should break upon all the parties, leading to
mutual recriminations? Harcourt, as if in triumph over the disappointed
Bertram, invites him to his house, presses, almost forces, him to come
and discovers, when too late, how matters are between the quondam
lovers. It was a delicate, difficult, and dangerous task to display the
feelings of man and wife upon the making of this discovery. Bertram
has taken his final leave of poor Caroline (a painful, passionate scene)
and immediately afterwards Harcourt, who has wind of it, comes to
demand an explanation. The scene increases in violence, the exasperated
husband uses language which no woman can tolerate or forget, and they
part for ever. What the issue is we will not divulge. We will only say
that the dénouement, saving only the suicide of Harcourt, who blows
his brains out in his dressing-room, very much like a gentleman, is not
to our liking—that sables, sables only, should have hung about the
memory of the great-hearted but weak-minded Caroline Waddington

The other pair of lovers are of a more homely class. Arthur Wilkinson the son of the Vicar of Hurststaple, is a very good young man, of small mental capacity, who falls in love with Adela Gauntlet, the daughter of a neighbouring Vicar, just after the humdrum fashion of ordinary people. On the death of his father the noble patron of the living gives it to him only on consent of his handing over the vicarage-house and the larger portion of the income to his widowed mother, which leaves him with only £150 a year, too little to marry upon, and this he tells poor Adela in a very business-like fashion—poor Adela, who would have gladly married him, and shared his fortunes if he had not a farthing. The character of this Arthur is truly and carefully drawn; but it is not an agreeable one. We grudge him his happiness at the end, agreeing with the summing up of the author:—'He was not worthy of her: that is, the amount of wealth of character which he brought into that life-partnership was, when counted up, much less than her contribution.' Yet there are women of this sort in the world, who, pure gold themselves, delight to gild and enrich mere lumps of lead.

The other characters introduced are of sufficient variety, and ably drawn. The old miser, Bertram, with his lingering affection for his nephew and granddaughter, struggling through the dross of his baser nature; his *vaut-riant*[1] but amusing brother, Sir Lionel, the father of hero No. 1; the faithful and confidential Pritchett; Baron Bawl, the jocular Judge; and Mr. Ststicks, the political economist M.P., are amongst the most prominent male personages. The females, in addition to those already mentioned, comprise a wonderful assemblage of old tabbies at Littlebath, who delight in card-playing and scandal. It will be seen, therefore, that the materials of this novel are sufficiently diversified. It may be observed in conclusion that the thought of the author often rises superior to the order of beings with whom he peoples his pages, and touches with becoming gravity upon many themes of the highest import in religion, morals, and policy.

[1] ' . . . *vaut-riant*': apparently a play on words combining *vaut rien* and *riant* to suggest a smiling good-for-nothing.

32. Unsigned notice, *Saturday Review*

26 March 1859, vii. 368–9

A long but humourless review taking Trollope to task for advocating early marriages regardless of consequences, and for a number of other failings, including lapses in history and ignorance of legal detail.

Considering the pace at which he produces his novels, Mr. Trollope is a very remarkable writer. Even if he wrote slowly, they would be exceedingly good, but that they come so fast certainly heightens our admiration. Whatever may be their faults, they fulfil the first great object of all novels—they give pleasure and amusement to the reader. It is the indispensable requisite—the one infallible test of success—that a tale should be entertaining. If a tale entertains, there is always some merit in it, although the entertainment may be of a low sort. It takes something beyond ordinary ability to make a good romance of horrors, or even a tale of facetious sentimentalism. But Mr. Trollope entertains us in a way that neither he nor we need be ashamed of. No one would say that there is anything very elevating, or deep, or pregnant with genius in his writings, but he always writes like a gentleman, and like an educated, observant, and kindly man. He is conspicuously clever, and all the strength and all the weakness that we attach to cleverness make the merits and the faults of his novels. He has the capacity, and has collected the materials, necessary for the delineation of detached sketches; but hitherto his sketches have been too much detached, and his tales have been in too great a degree mere bundles of fragments bound together by the slenderest possible fragment of a plot. In this respect the *Bertrams* is a great improvement on its predecessors. We confess that we like this new tale better than any that Mr. Trollope has written. The sketches are more subordinated to the evolution of a plot which is at once possible, interesting, and difficult to anticipate. Certainly the author has recourse to the violent expedient of making a superfluous husband shoot himself in order that the widow may marry the right

96

nan, and this is a liberty which the anticipating reader would not
resume to take. But otherwise the novel is all fair play, and our
nterest is not only excited and sustained, but legitimately satisfied.

It is curious that a successful plot should, like that of the *Bertrams*, be
n argumentative one. The drift of the tale is to support one side in a
ontroversy which a few months ago had a little life given it in the
ewspapers. The *Bertrams* is intended to advocate the expediency of
ove in a cottage.' Some of Mr. Trollope's critics remarked that his last
ovel, *Dr. Thorne*, preached the expediency of uncalculating love more
ecidedly than they thought proper. This is his reply. He has written a
ovel to show what are the practical consequences of sacrificing passion
o calculation. And this is done most ingeniously.

33. Unsigned review, *Examiner*

2 April 1859, p. 212

The Bertrams is a good novel. After the reader has once cleared Jerusalem, of which the stones rather obstruct progress through the early chapters, the story is so told as to maintain a lively interest. There is enough of purpose, plot, and character to fill the reader's mind, and make him live entirely in the artist's little world of fiction. The novel is not Mr Trollope's best; much of it is very diffusely written; but it is better than 'Three Clerks,' and far better than the majority of novels of the day. The construction of its plot is excellent, in this respect, indeed, it is superior to the preceding works by the same hand. Mr. Anthony Trollope has earned most fairly the place he deserves among contemporary novelists. Every new fiction, whether better or worse than its predecessors, has so far differed as to the nature of the ground it occupied, while showing mastery over its theme, as to have brought with it an increase of credit by the evidence it furnished of the author's power. Successive novels by this writer are not mere recombinations of a few ideas, but fresh extensions of the territory he claims as his own. They are substantial units of which one and one make two, and they contrast strongly with the work of some writers who produce only the substance of a single book, though they commit a dozen acts of publication.

34. Unsigned notice, *Leader*

2 April 1859, x. 431

Mr. Trollope has not diminished his reputation by 'The Bertrams': neither will he have increased it. There is the same amount of acute and sarcastic perception of life and character as distinguishes his former productions, but 'The Bertrams' wants something of the originality, the freshness, the probability, which are to be found, for instance, in his 'Barchester Towers.' . . . Mr. Trollope has in this work afforded another specimen of his keen perception of character, of his knowledge of life, and of his mastery over the strongest passion that finds place in the human breast. But his pen is dipped slightly in gall; his views of life are prone to the satiric, and sometimes, when he draws the character of a class, the portrait can only be regarded as that of an individual.

35. Unsigned notice, *Bentley's Quarterly Review*

July 1859, i. 456–62

. . . the success of this really clever book depends but little on our regard for its characters. It is impossible for our sympathy to be keenly wrought upon by the fortunes of persons who either have no fixed object at all beyond a general desire of making a figure in the world, or who are influenced solely by self-interest. The course of the hero, so to call him, is a perpetual conquest of the actual over the ideal—a continual abandonment of preconceived plans or aims to some present temptation; of which we have an early example suggested by the author's own experiences of travel. These he has incorporated into his novel, rather to the detriment of both, though the descriptions are given with much spirit. After a successful university career, Bertram recruits his powers by a journey to the Holy Land. Full of devout aspirations he approaches Jerusalem, but enters its sacred walls cursing and swearing from the discomforts of a Turkish saddle. This is a type of his course, and perhaps what Mr. Trollope would maintain is the type of many a real course which has begun in lofty aims and sunk under mean temptations. It prefigures in Bertram his lapse into infidelity, and his career of sceptical authorship into which he fell simply because things did not go smoothly in his long engagement with the heroine. . . .

It is part of the general want of method and plot that there are chapters of farce—and we have noticed this elsewhere in Mr. Trollope's writings—enacted by new characters, which do not advance the story a step, and which might be omitted by the reader without his being sensible of any hiatus. The flirtations of two widows in the homeward-bound steamer from Calcutta are of this sort, and give an impression of vulgarity quite at variance with the general tone of the book.

36. Unsigned notice, *National Review*

July 1859, ix. 187–99

The major part of this long essay is less concerned with Trollope and his novel than with the merits of the Bar over the Church as a vocation for young men. Trollope, the reviewer argues at length, unfairly stigmatizes the law and may encourage 'morbid and ill-founded scruples' in young men of promise against entering the profession.

This novel is inferior to Mr. Trollope's previous works. It wants something both of the firmness of conception and the delicacy of execution which made his two first essays rank among the pleasantest and wittiest of modern novels. We miss that satire, at once so gay and so trenchant, which laid its lash on Tom Towers and the *Times* newspaper; and find but little of that mixed acuteness and *bonhommie* which handled church dignitaries with so much boldness and so little offence. The lines are coarser, the reflection more forced, the sentiment, not in itself perhaps commonplace, but treated with a certain want of fineness of touch curiously in contrast with the nice lines by which foibles are traced, and the skill with which the lesser defects of character are turned inside out.

We do not mean to say that Mr. Trollope's right hand has forgot her cunning. If this book had been his first, there is enough in it of his characteristic excellencies to have attracted general attention; and our admiration is increased, not diminished, when we reflect that it is the fifth which he has produced within an incredibly short space of time, and find how much freshness and spirit his writings still contain. But in this novel he seems to us to trench on ground for which his genius is unsuited, and to deal with matters which do not easily submit themselves to that light crayon-like sketching of his.

. . . We think we may express our dislike of religious irony in general, and of Mr. Trollope's irony in particular, and say that there is a certain want of straightforwardness and boldness in the adoption of this elaborate ambush in order to 'hint a doubt and hesitate dislike,' instead of openly avowing any opinions he may entertain on the subject.

37. Unsigned review, *New Monthly Magazine*

July 1859, cxv. 500

Of value chiefly as a suggestive sample of perfunctory reviewing.

Success is a great incentive to exertion in literature as well as in other matters. 'The Bertrams', a novel, by Anthony Trollope, has followed quickly in the footsteps of its predecessor, 'Doctor Thorne.' Like it, too, it is a rattling, social novel, full of character, and replete with incident and scenery. The latter is a new feature imparted to the modern novel by increased facilities of locomotion: for 'The Bertrams' would, perhaps, not have gone off so buoyantly without the picnic at the Brook Kedron and the catastrophe in the Pool of Siloam. But the aspirations of George Bertram, as he sat upon the Mount of Olives, watching the stones of the Temple over against him, were doomed to a very Anglican and prosy dénouement—a wedding with a quiet, almost melancholy, widow. However, we have Cairo as a relief, and other couples in reserve, so the reader need not fear that the interest shall flag; it is well sustained, even to the last scene in Hadley Church—not a funeral—such is not the legitimate conclusion of the novel—but a marriage.

38. E. S. Dallas, *The Times*

23 May 1859, p. 12

This unsigned critique (attributed to E. S. Dallas in *The History of The Times* (1939), see Introduction, VII) is an important overview of Trollope's career through *The Bertrams*.

If Mudie were asked who is the greatest of living men, he would without one moment's hesitation say—Mr. Anthony Trollope; and Mudie's opinion is worth much. As Peel was the great Parliamentary middleman, Mudie is the great literary middleman. The wide world of authors and the wide world of readers alike regard him with awe; nay, even the sacred race of publishers have been known to kiss the hem of his garments and to invoke his favour. He is the mighty monarch of books that are good enough to be read, but not good enough or not cheap enough to be bought. He is the Apollo of the circulating library. He is the tenth Muse—the Muse of the three-volume novel. He is the autocrat of literature. Week by week and month by month he announces in various journals and magazines all the books which ought to be read; and authors run over the list with trembling to see whether Mr. Mudie esteems their volumes worthy of mention, and has purchased 2,500 copies or only 200. There are cases, indeed, in which a publisher, before he will condescend to treat with the author, must first take counsel with Mudie, whose bookshelves are a kind of literary barometer, showing the class of works that have been successful, the class that gluts the market, the class that nobody reads, and the class that everybody devours. To be unknown to Mudie is to be unknown to fame; to bask in the smiles of Mudie is to put on immortality, and feel all the future in the instant. This majestic personage, whom authors worship and whom readers court, knows that at the present moment one writer in England is paramount above all others, and his name is Trollope. He is at the top of the tree; he stands alone; there is nobody to be compared with him. He writes faster than we can read, and the more that the pensive public reads the more does it desire to read. Mr. Anthony Trollope is, in fact, the most fertile, the most popular, the most successful author—that is to say, of the circulating library sort. We believe there are persons who would rather not receive such praise, and who hold a circulating library success in great contempt, but they labour under a misapprehension. It is true that books which circulate without being cherished, which we read once and do not care to read a second time, which people borrow but never think of buying, are not the best of all books, and certainly are not the product of that mysterious something which we call genius. But genius is not everything in this world, and the presence of a few comets in the literary firmament need not make us blind to the existence of a good many stars. There are people who find Mr. Thackeray too thoughtful and Mr. Dickens too minute, who are tired of dainty fare and curious wines, who have had enough of the heavenly manna, and who long for the flesh-pots of Egypt. Mr. Trollope is the very man for them. There is no pretence about him, no shamming, no effort. He is always clever, often amusing, sometimes even great, or very near being great, but his predominating faculty is good sense. Belonging to the circulating library, Mr. Trollope's novels are free from those faults which we naturally associate with the circulating library—extravagance, trickery, false sentiment, morbid pictures. His style is the very opposite of melodramatic; it is plain and straightforward, utterly devoid of clap-trap. It is the style of a man who has a good deal to say, who can afford to say it simply, who does not attempt to astonish, and who is content to give his readers innocent and rational amusement. These novels are healthy and manly, and so long as Mr. Anthony Trollope is the prince of the circulating library our readers may rest assured that it is a very useful, very pleasant, and very honourable institution.

Perhaps Mr. Trollope carries his aversion from everything melo-dramatic to an extreme, and though he errs on the right side, still he errs. The essence of melodrama is surprise. The situations are unexpected; the characters are doing things for which we were not prepared; passions are evoked which are not justified by the facts, and sentiments are expressed which have no relation to the circumstances. Everything, in short, is a surprise. Mr. Trollope, on the other hand, has vowed that there shall be no surprises in his novels. The characters shall be naturally evolved; the incidents shall grow out of each other; the passion shall not be exaggerated, and the sentiment shall veritably belong to the event. But in determining thus to show cause for every effect, and a sufficient motive for every act and word, Mr. Trollope seems at times to be too anxious to avoid startling results; afraid lest the reader should be taken unawares, he lets out his secret too soon, and long before he has laid down his lines of action he forewarns us of what is to happen—what is to be the joyous consummation or the dismal catastrophe which is the intended result of all his plans. At the first mention of his heroine's name he says, ostentatiously, 'Now, this is to be my *prima donna*—the lady you must all love, the lady I am going to pet, the lady whom fortune is to favour, the lady who is to get the prime husband at the end of the third volume.' Here the story is at once told, all suspense is removed, and when we see the heroine afterwards under a cloud we know that the cloud means nothing, or is intended but to make the sunshine which afterwards bursts forth more bright. So of another personage, we are informed that his character is unsound and must inevitably end in misery and ruin. This is a sure way to prevent our being surprised when misery and ruin overtake the poor wretch; but it is also a method apt to damp our interest in the event, and to destroy all the excitement of suspense. It is the expression of a manly aversion to melodramatic art with which we cordially sympathize, but it is also an appeal to sources of interest which are more welcome to the student of philosophy than to the reader of novels. Mr. Trollope says virtually, 'I will do what novelists never yet have done; I will begin with the end of the story; I will have no secrets; I will sacrifice all the interest of cunningly devised situations and mysterious occurrences; I will, not perhaps formally, but virtually, give my readers the action of the piece as an accomplished fact, and if I cannot amuse them with what else remains—namely, with the rational pleasure of following the story in its details, tracing the gradual rise and progress of events, and describing the attendant circumstances,—then I may as well throw aside my pen altogether.' In making this resolve Mr. Trollope throws away, needlessly we think, some of the resources of his art; while, on the other hand, he wins our respect, and proves that a success which has not been purchased by vulgar methods must be due to merits of a sterling kind.

Mr. Trollope's first work was entitled *The Warden*, and when we give a skeleton of the story it will be seen that in the very outset of his career as a novelist he determined to shun the system of depending upon surprises. The Warden is appointed to the superintendence of a charity, something like that which Mr. Dickens described in one of his Christmas tales, and Mr. Whiston not long ago subjected to public criticism. The Warden pockets the greater portion of the emoluments, while those for whom the charity was intended divide among themselves a mere pittance. In the present instance the Warden, who is a soft-

hearted man, on being appointed to his sinecure, allows to the almsmen out of the mere goodness of his soul 2d. a-day more than the regulation of the charity gave them a right to expect. But a day comes when, just about the time that Mr. Whiston was urging his strong protest against the misappropriations of certain funds at Rochester, a surgeon named Bold created a disturbance in the cathedral town of Barchester, by suggesting that the Warden had no title to the very large income which he drew from the charity under his charge. The accused sees nothing for it but to resign. His resignation is a predetermined issue, and the rest of the novel is given to an exposition of the method by which his son-in-law tried to prevent that resignation, implying as it did the surrender of 800*l.* a-year. Nothing, however, can prevent the sacrifice. The Warden, who has usually no will of his own and allows his son-in-law to think for him, is in this matter of conscience firm as a rock. He resigns and the novel ends. Strange structure of a tale! The bloody villain and arch-diabolus of the story attacks the hero of the piece; the hero yields at once in his own mind; friends try to rouse his courage, but in vain he yields, and more than yields—he gives his daughter away to the enemy, and makes peace with him for ever. On this slight thread Mr Trollope has managed to hang a great deal of interest, limiting his tale to the dimensions of a single volume. The characters are well drawn— sketches rather than finished portraits, but still lifelike. There is the Bishop, incalculably sacred, stupid and senile; his son, the Archdeacon bustling, pompous, grasping, vigorous, the very type of an unpleasant but valuable church dignitary; the surgeon, bluff and bold, ardent and kind-hearted, but full of knight-errantry, and ready for the sake of a theory to hurl all his friends to perdition; the almsmen, with their paltry selfishness, their stupid prejudices, and their thin querulous style; the Warden himself, all goodness and meekness, soft and gelatinous; his daughter—one of those young ladies whom we seldom meet with in novels—a very ordinary young lady, with no peculiar gifts, but blessed with a pretty face, a sweet temper, and a little plain sense. Perhaps the Archdeacon is the best drawn character; and it may be amusing to learn how Dr. Grantley conducted himself within the hallowed recess formed by the clerical bed-curtains at Plumstead Episcopi. . . .
[The famous bed-curtain colloquy is quoted at length.]

Of Mr. Trollope's next novel, *Barchester Towers*, we gave some account when it appeared about two years ago. It is a continuation of the story of *The Warden*, the same characters being introduced with the addition of others, and the author depending for his success not so much on what is done in the way of action, as in showing vividly the manner in which it is done. We are interested in the characters, and for their sakes take pleasure in the action, which is, again, of the most common-place description. Mr. Trollope takes such action as occurs in the experience of every-day life—action which is so much the reverse of strange and improbable that any one leading the most placid existence must be able to trump it with something far more stirring from his daily life. But by the elucidation of character he invests his common-place incidents with remarkable attractions, and makes us all feel that we, too, must be acting such romances to intelligent on-lookers. In this case most of the personages with whom we form an acquaintance are of the tribe of Levi—bishops and priests, their wives and their children, their man-servant and their maid-servant, their ox and their ass. We are entirely in the clerical world, and are amused with its sacred loves and righteous hatreds, its canonical talk, its red-letter incidents, and its apostolical characters.

In the two years that have elapsed since the publication of this clerical novel, Mr. Trollope has sent forth three works written without diminution of power, notwithstanding the rapidity of production. Perhaps the greatest ability is displayed in the *Three Clerks*, a really brilliant tale of official life. It was difficult to handle the subject after Mr. Dickens, even if we allow that Mr. Dickens's account of the Circumlocution-office, with all its force, was not quite satisfactory. All that description of the Barnacles is very far from being in Mr. Dickens's best manner, and gives no real insight into the mysteries of the Government offices. It is too much of a caricature, and the caricature is too meagre to be very lifelike, while the sketch is sustained mainly by the author's extraordinary power of writing. If those who have been disappointed with that representation will turn to the picture of Mr. Trollope, they will at once see the difference between a funny sketch and a genuine photograph; and if the Administrative Reform Association is still in existence, we can confidently recommend to it the perusal of the *Three Clerks* as a very pleasant and profitable method of passing the time which must now hang heavy on its hands. Sir Gregory Hardlines is there, the distinguished secretary who imposed the system of competitive examinations; Sir Warwick Westend also, his faithful friend and coadjutor, together with the Rev. Mr. Jobbles, the prince of posers. Those who are curious in Parliamentary committees will be delighted with the investigation which one of these bodies conducts under Mr. Trollope's auspices. Those who are curious as to the habits of whippers-in should study the history of Mr. Whip Vigil and of his faithful fag, the Ho Undecimus Scott, familiarly known as Undy. If none of our reader have ever entered the office devoted to the Internal Navigation of th country, here they have an opportunity of studying the routine of the navvies—as the clerks in this department of the public service are playfully called. Those who admire the Woods and Works can enter into that mysterious abode; and those who love the Weights and Measures can here be introduced to their appointed guardians. From the Woods and Works, or the Weights and Measures, we retire when the day is done into the odorous parlour of the Magpie and Stump, or into the smoking-room of the Pythagorean Club, there to unbend after many hours of severe exertion. All these scenes are admirably depicted, and the story hangs on the adventures of a certain Alaric Tudor, one of the clerkly trio, who very early begins to speculate. From the moment of the first transaction, which is a dishonourable one, we know what is to follow—the downward course, until at length, in the heyday of his career, and amid all the prosperity that could be desired, Alaric Tudor turns to his own use trust money, falls upon evil days, is a defaulter, and ends with six months of Millbank prison. It is not very pleasant to follow the windings of such a story, in which we see the end from the beginning, and know that through each successive volume we are to be conducted down the facile descent to Avernus. It would be more agreeable to think, if but for a moment, that there is some chance left —there is some loophole to be discovered for an escape. The author is inexorable. We feel that after the first step there is no help for it, and we have the double disappointment of reading a tale of misery and tracing a career of folly which apparently it requires but a word or a sign to prevent. The disappointment is mitigated by the story of Charley Tudor, the third clerk, who begins life in the wildest way—haunts taverns, consults Jews, and kisses pretty barmaids, utterly regardless of consequences, until at length he is reformed and blest with an angel wife just about the time when Alaric Tudor is finally reduced to the manipulation of oakum. The whole novel is full of life and character, and gives perhaps the best idea of Mr. Trollope's power.

The other two novels—*Dr. Thorne* and *The Bertrams*—are of a less distinctive character, although they are not less interesting. In both we again trace the same sacrifice of the usual means of exciting interest; and the worst of it is that when we close the volumes we begin to think to ourselves,—'But, after all, how very stupid the people are to act in that way; they acted like idiots; they were to all appearance continually doing the very opposite of what they ought to have done, and with full knowledge running their heads against walls.' We are in the secrets of all hearts, and see the inevitable sequence of events in the passing thought. We gaze upon the personages with somewhat of the astonishment with which immortal spirits from the summit of their knowledge must look down upon the actions of men when they see us struggling for things that will end in our ruin, misjudging and hating our best friends, warming the viper in our bosoms, choosing the golden casket that contains the death's-head, instead of the leaden one that contains the pearl of price. To one who is deaf to the music a dance is very absurd; it is also absurd to those who hear a different music. Thus, readers who are lifted high above a tale, and in the plenitude of a superior knowledge removed from the silly fears and hopes that influence all-powerfully the personages below, are apt to lose their interest in what is taking place, and to see in the action nothing but a succession of follies. Mr. Trollope must beware of this danger. A good plot and a well-kept secret are not to be despised. Novel readers demand something more than the analysis of character, description of events, and humorous reflections, which it must be confessed that Mr. Trollope affords with no weak hand—in *Dr. Thorne* dwelling chiefly on life in the country, the life of great folks and little folks, of the hall and the hamlet; in the *Bertrams*, his latest novel, dwelling particularly on the choice of a profession and that unsettled period when a man with means at his disposal scarcely knows what to do with himself, and now thinks of entering the church, now studies law, now writes a heretical book, now sets off on a journey to Jerusalem and Mount Sinai. In all these scenes we detect the hand of a practised writer, a thoughtful man, and a kindly satirist. To those who are in the habit of reading novels it is unnecessary to say that Mr. Trollope is one of the most amusing of authors; and to those who in general prefer blue-books, statistics, and telegrams, but now and then indulge in the enormity of romance, we may report in a phrase which at this time of a new Parliament must be familiar to the British elector, that he is 'a safe man.'

39. Nathaniel Hawthorne, letter

11 February 1860

This letter to Joseph M. Field is quoted by Trollope in his *Auto-biography* (pp. 122–3), also in his article 'The Genius of Nathaniel Hawthorne', described in the headnote to No. 185.

It is odd enough that my own individual taste is for quite another class of works than those which I myself am able to write. If I were to meet with such books as mine by another writer, I don't believe I should be able to get through them. Have you ever read the novels of Anthony Trollope? They precisely suit my taste,—solid and substantial, written on the strength of beef and through the inspiration of ale, and just as real as if some giant had hewn a great lump out of the earth, and put it under a glass case, with all its inhabitants going about their daily business, and not suspecting that they were being made a show of. And these books are just as English as a beef-steak. Have they ever been tried in America? It needs an English residence to make them thoroughly comprehensible; but still I should think that human nature would give them success anywhere.

CASTLE RICHMOND

1860

In his *Autobiography* (pp. 131–2), Trollope remembered *Castle Richmond* as one of his failures. He had not looked at the book since it had first come out some sixteen years earlier, but 'poor as the work is', he said, he remembered 'all the incidents'.

Castle Richmond certainly was not a success,—though the plot is a fairly good plot, and is much more of a plot than I have generally been able to find. The scene is laid in Ireland, during the famine; and I am well aware now that English readers no longer like Irish stories. I cannot understand why it should be so, as the Irish character is peculiarly well fitted for romance. But Irish subjects generally have become distasteful. This novel, however, is of itself a weak production. The characters do not excite sympathy. The heroine has two lovers, one of whom is a scamp and the other a prig. As regards the scamp, the girl's mother is her own rival. Rivalry of the same nature has been admirably depicted by Thackeray in his *Esmond*; but there the mother's love seems to be justified by the girl's indifference. In *Castle Richmond* the mother strives to rob her daughter of the man's love. The girl herself has no character; and the mother, who is strong enough, is almost revolting. The dialogue is often lively, and some of the incidents are well told; but the story as a whole was a failure. I cannot remember, however, that it was roughly handled by the critics when it came out; and I much doubt whether anything so hard was said of it then as that which I have said here.

Castle Richmond was not, indeed, roughly handled by the reviewers, but few of them seem to have taken any notice of it.

---

40. Unsigned review, *Athenaeum*

19 May 1860, p. 681

'Castle Richmond' is a spirited novel; the characters are life-like, and the incidents real. There is a breadth of treatment, as painters call it, which gives a firmness and reality to the story, as well as to the people and things of which it treats. Three separate threads of interest are woven into the story; the famine in Ireland (for the story is Irish); the fortunes of the Fitzgeralds of Castle Richmond, in which the reader, after struggling in sandy shallows at the commencement of their history, is gradually embarked in a full tide of painful and absorbing interest; and, thirdly, the life and errors of Owen Fitzgerald, of Hap House, the real and only hero in the book, although his Cousin Herbert is the excellent young man, whose worth is recognized and virtue rewarded by the author, and who wins the prize. The reader throughout resolutely protests against the author's decision, and if the earnest sympathy of all who read his story could be any consolation to a man in sorrow, Owen Fitzgerald would have been recompensed long ago for his undeserved pangs of unrequited love; the author treats him basely, and every reader will resent it. The Countess of Desmond, the heroine's mother, and the evil influence of the story, is entirely detestable; not even the very gentlemanlike tone and manner in which the author speaks of her, abstaining from epithets against her, nor all the extenuating circum- stances which he tenderly brings to bear, can avail to mitigate the contempt and indignation she inspires; jealous of her own daughter, selfish, worldly, implacable,—playing with the happiness of three human creatures as with loaded dice,—she does not exhibit a trace of any quality to call forth esteem,—the author yet contrives to enlist pity in her behalf. Clara, the daughter and heroine, marries against the consent of the reader, who, however his judgment may be convinced, will have little sympathy with her choice. The only woman who draws any sympathy is Lady Fitzgerald, with her tragical secret, and the patient gentleness with which she carries it. The two Molloys, father and son, are very clever and well contrasted, so that the old rogue is softened when seen beside the young one; the redeeming touches are put in very skilfully. The remarks on the Irish famine are, on the whole, true and judicious, and the description of things, during that terrible time, very true and real. The story, however, as a story, is not so racy as 'Barchester Towers,' or 'The Warden;' there are no sketches in it equal to those of the Dean, or the Bishop, or Mr. Harding. The merest tyro in novel reading would have suspected the solution to the whole knot of difficulty and perplexity, which never occurred once to the astute lawyer, and which he is so slow to believe, even when it revealed itself of its own accord to him. 'Castle Richmond' is, however, a welcome addition to the novels of the season, and will remain a permanent boon to persons in search of a good, well- written novel, with plenty of genuine sense and interest in it; and the reader will be disposed to give more thanks than criticism to the author.

41. Unsigned notice, *Saturday Review*

19 May 1860, ix. 643–4

For the possibility that this review was influential in Trollope's taking up the shoemaker image as an analogy for himself as a prolific craftsman of the novel, see Introduction, VII. As the first sentence of this review reminds us, *Framley Parsonage* was already appearing in monthly instalments in the *Cornhill*.

Mr. Trollope is in the position of a man who, after becoming the father of an enormous family in a very short time, takes at last to having twins. For some years past he has written at least a novel a year; and now, whilst publishing one story in the *Cornhill Magazine*, he brings out another independently of it at the same time. . . . The remark which the whole fabric of the story suggests is, that Mr. Trollope has reached the stage in which he may justly claim the character of an excellent literary workman (though the style of his workmanship is certainly open to some criticism) but that he has also arrived at the point when he makes a novel just as he might make a pair of shoes, with a certain workmanlike satisfaction in turning out a good article, but with little of the freshness and zest which marked his earlier productions. The double bigamy artifice is an illustration of this. He brings it in openly and in a thoroughly businesslike way, but with as perfect a consciousness that he is going through a form as a lawyer feels when he puts in the usual covenants for title at the end of a conveyance. The legal simile suggests the observation that, according to his invariable habit, Mr. Trollope introduces a certain quantity of law, both civil and criminal, into his story. This time, however—yielding in some degree, let us hope, to the repeated representations addressed to him in this journal— he has contrived to get it substantially right. He need not, however, have antedated Sir John Stuart's elevation to the bench. He was not made Vice-Chancellor till long after 1847.

Perhaps the most curious part of the book is that which relates to the Irish famine. It is impossible not to feel that that was the part of it about which Mr. Trollope really cared, but that, as he had to get a novel out of it, he was in duty bound to mix up a hash of Desmonds and Fitzgeralds with the Indian meal on which his mind was fixed as he wrote. He really does know something, and really has something to say, upon this subject; and as a shoemaker who had served in the army might go on talking about his campaigns all the while that he was stitching away at the boot on his lap, Mr. Trollope constantly chats about the famine whilst he is making his novel. He has far more businesslike habits of thought, and a much fairer and more sensible mind than the great majority of popular novelists, so that what he does say upon the subject gives his readers cause to regret that he did not leave the loves of the mother, daughter, and two cousins unrecorded, to tell the world something more of what Mr. Trollope saw of Ireland in 1847, and afterwards, when pestilence and emigration had concluded that purgation of the country which famine began. It is of course impossible to persuade him to give up a practice which he appears to have adopted on principle, but the milk and the water really should be in separate pails. . . .

It would be unjust not to say, though it is a matter of course, that *Castle Richmond*, being written by Mr. Trollope, is very clever and amusing. It is needless to explain its merits. They are the same as those of his other novels.

Good wine needs no bush. We need not tell our readers that *Castle Richmond* is a clever and amusing novel, for its author's name is warrant enough for them of that fact. Critics may shake their sagacious heads at the dangerous rapidity with which book after book issues from Mr. Anthony Trollope's hand, but the books are all good, and the critics are silenced. But they are not beaten; it still remains true, notwithstanding one or another signal instance to the contrary, that hasty workmanship generally makes bad work; and Messrs. X., Y., and Z. may be assured that the odds are enormously against them if they be tempted to follow Mr. Trollope's example. Even he himself, with all his extraordinary nimbleness, cannot avoid paying some small forfeits to time. Capable as he is of writing pure, racy, and pleasant English, nothing but over-haste can account for the lapses into slovenly and ungrammatical language, of which he is habitually guilty. Such phrases as 'whether or no,' 'those sort of things,' 'to do other than,' are of frequent occurrence in all his novels. . . .

Mr. Trollope's new novel has its scene in the south of Ireland, in the year of the Famine; but none of its main issues are evolved out of that great calamity. Their connexion with it is casual, and just close enough to furnish in a suitable manner the secondary machinery and incidents of the story, to supply occasion for some of the comings and goings, the occupations and the talk of the dramatis personae, and to give to the story of the principal personages such a background of local and historical reality as serves to heighten its scenic illusion, and does not injuriously distract attention from the leading theme. The author's management of this portion of his materials is exceedingly judicious. He was in Ireland during the famine, travelling over its highways and byways in all directions, seeing everywhere the misery of the time, almost with the same fulness of opportunity as if he had been sent on a mission for its relief, but with a freedom of judgment which hardly any one could have retained amidst the distracting exigencies of such a position. Being, as everybody knows, not only a graphic writer but a man of approved administrative faculty, he must have a great deal to say about the terrible event of which he was so close an observer; but he is too good an artist to say it all in the wrong place. What he has said is eminently worthy of perusal, and will obtain it the more readily, and with the better effect, in consequence of the author's judicious reticence.

FRAMLEY PARSONAGE

1861

Framley Parsonage, published in the first sixteen issues of the *Cornhill Magazine* from January 1860 to April 1861 (in book form also in April of that year), brought Trollope a sharp increase in popularity (see Introduction, III) strongly reflected in the reviews of this novel, partly in protests against the excessive admiration he had been receiving from the public. Trollope himself (*Autobiography*, p. 121) felt that his plan for the novel was perilously slight, consisting 'simply of a girl refusing to marry the man she loved till the man's friends agreed to accept her lovingly'.

Nothing could be less efficient or artistic. But the characters were so well handled, that the work from the first to the last was popular,—and was received as it went on with still increasing favour by both editor and proprietor of the magazine. The story was thoroughly English. There was a little fox-hunting and a little tuft-hunting, some Christian virtue and some Christian cant. There was no heroism and no villainy. There was much Church, but more love-making. And it was downright honest love, in which there was no pretence on the part of the lady that she was too ethereal to be fond of a man, no half-and-half inclination on the part of the man to pay a certain price and no more for a pretty toy. Each of them longed for the other, and they were not ashamed to say so. Consequently they in England who were living, or had lived, the same sort of life, liked *Framley Parsonage*. I think myself that Lucy Robarts is perhaps the most natural, at any rate, of those who have been good girls. She was not as dear to me as Kate Woodward in *The Three Clerks*, but I think she is more like real human life. Indeed I doubt whether such a character could be made more lifelike than Lucy Robarts. And I will say also that in this novel there is no very weak part,—no long succession of dull pages.

43. Unsigned review, *Examiner*

20 April 1861, pp. 244–5

The *Warden* and *Barchester Towers* are the only novels of Mr. Trollope's better than *Framley Parsonage*. It has been said that every man, if he could write it, has one good novel in him. *Barchester Towers* is a sequel to the *Warden*, and *Framley Parsonage* is an appendix to them both. It is in as far as they resemble the *Warden* that the sequel and appendix claim pre-eminence because they contain the particular novel that seems to have been, according to this notion, in Mr. Trollope, or that which it was in his nature to write better than another man, however superior he might be in genius, could have written it. His sketches of clerical life are his own. When writing upon other topics he is always clever, lively, and observant, but the limits to his power are more clearly manifest.

Mr. Anthony Trollope is not in the highest sense a man of genius. In all his works, best and worst, perhaps, there is not a touch of original fancy; as far as it is possible for a novelist to be without invention he is without it. There is no ingenuity in the construction of his stories. The sketches of character on which they depend for their value are the result of shrewd observation cleverly expressed in every-day phrase; never of any subtle or peculiar insight into character. . . . Again, in the inability to represent strong passion Mr. Trollope shows his want of the insight that belongs to genius. The passion of Lucy Robarts in *Framley Parsonage*, when she pours out her secret misery of a baulked love to her sister-in-law, is an example of this. She speaks of herself as having been 'bowled over like a nine-pin,' when she was so sure that she 'should never be missish, and spoony and sentimental'; calls herself 'an unutterable ass,' and so forth; all which is of course very manly, and preserves the author from all risk of being himself considered to write 'spoony' love passages, but it does not represent the passion of a woman even when she, as Lucy is here doing, hysterically mocks at her own grief.

There is no want of hearty feeling in the book. A healthy human sense of what he has fairly seen and entered into with full understanding in the course of life, is no mean part of the strength of this as of all Mr.

Trollope's novels. The author is, no doubt, too much at the usual level of society in observation and expression to admit of pathos in his writings; they do not even contain any flashes of the wit with which not a few men who do not write are able to enliven social intercourse. But when he is at home with his subject and it represents a cause that has his sympathy, Mr. Trollope's clear expression of a wholesome human feeling makes its way home to the reader's heart. There is force then, and there is some force everywhere, in the literalness on which he depends necessarily for his power as a novelist; the literalness, let it be remembered, of a thoroughly quick-witted and observant man.

Mr. Trollope is at his best, we have said, when writing of the clergy; not of the bench of bishops, for his bishop is a feeble caricature, but of the lesser dignitaries of the cathedral close, their wives and daughters, and not of these only, as *Framley Parsonage* shows. The picture of Mark Robarts, the young country rector, too early possessed of a good living, who is tempted into the fast set of country society, beguiled by an embarrassed county member, and led through weakness of character to risk the very existence of a home to which he is attached with his whole heart, is excellent. The domestic side of his nature is well kept in view, and even when he is known in the county as a hunting parson, we are made to understand, together with his weakness, the domestic qualities and the religious nature underlying all. The sketch of the generous, impulsive wife, and a more elaborate study of the not less generous friend and neighbour, Lady Lufton, patroness of the living, whose son was Mark's schoolfellow and is his friend, are simply faultless. The little weaknesses, and the great strength of a refined womanly nature in Lady Lufton, the simple and good-hearted prejudices, the pleasant airs of patronage—always a part of the true dignity with which she is invested —the generous conquests of prejudice and temper, and the gentle sacri- fices that come of the love of a widow for her only son, are combined in the character of Lady Lufton with a delicacy of touch that is perhaps only the more admirably true and effective for that literalness of manner upon which we have just dwelt. Lord Lufton, her handsome and good- natured son, who falls for a short time into the hands of the Philistines; and Mr. Sowerby, the embarrassed county member whose estates are mortgaged, to whom little bills are a necessity of daily life, and who with unprincipled good-nature, never with malice, ruins himself and swindles his friends, represent also thoroughly well certain forms of life.

The weakest parts of the book are those which affect political satire. The meeting at Gatherum Castle; all that relates to the immensity of

Tom Towers, to the Jupiter, and to Mr. Harold Smith, who becomes Lord Petty Bag, or to the Parliamentary struggle described as a contest between the gods and giants, is feeble and confused. . . . Straightforward and sensible as he is, owing much of his popularity to the fact that he is the cleverest of novelists who, without being more subtle than most of their neighbours, speak to the world in their own way out of a shrewd head and a sound heart, Mr. Trollope still has affectations to be conquered. . . .

But we have laid too much stress on the drawbacks to our praise. The real and sound part of the book predominates so largely that we represent the strength not of a particular passage, but of *Framley Parsonage* itself, as one of the best novels of the day, when we quote at length—for to do justice to a writer whose strength is not in detached thoughts we must needs quote at length—part of the introduction to the reader of that story of the Crawley family which Mr. Trollope has written with the best feeling, and with his utmost skill. In it he has secured the sympathies and the respect of all his readers for the hardships borne by the thousands of high-hearted English clergymen who painfully endeavour to find gentle nurture for their families on incomes that do not exceed the hire of a mechanic. . . . The study of this poor clergyman and his household is, perhaps, the best of all Mr. Trollope's clerical sketches, and, as we have already said, they are the best that have been written in our day.

44. Unsigned notice, *Saturday Review*

4 May 1861, xi. 451–2

This critique is coloured, especially in the concluding paragraph, by the hostile attitude of the periodical toward the *Cornhill Magazine*. Thackeray as editor had lured away some of the *Saturday*'s most talented writers (see Bevington, pp. 28, 133, etc.).

Mr. Anthony Trollope has agreeably entertained for the last eighteen months that portion of society whose intellectual food is taken monthly in the shape of magazines. In looking back on the result of his labours we must confess that he writes as good a book as is often written by a clever and pleasant man in the intervals of business. With his love of fun and caricature he combines much kindliness and good feeling; he is always readable and pleasant, even if he does not assume to be severe; and few of his readers can complain of having ever risen from a chapter of *Framley Parsonage* in either too serious or too cynical a mood. If Mr. Mudie is 'a man,' and not merely the system that Madame de Staël pronounced the first Bonaparte to be, he has much reason to be grateful to Mr. Trollope. The author of *Framley Parsonage* is a writer who is born to make the fortune of circulating libraries. At the beginning of every month the new number of his book has ranked almost as one of the delicacies of the season; and no London belle dared to pretend to consider herself literary, who did not know the very latest intelligence about the state of Lucy Robarts' heart, and of Griselda Grantley's flounces. It is a difficult thing to estimate the exact position and merit of a book with which we are all so familiar, and which has diverted us so long. It seems a kind of breach of hospitality to criticise *Framley Parsonage* at all. It has been an inmate of the drawing-room—it has travelled with us in the train—it has lain on the breakfast-table. We feel as if we had met Lady Lufton at a country house, admired Lord Dumbello at a ball, and seen Mrs. Proudie at an episcopal evening party. How is it possible, after so much friendly intercourse, to turn round upon the book and its leading characters, and to dissect and analyse them as a critic should?

The best idea of Mr. Anthony Trollope's book is suggested by the skill of the artist who has illustrated it. Opposite the last page of the first volume is to be seen a picture by a well-known hand, the talent of which cannot be disputed. The subject of the plate is Lucy Robarts' crinoline, and the reader's eye following the folds of the crinoline, will come at last upon Lucy Robarts' face and shoulders, which have retired into a corner of the picture, in concession to the social claims of muslin and of lace. The expression on the heroine's handsome face is indicative of despair. She has lost her lover, as she believes, and has flung herself down to indulge her heart in its natural girlish grief. In the foreground the artist has placed one of the heroine's boots. In the background may be seen an oval mirror. The tableau is in all respects worthy of the novel. Mr. Millais, in a congenial moment of social inspiration, has been so fortunate as to hit off in this one illustration the whole spirit of the book. None of Mr. Trollope's figures in their wildest grief could be drawn except in their every-day dress. We should not know them out of it, any more than we should recognise an evening beauty in her morning costume. All are ordinary men and women, and their sayings and doings are neither above nor below the level of what we see in common and everyday life. Mr. Trollope himself nowhere pretends to do more than to write down what he sees going on around him. He paints from the outside. This does not make his painting for all ordinary purposes the less real. What we know of most people that we meet is the way they dress, their fortune, their manners in the world, their aims, the general tenor of their lives, and the kind of remarks that they make when they are talking to their acquaintances. Mr. Anthony Trollope tells us all this about his heroes and heroines, and tells it us with a strong dash of cleverness and fun. His business is simply to catch folly and fashion as they fly. We see Lady Lufton and Mrs. Grantley in the book just as we should see them if we were their neighbours in Barsetshire. We get tired of them as soon as, and no sooner than, we should get tired of Lady Lufton and Mrs. Grantley in real life, if they kept on calling once a month. We like to be amused, and we like to come across the characters that amuse us. We never become particularly intimate with any. Mr. Anthony Trollope has never encouraged his readers to suppose that he himself has much more than a ball-room acquaintance with his own heroines.

The subject-matter with which he deals is the same, or pretty nearly the same, as that with which others have dealt before. Though the author of *Barchester Towers* is no mere imitator, he probably owes something to the author of *Vanity Fair*. The latter, however, is, or rather has been, a far greater writer than Mr. Trollope has as yet proved himself, who never does more than caricature the fashionable vanities of society, and is satisfied to be the laughing philosopher of Rotten Row. Laughing philosophers are not only less sentimental than their weeping coadjutors—they do not pretend to be so profound. Mr. Trollope does not assert his claim to be considered an adept in the mysterious workings of the human heart; he does not despair, like the prophet, of everything but eating and drinking; he does not regret the time when he was birched at school; and he gives us merely the broad and salient points of human nature, mixed with a good deal of broad and occasionally brilliant fun. *Framley Parsonage* is not, however, either so brilliant or so well worth reading as *Barchester Towers*, of which it is too often merely a *réchauffé*. It stands to its predecessor very much as the *Newcomes* stands to *Vanity Fair*. With fewer faults of taste, with more polish and geniality of tone, it is infinitely less forcible and striking. It is a curious thing to notice how soon, in the words of the poet, a successful author 'rubs his social angles down.' As Mr. Trollope becomes more successful, he becomes more tame. He improves in the refinement and delicacy of his touch, at the expense of his brilliancy and his fun. Belonging as he does to the 'conversational' school, who address their readers from first to last in a tone of raillery and badinage, there is a slight danger that, with all his ability, he may at last degenerate into a mere *raconteur*, whose monthly mission is to gossip about things in general.

With some of the best characters in *Framley Parsonage* we are already acquainted. Mrs. Proudie, Miss Dunstable, the Greshams, and the Grantleys, are creations which belong to older and fresher works. It is astonishing how much a novelist loses in freshness and vigour by adopting the plan now so much in vogue, of borrowing from himself. It is at best a lazy and seductive artifice. It tempts the writer to save time by dispensing with new efforts and fresh draughts upon his own imagination, and the loss of interest to the reader is very great. We have several of these 'cyclic' novelists just at present. Mr. Trollope, it is true—whose art lies not in developing or creating character, but in depicting the behaviour of drawing-room company—suffers less than others might by his adoption of the practice. We are almost always glad to see Mrs. Proudie and Miss Dunstable in his book, just as we should be generally glad, for the sake of the fun, to go to an evening party if we knew they were to be there. But we simply are interested in them so far as they say something good to amuse us. About their inner life we have long known all that Mr. Trollope is able to tell us, and we do not care to watch them long unless they are going to be funny. Nobody, for example, at all wants to hear of the Greshams after they have been married and settled, except for the sake of politeness to their friend, Mr. Trollope. As for the Archdeacon and Mrs. Grantley, they may be tolerated because of Miss Griselda, but it is to be remembered that we have had them already at some length. If the present fashion continues, and the heroes of one novel reappear so constantly in the next, readers will begin to hope that funerals, and not marriages, may in future be made the *finale* in which all romances terminate. Even the gallant and moral Tom Brown, if he is wise, will beware of the Nemesis that follows on good fortune, and expire before he reaches a third work of fiction; and it is to be hoped that in the course of time some literary deluge may sweep away the whole generation among which the Newcomes moved. Writers who are really good damage their reputation and weaken their strength by relaxing their energies, allowing themselves to dress up their half-worn ideas, and living on their capital instead of coining fresh gold.

It is because we are only slightly interested in the character of the people in the story, that Mr. Trollope is driven continually to amuse us by caricature. To paint the ordinary doings of ordinary men and women would be a stupid and uninteresting performance, unless either a shade of mystery and romance, or of psychological interest, was added to the picture, or unless everything is cleverly turned into fun. A dash of exaggeration and emphasis is needed to convert a commonplace scene into an amusing comedy. Perhaps the two wittiest scenes in *Framley Parsonage* are Mr. Harold Smith's lecture, and Miss Dunstable's conversazione. There are very few living writers who could exaggerate and caricature with so delicate and ingenious a touch as Mr. Anthony Trollope in these two chapters. Mr. Dickens would convert these perhaps into a broad and humorous travestie. His great rival would turn them into a satirical narrative, mixed with an under-current of the philosophy of Ecclesiastes. Mr. Trollope simply sees the amusing side of the scene, and relates the history of the proceedings as a good story-teller might. In fact, he is far less of a novelist than a good diner-out. Any of Mr. Trollope's admirers who has a strong sense of fun may do for himself in imagination what it is Mr. Trollope's charm that he has done so well on paper. Given Mrs. Proudie and Mrs. Grantley in a room, who does not know what they would say to one another? The difference between Mr. Trollope and his readers is that he not only knows what Mrs. Proudie and Mrs. Grantley would say, and how they would look, but can seize upon the most amusing points and write them down. As of course it is only worth his while to write down the amusing part of their conversation, which after all must be a fractional portion of the whole, his narrative is a caricature.

The plot of *Framley Parsonage* is really extremely poor, and the abruptness with which the third volume concludes leads us to conjecture that the author was wearied of the society of the good people of Barsetshire, of whom, in the course of all his novels, he has seen so much. Mr. Trollope is not naturally a good constructor of plots, and writing month by month in a magazine is not the best way to make him so. It is not of course an inevitable result of the system of publishing in periodicals, that the plot becomes weak and unsubstantial. But it is no doubt difficult to keep the spine of a novel strong and healthy, if the novel is twelve times a year divided into minute portions, and joined together at the end like a piece of patchwork. All unity of conception in the book too often gives way—the chapters become fragmentary and disjointed—and the novelist does little more than stroll on from month to month—preaching and teaching his own particular philosophy —catering for the amusement of the public, and piously hoping that something interesting may ultimately happen to his own hero. It is not in this way that great works are written. Magazines may be floated by even the inferior works of famous pens; or sometimes by the mere names of once meritorious authors. Possibly it is right and proper to have an asylum for lazy or extinct genius. But the authors produce in almost every case what is unworthy of their own credit, and in some (with all submission be it spoken) what is not worthy of the attention of the public. A lazily-framed argument, and the *repetita crambe* of second-hand characters, do not stimulate curiosity. Mr. Trollope, if he is a prudent man, will consider his ways. When next the author of *Framley Parsonage* comes before the public—an event to which all of us look forward with pleasure—we trust that it may be with new heroes and new heroines, and a new plot; and that *Tom Towers*, and *the Jupiter*, the gods and the giants, Barchester and its Bishop, may all be sleeping in a common grave.

45. Unsigned notice, *London Review*

11 May 1861, ii. 544–5

Too many hundreds have read this beautiful novel, as it appeared monthly in *The Cornhill*, for it to be necessary to give any account of it as a story. . . . We know all the characters in the book as well as if we had been introduced to them at Miss Dunstable's grand party, had sat with them in Lady Lufton's state drawing-room, or had driven over to Barchester in the little basket-phaeton, or to Hogglestock, or to Plumstead; as if we had eaten at their boards and drunk from out their cellars; for Mr. Trollope has the art to incise all that he writes, and to cut, as if in granite, the very weakest of his lines. There is not a character in this story about the tracing of which is any blur or raggedness; all is cleanly drawn, sharp cut; definitely cleared; and we have made so many more actual friends and acquaintances in every person of the tale. Perhaps this exceeding definiteness and sharpness of delineation is Mr. Trollope's best quality as a mere workman. When a writer is able to make his characters live and breathe and move before us—when he lifts them out of mere names and endues them with personality—he has done the greatest thing that lies before him in that direction. After this may come the questions of the moral purpose of a book. . . .

We regard this work of Mr. Trollope as matchless in its way, being so perfectly pure and yet so manly, such fitting food for men, but with no odour and no savour that shall hurt the tenderest maiden. Perhaps one cause is, the highly 'respectable' station of his personages, and the fine flavour hanging even yet, in these degenerate Broad Church days, round the old High Church orthodox cathedral dignitaries, who rather patronize religion than live on it, and who are gentlemen before they are priests. One feels in eminently good society with Mr. Trollope. Not in the flashy, fashionable society of May Fair, with ruined gamesters and ruddled dowagers, but your steady, safe-going, port-wine, and county-family society, specially dear to the English nation at large, and giving a certain feeling of 'safeness' to the pages wherein they are depicted. . . . Mr. Trollope has no special theory to enforce. He cares to paint the world as he sees it—weaknesses, virtues, shortcomings, villanies—just as they flash across the mirror among the ordinary

virtuous and failing, and contents himself with delineating the everyday
men and women, who move about the world without special notice or
éclat. This is very delightful, and singularly refreshing. Mr. Trollope
has not the qualities of some of our ablest writers. He has not the intense
humour, nor the sweetness and pathetic tenderness of Dickens; he has
not Thackeray's inimitable irony; he has not George Eliot's breadth
and boldness; nor Kingsley's earnest genius; but he has his own special
qualities of strength and soundness, which make him as charming a
companion as any novelist extant. . . .

The clever son of a clever mother, Mr. Trollope has now got his foot
fairly in the stirrup. He has come to his full manhood before he has
come to his full fame, and the fame is all the deeper and richer and
sweeter-flavoured for the maturity of the nature. . . . Let other writers
claim their own special characteristics, and wear their own special
crowns; but let Mr. Trollope engrave on his the words health and
manliness, as the two qualities best expressing his intellectual condition.
'Framley Parsonage' is about the most healthy and most masculine book
that has been published in these later times, which, to our thinking, is
the highest term of praise to be awarded any work whatever.

46. Unsigned notice, *Eclectic Review*

July 1861, series 8, i. 126–8

We are not concerned to let our readers know what we think or have thought of Mr. Anthony Trollope's previous fictions; but we have certainly read *Framley Parsonage* . . . with pleasure. Mr. Trollope i not a writer to create in the reader feelings of delight; he is neithe learned, nor sentimental, nor metaphysical, but he is interesting, and real. Mr. Millais illustrates this fiction; and to the school of art repre- sented by Mr. Millais among artists, belongs Mr. Trollope among the writers of fiction. He is a Pre-Raphaelite; he draws the characters of life in hard lines; but the effect of this book is without doubt good the great moral of the story being, 'have nothing to do with friendly acceptances and accommodation bills.' There is plenty of material for reflection in these volumes upon the various strata of English society and especially while we would not have it thought that we speak in any wrath from 'the Sions and Ebenezers' Mr. Trollope speaks of, we think if there is anything true in the sketches of this book, there is something in what it unfolds touching the theory of Church of Englandism, which may well command attention; and when we re- member the tens of thousands who have probably read this tale, either in its original publication in the *Cornhill*, or in its present form, we trust that some will remember that the portrait of the Rev. Mr. Crawley, of Hogglestock, the starving, holy, faithful man of God, is a portrait to which innumerable counterparts may be presented from the life in most parts of England. . . .

We are sorry to give no more attention to a novel so thoroughly good as this is; certainly the best with which Mr. Trollope has favoured his readers. Lady Lufton and Lucy Robarts are most loveable creatures; so is the rector's wife; and the domestic scenes, and the social life upon its larger scale, alike entertain, without injuring; while the satire is smart without ever becoming morbid.

47. 'J.A.', *Sharpe's London Magazine*

July 1861, n.s. xix. 103–5

I have not discovered the identity of J.A., despite considerable searching. *Orley Farm*, with illustrations by Millais, mentioned in the concluding sentences of the notice, had been appearing in monthly parts beginning in March 1861.

It is as yet by no means decided what a novel should be. There is a growing inclination to restrict the domain of the novel within narrower and narrower bounds. Novels with a direct moral purpose, or a historic purpose, or a scientific purpose, are sure to be carped at by the critics. An essay, they say, is the right form in which to embody these high purposes; an author ought not to foist his speculations upon the public in a manner necessarily so untruthful and incomplete. Then, tragical subjects are said to be unfit for novels. To choose a tragical subject is instantly pronounced to be a mark of ill-taste. An intricate plot is decried as impossible in real life. Carefully elaborated characters are held up as burlesques of human nature. Altogether, it will be found that unfavourable criticisms generally point to the fact that the novel-writer has aimed at *too much*. His plot or his characters or his speculations are overdone. To say that the novel shall represent, without overstepping the modesty of nature, real human life, is no longer a sufficient definition. We are beginning to restrict it within very much narrower bounds. Some weeks ago we read in a critical journal a definition of what the novel should be, which, perhaps, most of our modern school of critics would accept. The writer stated that the only proper subject-matter for the novel was the *manners* of the time in which it was written. With great ingenuity he proceeded to show how invaluable such books would be to historians of later ages, who would thus have documents ready to their hands from which to cull those historical flowers which so pleasantly bestrew their heavier pages. 'Tom Jones' was cited as an example of this orthodox novel—'Tom Jones,' from which book we learn that swearing was more common in those days than in these, and that the lighter vices were not so strictly kept behind the veil as they now are. If we accept this definition of the novel, viz. that it shall represent solely the *manners* of the time in which it is written, then 'Framley Parsonage' is a model novel. This, with the other numerous works of Mr. Trollope, will be hailed by after-ages as a priceless possession. From its pages the future antiquary will learn, among other curious facts, that the contemporaries of Mr. Trollope were accustomed under all circumstances, whether of joy or grief, to dress for dinner. Surely, Mr. Millais, when he drew that personification of crinoline representing Lucy Robarts in a state of woe, was in an humour of grim satire. There could not be a better emblem of the book than this picture. The pretty woeful face and clasped hands and little pendant foot (though this must be booted in a horse-breaker fashion) squeezed into odd corners to give due prominence to that mountain of flounces, are as the touches of real human nature which Mr. Trollope has sparsely scattered on the outskirts of his huge mass of conventionalism. The story turns upon the inconveniences caused by a bill-acceptance, and the disquiets arising from a love-affair between a rich lord and the sister of his parson-friend. The bill, with all its attendant expenses, does not exceed a thousand pounds. Mark Robarts who accepts it has an income of fifteen hundred a-year; moreover, all his friends are rich and are eager to lend him or to give him the thousand pounds in question. One does not quite see why the affair should end in bailiffs taking possession of the parsonage furniture, save that the exigencies of the story demand that little piece of excitement, and that a moral is thus pointed how very much more shocking it is for a clergyman to suffer such misfortune than a layman. With regard to the love-passage between Lucy Robarts and Lord Lufton, the only difficulty is that Lady Lufton, his mother, is supposed to be hostile to the match. Lucy will not accept Ludovic until the consent of his mother is gained. The mother never could or did refuse Ludovic anything, and so, when he asks her to consent to the marriage, she does consent. Why Lucy should so often enter upon the scene woe-begone in crinoline does not sufficiently appear. There are the usual questions of conscience in the book—the struggles between duty and pleasure which lie at the bottom of all human stories. Here these take the form of casuistries as to what a parson ought to do or ought not to do. How far may he act against the wishes of his patroness? Ought he to visit a bachelor-duke? Does the presence of his bishop with him in questionable society render that society innoxious to himself? May he ride to the meet with a friend, and, if so, may he cross one field after the hounds, and, if one, how many more? By how much is the wickedness of having anything to do with a bill increased by the *party* being clerical instead of lay? . . . We have often wondered what he [Trollope] purposes in these constant mild satires. We get always now, in his books, a flourish of trumpets when he is going to trot out a parson. He has achieved fame for that trick, and it is always printed in his bills, in the largest letters. Mr. Trollope in his famous act of parsonship is received with loud applause at the threshold of the arena, and probably hisses would follow if he substituted any other performance for that time-honoured one. The lady-part of his audience, especially, appreciate this poking of fun at their pastors. Bishop Proudie turned into an old pantaloon is meat and drink to them. The wickedness of making fun of a bishop gives an exquisite edge to their delight. We could understand that applause of this performance would make Mr. Trollope repeat it, also that habit would make him repeat it—it must be very easy to do what he has been doing for half a life; but when we find him gravely hinting a high moral purpose in these exhibitions, and referring to his labours past and to come as giving him a claim to the gratitude of his countrymen, we recur with double force to our old wonderment—what is his object? Is he a special enemy or a special friend to the parsons? Did a parson ever injure him, or are all his relations in the church?

To say that there are no touches of nature in 'Framley Parsonage' would be untrue; but we do say that they are almost lost and swallowed up in the overwhelming floods of conventionality. Lucy is pleasantly drawn, and sometimes her satiric utterances against herself express as well as can be her bitterness of heart. The devotion of Mrs. Robarts in the bailiff-scene is touching. The spice of poetry that exists in Sowerby gains instant acknowledgment in every heart as true. The pride of Crawley, in its first conception, is excellent; but then Mr. Trollope has chosen to burlesque it with his flippant wit. There are passages in this book so truthful, so pathetic, so humourous, that they move those who are not admirers of the author to a tenfold impatience of the mass of twaddle in which they are buried. The standard which the story sets up for itself is a false one. There are no men and women in 'Framley Parsonage:' they are never viewed as men and women; but only with regard to their relations to Society. The only conscience in the book is, 'What will the world say?' the only morality, 'Such conduct does not become such a position.' Unfrock Mark Robarts and he does not exist. Deprive Lord Lufton of his title, Miss Dunstable of her wealth, and they cease to be. No doubt the accidents of life affect men greatly; but men do exist apart from these accidents. . . .

We have said enough about Mr. Trollope to show that we differ from all the world in our estimate of his novels. He is now, perhaps, the most popular of our modern novelists: his name (Heaven save the mark!) is coupled with the toast of English Literature at literary dinners. (Is novel-writing the highest branch of Literature? and have we no Dickens or Thackeray to represent it, if it is?) Rumour promises us another novel from his hand in the pages of the *Cornhill*. His Orley Farm, illustrated by an artist, once our first, is on every drawing-room table. Mr. Trollope is at the height of his fame. We prophesy that he will live to see his novels rated at their worth. That we should return to an admiration of the fashionable novel, long since buried beneath worthier fictions, now resuscitated in all its flimsy flippancy, is not a good sign.

J.A.

48. Unsigned notice, *Westminster Review*

July 1861, lxxvi. 282–4

It is a curious and not very satisfactory phenomenon that a novel so trivial and purposeless as 'Framley Parsonage' should have acquired the popularity it undoubtedly did during its appearance in the *Cornhill Magazine*. This can be attributed to no higher qualities than a certain facility, not to say glibness of composition peculiar to the author; there is an agreeable facility about Mr. Trollope's way of telling a story which reminds us of the kind of satisfaction we derive from a sensible after-dinner speech, the moral topics are as obvious and the remarks as well worn; we are never alarmed by an appeal to our powers of thought, but are supplied with observations on manners and society which few can have failed to have made at some time or other, and which are accepted as very true and descriptive, because they coincide with the first general and superficial reflections of most of his readers. The misfortune of this style of writing is that however pleasant it may be to listen to an after-dinner speech once a month, it is beyond human endurance to sit out some twenty such inflictions; the diffuse dead level which was even pleasant in detail, becomes tedious beyond description when we are forced to take the whole journey at a stretch. These remarks may, perhaps, appear unjust to many who have read the story from month to month, but any one who thinks so we invite to a re-perusal *in extenso* before coming to that conclusion. We do not think it very probable that the experiment will be made. The habit of writing a story in periodical instalments is almost always fatal to that coherence and proportion without which no work can lay claim to any really artistic merit. The consequence of this mode of publication is that 'Framley Parsonage' is rather a series of anecdotes than a well-knit tale. The central notion of the enormity of a young lady, without fortune or birth, aspiring to the hand of a young nobleman with twenty thousand a year, is hardly serious enough to support all that *entourage* of political life described in the words of *Times* leaders of a few years since; there is something ludicrous in the iteration with which this precious case of conscience is discussed by all the *dramatis personae*. We have the history of that tremendous offer of Lord Lufton's from at least five different persons, who can make nothing of it, nor in any way see their way out of such an astounding difficulty; the only conclusion we are allowed to come to—which after all it must be allowed is somewhat consolatory —is, that if two persons situated like his lordship and Lucy Robarts know their own minds, they have but little to fear from what may pass in those of their friends. Mr. Trollope gives way too in this and other of his novels to a weakness now very common with our writers of fiction, we mean in the return to characters which they have treated with more or less success in former works. This can hardly ever be accomplished successfully, and while it betrays a great poverty of invention, most commonly does but vulgarize, if not destroy, what may have been originally a happy conception. Few, we think, will be edified by the part which Dr. Thorne is made to play in the present novel. It would seem impossible for Mr. Trollope to invent a story without adding to his sketches of the clergy in their relations to general society. Mark Robarts and Mr. Crawley are new figures in this somewhat extensive gallery; his sitters have but little to thank him for, and it may be pleaded by them that there is a fundamental injustice in constantly treating a particular class of men from a point of view which is but accidental to their position.

The view, however, if partial cannot be said to be unjust; and Mr. Trollope adds greatly to the weight of the popular conviction, that a young man without external support can hardly be exposed to more severe moral trials in any walk of life than to those he must encounter if he adopts the Church as a profession. Society demands of clergymen a character and bearing for which it, like an Egyptian taskmaster, will not supply the absolutely necessary material conditions; the difficulties of the position, it must candidly be confessed, are, after all, far greater than the weaknesses of those who occupy it; and this truth is not sufficiently insisted on by the happy satirist of prebends, deans, archdeacons, and bishops. In 'Framley Parsonage' there is no evolution: the story progresses by constant aggregation of details; in this way novels may be manufactured like Manchester goods, and retailed at so much per yard so long as the colour and design retain their hold, or what after all is no better than a passing vogue.

Without thought it is impossible that any permanent literary work can be brought forth; and we think it as impossible that 'Framley Parsonage' should be remembered for a year, as that 'Silas Marner' should ever be forgotten.

49. Unsigned notice, *American Theological Review*

October 1861, iii. 765

Without any rare or exciting incidents, the interest of the reader in this new volume of Mr. Trollope, is kept up by the accurate delineation of the characters, the simple and regular movement of the story, and the naturalness and vivacity of the dialogue. The descriptions of scenes and events are uniformly good. It is a book that may be safely recommended, especially to young clergymen, who are solicited to indorse the notes of friends in an emergency.

How many admirers of 'Tom Browne's Schooldays' have managed to wade through the long succession of tedious chapters that profess to contain the history of Tom Browne at Oxford? An author who has once found a willing public, soon comes to have but too many inducements to make unfair trial of their good nature. If Mr. Trollope will write such dreary tales as 'Framley Parsonage,' even he must look to find himself sooner or later tumbled from his throne by the doom he has already done so much to provoke. For a writer who has made himself so widely agreeable to the novel-reading world, his last performance comes as near being utterly unreadable as any thing of his writing could. The twaddle, from which his former works were not always free, here colours every thing with its dull sickly hue; and the rambling tendency which he could never keep quite down, here drags him into fields of description neither fresh nor by any means entertaining. All that talk about 'gods' and 'giants,' and 'The Jupiter,' has been done before to weariness by the same pen; and who really cares to see the small party squabbles of the last few years fought over again in borrowed language in the pages of a novel which has properly nothing to do with mere politics?

The whole story in fact is blown out to its present size by a wonderful mixture of small talk and superfluous matter, partly filched from former novels. Half the characters are sheer excrescences, and even of those excrescences a great many lack the redeeming merit of being new. When are we to see the last of Bishop and Mrs. Proudie, of the Grantlys, of Tom Towers, of Dr. Thorne? This merciless reintroduction of old friends saves a novelist so much of the time and trouble needed for coining new ones; and is it not pleasant, too, for both reader and author to meet again as it were under the old roof amid so many memorials of past familiarity? And then how naturally the people all talk and act! Every thing, to their commonest thoughts, is set down with an unpretending minuteness that carries one back to the tales of one's early childhood! Mark Robarts is so sweetly simple in his money dealings with Sowerby, and writes such pretty natural letters home to his wife.

Lord Lufton talks so nicely to Lucy Robarts and behaves so like a dutiful son to his loving old mother. And how charmingly like the talk of humbler folk are the remarks exchanged with each other by the company assembled at Gatherum Castle! and how justly was Robarts punished for lending his name to a bill which he could not take up when it became due!

Of story, indeed, there is little enough in 'Framley Parsonage'; barely enough to give the successive chapters an air of distant cousinship with each other. You are shown, as it were, into a roomful of people known or unknown, with each of whom you exchange a mild remark or two in his or her turn, seldom pausing to learn more of the speaker's character than what may show itself at first glance, and still seldomer caring to improve the acquaintance thus casually begun. It is a book well suited to invalids, and all who cannot bear much intellectual or emotional rousing. It is a story without a hero, unless Mr. Sowerby can be accepted as such; without a heroine, unless Lady Lufton and Lucy Robarts between them may count for one. There is just one chapter which rises above the level of pretty commonplace, the chapter which records the earlier experiences of the poor, hard-working parson, battling for ten long years with the wretchedness resulting from a wife and family starved on an income of seventy pounds a year. As for the other characters, we may own to feeling a languid sort of amusement in following the various shifts and stratagems by which Sowerby tries still to keep his head above the waters of debt and social disrepute. For a while, too, a touch of languid sympathy with Miss Robarts tempted us on to see whether Lord Lufton would ever persuade his mother to accept a girl so quiet-looking and poor in worldly requirements for her daughter-in-law. Yet even Mr. Sowerby fails us towards the last; and for the lovers, we know that Lady Lufton will yield her gracious consent to their marriage long before she has done discussing the pros and cons of the matter with Mrs. Robarts. Aught drearier than the latter part of the book we have not for many a day tried to read, except, perhaps, the beginning. Compared with these shreds of flimsy finery, even 'Silas Marner' is a work of genuine art, and 'Tom Brown at Oxford' a masterpiece of noble workmanship.

THE STRUGGLES OF BROWN, JONES, AND ROBINSON

1862, 1870

This short work, surely the poorest of Trollope's forty-seven achievements in the novel, appeared in the *Cornhill Magazine* from August 1861 to March 1862. An unauthorized edition in one volume was brought out in the United States by Harper & Brothers in 1862; but Smith, Elder & Company did not choose to publish this novel in book form until 1870, when it seems to have fallen from the press almost unnoticed.

Trollope (*Autobiography*, p. 135) had no illusions about the reception accorded the work:

In August 1861 I wrote another novel for the *Cornhill Magazine*. It was a short story, about one volume in length, and was called *The Struggles of Brown, Jones, and Robinson*. In this I attempted a style for which I certainly was not qualified, and to which I never had again recourse. It was meant to be funny, was full of slang, and was intended as a satire on the ways of trade. Still I think that there is some good fun in it, but I have heard no one else express such an opinion. I do not know that I ever heard any opinion expressed on it, except by the publisher, who kindly remarked that he did not think it was equal to my usual work. Though he had purchased the copyright, he did not republish the story in a book form till 1870, and then it passed into the world of letters *sub silentio*. I do not know that it was ever criticized or ever read.

51. Unsigned notice, *Westminster Review*

July 1871, xcv. 574-5

We deeply regret, for Mr. Trollope's own reputation, that 'The Struggles of Brown, Jones, and Robinson' should have been published. It was universally felt, when the story first appeared in the 'Cornhill

Magazine,' that the whole affair was a blunder. Most people were un-willing to believe that the author of 'Framley Parsonage' could have written such unmitigated rubbish. The story is meant, we suppose, for a satire upon a certain class of unscrupulous tradesmen. No better subject could there be for a satirical tale. . . . But Mr. Trollope's satire is as coarse as the people whom he describes. . . . It is wasting time to say another word upon this miserable production.

52. Elizabeth Barrett Browning on *Framley Parsonage* and *Orley Farm*

From *The Letters of Elizabeth Barrett Browning*, ed. Frederic G. Kenyon (1897), ii, 377, 391.

(*a*) April 1860 to Miss Isa Blagden:
How good this 'Cornhill Magazine' is! Anthony Trollope [*Framley Parsonage*] is really superb.

(*b*) Probably March or April 1861, also to Miss Blagden. Kenyon gives 'about May 1860', but Mrs. Browning refers to reading one of the part issues of *Orley Farm*, which began to appear in one-shilling parts in March 1861:

How admirably this last [*Orley Farm*] opens! We are both delighted with it. What a pity it is that so powerful and idiomatic a writer should be so incorrect grammatically and scholastically speaking! Robert insists on my putting down such phrases as these: 'The Cleeve was distant from Orley two miles, though it *could not be driven* under five.' '*One rises up the hill.*' 'As good as *him*.' 'Possessing more *acquirements* than he would have *learned* at Harrow.' *Learning acquirements!* Yes, they are faults, and should be put away by a first-rate writer like Anthony Trollope. It's always worth while to be correct. But do understand through the pedantry of these remarks that we are full of admiration for the book. The movement is so excellent and straightforward—walking like a man, and 'rising up-hill', and not going round and round, as Thackeray has taken to do lately. He's clever always, but he goes round and round till I'm dizzy, for one, and don't know where I am. I think somebody has tied him up to a post, leaving a tether.

53. Trollope on his crowding the market, 1862-5

From *An Autobiography*, pp. 145-7

During the early months of 1862 *Orley Farm* was still being brought out in numbers, and at the same time *Brown, Jones, and Robinson* was appearing in the *Cornhill Magazine*. In September 1862 *The Small House at Allington* began its career in the same periodical. The work on North America had also come out in 1862. In August 1863 the first number of *Can You Forgive Her?* was published as a separate serial, and was continued through 1864. In 1863 a short novel was produced in the ordinary volume form, called *Rachel Ray*. In addition to these I published during the time two volumes of stories called *The Tales of All Countries*. In the early spring of 1865 *Miss Mackenzie* was issued in the same form as *Rachel Ray*; and in May of the same year *The Belton Estate* was commenced with the commencement of the *Fortnightly Review*, of which periodical I will say a few words in this chapter.

I quite admit that I crowded my wares into the market too quickly, because the reading world could not want such a quantity of matter from the hands of one author in so short a space of time. I had not been quite so fertile as the unfortunate gentleman who disgusted the publisher in Paternoster Row,—in the story of whose productiveness I have always thought there was a touch of romance,—but I had probably done enough to make both publishers and readers think that I was coming too often beneath their notice. Of publishers, however, I must speak collectively, as my sins were, I think, chiefly due to the encouragement which I received from them individually. What I wrote for the *Cornhill Magazine*, I always wrote at the instigation of Mr. Smith. My other works were published by Messrs. Chapman & Hall, in compliance with contracts made by me with them, and always made with their good-will. Could I have been two separate persons at one and the same time, of whom one might have been devoted to *Cornhill* and the other to the interests of the firm in Piccadilly, it might have been very well;—but as I preserved my identity in both places, I myself became aware that my name was too frequent on title-pages.

Critics, if they ever trouble themselves with these pages, will, of course, say that in what I have now said I have ignored altogether the one great evil of rapid production,—namely, that of inferior work. And of course if the work was inferior because of the too great rapidity of production, the critics would be right. Giving to the subject the best of my critical abilities, and judging of my own work as nearly as possible as I would that of another, I believe that the work which has been done quickest has been done the best. I have composed better stories—that is, have created better plots—than those of *The Small House at Allington* and *Can You Forgive Her?* and I have portrayed two or three better characters than are to be found in the pages of either of them; but taking these books all through, I do not think that I have ever done better work. Nor would these have been improved by any effort in the art of story telling, had each of these been the isolated labour of a couple of years. . . . Sometimes I have encountered what, in hunting language, we call a cropper. I had such a fall in two novels of mine, of which I have already spoken—*The Bertrams* and *Castle Richmond*. I shall have to speak of other such troubles. But these failures have not arisen from over-hurried work. When my work has been quicker done,—and it has sometimes been done very quickly—the rapidity has been achieved by hot pressure, not in the conception, but in the telling of the story.

ORLEY FARM

1862

Trollope (*Autobiography*, p. 140) could not agree with friends who were still (presumably in the middle eighteen-seventies) calling *Orley Farm* his best work.

Most of those among my friends who talk to me now about my novels, and are competent to form an opinion on the subject, say that this is the best I have written. In this opinion I do not coincide. . . . The plot of *Orley Farm* is probably the best I have ever made; but it has the fault of declaring itself, and thus coming to an end too early in the book. When Lady Mason tells her ancient lover that she did forge the will, the plot of *Orley Farm* has unravelled itself;— and this she does in the middle of the tale. Independently, however, of this the novel is good. Sir Peregrine Orme, his grandson, Madeline Stavely, Mr. Furnival, Mr. Chaffanbrass, and the commercial gentlemen, are all good. The hunting is good. The lawyer's talk is good. Mr. Moulder carves his turkey admirably, and Mr. Kantwise sells his tables and chairs with spirit. I do not know that there is a dull page in the book. I am fond of *Orley Farm*;—and am especially fond of its illustrations by Millais, which are the best I have seen in any novel in any language.

54. Unsigned notice, *Saturday Review*

11 October 1862, xiv. 444-5

Three concluding paragraphs—something over fifteen hundred words—of argument that Trollope is unfair to the 'working of the law' and to lawyers are omitted.

The numerous readers of Mr. Trollope will, we think, agree with us in considering this one of the best of his many novels. His power of producing novels is wonderful, and, as a mere literary feat, there has been scarcely anything equal to what Mr. Trollope is doing and has done lately. His *North America* was, indeed, to a great extent, book-making; but the novels are always well written, well contrived, and exceedingly entertaining. Nor are they copies of each other, and in *Orley Farm*, we are glad to say, even the well-known and established circle of Barchester and the neighbourhood are wholly avoided. Mr. Trollope, too, gives almost always a shilling's worth of story for our money. He does not make us pay the discount of philosophical reflections, or descriptions of his own mental state. He writes, from one end to the other, a tale which is meant to please and amuse, and which effects its object. Why a novelist pleases is generally beyond the reach of analysis to decide; nor, if it were possible, would it be worth while to bestow the requisite labour on an inquiry which would be fruitless. But there are one or two reasons for the success of Mr. Trollope's novels which are worth noticing, as they go far to fix his place among the novelists of the day. In the first place, he does the family life of England to perfection. No one has ever drawn English families better—without exaggeration, and without any attempt at false comedy. His gentlemen and ladies are exactly like real gentlemen and ladies, except, perhaps, that they are a trifle more entertaining. Mr. Trollope gives us two families in this new novel—one that of a judge, and the other that of a country baronet—and they are each excellent. The young ladies make love or receive it, and joke and have their little difficulties, in the most natural and lifelike way. They are not out of the ordinary way, and do very common things, and yet they have a distinct character, and behave with propriety and becoming reserve. How hard it is to sketch such persons in a story may be guessed by the fact that hardly any novelists have succeeded in it. The old ladies and gentlemen are equally natural in Mr. Trollope's books; and Lady Mason, the heroine of *Orley Farm*, is a masterpiece of one kind of delineation of character. Her mixture of guilt and innocence, her strength and weakness, and her power of making herself loved, whatever she does, constitute altogether one of the best-conceived types of mixed character, neither good nor bad, that modern English fiction has to show.

Mr. Trollope also excels in the creation of subsidiary comic characters. In his early novels he fell into the error of introducing characters merely to give a clever description of them. But practice has taught him to bring in those minor performers with the skill of an easy workman. In *Orley Farm* he has hit on a happy vein. He has described the bagman world, and his portrait of Mr. Moulder, who travels in the sugar line, and of Mr. Kantwise, who travels with the object of selling certain metallic chairs and tables, are quite revelations of the being and nature of commercial gents. Mr. Moulder is of the old school, and sticks to the rules of the commercial room, and has everything of the most comfortable. Kantwise is a little, wiry, pushing character, whose masters are by no means of the respectable sort, and who makes it his business, night and day, in season and out of season, to praise and advertise the horrid furniture by which he lives. A scene in which Kantwise has his boxes into the commercial-room and brings out a miserable wire-table, on which, to show its strength, he offers to stand, would be highly entertaining in itself, and its fun is much heightened by the very clever illustration in which Mr. Millais has set the scene before us. There is also a dinner which Moulder gives at home on Christmas day, which shows a sublime appreciation of the weak points of the bagman. Moulder has got a turkey, for which he has given a guinea, and to the cooking of which he has attended himself. This he carves in the most deliberate way, cutting off all the slices wanted from the breast, and then solemnly helping each person to as exactly the same amount in quantity and quality as he can manage. This seems rather a slight groundwork for the novelist to base his comic writing on, and we feel at once the wearisome exaggeration by which the sensation school would have tried to make it funny. Mr. Trollope goes through it with an easy and subdued humour that is a real comfort to his readers.

55. Unsigned review, *Spectator*

11 October 1862, xxxiii. 1136–8

It is probable, though not, so far as I have found, capable of
absolute proof, that this excellent critique represents Richard Holt
Hutton's first review of Trollope's novels for the *Spectator* (see
Introduction, VII).

Orley Farm is, in some respects, Mr. Trollope's greatest work; and in
some respects, perhaps, his most defective. It is the nearest approach that
he has made to the depth and force of tragedy, and for that very reason
the light ripple of his habitually tranquil manner, the wide shallows, the
arbitrary channels, and the ill-defined delta of this, as of nearly all his
stories, come out into stronger relief. Mr. Trollope's imagination is not
one that ever seems, to the critic's observation, at least, to brood long
over visions that task its full power. As, one after another, his men and
women pass out on to his literary stage, and become to us as the
acquaintances we meet every day, neither less distinct nor better known,
we gather the impression that his mind creates new varieties out of the
faces and characters that flash by him in society almost as easily as a
shaken kaleidoscope creates new patterns out of the same bits of
coloured glass, and yet always within the same general limits of form,
colour, and depth. There is nothing, apparently, of the agony of meditative travail about his mind. We know how Miss [Charlotte] Brontë
used to brood for months before she could satisfy herself about the life
of her imaginative offspring, when all at once the mist drew up before
her mind and she saw how to strike out a great scene or a new reach of
passion. No true critic, we think, who read Miss Brontë's novels, could
have failed to gather this impression long before it was confirmed from
her own pen. No one would gather it—though we are far from assuming that such impressions at all necessarily represent the real truth—
from Mr. Trollope's tales. There is an easy, sliding manner about Mr.
Trollope's imaginative delineations that, at least, disguises, if it does not
disprove, the birth-throes which ushered them into the world of art. In
short, Mr. Trollope does not give us so much the impression of conceiving and creating his own conceptions, as of very acutely observing

them as they pass along the screen of some interior faculty. In this respect he differs from almost all his greater brother artists.

His mode of writing is uniformly, and even in the critical scenes, that of a spectator. He never loses himself so much in any situation as to lose even the dialectic tricks of a narrator. Open any page anywhere in *Orley Farm* and you are almost certain to find several sentences in it beginning, 'And then,' in the true manner of a man who has minutely watched the succession of events, but not enough identified himself with any one character in the scene to make that so living a centre of interest that the little words which distinguish accurately the sequences of things almost become inappropriate. Take any of the greater situations in Sir Walter Scott, and you find the historian lost in the passion of the scene. When, for example, the Queen of Scots, in 'The Abbot,' is so abruptly reminded of the Holyrood murder that her excited and guilty imagination carries her into a passion of delirium, it would have been impossible for Scott to put this character so much at arm's length, as to interpolate Mr. Trollope's favourite conjunctive phrase. But in all the critical scenes of this book, Mr. Trollope never for a moment loses the nice discriminate style of 'articulately-speaking men,'—separating event from event, gesture from gesture, thought from thought, with the manner of a distinct witness who wishes to give the most perspicuous evidence, not of an artist the glow of whose conception has for the moment struck fire from his own mind. Mr. Thackeray and Mr. Trollope, though far as the poles asunder in many respects, resemble each other in being painters of social man rather than of man, in the wonderfully prolific variety of their genius within very narrow limits, and in the rather superficial character of the stratum from which they draw,—but they differ in nothing more than in this, that Mr. Thackeray is always more or less identifying himself, either as a satirist or as a man, with the men and women through whom he speaks, and that on occasions he kindles into a perfect forgetfulness of his own attitude as showman,—while Mr. Trollope (who is never, however, the showman so much as the spectator and describer) seems always narrating, not conceiving, telling you how the figures look as they pass along, but never seeming to have anything at all to do either with their appearance or their demeanour. Of course this is more or less an illusion. Sir Peregrine Orme and Lady Mason, and Moulder, and Kantwise, and the rest, whatever they may seem, *are* the creatures of Mr. Trollope's imagination and not the mere objects of his observing eye. But still the characteristic remains, and probably represents the fact that they are not so much offsprings of his heart, sentiment, and self-knowledge, as results of his alert, observing, and combining eye. No great novelist probably ever drew so little from the resources of his own visionary life,—so much from impromptu variations of the forms given by experience, as Mr. Trollope.

Yet in this novel Mr. Trollope has surpassed himself, and there are imperfect traces of a certain travail of the imagination in the conception —at times really powerful and tragic—of Lady Mason's criminal experience, and of the influence of her character and crime on the old baronet who falls under the spell of her stronger nature. There is not quite the same easy flow of event; there is a sensible gathering of the waters as against an obstacle, a temporary deepening of the channel, a straining of the eye into an interior almost beyond the artist's sight. Yet the effect is made with varying success. Sometimes Mr. Trollope seems to have desperately grasped at some trait in the dark, which scarcely belongs to the picture he wishes to set before us; sometimes he has really succeeded in finding the natural language of a deeper passion in the depths in which he sounds.

To illustrate what we mean more particularly in Lady Mason's case. We must premise that much of Mr. Trollope's secret charm generally consists in the spontaneous moderation with which he *limits* himself in regard to the leading characteristics of his *dramatis personae*, without in the least diminishing the emphasis or obscuring the meaning of his pictures, in the truthfulness with which he assigns a fixed verge within which the natural restraints of society and habit confine the swing of the individual passion or impulse he delineates. Thus, when he paints the cunning of a low attorney like Dockwrath, he confines it, and makes you feel his art in confining it, within the ordinary range of safe professional cunning; when he draws the vulgar domestic tyranny of a gross commercial traveller like Moulder, he marks clearly the conventional ideas of pecuniary equity to his wife and hospitality to his friends, within which it moves; when he sketches the slow obstinate vindictiveness of such a mind as Joseph Mason's, he outlines strongly and subtly the bounds of legal justice within which that vindictive fury is nourished. In no place does he paint a passion or eccentricity without making you see the outer margin and natural orbit of it; he never indulges himself with a vague, wasteful infinitude of any quality, like novelists in general, but scarcely hints a characteristic at all before he allows you to see its scope and boundary. Now the great aim of his art in *Orley Farm* is to paint a naturally strong, and even noble character, stained by a great crime, with the same studious moderation. Lady Mason has committed, from maternal passion, a great forgery and robbery, and Mr. Trollope is exceedingly anxious to paint the exact limits within which the effect of that crime is kept,—the effect it has, and the effect it does *not* have, in corrupting the other parts of her character. For the most part we think the picture, though the difficulty is for a long time evaded by a very cold external view of her demeanour to others,—very powerful. There is certainly much art in the added vividness which her own sense of guilt takes the moment the pressure of constant concealment is removed, and she sees it reflected back from the minds of friends whom she reveres. But there are grave faults, we think, in the earlier picture of the guilty woman's manner while the self-restraint is still exerted and the crime kept down. She is by no means meant, even then, to be an evil woman; the coldness of her manner expresses the sense of her solitary position—of her wish to retain that solitary position; otherwise the seed of evil is meant to be almost latent. But the conception of Lady Mason is fluctuating and (what is very rare with Mr. Trollope) indistinct before the confession of her guilt. The needless religious falsehood of the expressions used to Mr. Furnival and Sir Peregrine Orme, when told of the action brought against her, 'May the Lord give me strength to bear it!' 'By God's mercy I will endure it!' are not consistent with the general picture of the character. It is evident that Mr. Trollope could not quite make up his mind where to put the limits of the influence of this guilt upon her character, and that his outline was far less clear and certain than it usually is when dealing with more superficial characteristics. Indeed, in the last chapter he confesses plainly that Lady Mason has grown upon him as he wrote, that he has softened and deepened his own conception as he went on.

And, no doubt, in many places, the depth of colour and delicacy of the pathos are far beyond Mr. Trollope's usual manner. There is wonderful art, for instance, and truth, too, in the little touch with which Mr. Trollope aggravates Lady Mason's misery, when she has just confessed her guilt to Sir Peregrine Orme, and goes to her own room to be alone:—

Slowly and very silently she made her way up to her own room and having closed the door behind her sat herself down upon the bed. It was as yet early in the morning, and the servant had not been in the chamber. There was no fire there, although it was still mid-winter. Of such details as these Sir Peregrine had remembered nothing when he recommended her to go to her own room. Nor did she think of them at first as she placed herself on the bed-side. But soon the bitter air pierced her through and through, and she shivered with the cold as she sat there. After a while she got herself a shawl, wrapped it close around her, and then sat down again. She bethought herself that she might have to remain in this way for hours, so she rose again and locked the door. It would add greatly to her immediate misery if the servants were to come while she was there, and see her in her wretchedness. Presently the girls did come, and being unable to obtain entrance were told by Lady Mason that she wanted the chamber for the present. Whereupon they offered to light the fire, but she declared that she was not cold. Her teeth were shaking in her head, but any suffering was better than the suffering of being seen.

She did not lie down, or cover herself further than she was covered with that shawl, nor did she move from her place for more than an hour. By degrees she became used to the cold. She was numbed, and, as it were, half dead in all her limbs, but she had ceased to shake as she sat there, and her mind had gone back to the misery of her position. There was so much for her behind that was worse! What should she do when even this retirement should not be allowed to her? Instead of longing for the time when she should be summoned to meet Sir Peregrine, she dreaded its coming. It would bring her nearer to that other meeting when she would have to bow her head and crouch before her son.

This, simple as it is, has a depth beyond Mr. Trollope's usual range. Most artists would have made a mind in such a state quite insensible to the physical wretchedness of the cold and disordered bed-room; yet it was a true insight into the relaxed nerves and exhausted vital energy of a woman just cowering under the new sense of shame and exposure that painted this as a sensible aggravation of her misery.

We have dwelt so long on the general structure of Mr. Trollope's genius, and the deepest and most original of the characters he has here drawn for us, that we have little room left to criticize what scarcely needs criticism—the host of living men and women who scatter themselves in the loose grouping of real life about the diverging paths of this story. These groups are, indeed, in general so slightly connected both with the plot and with one another, that we may cherish a reasonable hope of not bidding them an eternal farewell as we close the book. The stately old baronet, indeed, whose chivalrous nature and warm heart we leave almost broken in the struggle of a generous affection with his keen sensitiveness to the slightest shade of dishonour, we may scarcely expect to meet again; but for all the others there is hope, for some we may say there is almost a certainty of prolonged existence, in the pages of Mr. Trollope's future works. The prosperous attorney, Mr. Matthew Round, who hardly cares quite enough about his business to make the most of his case, and who carries it with such a high dictatorial hand towards his client; the low cunning attorney, Mr. Samuel Dockwrath, who explains so emphatically to Mr. Joseph Mason at the failure of the suit, that 'he never came across a gentleman who behaved himself worse in a peculiar position;' these are, we venture to think, both of them too dear to Mr. Trollope's fancy to be absent for many years from the scene. And Mr. Moulder—in spite of those heartrending reflections of his before the Christmas turkey on his father's early apoplexy, it would be more than Mr. Trollope could bear to deprive Hubbles and Grease prematurely of Mr. Moulder's services. From him and Mr. Kantwise our heart assures us that we are not torn away for ever. Perhaps, indeed, —we are almost afraid that it must be so,—Mr. Kantwise will not be permanently engaged in the sale of that iron furniture of the Louis Quatorze pattern, on behalf of which he seems almost born to travel. That company of his,—we trust, Limited,—must, it is too clear, be short-lived. But in spite of the subtlety with which Mr. Trollope seems to incarnate the soul of a business in its commercial traveller, in spite of the maxim which he seems to have in his own heart that the 'commercial traveller *nascitur non fit*,' and is born, too, with a special organization for travelling on behalf of dry or soft or hard goods, as the case may be, and on behalf of substantial or hollow 'concerns,'—in spite of all this we will trust to the fertility of Mr. Trollope's genius to find some new concern not unsuitable for Mr. Kantwise, when the Iron Furniture Company shall collapse, and to give us the gratification of seeing him look over his shoulder at us again in new fields of labour.

We part from *Orley Farm* with real regret. With Mrs. Baker, and the housekeeper, far-sighted in her young mistress's feelings, who knows so well that 'bread sauce is ticklish'; with Mrs. Thomas and her pious peculations; with the strong-witted and metallic Miss Furnival, and her father, no longer wandering after strange goddesses; with his homely wife, and with Martha Biggs, lamenting her faithless friend in the exile of Red Lion Square Gardens; with Felix Graham, crotchetty and credulous, except where credulity is orthodox; with Mr. Joseph Mason, slow and savage in his resentments, slow and cautious in his daily affairs, we may or may not be permitted to meet again. But from the new types of *professional* character produced for us in *Orley Farm*, as from the old clerical faces in 'Barchester Towers,' Mr. Trollope will, we are sure, be slow to part. No English novelist has ever yet delineated the finer professional lines of English character with anything like his subtlety and power. The air and tone of a profession once caught, Mr. Trollope appears to possess some artistic Calculus of Variations, which gives him an infinite command over the shades and details of the different specimens.

56. Unsigned notice, *London Review*

18 October 1862, v. 344–5

Much of this review (which runs unabridged to over fifteen
hundred words) expresses judgements upon Trollope curiously
parallel to those of the *National Review* (No. 63, below), though
the two differ sharply on the interest of Trollope's comic scenes
involving Messrs. Kantwise and Moulder.

Mr. Trollope occupies in the world of novelists much the same position
as Mr. Frith does in that of painters. Both artists have achieved the very
best of second-rate reputations; both are universally popular, and their
popularity arises from the same cause. Everybody has read 'Framley
Parsonage,' just as everybody has been to see the 'Derby Day' or the
'Railway Station'; and no London diner-out would imperil his reputation by venturing into society without being thoroughly posted up in
the latest details of Sir Peregrine Orme's courtship, or the transcendental
inefficiency of Lucius Mason. And yet with Mr. Trollope and Mr. Frith
alike, the principal impression produced is that of the cheap rate at
which success has been purchased. 'Orley Farm,' for instance, is a
master-piece of easy writing. There is no appearance of effort, no profound sentiment, no searching observation from beginning to end; the
story is a shade, and only a shade, more entertaining than the commonplace lives of the most commonplace people. . . .

The rest of [Mr. Trollope's] complaints against society are equally
slight; he takes the world as he finds it, and is, on the whole, well content. There is a uniform cheerfulness pervading even his saddest scenes;
and he is evidently most in his element when he is describing the cheerful aspects of existence. Nothing can be better drawn than is the well-
to-do good-natured judge, his comfortable house, his amiable but rather
worldly wife, his idle son, his pretty daughter; Peregrine Orme again,
the heir to a baronetcy, a simple-minded, out-spoken country lad, full
of manliness, and prone to rats, is put upon the canvas with a few really
skilful touches, and is, we think, as attractive a character as Mr. Trollope

has ever conceived; nor, indeed, for people who like broad humour of the Mrs. Gamp order, can anything be broader or more humorous than the scenes in which the commercial gentlemen exchange sentiments, and Mr. Moulder, traveller for the great firm of Hubbles & Grease, Houndsditch, delivers himself of a number of oracular dicta. No one, as he reads, will be profoundly interested, or wrought up to any high pitch of feeling; no enthusiastic young lady will sit up shivering through the livelong night over Mr. Trollope's pages, nor will cabinet ministers, as was the case with 'Jane Eyre,' make them the apology for a late arrival; but every one will be entertained, and, with the help of Mr. Millais's pretty sketches, will realize in 'Orley Farm' a gaily coloured, well-composed tableau, in which the foibles of the day are playfully glanced at, the ordinary sentiments and opinions of mankind enunciated, and a number of commonplace individuals play out a drama, which derives its main attractiveness from its close and studied similarity to the domestic life of the nineteenth century.

57. Unsigned notice, *Examiner*

25 October 1862, pp. 677–8

A long review, occupying four full columns, but much of it taken up by quotation and a detailed but disappointingly routine re-telling of the story.

This is not only Mr. Anthony Trollope's best novel, it is one of the best novels of the day, and of its kind,—an excellent kind, honest and natural,—one of the best that has been written in any day. The reader, unaccustomed to recognize even in the single race of the novelists genius in many forms, will miss in *Orley Farm* that supreme energy of the imagination which can brighten every sentence with the aptest fancies or the happiest turn of phrase. Its author writes cleverly and pleasantly but at the simple level of the better sort of conversation, adopts in excess colloquial forms with which he may chance to have met more frequently than his neighbours,—an overuse for example of the word 'nice,' or the phrase 'all the same,'—and reproduces in his dialogues, never without an artist's purpose, and yet always without any obtrusive touch of art, the actual manner of every-day human talk. There is hardly a sentence in these two ample volumes,—admirable as they are and unquestionable as is the genius which makes them what they are,—there is, perhaps, not a sentence that could stand alone bearing the distinctive mark of Mr. Trollope's wit, or that is noticeable for originality of any sort. Nevertheless, *Orley Farm* is full of original power. Few books have contained, in a well contrived tale, studies of English life and character so perfect as those which are here grouped with unerring skill. Mr. Trollope has successfully endeavoured to paint men, women, and households, and to show of each person in his story, not that side of character which bears directly on the plot, but the whole character with all its lights and shades. This is not the one only way of telling a tale, but it is Mr. Trollope's way, and a very good one. His resolve is that he will interest us in the real; will look generously out on the actual world through an eye keen to observe, with a quick sense of all that is complex and, to one less intent, perplexing in the play of character. He will show the people of his drama, in their lives among each other and at home in their own households, acting and speaking naturally, so naturally that their dialogues would be tamely literal if he did not know also, as he does know, how to make every such transcript of the real manner of men's talk supply its colour to the scene he paints on his broad canvas. As the narrator he will himself also be absolutely natural in manner. There shall be no ambitious paragraphs, no twisted, knotted, or strained English. In all things, and above all things, the book is to be free from affectation. And so it is, in this our day of much strained writing and invention, a manly, unaffected, interesting English novel.

58. 'Mr. Trollope and the Lawyers', *London Review*

8 November 1862, v. 405–7

The anonymous writer devotes more than four columns (well over two thousand words) to a detailed but pedestrian analysis of Trollope's abuse of the law in *Orley Farm*.

Mr. Trollope is certainly one of the ablest novelists of the day, but he is infected with a fault which has become almost epidemic amongst gentlemen of his profession. He has become a reformer. He appears to think, like many others of his craft, that because he can arrange his own little world in his own way, and distribute rewards and punishments, good and bad fortune, as he thinks proper, he could also set to rights the real world outside him. This delusion appears, from its frequency, to be natural. Mr. Dickens and Mr. Charles Reade have both laboured under an exaggerated form of it, though in their later works they have given it up. Mr. Trollope is less vehement but more persistent. He hardly ever writes a book without some moral, social, or theological crotchet stuck into the middle of it. One of his heroes had peculiar views about the resurrection of the body, others on the distribution of livings in the Church, others afforded pegs on which to hang observations on the Irish famine. There is, however, one subject which Mr. Trollope pursues with unremitting zeal. He cannot bear a lawyer. They are all rogues, not by nature, but by profession; and one who becomes Solicitor-General at eight-and-twenty, has to shoot himself as an expiation for his guilt. In four or five of his tales the misdeeds of this unhappy class of men are dwelt upon, illustrations are given of their wickedness, and a quantity of law is introduced in different shapes to work the story. Voltaire used to boast of his acquaintance with the Bible, observing that a good advocate ought to know the case on the other side as well as his own. By the same rule Mr. Trollope ought to get his law right. As it is he always gets it wrong.

59. Unsigned notice, *Cornhill Magazine*

November 1862, vi. 702–4

The monthly survey of current literature for November 1862 was written by G. H. Lewes, J. F. W. Herschel, and J. W. Kaye (*Wellesley Index*). The proprietary tone of the notice, despite the fact that *Orley Farm* had not been published in the *Cornhill*, is understandable. The great success of *Framley Parsonage* had associated Trollope's name with the magazine, and *The Small House at Allington* had been appearing in monthly instalments in the *Cornhill* since September.

The completion of *Orley Farm* places in the hands of novel-readers a book to make them happy for a few hours, and, if read aright, to make them better for the rest of their days—a book not only stirring their interest, but enlarging their sympathies by its pictures of life. Original in conception, and sweetly human in its tone, we think it in some respects the finest of Mr. Anthony Trollope's works. Not that our praise must by any means be unaccompanied by objections on points of detail. For example, we think the book badly constructed, there being a large amount of wholly superfluous matter. The extent of his canvas has seduced him into episodes very imperfectly related to the main story, and not sufficiently interesting in themselves to excuse their irrelevancy. The desire to give variety has also led him to introduce characters which we regard as very far from successful—the Moulders, Kantwise, Mrs. Smiley, Martha Biggs, Mary Snow, and Albert Fitz-allen; the variety not having the comic gusto which might serve to relieve the more serious interest of the story. On the other hand the scenes at Noningsby and the Cleeve are touched with grace and cheerfulness. The young men, Peregrine, Lucius, and Augustus, are sketched with great verisimilitude; nor are Madeleine and her mother less felicitously handled. Without concealing our impression of the inequality of this long novel, we must still say that the sustained height of interest and the noble humanizing pathos of the main story leaves our final impression one of grateful admiration. Lady Mason's position is o singular interest, thrilling some of the deeper chords in the heart, and raising many questions respecting the charities of life, which it is well to have frequently brought home to us.

Mr. Anthony Trollope is no painter in black and white. His people are not angels and devils, but human beings, with good and evil strangely intermingled. Novel-readers (and we are sorry to add critic also, but these of the feebler sort) are very inconsequential in their demands. They require that the characters in a fiction should be 'true to nature'; and yet unless these characters markedly depart from the known truth of nature, by being either without vices, or without virtues, they pettishly declare that the author has 'forfeited their sympathies' by making the hero do this, or the heroine feel that; and upbraid him for endeavouring to confuse their moral judgments 'by engaging their sympathies in a man capable of,' &c. &c. . . . To move our sympathies and educate our charities it is absolutely necessary that the novelist should be true in his representations. The higher purpose of his art is frustrated by a substitution of faultless human beings, never to be met with on earth, for heroes and heroines such as may be met with; since by this substitution he directs our sympathies away from reality, and increases our tendency, already too strong, to judge actions by abstract standards. . . .

We expected that certain critics would raise the old foolish cry about making guilt interesting; and our expectations have not been deceived. But the guilt is *not* made interesting; it is the sinner we pity, not the sin we absolve. Never for a single instant is the reader's moral judgment in suspense. The author permits himself no sophistication as to the nature of the sin. Not one of the characters—not even the sinner herself—exhibits the least oscillation on this point. But nevertheless the sinner is lovable as a woman, and as a woman she is loved. We estimate the nature of her act; we estimate her temptation; we estimate her character; and the sum total of our judgment is that she sinned where a woman of stronger nature would have resisted temptation, but nevertheless apart from this she is pitiable, lovable. We do not murmur at her punishment, but we feel with her, feel for her. There is no false glare of melodramatic interest, there is none of the prurient curiosity awakened by celebrated criminals; but the feeling she inspires in Mrs. Orme, Sir Peregrine, and Mr. Furnival subtly indicates the charm of a woman in whose nature at least one serious flaw had been discovered. There can be little doubt that we should have been fond of this criminal had we known her in flesh and blood; why then should the novelist shrink from representing what is so true to life? If only as drawing forth the exquisite womanly tenderness of Mrs. Orme, this conception of Lady Mason would claim applause: a woman so firm in her moral judgments, so keen in her appreciation of what is becoming, may without suspicion show us the lesson of charity. We have endeavoured to rectify a widespread prejudice.

60. E. S. Dallas, *The Times*

26 December 1862, p. 5

This unsigned notice is attributed to E. S. Dallas in *The History of
'The Times'* (see Introduction, VII, and note 54).

Behold another law story, and Anthony Trollope the teller thereof. It is
one of the oldest traditions of our literature that between the study of
law and the exercise of imagination there is irreconcileable contrariety.
A poet might be a divine, a physician, a soldier, a statesman,—anything
but a lawyer. What are we to think now, when it appears that the most
popular source of amusement is to be found in the driest of all subjects,
and that the greatest scope for imagination is afforded by that study
which professes only to deal with facts and precedents? All our novelists
have suddenly become legal in their tastes. . . . Certainly the law
books and records make capital novels, and the one before us is as good
as any. Following the fashion of his tribe, Mr. Anthony Trollope
comes to us berobed and bewigged to tell the story of *Orley Farm*,
or (as in his first chapter he says he ought to have entitled it) *The Great
Orley Farm Case*.

When a voluminous author writes a work of sustained power, the
reader, fresh from the perusal of it, is apt to say, 'This is his best.' One is
strongly tempted to pronounce such an opinion on the present work,
seeing that in passages of it there is a tragic force, or something like it,
which is rare in Mr. Trollope's writings. As a whole, some of his other
novels may be better; but in parts he has attempted and he has achieved
something higher in *Orley Farm* than in any of his works. The character
of Lady Mason is an exceedingly difficult one to grasp, and the position
into which she is forced by her own acts is difficult to manage. She
commits a great crime; she is in effect a swindler; there is to be no
doubt as to the enormity of her guilt; and yet we are to love and admire
her, and like all her friends to part from her with kisses and benedictions.
During 20 years the lady bears in secret the load of her guilt and tries to
avoid the society of her neighbours; but at the end of 20 years, in the

prospect of her guilt being discovered, she is to break down, she is to court the society of her friends, and she is to get elderly gentlemen to fall in love with her, one of them even proposing to marry her. These contrasts are presented to the reader with power and plausibility, and the lady, who has committed a very daring piece of villany in order to gratify her maternal feelings, is depicted in all her weakness, the victim of remorse, of terror, of shame unspeakable. Here Mr. Trollope has room for the delineation of passion which is not over familiar to his pen. . . .

We cannot praise his theory as to the administration of the law. Mr. Trollope, in describing the progress of the suit, has attempted to awaken our interest in the question as to the right mode of conducting a trial. He has apparently taken up the idea expressed by one of his characters, that lawyers are all liars, and that the procedure of our courts is less adapted to elicit than to conceal the truth. He thinks that barristers should be judges rather than advocates, should say no more than they think, should refuse to accept a brief where they believe that their proposed client is guilty, and even after they have accepted the brief should throw it up, if circumstances should enable them to see that in defending the case they are hindering the ends of justice. These are notions which from time to time make their appearance in print, which have a thousand times been refuted, which come naturally enough in the pages of fictitious history, but which we are astonished to find in the fiction of an author who has generally so much regard as Mr. Anthony Trollope for hard facts and for common sense. . . .

He aims much higher when he attempts to interest us in the struggle going on in Lady Mason's mind. All that succession of scenes ending in the confession of her guilt, which none of her friends had suspected, and which she had kept secret for a score of years, is admirably conceived. At first, however, we have to get over the improbability of her sudden intimacy with the Ormes. She had been on friendly terms with them for 20 years; but in all that time we are told that their friendship had never ripened into intimacy, and that the cause of this reserve lay not so much with the Ormes as with Lady Mason herself, who had a burden on her mind and shunned society. Suddenly she hears of the charge which is to be brought against her; she is in terror that her secret is to be discovered, and, having previously avoided the Ormes because of her secret, she now courts them because it is about to be published to her disgrace. The real reason for the suddenness of the intimacy is, that it is necessary for Sir Peregrine Orme at this particular juncture to offer his hand to the widow. He has been her neighbour for 20 years without making love to her, but now, in order to work out the purposes of the story, he must needs, being threescore and ten years of age, propose to marry the widow. Knowing her position, she would rather not accept; but he will take no refusal, and she is forced into a consent. The proposed wedding creates much criticism and opposition. The son of Lady Mason is opposed to it; the son of Sir Peregrine Orme is bitterly opposed to it; and, worst of all, Lady Mason's chief legal adviser, who is himself very much in love with her, is opposed to it, and tells her plainly that if she marries Sir Peregrine Orme he will have nothing more to do with her case. Lady Mason is thus driven to set her affianced husband free. It must be done; there is no escape for her. But still Sir Peregrine will take no refusal, and overrides all objections. In a moment, seeing no other way before her, Lady Mason confesses her guilt and cuts the knot. This is the climax of the story, out of which arise some remarkable complications both of feeling and of incident. Sir Peregrine adores the woman in spite of her guilt; his daughter-in-law, Mrs. Orme, loves her with little less devotion; and the mingled grief and pride and love which are worked up in the scenes that follow have justice done to them by the author. Then the conflict that goes on between contrition and the necessity of secrecy, the determination to restore the property and the desire to avert an adverse verdict, bring about scenes that are full of interest, in which Mr. Trollope displays considerable mastery of the passions. In these portions of his book, we repeat, he has surpassed himself.

We doubt whether the great mass of his readers, however, will not be most interested in the quiet home life of Noningsby, as it is described by his pen. At Noningsby lives Judge Staveley with his wife, his son, and his daughter, and the pretty scenes which are enacted in dining-rooms and drawing-rooms there must not be told at second hand. There are the prettiest love scenes, in which all the gentlemen and all the ladies act with a correctness that is truly laudable. The correctness of Mr. Trollope's heroes and heroines in all their acts, but especially in lovemaking, does him infinite credit. None of them ever gets into a passion, or says anything foolish, or maunders, and the way in which they make love to each other without ever getting off the rails is a miracle of art. Especially do we admire the formulas which he has invented for persons who make proposals of marriage. It used to be said, but we don't know whether it is true, that in the performance of this interesting ceremony people are very much guided by novels as their book of fashion. The novelist suggests the proper attitudes, the tones of the voice, the gesture, the tender look, and the tender phrase, which are to have the most certain effect. We rather think that Mr. Trollope prides himself on his proposals of marriage, and we must give his formulas the double praise of being sufficiently varied and of having no nonsense in them; though it may be suspected that this is precisely the praise to which offers of marriage generally are not entitled. It may be suspected that where the heart is engaged most offers of marriage have a good deal of nonsense in them, and that one is very like another. However this be, all praise to Mr. Trollope for the amusement which he contrives to get out of these little scenes, and for the very pleasant pictures which he gives of domestic life in England. He has drawn nothing more attractive than his pictures of the household of Judge Staveley. And, speaking of pictures, we cannot conclude this notice without referring to the illustrations of Mr. Millais, which add considerably to the charms of the volume. The illustrations, it is true, are of unequal merit, and it is true also that we rather grudge to see so excellent a colourist working at mere sketches in black and white. Mr. Millais may lose in this way, but the book gains. We like best the pictures of out-of-door life, and next best the pictures of drawing-room life. The landscapes are beautiful, and the manner in which the peculiarly rich effects of drawing-rooms, with here their polished surfaces, and there their exquisite tissues, are displayed in these etchings is very clever.

61. Unsigned notice, *National Magazine*

January 1863, xiii. 48

When we take up a book of Mr. Anthony Trollope's, we may assure ourselves of two things: that nothing we shall find within its pages which either shocks our most delicate sense of the proprieties, or startles our susceptibilities by any alarming episode, or unforeseen adventure. . . . But as exceptions prove the rule, we have an exception in 'Orley Farm' (Chapman and Hall), the latest of Mr. Trollope's works. Here, for once, we have a break in the smooth landscape, a cloud on the calm horizon: a lady forger, and a perjurer to boot, is a character which might well become a 'sensational' feature in other hands; but the author, who disdains all clap-trap or stage trickery, softens even this down, and gives to the objectionable person the love of, perhaps the best one, in his book. The passion of an elderly gentleman of seventy is not, however, of that fierce and demonstrative nature which need disturb the halcyon progress of the tale, though the author does succeed unmistakably in interesting his readers in both these characters to a very great degree. In short, 'Orley Farm,' though certainly not the best of Mr. Trollope's works, is by no means the least amusing. Admirers of his style will find it well worth their perusal.

62. Unsigned notice, *Dublin University Magazine*

April 1863, lxi. 437

Chief among the writers of the class novel is Mr. Anthony Trollope; his faculty is really amazing. He sketches easy-going bishops, energetic archdeacons, quiet precentors, well-to-do rectors, starved perpetual curates, as if he had held a sinecure rectory all his life, and had spent the whole time in studying his brethren. He photographs the clerical exterior accurately; he does not go below the surface; does not introduce us to the man beneath the surplice. But so far as external habits go, Mr. Trollope is unsurpassed as a clerical painter; and his success arises from his carefully noticing the weaknesses of those he desires to sketch. Every class has its weaknesses; reproduce these, and the world will exclaim—What a likeness! If you attempt to paint the strength of a man your task is more difficult, and the public are less likely to recognize your subject. Mr. Trollope knows the limits of his power, and paints weaknesses only. His last triumph, in 'Orley Farm,' has been in a very unclerical direction. From bishops and archdeacons he has gone to commercial travellers; and really he describes all the bagman's little weaknesses as if he had been a bagman himself from infancy. He saturates you with the atmosphere of the commercial room; he leaves upon your palate the flavour of that fiery port which the bagman loves. Only by the doctrine of metempsychosis can we explain Mr. Trollope's singular faculty. In one of his previous existences he must have taken holy, and in another unholy, orders.

63. Trollope as the voice of the English middle class, *National Review*

January 1863, xvi. 27–40

Unsigned essay entitled simply 'Orley Farm'. E. D. Forgues's article 'Dégenérescence du roman' had appeared in *Revue des deux mondes* the previous August. The critic for the *National Review* points to Trollope's novels in general and *Orley Farm* in particular as evidence of the essential wholesomeness of the English reading public, in the face of M. Forgues's insinuations. Trollope's enormous popularity demonstrates both his considerable and significant virtues and his limitations as an artist.

Sir Cresswell Cresswell, mentioned in the first paragraph of the essay, had become first judge of the divorce court when it was created in 1858, and presided over it until his death in August 1863. The Windham Trial, also alluded to in the first paragraph, involved scandalous data on questions of breach of trust, breach of promise, and adultery. (See *The Times*, 5 December 1861, p. 8.)

M. Forgues has recently taken occasion, in the pages of the *Revue des Deux Mondes*, to express, under the unflattering title of 'Dégénérescence du Roman,' his views as to the present state of English fiction, and the future prospects of English morality. As he grounds his opinion in the one case on a survey of about a dozen of the most worthless stories of the day, and in the other on the revelations of Sir Cresswell Cresswell's court, it is natural enough that the account which he gives of us should be of a somewhat gloomy and humiliating character. With perfect good humour, and with a polite vindictiveness, the fruit evidently of prolonged provocation, he turns the laugh of his audience against the affected severity of our social code, the delicacy of our taste, and the boasted prudery of our literature. British mothers, he says, look upon a French novel as 'the abomination of desolation,' and British youths

166

veil their faces in pious horror before the innuendos of Paul de Kock, the eager voluptuousness of Dumas, or the ingenious impurity of Ernest Feydau. And yet, continues our frank monitor, England stands a good chance of descending from her pinnacle, and proving herself, in outward demonstration, no better than her neighbours. Such exposures as the Windham trial show that profligacy is much the same on one side of the Channel as the other, and the activity of the Divorce Court bespeaks an unhallowed restlessness in the matrimonial world. On the other hand, free trade is likely enough to extend from material to intellectual productions: along with the vintage of Bordeaux and the silks of Lyons, the sturdy Puritans are day by day imbibing the lax notions of less austere communities: and England, whose *métier* it has been to lecture the rest of Europe on improprieties, already possesses a race of novelists who want only the liveliness of their neighbours and the tricks of the trade, to be as viciously entertaining, and to gratify their own and their readers' improper cravings and unchastened sensibilities, by delineations as daring, a levity as complete, a license as openly avowed, as any thing that Eve's latest and most degenerate daughters can pluck from the fruit-trees of forbidden knowledge in the lending libraries of Paris.

Such a work as *Orley Farm* is perhaps the most satisfactory answer that can be given to so disagreeable an imputation. Here, it may fairly be said, is the precise standard of English taste, sentiment, and conviction. Mr. Trollope has become almost a national institution. The *Cornhill* counts its readers by millions,[1] and it is to his contributions, in ninety-nine cases out of a hundred, that the reader first betakes himself. So great is his popularity, so familiar are his chief characters to his countrymen, so wide-spread is the interest felt about his tales, that they necessarily form part of the common stock-in-trade with which the social commerce of the day is carried on. If there are some men in real life whom not to know argues oneself unknown, there are certainly imaginary personages on Mr. Trollope's canvas with whom every well-informed member of the community is expected to have at least a speaking acquaintance. The disappointment of Sir Peregrine, the boyish love of his grandson, the conceited transcendentalism of Lucius Mason,

---

[1] The writer's figures surely are exaggerated. Victorian families were, to be sure, large, and numbers of magazines were apt to be passed from family to family. The *Cornhill* started at 120,000 copies, but averaged 84,000 during the first two years (see Introduction, note 4). *Orley Farm* did not follow *Framley Parsonage* as a serial in the *Cornhill*, but came out instead in twenty monthly parts sold at one shilling each.

the undeserved prosperity of Graham, the matrimonial troubles of the Furnival establishment, and the high life below stairs to which Mr. Moulder and his travelling companion introduce us,—have probably been discussed at half the dinner-tables in London, as often and with as much earnestness as Royal Academies, International Exhibitions, the last mail from America, Sir William Armstrong's newest discovery[2] in the science of destruction, or any other of the standing conversational topics on which the conventional interchange of thought is accustomed to depend. The characters are public property, and the prolific imagination which has called them into existence is, without doubt, the most accurate exponent of the public feeling, and of that sort of social philosophy which exercises an unperceived, but not less actual, despotism over the life and conscience of every individual who forms a unit in the great aggregate of society. More than a million people habitually read Mr. Trollope, and they do so because the personages in his stories correspond to something in themselves: the hopes, fears, and regrets, are such as they are accustomed to experience; the thoughtfulness is such as they can appreciate; the standard of conduct just that to which they are prepared to submit. It becomes, therefore, an interesting inquiry to see what are the principal characteristics of an author in whom so large a section of the community sees as it were its own reflection, and who may himself unhesitatingly be accepted as the modern type of a successful novelist:—how far are we justified, with *Orley Farm* in our hands, in rebutting M. Forgues' accusations, and in maintaining that neither in literature nor morality has the period of English degeneracy as yet commenced.

One part of the charge may, we think, be very speedily disposed of. If the popularity of the portrait is the result of its truthfulness, and English life is at all what Mr. Trollope paints it, whatever its other failings may be, it is at any rate a very correct affair; writer and readers alike look at the performance from a strictly moral point of view: there is a general air of purity, innocence, and cheerfulness. The Bohemians that now and then flit across the stage are the tamest imaginable, and are only just sufficiently Bohemian to be picturesque without violating propriety. There are occasional villains of course, but they seem to belong to an outer world, with which the audience has so little in common that it can afford to treat their crimes as a matter of mere

---

[2] The effectiveness of inventor Sir William Armstrong's rapid-firing heavy artillery gun was being assailed for overheating and other problems (see, for example, *The Times* for 9 October 1861, p. 10).

curiosity. The low Jewish attorney, the brass-browed Old Bailey practitioner, Mr. Moulder in his drunken moods, Dockwrath in his revengeful spite,—are none of them models of what gentlemen and Christians should be; but they are never brought sufficiently near to display the full proportions of their guilt, or to suggest the possibility of contamination. The real interest of the story is concentred upon well-to-do, decorous, and deservedly prosperous people, who solve, with a good deal of contentment and self-satisfaction, the difficult problem of making the most both of this world and the next. The family of the Staveleys is in this way perhaps the most characteristic group which Mr. Trollope has as yet produced. They are thoroughly successful, and their success is well deserved; they have a calm, well-ordered, and healthily unobtrusive religion; they are quite above intrigue, shabbiness, or malevolence. Lady Staveley is a model as wife, mother, and mother-in-law; and Madeline, though she falls rather more precipitately in love than that *bien rangée* young lady should, is on the whole just such a daughter as a Lady Staveley would wish to have. The Christmas party at Noningsby could have been written only by a man who had experienced and appreciated the enjoyment of a well-ordered, hospitable, unpretentious country-house, where there are plenty of children, wealth enough to rob life of its embarrassments, simplicity enough to allow of a little romping and flirtation, and where every member of the family is on confidential terms with all the rest. Among the guests are a vulgar scheming young woman, the daughter of a London barrister; a nice simple lad, heir to a neighbouring baronet; and Felix Graham, clever, talkative, and agreeable, but ugly and penniless, and encumbered moreover with "an angel of light," in the shape of a young lady whom he has rescued from poverty, supplied with the rudiments of education, and promised, some day or other, to make his wife. Every thing is, however, perfectly innocent; and Graham, having been guilty of nothing but a generous indiscretion, proceeds forthwith to throw the angel of light into the background, and to fall in love with the young lady of the house. There are Christmas games in the evening for the children; and Graham is selected by one of them as her champion, and effects on her behalf a successful raid upon the snap-dragon, over which Miss Staveley is presiding as ghost and dragoness. . . .

All the point in this sort of scene depends on the innocence of the performers; and it is because Mr. Trollope can manufacture passages of the kind in any quantity required, that he has made himself the favourite writer of the day. The people on whose behalf he interests one are thoroughly sterling, warm-hearted, and excellent. Every body would be glad to spend Christmas at Noningsby, to go for a walk on Sunday afternoon with the good-natured old judge, to have a chat with Lady Staveley, and to receive a rap on the knuckles from Miss Madeline. What every body would be glad to do, every body likes to read about, and hence a universal popularity without either an exciting plot or forcible writing, or the least pretence at real thoughtfulness, to support it. Contrast Mr. Trollope in this respect with such a writer as the author of *Guy Livingston*, his superior certainly in melodramatic conception, in vivid scene-painting, brilliant dialogue, and in familiarity with several amusing phases of life. Not all the ability, however, of *Guy Livingston*[3] and its successors can force them into popularity against the steady dislike and disapproval which their loose tone excites. Throughout them there is an aroma of indelicacy, a half-admiration of profligacy, a familiarity with crime, which an English audience finds it impossible to forgive. There are, no doubt, sets of people whose proceedings and sentiments they correctly represent; but the great mass of readers regard them with aversion, and if they consent, for the sake of an amusing story, to make a transient acquaintance with the personages who play it out, accord them no welcome to their memories, and reject the whole picture as a libel upon modern society. When M. Forgues assures us that we are corrupt, and that our novels prove it, it would be enough, as regards this country, to contrast the fate of such books as *Sword and Gown* with that of *Orley Farm*, and, with respect to France, to remind him that such a volume as has within the last few weeks proceeded from the pen of M. Edmond About,[4] at one time the most decent as well as the wittiest of his profession, would be unhesitatingly refused admission to every English library or railway-stall, and would certainly forfeit for its author not only literary reputation and general popularity, but would make him an outcast from all respectable society.

But if we reject the imputation of one kind of degeneracy, it should be admitted that the success of Mr. Trollope's school of writing suggests the possibility of another. Such delineations are, to say the truth, but very low art; and while they do not corrupt the morals, they may degrade the tastes, and foster the weaknesses of those for whose edification

[3] George Alfred Lawrence (1827–76) was the author of *Guy Livingstone* (1857) and other sensational novels featuring a hero of enormous muscular strength and fierce passions—'a compound of pugilism and French sentiment', as a critic of the *Saturday Review* (14 April 1866, xxi. 439) was to say.

[4] Edmond About's *L'Homme à l'oreille cassée* (1862).

they are contrived. Mr. Trollope, it has been truly said, is a mere photographer; he manipulates with admirable skill, he groups his sitters in the most favourable attitudes, he contrives an endless series of interesting positions; but he never attains to the dignity of an artist. He has a quick eye for external characteristics, and he paints exclusively from without. He does not make us intimate with his characters, for the excellent reason that he is very far from being intimate with them himself. He watches their behaviour, their dress, their tone of voice, their expression of countenance, and he makes very shrewd guesses at their dispositions; but there is a veil in each one of their characters, behind which he is not privileged to pass, and where real conceptive genius could alone suffice to place him. Almost every nature has depths about it somewhere, with all sorts of moral curiosities at the bottom, if one has plummet deep enough to sound them. It is the inclination to do this, and the mental energy to do it with ability and discrimination, that constitute poetic power, and which give to writers like Charlotte Brontë or the authoress of *Adam Bede* so deep a hold over the interests and affections of the reader. When they have finished a portrait, one seems to have seen it through and through: it is a conception, created in their minds and brought visibly before their readers, by scenes so contrived as to bring the most secret passions into play, 'to try the very reins and the heart,' and to show the true nature of the actor more clearly even than he sees it himself. Mr. Trollope sets to work in quite another fashion. He arms himself, in the first place, with a number of commonplaces on religion, morals, politics, social and domestic philosophy. These supply his theory of life, and beyond them, in his most imaginative moments, he never raises his eye; but, accepting them as a creed, and as the ultimate explanation of all around him, he watches the society in which he lives, and elaborates a series of complications, which interest, partly from the sympathy one feels for pretty, nicely-dressed, and well-behaved young ladies, and partly from a natural curiosity to see how the author will get himself out of the scrape into which the evolution of the story has brought him. This sort of writing can never produce a profound emotion, and leaves us at last with a sense of dissatisfaction. Mr. Trollope himself seems to feel that it falls short of the requirements of a real emergency, and screens the defect by implying conversations, feelings, and expressions which he does not choose precisely to delineate. It is precisely these that we want to have, if we are to care in the least about the characters of the tale, and in their absence we feel a void exactly proportionate to the interest previously excited.

Take, for instance, the case of Lady Mason: nothing could be more exciting than the position assigned to her. She is beautiful, engaging, refined; an old country gentleman of high standing is her accepted lover, and she has just confessed to him that she has for twenty years been living on the proceeds of perjury and forgery, for which she is about, in a few weeks, to be brought into a court of justice. Sir Peregrine Orme, who was to have been her husband, sees of course the impossibility of his marriage; and Mrs. Orme, his widow daughter, and Lady Mason's confidential friend, proceeds to offer advice, consolation, and forgiveness. 'Many,' says Mr. Trollope, 'will think that she was wrong to do so, and I fear it must be acknowledged that she was not strong-minded. By forgiving her, I do not mean that she pronounced absolution for the sin of past years, or that she endeavoured to make the sinner think that she was no worse for her sin. Mrs. Orme was a good churchwoman, but not strong individually in point of doctrine. All that she left mainly to the woman's conscience and her own dealings with her Saviour, merely saying a word of salutary counsel as to a certain spiritual pastor who might be of aid. But Mrs. Orme forgave her as regarded herself.'

This seems to us about the most feeble way of getting through a striking scene that it is possible to conceive, and the suggestion of calling in the clergyman puts the finishing touch to the 'mildness' of the whole. Contrast it, for instance, with the description of Miriam and Donatello, in *Transformation*,[5] after the commission of the murder, or with that of the heroine of the *Scarlet Letter* after the discovery of her guilt. It is mere trifling to slur the scene over with hack religious phrases, to send for the parson just as one would for the parish engine, and calmly to pretermit the exact tragical *dénouement* to which the whole story has been leading up. Later on in the book we have a glimpse of the sort of consolation which, we suppose, the 'certain spiritual pastor' administered on his arrival. 'No lesson,' the author more than once informs us, 'is truer than that which teaches us that God does temper the wind to the shorn lamb.'[6] A shorn lamb! and this of a woman whose whole life has been one long lie, whose every act has been studied for a hypocritical purpose, and who is driven to reluctant confession at last, not from any sudden conviction of guilt, not because she finds the burden

---

[5] *Transformation* was the original English title for Hawthorne's novel *The Marble Faun* (1860).

[6] Trollope probably knew that he was quoting Sterne's *A Sentimental Journey* rather than the Bible; but the critic apparently did not.

of her solitary crime becoming absolutely intolerable, not because in an agony of fatigue and remorse she tears off the mask she has worn with such suffering endurance,—but because she is not wretch enough to incur the infamy of involving a noble old man in the disgrace and ruin which she knows, and which other people know, is shortly about to break upon herself.

There are, no doubt, people going about the world with secrets locked up in their hearts, to the safe custody of which, as of some ferocious wild beast, their whole existence is devoted. The Spartan lad with the hidden fox gnawing his flesh is probably no exaggeration of the agonies they endure, and the heroic self-restraint which concealment necessitates. . . . The tragedy of such careers is a dark one, and the artist who essays to paint it must be prepared with a courageous hand, intense colouring, and shades and lights in more striking contrast than are to be found in the mere conventional routine of ordinary society. Hypocrisy is a painful trade, and must make itself felt over an entire character, where once its employment has become essential. Lady Mason, after twenty years of it, would have been something very different from the calm, handsome, well-dressed, but impressible and half-coquettish woman to whom Mr. Trollope introduces us. Her experience would have put her beyond the reach of such gentle ministrations as Mrs. Orme's, and would have made it impossible for her in the crisis of her fate to behave like a silly impressible school-girl. Imposture 'should be made of sterner stuff,' and the sternness should be evidenced by a resolution, a courage, prepared nerves, a daring spirit, a readiness to run risk and encounter disaster, such as we find no trace of in Mr. Trollope's creation. Repentance, when it comes, must be the result of something more than accident, and remorse, if it is to be real, must require deeper comfort than little bits of texts, pet curates and pretty proverbs. . . . Lady Mason fades into indistinctness as soon as Mr. Millais's pretty sketches of a graceful sentimental woman, always *bien mise* and always in an appropriate attitude, have ceased to enlist our sympathies or arouse our curiosity.

But if Mr. Trollope's position in the artistic world is not very high, it is to this very circumstance that he probably owes much of his reputation. He travels with great agility, it is true, but never in a region where the million readers of *The Cornhill* find the least difficulty in following him. He paints life in its easy, superficial, intelligible aspects. Felix Graham and Lucius Mason, who are intended to be originals, deviate in no essential quality from the ten thousand other young men who might with equal propriety have been introduced to fill their place. Lucius is on the whole a greater fool than Graham, and being less of a gentleman, lets his folly escape in more disagreeable ways; but neither of them suggests any real rebellion against the actual constitution of society, the theories by which life is shaped, and the maxims which the majority at once obey for themselves and inflict upon others. The whole picture is full of sunshine; the tragedy of life, of which every man is conscious in his graver moments, and which at some particular crisis absorbs his thoughts,—the grave doubts, the painful struggles, the miserable anxieties, the humiliating defeats, all that makes the world something else than a mere playground for children or a bed of roses for idlers,— find no place in the cheerful, sanguine, well-to-do philosophy which feeds the perennial font of Mr. Trollope's fictions.

People like Charlotte Brontë speak out of the fulness of their heart, when they depict the sufferings of our existence, and they infect us with sympathy for vicissitudes, disappointments, or regrets, with which each of us has something in common. They go nearer the truth, and they teach us a worthier lesson than he whom a good-natured superficiality and a perilous influx of success prevent from looking into the gloomy caverns which surround him, from visiting the chamber where he, like his neighbours, has a skeleton on guard, and from indulging in the aspirations to which suffering flies for refuge, and which alone saves the miserable from despair.

A world of Lady Staveleys would be, after all, a poor concern, and angels like Madeline would be the inhabitants of a duller heaven than even that which conventional theology has depicted as the future residence of the blest. Contentment is a noble achievement, but it must not be the content of a mere material well-being, of shallow thought, of slight insight, of narrow scope. It is to this sort of mood that Mr. Trollope's stories are calculated to minister; and by fostering it, they perhaps do as much towards lowering the dignity, enfeebling the energies, and coarsening the prevailing taste of the times, as if they in any tangible particular violated the conventional standard of decorum. The mass of second-rate people is preserved from corruption only by a leaven of genius, and the world goes its way in peace only because a few men here and there are sensitive enough to appreciate its catastrophes, and bold enough to infringe its rules, question its methods, and attack its abuses. Without them we should degenerate into that Lilliputian congeries of petty interests, timid thoughts, and unworthy ambitions, which Béranger, with a gloomy mirth, depicted as the approaching condition of his countrymen. . . .[7] Some such danger seems to us, we confess, to impend over a generation for which such contrivances as *The Cornhill* secure an infinity of 'Orley Farms,' and which seduces an artist like Mr. Millais from his legitimate occupations to draw little commonplace sketches of commonplace life, with becrinolined young ladies fresh from the pages of *Le Follet*,[8] and incidents whose trivialities his pencil alone could rescue from being absolutely vulgar.

When we have said, however, that Mr. Trollope is incapable of conceiving a tragedy, or of doing justice to it when circumstances bring it in his way, we have well nigh exhausted the complaints that need be brought against him. It is a more agreeable task to touch upon the many excellent qualities which have concurred in recommending him to the good will of his countrymen. His pages are unsullied by a single touch of malice, unkindness, or revenge. His amusing sketch in *The Warden* of three bishops, given as a burlesque account of the three sons of the archdeacon, proves that he could, if he pleased, be personal to the greatest effect; and every author must have little spites and dislikes of his own, which only a resolute good feeling can prevent from intruding upon his canvas. Mr. Trollope never sins in this respect, and his immunity from this failing might well be accepted as an apology for a host of minor delinquencies. Another great charm is, that the author is for the most part kept well out of sight, and if he appears, shows himself thoroughly interested in the piece, and sincerely desirous that his audience should be so likewise. Mr. Thackeray's curious taste for careless, rambling, 'roundabout' writing, and the clever knack he has of making the most of 'an infinite deal of nothing,' has set the fashion to a host of imitators, who do not scruple to stop at every convenient point of their narration to indulge in a few personal confidences, and enunciate their views about their story, themselves, or the world in general. Mr. Thackeray, in particular, loses no opportunity of, so to speak, yawning in public; saying how dreadfully tiresome his novels are to him, how he falls asleep over them at the club, and strongly recommends his friends to do the same. Mr. Trollope has no touch of this affectation; he does his very best: he believes in the piece, he detests the villains, admires the heroes,

[7] The writer here takes space to quote the third and fourth stanzas of Pierre Jean de Béranger's *Les infiniment petits, ou la Gérontocratie*. He is fond of quotation and has already given his readers Thomas Hood's *Dream of Eugene Aram* (1846), p. 27, in the section omitted two paragraphs preceding. In the section omitted just previous to that, he quotes *King Lear*, III. ii. 51–7.

[8] The fashion magazine *Le Follet, journal du grand mond*, published in both Paris and London, 1846–1900.

and can scarcely refrain from caressing his pet heroine when she crosses his path. If he comes for a few moments on the stage, it is only to bustle about, to adjust the ropes, to hurry the scene-shifters, and to assure the beholders that no pains are being spared for their entertainment. Mr. Thackeray, on the contrary, lolls in dressed in a dressing-gown and slippers, stretches his arms, cries, 'Eheu! fugaces,—monsieur, mon cher confrère';[9] and acknowledges that he has often done vilely before, but never so vilely as on the present occasion.

Mr. Trollope does not, however, invariably preserve the wholesome rule of impersonality. Though a thorough optimist, and believing in his heart that the world is the best of all possible worlds, he has one or two little grievances which keep us just short of absolute perfection. With characteristic carelessness and high spirits, he points out the tiny flaw which he has discovered, and adds a scarcely serious murmur to the general chorus of complaint. One of his troubles, for instance, is, that there should be such wicked people as lawyers in the world, and he grows quite sentimental over the circumstance that gentlemen should put off their consciences when they put on their wigs, and consent, for the small remuneration of one guinea, to make the worse appear the better cause. In support of his views, he has constructed an elaborate trial scene, with a proper apparatus of bullying counsel, lying attorneys, frightened witnesses, and, finally, frustrated justice. A discriminating critic, who appears to write with professional enthusiasm,[10] has been at the pains to tear the whole thing to pieces, and to show that in every essential particular Mr. Trollope did not know what he was talking about, that no such facts as those on which he grounds his insinuation could possibly exist, and that all but a few black sheep in the profession do precisely what Mr. Trollope says that they ought. So much good labour seems to us in a large degree wasted upon a writer with whom instruction is necessarily subsidiary to amusement, and who scarcely pretends to any but the most superficial acquaintance with the evils of which he complains. Some of the details of the trial, especially the cross-examination by the counsel for the defence, are so ludicrously unlike real life, that it is evident Mr. Trollope's visits to a court of justice have been few and far between, and have left on his mind only a vague

[9] 'Alas, the fleeting [years]'—a common Latin tag from Horace (*Odes,* II. xiv. 1)—with 'my dear fellow' added in French, apparently to suggest a pretence of cynical informality on the part of Thackeray as narrator.

[10] Probably an allusion to the notice of *Orley Farm* in the *Saturday Review.* See the headnote to No. 54, above.

and indistinct impression, which nothing but the haze in which it is involved preserves from instant exposure. Ideas of this kind hardly admit of being definitely stated, but may be easily insinuated in the course of a story constructed for the purpose of exemplifying them. Witnesses, no doubt, are sometimes bullied into confusion and even forgetfulness; but Mr. Trollope cannot seriously mean that when a poor fool like Kenneby gets into the box to swear away another person's life or character, his capacity to remember any thing, and the degree in which he actually does remember the particular facts in question, ought not to be tested with the utmost severity. It is curious that, in the very case which Mr. Trollope frames in his own support, the performers do precisely that which justice required. Mr. Chaffanbrass, from the Old Bailey, may have been a great rogue; but he acted quite properly, and served the general interests of society in demonstrating that Dockwrath had private motives of the very strongest kind for supporting the prosecution, just as Mr. Furnival acted quite properly in showing that Kenneby had only half his wits about him, and had no such accurate recollection of a matter which happened twenty years before as to justify a conviction for perjury. Mr. Trollope probably meant nothing more than that barristers are sometimes vulgar and unscrupulous, and judges sometimes petulant and overbearing; but he should beware of discussing as a grievance that which is really a necessity, and of grounding on imaginary and impossible facts an imputation on the honour and good faith of a profession which certainly contains in its ranks as many scrupulous and high-minded gentlemen as any other.

It would be easy to multiply instances of the same sort of unsubstantial complaint thrown in without any real conviction, as a sort of sentimental garnishing to a matter-of-fact narrative. In his last tale, for instance, the author stops in the midst of the description of a village to contrast our present ideas of rural grandeur with those of our forefathers. In old times the good squire 'sat himself down close to his God and his tenants,' and placed his house so as 'to afford comfort, protection, and patronage' to those around him; nowadays 'a solitude in the centre of a park is the only eligible site; no cottage must be seen but the cottage *orné* of the gardener; the village, if it cannot be abolished, must be got out of sight; the sound of the church-bells is not desirable,' &c.; in fact, the present race of country gentlemen are a sad falling away from the traditional benevolence of their race. Does Mr. Trollope, we wonder, really believe this? What is the golden age with which the present iron epoch is contrasted? Does he look back with a loving eye upon feudal times and the 'droits de seigneurie'? or are we wrong in believing that the maxim, that property has duties as well as rights, has never been more thoroughly accepted than in our day, and that the squires of England, more perhaps than any other class of proprietors in existence, are alive to the responsibilities of their position, and struggling conscientiously 'to afford comfort, protection, and patronage' of the most substantial sort to their poorer neighbours?

We can afford to touch only upon one other characteristic of Mr. Trollope's writings, to which he would, we think, do well to pay attention,—their occasional broad vulgarity. He drops every now and then with suspicious ease into a society which is simply repulsive in its stupid coarseness; and as he has not the extravagant fun that Dickens pours over low life, and which has immortalized such personages as Mrs. Gamp, these parts of Mr. Trollope's writings are singularly tedious and unattractive. Some people have a genius for such descriptions: the authoress of *Adam Bede* can draw a set of countrymen drinking in a public-house so humorously that we forget every thing but the fun of the scene; but Mr. Trollope's commercial gentlemen, lodging-house keepers, and attorneys, are simply snobs, into whose proceedings one feels no wish to pry, and who might with great advantage be banished altogether from the picture. A stupid violent man like Moulder, coming home half tipsy, and proceeding to complete the process of intoxication before his wife and friends, must be very amusing indeed meanwhile, if we are to look on without disgust; in Mr. Trollope's hands he is any thing but amusing, and tries to atone for his dulness by being unnecessarily coarse. Mr. Trollope succeeds capitally in depicting nice young ladies like Madeline Staveley, and pleasant gentlemanly lads like Peregrine Orme; and he may contentedly resign the portraiture of Moulders, Kantwises, and Kennebys, to artists whose knowledge of life is more varied than his own, or whose conceptive ability enables them, as in some rare instances is the case, to dispense with the experience from which all but the very highest sort of artists are obliged to draw.

RACHEL RAY

1863

The publishing history of *Rachel Ray* (*Autobiography*, pp. 156–7) shows the perils of taking with undue literalness Trollope's picture of himself as a simple craftsman busily stitching shoes to order for his customers. The Reverend Dr. Norman Macleod, a Presbyterian minister and editor of the relatively liberal evangelical magazine *Good Words*, had asked Trollope to prepare for him a novel for serialization in his pages,

. . . explaining to me that his principles did not teach him to confine his matter to religious subjects, and paying me the compliment of saying that he would feel himself quite safe in my hands. In reply I told him I thought he was wrong in his choice; that though he might wish to give a novel to the readers of *Good Words*, a novel from me would hardly be what he wanted, and that I could not undertake to write either with any specially religious tendency, or in any fashion different from that which was usual to me. As worldly and—if any one thought me wicked—as wicked as I had heretofore been, I must still be, should I write for *Good Words*. He persisted in his request, and I came to terms as to a story for the periodical. I wrote it and sent it to him, and shortly afterwards received it back—a considerable portion having been printed—with an intimation that it would not do. A letter more full of wailing and repentance no man ever wrote. It was, he said, all his own fault. He should have taken my advice. He should have known better. But the story, such as it was, he could not give to his readers in the pages of *Good Words*. Would I forgive him? Any pecuniary loss to which his decision might subject me the owner of the publication would willingly make good.

Something in Trollope's nature other than the craftsman's instinct led him to create a novel that, from the evangelical view, was not only worldly but that went out of its way to caricature a dissenting minister and members of his flock along broadly comic lines. Trollope was obviously unrepentant.

There was some loss—or rather would have been—and that money I exacted, feeling that the fault had in truth been with the editor. There is the tale now to speak for itself. It is not brilliant, nor in any way every excellent; but it certainly is not very wicked. There is some dancing in one of the early chapters, described, no doubt, with that approval of the amusement which I have always entertained; and it was this to which my friend demurred. It is more true of novels than perhaps of anything else, that one man's food is another man's poison.

---

64. Unsigned review, *Athenaeum*

17 October 1863, pp. 492–4

In its unabridged form, this admiring but somewhat diffuse review runs to nearly three thousand words.

How comes it that at a time when a series of powerfully written novels —of which Mr. Trollope's 'Orley Farm' is a favourable example—have whetted the public appetite for tales of mysterious crime and startling surprises, this simple story of doings in a picturesque nook of Devonshire is as delightful as it is healthy? No full answer to the inquiry will be given on the present occasion; but we advise readers to put the question to themselves, as they laugh over the absurdities of the Tappitt family and kiss away the tears from Rachel Ray's pretty face. It will be enough for us to indicate a few of the good features which enable us to commend the story as a work that will do more than any number of critical protests to correct existing vices of public taste, and overthrow a school of artists whose extravagances have done no slight amount of harm, and are a cause of reasonable offence. . . .

The book, in short, is a portfolio of women's portraits, the like of which no artist but Mr. Trollope could produce. Many living novelists can describe women,—as they appear in ball-rooms and theatres, figuring a way under the eyes of society, and displaying just that small amount of personal character which can be shown by actresses on the stage of fashion. But to portray a woman, measuring her steps and framing her sentences according to the rules of conventional politeness, is one thing; to exhibit her in her parlour or her bedroom, sitting over her teapot or mending linen, and surrendering herself to the unrestrained gossip and quaint slovenlinesses of perfect domestic freedom, is another task. . . .

Who has not seen Mrs. Prime—zealous in good works to her inferiors, but very sparing of kind deeds and charitable thoughts to her
equals? Who has not seen her buy servility with the wealth allotted to
her by a turn of one of Fortune's smallest wheels? Who has not witnessed her anger towards brothers and sisters daring enough to oppose
her will or question her opinions? Such women are far from rare in a
world where much evil is wrought by persons thoroughly convinced of
their own moral excellence, though, thank Heaven! they are less numerous than the unobtrusive workers, whose goodness does more than
merely neutralize the influence of their strong-minded associates. But
though Mrs. Ray submits to the scoldings of this tyrannical daughter,
she has another child, on whom she lavishes the love of her womanly
heart. 'She had,' says the author, of the widow, 'one whom she feared
and obeyed, seeing that a master was necessary to her; but she had
another whom she loved and caressed, and I may declare that some such
object for her tenderness was as necessary to her as the master. She could
not have lived without something to kiss, something to tend, something
to which she might speak in short, loving, pet terms of affection.'

It is a strictly realistic novel, as we have already intimated; its most
striking positions and characters being the ordinary occurrences and
personages of country-town life; but it differs from the most memorable
specimens of recent realistic art in the merry lightness of heart and unaffected gaiety which animate its pieces of social description, and in its
entire freedom from scenes that either provoke indignation or rouse
deeply painful emotions.

65. Unsigned review, *Reader*

17 October 1863, ii. 437–8

Fortunately for the outside public, the author of 'Barchester Towers' cannot succeed in writing down to the level he has proposed to himself. The covert satire which runs through all his writings crops out constantly in 'Rachel Ray'; all the more so, perhaps, for his laborious attempt to divest the book of any originality. If report is true, and the proprietors of—let us say—'Social Sundays' did not consider the novelette exactly qualified for their peculiar public, we think they were wise in their generation. . . .

Still the book is not to our minds a pleasing one. Anybody we come across is, in his or her own way, selfish and self-seeking. The charge of cynicism, which is so often brought against the author of 'Vanity Fair,' might, we think, be imputed with greater justice to Mr. Trollope. The credit for good intentions, which he gives so liberally to all his characters, is too diffused to be of much value. The propositions that everybody is good and everybody is bad come to very much the same in the long run; the laughing and the weeping philosophers probably despised the world pretty equally. There is nobody that appears in these pages, or indeed, for that matter, in any one of Mr. Trollope's works, who has not a vague desire to do right, or a more or less distinct idea of duty; but then everybody, even the very best, is actuated by two motives. Luke Rowan is a very good, well-conducted, religious, young man; but he is hard to his partner, selfish to his mother, and cruel to his betrothed. Mrs. Prime is a woman who spends her life in works of charity, but makes everybody about her wretched, and refuses on any pretence to part with a penny of her money. Rachel is a loving, piously-bred girl; but she nearly breaks her mother's heart by refusing, after her own disappointment in love, to continue those marks of affection which cheered the widowed mother's lonely life. Mrs. Ray herself is very unhappy about her daughter; but chiefly so because her child's sorrow makes her own life so very dreary. The three clergymen of the parish—High Church, Broad Church, and Low Church—are each and all selfish in their several fashions; and, as for the Tappitts, we consider that the fact of their being respectable, moral, church-going people only serves to render their conduct even more inexcusable. The sketches of the Tappitt family are the cleverest, though the least pleasant, portions of the book. Mr. Thackeray, in his bitterest moods, could hardly have written a more cruelly true description than that given of Tappitt, the father, after he has been bullied by his family and partner into retiring from the brewery on an allowance. . . .

The truth is that Mr. Trollope seems oppressed throughout his work with a sense how dreary, and dull, and narrow is the life of a small English country town. This depression communicates itself to the reader. Balzac's scenes of provincial life are bad enough; but there, at least, you have the element of fierce desires and strong passions. The very idea of passion is carefully excluded from Mr. Trollope's pages, and the monotony of that dull round of life he describes seems unbroken by anything but death. There is a story in one of Mr. Dickens's works of an old clerk who had dined for fifty years at the same chop-house and posted the same books, till one evening it struck him that his life was hardly worth living for; so he went home and cut his throat.[1] We always wonder how, if such a life were possible as that of Baslehurst, the whole population does not cut its throat some fine Sunday morning.

[1] The reviewer is apparently recalling (imperfectly) the bachelor friend that Mr. Tulkinghorn of *Bleak House* (Ch. XXII) remembered, who, conceiving one summer evening that his life had grown too monotonous, gave his watch to his hairdresser and walked home and hanged himself.

66. Unsigned notice, *Saturday Review*

24 October 1863, xvi. 554-5

Mr. Trollope is quite a young lady's man. He devotes himself to painting the agitations, the difficulties, the tenderness, the dismay, and the happiness of the young female heart, and a natural insight and long practice enable him to succeed. His young women are capital—very like real young women, and yet distinct, ingenuous, and interesting. *Rachel Ray* is merely a story about a young lady, and it is a story of a very simple kind. The whole action is condensed within six months. The hero is introduced at the outset, and the young lady falls in love with him at once. The only hitch that arises is due to the circumspection of a neighbouring clergyman, an old family friend, who suggests that the engagement should not be permitted until the gentleman's means are clearly ascertained. In a month or two he is enabled to put all doubts at rest by setting up a brewery, and then the difficulties are over, and the young people marry and are happy. Mr. Trollope, therefore, has not much straw to make his bricks with, but he has taught himself to turn out a brick that really does almost without straw, and is a very good saleable brick of its kind. Even a young woman whose unhappiness is caused by her lover not setting up a brewery fast enough may have many anxious moments and display many fine feelings. Her love-making may have as deep an inner interest of its own as if it were going to end in her lover falling in a forlorn hope; and a novelist whose strength lies in imagining and representing how young women feel and behave when something a little out of the way happens to them can easily make something out of any heroine in any position. Rachel Ray has a mother and a sister, the former weak-minded and the latter strong-minded. The mother is deeply interested in Rachel's little affair, and longs to countenance it as much as she dare; but the strong-minded sister is against all young men on principle, as she considers them wolves, and she wishes the possible brewer sent about his business. The first volume shows how Rachel, impelled by an unacknowledged love, defies her domineering sister, and says Yes to the future brewer with her mother's sanction; but her mother then gets uncomfortable, and is guided, or misguided, by the old clergyman into ordering Rachel to return a very

iff, cold answer to the first love-letter she receives. The second volume
recounts the brewer's wrath, his establishment in business, his relenting
to Rachel and the final acquiescence of the domineering sister in the
marriage. Those who know Mr. Trollope's art will easily guess how
many conflicting emotions are felt by Rachel on receipt of the love-
letter, during the time before the answer is decided on and after it has
been sent. So far as we can guess, it seems to us very probable that a
young woman so placed as Rachel Ray would act and feel very much
as she is represented as acting and feeling. There is a brisk market for
descriptions of the inner life of young women, and Mr. Trollope is the
chief agent in supplying the market. This sample is quite up to the
mark, and that is all that need be said of it or can be said of it. But then
it must be remembered that, to supply this peculiar market creditably,
a novelist must not only have the gift of writing and the gift of devising
imaginary characters; he must also have tact, and discretion, and a
gentlemanly taste. It is because Mr. Trollope has all these in a high degree that his young women are successful.

Mr. Trollope has two minor strings to his bow besides this main one
of depicting the feelings of girls. He delights in drawing portraits of
vulgar or shabby-genteel life, and he also loves to sketch different types
of clergymen. There is a vulgar family in *Rachel Ray*, and there are two
or three clergymen, and more especially there is a Mr. Prong. We confess that we are a little wearied of these clerical people, and although
clergymen of the Prong type are much better in fiction than in real life,
yet there may be too much of them in novels, however cunningly they
may be described. Mr. Prong is a hard-working, zealous, vulgar, soft,
oily man, who preaches 'the gospel,' and firmly believes that every one
except himself and a few women of his flock are virtually condemned
already. There are plenty of men like this in England in whom, of
course, an optimist philosophy can see many virtues and a special use,
but whom it is desirable, if possible, never to see, speak to, or think of.
Nor do we even like to read of them. There is, indeed, something
comic in the love-making which Mr. Prong offers to Rachel Ray's
domineering sister, Mrs. Prime, and in the battles between them on the
great point whether the lady is to have all her money settled on herself.
We have no doubt that if a man of this sort were trying to marry a
widow with a little fortune, and if he were anxious to have her money
under his control, he would talk as Mr. Prong talks, and clothe his purpose under a mass of verbiage about 'greater usefulness in the vineyard,'
and so forth. It is also very probable that Mr. Trollope is quite right in

intimating that such a man need not be a hypocrite, and that there may be nothing very bad about him but his language. Mr. Prong is not an unfair representation of the lower order of clergymen in provincial towns. But the accuracy of the portrait does not make it pleasant to study it. The foolish language, the pert fanaticism, and the little petty tricks of the worst class of Evangelical clergy are not things that it is agreeable to study; and whatever there is of comic in them is soon exhausted, unless a glaring exaggeration of every symptom is used by the author to spice his description.

The Tappitts, who form the vulgar family of this novel, are only moderately successful. They are the established brewers of the town near which Rachel Ray lives; and the enterprising lover, when he, too, turns brewer, forces them to leave and retire on an annuity. The Tappitts go on in a very prosaic way. They first take up the young man who wishes to brew, because the mother hopes to marry him to one of her daughters; and she gives an evening party, in which he shines as a sort of hero of the house. But when it is obvious to all men that he is in love with Rachel Ray, the Tappitts turn against him, and Tappitt himself is furious beyond measure. The fun lies in the mode in which, after she has made up her mind that the best thing Tappitt can do is to retire, Mrs. Tappitt brings over her husband to her opinion. The fun is rather broad, for the final scene of her triumph is one in which Tappitt comes home drunk from an election dinner, and is put to bed by her, and partly through shame, and partly by having his clothes taken from him and so being forced to lie in bed, is brought to promise everything she wishes. These scenes in the Tappitt family are tolerably entertaining in their way, and a novelist who can paint vulgarity of this sort while he manages to inspire a constant conviction that he himself is not in the least vulgar, can do what very few people could do. Still, the humour of a henpecked, drunken country brewer is not of a very fascinating or elevated kind. *Rachel Ray* is poor when compared with Mr. Trollope's best works. It seems thin and slight, and about nothing, when judged by that standard. But it is never bad, and never dull, and is full of things which no one but Mr. Trollope could have written. It is his mission to keep on writing for ever about the inner life of girls, and the clergy, and vulgar families, and he always does it well. But sometimes he does it very well indeed, and sometimes only well; and *Rachel Ray* is an instance of the latter kind of success.

Mr. Trollope has, in fact, established his novels as the novels of the day, and his is the picture of English life which, for a brief space at least,

186

will be accepted as the true one by those who wish to see English life represented in fiction. It is impossible to say that the picture is wanting either in truth or in vigour. It comes quite as near the real thing as either of its two immediate predecessors—the family novel of Miss Yonge and the satirical novel of Mr. Thackeray. And yet those specimens of art were true enough to their originals. Country families of mild ecclesiastical principles, and living under circumstances which permitted a certain amount of enthusiasm to be found in the young ladies, were exceedingly like the families that appeared in the school of fiction to which Miss Yonge has given her name. Clubs were exceedingly like what Mr. Thackeray represented them to be—full of snobs, full of pretension, full of little exhibitions of petty selfishness. The different worlds that Mr. Thackeray revealed to us—the world of flunkies, and the world of artists, and the world of briefless barristers—were all photographed from life by a keen observer, who had been provided by practice and native ingenuity with the best of instruments. Mr. Trollope's novels also are true, but they are not more true, and all these different delineations of English life, each true in their kind and degree, make us feel what an inexhaustible thing the representation of any social life must be, and how slight is the truth to which a true representation attains. There is a vanity and a weariness even in truth of minute description. It seems as if it could hardly be worth while for an able man to go on, year after year, working off little likenesses, more or less exact, of provincial brewers retiring from business and of other provincial brewers coming into business. There is something unsatisfactory even in noticing for ever the shades of character which a young woman can display when she gets her first love-letter. It may seem rather hard that critics should read Mr. Trollope's novels and enjoy them, and then abuse them for being what they are. But this is, we believe, the exact combination of feelings which they would awaken in many minds. They are entertaining and very clever, but there is a satiety attending not only Mr. Trollope's representations of ordinary life, but all such representations, whoever may be the author. We wish fiction would do something for us besides giving us these accurate likenesses of the common run of those whom we see or know. We may hope that the next fashion in fiction will take us to something more exciting and poetical than the domestic sorrows of brewers' wives, although, while the present fashion lasts, we own that Mr. Trollope shows great skill in the mode in which he supplies the article in demand.

67. Unsigned notice, *London Review*

31 October 1863, pp. 467–8

Mr. Trollope is one of the few novelists who make us forget the labour
of criticism in our enjoyment of their books. He throws off his novels
with the ease of a man writing to some friend the latest gossip of his
circle; and seems as much amused with the foibles and humours of his
characters as if he were laughing at persons he had seen and heard, and
not at the creatures of his imagination. This characteristic of his writing
he has nowhere displayed more strikingly than in the novel before us.
It is almost a laugh from beginning to end, marked here and there with
touches of pathos effectively thrown in; and though at times verging on
caricature, only violating the truth of nature to the extent of a slight
exaggeration. Without plot and almost without incident, we are carried
through the book by the writer's exuberant spirits, and his way of turning to us the quizzical side of his characters; but still more by the power
with which he realizes the manners, the habits, and speech of English life
in their homeliest garb. They are real beings who play their part in his
story. We have met them, have spoken and lived with them. We have
sat with them in their houses, have walked with them over the fields,
watched with them the setting sun by the churchyard stile, and shared
their loves and jealousies, their weaknesses, and their virtues. We have
seen before this cottage interior, with its half-dozen books with gilt
leaves arranged in shapes on the small round table, where also is deposited the 'spangled mat of wondrous brightness, made of short white
sticks of glass strung together,' with its shells and china figures on the
chimney-piece, the birdcage without a bird, the old sofa, the old arm-
chair and carpet, and the old round mirror over the fire-place. We have
some experience of Mrs. Tappitt's manœuvres to convert a tea-party
into a ball, and win her lord and master by beautifully fine degrees to
consent to one expense after another, till the accumulation involves, as
an absolute necessity, a still further outlay for which he is to be consoled by one of her best beef-steak puddings. And who, that has not
been buried all his life in unredeemed bricks and mortar, has not met
Mrs. Sturt, the farmer's wife, who likes a young man who does the
thing that's honest, and is willing to lend her friendly aid to bring two

ung people together again who have been separated by the stupid
terference of soured or silly meddlers? With such traits does 'Rachel
ay' abound; and if it is not to be ranked, though we doubt this, with
Ir. Trollope's best works, he has written nothing which will give his
aders more thorough delight.

The design of his tale is to show how excessively mischievous over-
ood people may make themselves; and that there is a practical malig-
ity even about religion itself when it is pushed to an unnatural extreme.

Adam Bede and *Romola* are the best fictions that a woman has eve.
written; in Mr. Thackeray's masterpieces there is a profound philosophy endowed with charms to which philosophy in general has bu
little pretension; and Mr. Trollope, who travels on more level groun
as the novelist of common sense, writes with a shrewdness and a so-
briety, yet with a rush and fullness of thought that satisfies the intellec
while seeming but to tickle our curiosity. He is an immense favourit
with the most intelligent class of novel readers. He never soars ver
high, nor digs very deep, but he hardly ever disappoints; we can alway
rely upon him for a good story well sustained, full of life and not deficient in ideas. In one respect he reminds us more than any other write
of Defoe. It is a commonplace of criticism that Defoe wanted imagination, that never was there so great a writer of fiction who so palpabl
displayed such a deficiency. It would be difficult to define what is mean
by this, because nobody has yet been able to define what is meant b
imagination. . . .

Oddly enough the writer who displays this rough and ready, downright, prosaic, forceful style is, of all our novelists, the ladies' man of ou
time. His most celebrated men have belonged to the class clerical, whc
by reason of their cloth are not in the position of men proper. It is in th
portraiture of the fair sex that Mr. Trollope's great glory consists, and hi
success in this walk has made him the pet of our drawing-rooms. Th
women adore him. Nobody understands the gentle dames and damsel
of modern life half so well as this modern Anthony. We do not preten
to speak of him personally; we are only speaking of him as a book, anc
as a book, he is the great lady-killer of the age. He has attained thi
distinction chiefly by merit, but partly—we were going to say, b
demerit—we shall say, by an appeal to the prejudices of society. Hi
merit lies in his charming portraiture of the sex. He has studied all th
wiles of the feminine heart, and knows every fold of feeling—how ir
fashionable life Mamma thinks of the jointure, and how in humble lif
the worthy dame has thoughts of buttered toast. Emotions great anc
small he discusses with equal facility—the emotion of a lady who i

moving heaven and earth to circumvent her lord, and the emotion of a girl who in the midst of a ball discovers that her back hair threatens to fall loose upon her shoulders. . . .

By the rule of contraries we are reminded of this as we read Mr. Trollope's novel of *Rachel Ray*. It is a delightful tale, but with the simplest, smallest action that can be imagined. It is a tale in which women are the chief agents, then clergymen, then a brewer. The women being the chief agents, and being at the same time innocent and womanly, have nothing to do but to fall in love and marry, and to encounter in the process the strife of female tongues. The hero of the tale is a young brewer who means to reform Devonshire, to abolish cider-drinking, and to introduce good beer into that benighted land. While he is engaged in that laudable pursuit he sees Rachel Ray, falls in love with her, and the story hangs on the revolution which his love made in the cottage of Rachel's mother, and in the small gossip which ensued in the village up to the time of the wedding. A small village has an awful sense of propriety, and in relating the gossip of the neighbours Mr. Trollope has a rare opportunity of descanting on his favourite theme. The discourses which we listen to on what is correct and what is incorrect in love are most edifying; and, indeed, a considerable part of the action turns on the fact that Rachel Ray's elder sister quarrels with her upon a question of correctness of behaviour in this lovemaking. . . . We read the village gossip with as much concern as if the fate of the nation depended on it, and we take as much interest in a lawyer's poor daughter as if she were a peeress in her own right. Oh, happy art of fiction which can thus adjust the balance of fortune, raising the humble and weak to an equality in our hearts with the proud and the great!

69. Unsigned notice, *Westminster Review*

February 1864, lxxxi. 291–3

If Mr. Trollope's last novel falls short of some of its predecessors in variety of character and incident, it is inferior to none of them in many of the special qualities which have been their chief attraction, and must be read with pleasure by all who can appreciate a good design correctly drawn and coloured, though the subject may be homely and prosaic. There is not absolutely a single figure in the whole story fitted to play a great, a startling, or an intricate part; scarcely one that rises above the ordinary level of humdrum humanity; none that sink very deeply below it; but out of these common-place materials Mr. Trollope's practised hand has produced two pleasant, entertaining volumes, and a story which secures the reader the luxury of seeing his neighbours' follies and weaknesses in a thoroughly ridiculous light, without any tinge of malice.

THE SMALL HOUSE
AT ALLINGTON

1864

The Small House at Allington was widely popular during its run in twenty successive issues (from September 1862 to April 1864) of the *Cornhill Magazine*. Trollope (*Autobiography*, p. 150) was pleased at its success, but not, apparently, among the many admirers of his heroine. It is remarkable, too, that he does not mention Adolphus Crosbie, certainly among his most interesting creations, as his reviewers were quick to recognize.

The Small House at Allington redeemed my reputation with the spirited proprietor of the *Cornhill*, which must, I should think, have been damaged by *Brown, Jones, and Robinson*. In it appeared Lily Dale, one of the characters which readers of my novels have liked the best. In the love with which she has been greeted I have hardly joined with much enthusiasm, feeling that she is somewhat of a French prig. She became first engaged to a snob, who jilted her; and then, though in truth she loved another man who was hardly good enough, she could not extricate herself sufficiently from the collapse of her first great misfortune to be able to make up her mind to be the wife of one whom, though she loved him, she did not altogether reverence. Prig as she was, she made her way into the hearts of many readers, both young and old; so that, from that time to this, I have been continually honoured with letters, the purport of which has always been to beg me to marry Lily Dale to Johnny Eames. Had I done so, however, Lily would never have so endeared herself to these people as to induce them to write letters to the author concerning her fate. It was because she could not get over her troubles that they loved her. Outside Lily Dale and the chief interest of the novel, *The Small House at Allington* is, I think, good. The De Courcy family are alive, as is also Sir Raffle Buffle, who is a hero of the Civil Service. Sir Raffle was intended to represent a type, not a man; but the man for the picture was soon chosen, and I was often assured that the portrait was very like. I have never seen the gentleman with whom I am supposed to have taken the liberty. There is also an old squire down at Allington, whose life as a country gentleman with rather straitened means is, I think, well described.

70. Unsigned review, *Athenaeum*

26 March 1864, pp. 437–8

It is characteristic of this story, that the characters are all living, human beings; and there has been as much speculation whether Lily Dale would marry Johnny Eames, as about any 'marriage on the *tapis*' (as the *Morning Post* phrases it) in any town or village in Great Britain. Readers have made it a personal question, and there have been vehement discussions as to the probability of her forgiving Adolphus Crosbie, and being happy with him at last, after he had been punished sufficiently for the sake of the moral, and had profited by his sufferings so as to come to his right mind: Many hoped that he would break loose from his slavery to Lady Alexandrina and her family before the wedding-day, and go back to his lawful queen. Mr. Trollope has shown great skill in the management of the character of Adolphus Crosbie. He has kept the reader in charity with him, in spite of all his sins; even his faithlessness to Lily is made so natural that the candid reader cannot feel himself a Pharisee, and hug himself with complacency that he is not even like Adolphus Crosbie. The temptation to which he yielded was so suited to his weakness, and the point of view from which he saw things is given so fairly, that it is impossible not to understand how he fell from his own steadfastness under the enchantments of De Courcy Castle. There is no false excuse made for him, no palliation offered, except the truth, which appeals to each: 'consider thyself, lest thou also be tempted.' The whole of that passage of life in De Courcy Castle, under the high pressure got up for those distinguished visitors, Lady Dumbello and Mr. Plantagenet Palliser, is admirably true, as a sketch of manners and customs in a great house of that class, and true to the human nature of the different characters concerned in the story.

The gradual development of Crosbie's mistake, the recoil upon himself, the retribution which arises from the nature of things, and not from any machinery of human justice, are very subtly and skilfully indicated; it shows, too, what one is glad to have shown,—the genuine human conscience, that lives and moves under all the apparent selfish indifference of society to matters not immediately personal. The drawing of the characters in 'The Small House at Allington' is vigorous and lifelike:—the scene of Lord de Guest in his encounter with the bull, the family-scenes at the Gazebees' house in St. John's Wood, the buying of carpets and the other pre-matrimonial arrangements, are very clever. The scenes at Lily's home with Mrs. Dale, the squire and the two young ladies, are good; but the reader regards them with respect rather than with lively interest: whilst the scenes at the boarding-house are vulgar and absolutely unpleasant; except for poor Mrs. Roper, there cannot be the smallest interest. The secret of this falling off is, that in the picture of life in Burton Crescent Mr. Trollope has put no touches of kindly feeling like those with which he redeems the poor old worldly, ill-used Countess; and even mitigates one's detestation of Lady Alexandrina, by showing the very damp and dreary home to which she was brought. As for Johnny Eames himself, he is rather a bore; no woman could ever feel the smallest interest in him, unless it were a kind elderly woman like Lady Julia de Guest. His entanglement with Amelia Roper is fatal to all his pretensions as a hero, and he behaves as ill to her as he knows how. Mr. Trollope feels it necessary to apologize for two kisses bestowed on that young lady; but they are the only redeeming traits in the whole affair. With all his faults, the reader's sympathy is with Crosbie; he goes through his bad business with Lady Alexandrina in a dignified manner, accepting the consequences of his own fault with patience, and a manly endeavour to make the best of things. The story cannot be considered as concluded. In the interest of a wide circle of readers, we demand, with emphasis, of Mr. Trollope that he tells us the further fortunes of the characters in 'The Small House at Allington'; the only chapter we do not wish to have re-opened is that which concerns the inmates of Burton Crescent.

71. Unsigned notice, *Reader*

2 April 1864, iii. 418–19

Crosbie is especially unsatisfactory. We are sure, indeed, that he exists somewhere, and that Mr. Trollope knows him well. But we cannot help fancying that Mr. Trollope's information is defective, either as regards the disposition of his hero, or the incidents in his career. Either the plausible official has imposed upon our usually perspicacious friend and contrived to be taken for a much abler man than he really is, or his behaviour was not such as has been represented. The Crosbie described by Mr. Trollope is not the Crosbie who describes himself by the unspeakable folly and shabbiness of his acts. The former would not have broken his promise to Lily under the circumstances detailed to us. It is scarcely probable that he would have contracted the engagement at all; having once done so, the necessity of adhering to it would have been as evident to him as to Fowler Pratt. But, if we can imagine the false step, we may at least be sure that he would have accepted the consequences. Pride would have united him firmly to Lady Alexandrina; he would scarcely have borne to confess his error to himself, much less to the world. He would never have submitted to the shipwreck of his plans in life for the sake of his club. If he did, he was not the man Mr. Trollope thinks, and would lead us to think, whenever he discusses his hero's doings in his own character. His conception is throughout inconsistent and vacillating, which is much to be regretted, as Crosbie is the life and soul of the book. Wherever he appears we are sure of brilliant writing, of the finest indirect moral teaching, and of a degree of interest aroused by no one else.

Mr. Trollope has written nothing more true or entertaining than this admirable representation of our modern social world, with its special temptations, special vices, and special kinds of retribution. It is not so much a story, though it has a certain current of story quite sufficient to lead the reader on, as a fragment of complicated social strategy that he describes in these pages,—and describes with a delicacy of observation and a moral thoughtfulness which matters apparently so trifling probably never before received. The utter defeat of a man of the world in virtue of his too great worldliness, or rather in consequence of a dash of better and purer tastes being mixed up with that utter worldliness of purpose, the faint degree in which motives higher than merely worldly motives affect the feelings and estimates of worldly men, the stronger degree in which worldly thoughts and motives affect the feelings and estimates of unworldly men, the shades of advantage given by purely accidental circumstance and association to either combatant in a conflict for social ascendancy, the extent to which a defeated man may, if he has courage, even though he may not deserve it, save himself from utter ruin, and retire, not indeed with the honours of war, but without all the disgrace of defeat that the retributive appetite might demand for him, and with a prospect of partially retrieving his heavy losses in future,— these are the themes which Mr. Trollope embodies for us in pictures of wonderful skill, fidelity, and humour. There is scarcely a chapter in the book which does not in some way illustrate the laws of success and failure in what we may call social tactics,—from the great advantage given by perfect frigidity and utter heartlessness to the splendid strategy of Lady Dumbello, to the slight advantage gained by Lily in her little contest with Hopkins, the gardener, through the device of luring him out of the garden and the immediate vicinity of his plants into the over-awing neighbourhood of chairs and tables. 'I always like,' says Lily, 'to get him into the house, because he feels himself a little abashed by the chairs and tables; or perhaps it is the carpet that is too much for him. Out on the gravel walks he is such a terrible tyrant, and in the green-house he almost tramples on one.' And this subtle estimate of the strategical worth of a 'situation,' whether it be merely in trivial circumstance like this,—or one which depends on the moral claims which trouble and grief confer, such as the same young lady uses so playfully and yet tyrannically over her mother and sister,—or one which springs from superior courage, such as Eames gained over Cradell,—or one which arises from homage conceded to mere position and rank, such as the Countess de Courcy wields over poor Crosbie during the preparations for his wedding, where 'she throws her head a little back' as she accosts him, and he instantly perceives that he is 'enveloped in the fumes of an affectionate but somewhat contemptuous patronage,'—or one of a purely moral kind, such as Lady Julia de Guest gains over Crosbie for a moment at Courcy Castle, until his superior address and presence of mind redress the balance of advantage,—this subtle estimate of the value of the less obvious elements in the strategy of social life is, after all, what gives the chief humour as well as charm to this amusing book.

Mr. Trollope's intellectual grasp of his characters, so far as he goes (which is only now and then much below the surface), is nearly perfect; but then he chooses to display that grasp almost exclusively in the hold they get or fail to get over other characters, and in the hold they yield to other characters over them. It is in his command of what we may call the moral 'hooks and eyes' of life that Mr. Trollope's greatest power lies. And his characters are more or less interesting almost exactly in proportion to the degree in which their mode of influencing or failing to influence other people is unique and characteristic. For example, perhaps the most skilful chapters in this book are those which give an account of Mr. Plantagenet Palliser's faint attentions to Lady Dumbello, and of the Duke of Omnium's efforts to deter his nephew from advances in that quarter. And the reason is, that in Lady Dumbello's marble frigidity of nature and the Duke of Omnium's magnificent way of managing a menace through the hints of his man of business, Mr. Trollope has found almost a new medium for expressing the influence wielded by character over character, and one so exceedingly slight and indirect that no novelist but himself would have thought of availing himself of it at all. Indeed, Mr. Trollope's greatest power is, in this respect, in unison with the greatest power of cultivated modern society, namely, to make a great use of little means in expressing his meaning,— nay, to make more use, if one may so speak, of unused social weapons by faintly indicating their far-off existence than of those which are actually brought into play. There is nothing which Mr. Trollope draws with greater humour than the difference between the strategic value of a vague unexpended resource, and of the same resource if actually put into requisition. There is nothing which he loves better to paint than the wise self-restraint and reticence of true men or women of the world, in doling out gradually their doses of worldly motive to those whom they wish to influence, and their great caution and almost dread of expending that motive power. He evidently knows that the power of motives, like the power of money, is greatest in prospect, and even in his own art he always *hoards*, like the world, his rewards and penalties with the greatest care, adding to the sense of his power by the self-restraint with which he deals out his poetical justice. In this respect Mr. Trollope is like the Duke of Omnium himself;—he hints to his characters that if they do certain things there may be 'some change in the arrangements'; he uses that menace, however, most charily, reluctant to exhaust its power; and if at length he is compelled to make that 'change in the arrangements' he does so with studious moderation, relaxing his heaviest punishments almost immediately, and always reminding us of the great difference between the sharp moral retributions of fancy and the diluted moral sentences, modified by a hundred different counteracting circumstances, of actual life.

The story almost resolves itself into a series of moral engagements between the different characters,—first and foremost between the great Civil Service official, Mr. Crosbie, and his unworldly tempters at Allington, then between the same gentleman and his grander worldly tempters in De Courcy Castle and Portman Square,—in scenes which are, perhaps, the best artistic delineations in the book. His struggle with Squire Dale to get, if he may, a marriage-portion with his unworldly love is excellent,—but his encounters with the family of his worldly love, at considerable advantage before he has sold himself, at dreadful disadvantage afterwards, his loss of official dignity in the service in consequence of the bad odour of his conduct and the drubbing from his rival which that conduct entails, his struggles to regain his influence at the Board and his partial success, his complete discomfiture in domestic life, and especially the loss instead of gain in importance amongst people of rank which his distinguished marriage brings with it, are all told with a precision of social light and shade that only Mr. Trollope could give. It is impossible without much space to give any true idea of Mr. Trollope's delicacy of touch, and fortunately his story is too well known to make it necessary; but the following admirable sketch of the Countess's forlorn son-in-law on his first public appearance in the noble family to which he had allied himself, and his disgust for his brother in misfortune and brother-in-law by alliance, Mr. Mortimer Gazebee, will remind our readers of what we mean:

Crosbie had consented to go to the party in Portman square, but had not greatly enjoyed himself on that festive occasion. He had stood about moodily, speaking hardly a word to any one. His whole aspect of life seemed to have been altered during the last few months. It was here, in such spots as this, that he had been used to find his glory. On such occasions he had shone with peculiar light, making envious the hearts of many who watched the brilliance of his career as they stood around in dull quiescence. But now no one in those rooms had been more dull, more silent, or less courted than he: and yet he was established there as the son-in-law of that noble house. 'Rather slow work, isn't it?' Gazebee had said to him, having, after many efforts, succeeded in reaching his brother-in-law in a corner. In answer to this Crosbie had only grunted. 'As for myself,' continued Gazebee, 'I would a deal sooner be at home with my paper and slippers. It seems to me these sort of gatherings don't suit married men.' *Crosbie had again grunted, and had then escaped into another corner.*

It is impossible to express social humiliation and despair more delicately than that.

If the history of his rival John Eames is less effective, it is only because that young gentleman has not really gained any command of those social weapons, by their mode of wielding which Mr. Trollope chiefly delineates his characters, till towards the end of the story. He, too, is involved in a series of engagements with the vulgar people at whose house he boards, and there the manœuvring is too open and clumsy for Mr. Trollope's indirect mode of portraiture, while he has scarcely spent time and trouble enough upon them to bring his pictures up to the level of his coarser characters, such as Moulder and Kantwise in 'Orley Farm.' We are inclined to think the half-educated people suit Mr. Trollope less as a portrait-painter than either the wholly vulgar or the wholly refined people. He has more than his mother's power of comedy in painting broad vulgarities, and his own power in painting the perfect self-command, reticence, and innuendo of good society is still greater, —but in the mid-society he is not quite so happy. There is an uncertainty of touch about the Ropers, a visible mixing of colours, which is quite foreign to the general style of the book. And the same may be said about John Eames himself. The raw, impressible, bashful youth, not brought up in the most refined society, is capitally conceived, but the delineation is not quite equal to the conception. It is not till he begins to put off his hobbledehoyhood, and to do battle, like Crosbie, with a

ull knowledge of the value of small manœuvres, that we feel the full
ower of Mr. Trollope's pen. When he becomes aware of the import-
nce of asserting himself, and, as private secretary to Sir Raffle Buffle,
·f refusing to fetch his superior's shoes for him, we begin to appreciate
he sketch. Before that the execution is by no means equal to the con-
eption. Mr. Trollope is always great in sketching social diplomacy;
nd he can, as we said, be great also in broader humorous sketches, at
:ast when he is drawing from experience. . . .

But it would be impossible to exhaust the various merits of this
musing book. Perhaps there is nothing better in it than the character
·f the squire at Allington, hard, inarticulate, constant, patient, and,
·eneath all, latently generous and affectionate. Certainly there is very
ittle that is better in it than Lord de Guest, in whom the true farming
obleman, incapable of social *nuances*, yet capable of all that is, in its
·est sense, aristocratic except the intellectual culture of aristocracy, is
ketched with perfect knowledge,—Mr. Trollope not disdaining the
.rtistic help of one of Lord de Guest's prize bulls. What touch could be
·etter than his first question to John Eames when he finds him lying
sleep in his grounds,—'Have you got into trouble? You look as though
·ou were in trouble. *Your poor father used to be in trouble*,'—which
·xpresses with curious subtlety the rough sort of logic of an earl used
·o breed cattle, and evidently grounded on that deep belief in the
ereditary character of accidental qualities which he has learned from
iis breeding, and partly, also, on his belief in the hereditary character
·f habits of life, which he accepts as part of his aristocratic creed.
·inally, Mr. Trollope has never drawn better, if so good, heroines. Lily
)ale's pleasantry and tenderness are delightful, though one wishes for a
ittle more resentment of Crosbie's conduct; and Bell, though a slighter
ketch, is scarcely less perfectly drawn.

We have but one slight complaint to make. Why is so perfect a
naster of the English language so hasty and sometimes slovenly in his
grammar? We find him almost habitually making the blunder, 'if you
vere *me*' (Vol. II, p. 23), 'there were worse women than *her*' (Vol. I,
). 292), and occasionally misusing words, as 'predicate' twice used in
he sense of 'predict.' We have noticed some such errors in almost all
Mr. Trollope's novels. It is a pity that one who might write a really
:lassical style, if he chose, should ever admit annoying inaccuracies.

The bitterest pill, however, which the reader has to swallow is the provokingly unsatisfactory conclusion. No jury in a court of poetica justice would convict the author of anything less than a violent assault upon his reader's feelings in leaving Lily Dale unmarried; and the sentence upon him would probably be that he should make ample compensation in another tale. Whether he contemplates making this sort of amends of course we can have no means of deciding; but we imagine that a regard for his own character as a humane novelist will urge him to do so. The fact is, Lily Dale is one of the most charming creations that ever author devised; and flesh and blood cannot endure that she should be sentenced to lead the life of a 'widowed maid.' There is gall, moreover, in the reflection that henceforth Cœlebs [Bachelor] in search of a wife will look about him for a Lily Dale and will not be satisfied until he find one, before which time he will have most likely become greyheaded.

This, indeed, is Mr. Trollope's peculiar theme. He is far less successful when he seeks to delineate the boisterous and eccentric ways of that Bohemian region, where Pendennis and Warrington sojourned in their frank *cameraderie* upon town. On the other hand, Mr. Trollope is wonderfully well acquainted with the little politics of the ladies, their petty ambitions, jealousies, and tender affections, and with their confidential talk by themselves. The honest, maidenly conversations between the two sisters, Bell and Lily, about their respective lovers, contrasted with the combined manœuvres of Lady De Courcy and her daughters, who want to secure a husband for Alexandrina, and their subsequent behaviour towards him, when he cannot escape from the match, are related with that profound knowledge of womankind in which Mr. Trollope excels most other novelists of either the male or the female sex. Mrs. Dale, too, is a real, true woman in her virtues and her faults. A widow but forty years of age, with a pair of children, and left rather poor, she has fancied it her duty to renounce all the pleasures of life, and shut herself up in a proud humility, which gives offence to her late husband's brother, who wishes to bestow a part of his own fortune upon the girls, his nieces, and to provide them a handsome establishment in the world. The tenancy of the Small House at Allington, next to the jilting of Lily Dale by Crosbie, is the proper subject of the story. Mrs. Dale very naturally quarrels with her brother-in-law, the squire, who has sought to usurp something like a paternal authority over Miss Bell, with the benevolent design of compelling her to accept the heir to his estates. The daughters, like brave high-spirited girls, as they are, taking their mother's part and rebelling against the dictatorial patronage of their uncle, support her resolution to quit the Small House, in which he has allowed her to live rent-free. It is just one of those family disputes in which all parties have meant well, but some pique or scruple has arisen, and, being exaggerated by a warm temper, has set them at variance without any serious cause. Again, we remark that Mr. Trollope understands this sort of *imbroglio*, which is of the very essence of light comedy, more perfectly than it is understood by most other writers of fiction. He makes it, in fact, one of the principal motives in all his best stories; he develops the effects of *temper* in all the transactions of domestic life. Temper and woman are certainly two of the most important elements of the modern novel, and Mr. Trollope is master of both. . . .

Some of his tales, it must be confessed, have been quite unworthy of his genius,—clumsy and unmeaning daubs upon the canvas of farcical fiction, which requires a broader brush and more vigorous hand. In the genteel comedy style of painting, with finer strokes and on a smoother surface, the novel we have now before us is a masterpiece of art.

75. Unsigned notice, *Saturday Review*

14 May 1864, xvii. 595–6

Mr. Trollope has achieved another great success in his own peculiar line. It may not be the highest of all possible lines, but it is a very pleasant one, and suffices to show the great powers of the author. If the inner feelings of young ladies and young gentlemen are to be described as they display themselves in the bosom of comfortable and respectable English families, it would be impossible to describe them better than Mr. Trollope does. He sees a section of English life, and paints it with unerring truth, tact, and liveliness. Given a young lady and a young gentleman neither too high nor too low in the world, he can put down on paper what they would be likely to do if circumstances connected them in the ties of a close intimacy; and he can fill in all their belongings, their papas and mammas, their superiors and inferiors, their servants, dependents, and friends. He can do, in fact, what Miss Austen did, only that he does it in the modern style, with far more detail and far more analysis of character, although, perhaps, with less of lightness of touch and gentle pervading wit. In his new story he has hit on a happy idea. He has found a new subject. A girl jilted in a natural, easy way, with no worse result to herself than that she is not married, and with no worse result to the perfidious lover than that he is tied to a dreary stick of a wife from whom he is only too glad to separate six weeks after marriage, is, so far as we know, a new basis for the action of a novel. It is impossible to praise too highly the skill with which this sad history of jilting is told. Crosbie is one of Mr. Trollope's masterpieces—he behaves with such admirable consistency, and is so exactly the sort of man who would court and deserve the fate that overtakes him. The reader throughout is candidly told what a mean, hesitating, cowardly, gentlemanly snob he is. And yet he is the very personification of the cleverish, good-looking, shallow, popular man, rising in the world up to a certain point, but with nothing more than social cleverness in him, of whom London, as every great city, presents so very many examples. His young lady partly sees through him, but, not having been in love before, and being of an earnest and romantic nature, she gives herself up to the passion he offers her, and pours out her soul in tenderness for

the man whom she has to try hard not to despise in order that she ma
love him as much as she wishes. Perhaps he is too empty and hollow fo
the reader to have the proper amount of hope in him at the outset. Bu
he is by no means a man whose counterpart in real life would be un
likely to awaken the devotion of an ardent, affectionate girl. Al
devotion is rather the fruit of the mental gifts of the adorer than th
desert of the adored. Nor ought we to overrate the young woma
herself. Mr. Trollope is so true to life that he never takes for his heroin
a girl who would be thought superior in any way. The usual young
lady of *Punch*—the girl in a pork-pie hat and her hair in a bag—is th
sort of girl whom he likes describing; and it is quite true that such girl
may have deep feelings, and go through very interesting adventures
and make themselves the mark of much enlightened gossip.

Then, again, he can group together sets of people in no way remarkable, with no exaggerated peculiarities, with no strong or unusua
character, with no great claim on our admiration, and yet can make
them distinct, natural, and consistent. All the minor characters groupec
round Lily Dale strike us as excellent, and yet not one of them is in th
least superior, or in any way more interesting than the average o
people. She has, for instance, a mother and a sister. Mrs. Dale is nothing
more than the common sort of kind, gentle woman apt to take affront
guided by her daughters, a little overcome by their superior energy anc
vivacity, and yet able to think and in some measure to plan for them
Bell Dale is rather a disagreeable young person than otherwise—very
composed, reasonable, and affectionate, and yet with a certain strengtl
of character and with a power of pleasing which is judiciously ascribec
to her uniting good looks with a turn for silence, because, as a matter o
fact, pretty girls who hold their tongues are often made love to, anc
awake a tenderer passion than perhaps they deserve. The Squire o
Allington is even better. Mr. Trollope is able not only to conceive th
character of an elderly man who is very disagreeable in manner but ha
some warmth of heart, but he is able to see how such a man woulc
treat, and be treated by, his relations. The very success which Mr.
Trollope achieves in efforts of this kind sometimes provokes a sligh
impatience on the part of his readers. They are charmed by such a
contrast as that presented to them in Squire Dale. They see that th
basis of his character, the union of a melancholy gruffness with softnes
of heart under the heavier distresses of life, is exactly what makes him
at once a distinct and a natural person, but they hardly like that thi
contrast should be followed out to its probable results. Such a man is

likely to have little quarrels with his relations, for the precise reason that he is not understood. Nor does he deserve that his occasional and intermittent tenderness should alone be remembered, and his ungenial unsympathetic ways be altogether forgotten. Perhaps, if his lady relations were very wise, noble-hearted, superior people, they might see his good points, and let his bad points fade out of their view. But men cannot reckon on such relations as these. They are tolerably fortunate if they have such relations as Mrs. Dale and her daughters—ordinary people with ordinary faults, but with right principles, and with a fair share of what is graceful in thought and looks. Such ladies, however, would be very apt to treat the Squire as the ladies of the Small House treated him—take a little offence at his ways, and then think better of it, and determine to put their pride in their pocket and be good friends again. Mr. Trollope sees this, and what he sees he describes.

In the same way, objections might be made to Lily. It might be said that she allowed herself to love a trifling, foolish man very quickly and very deeply, that she makes love to him much more than he makes love to her, and that, when she finds out how he behaves to her, she does not get cured soon enough of an unworthy affection. At the end of the story she tells her mother that she cannot forget what has passed, that she remembers her love, all the outpoured confidence of her soul, all the caresses she has given and received, and that she feels bound to a man with whom she has been so intimate, and cannot forget him because he has forgotten her. She quite overcomes her mother, who is silenced, and does not attempt to reason with her. The same class of readers who wish to have the Squire at once harsh and tender, and at the same time to let him avoid the family differences to which his character gives rise, wish also that Lily Dale should have been corrected in this matter. They say that girls do, as a matter of fact, forget worthless men sooner or later, and that Mrs. Dale should have explained to her daughter that it was nonsense to attach so much importance to the remembrances of the effusions of her virgin affection, when she might know that before long her love for a man like Crosbie must grow faint. This, it is supposed, a judicious mother ought to have said, and then Lily would have been rebuked for her nonsense, and the reader would not have been led to imagine that Mr. Trollope himself thinks it right that a girl should vow a sort of romantic and eternal fidelity to a married man. The whole question of how novels ought to be written is raised by this objection. Is the novelist bound, after he has invented characters, to give them a twist, so as to produce the proper judicious moral effect? Many English novelists have answered in the affirmative, and some foreign critics, in their haste, do not hesitate to say that English novelists as a rule do this, and that character and probability are always sacrificed to the moral. Mr. Trollope, at any rate, works in a different way, and it must be owned that the result is interesting, even if it is faulty from the point of view of complete edification. He would doubtless ask his censors whether Lily Dale behaves in a consistent and natural way—whether it is likely or not that a girl, if of a romantic and earnest character, should have received an impression from the interchange of affection with her first lover which is not perhaps to be found in those excellent young women who, in a praiseworthy way, if they are jilted, transfer their innocent tenderness at the proper time from the naughty man who has been found out, to the new good man who has not been found out. And if this were conceded him, he might further ask whether it was more natural that a weakish, loving, ordinary sort of person, like Mrs Dale, should have been overawed by the vehement feeling of her daughter, or should have received it with the calm superiority befitting a judicious mother, and cleared up the young woman's position to her in a logical and sensible manner.

Mr. Trollope repeats in this tale all the faults and hobbies that usually mark his works. The faults are small, and the hobbies permissible, but still they are principally to be defended on the ground that even the best book cannot be good throughout. Once more Mr. Trollope amuses himself with breaking the thread of the story in order to introduce episodes connected with the characters of his former novels. This is all very good fun for him, but it is very poor fun for his readers. Having invented Mr. Harding, and Archdeacon Grantley, and Lady Dumbello, he naturally likes to recur to them, and to imagine what they would do under certain imaginary circumstances. It appears to have struck him that there would be something very droll in fancying Lady Dumbello being made love to by a man as hollow and proper and frigid as herself; and in order that he may have the gratification of working out this idea, all the story connected with the Dales and Crosbie stops, and we have a dreary passage about the loves of Lady Dumbello and a certain Mr. Palliser. Mr. Trollope also indulges in his customary pleasure of introducing scenes of that degree of low life which is scarcely to be distinguished from the shabby genteel. The woes and difficulties of a fifth- or tenth-rate London boarding-house furnish him this time with his theme, and we must own that all this boarding-house part seems to us equally vulgar and dull. It may be an accurate picture of the life led in the class which Mr. Trollope undertakes to paint, but the picture is scarcely worth painting. The same power of amplification which seems so masterly when Mr. Trollope has to give the details of the history of the main characters only leads to wearisome minuteness when we have to wade through the sad pleasantry of Mrs. Roper's establishment. Mr. Trollope also sets a very bad example to other novelists in the frequency with which he has recourse to the petty trick of passing a judgment on his own fictitious personages as he goes along, in order that the story may thus seem to have an existence independent of its teller, and to form a subject on which he can speculate as on something outside himself. Mr. Trollope writes so easily and pleasantly that probably only those who have been annoyed by this little device in minor novelists would notice it in the *Small House at Allington*. Lastly, he has perhaps sacrificed the story a little in order to bring in his favourite hobby of the advisableness of young people marrying without being too careful as to their future income. The point has been discussed too frequently to make it necessary to enter on it here; but whether Mr. Trollope is right or wrong, he evidently likes to show his opinion, and to let his readers know that he is on the side of what they would call imprudence. Obviously, however, as he has the complete control of the characters and events of the story, he cannot prove much by ordering matters as he likes. An imaginary Bell may marry an imaginary Dr. Crofts with complete impunity, and, as we know this, we regret that so much trouble should be taken to demonstrate it.

The most, however, that these little blemishes do is to make a very excellent novel unequal in parts. Nowhere has Mr. Trollope shone more in those conversations which are his peculiar strength. He can write out the talk of people as no one else can. He does not hesitate to give himself the great trouble of recording in full what, at a given crisis, his characters might be supposed to say. Very often there are three or four whole pages entirely filled with conversation, and this conversation is never dull, or forced, or epigrammatic. Nor is it trivial. It seems to come from the people as if it were inevitable it should come, and yet it is all coloured with the peculiarities of each individual, and all seems good, sensible, apt talk in its way. When all is excellent, one example is as good as another; but perhaps, as a triumph over difficulties, we might select the conversation of Lord de Guest and Johnny Eames, when the Earl asks his young friend to meet Colonel Dale. There really is hardly any basis for talk at all. There is very little that any of them can say that can be made to affect the story, and all that can come under this head might be easily got into a page or two. Lord de Guest is not made to wander into subjects foreign to the main plot, or to call up anecdotes and reminiscences, and things of that sort. He and Johnny talk about Lily Dale, but they talk at once so fully and so naturally that it seems as if a real conversation were going on; while yet what they say has an interest, and we do not find ourselves getting tired of their confidences. This shows that Mr. Trollope has a great gift for novel-writing. But it also shows how industriously he has cultivated this gift. It must be very hard work going through the trouble of writing out all these conversations; but Mr. Trollope never spares himself any trouble, and certainly his painstaking has its reward.

76. Unsigned notice, *North American Review*

July 1864, xcix. 292–8

A long but undistinguished review of the Harper & Brothers (New York) edition.

In the present book Mr. Trollope has produced several very good characters, and one very poor one, on which he seems most to pride himself.

We have two English country gentlemen, very well conceived and supported, the Lord de Guest and Squire Dale;—the Lord de Guest a short, thick man, a breeder of cattle, an amateur ox-rib-poker, stupid, moral, proud, and benevolent, 'every inch an earl,' such a character as England alone produces and Englishmen alone admire; the Squire a narrow-minded, caustic Englishman, with a kind heart, but wonderful skill in concealing it. The best characters by far in the book are the Misses Dale. Fresh and natural, they show in their conversation the vivacity, kindness, and foibles which are the charm of their sex. Trollope's characters from high life, like Mr. Palliser, are not, we think, well done, whether as caricatures or originals. As an original, Mr. Palliser is untrue, and it is not very amusing to caricature a mathematical formula, which he approaches as near as is possible in the present state of the science.

The great blemish in 'The Small House at Allington' is the character of its hero, Mr. Eames, whose development stopped at the asinine phase.

77. Unsigned notice, *Westminster Review*

July 1864, lxxxii. 251–2

And yet the story flags with all these merits, and the wholly unattractive character of the two men who figure as heroes renders the history of their career decidedly tedious when continued through thirty chapters. . . . Without Lily Dale and her uncle the squire, this book might be fairly described as a repetition of the 'Three Clerks' and 'Framley Parsonage,' with variations, but these two characters are both new, and both excellent enough to leaven a good deal of the heavy dough of vulgarity which surrounds them.

78. Trollope the man of business, *North British Review*

May 1864, xl. 369–401

This long, unsigned essay (well over ten thousand words), a relatively undistinguished piece, explains away, with much praise, Trollope's claims to being an artist.

The novelist *par excellence* of the moment is assuredly Mr. Trollope. His works can by no means be placed in the highest rank; but within their own range, nothing better ever came from an English novelist. In our view, it is no drawback to their merit that they are the books of a man whose peculiar temperament is scarcely that of the literary artist. If we may judge on such a point from his writings, we cannot help thinking it a happy accident that Mr. Trollope should have written books at all. The wit and liveliness of his story and dialogue, and the simplicity, ease, and vigour of his style—an admirable style—are unquestionably the graces of a master of his craft. But the whole tone and habit of mind implied in these novels is that of a man of activity and business, rather than of a man of letters. His books are the result of the experience of life, not of the studious contemplation of it. A rare degree of talent was required for their production, but the kind of talent which was required is not, perhaps, uncommon. Books like *Barchester Towers* are certainly not very numerous; and therefore it may be assumed that the writers are few, who possess such gifts as the author of *Barchester Towers*. And yet it is probable that the same powers of observation, the same shrewdness, good sense and humour, are expended every day on the common affairs and common amusements of life by people who never dream, or who only dream, of writing novels. . . .

We have probably said enough about an author who is so familiar to our readers. His name will not stand among the highest in his own department of literature; but some at least of his books deserve to live. Writers of fiction may be divided roughly into two classes, Cervantes being the unquestioned leader of the one, and Le Sage, though not so unapproachable in his greatness, being the leader of the other. Mr. Trollope is of the house of Le Sage. Incomparably inferior to the great master in power and genius, he yet resembles him in this, that he represents ordinary characters, and paints real life as it is, only omitting the poetry. The highest object of imaginative literature he neither attains nor aims at. His novels will not raise our minds very far above the weary trivialities of common life; but although they contain nothing very great or elevated, they are simple, natural, and moral, and if we can be amused with a picture of common life—as all people with any healthy curiosity of mind must be—he paints it for us, of the present generation, with an almost unrivalled delicacy and discernment. No novels are more pleasant than the best of Mr. Trollope's.

MISS MACKENZIE

1865

Trollope himself (*Autobiography*, pp. 157–8) is noncommittal about the merits of *Miss Mackenzie*.

Miss Mackenzie was written with a desire to prove that a novel may be produced without any love; but even in this attempt it breaks down before the conclusion. In order that I might be strong in my purpose, I took for my heroine a very unattractive old maid, who was overwhelmed with money troubles; but even she was in love before the end of the book, and made a romantic marriage with an old man. There is in this story an attack upon charitable bazaars, made with a violence which will, I think, convince any reader that such attempts at raising money were at the time very odious to me. I beg to say that since that I have had no occasion to alter my opinion. *Miss Mackenzie* was published in the early spring of 1865.

Critics of the twentieth century have generally dismissed the novel as 'amusing but faintly sordid' (Michael Sadleir) or 'very inferior' (Bradford Booth). Reviewers of 1865 did not award it great praise, but many of them found a fascination in the way Trollope coped with such an unlikely subject, marvelling, as *The Times* critic said, at the 'amount of amusement' Trollope managed to produce 'out of mere dulness'. The novel warrants further attention, if only as another means of exploring the anomalies in an author who professes to work for the market and yet is led to experiment with such intractable and out-of-the-way materials.

---

79. Unsigned notice, *Saturday Review*

4 March 1865, xix. 263–5

A great deal of Mr. Trollope's popularity is perhaps attributable to the care he has generally taken to fill his stories with nice people. He troubles himself very little about a plot, and never attempts to fathom subtleties of character, but he has an unrivalled knack of drawing attractive young ladies, well-mannered young gentlemen, and extremely agreeable persons of more mature age of either sex. Of course it is necessary to have a foil in the shape of artful, stuck-up, selfish, or vulgar people, but these have commonly been kept judiciously in the background, and only interest us incidentally on account of the vexation they inflict on their pleasanter friends. A dreadful story, it is true, was ascribed to Mr. Trollope, in which the chief characters, motives, and incidents were so odiously vulgar and stupid that the staunchest champions of realism were forced to give it up in disgust. It may be questioned whether any living being ever got to the end of *Brown, Jones, and Robinson*, or had any other sentiment than mingled loathing and despair towards that weary tribe of butchers and drapers, and their still more wearisome wives. *Miss Mackenzie* is a very different story from that memorable failure, but it is so far unlike the author's most successful books as that most of the persons who figure in it are intensely mean, dull, and generally disagreeable and uninteresting. And Mr. Trollope has made them mean and disagreeable intentionally. Deliberately and of set purpose, he has carried us into the midst of all these poverty-stricken gentry, dull old maids, unthrifty shopkeepers, and rapacious parsons. The principle on which he has selected so apparently unpromising a set of people is not new, but he has worked it out with an unflinching consistency which probably no other writer, even if he had the requisite knack, would venture to imitate. The old notion that in the dullest and most prosaic lives there is often buried a vein of unsuspected romance or pathos, has been the starting-point of more than one school of novelists. But Mr. Trollope expands the original force of the notion by contending that the ordinary idea of what romance or pathos means is far too limited, and that things commonly passed over as sordid cares or ignoble perplexities are, when rightly viewed, elements in life of the truest pathos. No other novelist, for instance, has made the various worries connected with want of money so prominent a feature in most of his stories—and this not from the comic, but from the most serious point of view. The troubles which money affairs bring upon Mr. Trollope's people are not like the troubles of Mr. Micawber or Mr. Skimpole. A bailiff in a house represents to Mr. Trollope nothing either funny or sordid, but a grave human care, and a thing, therefore, to be gravely and even tenderly written about. The anxieties of a lodging-housekeeper about her rent and taxes, or those of an insolvent tradesman about impatient creditors, are, in his eyes, neither mean nor amusing, but genuine sorrows which an artist who is not too grand to be content with human nature need not be ashamed of handling with sympathy.

In *Miss Mackenzie* the writer has attempted to draw, in the first place, an elderly lady who wants to be married, and, in the second, a number of gentlemen, all in want of her money, who wish to marry her. At first sight, and in the popular view, there is no room for sympathetic treatment in either case. A middle-aged woman hankering after a husband would commonly be looked upon as guilty of a weakness, or even impropriety, which could only be laughed at. A middle-aged gentleman hankering after eight hundred a year appears to be a simple type of mercenariness which every well-regulated novel-reader should hate or despise. Mr. Trollope has tried to show that, in both instances, the conventional notions are very superficial, and that we ought to view the supposed weakness of the poor elderly lady with genial sympathy, and to make large and kindly allowance for the selfishness of her still more elderly suitors. The whole story is an illustration, drawn from the very tamest and dullest kind of life, 'how wrong the world is in connecting so closely as it does the capacity for feeling and the incapacity for expression—in confusing the technical art of the man who sings with the unselfish tenderness of the man who feels.' The latter part of the sentence is sheer nonsense, because the man who sings must possess first the capacity for feeling. The singer feels at least as deeply and as tenderly as the man who is dumb, but he is so far superior as he is able to give effective utterance to what he feels. The world is wrong, Mr. Trollope really means, or ought to mean, not because it esteems the poet most highly, but because it refuses to recognize poetic depth and tenderness of feeling when unaccompanied by the faculty of poetic expression. Miss Mackenzie in her youthful days wrote poor verses, but, for all that, 'the romance and poetry of her heart had been high and noble.' We may all be wrong in regarding her as a prosaic and dowdy old maid, but Mr. Trollope's remark, so far as it means anything, blames us for mistaking the technical art of the man who sings, like Tennyson, for the true poetry of dumb but noble souls like Miss Mackenzie—as if feeling, and rhythmical expression of feeling, were for ever divorced and incompatible. Happily, the gist of *Miss Mackenzie* is not that people who write poetry are incapable of tender feeling, but that there may be abundant depth of feeling where there is least power of giving worthy expression to it. In order to illustrate this, Mr. Trollope has been almost excessive in his care to make the characters who have exceptional tenderness of feeling exceptionally dull in their lives, narrow in their motives, and contemptible in speech. Whether, in parts, the dulness is not often gratuitously dull may be questioned. It may safely be said that the author has pointed his moral by an extreme case, and nobody but Mr. Trollope would have dared to marry a heroine of some forty years to a widower of fifty with nine children. This is an enlargement of the popular notion of how a novel should end which is not likely to be very widely relished, although there is no absolute reason for objecting to a match of this kind, or for denying that it may be attended by as much romantic sentiment as if the heroine had been a lovely girl of eighteen and the hero a dashing fellow of five-and-twenty, who had gone through fire and water for his bride.

Miss Mackenzie is supposed to have been left pretty nearly alone in the world, at middle age, with an income of 800*l*. a year. All her youthful days were spent in tending an invalid brother in a house in one of the dullest streets off the Strand. She had honestly and patiently done her duty by her brother, and he had left her his fortune by way of recompense. In the dulness of Arundel Street she had written verses, and in various other ways allowed herself to think of brighter days and pleasanter companions than fell to her lot then; so, when her brother died, she hoped to get some of her visions realized. The comparative failure of her hopes, and the vexations she endured, the patience with which she bore all sorts of small perplexities, the unconscious generosity with which she strove to spare others, and the vitality of all the gentle aspirations of her youth, combine to make Mr. Trollope's heroine a very sweet and likeable woman. A reader with the strongest possible preference for the heroine of youth and beauty may still have a considerable amount of sympathy for Miss Mackenzie. But the heroes who beset her are strangely horrible. A vulgar dealer in oil-cloth is the first. He is called Rubb, goes to a tea-party in yellow kid gloves, and with his hair ludicrously be-curled and nauseously perfumed. The second is an insolvent curate in a fashionable watering-place. He is better bred than Rubb, but is disfigured by a frightful squint in one eye. The third is a cousin of Miss Mackenzie. He is ten years her senior, has nine children, and passes all his life in pinching and screwing to make both ends meet. All three want the heroine chiefly for her money, and she is fully aware of this, but, so far from resenting it, is only anxious to throw herself into the arms of any one of them who will in return give her a fragment of honest love. At first she refuses the widower, with his money troubles and his dull life. The poor gentleman's honesty, his plain account of all the heavy duties which would fall to her if she became his wife, and his no less plain statement of his need of her money, almost persuaded her to accept a position in which she should be able to do so much good. But then the recollection of the youthful verses, or of the feelings they embodied, became too strong, and the sight of her own still comely figure in the looking-glass determined her to reject a suitor with a bald head, and dull eye, and slow step. Then the contest lies between the vulgar dealer in oil-cloth and the squinting curate. Miss Mackenzie meets the two rivals at tea, and her indecision becomes ten times more undecided. The yellow gloves of Rubb and the appalling eye of the curate affect her with equal repugnance. Rubb talks with all the vulgar geniality of his order, and expatiates on the good sense of the French in banishing 'decorum.' The curate is no less unpleasant in his own way, and declares of his heart that 'it is a grievous sore that is ever running and will not be purified.' Miss Mackenzie was as angry with the curate for being a running sore as she was with Rubb for wearing yellow gloves and not being a gentleman, and she began to wonder whether, after all, the dull widower with the bald head and slow step was not the best of the three. How was she to realize the ideal of her verses out of such material as this? What tender sentiment could there be in any dealings with an underbred wretch like Rubb, or with a curate of tolerably good manners, but with a ghastly squint, and who talked of his heart being black, and a running sore? Of course Miss Mackenzie's mental perplexities, and the wavering of her choice between the suitors, are portrayed with an easy minuteness, and, it must be added, with an air of truthfulness, which are among Mr. Trollope's strongest points. But one cannot help wondering all the time how the author came to think it worth while to expend so much labour on such a set of people. Perhaps the truth that elderly ladies are often overflowing with pleasant visions and estimable aspirations has been neglected. Miss Mackenzie is a most worthy middle-aged person, and we are heartily pleased when she has finally fallen in love with the widower and accepted his hand. Her varying feelings towards the yellow gloves and the distorted eye respectively are perfectly natural, and we can quite understand them. Still there is no great depth in her perplexities, and, so far as they prove anything, they are of a kind to show that the world is not wrong in presuming that incapacity of expression is commonly a sign of comparative shallowness of feeling. That this is not really true is tolerably certain, but in Miss Mackenzie's case the world would probably have esteemed and respected her, and given her full credit for all the kindliness and earnestness of feeling which Mr. Trollope has brought out in her. In the same way, the old widower's faithfulness to Miss Mackenzie after he has ceased to need her eight hundred a year is natural enough, but did anybody ever suppose that tenderness of feeling was extinguished even in a dull old gentleman of fifty? Mr. Rubb, again, shows considerable staunchness and constancy in his suit, but neither yellow gloves, nor vulgarity, nor the retailing of oilcloth has ever been held inconsistent with disinterested affection. Mr. Trollope has taken the trouble to execute a very skilful photograph of a number of exceedingly tedious and unpleasant people, in order to show that vulgarity, and middle-age, and dulness are none of them incompatible with a good deal of sound sentiment. The indisputable truth of the implied conclusion scarcely compensates for the stupidity and downright unpleasantness of the people who have been introduced to us in order to illustrate the truth.

It need not be said that in *Miss Mackenzie*, as in all the rest of Mr. Trollope's stories, there is an abundance of good things. The pictures of the evangelical circle at Littlebath, of the manners of a popular pastor, of the craft and cant of the rapacious curate, are admirable. Miss Todd, an old maid who persisted in remaining among the wicked and unconverted sinners of Littlebath, says capital things against the saints, admitting, however, that 'there's a great deal in it, and only that some of them do tell such lies I think I should have tried it myself.' Her account of repentance, that 'it generally means much the same thing as forgetting all about it,' is eminently instructive. The satirical description of the fashionable bazaar at South Kensington for the benefit of the Negro Soldiers' Orphans' Fund is one which Mr. Trollope's fashionable readers would do well to ponder. As a satirist, Mr. Trollope is equally removed from the depth of Thackeray and the overdone grotesqueness of Mr. Dickens. There is a kind of satire which consists in the plainest possible statement of the obnoxious thing, and in this Mr. Trollope is perfectly skilled. It is far from being the most powerful kind, but it reaches a great many people whom anything like acrimony only repels. The silly swindling of a bazaar, however, will probably survive any number of attacks.

It is a pity Mr. Trollope continues that practice of coining stupid names for some of his characters of which Mr. Samuel Warren first set the example. In *Miss Mackenzie* we have a stiff young candidate for orders called Mr. Frigidy, a tardy attorney called Bideawhile, an insolent flunkey called Mr. Grandairs, and a fiery young man called Mr. Startup. And is there such a word as 'initionary'? Would any old maid who had not been brought up in the habit of speaking broken English reply to a question whether Rubb had mentioned the state of the business, that 'he did say some word as we came in the cab'? But occasional verbal tricks are less provoking, after all, than the needlessly ugly and disagreeable people who are so prominent in this monstrously prosaic version of Mariana in the moated grange.

Mr. Trollope is a novelist who requires space to bring out his conceptions to their full perfection; his longest novels are as a rule his best, and
the characters which have re-appeared oftenest on his stage are those
which give the keenest pleasure to the reader. He has never yet found it
in his heart, as far as we can remember, to kill off one of his multitudin-
ous types, unless it was the drinking railway contractor, Sir Roger
Scatcherd, in *Dr. Thorne*, whom not to have seen in the last stage of
delirium tremens, would scarcely have been to have seen at all. Even the
Warden, Mr. Harding, one of his very best and probably his finest
pictures, is not, we trust, yet dead, while Lady Hartletop, Mr. Plantagenet Palliser, the Duke of Omnium, and many others give ample
signs of life from year to year. Mr. Trollope was not the first to adopt
this practice of bringing his old characters on to the stage of a new story,
for Mr. Thackeray had adopted it before him, though less freely, and
without an equally happy result. We rather regret seeing Arthur Pendennis again, are vexed with Laura in her contracted matrimonial
goodiness, and thirst after fresh fields and pastures new. We believe the
reason of this to be that with Thackeray and perhaps most great novelists, the creative effort is spent upon the characters themselves, so that
when its first great impulse is exhausted there is a certain second-
handness about the repetition of the same imaginative picture. But with
Mr. Trollope, on the other hand, the creative effort is chiefly spent on
the construction of the little circumstances, the variation of the angles of
the little mental and moral reflectors in which we catch a new glimpse
of his characters' nature and essence. His characters themselves once
conceived never vary; they are always the same, and always affect us as
if they were data of Mr. Trollope's mind, the fixed, unalterable points
on his chart of operations, as if all that his imagination really had to
work at was to find out the little incidents which would best throw a
variety of lights *upon* these fixed centres of his thought and on their
relation to each other. We have noticed before, in reviewing *The Small
House at Allington*, how skilful he is in delineating the small manœuvres
and petty tactics of social life, how finely he calculates the effect of place,

of dress, of all the most trivial associations in modifying the mutual influence exerted by men and women over each other, how he makes a hair sometimes turn the scale between temporary failure or temporary success, and how admirably he understands a certain frugal artistic 'economy' which reveals to the reader only as much as, and no more than, ordinary social opportunities actually do reveal of the characters concerned. This great characteristic of his,—that his mind as an artist is engaged much more upon elaborating the infinitely varying social occasions for reflecting character than on creating character itself,—that he occupies himself with turning the social kaleidoscope in which the individual characters are always taking new relations to each other, rather than with penetrating to the core even of his best conceptions, has given him his power of perpetually bringing the old characters on the scene not only without fatiguing his readers, but even with new delight to them. And it is another way of saying the same thing to say that he requires ample space for his most effective pictures. A novelist who delineates best by a succession of varying circumstantial lights and shadows, whose happiest power is the reserve which he knows so well how to exercise in discussing the mental attitudes of frigid and self-restrained hauteur, who paints better in fact, the slighter the effect and the more of conventional knowledge and artificial custom goes to make up its medium (so long as it is a characteristic effect at all) which he wants to convey,—as, for example, the negotiations between the Duke of Omnium and his nephew, Mr. Plantagenet Palliser, through the Duke's agent, Mr. Fothergill,—a novelist in short who seems the more skilful the more minute and complex are the conventional *nuances* through which his characters express themselves, cannot but need ample space in which to delineate his conceptions. Those are almost always the best scenes in which the effective touches are apparently the slightest, and of course a great number of such scenes must go to make up a good story. In Thackeray, on the other hand, in whom a vein of strong feeling, whether satiric or pathetic, is almost always the basis of delineation, the finest scenes are those in which the conventional strata are broken through, such as that in which Becky half admires her husband for knocking down Lord Steyne, or Rawdon Crawley breaks out into tenderness over his little boy. Mr. Trollope is always strongest when painting individuals through the customary manners of a class, and even of classes he paints those manners best which are almost an artificial language in themselves, which it almost takes an art to interpret. The coarser manners which tell their own tale he paints admirably, but with the tone of something too loud a laughter, as if he were laughing not only at the false contrasts and ridiculous aims which all true vulgarity exposes, but almost at the spectacle of vulgarity itself, which is simply disagreeable, and not amusing. It is his great power of painting character in the very act of using or coping with minute social circumstances, of inventing little social circumstances to throw back a new meaning on character, which enables him to reproduce the same characters again and again with so much effect. He never exhausts them, because he never paints them directly, and if he can find a new store of situations for them his imagination goes to work as fresh as ever, not repeating itself, but only working with the more power because there is none of that new ground to break which Mr. Trollope does least effectively,—the first introduction of a character to his readers. And therefore in all his best artistic pictures Mr. Trollope needs ample room for gradual effect. There are few of his shorter stories anything like equal in impressiveness to the longer ones, because he has not space for his peculiar style.

To some extent, we think, *Miss Mackenzie* loses by being a tale in two volumes, and two short volumes, instead of being spread in his usual leisurely way over his usual long perspectives. It is very clever, and gives us one or two glimpses of some admirable old sketches of his, —Miss Todd and Miss Baker, who appeared in the *Bertrams*,—also the Duchess of St. Bungay and Lady Glencora Palliser, who appear in the tale still going on, *Can You Forgive Her?*—for which we are sincerely grateful,—but the new characters, many of them exceedingly able, are scarcely sketched in the variety of attitude and in the multiplicity of circumstances which are characteristic of Mr. Trollope's best style. There is Mr. Stumfold, of Littlebath, the *jolly* kind of Evangelical clergyman, who is cheery and jocular as well as Evangelical,—a sort of gentlemanly Spurgeon,—whom Mr. Trollope might well have painted for us with all the care with which he has painted Mr. Slope and Dr. Proudie. So far as the picture goes it is in his best style, but we regret to say that Mr. Stumfold disappears after a single Thursday evening's tea-meeting and re-appears on the scene no more. . . .

That Mr. Stumfold sang always, and that his lute had twenty strings, we feel no doubt at all; and therefore regret the more deeply that Mr. Trollope should only have given us the tune of one of them. Let us hope that he has kept his song with the trumpets and his song with the shawms,—by the way, it would be quite in Mr. Stumfold's line to explain the exact nature of a shawm, and make a cheery application thereof, which would have the advantage of instructing ignorant Christians all over England,—for some other book. Still we must reproach Mr. Trollope for giving us so brief a glimpse of so admirable a figure. Mr. Maguire, the curate, is somewhat less successful. Mr. Trollope harps too much on the squint, till it almost hides the picture of the man's pertinacious greediness and greasy Evangelicism. The libellous article which he writes in the *Littlebath Christian Examiner* against the other suitor for Miss Mackenzie's hand, or rather fortune, is handled with Mr. Trollope's usual skill in touching off the charlataneries of the press, and his relations to Mrs. Stumfold, or St. Stumfolda, as she is more appropriately termed, are skilfully hit off. Still, on the whole, Mr. Maguire, though he occupies much more space than Mr. Stumfold, is less vividly painted, being as it were almost pushed off the stage of Mr. Trollope's imagination by his own squint. It is the greater pity, because there is nothing in the sketch, except the terrible accentuation of the squint, which is not effective,—even to the name Jeremiah, which occurs to Miss Mackenzie as one of the great difficulties of accepting him, Jerry being so very ludicrous and unclerical for private use and Jeremiah so impracticable. The Ball family are well painted, and John Ball (who is a kindly and refined edition of Joseph Mason, of Groby Park, in *Orley Farm*), the slow, care-worn, stock-buying man, who nurses his grievances without losing sight of justice, and earns directors' guineas at the Shadrach Fire Office and the Abednego Life Office—(how happy is Mr. Trollope's humour in inventing names!)—for his nine children, is an admirable figure. But perhaps the most finished sketches in the book are those of Mrs. Tom Mackenzie and Mr. Samuel Rubb, Jun., though they are not the best of which Mr. Trollope is capable. We may note, by the way, that Mr. Samuel Rubb is made too vulgar for his education at Merchant Taylors' School, where, having learned a little Latin and a good deal, one would suppose, of the use of English words amongst fairly educated boys, he could scarcely have failed to learn that 'decorum' and 'ceremony' are not interchangeable terms, and that a man at an English watering-place would be making a blunder in complimenting ladies on having quite got rid of decorum. Still the man is admirably done, though there is evidently a slight increase in the vulgarization of his manners, and a slight change in the author's feeling towards him as the tale proceeds. Mrs. Mackenzie and the slavish captivity into which she goes to Grandairs, the man whom she hires to wait at her dinner-party, is very amusing. But we are sure no boastful woman, whose husband had 800*l.* a year, would have bought only a single bottle of champagne for such an entertainment as hers. She is not meant to be stingy, and was far more likely to have been lavish of her champagne than penurious; but excepting this slight touch of caricature, Mrs. Tom Mackenzie and her dinner-party are very amusing. We do not altogether appreciate the heroine. Mr. Trollope loves to delineate women *in a mess* with their love affairs, and scarcely knowing their own mind. But we doubt if he sketches these characters so well as those more determinate characters who fall in love in earnest. As a rule, his pictures are good almost in proportion to the definiteness of the character and the variety of the circumstances under which it is sketched. Miss Mackenzie's character is meant to be a fluid one, and the fluid characters are scarcely his forte. On the whole, however, the book, though too short and sketchy, is full of lively scenes, and shows no falling off in power, though there is somewhat too little fullness of execution.

81. Unsigned notice, *Athenaeum*

1 April 1865, p. 455

'Miss Mackenzie' is a study, rather than a novel, and a very clever study. There are few incidents of any kind, least of all are they sensational. Mr. Trollope has taken the most unpromising of characters so far as romance is concerned; they are personages for whom, at first sight, it would seem impossible to get up any interest, except by force of circumstances, and these circumstances are not invoked. The interest of the reader is nevertheless roused and sustained; he is obliged to take the individuals—beginning with an elderly maiden lady of moderate attractions and of no fascination, and a middle-aged widower, bald, unattractive and the father of nine children—into his friendship, and to feel genuine anxiety about the progress of their fortunes. This is a triumph of skill; but the genuine good taste and good feeling of the author have a great share in the pleasant result.

82. Unsigned notice, *London Review*

8 April 1865, x. 387

It is a bold undertaking on the part of a novelist to ask his readers to take an interest in the fortunes of such a heroine, especially as the hero to whom she attaches herself is a bald-headed gentleman of fifty, a widower with nine children; but Mr. Trollope revels in risk, and delights in surrounding himself with difficulties and dangers, for the sake of the pleasure he finds in ultimately overcoming them. In his present attempt he has thoroughly succeeded, and the skill with which he fights his battle deserves as much praise as the courage with which he enters upon it. He has invested with interest what might have appeared a dull subject; he has revealed the poetry which lay hidden in an apparently most prosaic life; and he has treated a theme which to many would have seemed ludicrous with such delicacy and feeling that he has rendered it singularly touching and pathetic. . . .

Even after [the reader] has laid the book down, a disagreeable impression is left upon his mind, so mean and ignoble are the thoughts and words of the people among whom he has lately been moving. But Miss Mackenzie's merits more than make up for the faults of her neighbours, and we strongly recommend our readers to make acquaintance with her. If they read her chronicle with care, they will not only while away a few hours in an agreeable manner, but they will increase their experience of life and their knowledge of human character.

83. Unsigned notice, *Reader*

27 May 1865, iii. 596

'Miss Mackenzie' is a novel that we believe no one but Mr. Trollope would have had either the hardihood to undertake, or the ability to write so as to be readable. . . . For ourselves, we cannot think that the line of art adopted by the author is of a high class, or that it produces either amusement or instruction. . . . As usual, again, the dull progress of the plot is redeemed by at least one really admirable scene. Mr. Trollope is always entertaining when he gets among clergymen; and the tea-party at the Evangelical parson's is a masterpiece of humour. To sum up, as a *tour de force,* 'Miss Mackenzie' is wonderful; as a novel, saving a few scenes, it seems to us dull.

84. Unsigned notice, *Dublin University Magazine*

May 1865, lxv. 576

Mr. Trollope presents details with his wonted inimitable skill, and we question whether there is in any of his works more evidence than here of those peculiar powers of observation in matters trifling of themselves, but yet full of character. No such touches are in Mr. Trollope's hand superfluous. They minister invariably to the growth of the interest or perfectness of the impersonation. Miss Mackenzie would not leave half the impression upon the mind if her little pruderies and old-maidish ways were not photographed; and her suitor, selfish and yet not bad at heart, as his constancy when her fortune was lost proved, would have been a mere shadow but for the same point of skill.

85. Unsigned notice, *Westminster Review*

July 1865, lxxxiv. 282–5

Our most popular novelist has devoted two volumes to the outer and inner history of an excellent spinster of five-and-thirty, who finds that the possession of eight hundred a-year has rendered her too attractive for her own peace, and whose life is a constant struggle to escape being run down and boarded against her will. With all a woman's instinctive readiness to trust herself to, and to take refuge with any man who would let her love him, she has to wage an unequal warfare against her own heart craving for affection, and her Scotch prudence that cannot be blinded to the greed of gold, which taught her to look upon her lovers 'as so many men to whom her income would be convenient, and to feel herself to be almost under an obligation to them for their willingness to put up with the incumbrance which was attached to it.' We all know with what mingled humour and kindliness Mr. Trollope can handle such a theme, and among his many female characters he has never drawn a better than this of Miss Mackenzie, with her homely face, her romantic heart, and her sterling uprightness—her innocent aspirations after the beautiful, and the desperately clayey nature of the fields wherein she dug for the treasure. From first to last she is admirable, and for her sake we bear with the odious company of her relations and admirers. But they are almost too much for mortal patience, and all Mr. Trollope's practised art hardly avails to carry the reader through chapter after chapter of too faithful description. It cannot be said that any of the story is badly done; good of their kind are the various members of the decayed family of the Balls; very good the religious world of Littlebath; and excellent the rival lovers, the Rev. Jeremiah Maguire, with his awful squint, and Mr. Rubb, with his greasy hair and yellow gloves; but there is a limit not easy to define, beyond which pictures of human nature distorted by vulgarity, cease to amuse and become simply offensive, and this limit, we are fain to say, is overstepped in 'Miss Mackenzie.' For, though the story is not a bad one, it becomes dull from the persevering consistency with which this one obnoxious image—that of a good, loving woman, hunted for the sake of her gold by one disagreeable man after another—is kept always before us, and, though we accept

231

thankfully the slight alleviation of such scenes as the Littlebath tea-parties, and Mrs. Tom Mackenzie's dinners *à la Russe*, even these are but a sorry diversion, and we have hardly patience to accompany the estimable heroine to the longed-for goal, when she becomes the wife of the least objectionable of her suitors.

86. Henry James, *Nation* (New York)

13 July 1865, i. 51–52

James was twenty-two and at the very beginning of his career when he wrote his three reviews of *Miss Mackenzie, Can You Forgive Her?* and *The Belton Estate* during a period of six months for the New York *Nation*. If young James was severe but searching in his judgements of Trollope's novels, he was no kinder to Dickens in a review of *Our Mutual Friend* for the *Nation* (21 December 1865), i. 786–7: '*Bleak House* was forced; *Little Dorrit* was laboured; the present work was dug out as with spade and pickaxe.' James congratulated Dickens 'on his success in what we should call the manufacture of fiction'.

We have long entertained for Mr. Trollope a partiality of which we have yet been somewhat ashamed. Perhaps, indeed, we do wrong to say that we have entertained it. It has rather usurped our hospitality, and has resisted several attempts at forcible expulsion. If it remains, therefore, in however diminished vigor, we confess that it will be through our weakness.

Miss Mackenzie is a worthy gentlewoman, who, coming at the age of thirty-six into a comfortable little fortune, retires to enjoy it at a quiet watering-place, where, in the course of time, she is beset by a brace of mercenary suitors. After the lapse of a year she discovers that she holds her property by a wrongful title, and is compelled to transfer it to her cousin, a widowed baronet, with several children, who, however, gallantly repairs the injury thus judicially inflicted, by making her his wife. The work may be qualified, therefore, in strictness, as the history of the pecuniary embarrassments of a middle-aged spinster. The subject has, at least, the charm of novelty, a merit of which the author has wisely appreciated the force. We had had heroines of many kinds, maidens in their teens, yea, even in their units, and matrons in their twenties, but as yet we had had no maidens in their thirties. We, for our part, have often been called upon to protest against the inveterate and excessive immaturity of the ladies in whose fortunes we are expected to interest ourselves, and we are sincerely grateful to Mr. Trollope for having practically recognized the truth that a woman is potentially a heroine as long as she lives. To many persons a middle-aged woman in love trenches upon the ridiculous. Such persons may be assured, however, that although there is considerable talk about this passion in 'Miss Mackenzie,' there is very little of its substance. Mr. Trollope has evidently been conscious of the precarious nature of his heroine's dignity, and in attempting to cancel the peril to which it is exposed, he has diminished the real elements of passion. This is apt to be the case in Mr. Trollope's stories. Passion has to await the convenience of so many other claimants that in the end she is but scantily served. As for action, we all know what we are to expect of Mr. Trollope in this direction; and the admirers of 'quiet novels,' as they are somewhat euphuistically termed, will not be disappointed here. Miss Mackenzie loses her brother, and assumes his property: she then adopts her little niece, takes lodgings at Littlebath, returns a few visits, procures a seat at church, puts her niece at school, receives a few awkward visits from a couple of vulgar bachelors, quarrels with her pastor's wife, goes to stay with some dull old relatives, loses her money, falls out with the dull relatives, is taken up by a fashionable cousin and made to serve in a fancy fair, and finally receives and accepts an offer from another cousin. Except the acquisition and loss of her property, which events are detailed at great length, she has no adventures. Her life could not well be more peaceful. She certainly suffers and enjoys less than most women. Granting, however, that the adventures entailed upon her by her luckless £800 a year are such as may properly mark her for our observation and compensate for the lack of incidents more dramatic, Mr. Trollope may consider that he has hit the average of the experience of unmarried English ladies. It is perhaps impossible to overstate the habitual monotony of such lives; and at all events, as far as the chronicler of domestic events has courage to go in this direction, so far will a certain proportion of facts bear him out. Literally, then, Mr. Trollope accomplishes his purpose of being true to common life. But in reading his pages, we were constantly induced to ask ourselves whether he is equally true to nature; that is, whether in the midst of this multitude of real things, of uncompromisingly real circumstances, the persons put before us are equally real. Mr. Trollope has proposed to himself to describe those facts which are so close under every one's nose that no one notices them. Life is vulgar, but we know not how vulgar it is till we see it set down in his pages. It may be said therefore that the emotions which depend upon such facts as these cannot be too prosaic; that as prison discipline makes men idiots, an approach, however slight, to this kind of influence perceptibly weakens the mind. We are yet compelled to doubt whether men and women of healthy intellect take life, even in its smallest manifestation, as *stupidly* as Miss Mackenzie and her friends. Mr. Trollope has, we conceive, simply wished to interest us in ordinary mortals: it has not been his intention to introduce us to a company of imbeciles. But, seriously, we do not consider these people to be much better. Detach them from their circumstances, reduce them to their essences, and what do they amount to? They are but the halves of men and women. The accumulation of minute and felicitous circumstances which constitutes the modern novel sheds such a glamour of reality over the figures which sustain the action that we forbear to scrutinize them separately. The figures are the generals in the argument; the facts are the particulars. The persons should accordingly reflect life upon the details, and not borrow it from them. To do so is only to borrow the contagion of death. This latter part is the part they play, and with this result, as it seems to us, in 'Miss Mackenzie.' It is possible that this result is Mr. Trollope's misfortune rather than his fault. He has encountered it in trying to avoid an error which he doubtless considers more pernicious still, that of overcharging nature. He has doubtless done his best to give us the happy middle truth. But ah, if the truth is not so black as she is sometimes painted, neither is she so pale!

We do not expect from the writers of Mr. Trollope's school (and this we esteem already a great concession) that they shall contribute to the glory of human nature; but we may at least exact that they do not wantonly detract from it. Mr. Trollope's offence is, after all, deliberate. He has deliberately selected vulgar illustrations. His choice may indeed be explained by an infirmity for which he is not responsible: we mean his lack of imagination. But when a novelist's imagination is weak, his judgment should be strong. Such was the case with Thackeray. Mr. Trollope is of course wise, in view of the infirmity in question, in devoting himself to those subjects which least expose it. He is an excellent, an admirable observer; and such an one may accomplish much. But why does he not observe great things as well as little ones? It was by doing so that Thackeray wrote 'Henry Esmond.' Mr. Trollope's devotion to little things, inveterate, self-sufficient as it is, begets upon the reader the very disagreeable impression that not only no imagination was required for the work before him, but that a man of imagination could not possibly have written it. This impression is fostered by many of Mr. Trollope's very excellences. A more richly-gifted writer would miss many of his small (that is, his great) effects. It must be admitted, however, that he would obtain on the other hand a number of truly great ones. Yet, as great effects are generally produced at present by small means, Mr. Trollope is master of a wide field. He deals wholly in small effects. His manner, like most of the literary manners of the day, is a small manner. And what a strange phenomenon, when we reflect upon it, is this same small manner! What an anomaly in a work of imagination is such a chapter as that in which our author describes Mrs. Tom Mackenzie's shabby dinner party. It is as well described as it possibly could be. Nothing is omitted. It is almost as good as certain similar scenes in the 'Book of Snobs.' It makes the reader's ear tingle and his cheeks to redden with shame. Nothing, we say, is omitted; but, alas! nothing is infused. The scene possesses no interest but such as resides in the crude facts: and as this is null, the picture is clever, it is faithful, it is even horrible, but it is not interesting. There we touch upon the difference between the great manner and the small manner; herein lies the reason why in such scenes Mr. Trollope is only *almost* as good as Thackeray. It can generally be said of this small manner that it succeeds; cleverness is certain of success; it never has the vertigo; it is only genius and folly that fail. But in what does it succeed? That is the test question: the question which it behooves us to impose now-a-days with ever-growing stringency upon works of art; for it is the answer to this question that should approve or condemn them. It is small praise to say of a novelist that he succeeds in mortifying the reader. Yet Mr. Trollope is master of but two effects: he renders his reader comfortable or the reverse. As long as he restricts himself to this scale of emotion, of course he has no need of imagination, for imagination speaks to the heart. In the scene here mentioned, Mr. Trollope, as we have said, mortifies the reader; in other scenes he fosters his equanimity, and his plan, indeed, is generally to leave him in a pleasant frame of mind.

This is all very well; and we are perhaps ill advised to expect sympathy for any harsh strictures upon a writer who renders such excellent service. Let us, however, plainly disavow a harsh intention. Let us, in the interest of our argument, heartily recognize his merits. His merits, indeed! he has only too many. His manner is literally freckled with virtues. We use this term advisedly, because its virtues are all virtues of detail: the virtues of the photograph. The photograph lacks the supreme virtue of possessing a character. It is the detail alone that distinguishes one photograph from another. What but the details distinguishes one of Mr. Trollope's novels from another, and, if we may use the expression, consigns it to itself? Of course the details are charming, some of them ineffably charming. The ingenuous loves, the innocent flirtations, of Young England, have been described by Mr. Trollope in such a way as to secure him the universal public good-will; described minutely, sympathetically, accurately; if it were not that an indefinable instinct bade us to keep the word in reserve, we should say truthfully. The story of Miss Mackenzie lacks this element of vernal love-making. The most that can be said of the affairs of this lady's heart is that they are not ridiculous. They are assuredly not interesting; and they are involved in much that is absolutely repulsive. When you draw on the grand scale, a certain amount of coarseness in your lines is excusable; but when you work with such short and cautious strokes as Mr. Trollope, it behooves you, above all things, to be delicate. Still, taking the book in its best points, the development of Miss Mackenzie's affections would not, in actual life, be a phenomenon worthy of an intelligent spectator. What rights, then, accrue to it in print? Miss Mackenzie is an utterly common-place person, and her lover is almost a fool. He is apparently unsusceptible of the smallest inspiration from the events of his life. Why should we follow the fortunes of such people? They vulgarize experience and all the other heavenly gifts. Why should we stoop to gather nettles when there are roses blooming under our hands? Why should we batten upon over-cooked prose while the air is redolent with undistilled poetry? It is perhaps well that we should learn how superficial, how spiritless, how literal human feeling may become; but is a novel here our proper lesson-book? Clever novels may be manufactured of such material as this; but to outweigh a thousand merits they will have the one defect, that they are *monstrous*. They will be anomalies. Mr. Matthew Arnold, however, has recently told us that a large class of Englishmen consider it no objection to a thing that it is an anomaly.[1] Mr. Trollope is doubtless one of the number.

[1] 'For the Englishman in general is like my friend the Member of Parliament, and believes, point-blank, that for a thing to be an anomaly is absolutely no objection to it whatever.'—Matthew Arnold, 'The Function of Criticism at the Present Time', *Essays in Criticism* (1865).

87. Unsigned notice, *The Times*

23 August 1865, p. 13

Mr. Trollope has written many novels which are far more attractive, which compel the attention more eagerly, which it is difficult not to go on with when once we have begun to read them. And yet, perhaps, he has written no novel which is more to his credit than this one of *Miss Mackenzie*. . . .

From young romance he turns to old common-place; and regarding the novel as a picture of life, he undertakes to show us life at its prosiest. 'It is good to remember,' he seems to say, 'that, amid all the romancing of passionate, young hearts, there is a more ordinary view of life in which there is no romance, and in which passion has been dulled into a colourless force. . . .'

We know not any other living writer of fiction who would have been so bold as to undertake the dealing with such a subject; and it would be impossible to name a living novelist who having buckled to such a work would have completed it with more success. It is not easy to make this sort of subject interesting, and we need not fear that it will be often selected for treatment; but once in a way we are pleased to have to do with it. Mr. Trollope touches it with his wonted ease and naturalness, and revels in the petty vulgarities of upstart existence which used to delight poor Thackeray. He gives us pictures which are not dull of dull lives, dull households, dull dinner parties, dull teas, and dull prayer meetings. The amount of amusement which he manages to get out of mere dulness is certainly remarkable, and is a striking proof of his vigour. Miss Mackenzie herself is drawn with rare accuracy, and her destined husband, Mr. Ball, the prosy widower, we seem to have known all our lives.

CAN YOU FORGIVE HER?

1865

Trollope had to some extent adapted his main characters and plot from the manuscript of *The Noble Jilt*, a drama that he had written in 1850. The novel was memorable for him, however, he tells us in his *Autobiography* (pp. 151–5), for characters unrelated to his play. *Can You Forgive Her?* was the first novel to present as fully formed characters Plantagenet Palliser and Lady Glencora, who were to become the central figures in his series of novels often referred to as the Palliser Novels (the last of them, *The Duke's Children*, appeared in 1880 after Trollope had written and laid aside his *Autobiography*).

. . . But that which endears the book to me is the first presentation which I made in it of Plantagenet Palliser, with his wife, Lady Glencora.

By no amount of description or asseveration could I succeed in making any reader understand how much these characters with their belongings have been to me in my latter life; or how frequently I have used them for the expression of my political or social convictions. . . .

In these personages and their friends, political and social, I have endeavoured to depict the faults and frailties and vices,—as also the virtues, the graces, and the strength of our highest classes; and if I have not made the strength and virtues predominant over the faults and vices, I have not painted the picture as I intended. Plantagenet Palliser I think to be a very noble gentleman,—such a one as justifies to the nation the seeming anomaly of an hereditary peerage and of primogeniture. His wife is in all respects very inferior to him; but she, too, has, or has been intended to have, beneath the thin stratum of her follies a basis of good principle, which enabled her to live down the conviction of the original wrong which was done to her, and taught her to endeavour to do her duty in the position to which she was called. She had received a great wrong,—having been made, when little more than a child, to marry a man for whom she cared nothing;— when, however, though she was little more than a child, her love had been given elsewhere. She had very heavy troubles, but they did not overcome her. . . .

Lady Glencora . . . is brought, partly by her own sense of right and wrong, and partly by the genuine nobility of her husband's conduct, to attach herself to him after a certain fashion. The romance of her life is gone, but there remains a rich reality of which she is fully able to taste the flavour. She loves her rank and becomes ambitious, first of social, and then of political ascendency. He is thoroughly true to her, after his thorough nature, and she, after her less perfect nature, is imperfectly true to him.

In conducting these characters from one story to another I realized the necessity, not only of consistency,—which, had it been maintained by a hard exactitude, would have been untrue to nature,—but also of those changes which time always produces. There are, perhaps, but few of us who, after the lapse of ten years, will be found to have changed our chief characteristics. The selfish man will still be selfish, and the false man false. But our manner of showing or of hiding these characteristics will be changed,—as also our power of adding to or diminishing their intensity. It was my study that these people, as they grew in years, should encounter the changes which come upon us all; and I think that I have succeeded. The Duchess of Omnium, when she is playing the part of Prime Minister's wife, is the same woman as that Lady Glencora who almost longs to go off with Burgo Fitzgerald, but yet knows that she will never do so; and the Prime Minister Duke, with his wounded pride and sore spirit, is he who, for his wife's sake, left power and place when they were first offered to him;— but they have undergone the changes which a life so stirring as theirs would naturally produce. To do all this thoroughly was in my heart from first to last; but I do not know that the game has been worth the candle. To carry out my scheme I have had to spread my picture over so wide a canvas that I cannot expect that any lover of such art should trouble himself to look at it as a whole. Who will read *Can You Forgive Her?, Phineas Finn, Phineas Redux,* and *The Prime Minister* consecutively, in order that they may understand the characters of the Duke of Omnium, of Plantagenet Palliser, and of Lady Glencora? Who will ever know that they should be so read? But in the performance of the work I had much gratification, and was enabled from time to time to have in this way that fling at the political doings of the day which every man likes to take, if not in one fashion then in another. I look upon this string of characters,—carried sometimes into other novels than those just named,—as the best work of my life. Taking him altogether, I think that Plantagenet Palliser stands more firmly on the ground than any other personage I have created.

---

88. Unsigned notice, *Saturday Review*

19 August 1865, xx. 240–2

Lady Glencora, a petulant and childish little lady, but excellently drawn, marries the frigid and haughty Mr. Palliser—whom the readers of the author's former novels are not particularly glad to meet again—without a particle of affection for him, and leads a wretched life for a time, but in the end gets to like her husband quite enough to make existence with him endurable. Alice Vavasor, too, is amply punished in various ways for not taking the leap boldly by marrying the man she loved when she could have got him, without any fuss about the importance of life. . . . However, his readers will forgive him a rather questionable doctrine of this sort, for the sake of those wonderful dialogues and imaginary letters which he goes on writing out with such amazing patience, and which are so exactly like the dialogues we hear and the letters we read in real life. The people do not let off epigrams at one another, nor make long speeches, each in his turn. They do literally talk. The conversations at dinner, in the drawing-room, at billiards, at Matching Priory, are perhaps the best specimens of Mr. Trollope's knack, unless we except the talk of the various members of the Roebury hunting club. And what can be more natural and more inimitable in its own way than Lady Midlothian's letter, imploring Alice 'to remember what she owes to God and man, and to carry out her engagement'? 'He has a right to claim you before God and man; and have you considered that he has probably furnished his house in consequence of his intended marriage?' This compound appeal to the female sense of religion and fear of public opinion, and dislike of a house being furnished to no purpose, is just in the tone that an old lady would use to a self-willed young one who was throwing away a good match.

The people of secondary importance in the story are more successful than minor people usually are. George Vavasor is the least so. The violent unscrupulous adventurer who is simply bent upon getting on at whatever cost is a character scarcely in Mr. Trollope's line. The gentlemanly unscrupulous adventurer, like Crosbie, is a more suitable subject for his peculiar talent. Burgo Fitzgerald, for example, the handsome, spendthrift, well-bred good-for-nothing, is admirable. 'He was beautiful, and never vain of his beauty; in the midst of his recklessness there was always about him a certain kindliness which made him pleasant to those around him. They knew that he was worthless, but nevertheless they loved him, and the secret of it was chiefly in this, that he thought so little of himself.' The touch of the difference between him and George Vavasor, the violent man, is capital. George Vavasor continually cursed his fortune with bitterness; but 'there remained about Burgo one honest feeling—one conviction that was true—a feeling that it all served him right, and that he had better perhaps go to the Devil at once, and give nobody any more trouble.' 'George Vavasor would have ground his victims up to powder if he had known how; but Burgo Fitzgerald desired to hurt no one.' The good points in a really worthless fellow of this stamp—a man so bad in one sense as deliberately to plan the carrying off of his neighbour's wife, and the sort of man too whom most of us are familiar with—have never been more delicately, or even sympathetically, brought out. Mr. Trollope does not scold and preach about his iniquities. He makes us feel quite tenderly for his good-for-nothing, and even when describing the preparations for his meditated villany he only fills us with the kind of pity for him we should have for a fallen woman. In another and much inferior way, the Norfolk farmer who is for ever bragging of the land on which he sits being his own, and of his rich piles of muck, and of the fearlessness with which he can walk into every bank in Norwich, is as good as anything Mr. Trollope has ever done. So is Mrs. Greenow, and so is John Vavasor, the type of men who live at clubs.

The defects of the book are those to which we are accustomed in Mr. Trollope's stories. There is, as usual, no plot. Of one of the most prominent characters we are told, 'And here George Vavasor vanishes from our pages, and will be heard of no more.' And a little further on, 'Here we must say farewell to Burgo Fitzgerald.' In neither case do we know in the least what becomes of them. If some of the pains which the author bestows on writing out endless little items and details were given to the careful conception of a plot and a story, his novels would have more pretension to art, and would therefore be more likely to live. Even if nothing were sacrificed for it, this infinite particularity of description is sometimes carried to a tedious extreme. Alice's vacillations, and the way in which she argued out all sorts of little points in her own mind, and the way in which John Grey and George Vavasor argued out little points in their own minds, are treated with a minuteness which at times becomes downright tedious. And one scarcely sees what is gained by letting us know how, after the Squire's funeral was over, Mrs. Greenow met the party with an invitation to lunch, and they all went into the dining-room and drank each a glass of sherry, and George took two or three glasses. Then we have what the doctor did, and after that we learn that the three gentlemen rose up and went across to the drawing-room, George leading the way. This kind of writing prolonged over page upon page makes us think that Mr. Trollope is right in publishing his book in monthly parts. A little of it once a month is just what everybody would like, and the story is far from being so fearfully absorbing that the break would leave us in too painful suspense.

89. Unsigned notice, *Month*

September 1865, iii. 319–23

His writings reflect admirably the manners and thoughts of the dominant classes in our society; they are full of brilliancy and good sense; and without the slightest pretence to any lofty philosophy of life, contain a good deal of quiet teaching in their way. He seems now to be in the prime of his career, in the full exercise of powers which he has taken many years of labour to develope. His greatest danger seems to lie in his facility; for he has usually two or three stories on hand at once. He may perhaps be content with the ambition of amusing his own generation, but he has enough in him to take his place among the greater writers of English fiction. . . .

Alice wins our forgiveness because she is Alice. Whether we shall have *Can you forgive* HIM? and Mr. Crosbie absolved in some future tale, remains to be seen. We never know when we have done with Mr. Trollope's characters, and Crosbie is too good a one not to come to life again some day. We are not disposed to quarrel with a system of reproduction which gives us so much amusement. The present novel owes quite as much of its interest to the fortunes of Lady Glencora Palliser and her husband as to those of Alice and Mr. Grey; in fact, Lady Glencora is the best character in the book. The 'villain' of the novel, George Vavasor, is very well drawn, and so is his sister.

90. Unsigned notice, *Athenaeum*

2 September 1865, pp. 305–6

The sorrows and temptations of Lady Glencora are very true to female human nature; her poor little struggles to do right are very touching, heroic, too, in their measure, for they are sincere, and cost her much. Alice is her guardian angel, and wiser for her than for herself. The good qualities of Mr. Palliser come out strong; he behaves generously, and he has the reader's sympathy when at last he wins the affection of his wayward, inconsiderate, but charming wife. . . .

We have noticed the general scope of the novel only; but there are incidental scenes and touches of character worthy of all praise; such are the Hunting Field, the Roebury Club, and the sketch of John Vavasor, the father of Alice. The account of the widow Greenhow and her lovers is coarse caricature, without redeeming fun. It is heavy and disagreeable. Mr. Trollope, however, has never written a story in which there is better workmanship, or more careful study of character, than 'Can You Forgive Her?'

91. Unsigned notice, *Spectator*

2 September 1865, xxxviii. 978–9

Can we forgive her? asks Mr. Trollope. Certainly, if it were worth while, but we scarcely care enough about her for either a forgiving or unforgiving spirit. . . . Alice Vavasor's type of character is uninteresting and unintelligible without much more of the scenery of inward emotion, of morbid distrusts, hesitations, self-analyses, and self-accusations of coldness, variableness, and exhaustion of feeling, than Mr. Trollope has attempted to give. . . .

Yet the tale is, in many respects, one of his best, in spite of a faint and misty centre. If Mr. Trollope has failed in Alice Vavasor, he has drawn a figure of unusual force in her cousin George Vavasor, and has not left his tale, moreover, without a true heroine. The moment she appears on the stage, Lady Glencora Palliser, a figure far better suited to Mr. Trollope's style of art than Alice Vavasor, takes the place of her friend in the reader's mind, and it is *her* fortunes rather than Alice's that we watch with the most interest during the chief part of the tale. We believe that Mr. Trollope meant to paint in Alice a woman of the most refined delicacy of nature guilty of an indelicacy simply owing to morbid distrust of her own feelings. In Lady Glencora Palliser he certainly does paint a woman with some little indelicacy of character from a nearly opposite cause,—a complete absence of reserve, combined with that kind of impetuosity which blurts out and even exaggerates, instead of as much as possible ignoring and repressing, the feelings of which she has most reason to feel ashamed. Lady Glencora is the sort of girl who, under unfortunate circumstances, might become even shameless and brazen, but could only become so by yielding impetuously to some half-generous feelings which might put her in conflict with the world's opinion, and make permanent defiance of its morality a part of her pleasure. There is something loveable and childlike in her which belongs to this impetuous nature, though she has none of the reserve in matters of feeling which generally marks children. In her restless love of strong exciting feelings Lady Glencora is almost bold, and Mr. Trollope takes her as near as he can find it in his heart to do—(she is evidently a great favourite of his)—to the edge of the abyss a plunge into which would

have made her what is called a 'bold' woman. We are not quite sure
that he is acting consistently with his own design and with the indications he throws out in the earlier part of the story in saving her from
this fatal plunge, but perhaps he would say that a certain irresolution is
a part of her character, and that it is strictly consistent to save her from
the fatal step of an elopement by interposing the same kind of circumstantial obstacles which were originally sufficient to make her marry
against her will and against the impulse of her affections. If Mr. Trollope
had had the heart (shall we say the nerve?) to ruin Lady Glencora, he
might have given (what is rare with him) a genuinely tragic interest to
his story,—but his artistic instinct seems to have an awe of tragedy, the
border of which he often brushes, touching it with no little insight and
ability, but also apparently with something of distrustful anxiety, and
leaving it again with a sense of relief. In Lady Glencora he has mixed
elements apparently almost intended to prepare us for feminine recklessness and that kind of desperation which cannot endure the condemnation it is so ready to brave. Her love of excitement, her yearning
for love, her half scorn for the prosaic plodder destitute of insight into
character who is her husband, the light effervescence of her spirits even
when she is most unhappy, her pleasure in *making faces* when her husband
preaches to her, her contumacious countermining of his little plans for
sobering her down, the mischievous spirit which makes her almost
mock her guest, the Duchess of St. Bungay, in Mr. Palliser's own house,
the devil in her which makes her unable to resist flirting before Mrs.
Marsham and Mr. Bott, or gaming in the gambling-rooms at Baden,
and which, even after she is happier, makes her tell the Duke of Omnium
when bending over her, that she hopes her child (his heir) may prove a
girl,—all these are traits which, taken together, would seem better
suited to prelude a great rashness and a tragic fate than those of any
other character Mr. Trollope has drawn. Nor can it be said that
her amenability to advice on occasion of her marriage would argue a
similar pliancy to the opinion of the world in greater matters after
marriage. Mr. Trollope clearly means us to understand that Lady
Glencora by marrying a man for whom she cared nothing has lost a
little of her delicacy and, with her delicacy, of her respect for the
opinions of others even on moral questions; and the longing she evidently feels to recover a sincerer position is only a new motive to leave
Mr. Palliser, her relation to whom she evidently felt insincere as well as
cold. On the whole we have a strong feeling that Lady Glencora was
in the earlier part of the book painted with a more or less unconscious

eye to a darker ending, but that Mr. Trollope shrank back from the picture, either because he distrusted his power to draw it, or because his instinct naturally leads him towards the play of lighter feelings. Something of the same tendency to run as close as he dare to the edge of tragedy without incurring the responsibility of delineating its darkest features, is shown in the masterly picture of George Vavasor's meanness and gloomy violence. Here Mr. Trollope does not shrink from delineating at least a murderous *heart*, but only from delineating the final consummation of its evil, and the general horror which a deliberately planned and executed crime of murder spreads around. Probably Mr. Trollope shrinks less from the imagination of dark thoughts, than from attempting that intensity of *style* required when dark thoughts come to a focus in dark deeds, and there is no room left for the play of those diffuse and piquant levities and elasticities of social life in the picturing of which he so much excels. George Vavasor vaguely contemplates getting rid of his grandfather, and very nearly succeeds in murdering John Grey, and in both cases the moody and savage state of mind of the sullen and ambitious man are admirably drawn, but as it comes to nothing in both cases, there is no occasion for any of that introverted intensity of tone which the picture of a great crime requires. George Vavasor, with that old scar on his face, which opens or closes according as he is angry or pleased with the course of events, with his cleverness, selfishness, and his capacity for conversation, his vehement ambition, his latent ferocity, his pride which makes the meanness of plundering Alice hateful to him, and his necessities, which nevertheless compel him to live on her without any sort of claim to do so, is a picture with far stronger lines and shadows than most of Mr. Trollope's heroes show. And never does Mr. Trollope paint him better than when he brings him, too, to the very edge of an abyss. . . . After giving us a character so powerfully drawn and so essentially dark in grain, it is almost a pity that Mr. Trollope should shrink from a province of his art which his tale almost goes out of its way to escape.

The less important characters in this novel are certainly not the least well executed. The fault of the vulgar group which centres in Mrs. Greenow is its very slender connection with the story itself, so that, like the side panels of some old-fashioned pictures, it seems to be connected mechanically only, and not naturally, with the subject of the principal painting. Mrs. Greenow and her two lovers are very amusing nevertheless, though it is not quite easy to account for so vulgar a person as the pretty widow belonging to the Vavasor family, of which all the other members are at least of good blood and good culture. As usual, however, with Mr. Trollope's novels the incidental humour shown in delineating cultivated society is the best, because it has more of the tone of irony, and because the stiff social decorums on which this humour is grafted enhances the absurdities so delicately observed. The Duchess of St. Bungay, Mrs. Conway Sparkes, Mrs. Marsham, Lady Midlothian, and above all Mr. Bott, the vulgar M.P. who tries to ingratiate himself with Mr. Palliser and rise with him to power, are the subjects for some of Mr. Trollope's most delicate humour. There is a self-restraint in these touches, and on the other hand a strong unrestrained appetite in the vulgarer fun, which makes the former far more really humorous than the latter. Taken as a whole, *Can You Forgive Her?* is certainly one of Mr. Trollope's best works, but its texture is more than usually loose and straggling; and its central point is far more faint and colourless than is the case in any of the group of tales with which it must be ranked.

92. Henry James, review, *Nation* (New York)

28 September 1865, i. 409–10

This new novel of Mr. Trollope's has nothing new to teach us either about Mr. Trollope himself as a novelist, about English society as a theme for the novelist, or, failing information on these points, about the complex human heart. Take any one of his former tales, change the names of half the characters, leave the others standing, and transpose the incidents, and you will have 'Can You Forgive Her?' It is neither better nor worse than the tale which you will select. It became long ago apparent that Mr. Trollope had only one manner. In this manner he very soon showed us his *maximum*. He has recently, in 'Miss Mackenzie,' showed us his *minimum*. In the work before us he has remained pretty constantly at his best. There is, indeed, a certain amount of that inconceivably vulgar love-making between middle-aged persons by which 'Miss Mackenzie' was distinguished; but the burden of the story rests upon the young people.

For so thick a book, there is certainly very little story. There are no less than three different plots, however, if the word can be applied to Mr. Trollope's simple machinations. That is, there is a leading story, which, being foreseen at the outset to be insufficient to protract the book during the requisite number of months, is padded with a couple of underplots, one of which comes almost near being pathetic, as the other falls very far short of being humorous. The main narrative, of course, concerns the settlement in life—it is hard to give it a more sentimental name—of a beautiful young lady. Alice Vavasor, well-born, high-spirited, motherless, and engaged to Mr. John Grey, the consummate model of a Christian gentleman, mistrusting the quality of her affection, breaks off her engagement, after which, in a moment of enthusiasm, she renews an anterior engagement with her cousin, George Vavasor, a plausible rascal. John Grey will not be put off, however, and steadfastly maintains his suit. In the course of time George's villany is discovered. He attempts, unsuccessfully, to murder Grey. Grey follows his mistress, pleads his cause once more, and is taken back again. The question is, Can we forgive Miss Vavasor? Of course we can, and forget her, too, for that matter. What does Mr. Trollope mean by this ques-

tion? It is a good instance of the superficial character of his work that
he has been asking it once a month for so long a time without being
struck by its flagrant impertinence. What are we to forgive? Alice
Vavasor's ultimate acceptance of John Grey makes her temporary ill-
treatment of him, viewed as a moral question, a subject for mere
drawing-room gossip. There are few of Mr. Trollope's readers who will
not resent being summoned to pass judgment on such a sin as the one
here presented, to establish by precedent the criminality of the conscientious flutterings of an excellent young lady. Charming women,
thanks to the talent of their biographers, have been forgiven much
greater improprieties. Since forgiveness was to be brought into the
question, why did not Mr. Trollope show us an error that we might
really forgive—an error that would move us to indignation? It is too
much to be called upon to take cognizance in novels of sins against
convention, of improprieties; we have enough of these in life. We can
have charity and pity only for real sin and real misery. We trust to
novels to maintain us in the practice of great indignations and great
generosities. Miss Vavasor's dilemma is doubtless considerable enough
in itself, but by the time it is completely unfolded by Mr. Trollope it
has become so trivial, it is associated with so much that is of a merely
accidental interest, it is so deflowered of the bloom of a serious experience, that when we are asked to enter into it judicially, we feel
almost tempted to say that really it is Miss Vavasor's own exclusive
business. From the moment that a novel comes to a happy conclusion,
we can forgive everything—or nothing. The gradual publication of
'Can You Forgive Her?'[1] made its readers familiar with the appeal
resting upon their judgment long before they were in a position to
judge. The only way, as it seems to us, to justify this appeal and to
obviate the flagrant anti-climax which the work now presents, was to
lead the story to a catastrophe, to leave the heroine *primâ facie* in the
wrong, to make her rupture with Grey, in a word, final. Then we might
have forgiven her in consideration of the lonely years of repentance in
store for her, and of her having been at any rate consistent. Then the
world's forgiveness would have been of some importance to her. Now,
at one for ever with her lover, what matters our opinion? It certainly
matters very little to ourselves.

Mr. Trollope's book presents no feature more remarkable than the
inveteracy with which he just eludes being really serious; unless it be

[1] It was published in twenty monthly parts at one shilling, from January 1864 to
August 1865.

the almost equal success with which he frequently escapes being really humorous. Both of these results are the penalty of writing so rapidly; but as in much rapid writing we are often made to regret the absence of that sober second thought which may curtail an extravagance—that critical movement which, if you will only give it time, is sure to follow the creative one—so in Mr. Trollope we perpetually miss that sustained action of the imagination, that creative movement which in those in whom this faculty is not supreme *may*, if you will give it time, bear out the natural or critical one, which would intensify and animate his first conception. We are for ever wishing that he would go a little further, a little deeper. There are a hundred places in 'Can You Forgive Her?' where even the dullest readers will be sure to express this wish. For ourselves, we were very much disappointed that when Alice returns to her cousin George she should not do so more frankly, that on eventually restoring herself to Grey she should have so little to expiate or to forget, that she should leave herself, in short, so easy an issue by her refusal to admit Vavasor to a lover's privilege. Our desire for a different course of action is simply founded on the fact that it would have been so much more interesting. When it is proposed to represent a young girl as jilting her lover in such a way as that the moral of the tale resolves itself into the question of the venality of her offence, it evinces in the novelist a deep insensibility to his opportunities that he should succeed, after all, in making of the tragedy but a simple postponement of the wedding-day.

To Mr. Trollope all the possible incidents of society seem to be of equal importance and of equal interest. He has the same treatment, the same tone, for them all. After narrating the minutest particulars of a certain phase of his heroine's experience he will dwell with equal length and great patience upon the proceedings of a vulgar widow (the heroine's aunt), who is engaged in playing fast and loose with a couple of vulgar suitors. With what authority can we invest the pen which treats of the lovely niece, when we see it devoted with the same good-will to the utterly prosaic and unlovely aunt? It is of course evident that Mr. Trollope has not intended to make the aunt either poetic or attractive. He has intended, in the first place, to swell his book into the prescribed dimensions, and, incidentally, to make the inserted matter amusing. A single chapter of it might be amusing; a dozen chapters are inexpressibly wearisome. The undue prominence assigned to this episode is yet not so signal an offence against good judgment as the subordination of Lady Glencora Palliser's story to that of Alice Vavasor's. It is a great mistake in speaking of a novel to be over-positive as to what ought to be and what ought not; but we do not fear to dogmatize when we say that by rights Lady Glencora is the heroine of the book. Her adventure is more important, more dramatic, more interesting than Alice Vavasor's. That it is more interesting is not a matter of opinion, but a matter of fact. A woman who forsakes her husband belongs more to the technical heroic than a woman who merely forsakes her lover. Lady Glencora, young and fascinating, torn from the man of her heart and married to a stranger, and pursued after marriage by her old lover, handsome, dissolute, desperate, touches at a hundred points almost upon the tragical. And yet her history gets itself told as best it may, in the intervals of what is after all, considering the *dénouement*, but a serious comedy. It is, to use a common illustration, as if Mr. Forrest should appear on the 'off-nights' of no matter what fainter dramatic luminary. It signifies little in the argument that Lady Glencora's adventure came also to an anticlimax; for in this case the reader rejects the conclusion as a mere begging of the issue. Of all literary sinners Mr. Trollope deserves fewest hard words, but we can scarcely refrain from calling this conclusion impudent. To a real novelist's eye, the story on which it depends is hardly begun; to Mr. Trollope, it is satisfactorily ended. The only explanation of all this is probably that the measure of his invention is not in his subject, in his understanding with his own mind; but outside of it, in his understanding with his publishers. Poor little Lady Glencora, with her prettiness, her grace, her colossal fortune, and her sorrows, is the one really poetic figure in the novel. Why not have dealt her a little poetic justice? Why not, for *her* sake, have shown a little boldness? We do not presume to prescribe to Mr. Trollope the particular thing he should have done; we simply affirm in general terms that he should have gone further. Everything forbade that Lady Glencora and her lover should be vulgarly disposed of. What are we to conclude? It is easy to conceive either that Burgo Fitzgerald slowly wasted his life, or that he flung it suddenly away. But the supposition is by no means easy that Lady Glencora either wasted hers or carefully economized it. Besides, there is no pretence of winding up Burgo Fitzgerald's thread; it is rudely clipped by the editorial shears. There is, on the contrary, a pretence of completing the destiny of his companion. But we have more respect for Lady Glencora's humanity than to suppose that the incident on which the curtain of her little tragedy falls, is for her anything more than an interruption. Another case in which Mr. Trollope had burdened himself, as he proceeded, with the obligation to go further, s that of George Vavasor. Upon him, as upon Lady Glencora, there hangs a faint reflection of poetry. In both these cases, Mr. Trollope, dealing with an unfamiliar substance, seems to have evoked a ghost which he cannot exorcise. As the reader follows George Vavasor deeper into his troubles—all of which are very well described—his excited imagination hankers for—what shall we say? Nothing less positive than Vavasor's death. Here was a chance for Mr. Trollope to redeem a thousand pages of small talk; the wretched man should have killed himself; for although bloodshed is not quite so common an element of modern life as the sensation writers would have us believe, yet people do occasionally, when hard pushed, commit suicide. But for Mr. Trollope anything is preferable to a sensation; an incident is ever preferable to an event. George Vavasor simply takes ship to America.

THE BELTON ESTATE

1866

Although Michael Sadleir, a half-century later, was to rank *The Belton Estate* among the very best of Trollope's novels, the author, from the vantage-point of the *Autobiography* (p. 163), agreed with the majority of his contemporary critics in placing the work among his poorer achievements:

It is similar in its attributes to *Rachel Ray* and to *Miss Mackenzie*. It is readable, and contains scenes which are true to life; but it has no peculiar merits, and will add nothing to my reputation as a novelist. I have not looked at it since it was published; and now turning back to it in my memory, I seem to remember almost less of it than of any book that I have written.

---

93. Henry James, review, *Nation* (New York)

4 January 1866, ii. 21–2

For James's later, much more favourable, opinion of Trollope, see No. 239.

Here, in the natural order of events, is a new novel by Mr. Trollope. This time it is Miss Clara Amedroz who is agitated by conflicting thoughts. Like most of Mr. Trollope's recent heroines, she is no longer in the first blush of youth; and her story, like most of Mr. Trollope's recent stories, is that of a woman standing irresolute between a better lover and a worse. She first rejects the better for the worse, and then rejects the worse for the better. This latter movement is final, and Captain Aylmer, like Crosbie, in 'The Small House at Allington,' has to put up with a red-nosed Lady Emily. The reader will surmise that we are not in 'The Belton Estate' introduced to very new ground. The book is, nevertheless, to our mind, more readable than many of its predecessors. It is comparatively short, and has the advantage of being a single story, unencumbered by any subordinate or co-ordinate plot. The interest of Mr. Trollope's main narrative is usually so far from being intense that repeated interruption on behalf of the actors charged with the more strictly humorous business is often very near proving altogether fatal. To become involved in one of his love stories is very like sinking into a gentle slumber; and it is well known that when you are aroused from your slumber to see something which your well-meaning intruder considers very entertaining, it is a difficult matter to woo it back again. In the tale before us we slumber on gently to the end. There is no heroine but Miss Clara Amedroz, and no heroes but her two suitors. The lady loves amiss, but discovers it in time, and invests her affections more safely. Such, in strictness, is the substance of the tale; but it is filled out as Mr. Trollope alone knows how to fill out the primitive meagreness of his dramatic skeletons. The three persons whom we have mentioned are each a character in a way, and their sayings and doings, their comings and goings, are registered to the letter and timed to the minute. They write a number of letters, which are duly transcribed; they make frequent railway journeys by the down-train from London; they have cups of tea in their bed-rooms; and they do, in short, in the novel very much as the reader is doing out of it. We do not make these remarks in a tone of complaint. Mr. Trollope has been long enough before the public to have enabled it to take his measure. We do not open his books with the expectation of being thrilled, or convinced, or deeply moved in any way, and, accordingly, when we find one to be as flat as a Dutch landscape, we remind ourselves that we have wittingly travelled into Holland, and that we have no right to abuse the scenery for being in character. We reflect, moreover, that there are a vast number of excellent Dutchmen for whom this low-lying horizon has infinite charms. If we are passionate and egotistical, we turn our back upon them for a nation of irreclaimable dullards; but if we are critical and disinterested, we endeavor to view the prospect from a Dutch stand-point.

Looking at 'The Belton Estate,' then, from Mr. Trollope's own point of view, it is a very pleasing tale. It contains not a word against nature. It relates, with great knowledge, humor, and grace of style, the history of the affections of a charming young lady. No unlawful devices are resorted to in order to interest us. People and things are painted as they stand. Miss Clara Amedroz is charming only as two-thirds of her sex are charming—by the sweetness of her face and figure, the propriety of her manners, and the amiability of her disposition. Represented thus, without perversion or exaggeration, she engages our sympathy as one whom we can understand, from having known a hundred women exactly like her. Will Belton, the lover whom she finally accepts, is still more vividly natural. Even the critic, who judges the book strictly from a reader's stand-point, must admit that Mr. Trollope has drawn few better figures than this, or even (what is more to the purpose) that, as a representation, he is an approach to ideal excellence. The author understands him well in the life, and the reader understands him well in the book. As soon as he begins to talk we begin to know and to like him, as we know and like such men in the flesh after half an hour of their society. It is true that for many of us half an hour of their society is sufficient, and that here Will Belton is kept before us for days and weeks. No better reason for this is needed than the presumption that the author does not tire of such men so rapidly as we: men healthy, hearty, and shrewd, but men, as we take the liberty of declaring, utterly without mind. Mr. Trollope is simply unable to depict a *mind* in any liberal sense of the word. He tried it in John Grey in 'Can You Forgive Her?' but most readers will agree that he failed to express very vividly this gentleman's scholarly intelligence. Will Belton is an enterprising young squire, with a head large enough for a hundred prejudices, but too small for a single opinion, and a heart competent—on the condition, however, as it seems to us, of considerable generous self-contraction on her part—to embrace Miss Amedroz.

The other lover, Captain Aylmer, is not as successful a figure as his rival, but he is yet a very fair likeness of a man who probably abounds in the ranks of that society from which Mr. Trollope recruits his characters, and who occurs, we venture to believe, in that society alone. Not that there are not in all the walks of life weak and passionless men who allow their mothers to bully their affianced wives, and who are utterly incompetent to entertain an idea. But in no other society than that to which Captain Aylmer belongs do such frigidity and such stupidity stand so little in the way of social success. They seem in his case, indeed, to be a passport to it. His prospects depend upon his being respectable, and his being respectable depends, apparently, on his being contemptible. We do not suppose, however, that Mr. Trollope likes him any better than we. In fact, Mr. Trollope never fails to betray his antipathy for mean people and mean actions. And antipathetic to his tastes as is Captain Aylmer's nature, it is the more creditable to him that he has described it so coolly, critically, and temperately. Mr. Trollope is never guilty of an excess in any direction, and the vice of his villain is of so mild a quality that it is powerless to prejudice him against his even milder virtues. These seem to us insufficient to account for Clara's passion, for we are bound to believe that for her it was a passion. As far as the reader sees, Captain Aylmer has done nothing to excite it and everything to quench it, and, indeed, we are quite taken by surprise when, after her aunt's death, she answers his proposal with so emphatic an affirmative. It is a pleasant surprise, however, to find any of Mr. Trollope's people doing a thing contrary to common sense. Nothing can be better—always from the Dutch point of view—than the management of the reaction in both parties against their engagement; but to base the rupture of a marriage engagement upon an indisposition on the part of the gentleman's mother that the lady shall maintain an acquaintance of long standing with another lady whose past history is discovered to offer a certain little vantage-point for scandal, is, even from the Dutch point of view, an unwarrantable piece of puerility. But the shabbiness of grand society—and especially the secret meannesses, parsimonies, and cruelties of the exemplary British matron—have as great an attraction for Mr. Trollope as they had for Thackeray; and the account of Clara's visit to the home of her intended, the description of the magnificent bullying of Lady Aylmer, and the picture of Miss Aylmer—'as ignorant, weak, and stupid a poor woman as you shall find anywhere in Europe'—make a sketch almost as relentless as the satire of 'Vanity Fair' or the 'Newcomes.' There are several other passages equally clever, notably the chapter in which Belton delivers up Miss Amedroz to her lover's care at the hotel in London; and in which, secure in his expression elsewhere of Belton's superiority to Aylmer, the author feels that he can afford to make him still more delicately natural than he has made him already by contrasting him, *pro tempore*, very disadvantageously with his rival, and causing him to lose his temper and make a fool of himself.

Such praise as this we may freely bestow on the work before us, because, qualified by the important stricture which we have kept in reserve, we feel that it will not seem excessive. Our great objection to 'The Belton Estate' is that, as we read it, we seemed to be reading a work written for children; a work prepared for minds unable to think; a work below the apprehension of the average man and woman, or, at the very most, on a level with it, and in no particular above it. 'The Belton Estate' is a *stupid* book; and in a much deeper sense than that of being simply dull, for a dull book is always a book that might have been lively. A dull book is a failure. Mr. Trollope's story is stupid and a success. It is essentially, organically, consistently stupid; stupid in direct proportion to its strength. It is without a single idea. It is utterly incompetent to the primary functions of a book, of whatever nature, namely—to suggest thought. In a certain way, indeed, it suggests thought; but this is only on the ruins of its own existence as a book. It acts as the occasion, not as the cause, of thought. It indicates the manner in which a novel should *not*, on any account, be written. That it should deal exclusively with dull, flat, commonplace people was to be expected; and this need not be a fault; but it deals with such people as one of themselves; and this is what Lady Aylmer would call a 'damning' fault. Mr. Trollope is a good observer; but he is literally nothing else. He is apparently as incapable of disengaging an idea as of drawing an inference. All his incidents are, if we may so express it, *empirical*. He has seen and heard every act and every speech that appears in his pages. That minds like his should exist, and exist in plenty, is neither to be wondered at nor to be deplored; but that such a mind as his should devote itself to writing novels, and that these novels should be successful, appears to us an extraordinary fact.

Mr. Trollope accustoms us to so high a standard of liveliness in his stories, that we are a little disappointed at the tameness of the *Belton Estate*. We do not remember any of his books in which the design was better, or the outlines of character more perfectly drawn, but there is not the usual amount of fixed air in the dialogue,—it does not bubble with humour and secondary points as Mr. Trollope's dialogue usually does. It keeps to the matter in hand, and discusses it very much as the people sketched would have discussed it in their ordinary moods. Now Mr. Trollope usually contrives to present us with his *dramatis personæ* if not in their best moods, yet in moods rendered more entertaining than usual to the spectator by the pressure of events. Lady Alexandrina de Courcy and Mr. Crosbie are not remarkable persons, but Lady Alexandrina cross-examining Mr. Crosbie about Lily, or discussing the new carpets with her sister in the upholsterer's shop, and Mr. Crosbie treated by the Countess as quite one of the family, and therefore privileged to run errands for her, or 'grunting again and escaping into another corner' when pursued by his brother-in-law, Mr. Mortimer Gazebee, the solicitor, at the Countess's party, are very entertaining persons indeed. The pressure of the social atmosphere under which they live and move makes them, if not amusing themselves, causes of amusement to others. Now this is not quite true of the *Belton Estate*. The characters are all admirably (though some of them incompletely) drawn,—but they are nearly as tame as the persons in English country life usually are. There are scarcely figures *enough* to bring out Mr. Trollope's special talent. The mutual influence of different social groups on each other is a department of his work in which he always excels. In this tale there is no room for any such influence. There is no variety of drawing-room life to speak of, no social finesse to paint. The consequence is that while all the figures strike you as real and some as powerfully drawn, there is a certain disappointment in the result. There is a feeling that they ought to interest us more deeply than they do, that they have all been a little out of spirits, and that yet their having been thus out of spirits has not been turned quite to the account to which this author usually turns it. Usually the want of spirits in his puppets would have been made to contribute to the spirits of his puppets' audience. In this case it is not so.

Perhaps the best figure in the book,—and yet the incompletest,—is Captain Aylmer, the cold, slow lover, who is half alarmed by being accepted, is inclined to think himself in a scrape, and never really wishes to marry the heroine again, till she has ceased to wish to marry him, and he knows it. His considerate but pallid regard, his half-and-halfness of all kinds, his faint obstinacy, his half disposition to take into account both his father's and his mother's advice, and his half disposition to reject it, his regard for the decencies of life, and his inability to get warm about anything, his dismay at finding a lady genuinely in love with him whom he had liked only just doubtfully enough to make her a hesitating proposal, all seem to us admirable. But what we want to see, and what we are only *told*, not made to see, is why a bright and clever woman like Clara Amedroz was first fascinated by Captain Aylmer. But Mr. Trollope, though he was bound to make us see why Clara had liked her tame lover so much, never does let us see the literary, sentimental, and mildly intellectual qualities he attributes to him. He is never made even 'soft in his manners, approaching nearly to the incipient tenderness of love-making.' There is nothing sentimental about him,—nothing like a love for reading Dante with young ladies, nothing in his demeanour to warrant Clara's feeling. Now whatever reaction his mind might have undergone under the chilling certainty that he had shut himself off from escape,—and we well appreciate the skill with which Mr. Trollope has drawn his disposition always to keep at the junction of two alternative courses, and not commit himself to either,—it is scarcely likely that the sentimental tenderness which he felt before his engagement should have deserted him so completely afterwards, as to leave no trace whatever of the man with whom Clara fell in love. Mr. Trollope scarcely does justice to his more energetic hero in delineating Will Belton's triumph over so very unengaging a rival as he has depicted here. While we think Captain Aylmer one of Mr. Trollope's most original, and, in *part*, best executed conceptions, we think he has failed, more than is at all usual with him, in so entirely suppressing the (to young ladies) attractive side of his pallid character, and *therefore* suppressing all occasion for real mental struggle in the mind of his heroine. There should have been Dante readings, and slight, pale flirtations, broken in upon by the misunderstandings inevitable between so ill-matched a couple, *after* the engagement, in order to carry out the artistic conception of the author.

Will Belton is a conception needing less delicate touches than Captain Aylmer, and is admirably sustained throughout. Mr. Trollope, as usual, shows himself quite alive to the value of those little outlying traits of character which enhance so infinitely the effect of the main drawing. The rough eagerness, impatience, and directness of all Mr. William Belton's impulses are the main features of his character, and almost any other novelist would have been content with ringing the changes on the effects which these characteristics suggest. But Mr. Trollope knows better. He draws also the great want of self-consciousness, or rather of self-recollection, which a man of this class is sure to display as to the former outbursts of passionate impulses once subsided,—the complete oblivion which is apt to descend upon him as to his former feelings towards obstacles since surmounted. . . .

The people of Aylmer Park and the Askertons are all well sketched, but even more slightly than is usual with Mr. Trollope. The heroine is good, but scarcely very interesting. She strikes us as a considerable improvement on the undecided young lady in *Can You Forgive Her?* the reasons and motives of her undecidedness being clearer, and the inward struggle more distinctly drawn. No doubt the type of character is different; Clara Amedroz is meant to have less of softness, less of natural morbidness, more of decision and frankness than Alice Vavasour, and therefore perhaps she is better drawn. Her difficulties are not so much of her own making, more made for her by unfortunate circumstances. She is in love with the wrong man before she sees the right man, and has to disentangle herself from a superficial and feeble sentiment in order to give herself to her natural master. And this she does with considerable energy and ability. Mr. Trollope is much more successful in drawing the feminine complexities of feeling which arise out of *circumstantial* embarrassments, than those which rise like a mist from a nature too inward and brooding for perfect health.

95. Unsigned notice, *Athenaeum*

3 February 1866, p. 166

The plot of 'The Belton Estate' turns, as so many of Mr. Trollope's plots turn, on the love of two men for the same woman, and on the way in which the characters of the two men are contrasted. This time there is a more pointed contrast than usual, as no two men could be further apart from each other than Will Belton and Capt. Aylmer. And the two men join issue very strongly in the scene at the Great Northern Hotel. The colourless politeness of Capt. Aylmer and the broad vigour of Will Belton make up a scene that is more than usually dramatic. But in working up this scene so vigorously, Mr. Trollope has gone a little too far. We agree with Capt. Aylmer in reprobating the swagger of Will Belton; but we do not understand how any nineteenth-century young lady could let her admiration of outspoken frankness predominate over natural, womanly instinct. Surely no young lady could either wish to be brawled for at an hotel dinner-table, or pardon an unsuccessful lover for parading his misfortune before his successful rival. Yet Mr. Trollope makes this scene the turning-point in the fortunes of his hero. It is his object to show us rude nature vanquishing tame conventionalism; but rude nature appears to some disadvantage when it can do nothing more than swagger. In the early days, when such defiance in word would have been succeeded by a combat *à l'outrance*, Will Belton would have been our own, as well as the lady's, hero. But when we have only the defiance, and the deeds of chivalry are confined to breaking a wine-glass, we are too sensible of the discrepancy.

The story drags during most of the first volume, and the verdict of periodical readers[1] was, we believe, unfavourable. But we have a decided improvement in the second volume, and there are detached scenes in 'The Belton Estate' which rise above Mr. Trollope's ordinary level.

[1] The novel had been published serially in the *Fortnightly Review*, 15 May 1865 to 1 January 1866.

96. Unsigned notice, *Saturday Review*

3 February 1866, xxi. 140–2

From a long, disparaging review detailing Trollope's sins in repeating situations from novel to novel.

The world is made up of commonplace, and it is his principle to stand by what is real, leaving the airy paths of imagination to be trodden by those superfine romancers for whom this world is not good enough. Still, admirable as the principle of realism in art may be, it is well worth considering whether there is not such a thing as a realism that is sordid and pitiful. Mr. Rubb, with his hands in staring yellow gloves, and his hair dripping with coarse bear's-grease, and his mind overburdened with an insolvent oil-cloth business, was a thoroughly well-drawn character. But what is gained by the careful portraiture of the meanest and most sordid set of human traits? Mr. Trollope may say that such things are, and that therefore they are the fit subjects of art. If a sculptor or a painter were to present us with one of these vulgar, smug, dull-eyed wretches, drawn exactly from the life as Mr. Trollope draws them, without so much as a hair of the creature's head idealized, people would see through the grossness of the fallacy. It is because readers and critics so seldom look upon prose fiction as a great art, with its own canons, that these photographs of what is meanest in life, without beauty or grace, without idea, without the faintest shade of significance, are allowed to pass muster. One cannot image anything much more pitiful than the last two pages of the *Belton Estate*. The hero and heroine have retired to rest, after entertaining Captain Aylmer, the defeated rival, and his bride. Clara, having secured Will Belton, might have been expected to display a decent magnanimity towards the lady who had taken the gentleman she had herself cast off. Mr. Trollope takes a different view. His heroine is an ordinary mortal, so she at once insists with her lord that Captain Aylmer's wife has a red nose. 'Don't you think she is very plain?' she continues. Then comes the unfortunate guest's age. 'If she's not over forty, I'll consent to change noses with her.' Another word or two of equal grace and delicacy, and then the climax. 'Will Belton was never good for much conversation at this hour, and was too fast asleep to make any rejoinder.' The heroine protesting that her old lover's wife is plain and over forty and has a horrid red nose, and the hero meanwhile turning his gigantic back and snoring—there we leave them. O sublime picture! This is what a crude half-considered notion of realism comes to.

97. Unsigned notice, *London Review*

3 March 1866, xii. 260

It is time . . . that Mr. Trollope should forbear from leading us through the same familiar scenes. We have followed him with docility, and not without much gratitude; but we begin at last to long for fresh fields and new pastures. A lady who cannot make up her mind whether to refuse a man or no, or whether, having accepted him, she shall keep her word and be miserable, or get rid of her promise and her troubles together, is an object worthy of all sympathy; but we cannot be constantly regarding her. Miss Mackenzie occupied a conspicuous position in that capacity; the heroine of 'Can You Forgive Her?' still more powerfully appealed to our feelings for a lady in deliberation; and now Miss Clara Amedroz comes forward to play the part with which her predecessors have rendered us so familiar. . . . But, whatever may be the faults of the story, Mr. Trollope has, as usual, contrived to make it interesting. No one can read his book without great pleasure, and, when that is the case, it seems ungrateful to criticize it severely. There are parts of it, also, which are worthy of all praise, as, for instance, the description of the dreary decorum of Aylmer Park, and the dull, colourless life led by its inmates. Lady Aylmer is an excellent sketch, and the chapters describing the contest between her and Miss Amedroz are among the best in the book.

NINA BALATKA

1867

For a more detailed account of Trollope's curious experiment in anony-mous publication at the height of his career, see Introduction, VI. Both *Nina Balatka* and *Linda Tressel* appeared as serials in *Blackwood's Magazine* (July 1866 to January 1867, and October 1867 to May 1868), and both were subsequently issued by Blackwood in two-volume form, without benefit of Trollope's name, as Trollope had stipulated.

98. Unsigned notice, *Athenaeum*

2 March 1867, p. 288

Nothing can be simpler than the invention of the story, which tells how a Christian girl of Prague, with an impoverished father and a rich, insolent aunt, fell in love with an opulent and respected Israelite, and so passionately that no prohibition nor contempt could shake her heart loose from its moorings. Anton Trendellsohn, her lover, was as devoted as herself, but not without his share of trials on the part of his family and friends, who could ill bear the thoughts of his separating himself from them to waste love on a Christian girl. The conflict of these sympathies and antipathies, involving little or no episode, and few subordinate characters, make up the story, which is told so clearly and tersely, and with so much real feeling, as to retain the reader to the last. . . .

To every thoughtful, not vacant, reader of novels,—to those especi-ally to whom the study of character is more interesting than the entanglements and extrications of a complicated and unnatural plot,—'Nina Balatka' may be safely commended.

99. Unsigned notice, *London Review*

2 March 1867, xiv. 266–7

The reviewer devotes two full columns to a redaction of the narrative and quotations from the novel.

One of the most charming stories we have read for a long time is 'Nina Balatka.' It is simple, interesting, and short—excellences not often to be met with in novels nowadays. Nina is a Christian, and the daughter of a Christian. The scene is cast in Prague; and in Prague the prejudice against the Jews not very long since was about on a par with the hatred evinced towards them by the Spaniards of the Inquisition era. Certain connections of Nina naturally contemplate her devotion to her Hebraic lover with profound disgust, and seek to oppose the marriage with the virulence that only unjust prejudice can inspire. . . . In the character of Anton Trendellsohn, the author seeks to vindicate the Hebrew from the numerous extravagant charges brought against him by those who endeavour to sanction their prejudices by appeals to that faith whose holiest precept is 'Love one another.' . . . Not that Anton is by any means one of those 'faultless monsters which the world ne'er saw,' so often set up by novelists as illustrations to support the dogmas of their fiction. He is a human being, neither very good nor very bad; possessed of middle qualities that neither exalt nor degrade—that neither awaken admiration nor excite contempt. . . . [The] characteristics of his disposition . . . not only furnish us with a just and clever type of the Hebrew nature, but render also apparent the author's knowledge of the human heart.

100. Unsigned review, *Spectator*

23 March 1867, xi. 329–30

Trollope was positive that this review was written by Richard Holt Hutton, his 'most observant, and generally . . . most eulogistic' critic (see Introduction, VI).

If criticism be not a delusion from the very bottom, this pleasant little story is written by Mr. Anthony Trollope. We have no external evidence for saying so, and there is the presumption against it that Mr. Trollope's name is worth a great deal in mere money value to the sale of any book. Still, no one who knows his style at all can read three pages of this tale without detecting him as plainly as if he were present in the flesh. Indeed, the present writer has applied what the scientific men call the best test of scientific knowledge,—the power of *prediction* given by the hypothesis that *Nina Balatka* is written by Mr. Trollope. The critic said to himself, 'if it is written by Mr. Trollope, I shall soon meet with the phrase, "made his way," as applied to walking where there is no physical difficulty or embarrassment, but only a certain moral hesitation as to the end and aim of the walking in question,' and behold within a page of the point at which the silent remark was made, came the very phrase in the peculiar sense indicated. And of such test-phrases we could indicate a dozen or so which, as far as we know, are found in Mr. Anthony Trollope's stories, and in those alone.

We do not know why the eminent novelist in question should have been unwilling to give his name to this little tale. It contains, to be sure, none of his English store of experience of society, and not much even of the social *nuances* of the country he describes; and its strong point is not Mr. Trollope's strongest point, namely, manners subtly described with a flavour of satirical humour; but for all that, and perhaps in consequence of the absence of this illimitable subject on which he refines so skilfully, there is a force in the main idea of the tale, and a grace in the picturesque framework of Prague scenery and customs, which adequately supply the place of the author's usual skill in tracing the refinements of English social habits. Most eminent novelists have felt, we suppose, at some time or other in their lives, a strong fascination in the subject which Sir Walter Scott took as the basis of his story in *Ivanhoe*, the struggle between love and that feeling, half of caste contempt, half of religious horror, which used to exist in old times between the Christians and the Jews. The intensity of Jewish pride in the midst of national humiliation has always given a grandeur to figures such as Scott's Rebecca, and where this is tempered by struggle with a passion for one of the oppressors' race, you have all the highest conditions of true romance without any unreality. Our author, with a true feeling for his own characteristic power, though he has taken the same general subject for his story, has taken it in its most modern shape, making Prague, where the old distinction between Jew and Christian still lingers in very much of its old intensity, the scene of his story, and showing us both the Jewish and the Christian feeling of alienation in its paralysis and decadence, fallen from its old persecuting fervour and its religious fanaticism, to mere social prejudice and religious *scruple*. He has so far varied the tale, too, as to make a Christian girl (a Bohemian) fall in love with a Jewish merchant and money-lender of Prague, with whom her father has business, and so interfere with the hopes of the Jewess—our author's Rebecca—to whom the fathers of both had intended that he should engage himself. The scene in which Rebecca Loth, the Jewess, appeals to Nina Balatka, the Bohemian (and Christian), heroine of the story, not to sacrifice her lover's position among the Jews of Prague, by persisting in an enagagement which must deprive Anton Trendellsohn of the confidence and regard of his own people, is one of great force and not a little pathos. Rebecca's pride and boldness and resolute defiance of all the motives for glossing over the truth, the unshrinking way in which she avows her own recent and scarcely extinguished hopes of marrying Anton Trendellsohn, the graphic minuteness of phrase with which at the same time she declares her knowledge of his profound passion for the girl with whom she is conversing, the complete absence of reserves even in language, the full, bold eye, as it were, which she fixes on delicacies of sentiment which any other girl would pass over with an allusion, are all made so as to bring out the Jewess, and the contrast between the Jewess and the Bohemian girl, with remarkable power. . . .

This contrast between Rebecca Loth and Nina Balatka, and the sketches of their mutual relations with each other, is the finest thing in the story, and, no doubt, the artistic object for which the story was written.

101. Unsigned notice, *Examiner*

11 May 1867, pp. 293–4

A long review made up chiefly of extensive quotations from the novel.

'Nina Balatka was a maiden of Prague, born of Christian parents, and herself a Christian; but she loved a Jew.' That is the first sentence of this novel, and the whole novel is a very simple and very charming history of the maiden's love, and the troubles into which it brought her, and through which it bore her. It is a love-story and nothing more; but, if we are tired of love-stories, we shall find the book delightful reading by reason of its lively pourtrayal of the ways of life, half mediæval and half oriental in the quaint old capital of Bohemia; and, if we want 'a novel with a purpose,' we shall find in it a very trenchant argument against the hundred-headed prejudice which would raise up barriers between the members of different religions, or different nationalities, or different social classes, instead of seeing bonds of universal sympathy and kindliness in the common virtues of our common nature.

LINDA TRESSEL

1868

['By the Author of "Nina Balatka" ' printed on the title page.]

102. Unsigned review, *Spectator*

9 May 1868, xli. 562–63

The author of *Nina Balatka*—and of not a few other works, we imagine, which are still greater favourites with the English public—has never written any study more striking,—or indeed anything that suggests so strongly the term of 'a study,'—as this vivid and minutely executed tale. The scene is laid in Nuremberg, but we do not know that there is any absolute reason why the main circumstances of the story should not have been laid in England, except that perhaps Englishwomen of the present day are a little in advance of young Bavarian women in their independence of action, and the liberty which they assume to judge for themselves as to what religious principle may require of them in the way of submission to their natural guardians with respect to marriage. The author's idea in *Linda Tressel* has been to work out, in the case of Madame Staubach, a really good woman of severe Calvinistic principles,—on the one hand, how terrible and powerful an engine for the torture both of others and herself, a stern Calvinistic creed, acting upon some arbitrary notion that God's will for the mortification of another's spirit is visible to her, may prove; and on the other hand, how illogically and imperceptibly this creed in the true religious woman will accommodate itself to her respect for the superiority of *men*, so as to except them from the law of mortification which she tries to impose upon even those whom she best loves among women. Thus much as regards the picture of the misery-inflicter. In Linda Tressel herself (Madame Staubach's niece) the author has still more carefully studied to draw the nature most susceptible of suffering from torture of this kind. Hers is a loving and grateful heart, full of real affection for her Calvinistic aunt, Madame Staubach, and yet not passive or gentle enough to yield her fate to the will of any other on a matter on which her own heart speaks strongly. She has neither independence enough to assert herelf so as to make her aunt feel her power, nor flexibility enough to be moulded by her into what the latter chooses. Linda Tressel has in her enough depth of tenderness to be simply *unable* to yield herself when her heart loudly asserts that the marriage proposed to her would be utterly shocking. . . .

What has made our author take Nuremberg as the scene of this story of tyrannical religious narrowness? There is something perhaps in the steady Protestantism of a place all of whose churches and other art monuments seem to speak the language of Catholicism—something of a conspicuousness in the Puritanic transformation of the interior religious life where the exterior thereof remains exactly what it was in the old Catholic days,—which suggests a conflict between Puritanic feelings and the instincts of easy, popular life. In a place such as Nuremberg, where the shell is the shell of the fifteenth century, and the kernel of religion in that shell is altogether modern, it no doubt may seem more natural to call up Protestantism to the bar, and ask whether it, too, does not often sin against nature with as much gravity as Catholicism did at the time it lost so much of its old ground and ascendancy. To arraign the bigotry of Protestantism where Protestantism is enjoying the fruits of another religion's labours, seems in some respects more natural, and perhaps more generous, than to arraign it in a locale where it has itself created all that it possesses. The quaint picturesque beauty of Nuremberg gives a certain charm to the tale, but it is not used as much, or with as much effect, as is the grandeur of Prague in *Nina Balatka*. Still, of the two stories, both of them hinging on certain kinds of religious persecution, this is, we think, on the whole, the more powerful.

103. Unsigned notice, *British Quarterly Review*
July 1868, xlviii. 281

Nina Balatka' was coloured through and through with Bohemian life and character. Written with great cleverness and power, it was chiefly remarkable for its delineation of the quaint, romantic old city of Prague, and of the many coloured archaic life that fills it. Those who had read it looked with interest for another story from the same pen. The scene of Linda Tressel' is the city of Nuremberg, almost as quaint, and, in its way, as unique as Prague. The spirit of the place is less vivid and pervading than in the former story; and there is a more restricted delineation of its forms of life, Linda, her aunt, Madame Staubach, and Peter Steinmarc being the only full length portraits in it. These are admirably drawn,—Madame Staubach with her strong Calvinistic Protestantism, not without conscience and kindness, but ready to sacrifice her niece for the discipline of her soul; and Peter Steinmarc, a mature man of fifty, neither religious nor refined, whom she seeks to force poor Linda to marry.

The development of the story turns entirely upon the coercion put upon Linda to induce her to accept Peter. We get very impatient with it. No sane woman who was not wicked would, in real life, act as Aunt Staubach acted; and no man who was not an utter knave would be such an ass as Peter was. The story is written with great ability; but so improbable and melancholy that it cannot be read with pleasure.

THE CLAVERINGS

1867

Reviewers of 1867 granted *The Claverings* unusual merit for its them
and its plotting, but were less willing to guarantee the reader any grea
rewards in entertainment. Trollope himself (*Autobiography*, pp. 164–5
felt that *The Claverings* was one of his good novels, though it had no
taken hold with the public.

In *The Claverings* I did not follow the habit which had now become very com
mon to me, of introducing personages whose names are already known to th
readers of novels, and whose characters were familiar to myself. If I remembe
rightly, no one appears here who had appeared before or who has been allowe
to appear since. I consider the story as a whole to be good, though I am no
aware that the public has ever corroborated that verdict. The chief characte
is that of a young woman who has married manifestly for money and rank,—s
manifestly that she does not herself pretend, even while she is making the mar
riage, that she has any other reason. The man is old, disreputable, and a worn
out debauchee. Then comes the punishment natural to the offence. When she i
free, the man whom she had loved, and who had loved her, is engaged to anothe
woman. He vacillates and is weak,—in which weakness is the fault of the book
as he plays the part of hero. But she is strong—strong in her purpose, strong i
her desires, and strong in her consciousness that the punishment which come
upon her has been deserved.

　But the chief merit of *The Claverings* is in the genuine fun of some of th
scenes. Humour has not been my forte, but I am inclined to think that the charac
ters of Captain Boodle, Archie Clavering, and Sophie Gordeloup are humorou
Count Pateroff, the brother of Sophie, is also good, and disposes of the youn
hero's interference in a somewhat masterly manner. In *The Claverings*, too, ther
is a wife whose husband is a brute to her, who loses an only child—his heir—
and who is rebuked by her lord because the boy dies. Her sorrow is, I think
pathetic. From beginning to end the story is well told. But I doubt now whethe
any one reads *The Claverings*.

104. Unsigned notice, *Spectator*

4 May 1867, xl. 498–9

The art of *The Claverings* strikes us as of a very high class. There are far fewer unconnected side-pictures than is usual in Mr. Trollope's novels. Indeed, almost every side-picture is calculated to heighten the effect of the principal subject of the story. Harry Clavering's rather weak openness to the influence of any attractive woman with whom he is much thrown, is brought out in strong relief against the ungainly curate's (Mr. Saul's) manly dignity and intensity of purpose. Mr. Trollope has contrasted his rather soft, though in relation to all but feminine affairs perfectly manly, hero, with one who in many respects seems but half a man, and yet is, in relation to the dignity, depth, and constancy of his affection, immeasurably Harry Clavering's superior; and the effect of the contrast is a new force both in the mere vividness of the picture and in the clearness and truthfulness of Mr. Trollope's moral. . . .

We fear that few readers will fail to find that, on the whole, there is more that is fascinating in Lady Ongar, in spite of her great, her unwomanly sin in marrying such a man as Lord Ongar for rank and money, than in Florence Burton;—a larger nature at least, capable of great sin and great magnanimity also. But in spite of this, Mr. Trollope draws with a sincerity that never fails him the true and natural punishment of her sin,—first of all, and perhaps deepest of all, the disappearance of that true delicacy which could scarcely survive so deliberate a sale of herself as Julia Brabazon's; then, as its external penalty, the gathering of mean intrigues and meaner intriguers round her, the dirty and rapacious little harpy, Sophie Gordeloup, the selfish and able Count Pateroff, the foolish good-for-nothing Archie Clavering. Archie Clavering's counsellor in his aspirations after Lady Ongar's fortune, Captain Boodle, is a picture of the highest humour and skill, and yet it is not in any sense a diversion from the main object of the story, as so many of Mr. Trollope's cleverest sketches in other tales have been. Many will read the coarse humour of the chapter, "Let her know that you're there," as if it were merely coarse humour, but in truth the coarse humour contains the highest moral in the story, showing, as it does, how just a retribution women who act as Julia Brabazon acted,

bring on themselves, by being made the subject of such coarse speculation. . . .

The Claverings has, as we believe, a higher moral, and a more perfect
artistic unity of the kind we have indicated, than any of Mr. Trollope's
previous tales. There is scarcely a touch in it which does not contribute
to the main effect, both artistic and moral, of the story, and not a character introduced, however slightly sketched, which does not produce its
own unique and specific effect on the reader's imagination.

11 May 1867, xiv. 547

Novelists are often apt to maltreat the puppets they create, but it is generally towards their bad characters only that they manifest an ill feeling. We do not remember ever to have met with a story in which the writer showed a thorough contempt for his hero and heroine, until we read 'The Claverings.' From the first to last Mr. Trollope takes little trouble to conceal from his readers the very poor opinion he has formed of the principal personages of his drama. He deliberately makes Harry Clavering misbehave himself, and then cynically girds at him from the heights of his philosophy; he paints Florence Burton in by no means flattering colours, and then sneers openly at the spectacle she presents. By way of moral to his fable, he seems to exclaim, 'What fools these men and women be!' and when he dismisses his actors from the stage, he lets the spectator know how little value he attaches to their personal character. In all this he may be right, but if so, we are inclined to hope that he will be wrong next time. A reader is apt to lose his interest in the fortunes of people whom even the author of their being despises, and he will feel inclined, after some time spent in their companionship, to turn aside to creations which may be less striking as works of art, but which are more capable of satisfying his cravings for the heroic and the ideal.

There is only one character in the whole book in whom we are really able to feel an interest. Lady Ongar is a very charming woman in spite of the mistake she makes in the early part of the history. She leaves the poor man she loves in order to marry the rich man she loathes. Brought up in a worldly school she mistrusts her own capacity for enjoying a simple life, and she acts according to the dictates of a cynicism which she fancies is natural to her, but which is in reality opposed to the whole current of her feelings. She commits a grave error, and she is severely punished. The wretched old *roué* whom she marries makes her life a burden to her, till at last death rids her of his hated companionship. She finds herself a rich widow, still young, and more beautiful than ever. At length the time has come, she fancies, when a little sunshine will be allowed to fall upon her path. It delights her to think that she can now enrich the Harry Clavering who had loved her so fondly in the days of old, and whom she had deserted although she loved him so well. All the better part of her nature makes itself felt under the influence of good fortune's genial warmth. Noble aspirations, generous sentiments, stir once more within the heart, which in the days of the past had seemed doomed to be crusted over with selfish indifference.

All her thoughts go forth to meet the hero of her earlier years, whom she now prepares to welcome back to his old place in her affections. But, in the meantime, Harry Clavering, who is one of the most insipid, well-intentioned, and weak-willed young exquisites who ever parted their hair in the middle, and didn't know their own minds, has consoled himself by falling in love with a girl of the most common-place order. Florence Burton is very good, and sweet, and well-behaved; she is naturally incapable of doing anything wrong, and has been admirably brought up; she has a genius for house-keeping, and she adores Harry Clavering. He recognizes her devotion, and, feeling himself lonely and dispirited after the loss of his first love, he takes her into the vacant place in his impressionable heart, and becomes formally engaged to her. For a time the incense which she is ever burning before his image is very grateful to him; but then Lady Ongar unexpectedly returns, and a cloud is interposed between the humble worshipper and the fickle deity. The old love re-asserts its rights, the power of the new one wanes away. The hero finds himself in a painful position between the two heroines, and, being of a feeble character, he is utterly at a loss how to extricate himself from it. Different influences draw him in opposite directions. He makes no effort to settle the question of his course, but leaves the whole matter to fate. On the one side there is Lady Ongar, whom he loves, beautiful, noble, majestic, and wealthy. On the other there is Florence Burton, whom he likes and pities, but whose prettiness is not enhanced by any other attractions than those which her virtues lend to her, and whose brother wears thick boots, and dusts them with his handkerchief.

Eventually the rich and noble lady resigns him to her lowly rival, and retires into obscurity, there to sorrow over his loss. Harry Clavering becomes heir to a large property, and the possessor of perfect bliss, and Mr. Trollope dismisses him with an undisguised sneer at his effeteness, and at the folly of the women who insisted upon regarding him in the light of a divinity. His character, although unsatisfactory, is admirably sketched, and the description of his constant vacillations is excellently managed. But by far the most powerful chapters in the book are those in which Lady Ongar's feelings are analysed, after the death of her husband, when she is attempting to get some satisfaction out of the money and lands for which she had sold herself. There is great vigour and real pathos in the account of her utter loneliness, and of the total failure of all her plans to obtain enjoyment, or even to do good.

The conversations throughout the story have the charm which Mr. Trollope knows so well how to impart to dialogue, and almost every scene has about it the air of reality and truthfulness with which he has such a wonderful power of investing all that he creates. The story of Fanny Clavering's love for Mr. Saul, the awkward curate, commencing with a contemptuous indifference, and terminating in a grave and almost solemn devotion, is capitally worked up; and a number of minor incidents are described, and a variety of subordinate characters are portrayed, with Mr. Trollope's usual ease and animation. Count Pateroff forms the subject of a very clever sketch, and so does his sister, the Russian spy, though she seems somewhat caricatured. On the whole, the story is certainly amusing and interesting; and, although it forms by no means one of the best of Mr. Trollope's works, it is well worthy of being read with attention.

106. Unsigned notice, *Saturday Review*

18 May 1867, xxiii. 638–9

People often complain that they cannot find out why it is that they like Mr. Trollope's novels so much, and are able to read so many of them without being bored. There is never very much movement in his stories. One is not excited by a violent plot, nor thrown into a pleasant meditative mood by light and subtle strokes of thought, nor strung up to an almost religious pitch of fervour by profound conceptions of human destiny and the diverse products of human effort. Perhaps there are two reasons which help to explain one's liking for Mr. Trollope's books. First, his pictures of life and manners and average human nature are exceedingly truthful, so far as they go. The author reproduces the world very much in those aspects which it wears in the eyes of most of us. It is a world where men and women play lightly at cross-purposes with one another about love and money, about sentiment and loaves and fishes; where on the whole, and in the long run, there is a very decently fair distribution of small worries and small bits of happiness; and where anybody who plays his cards as he ought to do can make sure of a competence of cash and a comfortable wife and a thoroughly respectable position before his fellows. In the second place, Mr. Trollope always writes in earnest. He never treats his people as if they were mere puppets, nor his incidents as if they were mere dreams. They are a reality in his own mind while he writes about them; he honestly feels for them as if they were actual neighbours in the flesh; and hence he talks of love-making without any levity, and of little meannesses and small ambitions in the matter of money without any sneering or snarling. The world of smallest things is still a serious place to Mr. Trollope. The tragic side is hidden from him, and the merely funny side he does not care to dwell upon. This simple earnestness, this plain sincerity of thought and vision, has a charm of its own which, added to the verisimilitude of his creations, is what lies at the bottom of the pleasure he gives us.

One of the most conspicuous of his characteristics is his strong belief in the general justice of things. He has a wonderful faith in respectability, and he would think ill of himself if he should write anything to make one suppose that iniquity is ever triumphant. This may be another reason why his stories are so pleasant. It is a comfort to believe that our suspicions as to the cruelty and injustice stalking around us are, after all, without foundation. In the *Claverings* this presence of the respectable god of social justice is perhaps more remarkable than in any previous book from the same hand. Everything turns out just as our belief in the general comfort of the universe requires that it should do. The heroine, one of the most charming women that even Mr. Trollope has ever drawn, in a very wicked manner marries a debauched peer for the sake of his money and his title, although she is in love all the time with a more interesting commoner, who, like the majority of interesting commoners, has only a very inadequate income. She never disguises her motives for a moment, either from herself or her lover. 'Our ages by the register,' she tells him, 'are the same, but I am ten years older than you by the world. I have two hundred a year, and I owe at this moment six hundred pounds. You have perhaps double as much, and would lose half of that if you married. . . . Now Lord Ongar has—heaven knows what—perhaps sixty thousand a year.' This is an example of Mr. Trollope's close reproduction of the actual way of the world. A novelist of the sentimental stamp would have made his heroine the heart-broken victim of cruel and rapacious parents, and very likely we should have been dreadfully moved by the young woman's sorrows. But then our emotion would have been fundamentally artificial; we should have felt that in ninety-nine cases out of a hundred parents do not drive their daughters into heart-breaking matches, and then we should have been ashamed of ourselves for being accessible to such sham pathos. Mr. Trollope's Pierian spring gives no beverage which leaves a remorse of this sort, but a sober and reasonable tipple, which pleases us at the time and does not bring repentance afterwards. So we are sorry that Julia Brabazon does a wrong and a wicked thing in marrying a lord who has delirium tremens from time to time, when she was in love with a healthy commoner who had no delirium tremens; still we are sure that it was a very probable thing for such a woman to do, and we know that Mr. Trollope, as the agent of the Providence of respectable virtue, will see that she is punished just enough, and not more than enough, to vindicate the ways of society to women. Hence, though very much interested in her, we are not under the influence of any artificial and unreal excitement. We know that she is in the hands of a writer who, though a fine artist in his own sphere, is never intoxicated by art. We know that a sober and reasonable vengeance will overtake her, of the kind which would overtake her in real life. Perhaps, if anything, she escapes too lightly. But then Mr. Trollope cannot bear to think of uncomfortable severity. Now and then, in his novels, he is obliged to bring some dreadful villain to thorough ruin; but he gets over it as quickly as ever he can, simply putting the villain out of doors and begging us to think no more about him. . . .

Some of the minor characters are photographs of the most perfect kind. The hard, selfish Sir Hugh, and his brother the soft, selfish Archie, and the feebly acute Boodle, are all excellent. Count Pateroff is only a shadow of a character, and his intriguing sister is more conventional and unreal than is usual with the author. The fun of Madame Gordeloup strikes us as forced. We should be disposed to doubt whether Mr Trollope knows a real Gordeloup; for, in drawing people who must have come under his actual observation, he seldom makes a wrong stroke or inserts a bit of unfitting colour. His characteristic humour is, in truth, only a very strong form of common sense reflecting known and observed realities. This may not produce the greatest works, but it always guarantees us works that are honest, truthful, and artistic.

107. Unsigned notice, *Athenaeum*

15 June 1867, p. 783

Not a stellar critique, but a convenient illustration of the divided attitudes more than one reviewer experienced toward this novel.

'The Claverings,' as a tale, is not so entertaining as some others that Mr. Trollope has written; but there are none of his books which show better or more artistic workmanship. . . . There are sketches of character and slight episodes which are masterpieces in their way, true to life and to human nature. Count Pateroff's little dinner at the Blue Posts is one of these; indeed the Count is altogether a sketch drawn with sharply incised lines, and Sophy Gordaloup, his sister, is a capital companion-piece; she has real humour in her too. . . .

There was room in 'The Claverings' for deeper studies in human nature; but the book in that case might not have been so pleasant to read.

108. Margaret Oliphant, 'Novels', *Blackwood's Magazine*

September 1867, cii. 275–7

This same general review of a number of novels by various hands includes a discussion of *The Last Chronicle of Barset* (given below as No. 114); also *Land at Last* and *Rupert Godwin* by the sensation novelist Mary Elizabeth Braddon, and Anne (Ritchie) Thackeray's *Village on the Cliff* (1865).

It is good to turn aside from these feverish productions—and we think it right to make as distinct a separation as the printer's skill can indicate between the lower and the higher ground in fiction—to the better fare which is still set before us. Though they seem to flourish side by side, and though the public, according to such evidence as can be obtained on the subject, seems to throw itself with more apparent eagerness upon the hectic than upon the wholesome, still we cannot but hope that Mr. Anthony Trollope has in reality a larger mass of readers than Miss Braddon, and we are very sure no sensational romancist of her school goes half so near the general heart as does the author of the 'Village on the Cliff.' There are still the seven thousand men in Israel who have not bent the knee to Baal, notwithstanding that mournful prophets in all ages will persist in thinking themselves alone faithful. Mr. Trollope writes too much to be always at his best. He has exhausted too many of the devices of fiction to be able to find always an original suggestion for his plot; but there is nobody living who has added so many pleasant people to our acquaintance, or given us so many neighbourly interests out of our own immediate circle. We are disposed to protest against the uncomfortable vacillation between two lovers which has been for some time past his favourite topic; but we do so only in the most friendly, and, indeed, affectionate way. High-pitched constancy is no doubt rare nowadays. On the one hand, it is by no means always a matter of certainty that the woman a man has been accepted by, or the man whom the woman accepts, are beyond dispute the best and most suitable for them. Friends of persons about to be married are on all hands agreed on that point. And, on the other side, we agree with Mr. Trollope that, as a matter of amusement, lovemaking is decidedly superior to either croquet or cricket. But the fact remains, that the man and the woman who, without very grave cause, change their minds in this important matter, are seldom satisfactory people. Harry Clavering, though not a bad fellow in the main, looks very foolish when his first love and his second love are squabbling over him—or at least, if not squabbling, mutually determining to resign, and sacrifice themselves to his happiness. It is not an elevated position for a man. The reader feels slightly ashamed of him when he has to tell his tale, and submit to everybody's comment, and realize that the part he has played has been a very poor one. We can forgive our hero for making a tragic mistake which ruins or compromises him fatally, or we can forgive him for the most stupid blunder in any other branch of his affairs; but a blunder which necessitates the intervention of three or four women in his lovemaking, and which is really arranged by them, he himself being very secondary in the matter, is humiliating, and goes against the very character of a hero. It seems to be Mr. Trollope's idea that, so long as he is faithful to her, a woman can see no blemish in a man whom she has once loved. But we fear this is far from being the fact. On the contrary, we should have been inclined to suppose that Florence Burton not only would never have been able to banish from her mind a certain (carefully suppressed, no doubt) contempt for her fickle lover, but that she would have indulged in a sound, reasonable, womanly hatred ever after, for all the kind intercessors who came between them. Women are neither so passive nor so grateful as they are made out to be; and a man's disdain for the girl who 'having known *me* could decline'[1] upon the lower heart and lower brain, is perhaps a few degrees less profound than the woman's contempt for the actor in a similar defalcation. It was mean of Florence Burton to have him again after he had forsaken her, and unspeakably mean of him to consent to the re-transfer, and to be happy ever after. The only person whom we have any sympathy with in the matter is the poor, faulty beauty, Julia, who was so dreadfully wrong in other respects, but yet not to blame in this. Here, however, is the vast difference between such a work as even the faultiest and least satisfactory of Mr. Trollope's and the best of the

---

[1] 'Is it well to wish thee happy?—having known me—to decline
On a range of lower feelings and a narrower heart than mine!'
—Tennyson's *Locksley Hall*, lines 43–44.

inferior school. Deep, tragic passion is not in them, although they are chiefly about lovemaking, and their perplexities and troubles and complications of plot all centre in this one subject. But the atmosphere is the purest English daylight; none of those fair women, none of those clean, honourable, unexalted English gentlemen, have any terrible secrets in their past that cannot bear the light of day. There may be unpleasant talk at their clubs, and they may make no exhibition of horror—but they don't mix it up with their history, or bring it into their intercourse with their friends. Now and then a woman among them may make a mercenary marriage, or a man among them be led into a breach of constancy; but they live like the most of us, exempt from gross temptation, and relying upon human natural incidents, contrariety of circumstances, failure of fortune, perversity of heart, for the plan of their romance. On this level we miss the primitive passions, but we get all those infinite shades of character which make society in fact, as well as society in a book, amusing and interesting.

109. Mrs. Proudie, *Saturday Review*

6 July 1867

Unsigned essay, 'Ambitious Wives', *Saturday Review* (6 July 1867), xxiv. 11–12. This essay, preceding by a week or more the reviews of *The Last Chronicle of Barset* given below, was, so far as I have found, the only notice that the *Saturday* was to give to the novel. Trollope must have been gratified to see his own vivid sense of Mrs. Proudie's reality confirmed; but he must also have been disappointed ultimately at being deprived of a full review in this influential and discriminating journal.

The recent death of Mrs. Proudie, who was so well known and so little loved by the readers of Mr. Trollope's novels, is one of those occasions which ought not to be allowed to pass away without being improved. To many men it will suggest many things. She was a type. As a type ought to be, she was perfect and full-blown. But her characteristics enter into other women in varying degrees, and with all sorts of minor colours. The Proudie element in wives and women is one of those unrecognized yet potent conditions of life which master us all, and yet are admitted and taken into calculation and account by none. It is in the nature of things that such an element should exist, and should be powerful in this peculiar and oblique way. We deny women the direct exercise of their capacities, and the immediate gratification of an overt ambition. The natural result is that they run to artifice, and that a good-natured husband is made the conductor between an ambitious wife and the outer world where the prizes of ambition are scrambled for. He is the wretched buffer through which the impetuous forces of his wife impinge upon his neighbours. . . . We are constantly being told of some aspiring man that he is, in truth, no more than the representative of an aspiring wife. He would fain live his life in dignified or undignified serenity, and cares not a jot for a seat in the House of Commons, or for being made a bishop, or for any of those other objects which allure men out of a tranquil and independent existence. But he has a wife who does care for these things. She cannot be a member of Parliament or a bishop in her own person, but it is something to be the wife of somebody who can be these things. A part of the glory of the man is reflected upon the head of the woman. She receives her reward in a second-hand way, but still it is glory of its own sort. She becomes a leading lady in a provincial town, and during the season in town she is asked out to houses which she is very eager to get into, and of which she can talk with easily assumed familiarity when she returns to the provinces again. She is presented at Court too, and this makes her descend to the provincial plain with an aroma of celestial dignity like that of Venus when she descended from Olympus. A bishop's wife is still more amply rewarded. Without being so imperious as the late Mrs. Proudie was, she has still a thousand of those opportunities for displaying power which are so dear to people who are fictitiously supposed to be too weak to care for power. Minor canons, incumbents, curates, and all their wives, pay her profound deference; or, if they do not, she can 'put the screw on' in a gushing manner which is exceedingly effective. . . .

As a rule, however, it is pleasant to think that with ambition in women, which is not their peculiarity, is yoked tact, which is their peculiarity emphatically. Hence, therefore, wives who are ambitious for their lords have often the discretion to conceal their mood. They may rule with a hand of iron, but the hand is sagely concealed in a glove of velvet. A man may be the creature of his wife's lofty projects, and yet dream all the time that he is altogether chalking out his own course. George II used to be humoured in this way by Queen Caroline. Bishop Proudie, on the other hand, was ruled by his wife, and knew that he was a mere weapon in her hands; and, what was even worse than all, knew that the rest of mankind knew this. This must be uncommonly unpleasant, we should suppose. The middle position of the husband who only now and then suspects in a dreamy way that he is being prompted and urged on and directed by an ambitious wife, and has sense enough not to inflame himself with chimerical notions about the superiority and grandeur of the male sex—this perhaps is not so bad. If the tide of ambition runs rather sluggish in yourself, it is a plain advantage to have somebody at your side with enthusiasm enough to atone for the deficiency. It is impossible to tell how much good the world gets, which otherwise it would miss, simply out of the fact that women are discontented with their position. Now and then, it is understood, the husband who is thus made a mere conductor for the mental electricity of a wife who is too clever for him may feel a little bored, and almost wish that he had married a girl instead. But enthusiasm spreads, and in a general way the fervour of the wife who aspires to distinction proves catching to the husband. Some ladies are found to prefer this position to any other. They are full of power, and have abundance of room for energy, and yet they have no responsibility. They get their ample share of the spoil, and yet they do not bear the public heat and burden of the day. It is only the more martial souls among them for whom this is not enough.

THE LAST CHRONICLE
OF BARSET

1867

Trollope, at the time of writing his *Autobiography* in 1875–6 and probably thereafter, considered *The Last Chronicle of Barset* his finest novel.

Taking it as a whole, I regard this as the best novel I have written. I was never quite satisfied with the development of the plot, which consisted in the loss of a cheque, of a charge made against a clergyman for stealing it, and of absolute uncertainty on the part of the clergyman himself as to the manner in which the cheque had found its way into his hands. I cannot quite make myself believe that even such a man as Mr. Crawley could have forgotten how he got it; nor would the generous friend who was anxious to supply his wants have supplied them by tendering the cheque of a third person. Such fault I acknowledge,— acknowledging at the same time that I have never been capable of constructing with complete success the intricacies of a plot that required to be unravelled. But while confessing so much, I claim to have portrayed the mind of the unfortunate man with great accuracy and great delicacy. The pride, the humility, the manliness, the weakness, the conscientious rectitude and bitter prejudices of Mr. Crawley were, I feel, true to nature and well described. The surroundings too are good. Mrs. Proudie at the palace is a real woman; and the poor old dean dying at the deanery is also real. The archdeacon in his victory is very real. There is a true savour of English country life all through the book. It was with many misgivings that I killed my old friend Mrs. Proudie. I could not, I think, have done it, but for a resolution taken and declared under circumstances of great momentary pressure.

[A paragraph at this point describes how Trollope overheard two men deploring his habit of carrying characters from novel to novel, with one of them declaring himself especially tired of Mrs. Proudie. Trollope thereupon broke into their conversation to reveal his identity and announce that he would kill Mrs. Proudie 'before the week is over'. It may be worth noting, however, that the *Saturday Review* had, in its reviews of the two previous Barsetshire novels, attacked Trollope for his habit of repeating characters and may have helped Trollope come to his decision. See Nos. 44 and 75. See also *Dublin University Magazine*, No. 50, and *London Review*, No. 97.]

I have sometimes regretted the deed, so great was my delight in writing about Mrs. Proudie, so thorough was my knowledge of all the little shades of her character. It was not only that she was a tyrant, a bully, a would-be priestess, a very vulgar woman, and one who would send headlong to the nethermost pit all who disagreed with her; but that at the same time she was conscientious, by no means a hypocrite, really believing in the brimstone which she threatened, and anxious to save the souls around her from its horrors. And as her tyranny increased so did the bitterness of the moments of her repentance increase, in that she knew herself to be a tyrant,—till that bitterness killed her. Since her time others have grown up equally dear to me,—Lady Glencora and her husband, for instance; but I have never dissevered myself from Mrs. Proudie, and still live much in company with her ghost (*Autobiography*, pp. 229–31).

---

110. Unsigned notice, *Spectator*

13 July 1867, xl. 778–80

Mr. Trollope is, after all, a little bit of a hypocrite. His title and his concluding page are put forward by him as merits for the sake of which readers may forgive slight defects. Now, all that his title and his concluding page tell us is, that we are to hear no more from him about the diocese of Barchester. Mr. Trollope knows well enough that this is not an announcement which any one will read with satisfaction, so, like a great speaker who, though all the world wishes to hear him as long as he can sustain the flow of his eloquence, makes it a merit to disappoint them, and sit down after a few words, Mr. Trollope promises, in return for our forbearance, that we shall hear of Barchester no more. The general effect of this announcement has been naturally enough very great discouragement. Men who do not go much into society feel as if all the society they had, had suddenly agreed to emigrate to New Zealand, or Vancouver's Island, or some other place, where they will never hear of them any more. 'What am I to do without ever meeting Archdeacon Grantly?' a man said the other day; 'he was one of my best and most intimate friends, and the mere prospect of never hearing his "Good heavens!" again when any proposition is made touching the dignity of Church or State, is a bewilderment and pain to me. It was bad enough to lose the Old Warden, Mr. Septimus Harding, but that was a natural death, and we must all bow to blows of that kind. But to lose the Archdeacon and Mrs. Grantly in the prime of their life, is more than I can bear. Life has lost one of its principal alleviations. Mr. Trollope has no right to break old ties in this cruel and reckless way, only to please himself, and then make a hypocritical merit of it.' We confess to feeling a good deal of sympathy with this gentleman. Even the present writer has found the loneliness very oppressive since he was told that he was never to meet almost the best known and most typical of his fellow-countrymen again, and has indulged some rash thoughts of leaving England for ever. What makes it worse is, that there is no sort of comfort in this case as to a future reunion. If we do not hear of Mr. and Mrs. Crawley again in this world, where else can we meet them, unless Mr. Trollope is condemned for his sin in thus abruptly cutting the thread of their mortal lives to continue their history for ever in another sphere? And that is not a contingency to which we can look with much hope. On the whole, it is a bitter and needless parting. If all the world prefer to hear about these Barchester people, whom they know so well, to hearing about other new people whom they do not know at all and care nothing for, and Mr. Trollope is the only person who knows about them, it is a selfish and cruel proceeding on his part to shut them off from their friends. It is hard enough to have the death of two of our old friends reported within a couple of months of each other. Mrs. Proudie's was, however, as she herself might have said, in some sense a 'merciful dispensation,' and Mr. Harding's occurred in the course of nature. But their deaths should have rendered Mr. Trollope only more tender of the feelings of those who have grown so fond of the Barchester set. It is positively heartless to wrench us away at one fell stroke from all of them—Mr. Crawley, old Lady Lufton, Mr. Robarts, Dr. Tempest of Silverbridge, Dean Arabin, Bishop Proudie, Mr. Thumble, the broken-kneed pony out of the Cathedral stables, and all! For our own part, and from a purely *naturalist* point of view, we feel the loss of Mr. Thumble almost as poignantly as any other. His behaviour at Mr. Crawley's after that unfortunate pony of the Bishop's had broken its knees under him, and when he wanted Major Grantly to take him back in his gig to Barchester, was such a delightful mixture of feeble impertinence to persons in misfortune and feeble servility to persons in prosperity, that we have lost in him a distinct type of human nature. Perhaps, however, *he* may leave the diocese of Barchester, and reappear elsewhere in Mr. Trollope's horizon. Nor can we give up the hope of meeting again Mr. Toogood the solicitor, Madalina Bangles, *née* Demolines, Sir Raffle Buffle, and other London characters. But that is poor consolation for parting from the circle at Plumstead Episcopi, and from Mr. Crawley—Mr. Trollope's noblest and most unique acquaintance.

To cease, however, from the mood of remonstrance and helpless lamentation,—this chronicle of Barset appears to us really the best, indeed, the richest and completest of Mr. Trollope's works. Mr. Crawley, the leading figure in it, is cast in a deeper and nobler, if also narrower, mould than most of Mr. Trollope's acquaintances. Both his sins and his virtues have a grander stamp upon them. There is nothing of the earth, earthy, about Mr. Crawley,—his savage spiritual pride being, at least, as intensely unworldly, as his devotion to the brickmakers at Hoggle End. Mr. Trollope has never before drawn a character either so full of (indicated rather than delineated) intellectual power, or so devoted to the diviner ends of life, or, again, so deeply involved in the strife of morbid personal feelings. The mixture of the three elements creates a picture of the highest interest and power. The pure intellect of Mr. Crawley is indeed chiefly shown in the acute criticisms he passes on other men's words or letters, and in the power of discerning with the utmost lucidity the limits within which his own memory or reason might have failed him, and in his thorough distrust even of his own clearest impressions to that extent. We are not shown at all as we should like to have been shown how Mr. Crawley's strength and weakness, both, conduced to his peculiar ecclesiastical views as a High-Church clergyman,—a High-Church clergyman, not, remember, of Archdeacon Grantly's worldly type, but of the true spiritual type, the true priestly type. There is but one passage in which you see for a moment the imagination of the man, and how it dwells on images of restless power fettered by what seems blind circumstance or dead necessity, but that passage certainly does not give a picture of an imagination as orthodox or as sacerdotal as Mr. Crawley's ecclesiastical views appear to imply that he was. It is a fine passage, and as it is one of the finest bits of intellectual delineation Mr. Trollope has ever written, we will extract it. We must remember that Mr. Crawley is at the time suffering agonies,—the more so for his feverish chafing under the burden,—from the unjust suspicion cast upon him as to the stealing of a lost cheque, and his own impotence, with all his talent, to account at all for his possession of it. Mr. Crawley is reading Greek with his daughter:

But before he commenced his task, he sat down with his youngest daughter, and read,—or made her read to him,—a passage out of a Greek poem, in which are described the troubles and agonies of a blind giant. No giant would have been more powerful,—only that he was blind, and could not see to avenge himself on those who had injured him. 'The same story is always coming up,' he said, stopping the girl in her reading. 'We have it in various versions, because it is so true to life.

> Ask for this great deliverer now, and find him
> Eyeless in Gaza, at the mill with slaves.

It is the same story. Great power reduced to impotence, great glory to misery, by the hand of Fate,—Necessity, as the Greeks called her; the goddess that will not be shunned! "At the mill with slaves!" People, when they read it, do not appreciate the horror of the picture. Go on, my dear. It may be a question whether Polyphemus had mind enough to suffer; but, from the description of his power, I should think that he had. "At the mill with slaves!" Can any picture be more dreadful than that? Go on, my dear. Of course you remember Milton's Samson Agonistes. Agonistes indeed!' His wife was sitting stitching at the other side of the room; but she heard his words,—heard and understood them; and before Jane could again get herself into the swing of the Greek verse, she was over at her husband's side, with her arms round his neck. 'My love!' she said, 'my love!' He turned to her, and smiled as he spoke to her. 'These are old thoughts with me. Polyphemus and Belisarius, and Samson and Milton, have always been pets of mine. The mind of the strong blind creature must be so sensible of the injury that has been done to him! The impotency, combined with his strength, or rather the impotency with the memory of former strength and former aspirations, is so essentially tragic!' She looked into his eyes as she spoke, and there was something of the flash of old days, when the world was young to them, and when he would tell her of his hopes, and repeat to her long passages of poetry, and would criticize for her advantage the works of old writers. 'Thank God,' she said, 'that you are not blind. It may yet be all right with you.'—'Yes, it may be,' he said.—'And you shall not be at the mill with slaves.'—'Or, at any rate, not eyeless in Gaza, if the Lord is good to me. Come, Jane, we will go on.' Then he took up the passage himself, and read it on with clear, sonorous voice, every now and then explaining some passage or expressing his own ideas upon it, as though he were really happy with his poetry.

That this type of mind is absolutely consistent with, nay, even in special harmony with, the sort of Church view Mr. Crawley takes, in spite of its apparent revolutionary fire of feeling, every thoughtful reader will feel. But Mr. Trollope might, without introducing theology into his novel, have indicated more than he has where the secret of the harmony lies. Mr. Crawley's mind is didactic and authoritative, loving to apply to others both the light and the force requisite to guide them; and, being also rather hasty in his assumptions, he would have been sure to catch at the idea of a Church authoritatively teaching the people, rather than helping the people to teach themselves. It is only when guidance and authority are applied to himself, and he feels deeply that the lights of those who try to guide are infinitely feebler than those of him who is bound to submit, that a chaos of conflict begins in his soul, the history of which is so finely traced in these pages.

Perhaps the most *delicate* piece of moral portraiture ever completed by Mr. Trollope is the inimitable sketch of the old warden, Mr. Septimus Harding, whose death in this story has drawn tears from many an eye to which tears are usually strangers. No more perfect delineation of high breeding, humility, self-forgetfulness, and faith was ever painted. That having painted two such pictures as those of Mr. Crawley and Mr. Harding, Mr. Trollope should be charged with a chronic disposition to libel the English priesthood, and make them a mere set of worldlings, is strange to us. No doubt Mr. Trollope sketches men chiefly as he sees them, whether in the Church or otherwise, and he does not see apparently very many men,—either in the Church or otherwise,— quite 'unspotted from the world.' Nay, even those who are unspotted by the *world* are sometimes otherwise not unspotted, like Mr. Crawley. But if such a man as Mr. Harding is seldom met with twice in any man's life, why should he be met with twice in any man's works? Again, nothing in its way can be finer than the picture of the Archdeacon's thorough practical worldliness, and the way it collapses before his impressionable and kind heart, when he comes to see a really pretty girl of high breeding in distress. Mr. Trollope has drawn nothing better than the Archdeacon's interview with old Lady Lufton, wherein he describes his worldly feelings about his son's proposed marriage in a very frank way indeed, and the immediately succeeding interview with the young lady, whom he visits in order to show her the wickedness of marrying his son, and to whom he has given, before the end of the interview, his hearty consent,—almost unconditionally,—in form even conditionally only on her father's proved innocence of the supposed theft,—to that marriage.

[The reviewer here quotes at length the memorable scene from Chapter LXVII in which Archdeacon Grantly confronts Grace Crawley only to be so impressed by the quality of her beauty and her spirited bearing that he quite reverses his attitude. 'He had gone to the parsonage hating the girl, and despising his son. Now, as he retraced his steps, his feelings were altogether changed.']

That is a perfect piece of truth and nature. What are we to do,—what *are* we to do, without the Archdeacon? Mr. Trollope *dare* not bereave us of the Archdeacon.

The minor excellencies of the story are far too numerous even to mention. We must say we think better of Mr. Trollope as an artist for making Lily Dale turn out a spinster. There is something anticipative of that fate even in her very way of falling in love at first, still more of her demeanour after the disappointment. And throughout *this* story, her whole manner, intense and *prononcé* without clingingness, has foretold the O. M. which she affixes to her name in the secrecy of her chamber. And yet (fools and blind that we were!) we believed till the very close that John Eames was to have her, and were proportionately relieved at the result. We have never cared very much for Lily Dale. Her character never interested us deeply after the first blow which deprived her of her lover. It knotted itself and stiffened off from that point. But then we have never cared very much, again, for John Eames, and there is always something unsatisfactory in seeing two persons you do not care for disposed of together in marriage. You resent marriage in such a case as an event which ought to be reserved for those who have the power to interest you. The vulgar people, as usual, are as good as the highbred and refined in the *Last Chronicle of Barset*. Madalina's last interview with John Eames, when her mother tries to bully him into a promise of marriage by locking him up till she can consult her cousin the Serjeant, and when Johnny begs a policeman to keep his bull's eye fixed on the room till he is released, and Madalina finally intervenes with, 'Let him go, mamma, we shall only have a rumpus,' is one of Mr. Trollope's best scenes of vulgar life. Of its own light kind there has been no better novel ever written than the *Last Chronicle of Barset*.

Mr. Anthony Trollope crowns with this work his labour upon that series of Barsetshire chronicles which is the best set of 'sequels' in our literature. Until of late, novelists hardly ventured beyond a second novel introducing persons of the first and carrying on the story of their lives. But in our day a new fashion has arisen, fostered in part by Mr. Thackeray's tendency to return to some of his old characters in a new story, and realize them more and more completely to himself and to his readers. Thus Sir Bulwer Lytton has dwelt also on his Caxton family, and we have more recent examples in Mr. Percy Fitzgerald's carrying of his Jenny Bell and some of her friends through three successive novels, and in the excellent series of the 'Chronicles of Carlingford.' Mr. Anthony Trollope has yielded, in fact, to a tendency inherent in the best form of the realism of modern fiction. In the combination of realism with great and exceptional crimes, a tale of passion when told must be done with. The complicated, highly-seasoned plot, once fairly wrought out, can have no sequel, except it be of depression after excitement. The Oresteia, and that old legend of the House of Œdipus, were complete stories, and thus the several plays of a Greek trilogy were but as volumes one, and two, and three of one grand fable. A chain of novels like Mr. Anthony Trollope's Barsetshire set is essentially a birth of our own time. . . . In justice to Mr. Trollope and to itself, the public should have these Barsetshire novels extant, not only as detached works, but duly bound, lettered, and bought as a connected series. Their author half apologizes for having lingered so long about one group of homes, but in doing so, as we have said, he simply followed to its natural end a form of fiction that is the true birth of our own day, and of which he is an accepted master. . . .

In Mr. Crawley, Perpetual Curate of Hogglestock, who is the hero of this last chronicle, a complex character is elaborated with great vigour; and here, as elsewhere, there is in the character painting a dramatic force that neither insight into character nor sympathy with men, and sense of the soul under the forms of life, can give, unless there be some gift also to the writer of an artist's genius. This it is that enables Mr. Trollope to retain the fixed interest of his readers when his plot, however cleverly constructed for his purpose of setting character in motion, is of the very simplest. Here the whole plot of two closely-printed octavo volumes only answers the question whether an eccentric clergyman of sensitive and noble nature, ground to the dust by poverty, did or did not, consciously or unconsciously, steal or use as his own a cheque for 20*l* that was not his.

No man could strongly interest educated readers, as Mr. Anthony Trollope does, through seven or eight hundred closely-printed octavo pages of a story with so simple a plot, if his sketches of English life were not true sketches, true in form and truly felt; if he did not write, as Mr. Trollope does, English as pure as it is unaffected; and if he had not the touch of genius that can give life to creatures of the fancy.

There can be but few of Mr. Trollope's readers in whose minds the first words of the book now before us will not inspire a gentle melancholy. It is really to be, he says, 'with some solemnity of assurance,' the last chronicle of Barset which we shall receive from his hands, and we cannot but feel grieved to have to say farewell to scenes which so many pleasant associations have endeared. To us, as well as to him, Barset has long been a real country, and its city a real city; and the spires and towers have been before our eyes, and the voices of the people are known to our ears, and the pavements of the city ways are familiar to our footsteps. Long ago we there, under Mr. Trollope's guidance, made acquaintances which have since then seemed to ripen into friendships, and now that we are told that we shall see their faces no more we are conscious of a genuine sensation of regret. Several of Mr. Trollope's Barsetshire characters have been from time to time so vividly brought before us that we have thoroughly accepted the reality of their existence, their shadowy forms have seemed to take equal substance with those of our living neighbours, and their fictitious joys and sorrows have often entered more deeply into our speculations than have those of the persons who really live and move and have their being around us. . . .

The character of Mr. Crawley is certainly one of the most powerful of Mr. Trollope's conceptions. There is a rugged grandeur and a harsh nobility about the man, both of which qualities are admirably brought out and rendered prominent in the course of the story. The wonderful ease with which Mr. Trollope writes, and the simplicity of the means by which he generally produces his effects, have induced some of his critics to underrate his powers, and to speak of him at times as if he were capable of doing little more than write excellent chit-chat, or analyse the mental vagaries of a young lady oscillating between two attachments. No one can rival him in investing commonplace with a winning charm; no one else can render airy nothings so acceptable as he succeeds in making them; but he has higher claims to be praised than these, and to their existence such a character as that of Mr. Crawley bears ample testimony. It cannot have been an easy one to depict, but the portrait is admirably executed. From first to last he is consistent with himself, and while his foibles are pointed out with genial humour, his native dignity is maintained, without any apparent difficulty, at a height to which in most cases it would have required a desperate effort to attain. There is something very grand about this ecclesiastical Titan, bowed down by troubles, and bound hand and foot by debt, while the vulture of poverty is ever gnawing at his side, but who yet defies the whole world, sets threats and persuasion equally at nought, and stubbornly maintains his own in spite alike of friends and foes.

113. Unsigned notice, *Athenaeum*

3 August 1867, p. 141

There is one advantage in writing a story as a serial[1]—the individual portions have an elaboration and finish which a novel written in the piece does not always obtain at the hands of the author. These 'Last Chronicles' are very carefully written, and the characters have remarkable substance and vitality. It is not given to every one to create characters out of the work-a-day world—neither better nor worse than persons whom we all meet every day—and yet to be able so to lay bare their hearts and stories that the reader accepts them as friends and acquaintances, follows their fortunes through the volume specially devoted to them, remembers the subordinate persons, and is glad to hear their story at length as soon as Mr. Trollope is pleased, like another Scheherazade, to take up one of the threads of the old story and weave a new one from it. The series of Barsetshire Chronicles have all been singularly real in their interest, and veraciously like Nature in the living characters introduced. Each chronicle has a central history, with slighter sketches grouped round it. The story of the subordinate personages has each in their turn been worked out at length. The interest has been kept up, the electric current has gone without break through the circle, from the days of the dear old Warden of Hiram's Hospital, at Barchester, to these last Chronicles of Barset, wherein Mr. Harding, full of years and goodness, drops into an honoured grave. In the meanwhile, all the personages of the town and country have, in their turn, appeared before the reader, and if the reader does not believe in Barsetshire and all who live therein—Lady Lufton, the Rev. Mr. Robarts, the great Duke of Omnium, and the still great Marchioness of Hartletop, the Dean of Barchester, the Archdeacon Grantley, the poor Bishop, and his wife the terrible Mrs. Proudie, along with others as numerous as a list of runners entered for the Derby—the fault is not in Mr. Trollope, but in himself. How many, both men and women, have desired to know the sequel to the story of Lily Dale! and what numerous sympathizers and well-wishers has not Johnny Eames had in his crossed love and

[1] The novel had first appeared in thirty-two parts at sixpence each, 1 December 1866 to 6 July 1867, an experiment that was not, it seems, very successful (*Autobiography*, p. 229).

constancy! But one has always felt that poor Johnny would never grow up into a marriageable hero; one only hoped he might not fall a victim to one of the designing young females with whom he had a curious tendency to perilous flirtation. Everybody who ever read 'The Small House at Allington' has bestowed many a passing thought on what would be the end of Crosbie—whether he would ever have the chance of marrying Lily Dale, and whether she could, would or ought to accept him. It tells of great gifts that Mr. Trollope should thus endow his characters with flesh and blood and individuality of interest; make their surroundings graphic and tangible, and yet make the men and women stand out from their background, and live and move like human beings; but it is evidence of still higher powers when the fortunes of these inhabitants of Mr. Trollope's county of Barsetshire obtain such a thorough hold on the interest of readers that they are anxious to hear more about them, more even than Mr. Trollope is willing to tell; for he declares on his title-page and in his closing paragraphs, that the present is the last word he will ever say about Barsetshire and its inhabitants. We only hope he will *not* keep his word; for he leaves 'distant wilds still opening to the view'; and we hope he will tell us a great deal *more* about many persons mentioned in the present 'Chronicle'. . . .

We have spoken heartily of all we liked in these 'Last Chronicles', but there are some four or five chapters which seem to have been introduced, neck and shoulders, apropos of nothing at all. Johnny Eames is taken out to dinner by an artist, Conway Dalrymple, and all that ensues is simply a disagreeable interruption to the course of the story, on which it acts as a patch unskilfully laid on, of incongruous colour and different material. Johnny Eames loses somewhat in the reader's regard, but Miss Clara van Siever, Madalina Demolines, with the two old harridans, their mothers, Musselborough, Bangles, Dobbs Broughton and Mrs. Dobbs Broughton, even Conway himself, and all the story of the mock loves of Madalina and Mrs. Dobbs Broughton are altogether out of place. No one ever wishes to hear of them further; their introduction is a mistake.

114. Margaret Oliphant, 'Novels', *Blackwood's Magazine*

September 1867, cii. 277–8

No. 108, above, was also part of this general review of novels of recent months.

Yet would we chide our beloved novelist for his 'Last Chronicle.' *We* did not ask that this chronicle should be the last. We were in no hurry to be done with our old friends. And there are certain things which he has done without consulting us against which we greatly demur. To kill Mrs. Proudie was murder, or manslaughter at the least. We do not believe she had any disease of the heart; she died not by natural causes, but by his hand in a fit of weariness or passion. When we were thinking no evil, lo! some sudden disgust seized him, and he slew her at a blow. The crime was so uncalled for, that we not only shudder at it, but resent it. It was cruel to us; and it rather—looks—as—if—he did not know how to get through the crisis in a more natural way. Then as to Lily Dale. Mr. Trollope's readers have been cheated about this young woman. It is a wilful abandonment of all her natural responsibilities when such a girl writes Old Maid after her name. She has no business to do it; and what is the good of being an author, we should like to know, if a man cannot provide more satisfactorily for his favourite characters? Lily will not like it when she has tried it a little longer. She will find the small house dull, and will miss her natural career; and if she should take to social science or philosophy, whose fault will it be but Mr. Trollope's? On the other hand, though he has thus wounded us in our tenderest feelings, our author has in this book struck a higher note than he has yet attempted. We do not know, in all the varied range of his productions, of any bit of character-painting so profound and so tragic as that of Mr. Crawley. Though there are scenes in 'Orley Farm' which approach it in intensity of interest, Lady Mason is not to be compared with the incumbent of Hogglestock. He is exasperating to the last degree—almost as exasperating to the reader as he must have been to his poor wife; and yet there is a grandeur about the half-crazed, wildered man—a mingled simplicity and subtlety in the conception—to which we cannot easily find a parallel in fiction. He has all the curious consistency and inconsistency of a real personage; we feel inclined to laugh and cry and storm at him all in a breath. His obstinate perversity—his sham sentiments and his true, which mingle together in an inextricable way as they do in nature, not as they generally do in art—his despair and confusion of mind, and quaint arrogance and exaggerated humility—make up a wonderfully perfect picture. The cunning of the craftsman here reaches to so high a point that it becomes a kind of inspiration. There is no high tone of colour, or garish light, to give fictitious importance to the portrait. Every tint is laid on, and every line made, with an entire harmony and subordination of detail which belongs to the most perfect art. Mr. Trollope's power of pleasing is so great, and his facility of execution so unbounded, that he is seduced into giving us a great many sketches which will not bear close examination. But so long as he continues to vindicate his own powers by such an occasional inspiration as this, we can afford to forgive him a great many Alice Vavasors and Harry Claverings.

The household at Plumstead, in its way, is almost as good. The Archdeacon's fierce wrath against his son, who is going to marry against his will—his suspicion of everybody conspiring against him to bring this about, and at the same time his instant subjugation by pretty Grace, and rash adoption of her on the spot—is altogether charming. Mr. Trollope is about the only writer we know (with, perhaps, one or two exceptions) who realizes the position of a sensible and right-minded woman among the ordinary affairs of the world. Mrs Grantly's perception at once of her husband's character and his mistakes—her careful abstinence from active interference—her certainty to come in right at the end—her half-amused, half-troubled spectatorship, in short, of all the annoyances her men-kind make for themselves, her consciousness of the futility of all decided attempts to set them right, and patient waiting upon the superior logic of events, is one of those 'bits' which may scarcely call the attention of the careless reader, and yet is a perfect triumph of profound and delicate observation. As for old Mr. Harding, our grief for his loss is yet too fresh to permit us to speak of him. We should like to go to Barchester and see his stall in the cathedral, and hear his favourite anthems, and linger a little by his grave. Honour to the writer who, amid so much that is false and vile and meretricious in current literature, beautifies our world and our imagination with such creations as these!

115. Unsigned notice, *British Quarterly Review*

October 1867, xlvi. 557–60

The old Archdeacon Grantly is perhaps the best-drawn character in this series of connected stories, and as he belongs to a past generation, and the next generation to ours will believe such a picture to border on gross caricature, it is nearly time for him to withdraw from contemporary observation. Did, however, any representative of the Liberation Society, any extreme political Dissenter, any tract issuing from a Winchester press, ever succeed in exhibiting the vulnerable points of our National Establishment, or the miserable weakness of the clerical order, as an order, so successfully as Mr. Trollope has done? With the exception of Mr. Harding and the Dean of Barchester, Dr. Arabin, how execrable is the style of man, how deplorable the type of character, how utterly unspiritual the ecclesiastical motive and government which he has portrayed! The particular interest of 'The Last Chronicle of Barset' is all made to turn on the defective memory of a poor, overworked incumbent, who cannot tell how he became possessed of a cheque which he had cashed and used for his own purposes. The mental struggle through which the good man passes is vehement and agonizing, and the secret is delayed till nearly the end of the second volume. At length he seems to believe that he must have stolen it, and judgment seems to be going against him. Surrounded with such friends, and seeing the fierce uprightness of the man,—the pride of his poverty, and his almost repulsive refusal of well-meant kindness,—no reader can get up much interest as to the result; and the elaborate means taken to prove his innocence and demonstrate it to a willing world, seem to us tedious and somewhat inartistic. There is not a hundredth part of the power with which Mr. Trollope depicted the parallel and contrasted scenes in 'Orley Farm', where Lady Mason's real forgery of her husband's will is made so long to look like innocence, and at length to take the reader with genuine surprise. The love-story of Grace Crawley and Captain Grantly is sweetly and tenderly done; but the whole of the London life, the painting of Jael and Sisera, the life and suicide of Dobbs Broughton, the preposterous love-making of Mdlle. Desmoulins, and other uninteresting matter connected with Conway Dalrymple and

Johnny Eames, might have been omitted with advantage. There does not seem to be anything more than a smart and lively reproduction of rather improbable circumstances in the life of a not very interesting set of people, to give them currency or popularity. When Mr. Trollope is pacing Barchester-close, or coming into quarters with Mrs. Proudie or the Archdeacon, or discussing foxes and county politics with the party assembled at the Duke of Omnium's, or when he is describing a simple-minded, high-principled girl, conquering her passion by her holier love or by another passion, he is uncommonly happy. He has given us an inimitable series of pictures, which reveal the *haut-ton* of English country life and the gossip of a cathedral town, and the reveries of some sweet damsels' boudoirs; but he has done nothing towards an exposition of the tendencies of modern society or of the deeper springs of human action. He writes most excellent English, though he seldom approaches eloquence. He neither wearies nor charms us either by descriptions of scenery or of persons, but he leaves a very deep impression of the reality and verisimilitude of many of his *personæ*, who are unquestionable men, women, and children. May he now devote his high and varied powers to some themes quite worthy of him, and be preserved from the fascination of French romance, towards which some of the scenes even in this volume, as well as in 'Can You Forgive Her?' lead one to fear he is tending.

PHINEAS FINN
1869

Apparently because the novel was part Irish and part urban political rather than rural English and clerical, *Phineas Finn* did not, so far as I have found, draw more than perfunctory attention in many places. Trollope himself had a good deal to say of *Phineas Finn* and its sequel *Phineas Redux* in his *Autobiography* (pp. 263–6); and both the *Spectator* and the *Saturday Review* gave the novel full treatment. The *Saturday*, to be sure, was by no means congratulatory on Trollope's change of scene. The *Dublin Review* (see No. 118) was enthusiastic, and the public seems to have found Trollope's Irish hero and his experiences in and out of Parliament more appealing than did the critics.

In writing *Phineas Finn*, and also some other novels which followed it, I was conscious that I could not make a tale pleasing chiefly, or perhaps in any part, by politics. If I write politics for my own sake, I must put in love and intrigue, social incidents, with perhaps a dash of sport, for the benefit of my readers. In this way I think I made my political hero interesting. It was certainly a blunder to take him from Ireland—into which I was led by the circumstance that I created the scheme of the book during a visit to Ireland. There was nothing to be gained by the peculiarity, and there was an added difficulty in obtaining sympathy and affection for a politician belonging to a nationality whose politics are not respected in England. But in spite of this Phineas succeeded. It was not a brilliant success,—because men and women not conversant with political matters could not care much for a hero who spent so much of his time either in the House of Commons or in a public office. But the men who would have lived with Phineas Finn read the book, and the women who would have lived with Lady Laura Standish read it also. As this was what I had intended, I was contented. It is all fairly good except the ending,—as to which till I got to it I made no provision. As I fully intended to bring my hero again into the world, I was wrong to marry him to a simple pretty Irish girl, who could only be felt as an encumbrance on such return. When he did return I had no alternative but to kill the simple pretty Irish girl, which was an unpleasant and awkward necessity.

In writing *Phineas Finn* I had constantly before me the necessity of progression in character,—of marking the changes in men and women which would naturally be produced by the lapse of years. In most novels the writer can have no such duty, as the period occupied is not long enough to allow of the change of which I speak. In *Ivanhoe*, all the incidents of which are included in less than

307

a month, the characters should be, as they are, consistent throughout. Novelists who have undertaken to write the life of a hero or heroine have generally considered their work completed at the interesting period of marriage, and have contented themselves with the advance in taste and manners which are common to all boys and girls as they become men and women. Fielding, no doubt, did more than this in *Tom Jones*, which is one of the greatest novels in the English language, for there he has shown how a noble and sanguine nature may fall away under temptation and be again strengthened and made to stand upright. But I do not think that novelists have often set before themselves the state of progressive change,—nor should I have done it, had I not found myself so frequently allured back to my old friends. So much of my inner life was passed in their company, that I was continually asking myself how this woman would act when this or that event had passed over her head, or how that man would carry himself when his youth had become manhood, or his manhood declined to old age. It was in regard to the old Duke of Omnium, of his nephew and heir, and of his heir's wife, Lady Glencora, that I was anxious to carry out this idea; but others added themselves to my mind as I went on, and I got round me a circle of persons as to whom I knew not only their present characters, but how those characters were to be affected by years and circumstances. The happy motherly life of Violet Effingham, which was due to the girl's honest but long-restrained love; the tragic misery of Lady Laura, which was equally due to the sale she made of herself in her wretched marriage; and the long suffering but final success of the hero, of which he had deserved the first by his vanity, and the last by his constant honesty, had been foreshadowed to me from the first. As to the incidents of the story, the circumstances by which these personages were to be affected, I knew nothing. They were created for the most part as they were described. I never could arrange a set of events before me. But the evil and the good of my puppets, and how the evil would always lead to evil, and the good produce good,—that was clear to me as the stars on a summer night.

Lady Laura Standish is the best character in *Phineas Finn* and its sequel *Phineas Redux*,—of which I will speak here together. They are, in fact, but one novel, though they were brought out at a considerable interval of time and in different form. The first was commenced in the *St. Paul's Magazine* in 1867, and the other was brought out in the *Graphic* in 1873. In this there was much bad arrangement, as I had no right to expect that novel-readers would remember the characters of a story after an interval of six years, or that any little interest which might have been taken in the career of my hero could then have been renewed. I do not know that such interest was renewed. But I found that the sequel enjoyed the same popularity as the former part, and among the same class of readers. Phineas, and Lady Laura, and Lady Chiltern—as Violet had become— and the old duke,—whom I killed gracefully, and the new duke, and the young duchess, either kept their old friends or made new friends for themselves. *Phineas Finn*, I certainly think, was successful from first to last. I am aware, however, that there was nothing in it to touch the heart like the abasement of Lady Mason when confessing her guilt to her old lover, or any approach in delicacy of delineation to the character of Mr. Crawley.

---

116. Unsigned notice, *Spectator*

20 March 1869, xlii. 356–7

Phineas Finn contains some of Mr. Trollope's best work, but it is not, as a whole, one of his very best tales. While far superior to the lower level of his novels,—stories like *Miss Mackenzie* or *Rachel Ray*,—it does not come up to the *Small House at Allington*, or *Framley Parsonage*, or *Can You Forgive Her?* and falls far short of the *Last Chronicle of Barset*. The run of the story is a little tame. Its most felicitous sketches, excepting only its most felicitous sketch of all, that of Lord Chiltern, are tame. The Irish hero is terribly tame,—if we may be allowed the bull. Of the four heroines, two at least are tame, and one, Lady Laura Standish, afterwards Lady Laura Kennedy, is scarcely a success. Even Madame Max Goesler, who is the best study of the four, wants definition. We scarcely feel that we know her even at the close, though we do feel a decided interest in her from her first appearance on the stage. Then the Parliamentary life is a little tame. Mr. Trollope sketches it too completely from the social side. As a mere reflex image of politics in London society it is as good as could be. But stronger political feelings than these go to make up a true politician, and we have only the faint drawing-room or club-room echo of those feelings. Even the political dinner-party at Mr. Monk's has no vivid life in it. There is a subdued tone about the conversation of all except Mr. Turnbull which is not natural. Mr Turnbull, offensive as he makes himself, would have been hit much harder than he is by any true politicians in such a discussion. And *prononcé* as Mr. Turnbull is, in his way, you see the hidden literary aim and purpose with which he is made to speak as he does, too clearly to accept the picture without hesitation. Like Dickens's pictures of American politicians in *Martin Chuzzlewit*, though, of course, less caricatured, Mr. Turnbull is seen at once by the reader to be a political puppet played off by the author for his own objects. Then of him, as of all the other fictitious politicians, it must be said that there is not enough told to define him. Mr. Monk has some affinities with Mr. Cobden, but he is a keen opponent of the ballot, and in other characteristics, too, is not Mr. Cobden. Yet enough is not told of him to make his image clear. Mr. Turnbull has some poor flavour of the worst parts of Mr. Bright, but neither in genius nor any other quality but popularity, is he really much like Mr. Bright. Mr. Gresham ignores the past, and is therefore certainly not meant for Mr. Gladstone, yet it is a problem what he is meant for. We want to hear more of these men, if they are to interest us deeply. The political life scarcely supplies the animation which so much of the tale seems to want.

It has been objected to Mr. Trollope that his creations are *too like* real life for literature,—that what one really wants in literature are men and women not so much *representative* of average men and women, as *typical* of them, with something, however, of intensity and force and clearness of outline, which belongs more to exceptional than to average men and women, but which is necessary in order to furnish keys to human nature in general. It is said that Mr. Trollope's sketches are so like to those whom one actually meets in society that one learns no more from them than we should learn from those whom we actually meet in society. We do not think that Mr. Trollope is fairly open to this charge. His characters are usually quite as marked and strong in relation to *modern* society, as are Fielding's in relation to the more sharply classified and more strongly contrasted types of character of a far less uniformly developed and far more localized and provincialized state of society. What we do think Mr. Trollope sometimes fails in, is in perceiving that there is, for most men at least, a depth of private character which barely gets to the surface of society at all, and which Mr. Trollope rarely ever indicates. Here, for instance, is Phineas Finn, who is an ambitious man and a warm politician, who is always in love with some lady or other, though the reader is always a little in doubt as to which, and who has apparently the intellect and heart to apprehend that there are plenty of considerations beyond that of mere success in life, and to look beyond it altogether. Yet we never see for a moment either the roots of his ambition, or the roots of his passions and affections, or the roots of his faith. We never see him as he would see himself even for a chapter. . . .

He must have had a private life of either self-recognition or self-mistake. He must have either known that he was not up to his high ambitious purposes, for instance, *or* at all events have deluded himself into throwing the blame on circumstances. So, again, of the four ladies amongst whom he flutters about, without distinctly knowing when he passed from one to the other;—we contend that he must have had some either true or false self-measurement in regard to this matter also. He must have either recognized that what he called love was not worth much, and was a faint watery sort of sentiment,—or he must have been a great adept in painting up the circumstances so as to excuse himself for his many transitions, and to persuade himself that there was a clear and well-marked water-shed dividing the opposite water-courses of his various loves. No man could have made those visits to Madame Max Goesler described towards the end of the story, while he was absolutely engaged to Mary Flood Jones, without a good deal of inward reckoning with himself of one kind or other as to whether or not he had anything in him that he could properly call love,—yea or nay. . . .

A man of such a type as his, in some of the circumstances of this story,—before the duel, for example, and still more perhaps in the last moments of indecision as to his political course on the Bill which led to his resignation,—must have gone down to the ultimate roots of human action, the deepest of all the considerations which actuate us. But if it was so with Phineas Finn, we never see it. Apparently, both in fighting the duel and in resigning his office, he was not only led by the poorest and most superficial motives,—*that* is not unnatural,—but was led by them without the forcible intrusion of better and higher motives. He does what is wrong and he does what is right alike without giving us any idea that such a thing as deep moral struggle can go on in the heart of man. Yet he is not a man without fine susceptibilities. He is meant to be a man, though of rather weak character, of some breadth of intellect and of much delicacy of sentiment. What, then, we regard as the true charge against Mr. Trollope,—to which this novel is more open than any of his more carefully written productions,—is that he gives us no strictly individual life,—no life beneath the social surface,—at all; that he never completes the outline of any character as it might be observed in society, by sketching it as it would be seen and appreciated or misconceived and falsely coloured by the inner self. This criticism applies most to Phineas Finn, as one always expects a deeper knowledge of the leading character than of any other; but it applies also to every character of any prominence,—particularly to Lady Laura Standish, and to Violet Effingham, in some degree even to Lord Chiltern, only that Lord Chiltern's rather violent, not to say ferocious nature, pierces the crust of social *convenances* almost as the cone of a volcano is upheaved through the surface of the earth, and tells you more of what lies beneath than is told us in any other case.

Lady Laura Standish was a fine conception, but we cannot but be dissatisfied with the way in which she is worked out. Her *amour propre*, her love of influence, her eager active nature, her generosity towards those she loves, the absence of compunction or even fear with which she marries a man whom she does not love for the sake of gratifying her wish for social and political influence, the repulsion of which she is sensible against Mr. Kennedy's formalism, the bitterer rebellion she nourishes against his attempt to lecture and govern her, are all finely conceived and strictly natural. But we find it very difficult to reconcile her final breach with him and ultimate horror of him,—which is an element in her nature akin to that of her brother Lord Chiltern's,—with the calm indifference with which she first married him when preferring another. The nature of Lady Laura Kennedy in the latter part of the book seems more passionate, as well as less ambitious, than is consistent with her early conduct. The girl who could patronize Phineas Finn so generously, while refusing him in order to make a marriage of *convenance*, would scarcely have broken with her husband and scandalized the world simply because she found her husband more didactic and obstinate and less considerate than she had hoped. Her soreness about Phineas Finn's forgetfulness of his love for her is natural; but the woman who could so successfully, so calmly, and with so much dignity repress his love when she intended to marry Mr. Kennedy, would scarcely have reproached him so openly with his desertion afterwards. As a whole, Lady Laura Kennedy is not to our minds a coherent picture. And if, as is possible, the artist *could* have vindicated the truth of his drawing by displaying the deeper, the more solitary, elements of her character, he has failed to do so.

But if Lady Laura is very imperfect, her husband, the Right Honourable Robert Kennedy, seems to us a great triumph of Mr. Trollope's art, less interesting and striking, indeed, but quite as perfect as the violent Lord Chiltern himself. The silent, stiff man, who is so taken by Lady Laura Standish's frank and eager manners before marriage, and so shocked by them after marriage; who makes such dull persevering efforts to tame down his wife, and who gets so sullen when he finds her wits too many for him; who was always master in small things in spite of her wits, and sickened her by the monotonous minutiæ of his arrangements; who wanted her to read all the books he named, and to read them in the precise times he named for them; who would have no guests and no novels on Sunday, and would read aloud dull sermons in the evening after the double attendance in church; who, when his wife was out of temper and out of spirits, would always propose to send for Dr. Macnuthrie; and who, when they came to quarrel with each other, seriously proposed to devote an autumn and winter 'to the cultivation of proper relations with his wife,'—studied, solemn, legal, decorous, pious Mr. Kennedy, with his terrible unconscious tyrannies, and his 'suit for the restitution of conjugal rights' after his wife had deserted him, is as wonderful a picture as Mr. Trollope has yet drawn. It was a great idea, in itself, to conceive an attempt made to garotte such a man as this; but it was a still greater stroke to picture him after Phineas Finn has saved him from the garotter's hands, as Mr. Trollope does, sitting for two or three days at home as stiff as a poker, and never speaking above a whisper,—absorbed in the shock to his throat and his self-importance, and in the danger to his life which he had so narrowly escaped. Mr. Trollope has never drawn any portrait more skilfully than the Right Honourable Robert Kennedy's.

Unless it be Lord Chiltern's. The savage and untamable element left in the English aristocracy, and in some of its very best specimens, was never so finely caught and painted as it is here. Lord Chiltern has something in him that reminds one of one of Mr. Trollope's most powerful sketches,—George Vavasour in *Can You Forgive Her?* But while George Vavasour is wholly selfish in his ferocity, Lord Chiltern is almost wholly generous, except so far as his ferocious self-will predominates over every other element,—his generosity included. There is something marvellous in the ease and rapidity with which, in a few love scenes, a few scenes of stormy altercation with his father and his friend and rival, and a hunting scene or two, the man's nature is delineated so fully on such slender materials. Except Mr. Kennedy, the reader knows no one so well as Lord Chiltern, and just as in the case of Mr. Kennedy, Lord Chiltern has scarcely uttered ten sentences before one becomes intimate with him,—in this case because his individual character breaks through all ordinary restrictions to express itself,—in Mr. Kennedy's case, because the individual character is identical with those restrictions, and is incarnate in them. Thus the contrast between the two is exceedingly striking, and adds to the power of each sketch. While there are many side-sketches of great skill and humour,—as, for instance, that of the money-lender Mr. Clarkson, who worries Phineas Finn to be 'punctual' with so much judicious torture,—the story of *Phineas Finn* will win permanent reputation for Mr. Trollope chiefly by the sketches of Lord Chiltern and Mr. Kennedy.

Reflecting on Mr. Disraeli's career, it would be rash to affirm that the professions of novelist and politician are incompatible. Mr. Disraeli, it is true, is like Juvenal's Greek. No trade comes amiss to him; no *tour de force* is too perilous or too extravagant for his courage and ingenuity. But Mr. Trollope is a steady-going, prosaic Englishman, and with the virtues possesses something of the ponderosity of that typically immobile character. On those who read to be startled, his performances will fall rather flat after those of the older novelist. He can go through a certain number of time-honoured tricks with variations, in the most unexceptionable manner; but he is not versatile and he is not brilliant, at least with the brilliancy and versatility of Mr. Disraeli. Nobody can draw a clergyman better, and he is perhaps the most trustworthy male lecturer living on the mental anatomy of young ladies. For these are subjects that seem to suit him exactly. For walking in dangerous places caution is more serviceable than agility. In dealing with women and with the Church an over-lively fancy is likely to become a snare. In either case a little wickedness and a little cynicism are expected of the novelist, but both must be duly watered with veneration and sentiment. If the infusion is too strong, he loses caste; if it is too weak, he loses readers. The proprieties must be observed, *ruat cælum*[1] and yet the most rigid sticklers for them do so love a little naughtiness. It is a great triumph to be able to gratify their tastes without incurring their displeasure; and that triumph has certainly been won by Mr. Trollope. From time to time his men have been wicked, but the wickedness has never been very unseemly. Once or twice a lady has been on the point of transgression, but something has always intervened to prevent the catastrophe; and though he has been quietly laughing at the parson for any number of years, he has never yet laughed at him in a manner unworthy of the most exemplary church-goer.

But the light castigation, coupled with an implied reverence for their order, which is so admirably in place where women or the clergy are concerned, is not the style of treatment of all others calculated to

---

[1] *ruat cælum*: though the skies should fall.

create an impression when applied to a contemporary statesman. Epigrams levelled at the sex or the cloth cannot be too carefully toned down. It is dangerous to laugh outright at the imbecility of a bishop, the follies of a fashionable woman, or the pretentious silliness of a young curate. In the one case the writer is set down by a great many good people as an unbeliever; in the other, as a misogynist. His book is damned if he does not contrive to get some fun out of his subject; but it will be excluded from every decent household if he does not keep his fun under proper control. With regard to our statesmen it is different. From time inmemorial a very considerable latitude has been permitted in this direction. Junius and Swift have been the most popular of our political writers. You may caricature to your heart's content; you may misrepresent, abuse, and insinuate, and the respectable will listen to you as eagerly as the ill-regulated. You are not generally supposed to be a person of peculiarly diabolical tendencies if you indulge in the wildest invective against Mr. Gladstone. You may call Mr. Bright Cleon,[1] and Mr. Disraeli Zamiel, and you need add no qualifying clause whatsoever. In point of fact, if you throw mud at them at all, you had better throw it vigorously, or nobody will notice you. And if you can manage to bring a little personality in you will show that you know your business as well as Artemus Ward's American journalist did, who wrote a series of letters in his paper ridiculing the appearance of a rival editor's sister, who had a cast in her eye. In one instance Mr. Trollope has availed himself pretty freely of the privileges accorded to a novelist in this direction, but for the most part he discourses of his political puppets with the same subdued chivalry and reverence with which he has for years recorded the sayings and doing of Church dignitaries and young ladies afflicted with the tender passion. Possibly the reason why he has allowed himself more freedom of speech than usual in his attack upon the Right Honourable President of the Board of Trade is to be found in the estimate—in some particulars the curiously inaccurate estimate—which he has formed of that gentleman's character. 'He was gifted,' says Mr. Trollope, in introducing his victim to us at a private dinner-party, 'with a moral skin of great thickness. Nothing said against him pained him; no attacks wounded him; no raillery touched him in the least. There was not a sore spot about him, and probably his first thought, on waking every morning, told him that he at least was *totus teres atque rotundus*.'[2]

[1] Cleon: the Athenian demagogue (d. 422 B.C.) satirized by Aristophanes in *Knights*.
[2] ' . . . *totus teres atque rotundus*': all smooth and round and whole (adapted from Horace, *Satires*, II. vii. 78).

If this is the case, though the fact is certainly new to us, he is not likely to be very angry with Mr. Trollope for the liberties taken with him. If his skin is really that of a rhinoceros, Mr. Trollope may of course belabour him till Doomsday, and never raise a wheal. Otherwise Mr. Bright might have taken it in bad part that his after-dinner conversations and habits should be sketched, whether from life or from imagination, for the amusement of the readers of the *St. Paul's Magazine*. For Mr. Trollope is cruelly careful that the veriest child shall not fail to recognize his pet aversion under the *alias* he has given him. With historical and needlessly elaborate minuteness he describes his robustness, age, hair, height, gait, complexion, eyes, nose, lips, coat, trowsers, and waistcoat. 'He always wore a black swallow-tail coat, black trowsers, and black silk waistcoat. In the house at least he was always so dressed, and at dinner-tables. What difference there might be in his costume, when at home at Staleybridge, few of those who saw him in London had the means of knowing.' Our sympathies are artfully alienated from him by the assertion that he is slow to perceive a joke. His heaviness is portentous, and his rudeness incredible. He is dictatorial to his host, quarrelsome and overbearing to his brother guests, and sermonizes persistently after dinner. . . .

By the side of this bold effort of a master's hand the portraits of the other Parliamentary leaders are inoffensive and colourless. Very little of this peculiar kind of banter is expended upon any of them. They speak and act for the most part like the great vague divinities that they are to most of us, and, if once and again we are favoured with any of their tricks of speech or personal foibles, it is manifest that their chronicler is not sneering, but merely detailing eccentricities which he thinks it may be interesting to his readers to be made acquainted with. It is only the contemplation of Mr. Bright that acts upon Mr. Trollope as a red rag upon a bull. He fights neither with small nor great, but only with Mr. Bright. He puts dull speeches in his mouth—surely an unpardonable solecism; he represents him invariably as solemnly arrogant and devilishly cunning, and introduces an amiable lady sighing for his death:

'My own impression is that nothing would save the country so effectually at the present moment as the removal of Mr. Turnbull to a higher and a better sphere.'
'Let us say the House of Lords,' said Phineas.
'God forbid!' said Lady Laura.

Mr. Bright and his brother statesmen are, of course, only the accessories to the story. *Phineas Finn*, unlike most of Mr. Trollope's works, is a novel with a hero, the impecunious son of a country doctor, who gets into Parliament at five-and twenty, is in the Ministry a year or two afterwards, fights a duel, rides an unmanageable horse, is fallen in love with three or four times by ladies of rank, saves a Cabinet Minister from the hands of garotters, is as strong as a coal-heaver, and as handsome as Apollo. Besides all this, he gives up a place of two thousand a year, and blights his prospects for ever, by a punctilious conscientiousness. He falls in love with the most charming facility, and is proposed to by a lady of great beauty and enormous fortune, who has lately refused the Duke of Omnium. Though ambitious, and with the certainty of a brilliant career before him in the profession which he prefers to all others, he leaves London at the call of duty, at the end of the novel, to settle down in contented obscurity at Cork with a poor Irish girl whose only merit is that she is more deeply in love with him than the rest of her sex. His personal adventures are in many respects entertaining, and his love complications, like most love complications invented by Mr. Trollope, are rather above than below the average, being narrated with that soberness of fancy, coupled with a copious variety of detail, which so often gives an air of reality of the most ordinary creations. Nobody has relied more persistently upon these two sources of attraction than Mr. Trollope has done, and it may be questioned whether any writer in any age has known how to make a more effective use of them. Put a character in plenty of situations, and it will be very strange if he is not likeable in one or two of them. Mr. Trollope thoroughly understands the art of putting his characters through their paces. If you don't care much for any of his men or women for a time, you may generally hurry on with the conviction that you will see something or other to like in them directly. Unfortunately the converse is too often true. Approval fades into dislike, and interest into tedium. If the highest aim of the novelist were to report of men and things as seen through the medium of a colourless imagination, it would be the highest praise that could be given to a writer to say that his characters seldom pleased or repelled you very much, but that they were not the kind of people it would be very desirable to be acquainted with; for the same reflection would apply to a vast majority of the people you meet in real life. Only unfortunately, we read a novel simply to be amused, while we associate with our fellows for a variety of other purposes. From a man of Mr. Trollope's powers we expect something more than the dexterous catching of a likeness. The periodic photographic school of novel-writing has its advantages. When once a tolerable proficiency is acquired, stories may be multiplied with amazing rapidity, none of them much better or worse than its predecessors. Provided each creature is tolerably like a human being, and has a different set of features from its companions, very little seems to be cared for grouping or the effects of light and shade. The last thing in the world apparently that is aimed at is the working out of a simple and harmonious whole. The multiplication of figures is the chief thing, and the system of continuing the story indefinitely to a certain extent baffles criticism. You can never say that the whole displeases you, because you can never be sure that you have got the whole. If the plan is pushed much further, clever novels bid fair to become as ephemeral as the daily papers. Several of Mr. Trollope's novels have risen beyond the level of *Phineas Finn,* especially one or two in which the clergymen and young ladies predominate. But, as regards the great mass of his stories, few of his admirers have any definite re-collection of any number of them. If *Phineas Finn* is remembered a few years hence, distinctly from the other tales in which many of its characters appear, it will owe its vitality to its political sketches, which are now comparatively devoid of interest, while the recollection of the events recorded is fresh and the excitement gone. The future historian may refer to it to discover what was the material of which Mr. Bright's waistcoats were made, and what was the bearing of the other Liberal leaders of the time in society; but the deplorable fact that it does not contain a single specimen of the parson of the period will very likely prevent its being read by the unprofessional dabblers in antiquities, who will betake themselves to Mr. Trollope's novels principally for the purpose of unearthing that extinct and interesting national curiosity.

118. 'Trollope's Irish novels', *Dublin Review*

October 1869, lxv. 361–7

In this unsigned seventeen-page essay dealing with several of Trollope's novels, but of interest chiefly in regard to the Irish novels, the overall tone of the writer is ironical and his political bias manifests itself throughout. His praise of Trollope for his understanding of Irish character and Irish problems, however, seems quite genuine.

The beauty, the skill, and the variety of Mr. Trollope's delineations of Irish character, his good taste in resisting the temptation to caricature, the yielding to which has been the bane of native Irish novelists, his rendering of the innocent *malice* (in its French meaning) of the humour of the peasantry, and his capital pictures of the out-at-elbow condition of the impoverished gentry, in whose poverty there is nothing sordid, and everything improvident and inconvenient, can hardly be thoroughly appreciated except by readers who know Ireland well. The English public with whom he is so popular would probably feel, without exactly analysing them, the truth and the cleverness, the quaintness, the humour, and the pathos of 'The MacDermots,' but we doubt whether they could appreciate 'Castle Richmond,' or realize the exact fidelity of the social relations set forth in 'The Kellys and the O'Kellys.' The difficulties and complications of the Fitzgeralds of Castle Richmond are totally unlike the difficulties and complications which sometimes beset English baronets, and are understood and discussed in a totally different spirit, and the small trading element in England has nothing in common with the proceedings of the widow Kelly, and her estimable but crafty and calculating son. The fun and ingenuity of the story every one can understand, but Anty Lynch and her brother, the young ladies at the widow's shop, and 'the lord' who is not an absentee, and is consequently beloved, but who is very poor, and therefore more beloved, are best tasted in the land of their growth. And herein is one of Mr. Trollope's greatest triumphs. That he should have written Irish stories with which English readers are much pleased and amused is not surprising, but that his Irish stories should be thoroughly satisfactory to Irish readers, who know the country and the people, this is an achievement which is to be measured by its extreme rarity. The rollicking country gentlemen, the absurdly lavish and insanely quarrelsome western magnates, the preposterous priests, the impossible lawyers, the flirting, ignorant, hoydenish horsewomen, the all-conquering military puppies, who performed Irish characters under the direction of Mr. Lever, and still occasionally make a dreary re-appearance in the quavering diatribes of Cornelius O'Dowd, amused English and Irish readers alike, partly because they were genuinely though coarsely amusing, and partly because English readers believed they were really something like people who had an actual existence in Ireland, while Irish readers knew they were not. Nobody was offended by them, they were too impartially absurd. The drunken, profane, and scheming Irish priest was no more unlike reality than the drunken, rollicking, loose-tongued English nobleman, whose viceroyalty was merely a saturnalia [sic] of feasting, singing, good stories, and low company. Baby Blake was not more unlike an ordinary Irish girl of good birth than Lady Charlotte Hilton was unlike a highly-placed English matron, or than Mrs. Paul Rooney was unlike any one who ever existed in any country. But though all these grotesque creations passed muster very well and annoyed nobody, they made it a more difficult and thankless task than before for a novelist who was not Gerald Griffin, or John Banim, or William Carleton, to please and amuse English readers without depicting Irish character as it is not, and to satisfy Irish readers by exhibiting it as it is. This task Mr. Trollope has accomplished, and from its execution he has passed to one of equal difficulty, in which his success has been quite as complete, and much more generally recognized. We allude to the combination of English and Irish life and character in his late novel, 'Phineas Finn.'

The recognition of the great ability displayed in 'Phineas Finn,' of the perfection with which Mr. Trollope's well-known characteristics are reproduced, and the exhibition of some new facilities and qualities, has been sufficiently general to give this novel a marked and singular place among the author's numerous works; but the especial cleverness of it, the distinctive feature which renders it unlike its predecessors, and an advance upon them all, has not, in our opinion, been sufficiently examined. Here are phases of Irish life—types of Irish character as perfect, as true, as exhaustive as any which he has portrayed. trans-

ported into the social and political atmosphere of England, blended
with those English 'interiors,' in the production of which he is un-
approached. . . .

But the triumphs of Phineas, political and social, were not, perhaps
happily for him, of long duration, and they ended in a way that is not
always characteristic of Irish Parliamentary aspirants. Phineas, in a very
simple, manly, and straight-forward fashion, sacrifices the Under
Secretaryship of the Colonies to his convictions in regard to the cause
of Irish Tenant Right. Let us hope that Mr. Trollope has not effected
that entirely original achievement, the writing of a historical novel in
the paulopost[1] future instead of the past tense, when he makes the crisis
of his hero's fortunes concur with the disruption of a Liberal ministry
on the Irish Land Question. . . .

It is evident that Mr. Trollope has studied the history of the Irish
Tenant League, and that he understands the principles and difficulties of
the land question in Ireland, in a way that not merely very few English
or Scotchmen do apprehend them, but more clearly, perhaps, than the
generality of Irishmen themselves. All good and sufficient reasons why,
as we suggested at the opening of this article, some Irish constituency
should do itself the honour of gratifying Mr. Trollope's unaccountable
desire to enter Parliament.

[1] ' . . . the paulopost future': *paulopost* means 'a little after' or 'somewhat later'—
usually relating to changes occurring in an igneous rock immediately after its solidifying.

HE KNEW HE WAS RIGHT

1869

Trollope, from the vantage-point of the *Autobiography* (pp. 266–7) some seven years later, was not happy with *He Knew He Was Right*.

I do not know that in any literary effort I ever fell more completely short of my own intention than in this story. It was my purpose to create sympathy for the unfortunate man who, while endeavouring to do his duty to all around him, should be led constantly astray by his unwillingness to submit his own judgment to the opinion of others. The man is made to be unfortunate enough, and the evil which he does is apparent. So far I did not fail, but the sympathy has not been created yet. I look upon the story as being nearly altogether bad. It is in part redeemed by certain scenes in the house and vicinity of an old maid in Exeter. But a novel which in its main parts is bad cannot, in truth, be redeemed by the vitality of subordinate characters.

In both the extended reviews and in briefer notices, the novel was awarded a mixed reception. In the United States, *Harper's New Monthly Magazine* (May 1869), which did not routinely praise novels because Harper and Brothers published them, approved the work for giving the transatlantic reader 'truth' about England: 'Perhaps no author gives the American reader a more correct picture of English society in its average aspect.' Edith Simcox in a review ultimately rejected for the first number of the *Academy* accused Trollope of raising 'a whirlwind of tragic passion' out of what was only 'the faintest breath of offence against the minor moralities' (see Diderik Roll-Hansen, *The Academy, 1869–1879* [1957], p. 237). The *Westminster Review* (July 1869) deplored Trollope's doling out 'the ordinary daily conversation of commonplace people at breakfast, dinner, or even when washing their hands or brushing their hair'. *He Knew He Was Right* had first appeared in thirty-two weekly parts (17 October–22 May 1868–9), sold at sixpence. *Public Opinion* (12 June 1869) commiserated with readers who had been obliged to wait from week to week and number to number to find what course events were to take in this tale possessed of an 'absorbing interest'.

119. Unsigned notice, *Saturday Review*

5 June 1869, xxvii. 751–3

A disparaging review of well over two thousand words which presents interestingly points that the *Saturday* had by now made several times in earlier reviews. Exigencies of space account for the drastic abridgement of it here, in order to make room for the fresher commentaries of the *Spectator* and *The Times*.

For the most part, we know not whether to wonder most at [Mr. Trollope's] marvellous abundance or at his strange uniformity of merit. If we were placed before the shelves which in some comprehensive library groan under the weight of his collected works (we imagine that in the British Museum there must be room for such a collection), we should revere one of the most singular monuments we know of human industry, directed to a good purpose; for certainly no one can deny that it is a good work to afford so much innocent amusement to so large a class of readers. The novel called *He Knew He Was Right* will add two more volumes to the existing Trollope Library, and we may say that it appears to us to be on the whole rather superior to the average. . . . [It] is only fair to add once more that the lovers of his style will find many descriptions excellently worked out, and many very clever subsidiary characters. Two American young ladies deserve honourable mention as excellent types of their countrywomen, though the Americans by whom they are surrounded strike us as resembling rather too closely the conventional Yankee, who has been at least sufficiently described.

120. Unsigned notice, *Spectator*

12 June 1869, xlii. 706–8

Mr. Trollope has chosen here a more than usually painful subject, and worked it out with a less than usually even hand. There are strokes of great power in the book; the history of the unhinging of Mr. Trevelyan's mind under the influence of vanity, jealousy, and suspense, and the sense of degradation involved in using low means to guard himself against deception is really one of great power, furnished with a common-place but a very striking moral. There has been little in our recent literature so good or so painful as the account of the ex-policeman, Bozzle, whom Mr. Trevelyan uses as a spy upon his wife's movements, and of the influence gained by the man's coarse assumptions over his employer's mind. In this part of the story, too, Mr. Trollope shows his usual strenuous moderation, if we may be allowed the paradox. He takes great care to show that though Bozzle is an object of disgust to us, he is so almost wholly through the degrading *circumstances* of his profession; that Bozzle himself is no worse, and possibly even a little better, than we have a right to expect from a man under such circumstances, and that it is, on the whole, possible for an ex-policeman and spy, with the vulgarest of natures and the meanest of trades, to be at least as little unworthy of individual respect as many of the less degraded characters through whose faults he gains his bread. It is characteristic of Mr. Trollope that he should write a tale about a truly tragic jealousy which has never even a reasonably adequate cause, the object of which jealousy is a man near sixty, old enough to be the heroine's father, too hollow as well as too old to do the sort of mischief attributed to him, and yet in a faint and unreal way hankering after mischief of that sort, and effectually doing a vast deal more mischief that he had ever contemplated, though after another sort. There is real genius in the conception of breaking a husband's heart and ruining his mind on so meagre a basis of fact as this,—using as the materials a proud, hard, wilful woman, with no trace of even the superficial flirt in her, and an elderly man of no real power of fascination, but a certain vanity which makes him feel pleasure in the reputation of wickedness. It is not only life, as Mr. Trollope so well knows it, but it is true tragedy to ground such a 'wreck', as poor Mr.

Trevelyan in the sullen moods which precede his death himself calls it, on the absurd foundation of an old gentleman's foppish vanity, a young lady's bitter wilfulness, and a self-occupied husband's angry, suspicious, and brooding sense of indignity. Mr. Trollope's power is exhibited at its highest,—his power as a shrewd observer, and his power as a satirist of that kind which springs from shrewd observation mingled with a *little* contempt for human nature,—in the scene where Colonel Osborne, the selfish old gentleman of sixty to whom we have referred, comes down after the separation between Mr. and Mrs. Trevelyan to Nuncombe Putney, where the wife is living with the mother of one of her husband's friends, simply to increase his reputation as a dangerous man by pretending a little sentiment for the injured wife. . . .

Not less severely real, and not less terribly tragic, is the picture of the influence gained over Mr. Trevelyan's mind by his spy, the ex-policeman, Bozzle, partly because Bozzle alone justifies his own jealousy by the black view which he takes of Colonel Osborne's relations to his wife, and because Trevelyan thirsts almost above everything for the assurance that he is only acting with the proper pride and authority of an injured husband,—partly because the familiarity with evil which Bozzle shows, and his unwavering assumption that everybody is much worse than they seem, so powerfully infects his own imagination, that his own secret estimate of his wife's innocence yields before Bozzle's assumption of her guilt. . . .

So far we have found no fault either with the art or the morality of Mr. Trollope's story. Indeed, throughout the first volume (except perhaps in relation to Nora Rowley, who is uniformly vulgar and uninteresting), Mr. Trollope impresses us with a power of conception he has rarely equalled in any of his novels, and gives us quite his highest style of execution. In the second volume, however, as it seems to us, the truth and power of the drawing, no less than the realistic morality of the tale, fail very rapidly. The picture of Mr. Trevelyan's breaking mind and overweening vanity, so powerfully commenced in the first volume, is spun out to wearisome length, and quite without any fresh artistic touches until the end is close at hand. The comedy touching Cammy French, with which Mr. Trollope seeks to lighten the story, becomes exaggerated and coarse. And worst of all, the conception with which, as we believe, Mr. Trollope clearly set out, of Mrs. Trevelyan,—the conception of a self-willed, haughty, steely woman, whose little feeling for her husband and easily wounded self-love were even more the cause of the whole tragedy than her husband's conceit and weakness,

melts away into something which it is almost impossible to define,
—for nothing can exceed her real hardness and self-occupation on
her husband's death-bed, and yet it seems the novelist's main effort
to make you regard her as a deeply injured woman, who has been
infinitely more sinned against than sinning. We entirely decline to take
this view, and even assert that Mr. Trollope in commencing his tale did
not take it himself. We are both astonished and displeased at the sympathy
which the novelist asks for on behalf of Mrs. Trevelyan as the tale
draws to its close, since he has drawn throughout a cold, self-willed,
high-tempered woman, who, though doubtless entirely free from any
imputation of the kind for which she suffers, never shows, till the end of
the tale, a particle of sympathy for her husband's sufferings, does do a
vast deal wilfully to provoke him, and is portrayed, even during his last
illness, as without a shadow of self-reproach for the obstinate heartlessness of her own conduct in the beginning of the troubles, and solely
occupied with the absorbing desire to extract her own complete
exculpation from her husband's dying lips. Mrs. Trevelyan is naturally
enough drawn, if we were never called upon to pity her, and were
permitted to condemn her as she deserves. But when Mr. Trollope tries
to lead us into wasting compassion upon her, and yet makes her so
unlovely as he does,—so utterly without remorse for conduct which
seems to us far worse than her husband's, though not in the way
imputed to her,—so concentred in self even in the most solemn
moments,—we not only rebel against the attempt, but have a right to
say that the art of the story is thereby spoiled. Let us see what account
Mr. Trollope himself gives of her proceedings. After her first natural
indignation against her husband for feeling any disposition to 'warn'
her about Colonel Osborne's attentions, she finds out for herself that
there *is* some necessity for caution; she finds Colonel Osborne anxious
to commit her to having a secret with him which she is not to impart
to her husband,—a secret which she is silly and disloyal enough to admit,—and she observes that his hand-pressure is too warm, and his
manner of calling her by her Christian name too affectionate, on parting
with her. All this makes her see that there is at least some colour for her
husband's warning,—and we must remember that Mr. Trevelyan had
at this time never even suggested anything against his wife, only against
Colonel Osborne and any close intimacy with him. She feels that her
husband is partially justified in his warning, and Mr. Trollope tells us
that if he had now gone to her and said a gentle word, all might have
been right. But he, in his annoyance at her private interview with

Colonel Osborne, does not make the advance, and she will not. 'If he chooses to be cross and sulky, he may be cross and sulky,' says Mrs. Trevelyan to herself, as she goes up to her baby. Then there comes a half-reconciliation, in which we are compelled to say that Mrs. Trevelyan makes herself as disagreeable as possible. Instead of admitting that there had been anything in Colonel Osborne's manners to justify her husband's dislike, as she had herself felt, she is haughty, resentful, and irritating, and Mr. Trevelyan shows the better temper of the two in admitting a reconciliation at all. After this reconciliation a note comes to her from Colonel Osborne at dinner-time. She does not open it, but hands it to her sister, with the irritating remark, 'Will you give that to Louis? It comes from the man whom he supposes to be my lover.' It comes from the man whom her husband thought to be trying to make mischief, and whom she had reason to know was not strictly loyal, and yet she does nothing but taunt her husband with his uneasiness. Mr. Trevelyan, feeling himself in a false position, now begs his wife to receive Colonel Osborne as usual, and let the whole thing be as if it had never been. 'He,' as Mr. Trollope himself remarks, 'was softer-hearted than she, and knowing this, was afraid to say anything which would again bring forth from her expressions of scorn.' We are carefully told, moreover, that Mrs. Trevelyan 'was still hard and cold, and still assumed a tone which seemed to imply that she was the injured person.' . . . After this Mrs. Trevelyan receives and destroys a note from Colonel Osborne (which contained nothing in particular), quarrels fiercely with her husband for being angry when he sees her note in reply to Colonel Osborne, which had not been shown to him, and herself proposes the separation. After the separation, she receives Colonel Osborne, as we have seen, without the slightest occasion to do so, and when the mere fact of doing so was, as she well knew, a deliberate insult to her husband, and then, for the rest of the book, becomes the injured wife and heroic sufferer,—at least, so Mr. Trollope wishes us to think her, though his delineation of her at the last is of one utterly self-seeking. We must say that though there is plenty of fault on both sides, the wife seems to us to have far more responsibility for her husband's alienation of mind and ultimate death than he has,—from her first admission of a secret with Colonel Osborne, to her obstinate pride in insisting upon receiving him when she is living apart from her husband. To our minds, Mrs. Trevelyan was meant at first by Mr. Trollope to be an unlovely character, and gradually became invested with a very false and hollow atmosphere of sentiment as the story grew towards its end. But we dislike her even more when she is wringing her exculpation from her dying husband, than when she is taunting him with his disapproval of the man in whose manners she had learned by her own experience to detect something unpleasantly familiar and tender.

We have no space left to remark on the wonderfully true and striking picture of the stiff, prejudiced, warm-hearted provincial character given in the sketch of old Miss Stanbury of Exeter and her various relations. That part of the book is absolutely perfect, and Dorothy Stanbury is the most delicate and fascinating of all Mr. Trollope's women. No doubt he has a little overdone the farcical element in the account of Mr. Gibson, the minor canon, and his wooing of Arabella and Camilla French. The history of the changes produced in Arabella's chignon by her desire to win Mr. Gibson is one of the most humorous of Mr. Trollope's petty strokes of humour; but the fierce war waged by 'Cammy' for her clerical prize is not comedy, it is farce. On the whole, we should say that while *He Knew He Was Right* contains some of Mr. Trollope's most powerful writing,—passing beyond the sphere in which he usually excels,—the latter part of the story drags on quite beneath the level of his ordinary execution, while the moral of it is distorted as we have rarely known any moral of Mr. Trollope's distorted before.

121. Unsigned notice, *The Times*

26 August 1869, p. 4

Much of this review, running to nearly three full columns, is taken up with long quotations from the novel and summary of the narrative.

Mr. Trollope has launched another novel, constructed on those well-known lines which secured for him long ago the reputation of a skilful book-builder. Like a literary prince as he is, he has not only a whole fleet of argosies at sea sailing smoothly down the trade winds, but every now and then a vessel fresh from the stocks, leaving harbour on the same prosperous voyage with guns firing and flags flying. To remark that *He Knew He Was Right* contains clever and natural writing, that it is generally very interesting, but sometimes very wearisome, that its story is in nothing forced or unnatural, but is as shapeless as a boned fowl, entirely without any skeleton of plot or incident, is saying no more than that it exemplifies in a rather eminent degree most of those merits and faults its author has from time to time made us all familiar with. A short recapitulation of these will therefore be the best introduction to the book itself. . . .

His writings have no aesthetic purpose; they mean nothing more than they say; they are not written *at* the reader; the author thinks of nothing but how his work may be made a correct copy, complete and minute; he looks at human nature as a man looks out of a window, painting exactly what he sees, up to the exact square of a pane. And the fact that he takes no trouble to devise plot or incident, but rather to avoid them, shows the strength of his pen. Ordinary sensation novelists require the stimulating and adventitious aid of a strange and startling fable; to bind Miss Braddon over to keep the Ten Commandments in a literary sense would be to tie her hands, but Mr. Trollope, by sheer fidelity of rendering carries us with him through stories in themselves for the most part thoroughly commonplace and uninteresting. And another reason of his success is that his novels can be fully enjoyed without the exertion of much mental activity; he leaves no gaps to be filled up by the reader's own independent imagination; he makes his characters think their every thought aloud, and if this occasions a quick mind some impatience, it at least saves a lazy one a great deal of trouble. And the simple fare he sets before us needs no educated taste, but only a healthy appetite. That charming work of Nathaniel Hawthorne's, *Transformation*, will always be caviare to the multitude, but *Framley Parsonage* is a delight to school-boys and scholars, young girls and men of the world. . . .

In *He Knew He Was Right* there is not a man or woman whom in real life we would greatly care to know, and there are certainly a great many we would rather not have anything to do with, and his readers would take it as a favour if Mr. Trollope would put a little vertebrate strength into his next literary creations, if he would give us a lover who is not like Issachar,[1] and a woman who has a mind of her own and knows it. Nor do we see why he should so frequently fly in the face of the proverb which associates gray hairs with wisdom; however often it may be the case in real life, there is in fiction a sort of impiety which should be seldom ventured on in making middle-age the synonym of silliness. Mr. Trollope's purpose, as we take it, is not satire; then why does he not show us a little more of the creditable side of human nature, instead of halting halfway between beauty and ugliness, and painting the commonplace? He gives us with ease and accuracy the pervading type, yet we cannot help wishing he would make a higher attempt at something, perhaps, less matter of fact, but certainly more alluring.

By dint of long practice Mr. Trollope has attained a wonderful facility of production; his novels almost tread each other down, and their rapid succession show that, at least in his case, what is always easy reading is easy writing too. Nelson sighed for a whole *Gazette* to himself, and got it; if Mr. Trollope has ever longed for a whole library, he is in a fair way of obtaining his wish. There is a sort of fascinating juggle in the rapidity with which his books follow each other; one is hardly 'at all the booksellers' before the next is half through the press, and we are reminded of the conjuror who draws tape out of his mouth, snipping it at intervals, as long as any one chooses to look at him. It is all the same, and cut in any lengths you please—collections of newspaper articles, collections of magazine articles, one and two volume novels; you pay your money and take your choice. . . .

Mr. Trollope has never given a better illustration of all he is and all he is not than *He Knew He Was Right*. The Barsetshire series show us his

[1] Issachar: one of the patriarchs (*Genesis* xxx. 18).

high merit; and they are so equal, so perfect in themselves, and so necessary to each other, that we wish for nothing else than they give us. But now that Barset, and the Bishop, and the Archdeacon, and all our old friends are done with, and we find Mr. Trollope still in the same vein, but with a little less vigour, and manifestly writing against time books that are pleasant reading for leisure hours, but are not such imperative claimants on the busiest lives as *Barchester Towers* and *Dr. Thorne* certainly were, we are apt to grow critical, and we think that most readers of *He Knew He Was Right* will agree with us when we say that, as coming from Mr. Trollope, there is something insufficient and unsatisfactory both in its conception and execution. . . .

There is one character however in the novel for which we really have to thank Mr. Trollope—that of Bozzle, the detective. Detective policemen have been a great deal too well treated hitherto. Novelists have delighted for the most part to surround them with an air of romance and mystery and gentility which in no way belongs to them. No doubt the public detective—if he will allow us to call him so—is a very useful functionary, and the usual preamble to his evidence in a police court, 'from information I received,' implies a great deal of keen energy and hard work; but for the private detective there is not much to be said— society would be better without him, and we are glad Mr. Trollope has given us in that character an ordinary vulgar rogue. Mr. Bozzle, no doubt, did his master's dirty work well, but his ingenuity in making out a bill amounts to a series of petty larcenies, and he is by no means the gentlemanly, quiet-looking man in plain clothes, with a marvellous eye and an iron hand, with whom, in a literary way, we are all familiar; but a sly, ungrammatical varlet, shrewd enough, but always ready to sacrifice his employers' interests to his own. As far as the private detective delusion is concerned, this is all very satisfactory and as it should be; but, at the same time, this very episode is one of the most irritating parts of the book. We are angry, and will not accept it even as a fiction that a scholar and an English gentleman should in the abominable indulgence of his ungrounded jealousy allow himself and his wife to fall into the hands of Bozzle, vulgar and h-less, who is for ever maddening Trevelyan by assuring him with respect to the colonel and Mrs. Trevelyan that 'he'll be down upon them together and no mistake;' and by making such observations as that 'I don't see as parsons are better than other folk when they has to do with a lady as likes her fancy-man.' . . .

It is undeniably a book well written and worth reading, wearisome now and then, either from the subject-matter failing in interest, or from the author's too free indulgence in the favourite habit alluded to before of making his characters think on paper. It also leaves the impression of being somewhat drawn out, but contains many happy instances of Mr. Trollope's peculiar and felicitous style. The fact is Mr. Trollope is one of the few novel writers the very excellence of whose work tends to produce hypercriticism. We cannot help wishing that a man who can do so much would do a little more; that he would give us something beyond a mere piece of realism; that, not content with the close and clear reflection of a square foot of the ground we all walk on, he would hold his mirror a little higher and include a larger area, some salient features of the country, and some sea and sky.

122. Unsigned notice, *British Quarterly Review*

July 1869, l. 263–4

The chief artistic study of Mr. Trollope's new novel is a psychological one—viz., the rise and development of a jealous monomania; its origin in wilful caprice, its strengthening through perverse obstinacy, and its consummation in misery, madness, and death. . . . Like all Mr. Trollope's writings, it is uncompromisingly realistic—the flaws of his heroes and heroines are remorselessly exhibited. It is no justification of this pre-Raphaelitism that it is true to life. A work of art should not be true to life, but should idealize—that it may elevate it. Why, too, we are constrained to ask, should so much of the story of modern fiction be made to turn upon the disordered relations of husband and wife? . . . We must utter an earnest protest against this morbid infatuation of modern novelists for plots and stories turning upon conjugal infidelity.

THE VICAR OF BULLHAMPTON

1870

Trollope felt that in *The Vicar of Bullhampton* he was meeting a new and difficult challenge by trying 'to create sympathy' for a fallen woman. He seems to have given himself so much to the problems of the scenes involving her and her family that he was not so deeply engaged as was usual with him in living the life of the more respectable personages that occupied his novel.

The *Vicar of Bullhampton* was written chiefly with the object of exciting not only pity but sympathy for a fallen woman, and of raising a feeling of forgiveness for such in the minds of other women. I could not venture to make this female the heroine of my story. To have made her a heroine at all would have been directly opposed to my purpose. It was necessary therefore that she should be a second-rate personage in the tale;—but it was with reference to her life that the tale was written, and the hero and the heroine with their belongings are all subordinate. . . .

I have not introduced her lover on the scene, nor have I presented her to the reader in the temporary enjoyment of any of those fallacious luxuries, the longing for which is sometimes more seductive to evil than love itself. She is introduced as a poor abased creature, who hardly knows how false were her dreams, with very little of the Magdalene about her—because though there may be Magdalenes they are not often found—but with an intense horror of the sufferings of her position. Such being her condition, will they who naturally are her friends protect her? The vicar who has taken her by the hand endeavours to excite them to charity; but father, and brother, and sister are alike hard-hearted. It had been my purpose at first that the hand of every Brattle should be against her; but my own heart was too soft to enable me to make the mother cruel,—or the unmarried sister who had been the early companion of the forlorn one.

As regards all the Brattles, the story is, I think, well told. The characters are true, and the scenes at the mill are in keeping with human nature. For the rest of the book I have little to say. It is not very bad, and it certainly is not very good. As I have myself forgotten what the heroine does and says—except that she tumbles into a ditch—I cannot expect that any one else should remember her. But I have forgotten nothing that was done or said by any of the Brattles (*Autobiography*, pp. 273–7).

The novel received no very cordial welcome from the Press. There was not much protest, and there was even some approval, at Trollope's rehabilitating Carry Brattle; but critics found much to complain about in the monotony of large parts of Trollope's story. The *Athenaeum* (30 April 1870) judged that on the whole Trollope had brought off his story of Carry Brattle's reinstatement, but had 'not unnaturally' sheered away from the history of her fall. Margaret Oliphant in *Blackwood's* (May 1870) confessed her disappointment in Trollope's abandoning Barsetshire and its inhabitants for less simple and innocent heroines like Mary Lowther, who in *The Vicar of Bullhampton* can 'engage herself to a man she cares nothing for' only a short time after breaking her engagement with the man she really loves. *Harper's Magazine* in New York (August 1870) dismissed the novel as another instance of Trollope's playing off one lover against another in his usual style 'through three hundred pages of what is called romance, probably for the all-sufficient reason that it contains neither history nor philosophy nor poetry enough to give it a right of classification any where else'.

---

123. Unsigned notice, *Saturday Review*

4 May 1870, xxix. 646–7

To the non-novel writing world Mr. Trollope . . . must always be a phenomenon; no novels going are better than his best—and how many good ones he has written! But now and then he furnishes us with a slight insight into the machinery of what is called the inventive faculty, which, if it does not make such speed intelligible, at least removes it out of the sphere of the supernatural. There is at any rate no reason in the *Vicar of Bullhampton* why a practised pen should not have held on at its most rattling pace, however that pace may be beyond our own experience or comprehension. A writer like Mr. Trollope cannot write without characteristic turns, occasional flashes of observation, felicitous hits —they are part of himself, but the rule here seems to be, the pen running on by its own impetus. We see that it knows its way over the paper. There is no suspense or hesitation. All the familiar tricks and mannerisms take their places unprompted; and long sentences form themselves about what *he* told himself, and what *she* told herself. Sometimes recapitulation in the epistolary form expands into whole pages while lagging thought is scarcely yet in sight. Such a pen is an instrument to be proud of, but we all know that the best of workmen need looking after and we are sure that Mr. Trollope's pen has had more of its own way than he at all designed at starting. . . . The fact is that the *Vicar of Bullhampton* is a story without a plot, and not only without a plot, but one showing no connexion whatever between the two trains of events and two groups of characters which occupy its pages. The chapters which tell of the one and those which relate the adventures of the other might be printed in separate volumes without a word of explanation or anything being missed. . . .

The atmosphere of the *Vicar of Bullhampton* constitutes a sort of 'black country' of manners. We think of its inhabitants together, not because the action ever brings them together, but because the same contradictious tone and temper pervade every scene. Nobody is pleasant; we find ourselves applying sibilant triads of epithets to one after another in turn. Surly, sulky, sullen, we see no reason why they should care for one another, or why we should care for any of them. We gather from the preface that Mr. Trollope has a moral design in his book. 'I have introduced in the *Vicar of Bullhampton* the character of a girl whom I will call—for want of a truer word that shall not in its truth be offensive—a castaway. I have endeavoured to endow her with qualities that may create sympathy, and I have brought her back at last from degradation at least to decency.' In the pursuit of his aim Mr Trollope cannot be reproached with making vice attractive. He tells us that Carry is pretty—an impression of which the illustrator has done his best to disabuse us[1]—and that a certain early charm had won the good will of the Vicar and his wife; but a less taking wrongdoer seldom demands our pity. We suppose she was led astray at first by her affections, though we are not told so, but her cool indifference whether the man she is afterwards engaged to is hanged or not shows that they were well under control by the end of the story. And her father and brother, who share the Vicar's regard, are as sour a pair as we ever knew time spent upon. Old Brattle is perhaps the best character as a work of art, the writer's mind has been most present in him; but no clownish rustic of fiction was ever a more ungracious piece of realism.

A sort of savageness pervades the book both in gentle and simple. We get used to anything, and it is only on a retrospect that we perceive

[1] The illustrations were engravings on wood produced by an artist designated on the title-page as H. Woods.

this singular species of harmony. Images of personal violence and broken bones are prominent. . . . The Vicar, who is the author's spokesman as it were, does the rudest things, either not knowing or not caring. The foolish fussy Marquis is misled by very suspicious appearances to believe the lout Sam Brattle guilty of murder, and insists that he ought to be shut up; but nothing he does or says can excuse the Vicar's solecism in bringing the Marquis's daughters into the argument; nor does the fact that these ladies were, in the author's words, old and ugly, form any excuse for dragging their names, by way of illustration, into a judicial investigation. . . . The Marquis in revenge builds a Methodist chapel at the vicarage gates, sharing the general ignorance that the site chosen is part of the glebe. The one civil person in the whole group of characters is the Marquis's son, who helps his father cleverly enough out of the scrape he has got into, and cheats the Vicar out of his cherished grudge without any damaging admissions; for which he gets called silky and soapy—so much is such peacemaking and filial respect out of keeping with the general tone.

We have said that there is no plot properly speaking, but there is much of the love-making on which a plot generally hinges. Mary Lowther has a lover of the constant sort, Squire Gilmore, the Vicar's friend. We do not wonder that this gentleman should have failed to make his proposals acceptable; there is nothing particularly persuasive either in himself or his love-making. His friends, however, the Vicar and his wife, are unwarrantably urgent that she should accept him, and Mary, who has a prudent eye to her own interest, would have him if she could; but she tells her friend, while her heart is still blank paper, that though she may have her doubts on this point behind his back, 'When I meet him face to face I cannot do it.' . . .

We have spoken freely of this not very satisfactory book; yet it is fair to add that not only are there good scenes and bright passages in it, but the Vicar himself has now and then a caustic humour, especially in his most charitable phase—his dealings with the Methodist minister (who, by the way, quotes the Church Catechism, seeming to suppose it Scripture)—which is in the author's true vein; all prompting the admission that, after all, Mr. Trollope's third-rate is more readable than most novelists' best.

124. Unsigned notice, *The Times*

3 June 1870, p. 4

Such is Mr. Anthony Trollope's latest clerical novel. No doubt it is interesting to see a good vicar struggling with the cares of parish life. But after all, parish life is dull and monotonous, especially when its description is a repetition. And this is just the fault we find with Bullhampton Vicarage, a great portion of the book is as flat as walking along the Trumpington road. It is a nice, easy, safe reading book for old ladies and young ladies, though we can fancy some of the latter class may be terribly provoked at Mary Lowther's high principle. Besides this the story skips about so from Loring to Bullhampton and back again, that no sooner is the reader comfortably settled in one place than he has to pack up and start off for the other. In our opinion the minor characters are much the best. . . . These and the general safeness of the story will make Bullhampton Vicarage welcome in all well-regulated families, but we do not think that either in construction or development this novel will add much to Mr. Anthony Trollope's reputation.

SIR HARRY HOTSPUR OF HUMBLETHWAITE

1870

This short novel, published in one volume of 324 pages, received almost universal approval. *Harper's Magazine* in New York (October 1871) declared it 'the saddest story, and at the same time the simplest, that Anthony Trollope has ever written' and attributed its effectiveness to its 'very simplicity'.

125. Unsigned notice, *The Times*

16 November 1870, p. 4

Nearly a four-column review occupied almost entirely by a detailed synopsis of the narrative.

In this short novel we are glad to recognize a return to what we must call Mr. Trollope's old form. If the spectacle of a young and innocent girl wasting her purest affections on a swindler and a scoundrel, and dying for love of one of the greatest reprobates known in novel life, be unpleasant to our feelings, it cannot be denied that the characters in this book are drawn with a vigour and boldness which have been wanting in Mr. Trollope's recent works. What was *Bullhampton Vicarage* but dulness itself! Very safe reading for ladies' schools, but anything but lively to the general reader. *Sir Harry Hotspur* certainly does not sin in this respect, but some of its revelations into the life of the black sheep at least are anything but fitted for the perusal of the young. It used to be printed on some French novels, '*La mère en défendra la lecture à sa fille*,'[1] and the same might be said of parts of *Sir Harry Hotspur*. But the reading world is not entirely composed of young ladies. This book may do good to many of both sexes more advanced in life.

[1] Mothers will forbid their daughters to read this novel.

126. Unsigned notice, *Athenaeum*

19 November 1870, p. 654

. . . It appears to us decidedly more successful than any other of Mr. Trollope's shorter stories. The author has shown in this brilliant novelette that he can interest his readers by rapid and direct sketching, as well as by the minute detail and patient evolution of little traits of character that mark his larger works. Of course the book does not contain any creation that for a moment can be classed with Mrs. Proudie, Mr. Crawley or Mr. Palliser. The best characters—the Baronet and Lady Emily—are given only in outline; but no reader who begins to read this book is likely to lay it down until the last page is turned.

Sir Harry Hotspur of Humblethwaite is one of Mr. Trollope's very best short tales. Mr. Trollope's genius demands space. He reels off his characters with almost unerring truthfulness, but then his touch is so light and his mode of portraiture so little intense, that you want the multiplication of details, the variety of situations, the change of lights, to make up for that *depth* of knowledge of them which Thackeray, or George Eliot, or sometimes Scott will contrive to give in a single scene and in a few sentences. Mr. Trollope's best figures are usually impressive in proportion to the scope he has had for painting them in a variety of different circumstances. Archdeacon Grantly appears in more than twice as many situations as Dean Arabin, and consequently Archdeacon Grantly is more than twice as vivid in our memories, though nothing could have been better than the sketch of Dean Arabin. Mr. Trollope's imagination paints not by intension, but by extension. Who can remember what Rachel Ray was like? Who can forget Miss Dunstable,—we should say Mrs. Thorne? But still there is a great difference between the excellence of Mr. Trollope's different short tales,—far more than between the excellence of his different long tales. And 'Sir Harry Hotspur of Humblethwaite and Scarrowby' is one of the very best of them. For the fundamental idea of the tale was one exactly suited to Mr. Trollope's genius, and one which, more than most others, was capable of complete delineation within a short compass. In it Mr. Trollope has sketched the conflict of feelings in the mind of a high-minded but proud man, who had always accustomed himself to consider his duty to the Estate and the Title, when that duty to the Estate and the Title comes into direct collision with his duty to his daughter in whom he is wrapt up. At his death the baronetcy would necessarily go to George Hotspur, the son of a first cousin, a very black sheep who had learned to gamble, and to incur debts of a decidedly dishonourable character, and whose manliness and veracity of character had long ago disappeared; but who, for the rest, was a man not without considerable ability; who knew how to make himself pleasant to women, and had some of that 'distinction' of *manner* which sometimes runs in the blood long after the true core and life of it has disappeared. Nothing can be more powerful than Mr. Trollope's delineation of the struggle in old Sir Harry Hotspur's mind between the sense of fitness which predisposes him to favour a match between this gentleman and his daughter, on the ground that it will reunite the title and the property and keep the estates still in the old family, and his love and duty to his daughter and the honourable aversion in his own mind towards the shade of dishonour attaching to this man's name. He vacillates between the two feelings; and when his daughter, not knowing the gravity of the imputations on her cousin, interprets her father's vacillation as a permission to fall in love and does fall in love with George Hotspur, Mr. Trollope's picture of the irresolution of the haughty and usually absolute old baronet, and of the see-saw of policy into which this irresolution plunges him,—now breaking off the match absolutely, and then again giving way to the will of his almost equally resolute and pertinacious daughter, and giving a half-sanction to the engagement, until at last the black sheep turns out to be so black that it becomes the father's duty rather to risk the death of his daughter and the ruin of all his hopes and plans, than to admit the possibility of the marriage,—is as good of its kind as any moral picture he has ever yet drawn for us. No subject ever suited Mr. Trollope better. He is, before all things, a man of the world, and as a man of the world he understands to the core every passion involved in this conflict,—the pride of blood, the sense of something like duty to the property and the title, the pride of honour, the sense of chivalry which compels Sir Harry to spurn a connection with a man of deficient honour, and then, again, the subtle twist which his wish to continue the old line through his daughter gives to his deep paternal love,—and he delineates these external effects with the most accurate and sure artistic touch. It is very nearly a new subject,—new, at all events, when touched with this fidelity and moderation;—for the ordinary novelists who have dealt with the pride of rank and wealth have either taken part against the worldly father who feels it, as if he were all but purely bad, or have made him the mere victim of some external necessity. Mr. Trollope does not make this mistake. Sir Harry Hotspur of Humblethwaite and Scarrowby is one of the highest-minded and highest-mettled of men. Willingly he will not sacrifice his daughter's happiness to any desire for prolonging the family name and title; nay, when his daughter herself is eager for it, he resolutely sets his face against it; but still, the convenience and external suitability of the arrangement fascinate his imagination in spite of himself, cause a slight vacillation, a tendency to exaggerate the hopes of the black sheep's reformation, a tendency to make the least of his evil qualities, and so produce a fatal hesitation and lead on the plot to a tragic end. No foil to Sir Harry Hotspur could be better than his feeble, submissive, amiable wife, Lady Elizabeth.

As to the black sheep himself, George Hotspur, we are not quite so sure that every line and touch are truthful. What we doubt about is whether there would not have been that in the evil of his character, not so much on account of his sins or vices, as on account of his knowledge that he had fallen below the moral level even of the fast society in which he lived, in short, that he was what even his own friends and associates would have called a cur,—which would have given some flavour of an air of caitiff to him certain to be detected and disliked by so high-spirited and keen a girl as Emily Hotspur. We are well aware that a triumphant *roué* might well have fascinated such a girl; that the qualities of a *roué* might only have added a new charm of self-confidence to his manners; but the self-confidence evidently was not in the least in George Hotspur's heart. From the first he can do nothing without clever advice to back him. He is a cur at heart. Would not this have spoiled the high-bred manner necessary to captivate such a girl as his cousin? Mr. Trollope knows the world better than his critics. But we confess a doubt whether such a nature as George Hotspur's,—dishonourable and cowardly in the conventional as well as the real sense, and known as such to himself,—could have been entirely consistent with the fresh, easy, high-bred manner which is described as winning the heart of his cousin. Emily Hotspur evidently loves mettle as much as her father. It was her cousin's apparent masterliness of manner, something which seemed to cover mettle, which took hold of her imagination. Could there have been exactly that kind of fascination about a character such as his,—a character base in every sense, the world's sense as well as the moralist's, to the very bottom? We do not say it could not be so, but we feel a serious doubt. Nothing can be better than the incidental sketches of George Hotspur's creditors and of their modes of persecution. In the sketches of Mr. Hart and Captain Stubber Mr. Trollope paints with as much power as ease.

Perhaps the least successful picture in the book is the drawing of Emily Hotspur herself. In that picture Mr. Trollope impresses us as attempting what is in some sense, not in the least beyond his *conception*, but beyond the resources of his artistic style, to execute adequately. Mr. Trollope can tell you what a girl of Emily Hotspur's passion of nature would *do*, and how she would do it, but he cannot tell you really what she feels. He needs an intensiveness of style to tell us this, on which he never ventures, and yet the picture is to our minds conspicuously incomplete without it. It is like the attempt of a geometrician to solve by plane geometry a problem which requires geometry of three dimensions. The figure of Emily Hotspur is really a very fine conception, but it is a conception which it needed something of Thackeray's power of condensing passion into words to delineate. Lest we should be supposed to be mystical and obscure, we will illustrate what we mean, by that great outburst of Lady Castlewood's in *Esmond*, where, after recognizing Henry Esmond at the evening service in the Cathedral, she welcomes him home again after their estrangement:

'I know how wicked my heart has been, and I have suffered too, my dear. I confessed to Mr. Atterbury.—I must not tell any more. He—I said I would not write to you or go to you,—and it was better even that, having parted, we should part. But I knew you would come back—I own that. That is no one's fault. And to-day, Henry, in the anthem, when they sang it, "When the Lord turned again the captivity of Zion, we were like them that dream"; I thought, yes, like them that dream,—them that dream. And then it went, "They that sow in tears shall reap in joy; and he that goeth forth and weepeth, shall doubtless come home again with rejoicing, bringing his sheaves with him." I looked up from the book and saw you. I was not surprised when I saw you. I knew you would come, my dear, and saw the golden sunshine round your head.'

Now that is the sort of intensity of style which seems to us to be needed for the painting of such a conception as this tragedy of Emily Hotspur's wasted passion,—the passion of a proud but devoted nature, wasted on a purely worthless object, and suffering as much from the sense of mere contamination in having been capable of giving such love to such a creature, as in the pain of separation and loss. Mr. Trollope has imagined most finely the sort of pang which killed Emily Hotspur, the sense of degradation of a proud nature, as well as the rebellion of a passionate love against God for not granting to her prayers the means of saving a nature too base to know its own need of salvation. But Mr. Trollope's art does not seem to command the symbols by which this could be adequately expressed. He has drawn a nature which needed portraiture by the expression of feeling as much as by action, and has failed to portray the intensity of feeling of which he has given us the sign. Consequently, he has left this central figure unfinished. He could depict the conflict of the father's hopes and passions. When he came to the daughter's the voice failed him. He needed the command of a 'lyrical cry' in addition to the ordinary resource of a great novelist, and he had it not at his disposal.

128. Unsigned notice, *Saturday Review*

10 December 1870, xxx. 753–5

A long review (approaching three thousand words), heavy on the anti-aristocratic bias it sees in the novel and in Trollope's characteristic attitude.

Sir Harry Hotspur is not a tragedy, though high hopes are overthrown; it is not even a sad story, though the heroine dies for love; for the author's sympathies are not with the hopes, and the reader's sympathies are never for an instant engaged by the lady's sorrows. . . . We here see one lover die, and really we would not hold out a straw to save her. No one can call the book pleasant reading, for throughout everybody is in the wrong, and everybody is going hopelessly to the bad; but it has thought, and a purpose. It is in fact a satire, veiling a very serious if not a fierce meaning. Mr. Trollope is never very friendly to an aristocracy. He has been all along at pains to show that blood and descent and great possessions are no safeguard against the lowest aims and meanest vices. He is much more alive to the dangers of luxurious idleness than to the stimulus to virtuous action which so many people delight to see in high place and its noble opportunities; but recent scandals seem to have spurred him to a keener sense of the mockery that too often attaches to hereditary honours, turning name and lineage into a machinery for wider exposure and aggravated disgrace. . . .

The style of *Sir Harry Hotspur* shows signs of greater care than Mr. Trollope always finds it worth while to take. Nature and practice generally enable him to say clearly what he wants to say with very little trouble, but we note perhaps fewer of certain tricks of rapid writing which weary the reader's ears in his recent stories.

RALPH THE HEIR

1871

Trollope placed *Ralph the Heir* low among his novels (*Autobiography*, p. 285), despite the fact that it had been welcomed by the reviewers as a notable success.

I have always thought it to be one of the worst novels I have written, and almost to have justified that dictum that a novelist after fifty should not write love-stories. It was in part a political novel; and that part which appertains to politics, and which recounts the electioneering experiences of the candidates at Percycross is well enough. Percycross and Beverley were, of course, one and the same place.[1] Neefit, the breeches-maker, and his daughter, are also good in their way, —and Moggs, the daughter's lover, who was not only lover, but also one of the candidates at Percycross as well. But the main thread of the story,—that which tells of the doings of the young gentlemen and young ladies,—the heroes and the heroines,—is not good. Ralph the heir has not much life about him; while Ralph who is not the heir, but is intended to be the real hero, has none. The same may be said of the young ladies,—of whom one, she who was meant to be the chief, has passed utterly out of my mind, without leaving a trace of remembrance behind.

129. Unsigned notice, *Athenaeum*

15 April 1871, p. 456

Those who like, at their leisure, to look for portraits in the costume of this period, will be amply rewarded by the perusal of this book. Every detail is marvellously true to modern life: the little self-deceptions of society are admirably exposed. Where this sort of workmanship is good throughout, it is difficult to select choice passages; but the whole description of Ralph's final settlement among the Eardhams,—notably the punt-scene at Cookham, with its deliciously false sentiment and innocent affection,—is certainly a masterpiece in its way. . . . [It is] a novel which we trust we appreciate, but cannot heartily admire.

[1] Trollope himself had stood for Parliament at Beverley in 1868. (See *Autobiography*, pp. 242–53.)

130. Unsigned notice, *Spectator*

15 April 1871, xliv. 450–3

To the mass of men, such a novel as *Ralph the Heir* brings not only a very large increase in their experience of men, but a very much larger increase than their own personal contact with the prototypes, if prototypes there be, of these personages, would ever have afforded them. Nor is the art of the book by any means deficient. We are not sure that we could name more than one or two of Mr. Trollope's tales in which the unity of the story is nearly as well kept up from the beginning to the close; and we doubt whether we could name any in which the studies of widely different types of character are so well adapted reciprocally to bring out, by similarity or by contrast, the force and significance of the other sketches. Take the contrast between the picture of the obstinate old squire, Gregory Newton, planning to put his natural son in possession of the estate which was entailed on his nephew by buying out the embarrassed heir, and throwing his whole heart so passionately into his plan that when he comes close upon fruition he is intoxicated and half-fay with his own success, and the picture of the breeches-maker, not more obstinate than old Squire Newton, for that would be impossible, but less capable of weighing what may be done and what cannot be done by pertinacity to achieve the object of an ambition, scheming in the same tenacious way for his daughter's advancement in the world, and thrown by his ultimate disappointment into a state of moral bitterness bordering on fury and despair, yet never for a moment passing the strict limits of that vulgar, narrow-minded vindictiveness which expresses resentment by trying to lower the object of it in the eyes of the world. Both ambitions ultimately fail; the squire's by his premature death, and Mr. Neefit's partly as a result of that premature death which sets Ralph the Heir at liberty to marry without any view to a fortune; but Mr. Neefit's parental ambition, indelicate and vulgar as it is, is dignified by its strong likeness to an ambition of a very similar sort, though of a higher and more noble form; while the squire's remorseful and passionate longing to put his son in the position which, but for the squire's own fault, ought to have belonged to him, gains instead of losing in dignity by its contrast with the ignorant and vulgar parental ambition that seeks to thrust a daughter up into a sphere above her parents, in which she would necessarily be ashamed of them and their manners and speech. Again, nothing can be happier than the contrast between the character of the shy, reserved, intellectual, fastidious lawyer, Sir Thomas Underwood, who can never manage to become intimate even with his own daughters, much less with any male friends, and who has lost by the want of *bonhomie* all he has gained for a moment by his intellectual gifts, and the other characters, with which he is brought into relation in this story,—his easy-going, pleasant, sociable ward, unstable of purpose, yet slipping through ill success and good success with equal facility by virtue of his agreeable manners, or Sir Thomas's vulgar-minded, unscrupulous, pushing colleague in the representation of Percycross, Mr. Griffenbottom, who sticks at nothing, and wins twice as much of the satisfactions of life by his purse and his coarse sagacity, as Sir Thomas Underwood can win by all his intellectual efforts and fastidious tastes. The picture of Sir Thomas Underwood,—a four-months' Solicitor-General, who when he went out with the Conservatives never gained another chance of office,—is one of Mr. Trollope's finest and best. As far as his social character goes, it is impossible to conceive a more carefully-finished picture. His sense of his own shortcomings in deserting his daughters (who are motherless) so much, and living to himself in chambers,—his slight peevishness with them in consequence,—the fruitless reproaches of his conscience, which make him miserable but do not make him mend,—his ineffectual attempts to enter into relations with the world,—the torture he undergoes in canvassing Percycross and winning his very temporary seat for that place,—his loathing for his colleague, Mr. Griffenbottom, who will call him familiarly 'Underwood,' and who despises him none the less for his incompetence as a man of the world,—his fretfulness when brought to the practical sense of a duty for which he feels himself incompetent, and his need of external stimulus even for purely intellectual work, are all drawn with consummate skill. All that Mr. Trollope fails in, is some picture or sketch at least of Sir Thomas Underwood's intellectual interests. We are told of his scheme of writing a life of Bacon, and of his various and hopeless attempts to immerse himself in it whenever the worry of the world became more than usually insupportable; but we are not told, and receive hardly any hint, of the real drift of Sir Thomas Underwood's intellectual life, of the direction in which his mind floated as he wandered about the Inns of Court after midnight, in the few hours when his thoughts were loosened;—in short, we have a man of high intellect sketched almost solely on his social, or rather unsocial side, whereas we seem to want for the completion of the picture some glimpse of the nature of the speculative life within him. Was he an imaginative man in the higher sense, or was his mastery of law due only to great powers of deductive reasoning? Was he a student of philosophy and science and history, or only of jurisprudence? These are questions to which we have no answer, or trace of an answer; and yet they are very naturally asked by the reader, as he studies this otherwise very fine and even noble picture of a fastidious intellect and conscience which have never really come to an understanding with themselves, but have half surrendered Sir Thomas captive to a subtle and negative kind of refined selfishness, whose disguise is the less easily penetrated because it yields him so few of the fruits of selfishness in any tangible happiness or pleasure. . . .

The picture of Mr. Neefit, the hunting-breeches maker, is absolutely perfect. How Mr. Trollope managed to know so much of him, so much of the out-of-the-way details of his life, as well as of his character, is one of the great mysteries of literature. It is natural enough that he should know that Mr. Neefit's manners to his customers contained a good working mixture of dictatorial assurance and subservience,—subservience to the opinions of his customers on all points except those involved in his own trade, and dictatorial assurance on that,—so much he has, no doubt, somewhere observed. He has doubtless known tradesmen who would 'take back anything that was not approved without a murmur,' but who 'after that must decline further transactions.' This interesting trait again has probably come within his observation:

It was, moreover, quite understood that to complain of his materials was so to insult him that he would condescend to make no civil reply. An elderly gentleman from Essex once told him that his buttons were given to breaking. 'If you have your breeches,—washed,—by an old woman,—in the country,'—said Mr. Neefit, very slowly, looking into the elderly gentleman's face, 'and then run through the mangle,—the buttons will break.' The elderly gentleman never dared even to enter the shop again.

But how did he come to observe a point so minute, yet so characteristic of the type of man, as the distinction between the answers given as to Mr. Neefit's whereabouts, to inquiries made between half-past twelve and one, and inquiries made between one and half-past one?—

From 9.30 to 5.15 were Mr. Neefit's hours; but it had come to be understood by those who knew the establishment well, that from half-past twelve to half-past one the master was always absent. The young man who sat at the high desk, and seemed to spend all his time in contemplating the bad debts in the ledger, would tell gentlemen who called up to one that Mr. Neefit was in the City. After one it was always said that Mr. Neefit was lunching at the Restaurong. The truth was that Mr. Neefit always dined in the middle of the day at a public-house round the corner, having a chop and a 'follow chop,' a pint of beer, a penny newspaper and a pipe.

Mr. Neefit's life, both at the shop at Conduit Street and at that un-happy Hendon villa which his wife in her ignorant ambition had in-duced him to take,—oblivious of the fact that, as Mr. Trollope puts it, to Mr. Neefit 'the legs of his customers were a blessed resource,' while she, when once they had left the shop in Conduit Street, had no re-source,—is a marvellous bit of at once strong and minute painting,—for no one can deny that Mr. Neefit's character, profoundly vulgar as it is, has a certain passion of tenacity in it which redeems it from insigni-ficance. As a contrast to the facile, gentlemanly, purposelessness of the man whom he has resolved and endeavoured to force into a marriage with his daughter, Mr. Neefit is really respectable.

Ralph himself is an admirable picture of shallow, agreeable, drifting sociability, without a grain of either high purpose or strong purpose. His easy loves and easy disappointments are beautifully drawn, nor can anything be more perfect as a bit of poetic justice than his ultimate fate in falling a prey to one of 'the Eardham girls,' and the manœuvring skill of their mamma. . . .

We might write on for another page or two, without exhausting the criticisms (almost all of appreciation) which a novel so full of life as this naturally suggests. But we must conclude, only remarking that, as usual with Mr. Trollope, his women are not equal to his men,—indeed, the only sketch of a woman in the novel which is really up to the studies of the masculine characters, is the picture of Polly Neefit. We should add, that no episode of Mr. Trollope's ever surpassed in ability the episode of the Percycross election and the election petition. Without it, the fine picture of Sir Thomas Underwood could not have been what it is, and therefore, though on the whole an episode, it is not without a very important bearing on the art of the tale.

131. Unsigned notice, *The Times*

17 April 1871, p. 6

A full two-column notice given almost entirely to an informal recounting of the story.

. . . The episodes of Sir Thomas Underwood's electioneering experiences down at Percycross, and the whole of the Neefit courtship are, in our opinion, really the strong points of the book. Probably no man alive, now that Charles Dickens has departed, can write on such subjects so humorously and so truthfully as Mr. Trollope. Sir Thomas Underwood and his clerk Stemm, Mr. Neefit and his daughter Polly, together with her lover Ontario Moggs, are creations of which any writer of fiction might be proud. Mr. Trollope has often written dully as well as brilliantly, but he need not be afraid lest his power should be leaving him if he always writes as well as in most parts of this his last novel, *Ralph the Heir*.

132. Unsigned notice, *Examiner*

22 April 1871, p. 419

Mr. Anthony Trollope is probably the most widely popular, as he is certainly the most productive, of living English novelists, and the same qualities that explain his popularity will also account for his uncommon productiveness. Always entertaining without being exciting, and instructive without being profound, his novels make but little demand on the attention, and still less on the intelligence of his readers. Easy writing has been pronounced to be emphatically hard reading, but the author of this epigram was obviously an exceptional man, and the sentiment to which he gave such forcible utterance is confined to a very limited class. It is quite true that no one can take pleasure in the works of a writer whose intelligence or information is inferior to his own, but with the vast majority a little superiority is not only sufficient, it is positively preferred; and should the superiority consist merely of a greater facility of expression, the appreciation is likely to be all the more complete and general. For one reader who is capable of relishing a new idea, or even a new fact, there are a hundred who will feel the keenest delight when they meet with a familiar thought or observation clothed in slightly better language than they have been accustomed to see it in. The perfection of easy reading cannot be provided by any writer who seeks to penetrate far below the surface of the subject with which he deals, for in that case it will inevitably cost the average reader an effort to follow him; and when a book is designed as a diversion or pastime the author should be careful to throw as little trouble as possible on the reader. Mr. Trollope's novels exactly suit the capacity of the bulk of the novel-reading public, and hence their great and well-merited success. But neither do they tax the powers of their author, and hence Mr. Trollope is enabled to furnish as regular a supply of works of fiction as if he had undertaken a contract. . . .

There can be little doubt that several of the characters in 'Ralph the Heir' have been studied from the life. Points of resemblance to men and women we have known are not infrequent, but the *tout ensemble* of none of the characters is entirely satisfactory. We feel, on laying down the book, that we do not know thoroughly any one of the individuals

352

whose career we have been following, and we doubt whether the author himself is better informed than we are. Only in the cases of Sir Thomas Underwood and Polly Neefit does Mr. Trollope seem to suspect that there is more to tell. The others profess to be finished and complete portraits, but are really little more than coloured sketches.

133. Unsigned notice, *Saturday Review*

29 April 1871, xxxi. 537–8

Mr. Trollope is always readable. Whatever may be the tone of his stories, he has qualities which secure him the regard and goodwill of the novel-reader; but we may with especial confidence recommend *Ralph the Heir* as being pleasant reading in a higher sense than some of his later productions. . . . Whatever or whomever the reader of it may forget —and who can anticipate an immortality for its ladies and gentlemen?— he will retain a distinct impression of Neefit the breeches-maker. . . . Eight chapters about the Neefits, Mr. Neefit's overtures and revenges and Polly's loves, would have been better than the sixteen in which they figure; but they will not the less figure among Mr. Trollope's creations. . . .

[This is] a story which, if not in his best style, is yet a marvel of freshness when we consider the prodigious number of its predecessors.

134. Unsigned notice, *North American Review*
(Boston)
April 1871, cxii. 433-7

A long, somewhat rambling causerie upon *Ralph the Heir*,
Trollope in general, and possible reasons for the inability of
Americans to write good novels.

Mr. Anthony Trollope we take as the most representative, if not the
best, specimen of the living English novelist. He was lately suspected of
having written himself out,—a suspicion which the 'Claverings' and
'He Knew He Was Right' did much to justify. . . .

When the question is asked in what Trollope's excellence particularly
consists, most persons answer that it is in the skill with which he
delineates the peculiarities of certain classes, and the example usually
given is clergymen of the Church of England. He certainly *has* made a
special study of parsons, as Miss Austen did before him, and as, to take a
parallel case in French literature, 'Droz' has made a special study of the
French priests. But to our mind his forte is not so much the peculiarities
of any one profession as the general walk and conversation of the upper
and upper-middle classes.

Why is it that such books can be written in England and cannot be,
at any rate are not, written in America? . . . Why, indeed? We are
sometimes told, because the English rejoice in lords and ladies and an
aristocratic society. . . . Miss Austen, to the best of our recollection,
seldom introduces any one of higher rank than a baronet, and in this
very 'Ralph the Heir' there is no lord at all and only one Sir. Again, the
writers of English novels (with few exceptions, and these exceptions not
including the best writers) do not belong to the nobility, hardly belong
in any sense to the aristocracy; therefore we have this anomaly and
contradiction that in England, with its tightly drawn class distinctions,
the men of one class can describe those of another as well as those of their
own; while in America, where it would be flat blasphemy to speak of
classes, the men and women of one set cannot describe either those of
their own or those of any other set in an accurate, natural, and amusing
way, except, as we have intimated, in mere sketches and studies.

135. Unsigned notice, *British Quarterly Review*

July 1871, liv. 126-7

Mr. Trollope's selection of types of characters and his successful delineation of them are equal even to his best work. Sir Thomas and old Neefit are not surpassed by Mrs. Proudie and Archdeacon Grantley. Every portrait is characteristic, and is most carefully finished. There are few things in fiction finer than the subtle admixture of excellencies and defects in Sir Thomas. We do not care much for 'Ralph the Heir'; we feel neither great indignation at his sins nor great satisfaction with his virtues. He will be as happy as a nature like his can be. Old Neefit is, in his way, as distinctive in drawing and indelible in impression as Pickwick himself, only, of course, far less agreeable. . . .

It is not the highest school of art, but Mr. Trollope is a master in it, and 'Ralph the Heir' is one of his greatest pictures. If one word may designate it, it is a novel of selfishness exhibited in various striking types, not pleasant, but unquestionably powerful, and likely to live when many things that Mr. Trollope has done are dead and forgotten.

THE GOLDEN LION OF GRANPERE

1872

Trollope had originally intended this short novel of life among the Vosges Mountains of Lorraine as a third of his experiments in publishing anonymously (see Introduction, VI).

136. Unsigned notice, *Spectator*

18 May 1872, xlv. 630–1

. . . But it is hardly possible to imagine anything slighter than the incident. The innkeeper's son is in love with the innkeeper's niece, or rather his wife's niece, and she returns his love. The innkeeper, an affectionate, active, masterful, hasty-minded man, commits himself hastily, and without the least consideration of the subject, to the view that such a match would be imprudent, and must not be permitted. His son, who has the same sort of masterful temper, goes off to Colmar, and takes a situation there in which he thrives rapidly. The innkeeper of Granpere in the meantime thinks his niece ought to be established in life, and favours the suit of a young linen merchant from Basle, who is thriving, well-looking, and a little effeminate. The whole story consists in narrating the efforts made by the innkeeper to force this suitor on his niece by the strenuous use of his great personal influence with her—she is almost as fond in a different way of her uncle as of his son—and of the mode in which he is foiled by his son after having nearly succeeded. And this is absolutely all. There is no incident of any kind beyond this. There is hardly any field at all for Mr. Trollope's humour as distinguished from his sketching power, and still the story is, we will not say one of Mr. Trollope's best,—his Nuremberg and Prague stories are both, we think, better, and of course all the stories founded on his knowledge of London and London society are much better,—but still lively and interesting, and of that kind that induces people who have read one number of it,—it was and still is appearing in periodical parts in *Good Words*, though now published as a whole,—to note in their minds when the next is due and obtain it as soon as it is out. . . .

Perhaps the best instance of all of this delicate appreciation of the value of social strategy is the picture of the wretched linen merchant's anxiety to get himself away from the girl to whom he had been betrothed, and who had broken off the engagement, without seeming to retreat in humiliation and in a manner involving ridicule on himself. The negotiation for the rather unseasonable October picnic as a mode of carrying off the parting with dignity, and with the appearance of a cheerful and voluntary retreat, is an admirable hit of the kind in which Mr. Trollope is so fertile. But we will leave that concluding bit of natural history for the reader's private enjoyment. Nothing can be more skilful too than the disgust which the sturdy innkeeper begins to feel at the young linen merchant's 'greasy hair' directly he feels the burden of his company really upon him, and sees that he is and is to be an unsuccessful suitor, though before, while he had hoped that all would go well, and while he was priding himself on the excellent match he had made for his niece, he had rather respected the young man's carefully got-up hair as indicative of the polish of city manners. It is by the multitude of details of this minute kind that Mr. Trollope makes one feel how great a social naturalist he is. His conception of character is good and strong, but its strength is not so much in the inward grasp he has of it, as in the marvellous accuracy with which he clothes it in appropriate circumstances. Many English authors have far surpassed Mr. Trollope in their imaginative command of the interior scenery of character, but no one ever knew so well as Anthony Trollope how what he does see would express itself in the externals of society,—and this almost whatever the society be, so long as he has had a glimpse of it.

137. Unsigned notice, *Athenaeum*

25 May 1872, pp. 652-3

When we add to the conception of two well-defined and original characters, a lifelike rendering of the subordinate parts, and occasionally, as in the *naïve* expedient of the picnic, a vein of humour more decided than is frequently the case with Mr. Trollope, we have indicated the principal merits of an excellent tale.

138. Unsigned notice, *Saturday Review*

29 June 1872, xxxiii. 833–5

A long, though somewhat condescending, review that recounts the story at considerable length.

. . . What so practised an observer sees he can report picturesquely. Given certain figures in costume, certain accessories, and the merest passing glimpse behind the scene helps him to arrange them into a semblance of foreign life and manners. But, in fact, there is no appearance in this story of Alsatian life of the author's knowing more of the mind, manners, and character of the Alsatians than could be gathered by one or two days spent at an hotel a little out of the main route. . . . There is the flimsiness of holiday work about it all; it requires more earnestness than he could put into the story to warm the reader into any strong interest in the difficulties of people who have one and all got themselves into the fix we find them in. Still Mr. Trollope's books are always pleasant reading; there is the touch of a master-hand even where the stroke is not in his truest and most confident style; his narrative is constantly enlivened by characteristic comments and reflections that come home, carrying his lightest efforts quite above the conventional novel. If we forget the story, there will still remain some flash of thought, some keen-eyed observation, to tell us that we have been engaged with an author worthy of the title.

139. 'The Novels of Mr. Anthony Trollope', *Dublin Review*

October 1872, lxxi. 393–430

Unsigned essay. This critique of well over fifteen thousand words attempts an overall view of Trollope's career to 1872. It is uneven in tone and in the quality of its observations (the point of view is specifically Catholic and Irish); but the opening paragraphs with their challenging claims and broader perspective seem well worth presenting. The assessment of Trollope's three Irish novels (only passing mention is given to *Phineas Finn*) seems also of special interest and value.

(*a*) 'The Leading Novelist of the Day'

Those who hold that the novelist's business is to delineate the manners of his own day, and to draw portraits of the people among whom he lives or whom he has opportunities of observing, those who, in fact, regard the novel as a product essentially distinct from the romance, will probably be disposed to agree with us in our estimate of Mr. Anthony Trollope as the first master of his craft now in existence. The name of George Eliot will rise to the lips of some in denial or remonstrance, but there is no contradiction in the opinion which awards to the wearer of that name a higher intellectual status than that of Mr. Trollope, but refuses to her precedence of him, in the class which they both elevate and adorn. The author of that series of close and philosophical studies of human nature, of which 'Scenes of Clerical Life' was the first, is much more than a novelist, as tested by the theory just indicated; and in so far as she is more, she is disqualified for competition with a writer who is not more, nor other. Some of the salient qualities of the works of Mr. Trollope are, like their aims, entirely out of the track of George Eliot; but those are precisely the qualities which are beside and above the needs of the novelist. A serious social revolution in England might render Mr. Trollope's books dull and difficult, if not unintelligible, to another generation of English people, as many novels which were excellent in their day have become dull and difficult to us; but 'Silas Marner' and 'The Mill on the Floss,' 'Adam Bede,' 'Romola,' and 'Middlemarch,' will be as much and as little to the taste and the comprehension of the coming as of the present race. In so far as Mr. Trollope's level is that of all decently educated and commonly thoughtful people, every one of whom can perceive and estimate the degree of perfection with which he does his work, while George Eliot's level is a much higher one, Mr. Trollope is a more complete type of the thoroughly successful and popular novelist. We do not think any other competitor for the very first rank in the crowded craft which, in our time, counts its ephemeral members by scores, could be proposed in a spirit of serious criticism, and the distance by which he surpasses those among his fellows who have achieved distinction tends to increase. No writer of note has written a novel of late which will bear comparison with those which won for him early distinction, as 'The Eustace Diamonds' will bear comparison with the first works of its author. The chronicler of Barsetshire is a veteran writer; but how hale, how hearty, how untired and vigorous, in comparison with others who have not done anything like the quantity of work he has accomplished! If, to take two of the prominent novelists whose books critics at all events are bound to remember, we compare him with Mr. Wilkie Collins or Major Whyte Melville, how striking is the difference! What a falling off is 'Poor Miss Finch' from 'The Woman in White,' or even its greatly inferior successor 'No Name'! In the ignoble pages of 'N or M' where shall we find any trace of the chivalry or the tenderness of 'The White Rose' and 'The Queen's Maries'; in the stiff and tawdry dulness, the stalking pomposity of 'Sarchedon,' how shall we be reminded of the scholarly grace, the fire, the feeling, and the depth of 'The Gladiators'! A considerable share in this remarkable difference is to be assigned to the fact that Mr. Trollope is a thoroughly consistent workman. He sticks to his last. He never strayed from the novel to the romance, as his brethren have strayed from the romance to the novel, thereby laying themselves open to having their attempts in the one direction judged by their achievements in the other. He has none of the versatility, none of the vagaries so commonly imputed to artists; he is a first-rate plodder; he has never mistaken the order or range of his powers, or been led by the suggestion of vanity to believe that because he can do certain things immeasurably better than any one else can do them, he must necessarily do other and opposite things well. He is in one sense the most serious of writers; though in another, that of solemnity or tragicalness, he is not serious at all beyond that seriousness necessary to the life-likeness of his fictions. His seriousness consists in his air and tone of absolute belief in the personages and the circumstances of his own creation. This it is which lends such form and persuasion to his realism: in this he is absolutely and pleasantly opposed to Mr. Thackeray. He never talks about having played out a play and shutting up the puppets, not only because he constantly requires to bring out the puppets again, that they may play other plays with a little more or less of difference in the situations, but also because he would not on any account acknowledge them to be puppets, but wishes them to be believed in with faith and recognized with knowledge like his own. He would not account for the adventures of any of the numerous families whose annals he gives with such simple, specious, convincing detail, by saying that he sauntered into a wood and dreamed them, as Mr. Thackeray accounted for his 'Newcomes,' and so did his best to destroy the effect of the reality that he had produced with so much skill and intensified with so much labour. There are no characters in fiction so real, as persons, to the world, as the creations of Mr. Trollope. We talk as familiarly, and perhaps more frequently, of some of Mr. Dickens's bright, fantastic fancies, but in a different way, and because of the exquisite, incomparable humour of them. But we talk of only a few, and of them for some special characteristic, and because they turn up in illustration of some particular quality or whimsical circumstance. We quote them when exceptions, oddities, vagaries are in question, and those we quote are not the people who play the serious parts in the stories in which they appear. But Mr. Trollope has given life, and speech, and motion to scores of portraits, has sent them to walk abroad and continue, and to have their names on men's lips when the actual every-day affairs and incidents of life are talked of, to rise up in one's memory in one's silent cogitations, to suggest themselves as matters of fact, the readiest, handiest, most suitable of comparisons, and illustrations. They come from all sides of his many-sided pictures of life; they are not his caricatures, for he rarely employs caricature; they are not his avowedly comic personages, for there is in all his stories no unmixed jester, no one who goes through life merely on the broad grin, or producing it; they are not his set, distinct types, for he has none. We do not find in all his long series of works, of the kind which would be called in the French language *actualités*, any special illustrations of ruling passions,—vices, virtues, or qualities. There is no one man who is avarice personified like Ralph Nickleby, or selfishness personified like Martin Chuzzlewit, or gambling personified like little Nell's grandfather. He avoids all exaggeration, in either good or evil, with such care and success, that sometimes one is almost provoked with him, especially in his later works, for his perfect, undeviating reasonableness; but his people, life-size and life-like, are all thoroughly real to his readers, as he forces his readers to feel they are to himself. We cannot conceive the possibility of Mr. Trollope's writing long interjectional letters to any one in the world, when he approaches the profoundly pathetic termination of the story of Emily Hotspur, proclaiming his misery at her inevitable death, and his doubts of his own fortitude, as Mr. Dickens wrote to Mr. Forster when little Nell's time had come. And yet the one is as real, as entirely true, as the other is theatrical, impossible; and that the girl lived and died, seriously and actually, a truth to the writer, is made evident by the perfection of the style of the narrative—plain, reticent, simple, almost to audacity. . . .

[The concluding paragraph of the essay:]

Great in small talk, unequalled in the dialogue of flirtation, skilful beyond praise in minutiæ, so just that he never makes any man or woman a monster of perfection, and has only once been tempted to produce, in George Vavasor, a monster of wickedness, and in that case has fallen short of his customary success; with the keenest powers of surface observation of any living novelist, and the finest humour, Mr. Trollope falls short in two of the attributes of a great writer. They are breadth and height. His landscapes of life are deficient in perspective; and his men and women are deficient in soul.

(b) Trollope's Irish Novels

That this writer should understand Ireland so thoroughly, and delineate it so faithfully, is truly astonishing. He lived in the country a long time, but so have many other clever Englishmen, who can and do write, lived there too, and learned nothing about it. That Mr. Trollope should have liked the place, as a good hunting country, and should have inquired into the statistics of its foxes and its packs of hounds, would have been but natural. But who would have supposed that any Englishman could have written such works as 'The MacDermots of Ballycloran,' 'The Kellys and the O'Kellys,' 'Castle Richmond,' and lastly, 'Phineas Finn,' though the scene of the latter story is the English capital and Parliament, and the perfect evenness of the effect of the other two is wanting in the more brilliant and happier narrative. If an Irishman had written the first of these books, the achievement would have been less surprising, but we cannot imagine any Irishman bringing to the task such unsoftened candour, such entire impartiality. Either love of his countrymen on the one hand, if he were of the class of Irishmen who do love their countrymen, or prejudice of social position and creed, if he were of the class who do not, must have interposed, in the one case to brighten and soften, in the other to darken and harden the picture. But this Englishman, keenly observant, painstaking, absolutely sincere and unprejudiced, with a lynx-like clearness of vision, and a power of literal reproduction of which his clerical and domestic novels, remarkably as they exhibit it, do not furnish such striking examples, writes a story as true to the saddest and heaviest truths of Irish life, as racy of the soil, as rich with the peculiar humour, the moral features, the social oddities, the subtle individuality of the far west of Ireland, as George Eliot's novels are true to the truths of English life, and rich with the characteristics of Loamshire. The English public, who so fully appreciate his clerical and domestic studies, have no means of learning how great is the merit of the Irish series, and probably consider them, for books by Mr. Trollope, rather heavy reading. If the author had made them lighter, he must have sacrificed some of their reality. They deal with heavy themes, and though they contain samples of Irish humour which prove that Mr. Trollope has thoroughly imbibed its spirit, and mastered its forms more completely than any other writer who ever studied them, the turmoil, the perplexity, the failure, the passion, the disjointedness which marked the period of which he wrote, in Ireland, are too faithfully delineated to permit the general effect to be anything but harsh and sombre. 'The MacDermots of Ballycloran' is one of the most melancholy books that ever was written. Its tone is subdued, quiet, matter-of-fact. The author has materials out of which almost any other writer would have constructed something more emotional and striking; but he uses them with a sober seriousness which is deeply impressive. There are only two persons introduced into this one tragedy of his upon whom the reader dwells with pleasure; one is Mrs. McKeon, the kindly woman who befriends to her unavailing utmost the wretched brother and sister whose fate is so awfully sad; the other is Father John Maguire, the exemplary priest, who is an easily recognized type by all who know what the priest is to his people in the remote Irish parishes. The Mac-Dermots, in the decadence of their fortunes, are drawn with a master's hand, the semi-idiotic old father; the harassed, ignorant, well-meaning, heavy-hearted son, little more than a peasant, but flattered by the peasants for the 'old blood,' and schemed for by the disaffected,—proud, sensitive, and honourable in his lumpish, uncivilized way, a born victim with his destiny in his face; the handsome, slatternly, novel-reading sister, motherless, without a defined rank in even the society of such a place, half a lady, but the companion of shopkeepers and servants, vain, passionate, but modest even in her fall, ashamed of her uncouth brother though uncouth herself, devoted to infatuation to the under-bred, manly, flirting, strong, brave, unfeeling, unprincipled man, who tempts her, to her swift destruction and his own. The plot of this story is very much superior to any other of Mr. Trollope's plots. Plots are not a strong point with him; he is indifferent about them, heeding sameness—even repetition—not at all, and relying, with reasonable confidence, upon his power of fixing attention upon the people in his books so firmly that it shall not stray to the incidents. But in this one instance he has bestowed equal care upon plot and personages. The book is as fine as a story, as it is perfect as a delineation of character; a book which must have produced supreme satisfaction to its author, though he was pro-bably aware that it would not find anything like universal appreciation. . . . The wedding party at Denis McGovery's is admirably described. The bridegroom, with his bashfulness, his anxiety about the 'thrifle iv change,' and his cunning, skilful aiding of the priest's desire that the merrymaking shall not be turned into a secret society meeting, is as perfect in his way as Pat Brady. The bride is inimitably amusing,—the fun of the whole affair, the strange mixture of classes, the odd little social features discerned by the author whom nothing escapes, render this portion of the work additionally remarkable. Here, too, the charac-ter of Father John begins to grow upon the reader in its homely truth-fulness; here, in his exercise of his sacerdotal functions, and in his close and anxious social relation with his people. How full the good man's heart is of troubles for his wayward flock, whose wrongs and cares he knows so well,—he who is raised above them only by his sacred office, but by that is raised so high that they are all equally his inferiors,—how earnestly he strives with them, never losing pity or patience, how perfect is his geniality, his sympathy with their pleasures, how completely he is one with them, and yet how dignified and authoritative on occasion. It is strange and interesting to a Catholic to observe how the author is, quite unconsciously, influenced in his delineation of the Catholic priest by that which has no place in his own life, or defined existence in his belief, the sacredness of vocation. He has drawn portraits in his clerical series of estimable and conscientious English clergymen. Mr. Harding and Mr. Crawley, for instance, have something more than the mere professional air about them; but there is an utter difference between the excellence and the dignity of those gentlemen and the excellence and dignity of Father John, who is not a gentleman at all, but around whom the author, true always to the truth, though he may not comprehend it fully, throws the grandeur of his awful privileges, his sublime authority. When Father John goes from the court-house, where Thady is being tried for the murder of Myles Ussher, to Feemy's deathbed, and thence to the prison cell, where is the roughness of manner, where is the homeliness of speech, where is the 'peasant in broadcloth and buckles'? The mingling of familiarity, fear, and reverence with which the people treat the priest, the important part he plays in their history, directly and indirectly, are comprehended and conveyed by Mr. Trollope as no other writer of fiction has ever comprehended or conveyed them. We may congratulate ourselves on his impartiality and fair-mindedness; to compliment him upon them would be to insult him. The less important persons in this sad story are equally well drawn and sustained. Perhaps Keegan's scoundrelism is a little too utter and unredeemed; but on this point the author is likely to be a better judge than his readers, for there is an intense individuality in the country attorney and beggar on horseback which powerfully suggests a portrait from life.

'The Kellys and the O'Kellys' is a different kind of story. It is more cheerful; it deals not so entirely with the lower classes; it introduces more numerous social grades and various pictures of manners, and, with only one hopelessly bad person in it, it presents some very peculiar and characteristic Irish ways of feeling and acting, and one type of character which we do not remember to have seen attempted elsewhere. This is Martin Kelly, a young farmer, whose mother keeps a little 'hotel' in the town of Dunmore. The widow Kelly is drawn with admirable humour, with all her excellences, her oddities, and her family pride, for are not the Kellys far-away cousins of 'the lord', young Frank O'Kelly, Viscount Ballandine, and as good as any one in county Galway, let alone the Lynches, who just rose, through roguery, from nothing at all? Martin is a fine, handsome, honest fellow,—a Repealer, of course; it is Repeal time, and the story opens with a picture of the Four Courts during O'Connell's trial, full of innumerable little cunning strokes of humour,—but a shrewd person, not likely to get into trouble for his politics. The mixture of honesty and cunning, of lawlessness, and an upright intention to do everything that is proper in the matter which brings him to Dublin, and which is simply the abduction of an heiress, is marvellously clever. He goes to his far-away relative, his actual landlord and friend, Lord Ballandine, to explain his intentions and 'get his lordship's sanction;' and nothing can exceed the cleverness and the humour of the roundabout way in which he explains the matter, making it evident that he must save poor Anty Lynch from her brother's wickedness and her own weakness; that he must run away with her; and yet wants to have her money properly settled upon herself, with power over it during his own lifetime; that he wants the young lord to have such a document drawn up ready for the signatures of the runaway couple, because any lawyer would do it for 'the lord,' but he might be regarded with suspicion. The simplicity and shrewdness, the candour of his acknowledgement that of course he would not marry Anty without the money, but equally of course that he would not marry her with it if he did not like her, are wonderfully delineated.

The family history of the Lynches; the strange wavering character of Anty, with her high sense of duty, her extreme sensitiveness, her forgiving spirit, her plain face, and her shy manner; the slow growth of her love for Martin; the sudden introduction of the tragic element in the horrid scene between her and her villainous brother; the strengthening and refining of her mind in the days of her expectation of death; and the gradual learning of her true worth and sweetness, which turns the honest but cool and interested suitor into the ardent, devoted lover; all these form a study of human nature which, we venture to think, surpasses any of the author's English stories whose scenes are laid among the upper classes. There is nothing in the latter to compare with the sketches of Irish peasants, their ways, and their talk, except it be the Brattle household in 'The Vicar of Bullhampton;' and that wonderful little bit in 'The Last Chronicle of Barsetshire,' in which Giles Hoggett addresses Mr. Crawley, and repeats that 'It's dogged as does it.' The O'Kellys are as cleverly handled as the Kellys; and Ballandine, with his duns, his debts, his racers, his confiding nature, his hot temper, his soft heart, his gusty pride, his chivalrous honour, is a far more charming person than any of Mr. Trollope's cautious, hesitating, worldly-wise young Englishmen, such as Mr. Clavering, Arthur Wilkinson, Lucius Mason, or Felix Graham. He is selfish, as all men are selfish who spend money on their pleasures irrespective of their duties; but he is more natural, more genial, more gentle, less deeply dyed with worldliness than any of the long list of young gentlemen who come after him. There is freshness in this book; there is impulse in it, and genuine charming humour—in the hunting scenes, in the conversations at Grey Abbey, in the gentle quizzing of the Protestant parsons and prejudices, and in the discomfiture of the Earl of Cashel in his little plan for taking Ballandine's lady-love—such a delightful Irish girl, and such a thorough lady—from poor foolish Frank, and wedding her to his son, Lord Kilcullen. The respective stories of the double conspiracy are carried on with great skill, and though the plot is not to be compared for weight and ability to that of 'The MacDermots,' the happy ending recommends it to the general taste, and the individuals and classes with which it deals can be more readily comprehended by the general reader.

'Castle Richmond' is a remarkable work, in a different sense from that in which its predecessors of the Irish series are remarkable. The chief portion of the plot is not good, and not original, and it is saved only by great skill in the treatment, by a straying out of the beaten track in particulars, from being a commonplace story. . . . There is not the smallest resemblance between the people who play the familiar parts in Castle Richmond,' and Sir Francis and Lady Clavering, Captain Altamont, and Madame Fribsby. The Fitzgeralds are perfectly Irish, and the love-story which is interwoven with the fortunes of the unhappy old Baronet and his son, is a striking one. Owen Fitzgerald of Hap House, is a far finer fellow than Lord Ballandine or Herbert Fitzgerald; and the author creates a genuine and warm liking for him, such as he rarely succeeds in awakening. One admires Mr. Trollope more than one likes his people; in general one is rather impressed by his realism, than attracted by the realities; but in the case of Owen Fitzgerald, the fire, the faith, the nobleness of the man command somewhat of the enthusiasm which the author in no other case feels or inspires. We do not care for the secure, happy, wealthy, commonplace future of Herbert and his bride, but we follow Owen out into his wanderings, and we linger beside the forlorn woman who so vainly loved him, and who, when he has long been forgotten in his county and his old home, 'still thinks of him, hoping that she may yet see him before he dies.' It is not, however, in his fine delineation of character, or in the humour, capital as it is, of Castle Richmond,' that the distinguishing merit of the third novel of the Irish series consists. It is in the description of the condition of Ireland in the years of famine, fever, and flight. Calm, unprejudiced, cool, but not unfeeling, looking at the unhappy land with the clear eyes of a stranger, and the unembarrassed judgement of a critical spectator who had no 'side' in the social, political, and religious questions which distracted Ireland,—for Mr. Trollope's Protestantism is not of the persecuting and partisan order,—he draws such a picture of those dreadful times as, in days to come, it will be justly difficult for the world to accept as free from exaggeration. Can such things have been, it will be asked, in incredulous good faith, as the things set forth here by the pen of an Englishman, a Government official, therefore trained to accuracy, not by any means a fanciful, romantic, or enthusiastic person, one whose other works, so true to a rather subdued view of facts, may be accepted as evidence of his entire credibility as the narrator of events which he witnessed? 'I was in the country, travelling, through the whole period,' says Mr. Trollope, in a chapter which it is hardly possible to praise sufficiently for its simple graphic force, its plain speaking, its genuine, kindly, awed compassion. . . .

In the same book, we find some of the drollest and most appreciative bits of Mr. Trollope's trenchant humour, sly, quiet, and good-natured. 'Castle Richmond' deals with the first days of the Anglican movement; and describes, with much pleasant quizzing, its *contrecoup* in Ireland, and the fillip given by that new, alarming, and perfidious device of the enemy, called Puseyism, to the contempt and dislike with which Irish Catholics are regarded by Irish Protestants.

The mixture of theoretical bigotry and practical benevolence exhibited by Miss Letty Fitzgerald, is one of the pleasantest of his sketches; and he admirably exemplifies the bigotry, without the benevolence, in the coarse, vulgar wife of the rector of Drumbarrow. The excellence of this portion of the book is also, we think, hardly to be discerned by purely English readers of the higher classes, because there is nothing in their own social experience which resembles it; but it is fully appreciated by those who know that in Ireland the ordinary laws of charity, the commonest rules of politeness, are habitually disregarded by persons of birth and breeding, where the bigotry of Irish Protestantism is aroused. If a convert to the Catholic faith be so well known not to be a fool, that he or she cannot be treated as a fool with general approval, then people who would resent any other imputation on the moral character of their relative or friend, will cheerfully make up their minds that he or she, being 'much too clever to believe in Popery,' is a pretender to that faith for some personal reason or interest. That he or she should be sufficiently wicked to lead a life of habitual sacrilege and hypocrisy, if the thing be true, and that, if it be not, there is any hardship in having it said of him or her by people who would really consider their lives and their spoons safe in the society of a convert, is odd and unreasonable; but it is one of the innumerable testimonies borne by our every-day life to the supernaturalness of the Church, and the Faith which is the gift of the Holy Spirit, not to be discerned in its simplest bearings by the heretical intellect. Mr. Trollope has portrayed these specialities of Irish character, life, and opinion in the upper classes with the same subtlety and humour which distinguish his studies of the peasantry and farmers.

THE EUSTACE DIAMONDS

1873

The Eustace Diamonds, though bearing 1873 on the title-page, was published in book form late in 1872. It was still running as a serial in the *Fortnightly Review*, where it appeared serially from 1 July 1871 to 1 February 1873.

Trollope conceded (*Autobiography*, pp. 285–6) the unusual popularity this work had enjoyed, but did not think it one of his best novels.

. . . But *The Eustace Diamonds* achieved the success which it certainly did attain, not as a love-story, but as a record of a cunning little woman of a pseudo-fashion, to whom, in her cunning, there came a series of adventures, unpleasant enough in themselves, but pleasant to the reader. As I wrote the book, the idea constantly presented itself to me that Lizzie Eustace was but a second Becky Sharpe; but in planning the character I had not thought of this, and I believe that Lizzie would have been just as she is though Becky Sharpe had never been described. The plot of the diamond necklace is, I think, well arranged, though it produced itself without any forethought. I had no idea of setting thieves after the bauble till I had got my heroine to bed in the inn at Carlisle; nor of the disappointment of the thieves, till Lizzie had been wakened in the morning with the news that her door had been broken open. All these things, and many more, Wilkie Collins could have arranged before with infinite labour, preparing things present so that they should fit in with things to come. I have gone on the very much easier plan of making everything as it comes fit in with what has gone before. At any rate, the book was a success, and did much to repair the injury which I felt had come to my reputation in the novel-market by the works of the last few years. I doubt whether I had written anything so successful as *The Eustace Diamonds* since *The Small House at Allington*. I had written what was much better,—as, for instance, *Phineas Finn* and *Nina Balatka*; but that is by no means the same thing.

The novel received much attention in the Press, most of it highly favourable. The *Athenaeum* (26 October 1872) awarded it only luke-warm praise, but did not think the work would harm its author's reputation. The *Examiner* (16 November 1872) judged that the novel showed Trollope 'at his best, both as a moralist and as a novelist'. In

New York, *Harper's Magazine* (December 1872) could not recall anything of Trollope's in which 'the characterization surpasses in vigor of drawing that of this his latest work'.

---

140. Unsigned notice, *Spectator*

26 October 1872, xlv. 1365–6

The Eustace Diamonds, though as full of good painting as most of Mr. Trollope's tales, has hardly fulfilled the promise of its commencement. We had supposed that in Lady Eustace we were to have Mr. Trollope's equivalent for Thackeray's 'Becky Sharp,' but we hardly think that we have got it; or if we have, Mr. Trollope's equivalent for Thackeray's 'Becky Sharp' is but a poor one. . . . There is something a little too suffocating for Art in this picture of the greedy cowardice and sly mendacity of a pretty woman without the vestige of a sense of right and wrong, without a vestige of passion, without a vestige of true anger, without a capacity even for any hatred rising above the level of spite. That Lizzie Eustace is a striking picture in this sense we will not deny. But it is a very unattractive picture, and we cannot help thinking that a writer with more of taste for the *inward* portraiture of character than Mr. Trollope, would have found some means to relieve the ignoble tone of the picture by something better than beauty and wealth. Seen from within, there must have been occasionally a sense of ignominiousness and degradation that would at least have enabled the reader to feel, what at present he cannot feel, something of pity for such a bit of living and breathing pretence and dissimulation as Lizzie Eustace. . . . If any one wants to know to what moral and social affinities such greedy cunning as Lady Eustace's tends, it is impossible to conceive a more striking picture than that of the loathsome meanness of the alliance with Mrs. Carbuncle, the interchange of false flatteries and of spiteful hostilities, the sickening attempt to sell Lucinda Roanoke to Sir Griffin Tewett, the elaborate huckstering about the value of the wedding presents to be given to Miss Roanoke, the relations of the whole set with that hard and cynical nobleman, who is something too good for them and very conscious of his contempt for them, Lord George De Bruce Carruthers (Lady Eustace's 'Corsair'), the scandals into which the robbery of the diamonds brings them all, and the utter baseness of the *dénouement*,—except indeed as regards Miss Roanoke, whose partial failure of reason in the prospect of her abhorred marriage has a true touch of the tragic. We do not in the least complain of this element of sordidness, which is the true moral of the book. It is the one powerful effect. But we do complain that there is so little to set it off, that the good characters are insignificant, the middling characters poor, and even the bad characters almost entirely sordid. We want a foil to Lady Eustace, Mrs. Carbuncle, and Sir Griffin Tewett. . . . The story of the two robberies and Lady Eustace's intricate and superfluous lies on the subject, are extremely skilfully manœuvred; indeed, Mr. Trollope has rarely managed a *plot* so well. The slight sketch of the Duke of Omnium's dotage is painfully vigorous, and the picture of Lord Fawn's official and personal weakness, and upright moral cowardice, is one of the most striking of Mr. Trollope's innumerable striking studies of modern life. Mr. Emilius, the sleek converted Jew preacher, who carries off Lady Eustace at last, is hardly so good. Mr. Trollope has there given too much rein to his pleasure in coarse painting, and has not quite produced upon his readers the sense of complete verisimilitude. . . .

It is a depressing story, in which all that is coarse and base is painted with lavish power, but where evil itself is not on a grand scale, and where the few good characters are so insignificant that you almost resent the author's expectation that you shall sorrow in their sorrows and rejoice in their joys.

Mr. Trollope has builded the tower of his literary achievements yet three volumes higher; still it shows no signs of tottering, for these last bricks laid upon its high battlements are well-nigh as good a sample as those which bear the weight of the structure. *The Eustace Diamonds* may fearlessly invite comparison with any of Mr. Trollope's earliest and best known novels. Indeed, one of the very few faults with which it can be charged is that there is too strong a family likeness between our old favourite, Lucy, in *Framley Parsonage*, and a certain very charming Lucy in these pages. When it has been further said that the story is rather too much spun out, and that it would have been better without the unpleasant episode of one Miss Roanoke's broken-off marriage, we have glanced at almost the only blemishes in this excellent novel. It is possible to give an idea of the plot of the story, but for its carefully filled in details, its ideal characters, who become to us as real acquaintances, nay, even friends, before we close the last volume—for all this and much more, the would-be readers must be referred to the book itself. . . .

One of the best-drawn characters in the book is that of Lord Fawn, and it is saying great things for Mr. Trollope's powers of such drawing when it can be declared that he has done one of the most difficult things in the world—he has made a respectable man interesting. Yes, Lord Fawn is interesting in spite of his small ideas, his slow perceptions, and, above all, his eminent respectability. He also may claim a place as a hero, inasmuch as he is a lover, and he has a fair share of proper pains and pleasures assigned to him. Then there are delightful glimpses of some friends of bygone days—of Lady Glencora Palliser, now a leader of fashion and politics; of the Duke of Omnium, sinking slowly into senility; of Mr. Palliser, distracted by the difficulty of finding a fitting name for a penny which is to be worth five farthings, and to do away with the necessity of a ready reckoner—and of many other familiar faces. But we will not imitate Mr. Trollope's frankness. He declares that he 'scorns to keep from his reader any secret that is known to himself.' Nevertheless, it would be rank theft, a theft almost as heinous as that of the Eustace Diamonds, if that reader were to be deprived of one jot or tittle of the pleasure and surprise which are in store for him if he choose to follow the fate of the famous necklace through these pages.

142. Unsigned notice, *Nation* (New York)

14 November 1872, xv. 320

'The Eustace Diamonds' is the name of Mr. Trollope's last novel, which fills a bulky volume of three hundred and fifty pages. Every one who reads novels has made up his own mind exactly how much merit this author has, exactly how far he sees into human nature, and how interesting his delineations are. That his popularity is declining we should explain as merely the weariness of the public at what formerly amused it. In his method, Mr. Trollope is singularly unchanged, and advancing years only give him more experience. This novel will, we think, be found very readable by those who are not appalled by the author's formal slowness and familiar mannerisms. There is something very ingenious in the account of the bad heroine's lies, and in her unreasonable devotion to her falsehoods. The book is dull at times, but it is clever and more entertaining than half a hundred of the parodies of sentiment which for ever attract hungry readers.

Mr. Trollope is himself again in *The Eustace Diamonds*, though perhaps it is his most cynical self. Having apparently set himself to draw a rival to Becky Sharpe, he has spared no pains, and has thrown his whole power of analysis into the delineation. His Lizzie stands out a distinct, strongly marked image and type, and will live among his characters. Whether she is worth the pains is another question. . . .

Lizzie certainly is well drawn. The attorney's summary of her character, 'a dishonest, lying, evil-minded harpy,' is not really too severe; but there is a companionableness, a life and spirit, about her which keeps her within the bounds of humanity. She likes talking and making confidences, and saying pretty things; she is capable of keen enjoyment in the exercise of her powers, whether she is abusing her absent acquaintances in select epithets, which is her notion of friendship, or following the hounds at the risk of her neck in the hunting-field. She longs to confide in her associates, only it is not in her nature to trust a woman. Her designs are not colossal. A secret is a real burden. She is not too clever; and the use she makes of her ignorance is a feminine feature. A great many women would have utilized their ignorance of law as she does, and stuck to the diamonds with a like pertinacity. Her lies are not always deliberate, 'only she would not have said a thing so often if she had fully believed it true.' Actress as she is, 'always bent on making things seem other than they are,' she is humble about her acting, and does not expect to be believed without a great deal of practice; being alive to the fact that her rivals' truth is more telling than her imitation, and wishing she could act better. It is probably natural that, being what she is, she should not be able to distinguish a gentleman from a 'cad', though the extent of her want of discernment is surely pushed to an absurdity. . . .

There is much not only to amuse, but to learn from, in *The Eustace Diamonds*, if people will accept the conduct of most of its actors as a warning; nor does Mr. Trollope formally put one of them forward in any other light. He only paints society as it shows itself to him.

144. Edward FitzGerald

1860, 1865, 1873

From *Letters of Edward FitzGerald* (London, 1907), II. 14, 71, 152, 158–9.

23rd February 1860:

I have been very glad to find I could take to a Novel again, in Trollope's Barchester Towers, etc.; not perfect, like Miss Austen: but then so much wider in Scope: and perfect enough to make me feel I know the People though caricatured or carelessly drawn.

1st November 1865:

Now this precious Letter can't go to-night for want of Envelope; and in half an hour two Merchants are coming to eat Oysters and drink Burton ale. I would rather be alone, and smoke my pipe in peace over one of Trollope's delightful Novels, 'Can you forgive her?'

March 1873:

I am hoping for Forster's second volume of Dickens in Mudie's forthcoming Box. Meanwhile, my Boy (whom I momently expect) reads me Trollope's 'He knew he was right,' the opening of which I think very fine: but which seems to be trailing off into 'longeur' as I fancy Trollope is apt to do. But he 'has a world of his own,' as Tennyson said of Crabbe.

1873 [no more specific date given]:

This is Sunday Night: 10 p.m. And what is the Evening Service which I have been listening to? The 'Eustace Diamonds'; which interest me almost as much as Tichborne [the famous Tichborne Claimant Trial]. I really give the best proof I can of the Interest I take in Trollope's Novels, by constantly breaking out into Argument with the Reader (who never replies) about what is said and done by the People in the several novels. I say 'No, no! She must have known she was lying!' 'He couldn't have been such a Fool! etc.'

PHINEAS REDUX

1874

For Trollope's comments upon *Phineas Redux* in his *Autobiography*, see the headnote to *Phineas Finn* (1869). Trollope considered the two works to be parts of a single novel, though nearly five years separated their dates of issue.

145. Unsigned notice, *Spectator*

3 January 1874, xlvii. 15–17

The rumour of Phineas Finn's return to the political world after his brief married life with Mary Flood Jones and his temporary exile in the Irish Civil Service, had long preceded even the appearance of the first number of this entertaining chronicle in the *Graphic*. Indeed, we all of us know those of Mr. Trollope's characters who appear and reappear in the main line of his social tradition, so much better than we know ninety-nine hundredths of our own friends, that if by any chance we can gather news of their future fortunes, however indirectly, from the one depository of the secret of their existence, there is none of us who would not avail himself of that opportunity far more eagerly than of any of the ordinary sources of social gossip. . . .

It seems to us indeed clear that Mr. Trollope gives a generally too 'loud' tone to the characters of his women, and that he succeeds best with those women who, like Lady Glencora, are distinguished by a preference for brusque and piquant rattle. Nothing can be, on the whole, happier than the picture of Lady Glencora in this book, wherein she becomes Duchess of Omnium, though her manners, when in the retirement of her private interviews with her husband the Duke, are surely a little too fast and bounceable. For instance, when she says to the Duke, 'I'll tell you what. If he [Phineas Finn] is passed over, I'll make such a row that some of you shall hear it,' we think there is more of slang than of piquancy in her language; and Lady Glencora, though brusque and piquant, should never be slangy. But when she threatens Barrington Erle that 'if this ends badly for Mr. Finn, I'll wear mourning to the day of my death. I'll go to the Drawing-room in mourning, to show what I think of it,' then she is the true Lady Glencora whom we have been taught to know ever since she was Lady Glencora M'Cluskie. . . .

The new story seems to us in every way even the superior of the old. There is more body in the plot, and more subtlety in the conceptions, though not perhaps more finish in the execution. The picture of Mr. Kennedy's rigid and conventional mind giving way under the pressure of shame and jealousy, till he attempts the life of the man whom he knows that his wife prefers to himself, is an exceedingly fine one. The cunning and vindictiveness, the mixed religious and personal gloom, the pride and the jealousy, the stupidly monotonous repetitions of his demand that his wife shall do her duty by returning to his roof, and the avarice which seems to grow upon him as his mind fails, are all painted with even more than Mr. Trollope's usual power. Nor is the picture of his wife and the unhappy growth of that passion by suppressing which in her youth, under prudential motives, she had grievously wronged both the man she rejected and the man she preferred, less powerful, though it is even more painful. We feel some doubt whether, in a character evidently so proud as was Lady Laura's originally, there could have been so repeated a confession of her state of mind to one who had long ceased to be her lover. The powerful scene in which she confesses her continued love to Phineas Finn near Dresden is natural enough. But after her husband's death, when she knew that Phineas had no thought whatever of renewing his suit to her, could she have continued to throw herself, as it were, at his feet in the way she here does? We believe Mr. Trollope knows a great deal more of human nature than the present reviewer, and he may be quite right in the delineation of what seems to us the fault of a very powerful picture. Unquestionably the drawing of Madame Max Goesler's comparative self-control and reserve,—we must remember that she, too, had, in the former tale, ventured on offering herself and her fortune to Phineas,—makes the portrait of Lady Laura Kennedy still more striking. Madame Max is one of Mr. Trollope's most graceful and carefully studied characters. With just enough of the adventuress to have an element of calculation in her nature, and quite sufficient resource and acuteness to be worth more in the ordinary concerns of life than almost any of the personages into competition with whom she comes, the tenderness of her heart gives a true fascination to the character. We may venture to hope that, though it will be difficult to recognize Madame Max under her new title as Mrs. Phineas Finn, we shall be made familiar with her in that new relation in some future story. The figure is altogether too good not to take its place in Mr. Trollope's regular gallery. We cannot say that, on the whole, we admire the hero more in this tale than we did in the last. There is great subtlety in the picture of his nervous break-down after his acquittal, and in the preparation for it before the accusation, when we see how morbidly susceptible he is to the attacks on him which result in his exclusion from office. We are perfectly aware that it is this sensitive element in him which both endears him to women, and, to some extent makes him fail in what we should call the manlier side of life. And we have nothing to say against the picture, which is altogether life-like and true. But while we thoroughly admire the painting, we cannot say that the man himself grows on us. The weakness in him is, very properly, made excessively prominent by the accusation, the trial, and its results. And it is therefore difficult to sympathize with the women in their very natural and dramatic enthusiasm for him.

Of some of the Parliamentary sketches it would be difficult to speak too highly. Mr. Daubeny's speech to his constituents, giving the first hint of his intention to 'educate his party' into a disestablishment of the English Church, and the way he brings his reluctant Cabinet—all but two members—round to his view of the case, may be a little exaggerated, but, if it be, it is an exaggeration of Mr. Disraeli's political tactique painted with so much humour as to be the better for the exaggeration. Nor is Mr. Gresham,—of course mainly intended for Mr. Gladstone,—less skilfully painted in the chief scene of the Parliamentary struggle. There is, however, a little too much of the various debates,—too much of the duller bits of them, which a novelist is bound *not* to paint unless he can make them amusing,—nor is there any indication given us of that ability in Mr. Finn's speech which would justify his friends in their congratulations. We differ, too, from Mr. Trollope as to his impression that competition for patronage,—an eager craving to have 'the slicing of the cake,' as he calls it,—is so great a mainspring in party politics as he thinks. Certainly last year Mr. Disraeli's party might have compelled him to take the cake and slice it, had they wished. As far as we know, they rather compelled him to refuse it.

We cannot leave this fascinating story without a special reference to the reappearance of our old friend, the Old-Bailey barrister, Mr.

Chaffanbrass, who defends Phineas Finn with even more than his traditional ability. There are one or two of Mr. Trollope's finest touches in the sketch of the skilful, dirty, old man, exerting all his powers to get Phineas Finn acquitted, while yet himself more than half convinced of his guilt. . . . These new lights on the character of our old friend Mr. Chaffanbrass, whom in previous novels Mr. Trollope has certainly not delighted to honour, are touches of real genius,—some few of the very many touches of genius which make the continuation of the story of Phineas Finn one of the most delightful as well as accurate of his marvellous pictures of our modern social life.

146. Unsigned notice, *Athenaeum*

10 January 1874, p. 53

It is not easy to say anything new of Mr. Anthony Trollope. He has been so long before the world, his success in his degree is so thoroughly acknowledged, his list of characters so thoroughly well known, that when we have said 'Phineas Redux' is a good specimen of his manner, all novel-readers will know what they have to expect. If there is little to stimulate the imagination, or suggest topics for reflection in the book, there is abundance of the light kind of intellectual gratification which may be drawn from seeing life-like portraits of common-place people.

147. Unsigned notice, *Saturday Review*

7 February 1874, xxxvii. 186–7

The only difficulty in the way of our pronouncing *Phineas Redux* an excellent novel is the doubt whether it can be called a novel at all. Does the question of the Disestablishment of the English Church, discussed at elections, by leaders of parties in the House, in Cabinet Councils, and Clubs, alternating with the grievances of a master of hounds on the poisoning of foxes, constitute material for a novel? Above all, can that be a novel where there is no plot, where everybody, with the exception of one insignificant couple, is on the shady side of thirty, and all the love-making is carried on by a widower and two widows of mature years? We imagine the youthful reader will hold a very decided opinion that it is not. We can only say then that it is far more amusing than most of the novels which it is our lot to criticize, and that our pleasure in it is derived, not from sympathy with the author's views and prepossessions, but from the play of qualities which are as essential to the novelist as either plot or lovemaking. . . .

Of course it is the thoroughness of his conception of characters that enables Mr. Trollope to make such large use of them. Take, for example, his Lady Glencora. How true to herself she shows on every occasion; how thoroughly he has realized in her case character, antecedents, and position in life, playing upon one another! One of the consequences of recurring again and again to the same *dramatis personæ* is that an author grows fond of them. Habit and their faithful service make him like them. He calls Lady Glencora's good nature in a great measure caprice; and we know it is so. She answers too well to our own experience to doubt it. But the person who does good-natured things, and thinks it worth while to bestow her wit and liveliness upon us, is loveable in spite of the questions which an analytical survey of character raises. And the author who finds her the ready vehicle for his own vivacity likes her on similar grounds. Lady Glencora is a general favourite, because she makes things pleasant; though her good nature is largely qualified by caprice, and her kindness by patronage, and in spite of the recklessnesss which is so apt to betray—even in ladies who are not quite duchesses—a sense of vast superiority to the lesser people for whom laws and rules are all very well. Such a personage fits in excellently with Mr. Trollope's cheerful portraiture of life. He certainly enjoys delineating that class of society which lives freest from the cares and anxieties that vex mankind at large, which consists of people who have the best of everything as a matter of course—state, rank, money, horses, and dogs, and the government of the country into the bargain. . . .

No novel of Mr. Trollope's will be wanting in an example of woman's constancy. The victim of the quality in this case is not attractive, nor intended to be so. Lady Laura Kennedy, separated from her husband, unhappy, faded, and unamiable, bestows upon her once-rejected lover, now her lover no longer, a great deal of embarrassing fondness. Artistically she may not be ill drawn, but the reader is always sorry when she comes on the scene, and is quite ready to agree with the Duchess (our old friend Lady Glencora), who, when the other fair widow, devoted to the hero's interests, sadly prophesies that his end will be to marry Lady Laura, exclaims, 'Poor fellow! if I believed that, I should think it cruel to help him to escape out of Newgate.' But he does not marry Lady Laura. It might indeed have been foreseen that two such names as that of the hero and Madame Max Goesler must come together at last and destroy one another like chemicals in combination. We have said nothing of Lord Chiltern and his standing grievance of Trompeton Wood, with which he troubles the last hours of the old Duke. It would be a greater injustice still to pass over the capital portrait of the ideal Master of Hounds drawn in a series of antitheses. There are many minor characters well sketched, and much animated description, but these the reader will not need to have pointed out to his attention.

148. Unsigned notice, *Nation* (New York)

12 March 1874, xviii. 174–5

A review running into well over two thousand words devoted mainly to generalizations upon Trollope that accuse him of, among other things, having failed to produce a single memorable character and leaving his readers without 'any vivid feeling of amusement'.

. . . But the easy solution of the problems of political life, that every man is actuated by motives of the basest self-interest, is certain to be acceptable to the mass of readers, not because it is true, but because it is intelligible, and this characteristic of easy intelligibility pervades all Mr. Trollope's views of life. That it is a good thing to be well off, that it is well to act honorably, that it is about the best of all things to be a well-to-do English gentleman, and that it is quite the best of all things to be at once a well-to-do English gentleman and a master of fox-hounds, are the sort of maxims which Mr. Trollope directly or indirectly presents for the acceptance of his admirers. The creed he holds is in fact that the life of an English gentleman is the most satisfactory kind of life which any man can spend. It is the creed of thousands, and the teaching of the teacher who propounds it is certain to be acceptable. The source, in fact, of Mr. Trollope's success is to be found in the satisfaction which he gives to the almost universal liking for accurate sketches of everyday life, and to the equally universal admiration for the easy optimism which sees in English society, as it now exists, the best of all possible arrangements in the best of all possible worlds. The generation of whom Mr. Trollope is a prophet are no doubt a generation who hate exaggeration and stilted sentiment; but an age which worships commonplace will be found, while free from some of the vices, also to lack some of the virtues of an age like that which pardoned a good deal of false sentiment in an author who could produce a character as lovely and natural as Clarissa.

LADY ANNA

1874

Trollope was aware (*Autobiography*, p. 288) that the public had found this short novel extremely unpalatable, but maintained that the vehemence of the public's reaction showed the merits of his story.

> . . . In it a young girl, who is really a lady of high rank and great wealth, though in her youth she enjoyed none of the privileges of wealth or rank, marries a tailor who had been good to her, and whom she had loved when she was poor and neglected. A fine young noble lover is provided for her, and all the charms of sweet living with nice people are thrown in her way, in order that she may be made to give up the tailor. And the charms are very powerful with her. But the feeling that she is bound by her troth to the man who had always been true to her overcomes everything,—and she marries the tailor. It was my wish of course to justify her in doing so, and to carry my readers along with me in my sympathy with her. But everybody found fault with me for marrying her to the tailor. What would they have said if I had allowed her to jilt the tailor and marry the good-looking young lord? How much louder, then, would have been the censure! The book was read, and I was satisfied. If I had not told my story well, there would have been no feeling in favour of the young lord. The horror which was expressed to me at the evil thing I had done, in giving the girl to the tailor, was the strongest testimony I could receive of the merits of the story.

George Saintsbury in the *Academy* (2 May 1874) declared that Trollope could not help being interesting, even if he were to write a novel in his sleep or while suffering 'an unbroken series of bilious headaches'. Nevertheless he makes it clear that he has seen all he wishes to see of Trollope's tailor hero. *Harper's Magazine* (July 1874) warned its American readers that it was hard for a democrat to understand why the Countess should object so strenuously to a tailor for a son-in-law, but pronounced *Lady Anna* 'a love-story of unusual interest'. The New York *Nation* (2 July 1874), on the other hand, found the two lovers possibly the two most boring characters in all Trollope's numerous novels. The *Examiner* (25 July 1874) declared for the psychological truth of Trollope's heroine and placed the novel among the best of Trollope's works.

149. Unsigned notice, *Saturday Review*

9 May 1874, xxxvii. 598–9

Mr. Trollope must have had an object very superior in his eyes to popularity, or even to general approval, when he indited a novel making Lady Anna, the daughter and wealthy heiress of an earl, marry a journeyman tailor (and, lest the reader should ever forget himself into the delusion that it is a master tailor, the full title is seldom spared him), carrying along with her, moreover, the author's sympathies in so doing. And he is a tailor who is nothing else than a tailor—not a prince in disguise, not a hero, not a poet, not even a demagogue, but a man who goes steadily to his work, coming home from it with hands hard and black with labour, and earning his thirty-five shillings a week; and withal an ill-conditioned tailor, with a 'coarse mouth' and a very uncivil tongue in it, selfish, surly, ill-tempered, and dangerous, whom the heroine (we use the term conventionally) fears at least as much as she fancies. This is a sort of thing the reading public will never stand, except in a period of political storm and ferment. There are Radicals in the abstract, but a man must be embittered by some violent present exasperation who can like such disruptions of social order as this. Not all the cleverness and admirable portrait-painting shown in *Felix Holt* could make that story popular, or overcome its unpalatable plot, which *Lady Anna* follows in too many points to allow us to regard the similarity as entirely accidental. And yet Felix Holt, as compared with our tailor, is Hyperion to a satyr, and Esther has nobody to please but herself. In the interest both of male and female novel-readers we protest against Lady Anna's match; for their sensibility's sake, we expose at once the main feature of the story, that they may not be betrayed unawares into reading what will probably leave a disagreeable impression. Fiction at least as much as poetry should be the art of instructing by pleasing. The most tragic catastrophe pleases something in us when human nature performs its part with credit; but who can be pleased here? Not middle-class readers midway between earls and artisans, determined at least to hold their own; not earls and countesses, unless they are disloyal to their order; not tailors, if they are wise men, for what sensible man wants a wife who is ashamed of him? and Mr.

Trollope knows his art too well to pretend that his tailor can talk or look or behave himself on any occasion at all like a gentleman. He has indeed shirked, which we think a little cowardly, showing us his hero in the posture and surrounding circumstances of his calling, but we see him distinctly, though the words are not written, sitting at the wedding-breakfast ill at ease on the edge of his chair, embarrassed in his new clothes, awkward and sullen.

We have heard it suggested that the plot of this story is the carrying out of a bet. Without accepting this solution, it is clear that for some reason or other Mr. Trollope set himself the task of marrying an earl's daughter to a tailor before he concerned himself with the how. The plot must have been an after-consideration.

150. Unsigned notice, *The Times*

24 July 1874, p. 5

A long notice devoted almost entirely to recounting the narrative.

The task which he had set himself to prove that an honest, hardworking tailor on 35s. a week is, after all, a man with a firmness and dignity of character that can first engage and then hold for life the affections of a high-born lady was not an easy one, and we are bound to say that he has performed it well. In love, as in so many things, the first step is the great difficulty, and in this respect the poverty of the Countess and her daughter gave Daniel Thwaite an opportunity which he seized, and never afterwards lost. But this would have been quite impossible had not the Lady Anna been a young woman as tenacious—though certainly at Yoxham she did waver for a moment—and affectionate as her lover was sturdy and faithful. Against their united wills all the coaxing of the Bluestones, all the eloquence of the Solicitor-General, all the advice of a great Lake poet, whom Mr. Trollope has brought into his story, and last, though not least, all the violence and interference of the Countess herself, recoiled as against a wall of iron. Into the general question whether such a marriage between a tailor and the daughter of a Countess is not so ill-assorted as to be ultimately productive of misery, and whether, as Miss Alice Bluestone asserted, there was not a great gulf fixed between the tailor and Lady Anna, we are not concerned to enter; sufficient unto a two-volume novel is the ending thereof, and the ending in this case is happiness to the two beings most deeply interested. While we pity the violent Countess in her loneliness, we trust that in after-life nothing may happen, even in Australia, to make Lady Anna regret that she married Daniel Thwaite, the Cumberland tailor.

HARRY HEATHCOTE OF GANGOIL

1874

This short novel first appeared in the Christmas number of the *Graphic* for 1873. The novel was published in book form in October 1874, but an illustrated edition was prepared later for the Christmas trade of 1874. Reviewers were almost uniformly pleased with *Harry Heathcote*, but somewhat condescending. The *Westminster Review*, indeed (October 1875), thought Trollope was trying his hand at a book for boys, a fact that proved his great versatility, though Henry Kingsley did that sort of work much better. The *Athenaeum* (7 November 1874) praised the book as a 'not unwelcome' variety, displaying Trollope's characteristic powers for minuteness of observation in a strange land. George Saintsbury in the *Academy* (19 December 1874) considered the book slight but pleasant, and the *Examiner* (3 April 1875) found in *Harry Heathcote* 'the double merit of being short and extremely interesting'.

151. Unsigned notice, *Saturday Review*

7 November 1874, xxxviii. 609–10

Mr. Trollope has presented us in this little story with some further results of his Australian experience. Though the story is a very short one and perfectly unpretending, we do not know but that it gives the pith of a large part of the information stated in a more statistical shape in the author's [book of] travels. . . .

There is a family of strolling blackguards in Mr. Trollope's story, who have abundant opportunities of making themselves disagreeable to well-conducted neighbours in a thinly settled country; but they are, we should say, inferior in vigour to the ordinary British rough, and even when a fight comes off, the only weapons used appear to be big sticks. . . . Mr. Trollope gives us a bush-fire and some weather of which we can hardly read without a desire to be sitting in our shirtsleeves. There is certainly a chance for the art of what is called word-painting. But Mr. Trollope never yields to the temptation . . . we may conclude by saying that lovers of Mr. Trollope's stories may have a pleasant hour's amusement in turning over the pages of this unambitious but thoroughly satisfactory little story.

152. Unsigned notice, *Spectator*

20 February 1875, xlviii. 247-8

Identified as Richard Holt Hutton's (see Introduction, note 39).

The two editions, one illustrated and one not illustrated,—we greatly prefer the latter, objecting, as we do on principle, to have an author translated into pictures by any less effective agency than that of our own imagination,—which Messrs. Sampson Low and Co. have already published of this graphic little tale, will probably have a good sale in Queensland, as well as in the other Australian colonies and at home. For slight as the story is, and it is exceedingly slight,—being as regards the love-story (if love-story it can be called) which the tale contains, no more than a brief mention of two very tepid interviews between the lovers, and a decidedly unromantic offer,—the author manages to make his tale the vehicle for a much more effective and interesting picture of the conditions of rural life in Queensland, of the different sorts of 'squatters,' of the 'free-selectors,' and the peculiar dangers to which the bush life is exposed, than could ever be got out of colonial manuals or colonial parliamentary debates. What Mr. Trollope sees with his eyes he can always embody in an animated story, and he has evidently seen with his eyes the peculiar conditions of rural life in Queensland.

153. Unsigned notice, *British Quarterly Review*

January 1875, lxi. 133

As might be expected, Mr. Trollope has turned his Australian experiences to account, and has found fresh fields and pastures new for his novel-writing genius; although Harry Heathcote is a tale of the slightest texture and of very little incident. Heathcote is a young settler renting extensive sheep runs. Frank, and somewhat imperious, he offends some of his men, who, leaguing with lawless marauders, seek to fire his grass. He is, moreover, angry with Mr. Medlicot, a sugar manufacturer, who, as a 'free selector,' has bought of the Government a portion of Heathcote's run. An attempt to fire his grass is made and defeated, largely by Medlicot's help. Heathcote and he get to understand each other; Medlicot marries Mr. Heathcote's sister; and that is all. The canvas is small, and the figures are slightly sketched in, but Mr. Trollope gives us a fair specimen of his level realistic writing, and a tolerably vivid picture of bush life in Queensland.

THE WAY WE LIVE NOW

1875

Beginning with Michael Sadleir, critics have generally considered *The Way We Live Now* one of Trollope's best works. Sadleir, indeed, could not ultimately make up his mind whether this novel or *Doctor Thorne*, so strongly contrasting with it in both subject and manner, represented the high point in Trollope's achievement. Trollope himself felt (*Autobiography*, pp. 293–6), as did most of his contemporary critics, that he had exaggerated the ills of his time in his satire; but he felt also that the book contained much that was 'as a satire, powerful and good':

. . . I began a novel, to the writing of which I was instigated by what I conceived to be the commercial profligacy of the age. Whether the world does or does not become more wicked as years go on, is a question which probably has disturbed the minds of thinkers since the world began to think. That men have become less cruel, less violent, less selfish, less brutal, there can be no doubt;— but have they become less honest? If so, can a world, retrograding from day to day in honesty, be considered to be in a state of progress. We know the opinion on this subject of our philosopher Mr. Carlyle. If he be right, we are all going straight away to darkness and the dogs. But then we do not put very much faith in Mr. Carlyle,—nor in Mr. Ruskin and his other followers. The loudness and extravagance of their lamentations, the wailing and gnashing of teeth which comes from them, over a world which is supposed to have gone altogether shoddy-wards, are so contrary to the convictions of men who cannot but see how comfort has been increased, how health has been improved, and education extended,—that the general effect of their teaching is the opposite of what they have intended. It is regarded simply as Carlylism to say that the English-speaking world is growing worse from day to day. And it is Carlylism to opine that the general grand result of increased intelligence is a tendency to deterioration.

Nevertheless a certain class of dishonesty, dishonesty magnificent in its proportions, and climbing into high places, has become at the same time so rampant and so splendid that there seems to be reason for fearing that men and women will be taught to feel that dishonesty, if it can become splendid, will cease to be abominable. If dishonesty can live in a gorgeous palace with pictures on all its walls, and gems in all its cupboards, with marble and ivory in all its corners, and can give Apician dinners, and get into Parliament, and deal in millions, then dishonesty is not disgraceful, and the man dishonest after such a fashion is not a low scoundrel. Instigated, I say, by some such reflections as these, I sat down in my new house to write *The Way We Live Now*. And as I had ventured to take the whip of the satirist into my hand, I went beyond the iniquities of the great speculator who robs everybody, and made an onslaught also on other vices,—on the intrigues of girls who want to get married, on the luxury of young men who prefer to remain single, and on the puffing propensities of authors who desire to cheat the public into buying their volumes.

The book has the fault which is to be attributed to almost all satires, whether in prose or verse. The accusations are exaggerated. The vices are coloured, so as to make effect rather than to represent truth. Who, when the lash of objurgation is in his hands, can so moderate his arm as never to strike harder than justice would require? The spirit which produces the satire is honest enough, but the very desire which moves the satirist to do his work energetically makes him dishonest. In other respects *The Way We Live Now* was, as a satire, powerful and good. The character of Melmotte is well maintained. The Bear-Garden is amusing,—and not untrue. The Longestaffe girls and their friend, Lady Monogram, are amusing,—but exaggerated. Dolly Longestaffe is, I think, very good. And Lady Carbury's literary efforts are, I am sorry to say, such as are too frequently made. But here again the young lady with her two lovers is weak and vapid. I almost doubt whether it be not impossible to have two absolutely distinct parts in a novel, and to imbue them both with interest. If they be distinct, the one will seem to be no more than padding to the other. And so it was in *The Way We Live Now*. The interest of the story lies among the wicked and foolish people,—with Melmotte and his daughter, with Dolly and his family, with the American woman, Mrs. Hurtle, and with John Crumb and the girl of his heart. But Roger Carbury, Paul Montague, and Henrietta Carbury are uninteresting. Upon the whole, I by no means look upon the book as one of my failures; nor was it taken as a failure by the public or the press.

The novel was first published in twenty monthly parts at one shilling, from February 1874 to September 1875. For a discussion at some length of Trollope's satire on literary critics in *The Way We Live Now*, see Introduction, VI.

154. Unsigned notice, *Athenaeum*

26 June 1875, p. 851

Easy as Mr. Trollope's style of writing appears to be, we suspect his best novels cost him a good deal of trouble. 'The Way We Live Now' is not one of his best novels; and apparently he has bestowed little pains upon it. That the story could have been made one that would sustain the author's reputation is doubtful; for a character like that of the swindler, who is the hero of the tale, requires to be sketched by a more powerful hand than Mr. Trollope's, and the choice of such a protagonist shows ignorance on the novelist's part of the limits of his capacities. But though Melmotte is a failure, the general plot and the secondary characters of the book would have been much better had Mr. Trollope given more heed to them. As it is, 'The Way We Live Now' is carelessly constructed and carelessly written. Characters are brought in only to disappear. For instance, the bishop introduced in the early part of the first volume plays no part in the subsequent development of the story, and the way in which he is dragged in at the end only serves to draw attention to the blunder. Mr. Trollope having created Bishop Proudie, may have become afraid of attempting to depict another bishop, and may have paused for that reason. But some of his other characters are similarly treated, and the tale is hurried to a close in a most inartistic fashion. Still, poor as the novel is, there are clever scenes in it. The Longestaffes are all excellent, and Georgiana Longestaffe's engagement to Mr. Brehgert is an episode worthy of Mr. Trollope in his best days.

155. Unsigned notice, *Spectator*

26 June 1875, xlviii. 825–6

The author is Meredith White Townsend, co-editor with Richard Holt Hutton of the *Spectator* (see Introduction, VI).

Mr. Trollope's novels are to us among the enjoyments of life, but it is with the greatest difficulty that we have read through *The Way We Live Now*. The author has made a mistake, which he made once before in the disagreeable story called *Brown, Jones, and Robinson*, and has surrounded his characters with an atmosphere of sordid baseness which prevents enjoyment like an effluvium. The novel, which is unusually long, is choked with characters, all of whom, with perhaps two exceptions, are seeking in dirty ways mean ends, working, playing, intriguing, making love, with the single object of obtaining, by dishonest means, either cash or a social position of the most vulgar and flaunting kind. The central figure, Mr. Melmotte, is a vulgar City swindler of the 'financial' sort, who floats great companies, gives enormous dinners, entertains the Emperor of China, gets elected for Westminster, bullies and seeks people with titles, and is at all times a possible bully of the lowest type. Such characters exist, but they are as unpleasant in a story as they would be as acquaintances, and the unpleasantness is not diminished by inartistic exaggeration. The kind of man who succeeds in attaining Melmotte's position is rarely a big brute who can hardly help insulting the friends his gold collects, who shakes and beats his daughter, who is an habitual forger, and who overbears his own Boardroom by direct insolence such as would excite rebellion among his own clerks. He would have some good quality at least, if it were only brain for business; but Melmotte has none, except a certain audacity, which is only half real, and does not prevent him from wanting over-doses of brandy in great crises, or from committing suicide when he thinks the game is up. He is left, moreover, almost entirely unaccounted for. Why does he forge the order to deliver the Pickering title-deeds *before* he has tried to get back the money he settled on his daughter, which would

397

make the forgery unnecessary? Why does he run such risks to get into grand society which he does not like? Or why, if that is his ambition, does he show none of the brain in that pursuit which distinguishes him in the City, or is supposed to distinguish him, for if he were real, we should call him a muddle-headed upstart. He is a mere brute, so little human as to excite less interest than one feels in watching an orang-outang. His daughter, beyond a certain affection for a well-dressed scoundrel of the feeble type, who is always drinking, yet wins heavily at cards—which no drunkard ever did yet—and a disagreeable sort of truthfulness to her own mind, has no good quality; proposes in writing to rob her father; bolts with her scamp for New York, stealing a cheque from her mother to go with; then accepts a man she knows she cares nothing about because it is convenient, then flings over her father to keep money which is not morally hers; then marries a Californian—the best character in the book—after a cautious inquiry about his means. She has 'spirit,' we suppose, but conducts herself in every scene except the elopement—which fails because she steals the cheque—like a plucky barmaid, and is at heart utterly sordid; thinks even as she is planning her elopement of her legal right over her father's money—he had put it in her name because he thought he could trust her—orders her wedding dress surreptitiously, and when threatened with the cheque gives up like any female pickpocket caught in the fact. She is base, though there is some strength in her, and so are all the women, except the dull heroine, Hetta Carbury. So is Mrs. Hurtle, the bright American, who is really in love with Paul Montague, but admires big dishonesty, is anxious in the very tumult of her passion first of all that her lover should be making money, declares her husband dead when he is alive, schemes and lies and dreams of vengeance like the worst specimen of the New York demi-monde. . . .

So is Georgiana Longestaffe, the vulgar daughter of an ancient house, who sells herself to a middle-aged, greasy Jew—whose excellence of character she knows nothing about—merely to live in London, breaks off with him when she finds he will not give her a double establishment; and finally, rather than not be married, bolts with a curate, who cannot give her a house anywhere. She is not even a consistent and competent worldling, like her friend Lady Monogram, whose hard talk, frank to cynicism, is amusing, but whose gospel is 'the way we live now,' and who will do any baseness if only society has settled it. Base even is Lady Carbury, for all her love to her son and her yearning for affection. She helps this son to run off with the heiress solely to get her money; she deceives and flatters every editor who she thinks can puff her novels; she is savagely hard on her daughter because she will prefer love to wealth; and at her very best is always more or less a liar. She gets too good a fate, as also does Marie Melmotte when she marries the imperious, half-honest Fisker, who is better than the other people in the book, only because though he plunders the public to make money, money does not dominate him, or make him a small cheat. As for the rest of the men, except Paul Montague, who is only weak, they are detestable. One, a Lord Alfred, is a crawling sycophant of the financier, who hates himself for sycophancy, and deserts his patron the moment he is ruined. Another, Lord Nidderdale, is a heartless fool, with just caste-honour enough to see that play-debts are settled, and so much good-nature that he protects a friend who cheats at cards because he would go straight if he had the money. The friend, Miles Grendall, is a poor cheat, no better than the steward of the Bear-garden Club, who with money to lend at call, cheats everybody, and bolts with the plunder. There is not a decently honest man in the book who is not a fool, except the squire, Roger Carbury, and he is an overbearing prig, who makes it his business to lecture everybody in season and out of season, preferring by some perversity the latter. Except Roger, everybody is always striving for money by every device except work, thinking of money, talking of money, till sordidness appears the mainspring of every character, and the reader is as tired as he would be if he waited too long in a dirty anteroom in a City office. There is no relief, no pleasantness, the subordinate comic characters even being disagreeable. Mrs. Pipkin, an old woman who watches over a pretty servant-girl whom Sir Felix Carbury feebly wishes to seduce, and who is intended to be comic, is made unintentionally as disagreeable as the rest,—her notion of governing her niece being to threaten her with the streets, and her idea of virtuous propriety to marry anybody, like him or not, if only he means marriage.

Nor can we say that the oppressive vulgarity of the characters is redeemed by many touches of Mr. Trollope's usual skill. Of course there is skill, for Mr. Trollope intended us to hate the greedy race he portrays, and we do hate them; and of course he cannot write a hundred chapters without some touches of his peculiar art, but they are very few, not enough to enliven the general atmosphere of the book. Perhaps the best of them is the gambling scene at the Bear-garden, where the Californian wins more than his adversaries can pay, and the two lords present, the nincompoop and the gorilla, take the trouble to pay for all, because,—because,—well, 'because a man should always have his money when he wins.' There is good enough in Lord Nidderdale to make him think cheating at cards objectionable, particularly if the cheated man is a stranger, and that is about the loftiest pinnacle of morality to which anybody in the book manages to attain. The scene is very clever, though too long for extract, but occasional clevernesses no more make the book pleasant than a few gas-lamps serve to make a London fog endurable. Mr. Trollope is so rarely inaccurate, that we suppose there is somewhere a world like that he describes; and so somewhere among the marshes there is a sewage-farm, and we would as soon go there for a breath of fresh air as to *The Way We Live Now* for entertainment.

156. Unsigned notice, *Saturday Review*

17 July 1875, xl. 88–89

The Way We Live Now. We must begin by quarrelling with the incivility of Mr. Trollope's title. 'The way *we* live!' We will not retort by requesting the author to speak for himself, for we do not for a moment suppose the picture here drawn is based upon close personal experience. The satirist has put all the vices attributed to society into a bag, shaken them together, and made a story out of them, and nothing else. His hero is a swindler, and by his audacity and the magnitude of his operations rises almost into respectability out of the base level of meaner worthlessness. Melmotte is always ably, and sometimes powerfully, drawn. His is a life of fraud demanding such constant vigilance, such habits of self-control, such foresight and preparation, such self-reliance and courage, that it is almost great. It is impossible not to sympathize in a degree with a struggle so manfully maintained; not to appreciate the power implied in bearing singly the weight of a terrible secret, the strength of endurance that dispenses with help, whatever the extremity, asks no counsel, and can live alone. The dramatist or the novelist finds in such perversion of strong qualities material worthy of his genius. But a character of this sort should be balanced by its contraries. Benevolence, frankness, simplicity, uprightness should have their representatives, or how are our compassion and indignation to be aroused? Such a satire as Mr. Trollope here favours us with loses all force by its indiscriminate onslaught. If there is a rogue to hate, there should be somebody to love and pity. Where all are knaves and fools guided by low aims, sordid desires, or merely animal instincts, we naturally side with the strongest. Nobody is wronged if nobody gets so much as his deserts. Where everybody else is mean, abject, toadying, sunk in sloth, gigantic knavery and boldness rise almost into virtues.

Let us look at the characters thus brought together. Lady Carbury, described as 'false from head to foot, but with much good in her, false though she was,' the good being her blind devotion to her son Sir Felix, to whom she sacrifices herself and everybody else. Sir Felix, handsome, but too low in the scale of moral intelligence to do anything even for himself but helplessly follow the base, low desire of the moment; lying, treacherous, remorseless, because he never had a conscience. The aristocratic brotherhood and their club the 'Bear Garden,' the best of whom gamble through all hours of the night, exchanging their tipsy I O U's at eight in the morning, while the worst are sharpers and blacklegs—all scrupulous in their non-performance of every duty. Their fathers, either wasteful, pompous fools, or baser, lower, more sordid than their sons, for being so much older; more intent on money, more regardless of honour in the modes of procuring it. And all, it may be observed, taking precedence in the scale of degradation according to their rank in the peerage. Thus it is a duchess who introduces the Melmottes to society. It is a duke's son, Lord Alfred, who allows himself to be bullied and ordered about by Melmotte (who had been 'obliged to buy him'), eating his dinners, drinking his wine, smoking his cigars, and always longing to kick him, but never doing it. It is a duke's grandson who conceals the ace in his sleeve at loo. It is the Marquess of Old Reekie who swears at his son for objecting to propose to a brewer's widow of forty immediately on the death of her husband, because he was reputed to have left her 20,000*l*. a year.

Nor does it fare better with ladies of condition. All the ill nature of Mr. Trollope's satire falls on those among the sex who have an undisputed standing in society and no mysterious antecedents—the wives and daughters of county magnates. There is a certain Georgiana Langestaffe, who sinks lower than woman ought to be degraded in fiction. She clamours to her parents for opportunities of settling in life; she bargains for these chances with acquaintance in almost set terms; she engages herself to a Jew—not merely by extraction, but by religion—a Jew, rich, fat, greasy, who is odious to her—rather than stay in the country through the London season. Then, finally—the Jew proving too good for her, and resenting a letter in which she makes the motive of her acceptance too clear—she runs away with the High Church curate who had declared himself a celibate. Nor do her mother and sister come much better out of Mr. Trollope's hands. The grounds of their objection to Georgiana marrying a Jew, that he *is* a Jew, seem to him futile. Christianity being what it is in society, why should not women marry Jews? Especially why should not the daughter of a country gentleman of long descent who holds his head higher than his neighbours? The whole picture of family life, the unblushing selfishness, the vulgar squabbles, the meanness of avowed motives and unconsciousness of anything better, the concentration of hope and aim on show and parade, is given in the same strain of bitterness towards recognized position.

We wish to do full justice to Mr. Trollope's extraordinary fertility and resource, but we suspect that after a time respectability as a condition to be made interesting to the reader, or to furnish sufficiently stimulating material to the writer, gets exhausted. Satire, of course, naturally turns upon its shams and pretences, but its credit and presentableness as such, its decorums and reserves, its fair show to the world, whether false or not, become in the course of time stupid and irritating to the jaded imagination. Some tinge of an opposite quality, either in character or surroundings, is required before it can rouse itself to its work. All the women on whom Mr. Trollope bestows the favour of a sympathetic interest in this picture of life we observe to have some discreditable mystery about them. Lady Carbury has gone through unmerited calumny, and is subject to the world's suspicions. Three others are classed by one of themselves as adventuresses, and the heroine of humble life, about whom gathers the comic interest of the story, does her very best to get classed among them. There is still the conventional exponent of the virtue of constancy, blameless and well behaved herself, yet who thinks everything may be forgiven in a man; but nobody can attribute any character to Hetta. She is simply a lay figure, saying precisely the same things in the same words we have heard so often before, just as there is the indispensable respectable admirer whom she stedfastly refuses in favour of the lover familiar to us all, who makes love to two women at once. Not that Mr. Trollope's adventuresses are as bad as they might be, only that respectable people would not care for them in their drawing-rooms. Mrs. Hurtle, the American beauty, who has killed her man, and divorced herself from her husband, has no doubt something to say for herself as to both acts, but her line altogether is at war with our prejudices. Marie Melmotte, the heiress, who has the members of the 'Bear Garden' at her feet, but can recall sordid want and ignominy, and has learnt some shrewd lessons in money matters from her varied experiences, makes love on her side on a plan as little congenial with received rules of propriety. She is a favourite with the author, and is drawn with spirit and freshness. One advantage of giving prominence to women bordering on the outlaw class must be particularly felt by Mr. Trollope, who has all the old romancers' taste for blows and fisticuffs, and never thinks a scene of passion complete without one party in it falling tooth and nail upon the other. Now in polite society, however low it has fallen in principles of action, he ought at least to be content to let the men knock one another about; but by escaping from the trammels of an effete civilization he can introduce women into the game, whether as doers or sufferers. Mrs. Hurtle is quite at home in the ferocities of passion, and threatens her lover with a horsewhip in round terms; while Marie Melmotte, who is used to be beaten by her father, lets him pound her to pieces rather than sign away the money he has settled upon her. This is neither the world we live in nor hear about, but it does not seem so very much out of place where it stands.

Two characters in this strange Vanity Fair stand out pleasantly enough; both members of the 'Bear Garden'—Lord Nidderdale, whose indomitable good humour gives a sort of grace even to his mercenary courtship, and Dolly (Adolphus) Langestaffe, whose shrewd common sense and easy cynicism, looming through a dense cloud of indolent inanity and vagueness of statement, show the hand of a master.

One subject on which our author justly relied for interesting many of his readers, and which to himself may have presented the attraction of a vein less worked than those of more common resort, is that of bookmaking without a vocation, which certainly may be pronounced one feature of the world we live in. The story opens with Lady Carbury —false in everything she touches—having just finished her *Criminal Queens*, now sitting at her desk inditing letters to three editors, imploring a friendly notice. Her letters are so fluent and plausible, they have run off Mr. Trollope's pen so easily, with so much of his own manner, that we almost wonder that the style of her book is not better than we are led to suppose it. Lady Carbury, humble in her falsehood, trusts much more to her powers of cajoling and coaxing than to the merits of her work. If Mr. Broune, the editor of the *Breakfast Table*, will but issue commands for a favourable notice; if Mr. Booker, of the *Literary Chronicle*, will accept a *quid pro quo*, and in return for her praises of his *New Tale of a Tub*, will celebrate her *Criminal Queens*; if Mr. Alf, in the *Evening Pulpit*, will only spare her, and say something civil instead of cutting her up after the more usual fashion of his paper, she reckons on a good sale. Money she wants in substantial coin—why should she not add 1,000*l.* a year to her income like the people she hears of? But she will be quite content with feigned praise. Mr. Trollope implies for himself a very exact and intimate knowledge of the editorial status and its chances. Mr. Alf, who is minutely described, makes 6,000*l.* a year out of the *Evening Pulpit*, which certainly proves savage, unsparing criticism a very profitable trade. The more tender-hearted and conscientious Mr. Booker, who would have been honest if his position would have allowed him to be so, makes but 500*l.* a year by his editorship. Mr. Broune's income is left to our own imagination; but he was powerful in his profession, and also 'he was fond of ladies,' which fact Lady Carbury, handsome still in her forty-third year, had had good reason to know. From him she succeeds in getting a flaming notice. Mr. Booker sadly submits to saying more for her *Queens* than they deserve. Mr. Alf does not depart from the system which has proved so profitable to him and so pleasing to the public; but in spite of the friendship between himself and the authoress, sets Mr. Jones, one of his most sharp-nailed subordinates, upon her book, who pulls it to pieces with rabid malignity. There is a certain sensitiveness in describing the accuracy of this Mr. Jones—his fine scent for misquotations, misdates, misrepresentations. 'The world knew him not, but his erudition was always there at the command of Mr. Alf—and his cruelty. The greatness of Mr. Alf consisted in this, that he always had a Mr. Jones or two ready to do his work for him. It was a great business, this of Mr. Alf's, for he had his Mr. Jones also for philology, for science, for poetry, for politics, as well as for history, and one special Jones extraordinarily accurate and very well posted up in his references, entirely devoted to the Elizabethan drama.' We can only see in Mr. Alf's staff an argument rather in favour of an anonymous press. It being a feature of the day that people write worthless books, wholly indifferent to their quality, solely to get money, it is well that there should be Mr. Joneses to analyse their worth and tell the truth about them; if it *is* the truth, that is all the public has to do with the matter. After her *Queens*, which, thanks to the *Breakfast Table*, had a respectable run, Lady Carbury sets about another work in the spirit thus represented:

It cannot with truth be said of her that she had had any special tale to tell. She had taken to the writing of a novel because Mr. Loiter had told her that, upon the whole, novels did better than anything else. She would have written a volume of sermons on the same encouragement, and have gone about the work exactly after the same fashion. The length of her novel had been her first question. It must be three volumes, and each volume must have three hundred pages. But what fewest number of words might be supposed sufficient to fill a page? The money offered was too trifling to allow of a very liberal measure on her part. She had to live, and if possible to write another novel—and, as she hoped, upon better terms—when this should be finished. Then what should be the name of her novel; what the name of her hero; and, above all, what the name of her heroine? It must be a love story of course; but she thought she would leave the complications of the plot to come by chance—and they did come. 'Don't let it end unhappily, Lady Carbury,' Mr. Loiter had said, 'because, though people like it in a play, they hate it in a book. And whatever you do, Lady Carbury, don't be historical—your historical novel, Lady Carbury, isn't worth a straw.'

The name of the story had been the great thing; she had fixed upon the *Wheel of Fortune*. She had no particular fortune in her mind, and no particular wheel; but the very idea conveyed by the words gave her the plot she wanted. We have had scruples in giving prominence to a recipe which may suit the needs of many an aspirant for literary distinction, who feels he could write if only he knew how to begin. The *Wheel of Fortune* gets praised by the *Breakfast Table*, but at the same time Lady Carbury is advised by the friendly editor to write no more novels. As she is a favourite with our author, as a woman, if not as a writer, he makes it up to her wounded feelings in a way the reader will not thank us for telling him.

Perhaps as far as Mr. Trollope is concerned he knows how to write novels only too well; his brain has acquired such a habit of construction, and shakes old ideas into new combinations so easily, that the action is scarcely voluntary, and effort is only called in for extremities, or to give point and weight to a few distinctive passages. While people will read his novels, it is of no use to advise Mr. Trollope to relax in his industry in writing them, merely for the sake of his high reputation. Where habit and a ready pen act together, to stay the hand is almost a physical impossibility—and it is almost as much so to regulate its speed. But till there is a pause we can hope for no more Archdeacon Grantlys, or Mrs. Proudies, or Dr. Thornes.

157. Unsigned notice, *The Times*

24 August 1875, p. 4

As has been observed in the Introduction, VII, *The Times* had itself been in recent months presenting something like satire on the manners and values of the age, and its reviewer seems only too glad to approve of the fierce portrait that Trollope has drawn.

'The Way We Live Now,' by Anthony Trollope . . . is only too faithful a portraiture of the manners and customs of the English at the latter part of this 19th century. For all its exactitude, however, it is neither a caricature nor a photograph; it is a likeness of the face which society wears to-day. There is its hollow smile, so often worn over tears and anxieties, its stereotyped expression of conventional politeness, its smoothness, and its falseness. Yet Mr. Trollope shows in his own inimitable way that this very conventionality is the price we pay for our high civilization, this instinctive repressiveness is the silent police which keeps the discordant social elements in order, and, like the air we breathe, is the quiet harmonizer of all things. Mr. Trollope's hand has not lost its cunning, nor his mind its habit of just observation. One of his distinguishing peculiarities as a writer is his extreme fairness. His great anxiety seems to deal an exact and even-handed justice to each of his characters. Does he describe a Melmotte, with his odious, purse-proud, pompous manners?—then he hastens to add some line or two, giving the man credit for powers of concentration, boldness of conception, and financial pluck. Are his readers growing indignant with Felix Carbury's selfish extravagance?—the portrait is straightway softened by a touch or two which brings out a bright light here and there, or the force of education and habit is pleaded for the lazy, dissolute young man. If it should be necessary to declare in two or three words Mr. Trollope's strongest points of delineation, there would be but one opinion—ladies of a certain age, and Bishops. Lady Carbury could never exist, except on Mr. Trollope's pages. That is to say, no other writer would dream of demanding our sympathy for a middle-aged woman who writes indifferent novels, and whose sorrows arise from the extravagance of her spoilt son and the determination of her daughter not to marry an eligible cousin. Yet our hearts are with Lady Carbury from the moment we first see her scribbling diplomatic little notes at her desk, until we take leave of her, a more sensible woman by far, kneeling at stout, elderly Mr. Broune's feet, his promised wife. Then, as to Bishops. Mr. Trollope's Bishops cut out the smartest Light Dragoon who ever clinked his sabre against his spur up and down Mr. Mudie's bookshelves. They are simply delightful 'all round,' as the slang phrase goes. Whether the veteran novelist has proposed to himself to wean novel-reading women's hearts away from frivolous guardsmen and smart but briefless barristers, can never be known, but it is certain that the Bishop of Mr. Trollope's stories is always the nicest man in the book. If there is no Bishop, then there is an affable Dean, or an Archdeacon, whom to know is to love. Nor is Bishop Yeld any exception to this rule, and it hardly needed the clever illustration which faces p. 104 to make us see what manner of man he is, how gentlemanly, how benignant, and yet how firm. There are young men, of course, in the book, and very headstrong and tiresome they are; but they each manage to secure the affections of damsels not so fortunate as Mrs. Yeld. The episode of the pretty American widow and Paul Montague is, perhaps, scarcely necessary to the construction of the story and is apt to distract attention from the central and admirable figures. As for Mr. Melmotte, the vulgar millionaire, he is hero and heroine both in one. After all, love affairs are but child's play compared to the excitement and interest of floating a loan or forming a company, and men of the Melmotte type, who shoot every now and then with meteor-like suddenness across the London sky, are only too familiar to us all. So true is Mr. Trollope to his theory that there is good under the least attractive surface, that Melmotte is no villain. He is a man with nothing to lose and everything to gain. The social risks which others run, the social deaths which others die, do not touch him, for he is sharp enough to know that though in society to a certain extent he is not of it, and can never be. Such a man compels a certain sort of grudging admiration from even the least sordid souls by his audacity, his courage, his resources, and—his success. Still the reader never loses the sense of how frail a bridge is gold after all, frailer than ice, and quite as slippery. Even when the star of the house of Melmotte culminates in a superb entertainment to the Emperor of China, one feels no envy of the fortunate host, only that Heaven-born compassion which it is no shame to feel even towards crime. The clouds are so black and so near, and there is no shelter anywhere for the wretched sinner, no loving arms to creep into, no sand-heap in which to hide his head. It is all so terribly true and real that the book would be altogether too sad were it not for those delightful touches of humour of whose value no one is so well aware of as Anthony Trollope. So close and keen an observer of human nature has always perceived the strange absurd jumble of irresistibly droll occurrences on the threshold of absolute tragedy. In real life a laugh often rises to lips quivering with suspense or anguish, and the reader is grateful to Mr. Trollope for the fidelity of the portrait which gives the lights as well as the shadows. With ruin and disgrace staring him in the face, Melmotte can still make a point of being presented to the Emperor of China; and, indeed, has an idea of discoursing with that illustrious Potentate, 'but the awful quiescent solemnity of the Celestial one quelled even him, and he shuffled by without saying a word.' The Longestaffe family are excellent in their several ways, from insipid Lady Pomona down to Dolly Longestaffe, the hopeful heir of the good old house. Dolly is a fool and a dissipated fool, but still he is a thorough gentleman and very good natured, though he relies implicitly on his valet for everything, ideas and all. Georgina Longestaffe's desire to be married becomes almost sublime, when one finds she is prepared to marry a Jew stockbroker sooner than return herself unbetrothed on her family's hands. In conclusion it may fairly be declared that this is one of Mr. Trollope's very best stories, and that it ought to accomplish more good in its generation than its ostensible mission of merely amusing or interesting its readers. It should make us look into our own lives and habits of thought, and see how ugly and mean and sordid they appear, when Truth, the policeman, turns his dark lantern suddenly upon them, and finds such a pen as Mr. Trollope's to write a report of what he sees.

158. Unsigned notice, *Examiner*

28 August 1875, pp. 384–5

As the title suggests, this new work of Mr. Trollope's is intended to be a satire on certain aspects of contemporary English life. The theme chosen is the insincerity and meanness of much that goes by the name of high life. Marriage-hunting in its coarsest and least scrupulous forms, the idolatry of the purse even by those who profess to respect nothing but gentle birth, the essential dishonesty of a great deal of splendid commercial success, the despicable aspects of youthful aristocratic dissipation, these are among the principal topics here dealt with by the novelist. Of Mr. Trollope's familiarity with the doings of the big world, so far as one can judge from the ease of the style, his readers do not need to be reassured. His mode of presentation is remarkably clear and direct. He makes the facts speak for themselves, and rarely attempts to increase the force of his satire by scathing invective. We miss perhaps that agreeable play of kindly humour which in Thackeray, Mr. Trollope's great predecessor in depicting the illusions of Vanity Fair, tones down the harsh judgment of the reader, and gives to the scenes and persons represented the appearance of a big child-world. Mr. Trollope is indeed, with all his incisive irony, rather deficient in genial humour, and we only once felt an irresistible impulse of laughter in perusing these two volumes, and that was when conceiving the sorry appearance of the naïf enthusiastic priest who has forced himself into the presence of the terrible millionaire for the purpose of ascertaining whether a donation given to a Catholic church as part of electioneering tactics indicates the great man's readiness to receive the grace of the church. Mr. Trollope does not seek to throw a transforming imaginative veil over his world. At the same time, the initiated are likely to wonder in places at the events described, and to ask, for example, whether indeed a vulgar *nouveau riche*, whose antecedents are in the highest degree suspicious, can so easily manage to force his way to the very front of English aristocratic society, securing even the presence of princes at his receptions. . . .

In the description of all the external phases of his story Mr. Trollope is highly successful. The several parts of conventional social life are sketched with a facile hand. The intricate schemings and plottings in which social ambition is wont to show itself—the methods of unscrupulous financiers, the details of Parliamentary candidature, together with all the petty splendours of balls and dinner parties, are here given as with the semblance of absolutely perfect knowledge. The eagerness of society to push into Melmotte's rooms while at the same moment it delights in every kind of vilification of its host, is told with the air of unsparing truthfulness. There are some very clever touches in this account of Melmotte's dinner; as when it is said that 'three tickets were to be kept over for presentation to bores endowed with a power of making themselves absolutely unendurable if not admitted at the last moment,' and again that 'only two Academicians had in this year painted royalty, so that there was no ground for jealousy there.' Mr. Trollope is no less at his ease in narrating the sayings and doings of home life, and his history of Hetta's wooings and of her mode of behaviour amid her embarrassing circumstances appears to be life-like and skilfully executed. The weakest element in the story seems to us to be the episode of village life, which is probably introduced as a relief to the tawdry displays of the fashionable world. Mr. Trollope's rustics are very unlike the convincing fictions of George Eliot, and have all the clumsiness of lay figures. . . .

The single character in the book that can lay claim to being a new psychological construction is that of Mrs. Hurtle, the American widow, who combines with a Southern ardour of passion and a Northern energy and force of will, a certain degree of feminine gentleness of nature. Mr. Trollope's attempts to sketch these heterogeneous motives in alternate play is on the whole successful, though we confess to being fairly baffled at understanding why the lady's almost fierce affection for Paul Montague should suddenly become sublimated into a self-sacrificing tenderness when she discovers that the vacillating young man, who has again and again given her ample assurance of her undiminished ascendancy over his heart, at length summons courage to tell her that he will not marry her. How this softness of feeling can manage to prevail against the tremendous impulses excited at this moment, such as wounded pride, tormenting chagrin, and intense disgust at discovering the utter feebleness of the man she had resolved to make a hero, we are at a loss to conceive. It is probably the first instance on record of a humiliating defection by a lover suddenly transforming a violent woman into an angel. Even in the slighter sketches we fancy we discover psychological improbabilities. One does not know how to reconcile Marie Melmotte's habitual shrewdness with her very silly supposition—unsupported even by an unambiguous verbal assurance—that the profligate young baronet, Sir Felix Carbury, cares a jot for her apart from her fortune. Still more striking is the inconsistency between Lady Carbury's long and absorbing devotion to her empty, tame-spirited, and thoroughly ignoble son during his more palmy days, and her sudden abandonment of him when he is overwhelmed by ruin and disgrace in order to indulge herself with a literary marriage. The literary impulse, too, in this lady seems to us to be very feebly worked out, so that the reader has the impression that the whole thing is a pure affectation. The characters of the well-meaning but feeble Paul Montague; the sober, practical, and honourable Roger Carbury; and the eminently English variety of virtuous young lady, Hetta Carbury, are rather too commonplace to exhibit any special power of characterization. The best, strongest, and most carefully finished character of the book is undoubtedly that of Melmotte, though its almost exaggerated simplicity of structure hinders it from being a notable creation. . . .

In any case, we do not think Mr. Trollope has succeeded in making his figures interesting. Melmotte is certainly the figure of the group which most powerfully arrests our attention, and we follow the stages of his certain ruin with considerable excitement. Mrs. Hurtle, from her character and her hard fate, enlists some portion of our admiration and our sympathy, though the effect would be much more powerful were the character more consistently drawn. As to Hetta Carbury, Marie Melmotte, Roger Carbury, and Paul Montague, they are, to our minds, in spite of their troubles and struggles, singularly uninteresting. We would suggest that their characters and their circumstances are alike too commonplace to awaken any pleasurable glow of affection or of sympathy. As to some of the other persons, the Longestaffes for example, they are simply and uniformly wearisome.

The story is singularly barren of fine observations and lively *mots*. One wonders whether it is possible for such a number of people to say so many things without rising sometimes to the level of intellectual respectability. Mrs. Hurtle is the one exception to this general intellectual torpidity. . . . Enough has been said perhaps to show that Mr. Trollope's last book, while it manifests many clear traces of his characteristic skill, can make but few pretensions to value as a work of art. It bears all the marks of haste both in conception and in execution. It looks indeed as though the writer's facility in reproducing conventional life in all its finest details were a dangerous gift.

159. Unsigned notice, *Nation* (New York)

2 September 1875, xx-xxi. 153-4

A lengthy but diffuse critique that ultimately concludes that Mrs. Hurtle is with all her eccentricities 'perhaps the nicest person in the book'.

The good American will find in this novel not only an entertaining story of modern life, but also a justification for his love of country. Whatever hard things have been said in times past of America by English travellers, English newspapers, and English writers, no description of ordinary American life at their hands was ever made blacker than this picture of English civilization by Mr. Trollope. Whether it is a fair picture or not, we do not undertake to say, but Mr. Trollope is not a satirist, and hitherto his descriptions have been always accounted truthful. Moreover, in the great international controversy which has been raging so long between England and the United States as to which is the worse country of the two, we, on this side of the water, are certainly entitled, black as we may be, to the presumption that such a state of society as Mr. Trollope here describes could not have been absolutely invented, even by so clever a novelist as Mr. Trollope.

160. Unsigned notice, *Harper's Magazine* (New York)

October 1875, li. 754

Mr. Anthony Trollope's novels are not only 'among the enjoyments of life,'[1] they are also among its instructors; for no modern novelist, and perhaps no novelist of any time, has depicted with such scrupulous fidelity to the truth the actual facts of society, the phases of our national and social life which almost inevitably escape the historian, and which are rarely caught even by the tourist or the essayist. There is nothing false about *The Way We Live Now* (Harper and Brothers) but the title. There is a flavor of cynicism about that which is quite unlike Mr. Trollope. That Mr. Melmotte represents the ordinary type of enterprising capital or moneyed aristocracy, or Lady Carbury the average literary woman, or her worthless son the young man of the present age, or Miss Melmotte or the Longestaffe girls the best or even the average product of modern society, no one, we think, will be inclined to allow; and that Mr. Booker, Mr. Alf, or Mr. Broune fairly answers to the modern literary critic no reviewer could for an instant concede. It is true that the atmosphere of such a society as that which Mr. Trollope depicts is any thing but healthy. It is true that, with perhaps two exceptions, there is not a noble character in the book. But it is also true that the vices which Mr. Trollope so effectually uncovers are not only common, but, in their thin disguise, get ready admission and not infrequent respect in the society of both England and America.

[1] Apparently quoting the first line of the *Spectator* review, No. 155, above.

161. Unsigned notice, *Westminster Review*

October 1875, civ. 529–30

All novelists should read 'The Way We Live Now,' if only for the sake of Lady Carbury. Lady Carbury writes both novels and history, but her history may from its blunders be also regarded as fiction. There are few reviewers, who in their time have not received notes from Lady Carbury. Lady Carbury successfully wheedles two editors into praising her wretched historical work, 'Criminal Queens.' But there is a third editor, a Mr. Alf, 'a stern man,' as Thackeray said of his successor on the *Cornhill*, who will not be won over by flattery or dinner-parties. He keeps a staff of Joneses, men of vast erudition and great powers of sarcasm. One of the Joneses crushes poor Lady Carbury's book without mercy, fastens on the wrong dates, exposes the bad grammar, shows that all her knowledge is third-hand, and her style third-rate, and makes himself as disagreeable as his powers of sarcasm and the law of libel permit. We certainly feel no pity for Lady Carbury. We can only wish that there were more editors like Mr. Alf, and more reviewers like Mr. Jones. We should then have fewer Lady Carburys. Of Mr. Trollope's own novel we also feel inclined to wish that it was reviewed by his own Jones, that particular Jones who writes such slashing reviews on novels. We fear, however, that in Mr. Trollope's case criticism, however severe, would have no effect. Still we think that Jones might fairly point out how closely Mr. Trollope himself resembles Lady Carbury—how he too has written all sorts of books, a hack translation of Cæsar, a scratch volume of hunting sketches, a boys' Christmas book of Australian adventure, all of them with no higher aim than Lady Carbury's. Jones, too, might very fairly proceed with a comparison between 'The Way We Live Now' and 'Vanity Fair.' He might contrast Mr. Trollope's flabby sentences with the terse epigrams of Thackeray. He might con-contrast that grand adventuress, Becky, against the literary adventuress, Lady Carbury, and Rawdon Crawley against Sir Felix Carbury, Cohenlupe and Melmoth, with what results we can imagine. However, we are not disposed to play Jones's part just now. We will merely say that Mr. Trollope, like Lady Carbury, writes up to what may be called the paying point. He has taken a good subject, and has made it fairly interesting, but nothing more. We look in vain for any flash of Juvenalian satire. We look in vain for any nobleness of character to compensate for all the rascality against which we rub shoulders. In short, we look in vain for any of those higher artistic touches which give life to a work of fiction.

THE PRIME MINISTER

1876

The novel was appearing in parts but had not yet been published as a book when, early in 1876, Trollope recorded (*Autobiography*, pp. 299–300) what he had attempted in portraying Plantagenet Palliser as Prime Minister:

He should have rank, and intellect, and parliamentary habits, by which to bind him to the service of his country; and he should also have unblemished, un-extinguishable, inexhaustible love of country. That virtue I attribute to our statesmen generally. They who are without it are, I think, mean indeed. This man should have it as the ruling principle of his life; and it should so rule him that all other things should be made to give way to it. But he should be scrupu-lous, and, being scrupulous, weak. When called to the highest place in the council of his Sovereign, he should feel with true modesty his own insufficiency; but not the less should the greed of power grow upon him when he had once allowed himself to taste and enjoy it. Such was the character I endeavoured to depict in describing the triumph, the troubles, and the failure of my Prime Minister. And I think that I have succeeded. What the public may think, or what the press may say, I do not yet know, the work having as yet run but half its course.

That the man's character should be understood as I understand it—or that of his wife's, the delineation of which has also been a matter of much happy care to me—I have no right to expect, seeing that the operation of describing has not been confined to one novel, which might perhaps be read through by the majority of those who commenced it. It has been carried on through three or four, each of which will be forgotten even by the most zealous reader almost as soon as read. In *The Prime Minister*, my Prime Minister will not allow his wife to take office among, or even over, those ladies who are attached by office to the Queen's court. 'I should not choose,' he says to her, 'that my wife should have any duties unconnected with our joint family and home.' Who will remember in reading those words that, in a former story, published some years before, he tells his wife, when she has twitted him with his willingness to clean the Premier's shoes, that he would even allow her to clean them if it were for the good of the country? And yet it is by such details as these that I have, for many years past, been manufacturing within my own mind the characters of the man and his wife.

I think that Plantagenet Palliser, Duke of Omnium, is a perfect gentleman. If

417

he be not, then am I unable to describe a gentleman. She is by no means a perfect lady; but if she be not all over a woman, then am I not able to describe a woman. I do not think it probable that my name will remain among those who in the next century will be known as the writers of English prose fiction;—but if it does, that permanence of success will probably rest on the character of Plantagenet Palliser, Lady Glencora, and the Rev. Mr. Crawley.

I have now come to the end of that long series of books written by myself, with which the public is already acquainted. Of those which I may hereafter be able to add to them I cannot speak; though I have an idea that I shall even yet once more have recourse to my political hero as the mainstay of another story.

Later he added a note to the paragraphs of his manuscript just quoted:

> Writing this note in 1878, after a lapse of nearly three years, I am obliged to say that, as regards the public, *The Prime Minister* was a failure. It was worse spoken of by the press than any novel I had written. I was specially hurt by a criticism on it in the *Spectator*. The critic who wrote the article I know to be a good critic, inclined to be more than fair to me; but in this case I could not agree with him, so much do I love the man whose character I had endeavoured to portray.

And to a later sentence in the last paragraph he added another note. Apparently Trollope had been so deeply hurt by adverse criticism of *The Prime Minister* as to wonder if, at sixty-one, he had lost his power of writing effectively.

> *The American Senator* and *Popenjoy* have appeared, each with fair success. Neither of them has encountered that reproach which, in regard to *The Prime Minister*, seemed to tell me that my work as a novelist should be brought to a close. And yet I feel assured that they are very inferior to *The Prime Minister*.

It is possible that the *Saturday Review* with its cruelly blunt diagnosis of what it saw as 'a decadence in Mr. Trollope's powers' (see below) was more disturbing to Trollope even than the comments of the *Spectator*.

Reviews of *The Prime Minister* had been, indeed, almost universally unfavourable. The *Athenaeum* (1 July 1876) declared it could feel only a languid interest in Trollope's politicians, whether the case in point was Phineas Finn or the Duke of Omnium. The *Illustrated London News* (8 July 1876) considered the political chapters the weakest parts of a novel that it had finished 'with a sigh of relief'. The *Nation* in New York (20 July 1876) dismissed *The Prime Minister* as a work 'as good, or as bad, or as indifferent as some twenty others of [Trollope's] less successful novels' and as monotonous as the bricks in a series of non-descript city houses. The *Examiner* (22 July 1876) found Trollope's politicians in general 'not very interesting' and chiefly commonplace, though it admitted a certain charm about them nevertheless because they were portrayed in action and imparted to the reader a notion of what went on in Parliament. R. F. Littledale in the *Academy* (29 July 1876) praised Trollope as the only English novelist since Jane Austen to 'fathom the resources of the entirely commonplace' and judged that the portrait of Plantagenet Palliser was developed 'with a higher degree of artistic skill and insight than many critics will have been prepared to expect from Mr. Trollope'. The rest of the story, however, was below the quality of Trollope's earlier work. *Harper's Magazine* (August 1876) considered *The Prime Minister* a 'photograph' useful for giving Americans some idea of the secrets of a Parliamentary career, but on the whole a book that was both 'commonplace and sombre'.

162. Unsigned notice, *Spectator*

22 July 1876, xlix. 922–3

This review was written not by Richard Holt Hutton, as Trollope thought, but by Meredith White Townsend (see Introduction, Section VI).

This is not one of Mr. Trollope's pleasanter novels. It contains some pleasant chapters, full of characters whom we have all met, of incidents so natural as almost to seem undeserving of record, and of acute and humorous observations; but the book, as a whole, is tainted with the defect which characterizes its author's more recent stories, the disposition to attribute to the majority of mankind an inherent vulgarity of thought. Lopez, the hero, is simply intolerable, not because he is a criminal, for his criminality is not made prominent, but because he is such a 'cad,' that it is nearly impossible the heroine should have loved him, and quite impossible that he should ever have been mistaken for a gentleman. In his love-making and his jealousy, his efforts to bully, and his intercourse with his friends, he is always a 'snob' of the lowest type, who excites no feeling but loathing of the most contemptuous and irritated kind. We should respect him more if he struck his wife, or went in for some bold swindle. We can hardly believe in such a man entering good society, or standing for Parliament, or winning any decent girl, much less one intended to be so charming and oversensitive as Emily Wharton. He is not redeemed by any single trait,—for the love he is said to bear his wife never evinces itself in any act,—not even the poor one of capacity to endure the failure of his own schemes. He is a mere rogue, and a rogue of the most ordinary and feeble type, scarcely better worth analysis than the last 'welsher' who complains that the mob have torn his coat to 'ribbins.' The reader is glad when he is dead, not merely from dislike to the man, but from relief that Mr. Trollope cannot employ so coarsely-conceived a character again, or weary us any longer with his sordid and ill-planned schemings for cash, or position, or respect. We feel no sympathy with him even when he dies, for we perceive instinctively that he never would have killed himself, or killing himself, would have carefully avoided a moment when his death was such a convenience to all. The heroine is not much better. She is not vulgar, indeed, in speech or thought, but she must have had a trace of vulgarity in her to worship such a man; she finds him out very easily, and her repentance for her blunder, when he has been removed from her path, is overstrained and silly. It is impossible to feel any interest in her woes or those of her father, who, after violent opposition to the match, permits her to marry without an inquiry into her lover's means; who, utterly distrusting this lover, believes all he tells him about a favourite son; and who, loving his daughter as the apple of his eye, is perpetually treading on her mental corns. He discusses her future with her good lover as if she were an acquaintance, and urges her marriage as if his own object were to be rid of a burden.

The Whartons and Lopez are, however, new characters, and the reader who dislikes them has lost nothing except the pleasure of believing that Mr. Trollope could create pleasant people for ever; but he has chosen also to smirch old characters, people who have become a possession of the reading world, and whom he had no right to degrade in its estimation. Mr. Palliser has become Duke of Omnium and Prime Minister, and is in the process changed for the worse to a degree which could never have occurred. He was always over-sensitive and over-fidgetty, but he never before was over-bearing, unjust, and as far as he can be—for he retains a certain dignity of demeanour—vulgar. His entire bearing towards his leader in the House of Commons, Sir

Orlando Drought, is vulgarly insolent. It is true, Sir Orlando provokes this treatment, for he is a man who, being an old politician and leader of the House, and full of ideas of his own importance, still condescends to complain formally to the Premier that the Premier's wife does not ask him to dinner—a simply impossible incident—and in all political interviews is a pretentious 'snob;' but still, no Premier ever snubbed his first colleague as the Duke of Omnium snubs poor Sir Orlando, when he ventures to suggest that the Cabinet should have a policy in regard to county suffrage. There is bad drawing in the whole scene, and entire failure to perceive what relations are and are not possible among English political men. The Duke treats his own leader as if the latter were some led captain. The intention is, no doubt, to point out the incapacity of the victim, but the effect left on the reader is that no Premier could have been so insolent to a powerful colleague, and least of all the Premier whom he had known so many years as Plantagenet Palliser. The still more extreme scene in which the Duke—a man of sensitive refinement, and habitually forbearing—tells one of his wife's guests he is an impertinent, and orders him out of his house, because he had ventured to ask for support at an election, is almost an insult to the reader's social sense. The thing could not have occurred. Major Pounteney was presuming, and the Duke was sensitive; but no sensitive gentleman ever punished a bit of presumption, not intended as a presumption, with that ungentlemanly brutality. The real 'Planty Pall' would have uttered some dry or humorous excuse, avoided his guest for the term of his stay, and perhaps have taken care that he never met him again; but he would have left the course suggested by Mr. Trollope to the class of titled roughs to which, less than any man, he himself belonged. His sensitiveness, too, under the attacks of Quintus Slide, a man who is to Tom Towers what a beggar's chalking on the pavement is to a fine picture, must surely be exaggerated. Something of the aristocratic habit of mind must have existed even amidst his sensitiveness, to afford him some support; he must have derived at least some little strength from his contempt. He is vulgar in his unreasoning and exaggerated dread. Lady Glencora's vulgarization is perhaps more natural, for Mr. Trollope, whenever he has presented her, has suggested that her charming qualities covered some faint tinge of vulgarity inherent in her nature; but then her vulgarity was of the audacious, or, at the worst, of the slightly fast kind,—the vulgarity of a nature too truthful, too daring, too irreverent for an ancient society, not vulgarity of the pushing, perspiring kind. Lady Glencora in the *Prime*

Minister pushes like any parvenue who wants to become a personage, courts objectionable people, flatters politicians she hates, and turns her house into a menagerie of members, under the belief that fed beasts are grateful to the hand that feeds them. Many a woman has played that part, but not Lady Glencora; nor, supposing Lady Glencora to have tried it, would she have been so ordinary, or so unsuccessful. She descends, in fact, to an impossible degree, and perspires with effort in the vulgar crowd till she is utterly unrecognizable, or would be, were it not that in a few scenes, notably one between herself and the Nestor of the party, the Duke of St. Bungay, she is her old self once more. Her very mind has deteriorated, and her talk, even with Mrs. Finn, has lost much of the racy verve which formerly redeemed its vulgarity. . . . The motive has deteriorated, like the language, and Lady Glencora, whose specialty it was always to be herself, who was a great lady unconsciously, unable to plot or to dissimulate, is in the *Prime Minister* actuated by a thoroughly ill-bred ambition, in seeking which, again, she shows none of her instinctive knowledge of the world. She fights for place as if she had had no place before. She believes that she can make her husband's career easy by, as she says, 'preparing food and lodging for half the Parliament and their wives,' and prepares them like a cook. That is not the woman whom so many of Mr. Trollope's readers have admired, and not the woman into whom Lady Glencora would have degenerated. Her manners, as an American once said to us, were always 'large in proportion' but till this time, the caste stamp was on her.

This vulgarization of Mr. Trollope's old characters spoils the book, to our taste, nor can we see that it is redeemed by the political sketches. None of them are new, and though the reluctance of the Duke of Omnium to give up power is well painted, we gain no clear idea of the causes of his reluctance, the reasons for the growth of ambition in so unambitious a mind. We should, in fact, be half-inclined to believe that Mr. Trollope's power itself had declined, that he was positively unable to give us the sketches in which we have taken such delight, were it not for the exquisite delicacy and skill with which he has painted the relations between the Duke of St. Bungay, the calm, reasonable old politician, whose party management is so influenced by his goodness of heart and his personal affections, and his sensitive and obstinate colleague. The analyses of his feeling for the Duke of Omnium, the entire respect for him as a man and faint contempt for him as a politician, the weariness of his scruples, yet honour for his scrupulosity, the deep affection for him personally, yet the sense that it will be a relief when he is no longer of use to the country, are all admirably portrayed,—so admirably, that when the story ends the Duke of St. Bungay, though so subordinate throughout it, is added to the gallery of portraits with which Mr. Trollope has enriched his readers' circle of acquaintance, and acknowledged as one of the men who are more real to us than half the people we shall meet to-morrow. He is as solid to the mind's eye as any man in *Barchester Towers*, and much more agreeable.

163. Unsigned notice, *The Times*

18 August 1876, p. 4

The capacity for making your characters so life-like that your readers grow into their intimacy and are always eager to meet them again, seems to us one of the surest tests of a really gifted novelist. . . . The feeling we entertain towards Mr. Trollope's best-known personages shows at once the truthfulness and the geniality of the clever art to which they owe their existence. They are real enough to us; we repeatedly have their features recalled to us by the people we are habitually meeting in the world; and yet there is scarcely one of them, with all their faults and their failings, for whom we have not something of a kindly feeling. We even give a sigh to the memory of Mrs. Proudie for her own sake when she at length comes to her end in 'The Last Chronicles of Barset,' although ever since our first introduction to her in 'Barchester Towers,' she has been figuring as a noxious specimen of the most objectionable type of female. But, perhaps, Mr. Trollope has never given more convincing proof of his easy command of materials that are apparently anything but plastic than in developing the Duke of Omnium into the Prime Minister. Plantagenet Palliser, when we first met him, was as little interesting and almost as disagreeable as a man could be, who had the manners and feelings of a gentleman. We felt towards him as Arthur Pendennis felt towards Mr. Pynsent, when he remarked that he disliked that gentleman as he disliked cold boiled veal; and we feared that there was much of the tragic in the arrangement that had mated him with the impulsive, light-headed, and warm-hearted Lady Glencora. In 'Can You Forgive Her?' we began to suspect Mr. Palliser has a heart, although we doubted whether he could ever win his wife, with his chilling rigidity of manner and prim correctness of feeling. In 'Phineas Finn' and its sequel we slowly learnt to respect him, as an intelligent and indefatigable man of business, and a politician of punctilious honour and considerable patriotic ambition. If he could not mould men easily and pleasantly to his purpose, at least he had some art of commanding them and making them follow his lead at a respectful distance. So that, considering the social position of the Duke, his immense landed stake in the country, and the cool temperament that

424

kept him clear of perilous extremes, there was nothing unnatural in his being chosen as the head of a Ministry of compromise. But we were scarcely prepared to find that Mr. Trollope should actually make us know him and like him better in that exalted post than we had ever done before.

All is managed simply and naturally, but his very isolation admits us to his closest confidence and lays bare his innermost feelings to us. Accepting the Premiership with many misgivings, he feels morbidly conscious of the shortcomings which he exaggerates. He smarts bitterly under the stings of obscure journalists and orators. He knows he has not the knack of dealing with his colleagues or subordinates, although the few who are personally attached to him are willing to make many allowances. Pride and temperament keep him silent as to the anxieties he is brooding over; yet sometimes he must speak, or the suffering would become intolerable, and it is then we get glimpses at his innermost heart. The more habitual the represssion and constraint, the greater the outpouring of his unreserve in these rare outbursts. The Duchess, too, comes out in more engaging lights, which, at the same time, are in no way inconsistent with all we have hitherto known of her. She is not only proud of her husband as Premier, but all the fonder of him. She is still wayward, and seems often unfeeling, though she softens to him and pities him, when she sees him evidently afflicted. But her nature is so unsympathetic with his; it is even so antagonistic, that she is moved to impatience when she means to console, and spoils her caresses by some sneer that accompanies them. She sets herself to play the political game in her own way in her husband's interests, and thereby does him incalculable injury, he being what he is. While she is penitent for the results, she cannot help thinking how different it might all have been had her husband had less of that unfortunate sensitiveness. The Duke shakes himself clear of his harness, but he is already regretting the office he has resigned before we take leave of him; and, as for his wife, her taste of political supremacy has spoiled her altogether for retiring with him to their estates to cultivate their cabbages. The rest of the story hardly seems up to Mr. Trollope's usual mark. . . .

'The Prime Minister' is a novel that will be greatly enjoyed by people who can take an interest in its public personages, and who appreciate clever studies of political character; but we doubt whether it will ever be numbered among the favourites of those who delight in Mr. Trollope for his love stories.

164. Unsigned notice, *Saturday Review*

14 October 1876, xlii. 481–2

We can pardon any degree of dulness in the theme so long as the artist's method remains delicate and true, and there is no depth of vulgarity in the kind of life presented that may not be overcome by a refined and searching perception of the most significant truth. When therefore we find that an author's work leaves the final impression of vulgarity, we may assume that the fault lies with him, and not with his subject, and it is on this ground we are forced to the conclusion that *The Prime Minister* represents a decadence in Mr. Trollope's powers. Such a decadence, however, was in the nature of things inevitable. The vision of the novelist, no matter how limited its scope, can only be kept fresh and strong by the constant help of imagination. 'Minds that have nothing to confer,' to quote the judgment of Wordsworth, 'find little to perceive,' and the artist who places himself entirely at the mercy of his material, without the support of an independent invention, must discover sooner or later that he is unable even to present a complete and vivid picture of the mere outward facts of life. Mr. Trollope has at last been overtaken by this fate. The want of imagination, always sufficiently manifest in his treatment of the deeper problems of fiction, is now beginning to tell upon the execution of details; the hand begins to falter where it once was cunning, and even as a picture of manners the work is no longer free from reproach. To whatever part of the story he may turn, the reader of *The Prime Minister* is unable to escape the all-pervading sense of artistic vulgarity. The impression is stamped as strongly upon the doings of dukes and duchesses as upon the petty existence of the avowedly plebeian actors in the drama, and even the portentous dulness of the Wharton family does not serve to protect them from the general infection. It is, in short, the incomplete vision of the author and not the dulness of the material that begets such a result as this; but at the same time it must be confessed that the artistic shortcomings of the work might have been partly concealed had Mr. Trollope been able to make choice of a more attractive theme. . . .

We have not devoted any attention to the purely political parts of the novel, partly because the persons who here support the action are already known to Mr. Trollope's readers, and still more because very much of this political gossip does not seem to be successfully subdued to the requirements of fiction. It might serve for a somewhat tame account of events that actually happened, but it can scarcely claim to possess any sort of imaginative value.

THE AMERICAN SENATOR

1877

165. Unsigned notice, *Athenaeum*

16 June 1877, pp. 766–7

'The American Senator' is not one of Mr. Trollope's best books. In the first place, as he himself admits, it might just as well have been called 'The Chronicle of a Winter at Dillsborough,' and most readers will probably wish there had been no ground for calling it by its present title. The Senator might be cut out of the book almost without affecting the story; and his lecture on British institutions, thrust in at the end by way of giving him a little prominence, is as near to being a bore as as anything Mr. Trollope could write. . . .

Turning to Dillsborough, the mere name will conjure up to readers of Mr. Trollope's books (and that means everybody) a picture full of pleasant recollections. Dillsborough is not, it is true, a cathedral city, nor even an assize town; but it is buried away in the depths of the country, and apparently exists for no purpose whatever. This is Mr. Trollope's own proper ground. He has made it familiar to his readers, but they see it again and again without weariness. Those who try to analyse the charm will fail to detect in what it consists. The detail is minute, often, as it seems, irrelevant, but there is an indefinable humour running through it, and all helps to produce the general effect. The first chapter of the book is an excellent specimen of this skill. An attempt at a *réchauffé* of this description could only read like an extract from a guidebook. An attempt to point out how it comes to make an excellent picture in Mr. Trollope's hands could only lead to an essay on his manner. Fortunately, perhaps, for him, it is a dangerous style to copy. In this it reminds us of Macaulay's remark about his own style. It is a good style, but very near to being a very bad one. In the characters there is nothing new, but the reader meets a great many old friends under other names.

166. Unsigned notice, *Saturday Review*

30 June 1877, xliii. 803–4

We have a great deal of flirtation and love-making, and there are men and women who remain through the three volumes distressingly embarrassed as to their ultimate choice; while the American Senator, Mr. Gotobed, is introduced to play the part of the candid censor on 'institutions' which are fair subjects of political criticism and discussion. And lest we should grow weary, as to tell the truth we are inclined to do, of discussions on the social and political subjects which are practically settled for us, we have hunting and other rural matters of interest in ample variety by way of counterpoise. . . .

The American Senator is unquestionably pleasant reading, but we must own that we should have liked it quite as well if the part of the Senator had been left out.

167. Unsigned notice, *Examiner*

21 July 1877, pp. 916–17

Mr. Trollope has not yet recovered from the attack of misanthropy from which he was suffering when he wrote 'The Way We Live Now.' He seems still to keep a special inkstand supplied with gall, for use when describing fashionable society, against which his rancour appears to be unbounded. When he penned the character of the heroine of his present story, for instance, the very paper must have blanched under the withering impress of his quill. Arabella Trefoil is the name of this young lady, the conventional ball-room beauty of fiction. Mr. Trollope is not content with painting her heartless, mercenary, and unfilial, but, to make her moral deficiencies the more hideously glaring, contrasts with her the equally familiar character of the stereotyped country maiden, innocent and simple-minded to an almost imbecile pitch, the uncomplaining victim of maternal harshness. The chequered courses of the love affairs of each of these damsels, in alternate chapters, make the story. . . .

We can only hope that a tropical sun will reopen the petals of Mr. Trollope's imagination and elicit something more worthy than the 'American Senator'.

168. Unsigned notice, *The Times*

10 August 1877, p. 3

. . . We are introduced to all classes of people, from dukes and duchesses downwards, and they all fall easily into their parts, making up one of those pictures of English society with which Mr. Trollope has made us familiar. But the Senator himself is an excrescence on the work to which he gives his name, and has nothing whatever to do with the actual double story. He comes in, like the chorus in a Greek play, to make running comment on our manners and customs. But the shrewd Mr. Gotobed's outspoken criticisms prove nothing more than his incapacity for rightly understanding our 'institutions'; while he is too commonplace, too much of an American gentleman, perhaps, to lend himself to the grotesque caricature which made the fun of studies by humourists like Dickens. In short, his long-winded talk, though often reasonable, is always dull; nor is there much amusement to be extracted from his inveterate want of tact. All that can be said of him is that he is made to place English hospitality in a most pleasing light, since it gave a general welcome to so objectionable a guest. On the other hand, the society of Dillborough and the neighbourhood is in Mr. Trollope's most entertaining manner. We are introduced to the notabilities of the little town in the club that assembles weekly at the Bush, under the mild despotism of Mr. Runciman, the landlord. All of the members, of course, are deeply interested in the events that are passing under their curious eyes. We hear a great deal of the fox-hunting mania that shocks the common sense of the American visitor. Mr. Trollope, with all the enthusiasm of a hunting man, carries us through one or two capital runs, and throws us into the bitterness of the local excitement caused by an aggravated case of fox poisoning. Mr. Gotobed, during his visit to Bragton Hall, has opportunities of studying and marvelling at types that are absolutely new to him—at the wealthy and good-humoured Lord Rufford, who, lightly discharging the responsibilities of his station in a liberal but perfunctory manner, devotes the whole of his energy and income to the business of unceasing amusement and, more astounding still, at those tenant farmers who positively wel-

431

come the flying squadrons who charge over their wheat and go crashing through their gates and fences.

But decidedly the most exciting part of the book is the chase of his lordship himself by Miss Trefoil, though that mature young beauty and her scheming mother strike us as playing a more unblushing game than is even compatible with 'the way we live now.' We can understand her not sticking at trifles, had she fancied that boldness would serve her ends; but surely Lord Rufford, who was anything but a fool, would have refused to follow her lead, since he clearly saw his danger. The situation is as exciting as delicate when, after a long run, she has been driven home with him *tête-à-tête* in a post-chaise, where she sank down on his shoulder, while he beguiled the way with kisses. His good-humoured Lordship behaved very badly, but we feel sensibly relieved when he saves his brush, although the lady does in some measure redeem herself afterwards by her concern for the death of a benefactor she has jilted. The wooing of Mary Masters is divested of some of its romance by the circumstances of the rival aspirants. But Mr. Trollope has used his materials with his accustomed skill, so that we have sympathy to spare for the rejected lover, while we fully enter into Miss Masters' feelings when the hero she has idealized speaks out at last. For herself, though the daughter of a small country attorney and under the wing of a very vulgar stepmother, she is made an exceedingly charming girl; and altogether a perusal of the book leaves very pleasant impressions behind.

169. Unsigned notice, *Nation* (New York)

23 August 1877, xxv. 122–3

The Hon. Elias Gotobed, Senator of the United States from the State of Mikewa, has made the acquaintance in Washington of John Morton, one of the heroes of the novel, a rising young diplomatist. On his return to England the Senator accompanies him to study English institutions, and digest his information into a lecture, to be delivered first in London and ultimately in America. The part he plays in the plot is not very important, and the author confesses at the end that the book might as well have been called by some other name. But the senator's part is the most elaborately written, and, fair or unfair in its satire, the pleasantest to read. The rest is chiefly a couple of matrimonial affairs, one with and one without heart, not unamusing, but very conventional, and in parts disagreeable, not to say repulsive. The style of these chapters strongly confirms the hint which has reached us from England, that Mr. Trollope is beginning to 'let out' portions of his novels to less renowned assistants.

170. Unsigned notice, *Harper's Magazine*

October 1877, lv. 790

If the portrait had been that of an Assemblyman, we should not have objected; we could even have borne with him as a member of the House of Representatives; but to make him a Senator! Surely the body which has given to the political world a Calhoun, a Webster, a Clay, a Sumner, and a Seward deserved some different typical man to represent it to the readers of English romance than Mr. Gotobed. The story is an entertaining one, and even the caricature is clever.

171. T. W. Crawley, *Academy*

24 November 1877, xii. 487–8

It strikes us that, throughout the book, Mr. Gotobed is represented as almost too sweeping in his denunciation of all things British even for an American, and his plain speaking is often unmitigated rudeness. Turning to the fictional part of the work we find, as is usual in Mr. Trollope's novels, capital descriptions of life in official circles and in country houses. The unsuccessful love of Larry Twentyman, an English yeoman of the good old sort; Arabella Trefoil's persevering attempts to secure a rich husband, in spite of all rebuffs; and, lastly, the idyllic courtship of Reginald Morton and Mary Masters, all combine to counteract the unpleasant obtrusiveness of the blatant American.

172. Unsigned notice, *Spectator*

31 August 1878, li. 1101–2

Mr. Anthony Trollope rarely writes a bad book, and almost as rarely now writes one which may be distinctively called good. We take his more recent novels very much as we take English weather,—as something good in the main for health and amusement, though rarely affording special opportunities for either. . . .

'The American Senator' is a gentleman who comes over to England to examine English institutions, and to try and discover the reason that his countrymen, while speaking of England, on the whole, as a decayed, worn-out country, yet evidence the greatest respect for English institutions, English manners, and English customs. Now, it may easily be imagined that in competent hands—and for a task of this kind Mr. Trollope's are very competent—this might be made a most entertaining and original book—and the part of it which is devoted to explaining and describing Mr. Gotobed's impressions of England is excessively clever and interesting. But unfortunately, Mr. Trollope was tempted by his tremendous facility of writing, and the consequence is that he has spun out what should have been a *jeu d'esprit* in one volume, into a three-volume love-story, where the American Senator appears every now and then for a short time, when he is wanted to fill up the gaps. This is the more irritating as, considered in the light of a story, the work is perhaps the least interesting our author has ever written. The hero is a young man named Laurence Twentyman, who passes his life, or, at all events, that portion of it which appears in this book, in proposing to a young lady called Mary Masters, daughter of a county-town solicitor. . . .

There is, however, another love-story, which occupies at least as large a portion of the book as this one,—we mean the account of how the Honourable Miss Trefoil is engaged to a Foreign-Office gentleman, lately Plenipotentiary at Washington, and at the present time living on his estate of £7,000 a year in the country; and how this young lady, not satisfied with her *fiancé's* financial and social position, endeavours to capture and hold fast a certain Lord Rufford, whose estates are worth

£40,000 a year. The description of this attempt is the only interesting part of the book, apart from the American's sayings and questions, of which, as we have said, there is comparatively little, the Senator disappearing occasionally even for a volume at a time. There is also a fourth thread of interest, almost entirely of the padding order, connected with the poisoning of a fox in one of the favourite hunt coverts.

173. 'Mr. Anthony Trollope's Novels', *Edinburgh Review*

October 1877, clxvi. 455–8

Unsigned essay. This extended essay on Trollope's chief novels from *The Warden* to *The American Senator* runs to thirty-four pages, or around fifteen thousand words. The author was Alexander Innes Shand, who was in all probability the original for Trollope's Mr. Booker in *The Way We Live Now*—a competent, scholarly writer who nevertheless felt he was obliged to play the game of mutual puffery with Lady Carbury (see Introduction, Section VI). Shand's critique in the *Edinburgh* gives moderate praise to Trollope as serviceable but never in danger of dazzling his audience. He adds (with a touch worthy of Mr. Booker) that Trollope on the other hand shows no signs of wearing out what talent has been vouchsafed him. The essay is pleasant reading, though the judgements do not seem especially original or acute. Limitations of space prevent giving it at length. A sample of both its tone and its point of view is provided by its opening paragraph.

We have little hesitation in asserting that the present generation owes a larger debt of gratitude to Mr. Trollope than to any other writer of fiction, living or lately dead. In saying this, we believe that Mr. Trollope with his sound sense and professional intelligence is the last man to misunderstand us, or to imagine that we mean extravagant exaggeration of his merits. If he has laboured long and successfully in his special sphere he has learned where that sphere has its limits. He has seldom attempted to go beyond the powers he is conscious of, or to soar a sustained flight in an atmosphere too refined for his pinions. He has not the genius either of pathos, or of humour, or of satire, though he is very far from being deficient in any of these invaluable gifts. He has never written a great work of romance that will survive as the lasting monument of his fame; but then again, under the influence of too ambitious aspiration, he has never advanced to the brilliant authorship that chills and dazzles the reader with its cold, hard polish; or puzzles him with its perpetual mystery of inscrutable moral enigmas. Unlike more eminent authors, too, whom it is unnecessary and might be invidious to name, Mr. Trollope has never 'written himself out,' and, as we are glad to flatter ourselves, he shows no signs of doing so. His talent is emphatically of the serviceable order, and wears wonderfully well. There must obviously be a good deal of the mechanical about his assiduous literary toils, since he has been in the habit of delivering a regular supply of his work with most methodical precision. No doubt that must be essentially an affair of sound stamina and healthy temper. There are novelists of the highest rank who, as we know, have been able to count on themselves at all times with the confidence of experience. Walter Scott and Alexandre Dumas—we do not place the brilliant Frenchman on a par with the Magician of the North—are instances that will naturally suggest themselves. Scott in the plenitude of his power threw off the pages of 'The Antiquary' apparently with the ease of a clerk or a copying machine; while Dumas dashed off the multitude of his literally historical 'romances' in the longer or shorter intervals of a life of bustling distractions. But Scott and Dumas, in their several ways, were geniuses of very singular capacity, and such rare exceptions merely serve to prove an almost universal rule. Mr. Trollope long pursued a regular occupation, and could only devote his official leisure to his voluminous literary work. The result is what might have been expected. His work is necessarily unequal; occasionally, in the urgency of rapid invention, he has been hurried away after some hastily conceived idea which almost foredoomed him to failure, since he would persist in following it up. But taking the broad average of the library of fiction he has written, we can only admire its sterling merit.

IS HE POPENJOY?

1878

Though Trollope felt that *Is He Popenjoy?* had met with 'fair success' (see above, headnote to *The Prime Minister*), the reviews I have seen are, if anything, less favourable than those dealing with *The Prime Minister*. The *Athenaeum* (4 May 1878) found many scenes far from pleasing, but granted that there was 'much that is readable' in the novel. R. F. Little-dale in the *Academy* (8 June 1878) judged that the book was representa-tive of Trollope's 'least pleasant' manner and belonged among his satires that demonstrated uncomfortably 'how very slight are the barriers which part modern civilization from ancient savagery'.

174. Unsigned notice, *Saturday Review*

1 June 1878, xlv. 695–6

Mr. Trollope's present story reminds us of a copper-plate by a good artist at its last stage. All the finer touches, the tender, subtle gradations are worn out, and strength is supplied by a hardening of the strongest lines. We are among people who in a certain way recall *Barchester Towers*, and pleasant Barsetshire circles; but they are defined by very black lines indeed—all the delicacy and nicety of touch is gone. The author used to be fond of his characters; but such lovingness finds no place here. He stands outside and shows a world intent on the world's good things. Some are malignant, some good-natured, but in the greater part a moral sense is wanting. Where it shows itself it is under a form designedly not made attractive. It is the heroine's trial (and a very real one) that, whereas 'what suited her was to sit well dressed in a lighted room and have nonsense talked to her,' her marriage subjected her to the sole intercourse of four old-maid sisters of her husband's, who possessed his confidence, and to whose manners and pursuits, especially the stitching at petticoats for the poor and going to church twice on the

Sunday, he wished his pretty young bride to conform herself. The author justifies the lady's rebellion on the ground that her love of pleasure is innocent, that she is within her rights, and that through it all, and notwithstanding her obstinate resolution to amuse herself in spite of her husband, her feeling for him increases into a real affection, though he is the very opposite of her early ideal. But the reader does not see the likelihood of this growth of tenderness. Lord George is not the person to gather affection about him; in fact, he makes a poor figure throughout, and, as personating a form of virtue, shows a very low standard, though perhaps as high a one as Mr. Trollope can allow to a scion of nobility. . . .

The character in the book on which the author has bestowed most pains is that of the Dean, Mary's father. It is drawn with vigour, but with a coarse, hard vigour which unpleasantly contrasts with Mr. Trollope's earlier manner. Archdeacon Grantly is worldly; but Dean Lovelace sets himself with a directness of bent towards his aims which is not human in the truest sense. There is a hesitation, a misgiving, interposing at intervals in all human endeavours; but that his daughter should be a Marchioness and his grandson the real Popenjoy, is as fixed an object with the Dean as it is with a beaver to construct a dam. He supports his daughter in her rebellion against authority, because, as it seems, it belongs to marchionesses to be worldly, and to lead society as they choose. On this account he throws over all the conventional teaching of her youth; that sort of thing suited the daughter of a cathedral magnate, but is out of place among great ladies.

There is one odious character pre-eminent in this story. It is lawful to the novelist to have a villain of a purely animal type, and the Marquess, father of the infant Popenjoy, who is to be superseded, is of this kind. Only an aristocracy could have produced such a monster, as only aristocratic surroundings could enable him to carry out the 'resolution of his life to live without control' on a gigantic scale. His practised powers of insolence are brought to bear on the Dean in an heroic encounter, each using the weapons most congenial to his nature. The Marquess requests the Dean to call on him, and tells him when they meet that his father was a livery-stable keeper and his daughter what printed words must not define. The Dean follows the instinct of all Mr. Trollope's favourites. He lifts the decrepid Marquess in his arms, half throttles him, and flings him into the empty fire-grate. The insult justified almost anything; but it is difficult to imagine a Church dignitary taking such a step. After all, it is death and not the Dean who removes out of the way the so-called Popenjoy, whom it would have been difficult to displace, and makes way for the grandson to be born in all the honours of the purple. As an instance of Mr. Trollope's new views of the fitnesses and probabilities of social life, he attaches a joke to the smaller hero of the piece which might better have been spared. A certain aunt of the Dean's, Miss Tallowax, as great a lover of rank as himself, whose name indicates the method by which her fortune has been got together, is introduced in the beginning of the story and apparently forgotten by the author until the very end, when she is brought forward again as bribing the new Marquess—the rigid Lord George—to admit her to the honours of sponsorship to the illustrious infant, on the payment of twenty thousand pounds down, providing he is called after her—Tallowax. There was strong objection at first to the proposal, but all scruples were over-ruled by the Dean; the twenty thousand pounds were important, and all other things were not. . . .

Such pictures of life cost Mr. Trollope, we suppose, very little trouble, and perhaps he does not expect them to be seriously taken as representing his views. But we are sure that his happier efforts were carried through under a stronger sense of the duties of his calling and of the office and uses of fiction in gifted hands. We regard the present caricature of a corrupt state of society as an instance of the ill effects of over-writing, and of its deadening influence on the finer perceptions. All the temptations of life become only so much material to the mechanical facility of long practice, and what will catch the attention of the least critical readers and keep within the bounds of the easiest conventional decorum becomes the measure of literary merit and social propriety.

175. Unsigned notice, *The Times*

14 September 1878, p. 4

'Is He Popenjoy?' would more than pass muster had it appeared anonymously, but it is by no means worthy of its author. The plot is slight, the characters are weak, and the general impression is unpleasing. It is not to be expected that one of the most indefatigable novel-writers of the time should invariably come up to the expectations he has excited. He may have been unfortunate in the keynote of his story, or he may have been labouring against the grain. But he owes the public a reasonable amount of care, and 'Is He Popenjoy?' shows signs of haste and carelessness. The title strikes us as untempting, though that is a matter of taste.

176. Unsigned notice, *Spectator*

5 October 1878, li. 1243–4

Mr. Trollope has done so much good and healthy work in his time, that when he writes a tale which is poor as a work of art and to some extent unwholesome in tone, the reviewer's first inclination is to let the book alone. And yet it would not be well that a popular and justly popular novelist like Mr. Trollope should trade on his reputation, and write inferior tales, without some critical protest. . . .

With the exception of the heroine, Lady George Germain, and of her father, the Dean, there is not a character in the story which excites a pleasurable interest; and there are several characters so vulgar, coarse, or wanting in self-assertion that they excite nothing but contempt. No doubt this is a feeling which a novelist may call forth legitimately enough. In order to produce a true picture, men and women with low worldly aims or vicious propensities must be represented, to some extent, as they are, but the artist has the choice of his materials; he can let us see the blue sky over all, he can let us breathe the sweet breezes of heaven, he can invigorate instead of depressing us by his representation of life. Mr. Trollope has done this in former days, but he has not done it in this novel.

AN EYE FOR AN EYE

1879

Save for one remarkable exception (No. 177), *An Eye for an Eye* was to be dismissed as another of Trollope's uncomfortable stories, devoid of his earlier charm. The *Athenaeum* (11 January 1879) gave the novel only brief attention as a slight story about commonplace people. R. F. Littledale in the *Academy* (8 February 1879) decided that Trollope was prolonging the perverse fit that had seized him in *Is He Popenjoy?* Specifically he was reviving the 'pre-eminently painful' mood of another story of Ireland, *The Macdermots of Ballycloran*. The *Illustrated London News* (12 April 1879) speculated on what could have made an established author select such an unpromising subject as a homily on seduction and then let the world see 'so very moderate a specimen of his great powers'. The New York *Nation* (24 April 1879) considered the story on the whole well told, but ultimately weak rather than tragic in its impact.

177. Unsigned notice, *Spectator*

15 February 1879, lii. 210–11

One is tempted to assign this review to Richard Holt Hutton (see Introduction, VII), but there is no really solid evidence for doing so. There is, indeed, more than a suggestion of Hutton's style; and there is also the author's confidence in his ability to detect 'certain obvious peculiarities of mere language' in Trollope's writing (as Hutton had apparently done in identifying the anonymous *Nina Balatka* as Trollope's).

This story will take a high place among Mr. Trollope's works. Indeed, there is something in the atmosphere of Ireland which appears to rouse his imagination, and give force and simplicity to his pictures of life, though no doubt the stories by which he will, in the future, be most generally remembered will hardly be his Irish stories. The Barchester series of clerical sketches, including those which contain his shrewd delineations of the political coteries of London,—from *The Warden* to *Phineas Redux*,—are more completely out of the sphere of any other writer, and fuller of careful and complex observation, than any which he has written. But for that very reason, they are never as classical, as single in their interest, as intense in their vividness, as his Irish tales. And when compared with any but the very best of his English stories, such a tale as this is entitled to take precedence even of Mr. Trollope's clever clerical and political fictions. Except for certain obvious peculiarities of mere language, *An Eye for an Eye* hardly seems to be written by the same author as *The Way We Live Now*. To one emerging from the over-laden atmosphere of that sordid world, this tragic story of mastering passion and over-mastering prejudice,—of a great sin, a great wrong, and a great revenge,—is like the breath of that Atlantic to the shores of which it carries us, after the stifling atmosphere of a London alley. There is something simple and great in the story, and we turn to it with the more pleasure, that Mr. Trollope has too much accustomed us of late to the delineation of moral malaria, and of endless varieties of what we might almost term middle-class squalor,—thereby meaning, of course, to use 'squalor' metaphorically, not for what offends the senses, but for what oppresses almost to nightmare the little moral ideality left to our age. Here, at least, there is no nightmare of the kind. The guilt, the grief, and the crime all have their roots in the natural instincts of man, as these are known to us in such a society as our own; and all appear to be just what they are, without any artificial disguises. Nothing can be more striking than the picture of the manner in which hereditary pride takes hold of the heir to the old English earldom, almost without his own con-sent, and against his own better nature and feelings, and yet assumes to itself the air of disinterested duty and high necessity, driving him to do what he is ashamed of, and yet only ashamed of as a man; while as the head of a house and the heir to a great name, he seems to himself to owe more to society than he owes even to his own conscience and his God. Mr. Trollope has hardly ever painted anything so striking as the mode in which the promise not to disgrace his house and name grows un-consciously and involuntarily in the young Lord Scroope's mind, till it takes all the life out of the more binding and far more sacred promise under the faith of which he has gained from Kate O'Hara all she has to give; and this, though far from wishing to desert her, though he is

really willing to give all he has to give in the world, except his rank
and social position, to make atonement to her for what has been done.
Of all the strange perversions of which the moral nature of men is
capable, probably none is stranger than the tendency of certain so-
called 'social obligations' to over-ride entirely the simpler personal obligations in certain men's breasts, and yet to work there with all the force
of a high duty, and all the absoluteness of an admitted destiny. Of
course, in the case of the Lord Scroope whose tragic fate this story tells
us, a certain contempt for the girl who has yielded to his passion co-
operates with the growing, and at first quite unsuspected, pride of rank,
to harden him in his determination not to fulfil his promise of making
her his wife. But the subtlety of Mr. Trollope's insight is shown by his
clear perception that this contempt for her, though fatal to his sense of
justice to her, so far as regards the promise to make her his true wife,
is yet not fatal to the same sense of justice to her,—for it is hardly less,
—so far as regards his promise to be to her all that a husband should be,
except her lawful husband,—that it is not fatal to his conviction that he
may not desert her for any other woman, and that he is bound to give
up his life, so far as, within such conditions, he can, to her happiness.
The mode in which this sense of family pride, which appears to be at
first quite wanting in Fred Neville's not very passionate and not very
strong character, grows and grows almost without his own knowledge,
until, when it is at length reinforced by a touch of scorn for the object
of his tenderness, it hardens him, as if it had the combined force of a
spurious conscience and of hereditary prejudice acting in unison, is
painted with extraordinary vividness and extraordinary simplicity. You
are made sure that the picture is a true one, and yet it takes you by surprise,—so little of the root of this family pride has been shown to you
in the earlier pictures of the hero.

Equally powerful is the slight sketch of the uncle whose sad and
austere life gives you the key to the family character on its highest side;
and but little less so of the aunt, whose aristocratic feeling is made the
unhappy instrument of rivetting the claims of family on her nephew's
mind. But the finest picture in the tale,—after that of the idle-minded
young officer who makes the principal figure in it,—is that of the Irish
priest, Father Marty,—who is so closely implicated in the tragedy.
Nothing truer or stronger in drawing has ever proceeded from Mr.
Trollope's pen than this vigorous sketch,—dashed off in a very few scenes,
—of the too rash and yet thoroughly noble and faithful priest of Lis-
cannor. If the sketch of the unhappy mother, whose crime is expiated

by hopeless madness, is not quite equal to that of any of the other leading figures, it is rather that we are told something too little of her, than that any touch is put in which is out of keeping with the progress and ending of the tale. One feels that here a little more should have been told. Something of her relations with her disreputable husband,—something that would throw a light on the intensity of her passions,—is wanted, in order to make the figure as striking as is that of the other chief actors of this simple and tragic story. It is not a story for which we can do anything by extract. It is too short and too classical in its simplicity, to be illustrated effectively by any specimen-passage. But it is a story which no man without a very powerful imagination could have written. And as Mr. Trollope's imagination has lately but too frequently lost itself in sands and marshes and all kinds of muddy fen-countries, we welcome cordially this flashing-up of his higher power, in the present striking tale.

But one trivial remark more. What makes Mr. Trollope put into the mouth of his hero the assertion that on the cliffs of Moher—the cliffs where Clare meets the Atlantic—'the gulls never show themselves' in hot summer weather? The present writer can answer for it that he has seen the air thick with them, under the bluest sky and the serenest heaven of a brilliant August day.

178. Unsigned notice, *Saturday Review*

29 March 1879, xlvii. 410–11

As usual in its reviews of Trollope's novels, favourable or not, the *Saturday* allotted more than two columns (over two thousand words) to *An Eye for an Eye*, much of the space devoted in this instance to retelling the story and quoting from the novel.

. . . The work has been carried through without that intimate partnership between heart and soul and hand, which is apparent in the past efforts of genius, whether the thing be handicraft or headwork. . . . We do not suppose it possible to be keenly interested in any story which has not awakened an intensity of feeling in its narrator. Such intensity is certainly wanting in the tragical story before us; and therefore the reader takes the calamities of its leading characters not only dry-eyed, but with an easy composure which would in its turn be tragical to the writer were it his first novel—though this is an impossible supposition. . . .

When novel writers are no longer inspired by a moving story to tell, which is the first motive setting the pen to work, their next resource is a principle to advocate or an abuse to expose and illustrate. It is not very easy to divine what is the especial grievance against society in an *Eye for an Eye*, unless it be the deleterious effect of rank on the moral character. The hero starts as a very poor fellow, but pretty much on a par with other merely self-indulgent young men till he comes to the earldom, when the weight of a coronet and the sense of *noblesse oblige* makes him a stolid traitor to the more natural sense of honour which had previously had some influence with him.

JOHN CALDIGATE

1879

---

179. Unsigned notice, *Athenaeum*

14 June 1879, p. 755

The same strength and the same weakness distinguish 'John Caldigate' and 'Barchester Towers.' The same characters with which we have so long been familiar reappear in the later story, though under different names. We meet once more with almost the identical scenes, illustrations, and turns of expression, which made Mr. Trollope's first efforts so racy and so successful. . . . 'John Caldigate' is an interesting story, but its art is neither specially elaborate nor very well sustained.

180. E. Purcell, *Academy*

5 July 1879, xvi. 5

[Mr. Trollope] has for once given his old favourites a holiday, and has applied all his resources to the careful delineation of a new hero. John Caldigate, the successful gold-digger—shrewd, sensible, honourable, and strong-willed, yet hiding under his firmness some lingering weaknesses and passions—would hardly have interested us much without those early chapters in which Mr. Trollope analyses and accounts for the unsuspected strength and capacity latent in the good-for-nothing college youth. Here, as again in the sudden transition by which he avoids the dubious part of the young man's story, his construction is both masterly and judicious.

181. Unsigned notice, *Spectator*

19 July 1879, lii. 916–17

With one recent exception, we mean the little Irish tale, *An Eye for an Eye*, there has been so great a falling-off in Mr. Anthony Trollope's recent novels from the level excellence of his works up to a certain period, that we have ceased to welcome the announcement of a new book by the author of so many stories in which we have taken delight in their time, with the fearless confidence of former days. This falling-off dates from the *Prime Minister*, in which the grind of the barrel-organ, the mere mechanism of the author's performance, made itself felt; and since then Mr. Trollope has declined still farther, in *The Way We Live Now*, *Lady Anna*, and *The American Senator*. The group of Irish novels, which included *The Kellys and the O'Kellys*, *The Macdermots*, and *Castle Richmond*, was a very remarkable achievement, and is not to be confounded or compared with the two celebrated stories, *Phineas Finn* and *Phineas Redux*, which are not Irish in a similar sense at all, in which, in fact, there is nothing Irish except the hero of them both; and we think it likely that when Mr. Trollope's works come under the judgment of the future, the Irish novels will be regarded as the high-water mark of his ability. They have not the wide popularity of his other books, just because the country, the people, and the life represented in them, with such subtle and sympathetic realism, are all unknown to the great mass of English readers; but we do not think they could be read by anybody, although Ireland and the Irish were as strange to that reader as Africa and its tribes, and not convey the sense that they are absolutely real and perfect presentments of character, of types, and of events. . . . This story exhibits a good deal of the same kind of power as that which characterizes the author's Irish novels. It transports the reader to a distant country, to Melbourne and the Victorian gold-diggings, introducing him to strange, rough company, in those unfamiliar scenes; and so doing, conveys an impression of complete likeness and realism. . . .

The great achievement of the novel is Hester Caldigate. We do not think Mr. Trollope has ever drawn so fine, impressive, interesting, and sympathetic a character as this wifeliest of wives and womanliest of women. She is charming throughout,—in her simple and picturesque girlhood; in her first bloom of happy marriage, when trouble comes and doubt, but not doubt of *him*; in her full, free pardon of that hardly comprehended sin which he confesses; in her fearless fight for him, and steady abiding by him; in that hard contest with her parents, which forms one of the most striking features of the story; in the final victory, and the hard-won peace. It would be difficult to praise too highly the ingenuity of Mr. Trollope's working-out of the detective portion of a plot of a much more complicated nature than usual with him, and it is due to him to observe that the accessories of the drama are studied with minute carefulness. The gradual winning of John Caldigate's father by his son's sweet wife is beautifully conveyed, but never obtruded, and in the by-play of the family history there is much humour, a quality in which the author's recent works have been wanting.

182. Unsigned notice, *Examiner*

2 August 1879, p. 1000

We have not so many writers of fiction of the first class that we can afford to witness the decadence of any of them. The novel now before us, though we admit at once that it is much better than two-thirds of the stories published, certainly does not afford a favourable specimen of Mr. Trollope's powers. Indeed, were a reader who had no previous acquaintance with the author to take up this story before any of its predecessors, he would be puzzled to account for its writer's great popularity. . . . There are not a few improbabilities in the story and the author is scarcely to be congratulated upon his plot. . . . Altogether, although this novel contains some good things, it can scarcely be said to maintain Mr. Trollope's reputation.

183. Unsigned notice, *The Times*

8 August 1879, p. 3

'John Caldigate' is a good novel expanded into a dull one. The promise of the opening is excellent, and the interest rises rather than otherwise towards the close of the first volume. But then Mr. Trollope falls into that methodical and detailed narrative which we should say had been growing into a habit with him, did he not every now and then break away into a book which reminds us of his 'Doctor Thorne' or the 'Last Chronicles of Barset.' The fact is that a business-like tendency to routine and method is Mr. Trollope's bane. With all his literary talent and his happy fertility of fancy, he will carry business habits into novel writing, till his very facility becomes a snare to him. In 'John Caldigate' we have the materials for an exciting and pathetic romance, and there is very sufficient sensation, with a variety of pathos, in the volumes. But it would have been more moving, not to say more pleasant, had it been more briefly told; especially as two or three of the principal characters are meant to be gloomy, dull, and repulsive. The keynote to the impression on the reader is struck in the cheerless aspect of the country where the scenes are chiefly laid. . . . The parts of the story that are the pleasantest and most lively reading were pregnant with grief and misery to the Boltons. Caldigate goes to Australia to retrieve the past and come back with a competency. He not only makes a competency but a fortune, and the scenes at the gold-diggings are described with a truth and spirit which remind us that Mr. Trollope went on a tour in the Australian Colonies. But Satan, who finds mischief for idle men, tempted Caldigate to his future misery on the tedious voyage to the Antipodes.

16 August 1879, xlviii. 216–17

Bigamy has been found of late years so fertile a subject for the novelist's handling, and lends itself so readily to the turn of Mr. Trollope's genius, and his dramatic, many-sided treatment of social questions—he throws himself in the volumes before us with such zest and revival of power into all its aspects, whether viewed on its legal, moral, domestic, or gossiping side—that, instead of regretting that he should have meddled with so questionable a topic now, we may rather wonder that he has not taken it up before. . . .

Life at Nobble, the gold-digging town (reached from Melbourne), 'the foulest place ever seen,' 'the beastliest hole man ever put his foot into,' with its 'old stick-in-the-mud soft goods store,' its delicacies of the table condensed into 'grub' three times a day, its abandonment of all the restraints of civilized life, its ignorance of every man's ante-cedents and of all surnames borne in the old country, is only too natural a source of the scrapes, including one pre-eminent scrape, into which John Caldigate, being the man he is, has to fall. It does not seem the same thing to him as it would be at home to call the woman who is already in possession of two names—one for shipboard use, the other placarded on the walls of Sydney in theatrical posters with a portrait encumbered with as few garments as may be—by a third; to address an envelope to her as Mrs. Caldigate, and to call her his wife. In fact, the author so far excuses him under the circumstances that, though he punishes him through the law of the land which mistakenly, and therefore unjustly, convicts him, he never inflicts on him the novelist's true punishment—the disapproval of the honest conscientious characters of the story. Those who visit John Caldigate's conduct with their hearty disapproval are under the cloud of the author's dislike or contempt; those who stand by him through thick and thin are the good fellows of the piece; and the pure Hester takes this episode of his life as belonging to him merely as one of a class with whom similar episodes are universal; and therefore without any feeling of protest or repulsion. . . . We hope that in his next story Mr. Trollope, while retaining his varied powers of amusing his readers and imparting to them the conclusions of his own insight into character, will choose a theme that may engage our sympathies undisturbed by protest.

185. 'Trollope, Hawthorne, and the New Aestheticism', *Dublin University Magazine*

October 1879, iv. 436–42

Unsigned essay, 'Polar Opposites in Fiction'. For the September issue of the Boston *North American Review* (cclxxiv. 203–22), Trollope had written an essay entitled 'The Genius of Nathaniel Hawthorne'. It is an unpretentious, low-density, somewhat rambling discussion of Hawthorne's novels; and it strongly suggests, to be sure, that whereas Hawthorne in his terse critique of Trollope (see No. 39) had penetrated to essential values of the English novelist, Trollope did not in turn see very deeply into Hawthorne's novels.

In the September number of the *North American Review* is an article entitled 'The Genius of Nathaniel Hawthorne,' which possesses a peculiar interest for all admirers of that genius, being written by one who dwells content in the opposite pole of mind. It requires some effort, at first, to convince oneself that there is before one an elaborate critique upon Hawthorne written by so unlikely a person as Anthony Trollope. But the result of this strange combination is particularly instructive. Trollope has made a noteworthy attempt to understand and admire Hawthorne, and in so doing has afforded a charming illustration of the fact that between the realist and the idealist there is a great gulf fixed, which the former can no wise cross unless he learn to fly.

Mr. Trollope is very anxious to make us clearly understand, at starting, that he and Hawthorne were great admirers each of the other. Mr. Trollope appreciates the 'Marble Faun' because, or in spite, of its being so unlike anything which he could himself have produced; while he acquaints us also with Hawthorne's feelings towards himself, which are thus expressed in his own words, in a quotation from a letter to a friend. . . .[1]

---

[1] At this point the reviewer quotes Hawthorne's comment in a letter of 1860 upon Trollope's novels (given above as No. 39).

Mr. Trollope seems inclined to accept this as a kind of praise given by one artist to another of a different order. Truth to tell, we see little but the amused interest and humorous regard of an ideal artist for a worker in earthen pots. Mr. Trollope does not seem to suspect that his work may stand in the same relation to the intense imagination of Hawthorne, as the veriest trash to the tired thinker, to whom it sometimes affords the relief of cessation of thought. What is a work of art? Is it solid and substantial, as if some giant had hewn a great lump out of the earth? . . . The actual marble of the statue, the touchable canvas and paint of the picture, the piece of reality which is used as scaffolding for the artist's work, this Mr. Trollope can appreciate, and does appreciate heartily: the Turneresque atmosphere which Hawthorne could fling about his characters, is to him but a 'preserved extract of moonshine and mist.' Just that part which, instead of being built out of beef and ale, is produced from strength of spirit and inspiration of soul, misses his apprehension. . . .

Mr. Trollope has one great advantage over many of his brother authors; he deals in the respectabilities of life. Church dignitaries and commonplace housewives adorn his pages. These people are as intelligible as poor Hephzibah. But a crazed soul like Clifford Pyncheon, who, though a grown man, can find strange childlike joy in a gleam of sunshine, and cowers in childish fear before the superior cunning of his stern kinsman—such a soul he wots not of. Yet even his favourite, poor rusty Hephzibah, though she had to guard her brother like a baby, recognized dimly that his mind reached into regions to which she could not raise her own. . . .

Mr. Trollope chooses some others of Hawthorne's most trivial stories to dissect, such as 'Mrs. Bullfrog' and 'P.'s Correspondence,' the mere quips and quirks of a productive pen. But he says nothing of that marvellous story, 'The Artist of the Beautiful,' in which Hawthorne's peculiar powers are so markedly visible. Is it too much to expect a writer who avowedly reproduces the commonplace characters in life with the fidelity of the photographer, and who is so devoid of all sense, both of the absurd as well as of the artistic, as to entitle a book, 'Is he Popenjoy?' to study a story which is full of the purest artistic feeling? What cares he for the useless butterfly wings? he loves what Hawthorne somewhere calls the solid unrealities of life. Art is outside of these; she is not solid, she is often unintelligible, but she is real. 'If there were nothing mystical in human destiny, if mere instincts and the impulses of sheer emotion never struck truer than cool common sense,'[1] then perhaps we might accept Mr. Trollope as our prophet, and put aside the inner longing for something less intelligible than Archdeacon Grantly or Mrs. Proudie. But we cannot; man does not live by beef and ale alone.

[1] The writer cites in a note: '*Daily News*, Jan. 17, 1874.'

COUSIN HENRY

1879

---

186. Unsigned notice, *Athenaeum*

18 October 1879, lii. 1319–21

The present story excels both in minuteness and commonplace. Cousin Henry . . . occupies the greater part of two meagre volumes with his doubts on the question whether or not he shall destroy a will unfavourable to his interests. . . . That the story is written with much fluency goes without saying; from a less skilful pen so much ado about nothing would be intolerable.

187. Unsigned notice, *Spectator*

18 October 1879, lii. 1319–21

But what other novelist besides Mr. Trollope would venture to begin a story as he begins this? What other novelist, besides him, could make it interesting? Nay, how does Mr. Trollope himself make it interesting? To us, it is a mystery; all we know is that we read on and on, and do not get tired, and this, too, despite the fact that we know, in a sense, just what is in store for us, or rather, we know what is not in store for us; no breathless astonishment, no curdling horror, no consuming curiosity. There may be, for aught we can say, as many murders, forgeries, abductions, foundlings, missing wills, in Mr. Trollope's novels as in any others; but they are not told about in a manner to alarm us, we accept them quite philosophically; we come upon many a paragraph in our morning newspaper that excites us far more. And yet they are narrated with admirable art, and with fully as much dramatic effect as we are accustomed to look for in real life. They are interesting, but not uncourteously, not exasperatingly so; and the strangest part of it is that the introductory and intermediate passages, such as we have just been reproducing, are no less interesting, under Mr. Trollope's treatment, than are the murders and forgeries. Not only does he never offend the modesty of nature,—he encourages her to be prudish, and trains her to such evenness and serenity of demeanour, that we never know when we have had enough of her. His touch is eminently civilizing; everything, from the episodes to the sentences, moves without hitch or creak; we never have to read a paragraph twice, and we are never sorry to have read it once. He is the most unique and indispensable of fiction-writers, for the very reason, as it seems, that he tells his stories with the most common-place possible air, and never tells anything that we might not have heard somewhere else.

188. Unsigned notice, *Examiner*

25 October 1879, p. 1382

No subject for a plot is, we think, so entirely worn-out as the loss of a last will and testament. Dozens of novels and plays have been constructed on this basis, and no experienced author except Mr. Anthony Trollope would, we think, now venture again on this well-trodden path. Trite as is the theme, the fertile novelist has by its very triteness and the extreme slightness of the plot proved once more his great powers. No one knows so well as Mr. Trollope how to fit together the very slender materials of which most novels are constructed; and those he has chosen for this, his last production, are far slighter and weaker than even he generally employs. The two thin volumes comprising the book are devoted almost entirely to an elaborate history of the operations of Cousin Henry's mind under great temptation. The hero (for we suppose that we must call him so) is a weak and vacillating character, without any redeeming, still less attractive, features. The heroine, who is sketched, rather than worked out, loathes him, and the only other character of any importance, the family lawyer, is busy throughout the work trying to expose him. How he succeeds, and how the heroine comes to her rights, we shall not betray. But, as we have said, the story is of the very slightest, and if told by anyone else would probably prove totally insufficient to keep the reader's interest alive even for the short time required to peruse it. Mr. Trollope, however, succeeds in making us anxiously wonder from page to page, not whether Isabel will accept Mr. Owen (for we do not care much about that); not whether the will has been lost, for we are at the very beginning of the book put in possession of the secret, but simply what phase Cousin Henry's weakness will next assume.

The workings of his mind and the vacillations of his purpose, his self-communings and self-reproaches, are followed with wrapt attention, although there is, in fact, nothing in them, and every experienced novel reader would have been able to foretell the end from the opening chapter. This subtle web, woven of such thin materials, is not, perhaps, the highest style of art, and the mechanical execution of the work, suffering as it does from the mannerisms of language which have become a part of Mr. Trollope's nature, leaves very much to be desired. Yet, stilted as the English often is, it is always pure and grammatical, and although the reader dislikes Cousin Henry cordially, and may occasionally say to himself that he does not really care at all what the odious man thinks and how much he suffers, he is yet carried on almost against his will to turn page after page with increasing attention, till, when the end is reached, he is inclined to ask himself by what means Mr. Trollope has succeeded in making a couple of hours fly so rapidly. This, we take it, is a sufficient proof that the novel—if novel it be—is a success; not as a great novel, but as an elaborate, though small, study of human nature.

189. Unsigned notice, *Saturday Review*

25 October 1879, xlviii. 515–16

This is not a novel exactly, but rather a study, and a very able one. One character occupies both the author's space and his—we may almost say —undivided attention. The story lends itself to the development and exhibition of Cousin Henry. The other characters are shadows or repetitions of what the author has given us before; but we cannot recall among Mr. Trollope's creations another Cousin Henry. There is very little love-making; so what there is has to be condensed, in the summing up of the story especially, into a somewhat overpowering essence. We know at once that Cousin Henry, though pressed upon, and pressing himself upon, the heroine, though not evil to the eye but tall and with well-formed features, and even though in the first scene she tells him he is odious to her—which, according to our experience of fiction, is generally a sign full of promise—has no chance. 'I don't care a bit for his wild oats,' says the lady to her old uncle; 'but why can't he look me in the face?' This objection we feel to be conclusive. There is, in fact, another reason for this impossibility of Isabel Brodrick ever marrying her cousin, Henry Jones, in the person of William Owen of Hereford, a Minor Canon attached to the cathedral. Minor Canons, it may be observed by the way, have risen lately in the market of fiction as *jeunes premiers*. Property, not love, is the real theme of the story. The trials, the temptations, the conflict between duty and inclination, all relate, not to the hearts of impressionable young people, but to the holders, in possession or in prospect, of real property—property of solid, not dazzling, value; the merits of fifteen hundred a year appealing rather to the judgment than the imagination of the reader.

190. William Wallace, *Academy*

1 November 1879, xvi. 316

Cousin Henry is a story of petty and linked misery most unconscionably long-drawn out in Mr. Trollope's characteristic manner. No other novelist could have racked through two volumes a shivering coward who has not the courage either to destroy or to give up a will unfavourable to himself which he has accidentally discovered. Miss Isabella Brodrick, the cousin of this fly which Mr. Trollope takes such a time in breaking on his wheel, is an old friend with a new name, one of those sensible, tantalizing young women who, when they give their hearts away, are not, as one of them says, 'missish or coy in their love,' but who must surrender only after all relations with their social circle have been satisfactorily adjusted and with the family banners flying.

191. Unsigned notice, *The Times*

6 November 1879, p. 6

Mr. Trollope has described so many types of the middle-class Englishman that he must be sorely puzzled to avoid plagiarizing from himself; but, happily for him, on the strength of his reputation he can afford to risk hazardous experiments. No novice with sound literary instincts would have dared to stake his credit on the despicable 'hero' whom Mr. Trollope, with practised skill, has made the subject of a readable little novel.

THE DUKE'S CHILDREN

1880

For this last novel of the Palliser series, Michael Sadleir could express only mild approval; but more recent critics, including both Arthur Mizener and Bradford Booth, place the work among Trollope's finest achievements, as a subtle and profound view of the Duke's last years in a time of change.

192. Unsigned notice, *Athenaeum*

29 May 1880, p. 694

There is a school of detractors who urge that Mr. Trollope does nothing to lead his readers to see the beauties of a higher life, but such criticism altogether misses the conditions and requirements of art. No doubt Mr. Trollope is not an artist according to the modern school of high art, which is, after all, a very didactic and formal thing. His work is of a freer kind. He takes life as he sees it, and works in a broad and genial spirit. He has no esoteric doctrines. His lessons are plain to all the world, and, above all things, he knows that the first thing required of a novelist is that he should seize the attention of his readers by interesting and amusing them. In this he is successful in 'The Duke's Children.'

We cannot say that we care very much for the sorrows and loves of the young people whose function it is to exercise the temper, to try the patience, to test the principles of our old friend, now Duke of Omnium; but they do effect these necessary ends. The Duke represents the struggle between the old aristocratic sentiment and modern liberalism. The conflict in his case is between pride of birth, the sense of nobility, a long ancestry, a great historical position, and the opposition to all these feelings which distinguishes the party of which he is nominally the head, and whose principles he has to advocate. . . . The reader feels really grateful to Mr. Trollope that his tenderness towards his own creation prevents him from exposing the Duke to deeper trials than he encounters in the present story. Tregear is a gentleman. Lady Mary is quite as determined a character as that Lady Anna of one of his recent novels who married a tailor; and on whomsoever her choice had fallen the Duke would have had to give way.

The scrapes of the Duke's sons are more in the ordinary course of things. Silverbridge loses seventy thousand pounds, and the younger brother four thousand, by betting and gambling. A Major Tifto who assists in these affairs is drawn with knowledge, and gives point to several of the scenes. Whether in the club, or the racecourse, or the hunting field, he is recommended to the reader as something above a mere swindler by becoming the victim of a more thorough rogue than himself. The sons very properly pronounce their father a brick and tip-top, for he pays their gambling debts at the expense of stern lectures, softening off at the end into Latin quotations. 'You should have heard the Governor spouting Latin,' writes Lord Gerald to his brother, congratulating himself at having gone slap at his confession. 'If there is anything that never does any good it is craning. I did it all at a rush, just as though I was swallowing a dose of physic.' And thus the young men escape the insidious blandishments of Messrs. Comfort and Criball. There is no doubt that the Duke under a cold exterior is the most amiable of men, superior in all respects to his children, and finding very little pleasure or prospect of satisfaction in them; so that the main interests of the story are more or less sad. He is throughout a sufferer. Therefore, whatever the views of the reader, none will grudge him his return to power as the story closes, or will seriously object to Silverbridge's penitent return to the family politics, after starting in political life in direct opposition to his father, though he comes round at last upon no higher ground than that his leader, Sir Timothy Beeswax, is 'such a beast, you know.'

194. Unsigned notice, *Spectator*

12 June 1880, liii. 754–5

In the present work, we find him not quite at his best. But the writer's familiarity with his characters communicates itself imperceptibly to the reader; there are no difficult or awkward introductions; the toning of the picture, to use an artistic phrase, is unexceptionable; and if it is rather tinted than coloured, the tints are so handled that only the masters of colour could produce anything more likely to recall reality.

The story is concerned with the recent adventures of the present Duke of Omnium, his two sons, and his daughter. No novelist of whom we have any knowledge seems to possess so sane a comprehension of the mode of life and thought of the British aristocracy as Mr. Trollope.

For this dramatic essay, if we may so term it, upon the aristocratic principle, in its relation to politics, society, and morality, possesses an interest which few or none besides Mr. Trollope could have imparted to it; it is the thoughtful and sensible judgment of an able and comparatively impartial mind upon one of the quaintest of modern problems. The Duke of Omnium himself is the best and highest type of the surviving aristocracy of the last generation; but his children are also the children of progress; more emancipated than he from the traditions of the past, but forfeiting, as Lady Glencora's children should, along with these, a good deal of dignity and self-respect. The Duke has the worst of the logic throughout; but the occasional shortcomings of the best logic are very clearly indicated by the novelist. Two principal considerations stand in the way of the Duke's squaring his concrete practice with his intellectual theories. In the first place, he is the representative and, as it were, responsible curator of the traditions and the honour of an ancient and noble line. It is his duty to see that it suffers no diminution of quality or prestige at his hands. In the second place, he is, from a personal or individual point of view, one of the foremost figures of his order; and there is an ever-present conflict going on in his mind between his gentleness and charity as a human being, and his pride and punctiliousness as one of the leaders of an august and artificial social oligarchy. He cannot satisfactorily divide himself between the claims of these opposing interests; and the struggle, which is admirably pourtrayed by Mr. Trollope, in various amusing and pathetic scenes, involves much incidental anxiety and distress, both to

470

the Duke and his children. The story ends happily, in the conventional sense; but the total impression upon the reader's mind is somewhat depressing; the Gordian knot which puzzled the poor old Duke is cut, rather than untied; the bonds of the past are arbitrarily broken; they are not modified into picturesque appendages. Mr. Trollope appears to suggest that the religion of caste is hopelessly and helplessly incompatible with the creed of progress, when, nevertheless, caste is the very root of the tree of the political English oak, and can be interfered with only at the risk of destroying the entire organism. . . .

Among the materials which Mr. Trollope uses in the evolution of his tale is a young American heiress, Miss Isabel Boncassen. She is so deficient in the matter of family as to be the granddaughter of a labourer, but by way of compensation she possesses a learned and intelligent father, who is 'spoken of' as a possible President of the United States; an ample fortune, and superlative attractions of mind and person. The Duke's eldest son falls in love with this young republican, and she with him. Her character, speech, and manners are so carefully and justly presented by Mr. Trollope, that few even of his most critical American readers would, we fancy, be inclined to raise objections to the portrait. In one point only does it seem to us that the author has failed adequately to apprehend this young lady. . . . Mr. Trollope has made his republican heiress lay aside her republican irreverence altogether too easily and too soon. In as far as Plantagenet Palliser was Plantagenet Palliser, she would doubtless love him and respect him; but in so far as he was Duke of Omnium, she would inevitably make fun of him, and even look down upon him, as the victim of a solemnly ludicrous piece of mummery. That she herself should come to be Duchess of Omnium would strike her in the light of a preposterous joke,—a state of things to be mischievously enjoyed, perhaps, in proportion as other people might be taken in by it; but, on the whole and in the long-run, a state of things to be ashamed of, as unworthy the tolerance of a sane and honest young woman. Miss Boncassen is a charming girl, and her vivacity and her smartness are doubtless as un-English as her parentage; but essentially and at bottom she is as English as the Duke himself, and not American at all.

We have not space to analyse this novel farther; but it appears to us, from first to last, to be thoroughly readable and one of the most edifying that Mr. Trollope has yet produced. It is of more than average length, but full of matter, and capable, in spite of its perspicacious style, of being read more than once.

195. Unsigned notice, *Illustrated London News*

26 June 1880, lxxvi. 622

Society is probably very like the representation of it which is to be found in *The Duke's Children* by Anthony Trollope . . . a novel abounding, as life itself abounds, with conversation, gossip, and much ado about nothing, from the philosophical point of view. To the world, however, it is all extremely interesting; and, for that reason, the novel, exactly reproducing the sort of fuss of which daily existence in the higher social circles is understood to be made up, is sure to be read with interest, if not delight, by a large number of readers. It is certainly a very readable novel; for the author has a singular gift of readability, a wonderful power of story-telling, though his stories may be deficient in what is called action. . . .

196. Unsigned notice, *Nation* (New York)

19 August 1880, xxxi. 138–9

As a whole it is one of Mr. Trollope's most successful novels. It is pitched in the usual quiet key which all readers of his books know so well, and which is maintained with the hand of a master to the end. . . . If any one will examine such a chapter as the one which describes the breakfast-table of the duke and his two sons, and ask himself when he has read it how any detail could be altered so as to increase the reality of the scene, he will find that it is almost impossible to change a word without impairing the effect. This is something, too, which can be said of hardly any other novelist, living or dead. Whole pages and chapters might be expunged from Thackeray and Dickens with vast improvement of the general result. . . . He is, unless we are greatly mistaken, the last of the realists, and, like a true Englishman, not even that on any theory. He paints the world as he sees it, but he sees it with just that amount of artistic vision which saves his picture from having the dull flatness of every-day life, and yet never makes the light and shade any lighter or any darker than everybody feels to be within the bounds of naturalness. No one ever, we fancy, read a novel of his without wishing that he might soon write another, and it is only born story-tellers who leave us in this frame of mind.

197. Unsigned notice, *Westminster Review*

October 1880, cxiv. 574

Those who fancied that Mr. Trollope had been falling off will be delighted to read 'The Duke's Children,' and to meet again their old friend the Duke of Omnium, the only duke whom all of us know. Mr. Trollope is upon old ground, and describes it with all the ease of his best days. The death of the Duchess so early in the tale will be a great shock to many worthy people, but even duchesses must die that novels may be written.

DR. WORTLE'S SCHOOL

1881

A. O. J. Cockshut provides a rewarding analysis of *Dr. Wortle's School* as a study in a special kind of grotesque art. (Michael Sadleir also considered this novel among Trollope's best.)

198. Unsigned notice, *Athenaeum*

15 January 1881, p. 93

Mr. Trollope's last novelette is happier than some that we have read of his, partly because its length is not unsuitable to his lucid commonplace, which occasionally outruns the patience of the reader, and partly in consequence of a novelty of method, for which he very unnecessarily offers a sort of apology. The mystery which shrouds the connexion between Mr. and Mrs. Peacocke, which so severely exercises the consciences of sundry spinsters, matrons, and clerical gossips, and drives the warm-hearted and domineering Dr. Wortle to the verge of lunacy, is revealed at the outset, and the remainder of the book is occupied in describing, with much skill and a good deal of quiet pathos and humour, the effect produced by the discovery on a number of average, but by no means equal or identical, minds.

199. Unsigned notice, *Critic* (New York)

12 February 1881, i. 35

There is originality as well as ingenuity in the idea of developing all the characters of the story simply by their relation to a single event not in itself important to any but the chief actors. By their approval or disapproval of Mr. Peacocke's course, we may even say by their manner of approving or disapproving, we gain a complete photograph of the mental and moral qualities of all the persons in the story. But Mr. Trollope's tale is more than interesting, more than ingenious; it is bracing, which is much to say of a story dealing with delicate conjugal relations.

200. Unsigned notice, *Nation* (New York)

10 March 1881, xxxii. 172–3

The English part of the story is simply perfect; the picture of the process by which the world becomes estranged from and suspicious of Dr. Wortle is as good a piece of work as Mr. Trollope has ever done. The American scenes are naturally not quite so true to life, but they will be found, perhaps, by American readers all the more amusing on this account. The adventures of Mr. Peacocke and Lefroy at Chicago are particularly entertaining. The two men are at a quiet boarding-house kept by a Mrs. Jones. In this boarding-house we find Lefroy 'seated in the bar' drinking, chewing a cigar, and 'covering the circle around him with the results.' In the course of conversation both men get out their pistols, but are interrupted by a stranger, who enquires: 'What are you men doing with them pistols?' and suggests that if they are 'a-going to do anything of that kind,' they had better go and do it elsewhere. He then adds: 'It's a decent widow woman as keeps this house, and I won't see her set upon.' The whole scene has an antique flavour which carries one back to the days of 'Martin Chuzzlewit'.

201. Unsigned notice, *The Times*

16 April 1881, p. 10

Scandal whispers that the quiet and retiring Mrs. Peacocke is not Mr. Peacocke's lawful wife. Scandal for once is right, though the explanation, in the doctor's opinion, is morally, if not technically, satisfactory. The pair had committed unconscious bigamy, believing that the lady's first husband was dead. The doctor's chivalry is excited. He sympathizes with their trouble, and declares he will stand by them; declining to dismiss his assistant, whom he has not ceased to respect. Naturally, such a man as the doctor has made enemies in abundance, and they nearly succeed in ruining the model school, which is at once his pride, pleasure, and profit. The strong-willed victim of his own generosity is sorely tried, but he never falters in his resolution, whatever the probable sacrifice. And we are glad when he is finally rewarded for his disinterestedness, by being restored triumphantly to more than his former prosperity.

202. Unsigned notice, *Saturday Review*

22 January 1881, li. 121–2

Dr. Wortle's School hardly deserves the position of a full-grown novel, and its two slim volumes do not contain much more than half or a third of the quantity usual in such novels. But the earlier part of it at least is as brightly and pleasantly written as anything that the author has done, and exhibits his mannerism—limited and somewhat tricky as that mannerism is—in a very favourable light. The end is not good, and seems somewhat huddled up; but the story goes off with great spirit, and, as Mr. Trollope ingenuously tells his readers all about it in the first few score pages, the usual bashfulness which prevents reviewers from giving arguments of novels hardly applies here. Dr. Wortle is a sufficiently distinguished scholar with a will of his own, and a consciousness of the side on which his bread is buttered. He has left his college, has taken a living, and has combined with that living a preparatory school where the charges are very high, and of which the reputation is proportionately great. When the story opens, twenty-eight happy youths are boarded, lodged, washed, &c. under Dr. Wortle's roof, and their pleased parents requite the Doctor with sums varying from two hundred to two hundred and fifty pounds yearly. Nor let any reader suppose that this ingenious combiner of the cure of souls with the care of youth is a charlatan. Dr. Wortle is represented as a somewhat worldly but thoroughly honest and honourable man, giving everybody full *quid* for their *quo*; of a generous spirit, and capable of making his parish a model parish at the same time that he makes his school an exceedingly profitable school. Only he has a certain affectation of contempt for spiritual zeal which brings him into loggerheads perpetually with his bishops, whom he invariably routs, and who naturally do not love him any the more therefore. Nor is he without other enemies, notably a certain Mrs. Stantiloup, with whom he has had to fight in her capacity of parent, and who hates him with a deadly hatred. Now the experienced reader who knows the ways of schoolmaster-parsons will perceive at once that it is an object with Dr. Wortle to unite as far as possible the two kinds of assistants that he requires, assistant-master and curate, in one person, and that it is not easy for him to do so, more

479

especially as he also desires to get out of this assistant's wife certain other assistance of the matron character. At the date of the story he has got a phœnix, or a pair of phœnixes, if that were possible. Mr. Peacocke has been a Fellow of his college; he has taken the highest honours; he has an American wife who is not only a charming lady, but who is quite willing to look after the boys maternally and spare Mrs. Wortle. The Doctor would be able to say *quis me uno felicior?*[1] but for a little hitch about the curacy. Mr. Peacocke is rather shy of this complication of duties, and it shortly becomes apparent that if he were not shy the reigning Bishop would see in the circumstance an opportunity for playing a return match with Dr. Wortle. Between the time of his leaving Oxford and the time of his coming to Dr. Wortle, Mr. Peacocke has spent five years in America, and of his history during those five years, of the antecedents of Mrs. Peacocke, &c. &c., nothing whatever is known. The Bishop puts it to Dr. Wortle whether he can be expected to license a man in whose *livret* there is such a singular gap, and suggests with a proper episcopal mixture of mildness and severity that the gap shall be filled. The reasonableness of this point of view is insisted upon by Mr. Puddicombe, the parson-confidant of somewhat narrow mind, but upright and not unkindly disposition, whom also we have met a few times in Mr. Trollope's books. So the Doctor very unwillingly requests his phœnix to give an account of himself during his last stay in the desert, and the phœnix acknowledges with commendable frankness that he is unlike the knife-grinder, and has a story to tell. A delay of a few days is agreed upon, during which it is to be decided whether this story is to be told or not. What the story is, Mr. Trollope very obligingly tells his readers at once—a frankness in which we shall not imitate him. . . . But both Dr. Wortle and Mr. Peacocke—the former altogether undeservedly, the latter with a proportion of desert which will be judged differently by the strait-laced and the loosely girt in matters ethical—have to undergo a period of considerable tribulation. This involves a sharp fight with the Bishop, and the preliminaries, at least, of a sharp fight with a London newspaper of the scandal-mongering sort. . . .

The weakest part of the book is the love affair between Lord Carstairs and Mary Wortle. It is the weakest not because it is episodic—for, as a matter of fact, it has a good deal to do with the *dénouement*—but because there is not sufficient space given to the display of the characters and fortunes of the lovers.

[1] *quis me uno felicior*: Who could be happier?

. . . There is nothing about the worthy doctor and his wife, nor his daughter and her wooer, Lord Carstairs, nor in his assistant, Mr. Peacocke, and the woman who is and is not his wife, to greatly attract the ordinary novel reader. But Mr. Trollope endows them with a true vitality, with a distinct reality, which compels us to follow their fortunes with interest, and to take some concern in their actions and their speech, as we should if we had lived with them and sympathized with their troubles. It is told of Mr. Trollope that he considers his own method of art to be purely mechanical, and that he has declared that he could teach easily any one to write as good books as his own in a short space of time. If this is so, we sincerely hope that Mr. Trollope will instruct some able pupil in the secret of the method which in his hands has produced such good work. If Mr. Trollope's novels are not of the highest order of art, they are singularly valuable and faithful pictures of some portions of the age they delineate.

AYALA'S ANGEL

1881

---

204. Unsigned notice, *Athenaeum*

21 May 1881, p. 686

The main story—that of Ayala—includes several others, all more or less alike, inasmuch as money troubles in each case are the difficulty which makes a story possible. In Ayala's own case there is something more. She has an ideal. That is the explanation of the title of the book. She has formed an idea of perfection, an angel of light, as Mr. Trollope calls him over and over again in his well-known and very pleasant manner. A sort of point and a dash of humour are given to the story by the nature of the man who is ultimately successful.

205. Unsigned notice, *Illustrated London News*

28 May 1881, lxxviii. 526

Not a noble thought, not a striking incident, not a scrap of plot, worthy of the name, is to be found, if it be not rash to make such an assertion, throughout the story. And yet the story has the singular charm of undeniable reality, as regards the sayings, and doings, and correspondence of the various personages; and the style of writing is pleasant, chatty, sprightly, amusing; though the tone may awaken reminiscences of Houndsditch.

206. Unsigned notice, *Saturday Review*

11 June 1881, li. 756-7

Ayala is pretty and fascinating, no doubt; she tempts her suitor on by
the unpleasant surprises she prepares for him when he believes himself
tolerably sure of a gracious reception. But we agree with the Colonel's
good friend and cousin Lady Albury, that Miss Dormer hardly deserves
the trouble she causes him. She is no Lily Dale or Grace Crawley. So
far as we can see, there is little in her. She has perversity and fits of
obstinacy, but no real decision of character; while the Colonel is perhaps as masterly a male character as Mr. Trollope has drawn in any
recent book. He is the sort of good fellow who seems to be born to go
through the world with the regard of all whose regard is worth having.
Like Thackeray's Dobbin in *Vanity Fair*, he gradually impresses you
with a sense of his power as well as of his sterling worth. . . .

We shall only add that, in our opinion, Mr. Trollope has never
showed to more advantage than in those dialogues which he generally
succeeds in making extraordinarily lifelike.

207. Unsigned notice, *Spectator*

18 June 1881, liv. 804–5

Mr. Trollope is undoubtedly an adept at describing society in its every-day life. He reveals the motives of the most trivial actions. . . . By dint of subtle appreciation of character and of these arts, which must surely result from unusual quickness in feeling the social pulse, he accomplishes a feat that no less able writer could perform, and takes his readers pleasantly through three volumes, without the usual aids of plot and incident; the thread of story in *Ayala's Angel* is too slight to be called a plot, yet the book is amusing, in spite of that deficiency.

208. Unsigned notice, *The Times*

16 July 1881, p. 5

The heroine herself is shallow, although both pretty and fascinating; and everybody about her is either assiduously set upon pleasure or absorbed in making a creditable appearance on very inadequate means. Nor has 'Ayala's Angel,' although a purely ideal being, anything to do with the world of spirits. The angel is, in reality, a gentleman 'in the clouds,' whom a romantically-minded young woman dreams one day of marrying. She has gifted this bright vision of her fancy with perfections that should make him something more than a demigod, and in the meantime is expecting his appearance with more or less impatience. Ayala has more and far better proposals than fall to the lot of most portionless girls; but among the very different rivals who lay their fortunes at her feet, nobody can by possibility be mistaken for the angel. Indeed, in presenting to us the three most prominent competitors, Mr. Trollope's nervous portraits verge upon caricature. Captain Batsby is preternaturally dull and uninteresting; Mr. Thomas Tringle is preternaturally vulgar; and Colonel Jonathan Stubbs is preternaturally ugly. We foresee from the first that Colonel Stubbs is destined to be the happy man; and although we have serious doubts whether Ayala will prove worthy of him, we are persuaded that she cannot possibly do better for herself. Stubbs must rank among Mr. Trollope's best male studies, although he has rather been dashed in roughly than finished in detail....

The novel, as we have said, in spite of some of the leading characters being caricatured, is a very good one; but it is a pity that Mr. Trollope should have gratuitously encumbered his plot with episodes and people which have nothing to do with it.

THE FIXED PERIOD

1882

The Fixed Period was published anonymously in *Blackwood's Magazine*, from October 1881 to March 1882. During these months the *Illustrated London News* in its column of comment on serial fiction then running in various magazines praised the tale as a contribution in *Blackwood's* 'best style' (8 October 1881); as a 'remarkable contribution' (5 November 1881); and as a story that continued to prove both quaint and humorous (7 January 1882). On the surface the work appears, as the reviewers of the time remarked, a *jeu d'esprit*, a species of cumbrous joke. But then one might well ponder Trollope's telling a friend (see No. 214, below), 'It's all true—I *mean* every word of it.'

209. Unsigned notice, *Athenaeum*

11 March 1882, p. 314

Mr. Trollope has agreeably varied his series of intensely nineteenth-century tales by projecting his imagination into the future. 'The Fixed Period' is an amusing *jeu d'esprit*. . . . But what is the 'fixed period'? It is a social institution for which the world was not quite ripe in *1980*, and for its features of academic interest we refer to its author's account of it.

210. Unsigned notice, *Spectator*

18 March 1882, lv. 360–1

Richard Holt Hutton is the author (see Introduction, note 39), though the critique is hardly among his most distinguished contributions.

The Fixed Period is a humorous sketch of life towards the end of the twentieth century, as it might be affected by an attempt to reconstruct the conditions of human existence so as to cut off altogether from it the period of dwindling and decaying powers, and fix an inevitable limit to the age of men. Mr. Trollope supposes that one of the Pacific Colonies of Great Britain, which he calls Britannula, has thrown off her connection with the mother-country, established a Republic, and passed a law that the age of her citizens shall never exceed sixty-eight years,— and that the last year between sixty-seven and sixty-eight is to be passed meditatively in a kind of honourable seclusion, in a College established for that purpose, where the old shall be 'deposited' at sixty-seven, and receive euthanasia a year afterwards. The law has, it is supposed, been passed by large majorities, but majorities of the young only, for the island, which had been peopled from New Zealand, was peopled almost wholly by the young, while the few who were really old at the time of the settlement were exempted from its operation. . . .

The joke is a somewhat grim one, but we need hardly say that Mr. Trollope treats it from the laughing rather than the grim point of view. . . . This little story is rather an amusing exposure of doctrinaire audacity and folly, than a serious apology for the time and thought and care devoted to weakness, helplessness, and decay. . . . But it is not, perhaps, very easy to prevent the satire of the situation, from occasionally passing into extravagance. Nor in a *jeu d'esprit* like this ought we to object to it. The only fault we have to find with the story is that the subject is somewhat too grim for light treatment, and that, in consequence, genuinely religious creeds are occasionally very lightly handled. A novel the book hardly is, unless *Erewhon* and Lord Lytton's story, called *The Coming Race*, are novels also. But a clever, if not altogether agreeable, flight of fancy it certainly is.

211. Unsigned notice, *Saturday Review*

8 April 1882, liii. 434–5

While this story was gradually unfolding itself in the pages of *Black-wood*, reader and author were, we suspect, often at odds. The subject was an amusing one; but what did it all mean? The leisurely self-possession of the narrator, whoever he might be, showed the practised writer, thoroughly at his ease, and accustomed to carry his reader along with him in willing subjection; the reader, however, on this occasion, always looking for something that did not come, and reading on, therefore, in a state of unfulfilled expectation. Was it a political squib—a satire on human nature, after the manner of Swift? . . .

The name of the author, however, throws a stream of light on any such perplexities. When we once know the tone to expect, things arrange themselves in accord with it. No change of circumstances can make Mr. Trollope's personages act otherwise than naturally in the commonplace acceptation of the word. And for the motive the reader need go no further than to consider the author's favourite quality, the power that keeps the world going. The story may be regarded as a sort of epic intended to exhibit dogged obstinacy in heroic proportions.

212. Unsigned notice, *The Times*

12 April 1882, p. 3

Prolific writers must be often at a loss for subjects; but it must always be more or less of a hazardous speculation when they pass the limits of the fanciful into the realms of the fantastic. Nor is it possible to excite any very likely interest in the beings of a society as far removed from our actual experience as from our times. Moreover, the main idea of Mr. Trollope's novel, whence it takes its name of 'Fixed Period,' is essentially ghastly. . . .

The discussions in which the zealous President strives to bring the reluctant Crassweller to a patriotic sense of his duty have a good deal of grim humour in them, but the details of the arrangements of the 'College' where Mr. Crassweller was to be sequestered, previously to being put out of the way and cremated, savour, to our mind, decidedly too much of the dead-house.

For satire there must be somewhere a serious foundation of belief to be ridiculed and made light of. Here there is just the opposite. The result is that this book is like an elaborate elephantine attempt at a joke by a person without any sense of humor. As admirers of Mr. Trollope we feel that we must beg him to stop and not be deluded into imagining that the 'Fixed Period' is a success. The satire involved in the general conception of the story is weighed down and rendered still more ponderous by some cyclopean specimens of incidental humor. Everybody travels on bicycles going at the rate of a railroad train, and lighted with electric lamps; cricket matches are played with steam bowlers and catapults; telephonic communication between sea and shore is maintained by means of 'hair' telephones, etc. All this is rather labored than amusing.

214. W. L. Collins, 'Autobiography of Anthony Trollope', *Blackwood's Magazine*

November 1883, cxxxiv. 577–96

It had been his constant prayer that he might not survive his powers of work, without which, he says in the closing chapter—'there can be no joy in this world.' And it was at this time that he conceived the idea embodied in that curious story 'The Fixed Period,' which first saw light in the pages of 'Maga.' The law of his imaginary republic of Britannula was to provide that 'men should arrange for their own departure, so as to fall into no senile weakness, no slippered selfishness, no ugly whinings of undefined want, before they shall go hence and be no more thought of.' In their sixty-seventh year they were to be 'deposited' in a kind of college, and after the interval of a twelvemonth be put to a painless death. When an intimate friend once ventured to refer to this Utopian euthanasia as a somewhat grim jest, he stopped suddenly in his walk, and grasping the speaker's arm in his energetic fashion, exclaimed: 'It's all true—I *mean* every word of it.'

MARION FAY

1882

---

215. Unsigned notice, *Athenaeum*

24 June 1882, p. 793

In Mr. Trollope's latest novel the reader will recognize with pleasure
much of the brightness and lightness of touch which characterized his
early work, and there is a good deal of real pathos in the love story of
Lord Hampstead and Marion Fay. Marion's strength of moral purpose
is equal to her tenderness, and she is immovable when her sense of duty
compels her, knowing herself doomed to consumption, to refuse her
lover's passionate desire for marriage. The lover, the Radical son of a
marquis who has been Liberal in his day, has been shaken by Marion's
grace and the contrast her Quaker quaintness presents to the ways of
his own world, in the purpose he has formed (at one-and-twenty!) of
retaining his republican virtue as a bachelor, and allowing his stepmother's children to carry on the line of Trafford.

216. Unsigned notice, *Saturday Review*

8 July 1882, liv. 64–5

In *Marion Fay* Mr. Trollope has reverted to his characteristic manner, to the topics with which he is familiar, and the line of treatment into which his pen naturally falls. In *Marion Fay* we have plenty of lords and ladies, and the democratic element fighting against the aristocratic in fierce defiance. We have a young Earl ashamed of his title, and falling headlong in love with a pretty Quakeress in the prim garb of her sect; his sister, Lady Frances, engaging herself to a Post Office clerk; and both of them, as far as mortals can obtain success, carrying their point. And yet all the while that preference inherent in human nature for fine manners and fine living is never too grossly outraged. Politically, Mr. Trollope favours the democratic side; but he evidently appreciates the charm of finished manners and of the antecedents and surroundings that form them. . . . The young lord is a faithful lover, and is resolved to marry the Quakeress, as she is resolved, on the ground of her health, not to marry him. There is a great deal of talk on both sides on the snip-snap method 'of course I shall,' 'certainly I shall not,' 'that is nonsense,' &c., as there are many chapters expended on the question whether the Post Office clerk whom we know as George Roden should or should not call himself by the Italian title which it turns out was his father's before him. These young democrats, however, do not get much beyond the fact of their opinions, and the inconvenience they cause to their friends; they do not even begin to regenerate the world. In fact, neither of them is the author's real hero; there is another much more congenial to his humour. Crocker, also a Post Office clerk, is vulgar almost beyond an author's licence, but he has life. The various degrees in that office, from high to low, the dialogues between heads and subordinates, are all given with spirit, and are accepted by the reader as dealing with matter on which the writer is an authority.

217. Unsigned notice, *Critic* (New York)

29 July 1882, ii. 201

It is a disappointment to find that Mr. Trollope can be tiresome; but very, very tiresome and unnatural he is in the story of 'Marion Fay.' He not only resorts to the old-fashioned device of having his young plebeian prove to be a duke, but he indulges in an excess of feeble sentiment which makes the whole thing ridiculous.

218. Unsigned notice, *Spectator*

19 August 1882, lv. 1088–9

We have a good deal of 'good society,' for those who like it, some pleasant hunting experiences, and a great deal of fun from the irrepressibility of the 'irrepressible Crocker,' also a clerk in the Post Office, who sits at the same desk with Roden. We cannot help being rather disappointed that Mrs. Roden's unknown husband should turn out to be a somebody, and that in consequence George's marriage with Lady Frances should be made more palatable to her big relations. This conclusion leaves on the mind rather an impression of incompleteness and want of art. The story is, however, amply interesting and entertaining, as Mr. Trollope's writing is sure to be, and many readers will probably prefer the end as it is; for it has the merit of shocking no one's prejudices, is a happy compromise of principles, and makes it more probable that Mr. George and Lady Frances Roden will live happily ever afterwards.

KEPT IN THE DARK

1882

A part of the reviews were written after the death of Anthony Trollope on 6 December 1882 and are coloured by an awareness of that event.

---

219. Unsigned notice, *Athenaeum*

18 November 1882, p. 658

'Kept in the Dark' is an amusing 'society' story, told in the well-known style of the author about whose health society is now genuinely anxious. Sir Francis Geraldine is an ill-conditioned baronet (his baronetcy is quite an inseparable accident of the man). When he is thrown into contact with the spirited, rather fastidious Cecilia, the blending of oil and vinegar, according to the poet, has been attempted. So they part; but the baser lover is determined the world shall not say he was jilted, and when the lady is married to an honest, rather jealous and pig-headed adorer, he makes mischief in revenge.

220. W. E. Henley, *Academy*

25 November 1882, xxii. 377–8

The hero and heroine of Mr. Trollope's new novel are the average man and woman of society. He is a son of Adam, She is a daughter of Eve. But refinement and respectability, and stays and the Established Church, are too much with them; and, in the interests of civilization, they make themselves as inhuman as they can, and suffer in each other almost as much as they deserve. . . .

This is the story of *Kept in the Dark*. It has a pleasant and amusing underplot besides; it is told with the ease, the lucidity, the plain good sense peculiar to its author; and it is interesting from the first line to the last.

221. Unsigned notice, *Graphic*

23 December 1882, xxvi. 710

In almost all respects, 'Kept in the Dark' is typically characteristic both of the special topics of its author and of his manner of dealing with them, and might be made the text of a criticism upon his style and process generally. He has taken for his central situation the trouble of a young wife whose happiness, as well as her husband's, a most natural timidity in facing the confession of a most innocent and open secret very nearly destroys. A tragedy of two lives is developed from the most trivial want of complete openness; and the supreme importance of moral courage in seemingly immaterial trifles has seldom been illustrated so clearly as in Cecilia Western, who must in all respects retain a high place in Mr. Trollope's gallery of heroines. 'My real mission is to make young ladies talk,' is one of his reported self-criticisms, and he has certainly not often made young ladies talk better than in these pages. It is to be hoped that his experience did not include many such young ladies as Miss Altifiorla, but she is an excellently finished portrait of a very actual, if happily exceptional, nature.

222. Unsigned notice, *Spectator*

20 January 1883, lvi. 88–9

Though *Kept in the Dark* is one of the least important of Mr. Trollope's works, the fact that it is probably almost the last he has written must invest it with a particular and regretful interest in the eyes of all readers. It is a simple little story, with few characters and few events, but full of truth and touches of nature, like all his writings. The incident is so slight, that if the heroine had not put off a little too long the telling her husband of a former engagement, or if he had only heard of it from general report, like any one else, there would have been no story at all. . . .

It is a very pleasant little book, altogether; we feel intimately acquainted with all the characters, we sympathize throughout with the heroine, and are spitefully delighted when Miss Altifiorla meets her match, but it is perhaps a little disappointing that Sir Francis Geraldine comes off so easily at the end. We cannot lay the book aside without a strong feeling of sadness that Mr. Trollope, who has given his readers so many happy hours of amusement and enjoyment, should have passed away from among us.

To us, it really seems 'much ado about nothing,' and is in many respects incredible, unless Mr. Trollope meant to write a satire on the weakness even of strong, independent-minded men in relation to the mean, malicious side of society. The sketching of some of the minor characters is good. Dick Ross and Miss Altafiorla, with her family tree of Fiascos and Disgrazias, are clever; and the people of the Close at Exeter would be fresh were it not that Mr. Trollope has so often done this kind of life. On the whole, the novel shows both Mr. Trollope's strength and weakness, and bears no mark of progress in any respect. He is powerful in little bits of photographic portraiture, and shows his immense knowledge; but his success has made him disinclined to take pains, and he fails precisely where he has failed before—to get at the truth below the surface, even when he himself suggests depths. Cecilia Holt we never really see, but only some shadow made by a fine nature on Mr. Trollope's mind, which contents itself with a process of reflection and lazy analysis, instead of patient and devoted comprehension and dramatic presentation.

We little thought when writing the above that before it saw the light Mr. Trollope would be removed from the sphere of human praise or blame. In him our lighter literature has lost a man of distinctive gifts, whose place in it has not only been large but distinguished. Perhaps he wrote too much, but some of his work will live—a vivid and clever representation of interesting phases of nineteenth century life.

A SUMMING-UP
1882

224. Unsigned essay, *The Times*
7 December 1882, p. 9

By the death of Mr. Anthony Trollope multitudes of English-speaking people will feel that they have lost a friend. . . . And if ever a novelist had a claim to this kind of widespread affectionate remembrance, it is Mr. Trollope. He will scarcely rank in the future beside the great novelists of the century. Scott, Balzac, Dickens, George Sand, George Eliot, Charlotte Brontë, Thackeray, Turguenieff, these at least must be put in a first class to which posterity will hesitate to admit him in spite of his range and facility. Neither, we believe, will it admit Miss Austen, great as she is. She and Mr. Trollope, and, perhaps, Mrs. Gaskell, stand at the head of the second order. From their labour has sprung a tribe of novels in which the ways of the English middle class are described with an ease, a humour, and a tenderness of feeling which are only not the best of what the novelist's art can produce because there are certain rare and in-born gifts of genius which as it were take the heaven of our praise by force and conquer for themselves a place apart whenever they appear. Miss Austen drew the middle class of the England of Napoleon's day; her country squires, her fashionable ladies, above all her clergy-men, are as real as they can be made by the most delicate observation, expressed in a style which for its mixture of crispness, pliancy, and a kind of rippling gaiety has no rival in English. Thirty eventful years or more divided her death from the beginning of Mr. Trollope's career as a novelist. But still his world is the heir of Miss Austen's. There is nobody with whom Mr. Collins may be better compared than with Mr. Crawley; and Anne Eliot, Catherine Morland, Emma and the delightful Elizabeth Bennet herself, are conceived in substantially the same mood, allowing for the difference of two generations, as Mary Thorne, Lucy Robarts, or Lady Lufton. . . .

His realistic studies of English domestic life will be read and enjoyed for many years to come, when all his other books and the much more ambitious work of other men will be forgotten.

225. Unsigned essay, *Saturday Review*

9 December 1882, liv. 755–6

Much of the *Saturday*'s farewell essay is unfortunately taken up by an ill-judged and ill-mannered attack upon the critic of *The Times*.

The death of Mr. Anthony Trollope will be at once more widely and more personally felt than that of any writer of equal eminence who has died for many years past. Mr. Anthony Trollope had the singular faculty of appealing at once to the widest and the nicest circle of readers; he had the keenest perception and intellect; and he had, with these gifts, the power of so clothing his thought and penetration in words that they could be understanded of the general reader, while they had also an instinctive revelation of life which delighted the most fastidious critic. He was at once, in a word, universal and particular, both as an author and as a man. . . . Among many signal merits of Mr. Trollope's genius was this—that he could handle at will and with equal success the masculine and the feminine nature and bent. The stupid critic, while he places Miss Austen and Mr. Trollope together in the second rank of novelists, probably also infers that the steady regularity of Mr. Trollope's method of work is incompatible with genius. Yet there was once a novelist named Balzac, and there is now living a novelist, to say nothing else of him, who wrote *Notre Dame de Paris* under conditions as 'mechanical' as could well be devised. . . . The Warden, Arabin, Mr. Crawley, Squire Thorne, the Signora Vici-Neroni, Mr. Kantwise, and a host of other characters, to say nothing of those involved in the Phineas Finn series, will live in the memory of that very useful and much-abused creature, the general reader, and will help to keep alive Mr. Trollope's memory as one of the very first of English novelists. . . . His loss to the large reading public which delighted in his works may be estimated. His loss to those who were privileged to know him is inestimable.

226. Unsigned essay, *Spectator*

9 December 1882, lv. 1573-4

Richard Holt Hutton is the author (see Introduction, note 39).

The death of Mr. Anthony Trollope, without a familiar knowledge of whose works no historian who emulated the style of Macaulay would even attempt to delineate English society in the third quarter of the present century, marks almost the close of an era. We can never again recall the endless gallery of his social pictures, without associating with them the thought that he whose imaginative world they peopled—he whose offspring, indeed, they in some sense were—has passed away, and that more and more from the present date they will represent the figures, not of the present, but of a former age. For some time past, indeed, many of his best-known figures have been assuming a slightly remote aspect, not only to the world as it is, but even to the world as he himself more recently pictured it. Even in his own pages, the old order has changed, giving place to new. His second Duke of Omnium was a very different figure from his first, and a much nobler one; while in the third generation, Lord Silverbridge, with more, perhaps, of generous impulse than his father, had far less of his dignity and of his profound sense of public duty. Again, the clergymen who abounded to the great delight of the reader, in Mr. Trollope's earlier and middle period, have grown fewer and less interesting of late years,—in 'The Duke's Children,' if we remember rightly, there was not one. Probably the type of the modern clergyman had changed, and become less intelligible to Mr. Trollope. Septimus Harding seems to have lived quite a long time ago, even Archdeacon Grantley has an old-fashioned air, and Dean Arabin himself must have gone, though Mr. Trollope never told us of his decease. Natural selection had brought speculating stockbrokers, American senators, and American heiresses into the foreground of Mr. Trollope's pictures before he left us, and the advance of both plutocratic and democratic ideas might have been steadily traced in the vivid social pictures with which he so liberally supplied us. We shall still, we imagine, have posthumous children of Mr. Trollope's, though the fancy which produced them has passed to other worlds than ours; for his was a wonderfully prolific mind, always beforehand with the world, and we believe that there is more than one complete story of his writing of which not a page has yet seen the light. Still, now that he himself is gone, the changes creeping rapidly over the outlines, lights, and shadows of the social diorama with which he presented us, will seem to be more conspicuous than usual as we gaze at his lively scenes; and before another generation passes away, Mr. Trollope's works will rank with those of other great novelists rather as works helping us to revive the past, than as works of which it is the great merit to interpret the relations in which we actually live.

That Mr. Trollope's name will live in English literature follows at once from the fact that his books are at once very agreeable to read, and contain a larger mass of evidence as to the character and aspects of English Society during Mr. Trollope's maturity than any other writer of his day has left behind him. It is too soon, and would be a mistake at the present moment, when he has only just vanished from amongst us, to fix what his place in English literature is likely to be. But we cannot think of him at all without remembering the greater features of his literary work,—the ardent admiration with which he always painted humility and unworldliness, like Mr. Harding's, or even Dean Arabin's, in the rare instances in which he represented them, and the sense of something like moral wonder with which he regarded them;— the profound respect which he entertained for public spirit like that of his second 'Duke of Omnium,' and the charity with which he regarded the authority of family traditions, even when waging war against the sense of justice in a radically just mind;—the scorn which he felt for all the knavery of commercial Rings, and, at the same time, the keen insight with which he contemplated the snares and toils of the speculative commercial life;—the thorough appreciation which he evinced in such stories as 'Phineas Finn,' for the ties of party, as well as for the obligations of individual honour, and the zest with which he analysed the conflicts which arise between them;—the strength of his impression that almost every young man of his day has a vacillating heart, and that almost every young woman is in danger of overruling, for some strategic reason or other, whether interested or disinterested, the strong instincts of her own heart;—the loathing with which he regarded the passion of jealousy in men, and the dread which he evidently entertained for the craftiness of women;—the deep study he had given to all the tactics of social life, and the little account which he made of the results of even the most skilful of these tactics, when matched against the stronger passions and interests of human nature. All these are features which appear and reappear for ever in his stories, representing evidently impressions which had been gaining ground with him, day by day, in his shrewd study of life.

On the other hand, it is clear that there was little or no disposition in Mr. Trollope to pierce much deeper than the social surface of life. It is not often that he takes us into the world of solitary feeling at all, and of the power of the positive influence of their religion over men, you would hardly gain more knowledge from Mr. Trollope's stories than from those of the old-fashioned *régime*, when religion was thought too sacred to be touched-on at all as a real part of human life. The nearest thing which we can recall to any touch of a deeper kind in Mr. Trollope, is his pathetic picture of Bishop Proudie, after his wife's death, saying the little prayer which he thus describes:—'It may be doubted whether he quite knew for what he was praying. The idea of praying for her soul now that she was dead would have scandalized him. He certainly was not praying for his own soul. I think he was praying that God might save him from being glad that his wife was dead.' But touches as deep as that are very rare in Mr. Trollope.

That Mr. Trollope's humour has played a great part in the popularity of his novels, is evident enough, and yet his humour may be called rather a proper appreciation of the paradoxes of social life, than any very original faculty of his own. Mr. Trollope did not heighten, as Miss Austen does, the ludicrous elements in human life by those quaint turns of expression and those delicate contrasts which only a great genius of satiric touch could invent. Mr. Trollope's humour lay in his keen perception of the oddity of human motives, pursuits, and purposes, and his absolute truthfulness in painting them to the life. This humour is shown in such descriptions as that of the sportsman, Reginald Dobbes, who, making it his ambition to obtain the largest bags of game in the Highlands, regards Lord Silverbridge's defection from his shooting party, when once he had joined it, as a moral treachery.[1] 'It is hardly honest, you know,' said Reginald Dobbes. The humour there is not inventive, but perceptive. Reginald Dobbeses really do exist, and Mr. Trollope saw with the keenest enjoyment the absurdity of that view of sport, and yet its complete naturalness also in a man who had once thrown his whole energy into an amusement, so as to make it the

[1] The scene occurs in Chapter 38 of *The Duke's Children*.

business of his life. These really existing paradoxes Mr. Trollope was the first to see, and as keen as possible to delineate. So, too, he makes Archdeacon Grantley insist, when he wants to break off the engagement between his son and Grace Crawley, that his son is dependent upon himself for the greater part of his income, and that *therefore* he feels 'the greatest possible concern in his future prospects.' 'The Archdeacon,' remarks the novelist, 'did not know how to explain clearly why the fact of his making a son an annual allowance should give him a warmer interest in his son's affairs than he might have had, had the Major been altogether independent of him; but he trusted that Grace would understand this by her own natural lights.' That is a kind of humour which comes wholly from the keen insight into the little unconscious hypocrisies of worldly men's feelings. Mr. Trollope saw through all these little make-beliefs with the clearest vision, and his humour depended on the clearness of that vision. But he did not add to the humour of the facts, when seen, by any very unusual art in their presentation. What was absurd in the tactics of society, he seized and defined, but hardly ever heightened. Only there is so much that is absurd in the tactics of society, that to see and define all that is absurd therein makes a man a humorist of no common power. Perhaps Mr. Trollope never showed this humour more effectually than when he delineated the romantic vein in very vulgar and very selfish people,— like Mrs. Greenow, in 'Can You Forgive Her?' when she treats herself to a husband of a romantic kind, or when Miss Dunstable forces her aristocratic suitor to remember that her fortune is made out of the sale of a quack ointment. Mr. Trollope's humour is thoroughly realistic. He sees the coarseness of human life in its close contrast with its ambitiousness, and simply shows us what he sees.

For a writer who dealt, and always professed to deal, chiefly with the surface of society, Mr. Trollope has been singularly sincere, never seeking to hide from us that there are deeper places of human nature into which he does not venture; nor his impression that the world and the motives of the world also penetrate into those places, and have perhaps as much to say to the practical result in conduct, as the higher motives themselves. Still, he cannot be called a satirist. He paints only a part of human life, but he paints that part precisely as he sees it, extenuating nothing and exaggerating nothing, but letting us know that he does not profess to see all, and does not try to divine by imaginative power what he cannot see. Probably no English writer of his day has amused Englishmen so much as Mr. Trollope, or has given them that amusement from sources so completely free from either morbid weaknesses or mischievous and dangerous taints. His name will live in our literature, and though it will certainly not represent the higher regions of imaginative life, it will picture the society of our day with a fidelity with which society has never been pictured before in the history of the world.

227. 'From Miss Austen to Mr. Trollope', *Spectator*

16 December 1882

Unsigned essay. Richard Holt Hutton is the author (see Introduction, note 39).

The loss of Mr. Anthony Trollope makes us turn back from his long series of elaborate pictures of English society during the third quarter of the present century, to those in which Miss Austen painted the rural society of England during the end of the last and the beginning of the present century, with a quite new sense of the magnitude of the change which had taken place in the transition from the one to the other. Miss Austen's works have just been republished by Mr. Bentley, in six handsome volumes, sadly injured, to our eyes, by the unfortunate redness of the ink with which the admirable type has been printed. . . . But even the special unfitness which there seems to be in this tint of the new edition of Miss Austen's stories, reminds us at once of the greatest of all the social changes between the rural life of Miss Austen's pictures and the rural life of Mr. Trollope's. The former is, above all things, mild and unobtrusive, not reflecting the greater world at all, and giving us the keenest sense of how easy it would be to drive oneself, even in a short drive, quite out of reach of all the characters described in any one story; while the latter is, above all things, possessed with the sense of the aggressiveness of the outer world, of the hurry which threatens the tranquillity even of such still pools in the rapid currents of life as Hiram's Hospital at Barchester, of the rush of commercial activity, of the competitiveness of fashion, of the conflict for existence even in outlying farms and country parsonages. Miss Austen's clergy are gentlemen of such leisurely habits of mind, that even the most energetic of them suggests a spacious and sequestered life. Mr. Trollope's clergy are the centres of all sorts of crowding interests, of ecclesiastical conflicts, of attacks of the Press, of temptations from the great London world, of danger from Courts of Justice. The difference between Mr. Elton, empty, conceited, easy-going, under-bred, and Mr. Slope, ambitious, audacious, prompt, and vulgar, is the difference between the whole world of the two novelists. Everybody in Miss Austen, from the squires and the doctors down to the lovers, is leisurely, giving one a great sense of perfect seclusion, ample opportunity, plenty of space, and plenty of time. Everybody in Mr. Trollope is more or less under pressure, swayed hither and thither by opposite attractions, assailed on this side and on that by the strategy of rivals; everywhere someone's room is more wanted than his company; everywhere time is short. Mr. Woodhouse's quiet apothecary, Mr. Perry, of Highbury, in 'Emma,' and the pompous physician, Dr. Fillgrave, of Barchester, who telegraphs for a consultation with Sir Omicron Pie whenever a distinguished patient is in danger, in 'Barchester Towers,' are not more different from each other, than the whole spirit of Miss Austen's country life from Mr. Trollope's. Compare two even of their stupidest clergymen. . . . [In Mr. Thumble of *The Last Chronicle of Barset*] you see a clergyman almost as stupid as Mr. Collins, and quite as full of his own small affairs; but instead of seeing him, as you do Mr. Collins in 'Pride and Prejudice,' swelling out like a shrivelled apple under an air-pump to its full size, and much more than its full importance, you see Mr. Thumble jostled and fidgetted by the impact of the world, and crumpled up, as it were, into the insignificant man he is. In Miss Austen's novels,—it is one of their chief attractions,—this is never so. Every one is what he is by the natural force of his own nature and tastes. You hardly ever see the crush of the world on any one. The vain man's vanity sedately flowers; the dull man's dullness runs to seed; the proud man's pride strikes its roots deep; even the fidgettiness of fidgetty persons appears to come from within, not from the irritation of external pressure. Half the distinctiveness, for instance, of such sketches as those of Mrs. Jennings and the Misses Steele in 'Sense and Sensibility' arises from the circumstance that the active good-natured vulgarity of the one, and the furtive restlessness of the others, are so entirely self-prompted, so entirely unforced from outside. Turn to Mr. Trollope, and everything is changed. The atmosphere of affairs is permanent. The Church of the world, or the flesh or the devil, seems always at work to keep men going, and prevent them from being exactly themselves. Miss Austen's people are themselves alone. Mr. Trollope's people are themselves so far as the circumstances of the day will allow them to be themselves, but very often are much distorted from their most natural selves.

Then, again, in Miss Austen's world, how little you see of London, even in the effect the metropolis has upon the country. In 'Northanger

Abbey' and in 'Persuasion,' you see a good deal of the local capital of pleasure, Bath. In 'Mansfield Park,' and in 'Pride and Prejudice,' a very small portion of the by-play of the story takes place in London. In 'Sense and Sensibility' alone, there is an important London episode. In 'Emma,' if we recollect rightly, London is hardly mentioned at all. In Mr. Trollope's novels—the Irish ones, of course, excepted—nothing can be done without London. Even 'The Warden' depends wholly for its plot on the articles of Tom Towers in the 'Jupiter,' and poor Mr. Harding's visit to London is the turning-point of the story; while ten out of every dozen of Mr. Trollope's stories turn chiefly upon London life. Even his evangelical Bishops go up to London, while his statesmen, politicians, Civil servants, money-lenders, commercial travellers, barristers, boarding-house keepers, and policemen, all, of course, live there. Nothing is more remarkable, in reading the two series of novels together, than the self-centredness of the country in Miss Austen, and the constant reference to London in Mr. Trollope. One might read Miss Austen's books through and never know that there was a Parliament sitting in Westminster at the time, so little are the doings of the Legislature ever referred to in her country houses. One might read them through, and never know that there were Courts of Law in London. One might read them through, and never suspect that there was better medical advice to be had in London than in the country. In Mr. Trollope's tales you never forget these things. Indeed, you see a good deal of the machinery of Parliament and of the greater administrative offices of the State. You are constantly hearing of the Bar, of the various kinds of solicitors, and of the mighty physicians by whose fiat it is supposed to be known whether a man shall live or die. In a word, the society which in Miss Austen's tales seems to be wholly local, though it may have a few fine connections with the local capital, is in Mr. Trollope's a great web of which London is the centre, and some kind of London life for the most part the motive-power. The change from Miss Austen to Mr. Trollope is the change from social home-rule to social centralization. And, to read about, at all events,—though both are most entertaining,—one prefers the home-rule.

MR. SCARBOROUGH'S FAMILY

1883

Critics from Michael Sadleir to A. O. J. Cockshut and Bradford Booth place this work, the last of Trollope's satires, among his more impressive novels.

228. Unsigned notice, *Athenaeum*

12 May 1883, p. 600

. . . There is the same immense elaboration and minuteness of narrative, the same mastery of little turns of expressive dialogue, the same cheerful mixture of cynicism and kindliness, the same prosaic level of commonplace characters. Not that Mr. Scarborough is commonplace in his actions. He is an ingenious old gentleman who, taking a very long look ahead, has the prudence to cause himself to be twice married to the same lady, before and after the birth of his eldest son, in order that he may declare for the offspring of either marriage as his legitimate successor in his entailed estate. When of his two sons, Mountjoy and Augustus, the elder proves to be hopelessly in the hands of the Jews, Mr. Scarborough promptly proclaims him illegitimate; and when the latter shows nothing but insolence in return for his promotion to the succession, his father produces the evidence of his first marriage, and re-establishes his favourite son. This result is considerably hastened by the ill-considered action of Augustus in compounding with Mountjoy's creditors, and thus completing the purposes of his wily father. It may be supposed how well a plot of this kind lends itself to Trollopean treatment. There is a spark of good in Mountjoy, who will not hear his mother abused, and the defeat of the too-suspicious Augustus will commend itself to the conscientious reader. Not the least of the suffering inflicted by the eccentricities of Mr. Scarborough is the perplexity and horror he entails upon his solicitor, an upright gentleman, who finds himself regarded as an accomplice in the frauds perpetrated by his client.

229. Unsigned notice, *Spectator*

12 May 1883, lvi. 612–13

Mr. Trollope's first posthumous novel—we believe there are others to come—differs from the ruck of his novels only in this, that he has endeavoured to use a very singular character as his *deus ex machina*. 'Mr. Scarborough's Family' and their friends are for the most part very ordinary people, less carefully described than was Mr. Trollope's wont; and their adventures, though readable, are described at too great length. . . .

The description is in parts fine, you catch the impression of a powerful Voltairian personality; but Mr. Trollope had not thought-out his new character fully, and Mr. Scarborough is, therefore, from first to last a mere bundle of discordant qualities, which are hidden a little by the writer's art, but are always there, and always affecting the story in some unexpected way. The portrait, on which the novel depends, though, of course, there is plenty of amusing writing, must be pronounced a failure.

230. William Wallace, *Academy*

19 May 1883, xxiii. 344

Mr. Scarborough's Family is a very enjoyable novel. Mr. Trollope has never given us two stronger or less commonplace characters than that terrible old pagan, John Scarborough, and his attorney, Grey, whom we agree with his employer in describing as 'the sweetest and finest gentleman' we ever came across. The Machiavellian plots by which Scarborough, on his death-bed and tortured by disease, first discovers and then baffles the designs of his own son Augustus occupy three volumes. But the reader never wearies of them, because they bring him perpetually into contact with Grey, to whom love of justice is as much a passion on a small, as it was to Bayard on a great, scale, and with his daughter Dolly, who declines to marry because she can find no man to compare otherwise than unfavourably with her father. Mr. Trollope has always shown great skill in providing foils to his good characters; and Amelia Carroll, Dolly's vulgar cousin, who feels honoured by the insolent familiarity of a Russian Prince, and who, after failing to secure a Newmarket swindler for a husband, contents herself with a poor clergyman, is certainly an admirable foil to her. . . .

Mr. Trollope's peculiar art in sketching vulgar characters is well illustrated by his portraits of the Harts, Junipers, and other money-lending harpies who prey upon Mountjoy, and find their Jeremy Diddler[1] in Augustus Scarborough. There is only one white tie in *Mr. Scarborough's Family*—that of Annesley's father, and it plays a very modest part. This fact will in the eyes of not a few of Mr. Trollope's admirers be considered not so much a fault as an excellence.

[1] Jeremy Diddler, the main character in *Raising the Wind* (1803), a farce by James Kenney, makes a habit of borrowing small sums and evading repayment.

Mr. Trollope, as we have repeatedly observed, was of course an unequal writer; nor could it have been otherwise with one who was so singularly prolific. But then he had the root of the matter in him; and he possessed an inherent vitality and freshness which always gave us assurance that he would rally after a collapse. 'Nil de mortuis nisi bonum' can hardly apply in the case of any piece of honest criticism; and we are bound to say that *Mr. Scarborough's Family* must be ranked among its author's comparative failures. At the same time it is as far above the most disappointing of his works as it is beneath his *Barchester Towers* or *The Last Chronicles of Barset*. There is abundance of 'go' in it; there are many striking scenes; and there is one character at least which is original, almost to incredibility. There are light sketches of social life, one or two of them nearly in the author's best manner, and many chapters which are extremely entertaining. We might have supposed that the novel had been left unrevised, and that it had received the final polish from some friendly hand which unfortunately was uninspired by the brain of the creator. But we fancy that we know enough of Mr. Trollope's manner of writing to believe that he not merely blocked out his work, but finished it as he went along. The chief fault in *Mr. Scarborough's Family* is excessive and superfluous reiteration. The same story of the mysterious underhand dealings of the most conspicuous personage is repeated time after time with very insignificant variations; although already we have been informed of all that can be easily explained as to an individuality which in reality is inexplicable. And yet when everything has been said in the way of detraction or fault-finding, the story is so lifelike and so extremely readable that we lay it down with a pleasure largely leavened by regret. . . . What is more—and we know not whether it is morally to the author's credit or not—Mr. Scarborough wins us, with most of the people who come about him, in a measure over to his own way of thinking. Though he sets all the ordinary laws of morality at defiance, as we have said, he really appears to be at peace with his own most peculiar conscience. Heroic he is, so far as his calm attitude in presence of death is concerned, considering that he is supposed to believe in a future state and is prepared to submit himself to a coming judgment. Compared to that, it is a small matter indeed that he supports atrocious surgical operations with the constancy of a stoic, and can summon to his service all his firmness of will when his strength has been shattered by protracted suffering. The question is whether a character so inconsistent is credible; and whether Mr. Trollope did not outrage the canons of his art in seeking to impose on our intelligence such a caricature of humanity. . . .

Altogether, if the novel shows no great originality, its pictures of life are at least as full of variety as usual; and reading it we can only regret the more that we have lost a novelist of extraordinary versatility, who could ring fresh changes almost indefinitely upon all that he had made most familiar to us.

232. Unsigned notice, *Westminster Review*

July 1883, cxx. 301

'Mr. Scarborough' himself is an admirable and original creation; and in him the main interest of the story centres from first to last. But the book contains some other remarkable studies of character, as, for instance, Mr. Grey, the solicitor, and his daughter, the two sons of Mr. Scarborough, and Mr. Prosper of Burton Hall. Florence Mountjoy is such a heroine as Mr. Trollope loved to paint, and deserves to rank with his most successful delineations of female character. The plot, which we purposely abstain from forestalling, is ingenious, and keeps the reader's curiosity alive to the very last chapter.

THE LANDLEAGUERS

1883

Trollope at the time of his death had completed only forty-eight of the sixty chapters he had planned for *The Landleaguers*. No one at the time of publication or since has shown any great enthusiasm for the work. William Wallace in the *Academy* (17 December 1883) dismissed it as a mere rewarming of news from Ireland during the last three years in the daily papers. The *Athenaeum* (24 November 1883) maintained half-heartedly that the story showed no falling off in 'Mr. Trollope's peculiar power', but did not labour unduly to try to convince its readers.

233. Unsigned notice, *Spectator*

15 December 1883, lvi. 1627

. . . As it is, the forty-ninth chapter is left unfinished. Under these circumstances, the form of the three-volume novel is a little out of place. It gives an air of completeness which is not real. For the rest, it is characteristic of the author, but not of his best style or his happiest mood. . . . Any policy that had any semblance of the heroic was utterly distasteful to him; and most people are agreed that in Irish affairs there was need of the heroic. Now, *The Land Leaguers* is really a long pamphlet, under the guise of fiction, upon Irish troubles, and the remedies which have been lately employed for them. If the pamphleteer had possessed consummate wisdom and insight, the novelist must not the less have made a failure. As it is, both pamphleteer and novelist fail. Yet, as need hardly be said, there is plenty of good work in these volumes. . . . Humorous, easy, clever dialogue, shrewd remarks on matters of the day, lively sketches of character, are to be seen in almost every chapter. . . . Still, on the whole, the book is a disappointment.

234. Unsigned notice, *Westminster Review*

January 1884, cxxi. 276

The purpose of the book is to depict the actual life of dwellers in Ireland during the tragic and shameful years of 1880–1882, and this purpose it fulfils completely. Any one who has read 'The Land-Leaguers' will have a more lively and vivid idea of how life, especially that of middle-class landowners and their families, was disturbed and distorted by that hideous reign of terror, than could be obtained from all the newspaper reports of the time. . . . But, apart from its politics, the story is in itself full of interest, and, though the final chapters are wanting, the *dénouement* is clearly foreshadowed.

AN OLD MAN'S LOVE

1884

---

235. C. E. Dawkins, *Academy*

29 March 1884, xxv. 220

The last completed novel that Mr. Anthony Trollope left—for *The Land-Leaguers* was unfinished—is in every way slighter than his best work, but there is no falling off in the vigour and sincerity of the style. The characters are few, and the construction of the plot is simple. . . . There are stronger and more elaborate pictures drawn by the same hand, but the Rev. Montague Blake is an addition to the author's long portrait-gallery of country and cathedral clergy; and, though we have known old housekeepers like her before, we are glad to meet Mrs. Baggett and listen to her lectures. While written with vigour and directness, the almost total absence in the two volumes of those shrewd and half-humorous disquisitions about men and things which the author loved shows that the stream was getting dry.

236. Unsigned notice, *Saturday Review*

29 March 1884, lvii. 414–15

The volumes before us contain work which, as was explained in the preface to the author's Autobiography, was written before *The Land Leaguers*, but which, unlike *The Land Leaguers*, was finished and perfect. *An Old Man's Love*, moreover, is, in more than the mere mechanical sense, a more finished book than *The Land Leaguers*. It is very much shorter, and deals with a much more confined set of situations; indeed the whole really important part of the action is comprised within a space of time very little longer than the twenty-four hours of the venerable Unities. It is also more original in design and *donnée*, not only than *The Land Leaguers*, but than any of its author's more recent work, with the doubtful exception of *The Fixed Period*, which was not so much a novel as a *jeu d'esprit*. There are a few slips here and there, pretty evidently due to failing memory and other physical weaknesses. A personage is named Furnival in one place and Hall in the rest of the book; a sentence or two here and there has a slight slovenliness which he would certainly not have committed in his earlier days. But, on the whole, the book is not an unfitting finale to an almost unparalleled series of works in fiction; and there is something in its pathetic motive which may be thought without much fancifulness appropriate to a *pièce d'adieu*.

237. Unsigned notice, *Athenaeum*

5 April 1884, p. 438

'An Old Man's Love' is interesting not only for itself, but because it is the last complete work of its lamented author. Mr. Whittlestaff's chivalry, in resigning to an earlier and younger lover a lady whom gratitude compelled to accept himself, is not a superhuman effort, but a very creditable one as times go. . . .

A melancholy interest attaches to the last story we shall ever have from Anthony Trollope, and its excellence reawakens our regrets for his loss. 'An Old Man's Love' is rather a novelette than a novel, and perhaps Trollope has seldom done himself justice in his more sketchy productions. He needed elbow-room for the effective display of his powers, and the most elaborately painted of his characters became our greatest favourite. But 'An Old Man's Love' is unusually compact and complete; and we fancy that, with his practical turn of mind, he may have felt when he had finished it that he had been recklessly wasteful of good material. In the little group of personages who play their parts, there are two at least of rare capabilities; nor do we remember that in any of his equally unpretentious books he has shown so striking a command both of humour and pathos. As he might have written himself in his autobiography, in the old housekeeper, Mrs. Baggett, 'I think there is a great deal of good comedy,' while Mr. Whittlestaff, the elderly gentleman who falls in love, is very nearly a masterpiece in his marvellous truth to nature. And it was the more difficult to evolve real pathos from Whittlestaff's love affair that he is represented throughout as almost perversely prosaic. He is old beyond his years, for he is only 50; and he is made more of a prig in manners and deportment than he need have been. To appreciate the true grandeur of the man's nature, to understand the extent of the sacrifice to which he resigns himself, we must realize all the circumstances of his life and character. Mr. Whittlestaff is a bachelor of easy means, living quietly by himself in a retired Hampshire village. His life has been one long education in self-indulgence; his housekeeper, though she scolds, makes it her pleasure to spoil him; and all his thoughts have naturally been concentrated on himself. Besides, he is shy and morbidly sensitive; and the one great sorrow and humiliation of his life has been that a woman he once loved had thrown him over. He has always been smarting under the sense that people think scornfully of the man who has been jilted.

There may be some unconscious selfishness underlying the generous charity with which he welcomes the daughter of an old friend under his roof and adopts her as a daughter of his own. Mary Lawrie is pretty and attractive, and brightens the lonely house. So very speedily the character of his feelings changes, and the father turns into the bashful lover. . . . When he does screw himself to his great decision at last, it is difficult, as he said, to gauge the greatness of his sacrifice, and so sorely does he dread the imputation of having been thrown over a second time that nothing but his principles restrains him from suicide. There is an exquisite truth to nature in the altered bearing of this mild-mannered man, when, his mind having been once painfully made up, Mary generously tries to shake his purpose. He is blunt and irritable in his language towards the girl he adores—blunt almost to brutality towards his rival. And naturally the one comes to love him as she could never do while he desired her love, as he rises in the regard of the other with each plain-spoken personality. As for Mrs. Baggett, the comic old housekeeper to whom we alluded, Trollope has shown all the familiar versatility in the completeness with which he has identified himself with the crusty but warm-hearted old woman who speaks her mind in season and out of season, both to her master and to the young intruder whom he admires. Yet, vulgar and coarsely indifferent to feelings as she is, Mrs. Baggett shows herself almost as self-sacrificing as her noble-minded master. So altogether, and notwithstanding our regrets, we are glad to think that the last of Trollope's works should leave us with agreeable memories of its lamented writer almost at his very best.

239. Henry James, 'Anthony Trollope', *Partial Portraits*

1888, pp. 97–133

This essay was first published in the New York *Century Magazine* (July 1883), n.s. iv. 385–95.

When, a few months ago, Anthony Trollope laid down his pen for the last time, it was a sign of the complete extinction of that group of admirable writers who, in England, during the preceding half century, had done so much to elevate the art of the novelist. The author of *The Warden*, of *Barchester Towers*, of *Framley Parsonage*, does not, to our mind, stand on the very same level as Dickens, Thackeray and George Eliot; for his talent was of a quality less fine than theirs. But he belonged to the same family—he had as much to tell us about English life; he was strong, genial and abundant. He published too much; the writing of novels had ended by becoming, with him, a perceptibly mechanical process. Dickens was prolific, Thackeray produced with a freedom for which we are constantly grateful; but we feel that these writers had their periods of gestation. They took more time to look at their subject; relatively (for to-day there is not much leisure, at best, for those who undertake to entertain a hungry public), they were able to wait for inspiration. Trollope's fecundity was prodigious; there was no limit to the work he was ready to do. It is not unjust to say that he sacrificed quality to quantity. Abundance, certainly, is in itself a great merit; almost all the greatest writers have been abundant. But Trollope's fertility was gross, importunate; he himself contended, we believe, that he had given to the world a greater number of printed pages of fiction than any of his literary contemporaries.[1] Not only did his novels follow each other without visible intermission, overlapping and treading on

[1] Trollope's *Autobiography* (p. 301): 'And so I end the record of my literary performances,—which I think are more in amount than the works of any other living English author. If any English authors not living have written more—as may probably have been the case—I do not know who they are.' (But James's essay preceded publication of *An Autobiography* by three months and is not a probable source.)

each other's heels, but most of these works are of extraordinary length. *Orley Farm, Can You Forgive Her?, He Knew He Was Right*, are exceedingly voluminous tales. *The Way We Live Now* is one of the longest of modern novels. Trollope produced, moreover, in the intervals of larger labour a great number of short stories, many of them charming, as well as various books of travel, and two or three biographies. He was the great *improvvisatore* of these latter years. Two distinguished story-tellers of the other sex—one in France and one in England—have shown an extraordinary facility of composition; but Trollope's pace was brisker even than that of the wonderful Madame Sand and the delightful Mrs. Oliphant. He had taught himself to keep this pace, and had reduced his admirable faculty to a system. Every day of his life he wrote a certain number of pages of his current tale, a number sacramental and invariable independent of mood and place. It was once the fortune of the author of these lines to cross the Atlantic in his company, and he has never forgotten the magnificent example of plain persistence that it was in the power of the eminent novelist to give on that occasion. The season was unpropitious, the vessel overcrowded, the voyage detestable; but Trollope shut himself up in his cabin every morning for a purpose which, on the part of a distinguished writer who was also an invulnerable sailor, could only be communion with the muse. He drove his pen as steadily on the tumbling ocean as in Montague Square; and as his voyages were many, it was his practice before sailing to come down to the ship and confer with the carpenter, who was instructed to rig up a rough writing-table in his small sea-chamber. Trollope has been accused of being deficient in imagination, but in the face of such a fact as that the charge will scarcely seem just. The power to shut one's eyes, one's ears (to say nothing of another sense), upon the scenery of a pitching Cunarder and open them upon the loves and sorrows of Lily Dale or the conjugal embarrassments of Lady Glencora Palliser, is certainly a faculty which could take to itself wings. The imagination that Trollope possessed he had at least thoroughly at his command. I speak of all this in order to explain (in part) why it was that, with his extraordinary gift, there was always in him a certain infusion of the common. He abused his gift, overworked it, rode his horse too hard. As an artist he never took himself seriously; many people will say this was why he was so delightful. The people who take themselves seriously are prigs and bores; and Trollope, with his perpetual 'story,' which was the only thing he cared about, his strong good sense, hearty good nature, generous appreciation of life in all its varieties, responds in perfection to a certain English ideal. According to that ideal it is rather dangerous to be explicitly or consciously an artist—to have a system, a doctrine, a form. Trollope, from the first, went in, as they say, for having as little form as possible; it is probably safe to affirm that he had no 'views' whatever on the subject of novel-writing. His whole manner is that of a man who regards the practice as one of the more delicate industries, but has never troubled his head nor clogged his pen with theories about the nature of his business. Fortunately he was not obliged to do so, for he had an easy road to success; and his honest, familiar, deliberate way of treating his readers as if he were one of them, and shared their indifference to a general view, their limitations of knowledge, their love of a comfortable ending, endeared him to many persons in England and America. It is in the name of some chosen form that, of late years, things have been made most disagreeable for the novel-reader, who has been treated by several votaries of the new experiments in fiction to unwonted and bewildering sensations. With Trollope we were always safe; there were sure to be no new experiments.

His great, his inestimable merit was a complete appreciation of the usual. This gift is not rare in the annals of English fiction; it would naturally be found in a walk of literature in which the feminine mind has laboured so fruitfully. Women are delicate and patient observers; they hold their noses close, as it were, to the texture of life. They feel and perceive the real with a kind of personal tact, and their observations are recorded in a thousand delightful volumes. Trollope, therefore, with his eyes comfortably fixed on the familiar, the actual, was far from having invented a new category; his great distinction is that in resting there his vision took in so much of the field. And then he *felt* all daily and immediate things as well as saw them; felt them in a simple, direct, salubrious way, with their sadness, their gladness, their charm, their comicality, all their obvious and measurable meanings. He never wearied of the pre-established round of English customs—never needed a respite or a change—was content to go on indefinitely watching the life that surrounded him, and holding up his mirror to it. Into this mirror the public, at first especially, grew very fond of looking—for it saw itself reflected in all the most credible and supposable ways, with that curiosity that people feel to know how they look when they are represented, 'just as they are,' by a painter who does not desire to put them into an attitude, to drape them for an effect, to arrange his light and his accessories. This exact and on the whole becoming image, projected upon a surface without a strong intrinsic tone, constitutes mainly the entertainment that Trollope offered his readers. The striking thing to the critic was that his robust and patient mind had no particular bias, his imagination no light of its own. He saw things neither pictorially and grotesquely like Dickens; nor with that combined disposition to satire and to literary form which gives such 'body,' as they say of wine, to the manner of Thackeray; nor with anything of the philosophic, the transcendental cast—the desire to follow them to their remote relations—which we associate with the name of George Eliot. Trollope had his elements of fancy, of satire, of irony; but these qualities were not very highly developed, and he walked mainly by the light of his good sense, his clear, direct vision of the things that lay nearest, and his great natural kindness. There is something remarkably tender and friendly in his feeling about all human perplexities; he takes the good-natured, temperate conciliatory view—the humorous view, perhaps, for the most part, yet without a touch of pessimistic prejudice. As he grew older, and had sometimes to go farther afield for his subjects, he acquired a savour of bitterness and reconciled himself sturdily to treating of the disagreeable. A more copious record of disagreeable matters could scarcely be imagined, for instance, than *The Way We Live Now*. But, in general, he has a wholesome mistrust of morbid analysis, an aversion to inflicting pain. He has an infinite love of detail, but his details are, for the most part, the innumerable items of the expected. When the French are disposed to pay a compliment to the English mind they are so good as to say that there is in it something remarkably *honnête*.[2] If I might borrow this epithet without seeming to be patronizing, I should apply it to the genius of Anthony Trollope. He represents in an eminent degree this natural decorum of the English spirit, and represents it all the better that there is not in him a grain of the mawkish or the prudish. He writes, he feels, he judges like a man, talking plainly and frankly about many things, and is by no means destitute of a certain saving grace of coarseness. But he has kept the purity of his imagination and held fast to old-fashioned reverences and preferences. He thinks it a sufficient objection to several topics to say simply that they are unclean. There was nothing in his theory of the story-teller's art that tended to convert the reader's or the writer's mind into a vessel for polluting things. He recognized the right of the vessel to protest, and would have regarded such a protest as conclusive. With a considerable turn for satire, though this perhaps is more evident in his early novels than in his later ones, he had

[2] '*honnê e*': seemly, decent.

as little as possible of the quality if irony. He never played with a subject, never juggled with the sympathies or the credulity of his reader, was never in the least paradoxical or mystifying. He sat down to his theme in a serious, business-like way, with his elbows on the table and his eye occasionally wandering to the clock.

To touch successively upon these points is to attempt a portrait, which I shall perhaps not altogether have failed to produce. The source of his success in describing the life that lay nearest to him, and describing it without any of those artistic perversions that come, as we have said, from a powerful imagination, from a cynical humour or from a desire to look, as George Eliot expresses it, for the suppressed transitions that unite all contrasts, the essence of this love of reality was his extreme interest in character. This is the fine and admirable quality in Trollope, this is what will preserve his best works in spite of those flatnesses which keep him from standing on quite the same level as the masters. Indeed this quality is so much one of the finest (to my mind at least), that it makes me wonder the more that the writer who had it so abundantly and so naturally should not have just that distinction which Trollope lacks, and which we find in his three brilliant contemporaries. If he was in any degree a man of genius (and I hold that he was), it was in virtue of this happy, instinctive perception of human varieties. His knowledge of the stuff we are made of, his observation of the common behaviour of men and women, was not reasoned nor acquired, not even particularly studied. All human doings deeply interested him, human life, to his mind, was a perpetual story; but he never attempted to take the so-called scientific view, the view which has lately found ingenious advocates among the countrymen and successors of Balzac. He had no airs of being able to tell you *why* people in a given situation would conduct themselves in a particular way; it was enough for him that he felt their feelings and struck the right note, because he had, as it were, a good ear. If he was a knowing psychologist he was so by grace; he was just and true without apparatus and without effort. He must have had a great taste for the moral question; he evidently believed that this is the basis of the interest of fiction. We must be careful, of course, in attributing convictions and opinions to Trollope, who, as I have said, had as little as possible of the pedantry of his art, and whose occasional chance utterances in regard to the object of the novelist and his means of achieving it are of an almost startling simplicity. But we certainly do not go too far in saying that he gave his practical testimony in favour of the idea that the interest of a work of fiction is great in proportion as the people stand on their feet. His great effort was evidently to make them stand so; if he achieved this result with as little as possible of a flourish of the hand it was nevertheless the measure of his success. If he had taken sides on the droll, bemuddled opposition between novels of character and novels of plot, I can imagine him to have said (except that he never expressed himself in epigrams), that he preferred the former class, inasmuch as character in itself is plot, while plot is by no means character. It is more safe indeed to believe that his great good sense would have prevented him from taking an idle controversy seriously. Character, in any sense in which we can get at it, is action, and action is plot, and any plot which hangs together, even if it pretend to interest us only in the fashion of a Chinese puzzle, plays upon our emotion, our suspense, by means of personal references. We care what happens to people only in proportion as we know what people are. Trollope's great apprehension of the real, which was what made him so interesting, came to him through his desire to satisfy us on this point—to tell us what certain people were and what they did in consequence of being so. That is the purpose of each of his tales; and if these things produce an illusion it comes from the gradual abundance of his testimony as to the temper, the tone, the passions, the habits, the moral nature, of a certain number of contemporary Britons.

His stories, in spite of their great length, deal very little in the surprising, the exceptional, the complicated; as a general thing he has no great story to tell. The thing is not so much a story as a picture; if we hesitate to call it a picture it is because the idea of composition is not the controlling one and we feel that the author would regard the artistic, in general, as a kind of affectation. There is not even much description, in the sense which the present votaries of realism in France attach to that word. The painter lays his scene in a few deliberate, not especially pictorial strokes, and never dreams of finishing the piece for the sake of enabling the reader to hang it up. The finish, such as it is, comes later, from the slow and somewhat clumsy accumulation of small illustrations. These illustrations are sometimes of the commonest; Trollope turns them out inexhaustibly, repeats them freely, unfolds them without haste and without rest. But they are all of the most obvious sort, and they are none the worse for that. The point to be made is that they have no great spectacular interest (we beg pardon of the innumerable love-affairs that Trollope had described), like many of the incidents, say, of Walter Scott and of Alexandre Dumas: if we care to know about them (as repetitions of a usual case), it is because the writer has managed, in his candid, literal, somewhat lumbering way, to tell us that about the men and women concerned which has already excited on their behalf the impression of life. It is a marvel by what homely arts, by what imperturbable button-holing persistence, he contrives to excite this impression. Take, for example, such a work as *The Vicar of Bullhampton*. It would be difficult to state the idea of this slow but excellent story, which is a capital example of interest produced by the quietest conceivable means. The principal persons in it are a lively, jovial, high-tempered country clergyman, a young woman who is in love with her cousin, and a small, rather dull squire who is in love with the young woman. There is no connection between the affairs of the clergyman and those of the two other persons, save that these two are the Vicar's friends. The Vicar gives countenance, for Christian charity's sake, to a young countryman who is suspected (falsely, as it appears), of murder, and also to the lad's sister, who is more than suspected of leading an immoral life. Various people are shocked at his indiscretion, but in the end he is shown to have been no worse a clergyman because he is a good fellow. A cantankerous nobleman, who has a spite against him, causes a Methodist conventicle to be erected at the gates of the vicarage; but afterward, finding that he has no title to the land used for this obnoxious purpose, causes the conventicle to be pulled down, and is reconciled with the parson, who accepts an invitation to stay at the castle. Mary Lowther, the heroine of *The Vicar of Bullhampton*, is sought in marriage by Mr. Harry Gilmore, to whose passion she is unable to respond; she accepts him, however, making him understand that she does not love him, and that her affections are fixed upon her kinsman, Captain Marrable, whom she would marry (and who would marry her), if he were not too poor to support a wife. If Mr. Gilmore will take her on these terms she will become his spouse; but she gives him all sorts of warnings. They are not superfluous; for, as Captain Marrable presently inherits a fortune, she throws over Mr. Gilmore, who retires to foreign lands, heart-broken, inconsolable. This is the substance of *The Vicar of Bullhampton*; the reader will see that it is not a very tangled skein. But if the interest is gradual it is extreme and constant, and it comes altogether from excellent portraiture. It is essentially a moral, a social interest. There is something masterly in the large-fisted grip with which, in work of this kind, Trollope handles his brush. The Vicar's nature is thoroughly analysed and rendered, and his monotonous friend the Squire, a man with limitations, but possessed and consumed by a genuine passion, is equally near the truth.

Trollope has described again and again the ravages of love, and it is wonderful to see how well, in these delicate matters, his plain good sense and good taste serve him. His story is always primarily a love-story, and a love-story constructed on an inveterate system. There is a young lady who has two lovers, or a young man who has two sweet-hearts; we are treated to the innumerable forms in which this predica-ment may present itself and the consequences, sometimes pathetic, sometimes grotesque, which spring from such false situations. Trollope is not what is called a colourist; still less is he a poet: he is seated on the back of heavy-footed prose. But his account of those sentiments which the poets are supposed to have made their own is apt to be as touching as demonstrations more lyrical. There is something wonderfully vivid in the state of mind of the unfortunate Harry Gilmore, of whom I have just spoken; and his history, which has no more pretensions to style than if it were cut out of yesterday's newspaper, lodges itself in the imagina-tion in all sorts of classic company. He is not handsome, nor clever, nor rich, nor romantic, nor distinguished in any way; he is simply rather a dense, narrow-minded, stiff, obstinate, common-place, conscientious modern Englishman, exceedingly in love and, from his own point of view, exceedingly ill-used. He is interesting because he suffers and because we are curious to see the form that suffering will take in that particular nature. Our good fortune, with Trollope, is that the person put before us will have, in spite of opportunities not to have it, a certain particular nature. The author has cared enough about the character of such a person to find out exactly what it is. Another particular nature in *The Vicar of Bullhampton* is the surly, sturdy, sceptical old farmer Jacob Brattle, who doesn't want to be patronized by the parson, and in his dumb, dusky, half-brutal, half-spiritual melancholy, surrounded by domestic troubles, financial embarrassments and a puzzling world, declines altogether to be won over to clerical optimism. Such a figure as Jacob Brattle, purely episodical though it be, is an excellent English portrait. As thoroughly English, and the most striking thing in the book, is the combination, in the nature of Frank Fenwick—the delightful Vicar—of the patronizing, conventional, clerical element with all sorts of manliness and spontaneity; the union, or to a certain extent the contradiction, of official and personal geniality. Trollope touches these points in a way that shows that he knows his man. Delicacy is not his great sign, but when it is necessary he can be as delicate as any one else.

I alighted, just now, at a venture, upon the history of Frank Fenwick; it is far from being a conspicuous work in the immense list of Trollope's novels. But to choose an example one must choose arbitrarily, for examples of almost anything that one may wish to say are numerous to embarrassment. In speaking of a writer who produced so much and produced always in the same way, there is perhaps a certain unfairness in choosing at all. As no work has higher pretensions than any other, there may be a certain unkindness in holding an individual production up to the light. 'Judge me in the lump,' we can imagine the author saying; 'I have only undertaken to entertain the British public. I don't pretend that each of my novels is an organic whole.' Trollope had no time to give his tales a classic roundness; yet there is (in spite of an extraordinary defect), something of that quality in the thing that first revealed him. *The Warden* was published in 1855. It made a great impression; and when, in 1857, *Barchester Towers* followed it, every one saw that English literature had a novelist the more. These were not the works of a young man, for Anthony Trollope had been born in 1815. It is remarkable to reflect by the way, that his prodigious fecundity (he had published before *The Warden* three or four novels which attracted little attention), was enclosed between his fortieth and his sixty-seventh years. Trollope had lived long enough in the world to learn a good deal about it; and his maturity of feeling and evidently large knowledge of English life went for much in the effect produced by the two clerical tales. It was easy to see that he would take up room. What he had picked up, to begin with, was a comprehensive, various impression of the clergy of the Church of England and the manners and feelings that prevail in cathedral towns. This, for a while, was his speciality, and, as always happens in such cases, the public was disposed to prescribe to him that path. He knew about bishops, archdeacons, prebendaries, precentors, and about their wives and daughters; he knew what these dignitaries say to each other when they are collected together, aloof from secular ears. He even knew what sort of talk goes on between a bishop and a bishop's lady when the august couple are enshrouded in the privacy of the episcopal bedroom. This knowledge, somehow, was rare and precious. No one, as yet, had been bold enough to snatch the illuminating torch from the very summit of the altar. Trollope enlarged his field very speedily—there is, as I remember that work, as little as possible of the ecclesiastical in the tale of *The Three Clerks*, which came after *Barchester Towers*. But he always retained traces of his early divination of the clergy; he introduced them frequently, and he always did them easily and well. There is no ecclesiastical figure, however, so good as the first—no creation of this sort so happy as the admirable Mr.

Harding. *The Warden* is a delightful tale, and a signal instance of Trollope's habit of offering us the spectacle of a character. A motive more delicate, more slender, as well as more charming, could scarcely be conceived. It is simply the history of an old man's conscience.

The good and gentle Mr. Harding, precentor of Barchester Cathedral, also holds the post of warden of Hiram's Hospital, an ancient charity where twelve old paupers are maintained in comfort. The office is in the gift of the bishop, and its emoluments are as handsome as the duties of the place are small. Mr. Harding has for years drawn his salary in quiet gratitude; but his moral repose is broken by hearing it at last begun to be said that the wardenship is a sinecure, that the salary is a scandal, and that a large part, at least, of his easy income ought to go to the pensioners of the hospital. He is sadly troubled and perplexed, and when the great London newspapers take up the affair he is overwhelmed with confusion and shame. He thinks the newspapers are right—he perceives that the warden is an overpaid and rather a useless functionary. The only thing he can do is to resign the place. He has no means of his own—he is only a quiet, modest, innocent old man, with a taste, a passion, for old church-music and the violoncello. But he determines to resign, and he does resign in spite of the sharp opposition of his friends. He does what he thinks right, and goes to live in lodgings over a shop in the Barchester High Street. That is all the story, and it has exceeding beauty. The question of Mr. Harding's resignation becomes a drama, and we anxiously wait for the catastrophe. Trollope never did anything happier than the picture of this sweet and serious little old gentleman, who on most of the occasions of life has shown a lamblike softness and compliance, but in this particular matter opposes a silent, impenetrable obstinacy to the arguments of the friends who insist on his keeping his sinecure—fixing his mild, detached gaze on the distance, and making imaginary passes with his fiddle-bow while they demonstrate his pusillanimity. The subject of *The Warden*, exactly viewed, is the opposition of the two natures of Archdeacon Grantly and Mr. Harding, and there is nothing finer in all Trollope than the vividness with which this opposition is presented. The archdeacon is as happy a portrait as the precentor—an image of the full-fed, worldly churchman, taking his stand squarely upon his rich temporalities, and regarding the church frankly as a fat social pasturage. It required the greatest tact and temperance to make the picture of Archdeacon Grantly stop just where it does. The type, impartially considered, is detestable, but the individual may be full of amenity. Trollope allows his archdeacon all the virtues he was likely to possess, but he makes his spiritual grossness wonderfully natural. No charge of exaggeration is possible, for we are made to feel that he is conscientious as well as arrogant, and expansive as well as hard. He is one of those figures that spring into being all at once, solidifying in the author's grasp. These two capital portraits are what we carry away from *The Warden*, which some persons profess to regard as our writer's masterpiece. We remember, while it was still something of a novelty, to have heard a judicious critic say that it had much of the charm of *The Vicar of Wakefield*. Anthony Trollope would not have accepted the compliment, and would not have wished this little tale to pass before several of its successors. He would have said, very justly, that it gives too small a measure of his knowledge of life. It has, however, a certain classic roundness, though, as we said a moment since, there is a blemish on its fair face. The chapter on Dr. Pessimist Anticant and Mr. Sentiment would be a mistake almost inconceivable if Trollope had not in other places taken pains to show us that for certain forms of satire (the more violent, doubtless), he had absolutely no gift. Dr. Anticant is a parody of Carlyle, and Mr. Sentiment is an exposure of Dickens: and both these little *jeux d'esprit* are as infelicitous as they are misplaced. It was no less luckless an inspiration to convert Archdeacon Grantly's three sons, denominated respectively Charles James, Henry and Samuel, into little effigies of three distinguished English bishops of that period, whose well-known peculiarities are reproduced in the description of these unnatural urchins. The whole passage, as we meet it, is a sudden disillusionment; we are transported from the mellow atmosphere of an assimilated Barchester to the air of ponderous allegory.

I may take occasion to remark here upon a very curious fact—the fact that there are certain precautions in the way of producing that illusion dear to the intending novelist which Trollope not only habitually scorned to take, but really, as we may say, asking pardon for the heat of the thing, delighted wantonly to violate. He took a suicidal satisfaction in reminding the reader that the story he was telling was only, after all, a make-believe. He habitually referred to the work in hand (in the course of that work) as a novel, and to himself as a novelist, and was fond of letting the reader know that this novelist could direct the course of events according to his pleasure. Already, in *Barchester Towers*, he falls into this pernicious trick. In describing the wooing of Eleanor Bold by Mr. Arabin he has occasion to say that the lady might have acted in a much more direct and natural way than the way he attributes to her. But if she had, he adds, 'where would have been my novel?' The last chapter of the same story begins with the remark, 'The end of a novel, like the end of a children's dinner party, must be made up of sweetmeats and sugar-plums.' These little slaps at credulity (we might give many more specimens) are very discouraging, but they are even more inexplicable; for they are deliberately inartistic, even judged from the point of view of that rather vague consideration of form which is the only canon we have a right to impose upon Trollope. It is impossible to imagine what a novelist takes himself to be unless he regard himself as an historian and his narrative as a history. It is only as an historian that he has the smallest *locus standi*.[3] As a narrator of fictitious events he is nowhere; to insert into his attempt a back-bone of logic, he must relate events that are assumed to be real. This assumption permeates, animates all the work of the most solid story-tellers; we need only mention (to select a single instance), the magnificent historical tone of Balzac, who would as soon have thought of admitting to the reader that he was deceiving him, as Garrick or John Kemble would have thought of pulling off his disguise in front of the foot-lights. Therefore, when Trollope suddenly winks at us and reminds us that he is telling us an arbitrary thing,[4] we are startled and shocked in quite the same way as if Macaulay or Motley were to drop the historic mask and intimate that William of Orange was a myth or the Duke of Alva an invention.

It is a part of this same ambiguity of mind as to what constitutes evidence that Trollope should sometimes endow his people with such fantastic names. Dr. Pessimist Anticant and Mr. Sentiment make, as we have seen, an awkward appearance in a modern novel; and Mr. Neversay Die, Mr. Stickatit, Mr. Rerechild and Mr. Fillgrave (the two last the family physicians), are scarcely more felicitous. It would be better to go back to Bunyan at once. There is a person mentioned in *The Warden* under the name of Mr. Quiverful—a poor clergyman, with a dozen children, who holds the living of Puddingdale. This name is a humorous allusion to his overflowing nursery, and it matters little so long as he is not brought to the front. But in *Barchester Towers*, which carries on the history of Hiram's Hospital, Mr. Quiverful becomes, as a candidate for Mr. Harding's vacant place, an important element, and the reader is

---

[3] *locus standi*: a place to stand (i.e. where one can claim the right to stand).

[4] Wayne C. Booth's comment on this passage in *The Rhetoric of Fiction* (1961), pp. 204, 206, seems legitimate. It is extremely rare for Trollope to intimate that he has the power of actually altering the events in the lives of his characters. As narrator he can, Trollope implies, choose his *manner of telling* what has happened; but the events themselves are, in all but rare instances, viewed as actual and inviolable.

made proportionately unhappy by the primitive character of this satiric note. A Mr. Quiverful with fourteen children (which is the number attained in *Barchester Towers*) is too difficult to believe in. We can believe in the name and we can believe in the children; but we cannot manage the combination. It is probably not unfair to say that if Trollope derived half his inspiration from life, he derived the other half from Thackeray; his earlier novels, in especial, suggest an honourable emulation of the author of *The Newcomes*. Thackeray's names were perfect; they always had a meaning, and (except in his absolutely jocose productions, where they were still admirable) we can imagine, even when they are most figurative, that they should have been borne by real people. But in this, as in other respects, Trollope's hand was heavier than his master's; though when he is content not to be too comical his appellations are sometimes fortunate enough. Mrs. Proudie is excellent, for Mrs. Proudie, and even the Duke of Omnium and Gatherum Castle rather minister to illusion than destroy it. Indeed, the names of houses and places, throughout Trollope, are full of colour.

I would speak in some detail of *Barchester Towers* if this did not seem to commit me to the prodigious task of appreciating each of Trollope's works in succession. Such an attempt as that is so far from being possible that I must frankly confess to not having read everything that proceeded from his pen. There came a moment in his vigorous career (it was even a good many years ago) when I renounced the effort to 'keep up' with him. It ceased to seem obligatory to have read his last story; it ceased soon to be very possible to know which was his last. Before that, I had been punctual, devoted; and the memories of the earlier period are delightful. It reached, if I remember correctly, to about the publication of *He Knew He Was Right*; after which, to my recollection (oddly enough, too, for that novel was good enough to encourage a continuance of past favours, as the shopkeepers say), the picture becomes dim and blurred.[5] The author of *Orley Farm* and *The Small House at Allington* ceased to produce individual works; his activity became a huge 'serial.' Here and there, in the vast fluidity, an organic particle detached itself. *The Last Chronicle of Barset*, for instance, is one of his most powerful things; it contains the sequel of the terrible history of Mr. Crawley,

[5] Toward the end of this long paragraph, James gives 1856–69 as the dates of Trollope's most memorable period of creating novels. Apparently James's memory tells him that he had stopped reading Trollope regularly with the publication of *He Knew He Was Right* in 1869. In the remainder of the essay, James shows familiarity with *The Vicar of Bullhampton* (1870) and *Ralph the Heir* (1871) and some acquaintance (not a pleasant one) with *The Way We Live Now* (1875).

the starving curate—an episode full of that literally truthful pathos of which Trollope was so often a master, and which occasionally raised him quite to the level of his two immediate predecessors in the vivid treatment of English life—great artists whose pathetic effects were sometimes too visibly prepared. For the most part, however, he should be judged by the productions of the first half of his career; later the strong wine was rather too copiously watered. His practice, his acquired facility, were such that his hand went of itself, as it were, and the thing looked superficially like a fresh inspiration. But it was not fresh, it was rather stale; and though there was no appearance of effort, there was a fatal dryness of texture. It was too little of a new story and too much of an old one. Some of these ultimate compositions—*Phineas Redux* (*Phineas Finn* is much better), *The Prime Minister, John Caldigate, The American Senator, The Duke's Children*—betray the dull, impersonal rumble of the mill-wheel. What stands Trollope always in good stead (in addition to the ripe habit of writing), is his various knowledge of the English world—to say nothing of his occasionally laying under contribution the American. His American portraits, by the way (they are several in number), are always friendly; they hit it off more happily than the attempt to depict American character from the European point of view is accustomed to do: though, indeed, as we ourselves have not yet learned to represent our types very finely—are not apparently even very sure what our types are—it is perhaps not to be wondered at that transatlantic talent should miss the mark. The weakness of transatlantic talent in this particular is apt to be want of knowledge; but Trollope's knowledge has all the air of being excellent, though not intimate. Had he indeed striven to learn the way to the American heart? No less than twice, and possibly even oftener, has he rewarded the merit of a scion of the British aristocracy with the hand of an American girl. The American girl was destined sooner or later to make her entrance into British fiction, and Trollope's treatment of this complicated being is full of good humour and of that fatherly indulgence, that almost motherly sympathy, which characterizes his attitude, throughout toward the youthful feminine. He has not mastered all the springs of her delicate organism nor sounded all the mysteries of her conversation. Indeed, as regards these latter phenomena, he has observed a few of which he has been the sole observer. 'I got to be thinking if any one of them should ask me to marry him,' words attributed to Miss Boncassen, in *The Duke's Children*, have much more the note of English American than of American English. But, on the whole, in these matters Trollope does very well. His fund of acquaintance with his own country—and indeed with the world at large—was apparently inexhaustible, and it gives his novels a spacious, geographical quality which we should not know where to look for elsewhere in the same degree, and which is the sign of an extraordinary difference between such an horizon as his and the limited world-outlook, as the Germans would say, of the brilliant writers who practise the art of realistic fiction on the other side of the Channel. Trollope was familiar with all sorts and conditions of men, with the business of life, with affairs, with the great world of sport, with every component part of the ancient fabric of English society. He had travelled more than once all over the globe, and for him, therefore, the background of the human drama was a very extensive scene. He had none of the pedantry of the cosmopolite; he remained a sturdy and sensible middle-class Englishman. But his work is full of implied reference to the whole arena of modern vagrancy. He was for many years concerned in the management of the Post-Office; and we can imagine no experience more fitted to impress a man with the diversity of human relations. It is possibly from this source that he derived his fondness for transcribing the letters of his love-lorn maidens and other embarrassed persons. No contemporary story-teller deals so much in letters; the modern English epistle (very happily imitated, for the most part), is his unfailing resource.

There is perhaps little reason in it, but I find myself comparing this tone of allusion to many lands and many things, and whatever it brings us of easier respiration, with that narrow vision of humanity which accompanies the strenuous, serious work lately offered us in such abundance by the votaries of art for art who sit so long at their desks in Parisian *quatrièmes*.[6] The contrast is complete, and it would be interesting, had we space to do so here, to see how far it goes. On one side a wide, good-humoured, superficial glance at a good many things; on the other a gimlet-like consideration of a few. Trollope's plan, as well as Zola's, was to describe the life that lay near him; but the two writers differ immensely as to what constitutes life and what constitutes nearness. For Trollope the emotions of a nursery-governess in Australia would take precedence of the adventures of a depraved *femme du monde* in Paris or London. They both undertake to do the same thing—to depict French and English manners; but the English writer (with his unsurpassed industry) is so occasional, so accidental, so full of the echoes

---

[6] *quatrièmes*: attics (fourth floors, as the French count floors, omitting the ground-level).

of voices that are not the voice of the muse. Gustave Flaubert, Emile Zola, Alphonse Daudet, on the other hand, are nothing if not concentrated and sedentary. Trollope's realism is as instinctive, as inveterate as theirs; but nothing could mark more the difference between the French and English mind than the difference in the application, on one side and the other, of this system. We say system, though on Trollope's part it is none. He has no visible, certainly no explicit care for the literary part of the business; he writes easily, comfortably, and profusely, but his style has nothing in common either with the minute stippling of Daudet or the studied rhythms of Flaubert. He accepted all the common restrictions, and found that even within the barriers there was plenty of material. He attaches a preface to one of his novels—*The Vicar of Bullhampton*, before mentioned—for the express purpose of explaining why he has introduced a young woman who may, in truth, as he says, be called a 'castaway'; and in relation to this episode he remarks that it is the object of the novelist's art to entertain the young people of both sexes. Writers of the French school would, of course, protest indignantly against such a formula as this, which is the only one of the kind that I remember to have encountered in Trollope's pages. It is meagre, assuredly; but Trollope's practice was really much larger than so poor a theory. And indeed any theory was good which enabled him to produce the works which he put forth between 1856 and 1869, or later. In spite of his want of doctrinal richness I think he tells us, on the whole, more about life than the 'naturalists' in our sister republic. I say this with a full consciousness of the opportunities an artist loses in leaving so many corners unvisited, so many topics untouched, simply because I think his perception of character was naturally more just and liberal than that of the naturalists. This has been from the beginning the good fortune of our English providers of fiction, as compared with the French. They are inferior in audacity, in neatness, in acuteness, in intellectual vivacity, in the arrangement of material, in the art of characterizing visible things. But they have been more at home in the moral world; as people say to-day they know their way about the conscience. This is the value of much of the work done by the feminine wing of the school—work which presents itself to French taste as deplorably thin and insipid. Much of it is exquisitely human, and that after all is a merit. As regards Trollope, one may perhaps characterize him best, in opposition to what I have ventured to call the sedentary school, by saying that he was a novelist who hunted the fox. Hunting was for years his most valued recreation, and I remember that when I made in his company the voyage of which I have spoken, he had timed his return from the Antipodes exactly so as to be able to avail himself of the first day on which it should be possible to ride to hounds. He 'worked' the hunting-field largely; it constantly reappears in his novels; it was excellent material.

But it would be hard to say (within the circle in which he revolved) what material he neglected. I have allowed myself to be detained so long by general considerations that I have almost forfeited the opportunity to give examples. I have spoken of *The Warden* not only because it made his reputation, but because, taken in conjunction with *Barchester Towers*, it is thought by many people to be his highest flight. *Barchester Towers* is admirable; it has an almost Thackerayan richness. Arch-deacon Grantly grows more and more into life, and Mr. Harding is as charming as ever. Mrs. Proudie is ushered into a world in which she was to make so great an impression. Mrs. Proudie has become classical; of all Trollope's characters she is the most often referred to. She is exceedingly true; but I do not think she is quite so good as her fame, and as several figures from the same hand that have not won so much honour. She is rather too violent, too vixenish, too sour. The truly awful female bully—the completely fatal episcopal spouse—would have, I think, a more insidious form, a greater amount of superficial padding. The Stanhope family, in *Barchester Towers*, are a real *trouvaille*, and the idea of transporting the Signora Vesey-Neroni into a cathedral-town was an inspiration. There could not be a better example of Trollope's manner of attaching himself to character than the whole picture of Bertie Stanhope. Bertie is a delightful creation; and the scene in which, at the party given by Mrs. Proudie, he puts this majestic woman to rout is one of the most amusing in all the chronicles of Barset. It is perhaps permitted to wish, by the way, that this triumph had been effected by means intellectual rather than physical; though, indeed, if Bertie had not despoiled her of her drapery we should have lost the lady's admirable 'Unhand it, sir!' Mr. Arabin is charming, and the hen-pecked bishop has painful truth; but Mr. Slope, I think, is a little too arrant a scamp. He is rather too much the old game; he goes too coarsely to work, and his clamminess and cant are somewhat overdone. He is an interesting illustration, however, of the author's dislike (at that period at least) of the bareness of evangelical piety. In one respect *Barchester Towers* is (to the best of our recollection) unique, being the only one of Trollope's novels in which the interest does not centre more or less upon a simple maiden in her flower. The novel offers us nothing in the way of a girl; though we know that this attractive object was to lose nothing by waiting. Eleanor Bold is a charming and natural person, but Eleanor Bold is not in her flower. After this, however, Trollope settled down steadily to the English girl; he took possession of her, and turned her inside out. He never made her a subject of heartless satire, as cynical fabulists of other lands have been known to make the shining daughters of those climes; he bestowed upon her the most serious, the most patient, the most tender, the most copious consideration. He is evidently always more or less in love with her, and it is a wonder how under these circumstances he should make her so objective, plant her so well on her feet. But, as I have said, if he was a lover, he was a paternal lover; as competent as a father who has had fifty daughters. He has presented the British maiden under innumerable names, in every station and in every emergency in life, and with every combination of moral and physical qualities. She is always definite and natural. She plays her part most properly. She has always health in her cheek and gratitude in her eye. She has not a touch of the morbid, and is delightfully tender, modest and fresh. Trollope's heroines have a strong family likeness, but it is a wonder how finely he discriminates between them. One feels, as one reads him, like a man with 'sets' of female cousins. Such a person is inclined at first to lump each group together; but presently he finds that even in the groups there are subtle differences. Trollope's girls, for that matter, would make delightful cousins. He has scarcely drawn, that we can remember, a disagreeable damsel. Lady Alexandrina de Courcy is disagreeable, and so is Amelia Roper, and so are various provincial (and indeed metropolitan) spinsters, who set their caps at young clergymen and government clerks. Griselda Grantly was a stick; and considering that she was intended to be attractive, Alice Vavasor does not commend herself particularly to our affections. But the young women I have mentioned had ceased to belong to the blooming season; they had entered the bristling, or else the limp, period. Not that Trollope's more mature spinsters invariably fall into these extremes. Miss Thorne of Ullathorne, Miss Dunstable, Miss Mackenzie,[7] Rachel Ray (if she may be called mature), Miss Baker and Miss Todd, in *The Bertrams*, Lady Julia Guest, who comforts poor John Eames: these and many other amiable figures rise up to contradict the idea. A gentleman who had sojourned in many lands was once asked by a lady (neither of

---

[7] James in 1865–6 had written reviews of *Miss Mackenzie* (1865), *Can You Forgive Her?* (1866), and *The Belton Estate* (1866) for the New York *Nation*. See above, Nos. 86, 92, and 93.

these persons was English), in what country he had found the women most to his taste. 'Well, in England,' he replied. 'In England?' the lady repeated. 'Oh yes,' said her interlocutor; 'they are so affectionate!' The remark was fatuous, but it has the merit of describing Trollope's heroines. They are so affectionate. Mary Thorne, Lucy Robarts, Adela Gauntlet, Lily Dale, Nora Rowley, Grace Crawley, have a kind of clinging tenderness, a passive sweetness, which is quite in the old English tradition. Trollope's genius is not the genius of Shakespeare, but his heroines have something of the fragrance of Imogen and Desdemona. There are two little stories to which, I believe, his name has never been affixed, but which he is known to have written, that contain an extraordinarily touching representation of the passion of love in its most sensitive form. In *Linda Tressel* and *Nina Balatka* the vehicle is plodding prose, but the effect is none the less poignant. And in regard to this I may say that in a hundred places in Trollope the extremity of pathos is reached by the homeliest means. He often achieved a conspicuous intensity of the tragical. The long, slow process of the conjugal wreck of Louis Trevelyan and his wife (in *He Knew He Was Right*), with that rather lumbering movement which is often characteristic of Trollope, arrives at last at an impressive completeness of misery. It is the history of an accidental rupture between two stiff-necked and ungracious people —'the little rift within the lute'—which widens at last into a gulf of anguish. Touch is added to touch, one small, stupid, fatal aggravation to another; and as we gaze into the widening breach we wonder at the vulgar materials of which tragedy sometimes composes itself. I have always remembered the chapter called 'Casalunga,' toward the close of *He Knew He Was Right*, as a powerful picture of the insanity of stiff-neckedness. Louis Trevelyan, separated from his wife, alone, haggard, suspicious, unshaven, undressed, living in a desolate villa on a hill-top near Siena and returning doggedly to his fancied wrong, which he has nursed until it becomes an hallucination, is a picture worthy of Balzac. Here and in several other places Trollope has dared to be thoroughly logical; he has not sacrificed to conventional optimism; he has not been afraid of a misery which should be too much like life. He has had the same courage in the history of the wretched Mr. Crawley and in that of the much-to-be-pitied Lady Mason. In this latter episode he found an admirable subject. A quiet, charming, tender-souled English gentlewoman who (as I remember the story of *Orley Farm*) forges a codicil to a will in order to benefit her son, a young prig who doesn't appreciate immoral heroism, and who is suspected, accused, tried, and saved from conviction only by some turn of fortune that I forget; who is furthermore an object of high-bred, respectful, old-fashioned gallantry on the part of a neighbouring baronet, so that she sees herself dishonoured in his eyes as well as condemned in those of her boy: such a personage and such a situation would be sure to yield, under Trollope's handling, the last drop of their reality.

There are many more things to say about him than I am able to add to these very general observations, the limit of which I have already passed. It would be natural, for instance, for a critic who affirms that his principal merit is the portrayal of individual character, to enumerate several of the figures that he has produced. I have not done this, and I must ask the reader who is not acquainted with Trollope to take my assertion on trust; the reader who knows him will easily make a list for himself. No account of him is complete in which allusion is not made to his practice of carrying certain actors from one story to another —a practice which he may be said to have inherited from Thackeray, as Thackeray may be said to have borrowed it from Balzac. It is a great mistake, however, to speak of it as an artifice which would not naturally occur to a writer proposing to himself to make a general portrait of a society. He has to construct that society, and it adds to the illusion in any given case that certain other cases correspond with it. Trollope constructed a great many things—a clergy, an aristocracy, a middle-class, an administrative class, a little replica of the political world. His political novels are distinctly dull, and I confess I have not been able to read them. He evidently took a good deal of pains with his aristocracy; it makes its first appearance, if I remember right, in *Doctor Thorne*, in the person of the Lady Arabella de Courcy. It is difficult for us in America to measure the success of that picture, which is probably, however, not absolutely to the life. There is in *Doctor Thorne* and some other works a certain crudity of reference to distinctions of rank—as if people's consciousness of this matter were, on either side, rather inflated. It suggests a general state of tension. It is true that, if Trollope's consciousness had been more flaccid he would perhaps not have given us Lady Lufton and Lady Glencora Palliser. Both of these noble persons are as living as possible, though I see Lady Lufton, with her terror of Lucy Robarts, the best. There is a touch of poetry in the figure of Lady Glencora, but I think there is a weak spot in her history. The actual woman would have made a fool of herself to the end with Burgo Fitzgerald; she would not have discovered the merits of Plantagenet Palliser—or if she had, she would not have cared about them. It is an illustration of the business-like way in which Trollope laid out his work that he always provided a sort of underplot to alternate with his main story—a strain of narrative of which the scene is usually laid in a humbler walk of life. It is to his underplot that he generally relegates his vulgar people, his disagreeable young women; and I have often admired the perseverance with which he recounts these less edifying items. Now and then, it may be said, as in *Ralph the Heir*, the story appears to be all underplot and all vulgar people. These, however, are details. As I have already intimated, it is difficult to specify in Trollope's work, on account of the immense quantity of it; and there is sadness in the thought that this enormous mass does not present itself in a very portable form to posterity.

Trollope did not write for posterity; he wrote for the day, the moment; but these are just the writers whom posterity is apt to put into its pocket. So much of the life of his time is reflected in his novels that we must believe a part of the record will be saved; and the best parts of them are so sound and true and genial, that readers with an eye to that sort of entertainment will always be sure, in a certain proportion, to turn to them. Trollope will remain one of the most trustworthy, though not one of the most eloquent, of the writers who have helped the heart of man to know itself. The heart of man does not always desire this knowledge; it prefers sometimes to look at history in another way—to look at the manifestations without troubling about the motives. There are two kinds of taste in the appreciation of imaginative literature: the taste for emotions of surprise and the taste for emotions of recognition. It is the latter that Trollope gratifies, and he gratifies it the more that the medium of his own mind, through which we see what he shows us, gives a confident direction to our sympathy. His natural rightness and purity are so real that the good things he projects must be real. A race is fortunate when it has a good deal of the sort of imagination—of imaginative feeling—that had fallen to the share of Anthony Trollope; and in this possession our English race is not poor.

APPENDIX

Trollope informs us that with one exception (No. 251, below), he did not see reviews of his first three novels. For a discussion of the subject, see Introduction, II. Unless otherwise noted, reviews given below are presented in abridged form. Nos. 243, 246–50, and 252–3, are, so far as I have discovered, printed here for the first time since their original publication.

THE MACDERMOTS
OF BALLYCLORAN

1847

For an interesting article on reviews of the *Macdermots*, see Lance O. Tingay, 'The Reception of Trollope's First Novel', *Nineteenth-Century Fiction* (1951), vi. 195–200. See also No. 139 (*b*) above.

---

240. Unsigned notice, *Critic*

1 May 1847, v. 344

As its title implies, an Irish story, of which the plot is the only part to be commended. *That* is interesting and ingenious, proving that the author possesses some invention. But the composition is very bad indeed. Seldom have we seen such slovenly writing. Every page is crowded with tautologies. Whether Mr. Trollope be boy or man, we know not; but we suspect, nay, for his own sake we hope, the former, and that he has perpetrated the publication of this juvenile essay without consulting his friends. Years will in such case bring both discretion and improvement, and at some future time, after much labour and study, we may have to welcome him to a respectable place among the novelists of the age. But if he have already reached maturity of years, his case is hopeless.

241. Unsigned notice, *Spectator*

8 May 1847, xx. 449

[This is] such a subject as Mrs. Trollope herself might have chosen, or advised; and the treatment has a literal kind of naturalness, without producing the usual effects of nature. There is, however, more of mellowness in the composition of Mr. A. Trollope, and less of forced contrivance in the management of his story, than the fluent lady has ever displayed. . . .

There is reality in *The Macdermots of Ballycloran*; and Mr. Trollope displays a knowledge of Irish character and an aptitude for developing it in dialogue. The subject is also well treated. The characters are natural, without much of book exaggeration: they are human in their vices, not mere abstractions of unalloyed folly, villany, weakness, or virtue. But the subject is not well chosen, and is too elongated. . . . The matter of the story should excite an interest which we cannot feel for the characters, either as gentry or peasants, because they belong to neither. The story, too, is overdone in either point of view, not by tedious elaboration, but by needless minutiae.

242. Unsigned notice, *Athenaeum*

15 May 1847, p. 517

The first of the heap which comes to hand is unfortunate only in the name of its author; who comes before the public with the disadvantage of *not being* the popular writer for whom careless readers might have mistaken him. We are sorry for the second Mrs. Butler—for the second Mr. Browning; and for like reasons, had we been Mr. A. Trollope, we would have written under some *Beville* or *Lovel* disguise, if we were able to write so clever a novel as his 'Macdermots of Bally-cloran.' Clever as this tale is, however, it does not produce a pleasant impression. . . .

Twenty years ago 'The Macdermots' would have made a reputation for its author. Now, those who read it will join, we have little doubt, in our verdict: but their number will be fewer. If we meet Mr. Trollope again, we hope that it will not be on 'Mount Misery.' He seems to possess a vein of humour—*vide* the description of Mary Brady's wedding—which, if duly reined in (our caution is not needlessly prudish), might win him success among those who prefer 'the quips and cranks' of Mirth's crew to the death-spasms of Crime and Sorrow.

243. Unsigned notice, *John Bull*

22 May 1847, xxvii. 327

Mr. Trollope has produced a work of rare and singular merit, for, with almost a single incident of domestic life, and embracing a period of time not exceeding twelve months, he has constructed a story of surpassing and increasing interest to its close. The scene is laid in Ireland, in the County of Leitrim, and the events are made to bring out all the peculiar features of Irish life among the peasantry, with a fidelity of description and knowledge of character equal to anything in the writings of Miss Edgeworth. There is no extravagance, no caricature, none of the hacknied circumstances which raise a laugh at the expense of truth. The reader lays down the work at the end with the impression that he has visited Ireland, conversed with the individuals who are introduced, witnessed the scenes in which they are engaged, listened to their language, and watched the progress of their actions. All the characters are admirably discriminated, and some of them are portrayed with a dramatic power akin to that which we find in Sir Walter Scott's novels. Among the latter we would name Larry Macdermot, his son Thady and daughter Feemy (the hero and heroine of the work), Hyacinth Keegan (the rascally lawyer), Pat Brady, Myles Ussher, and Father John. The last is an admirably conceived and admirably sustained character; and happy would it be for Ireland if she had many such parish Priests as the Rev. John M'Grath. The trial of Thady Macdermot, his execution, and the death of his sister Feemy, are described with great power. Mr. Trollope is not only well acquainted with the peculiarities of Irish character, but he knows how to seize upon those which most vividly exhibit the social features of the people. He is, too, an acute observer of human nature, and it is because he never violates its genuine impulses that his work, from the first page to the last, lays so firm a hold upon the sympathy of the reader. The idiotic imbecility of Larry Macdermot, its earlier symptoms, their gradual development, and the final wreck of the old man's mind, are finely described.

244. Unsigned notice, *Howitt's Journal*

19 June 1847, i. 350

If this work be, as is said, by the son of Mrs. Trollope, then the son assuredly inherits a considerable portion of the mother's talent. It is a story of intense interest, and is written by a bold and skilful hand. To give a slight idea of the unfortunate Macdermots, the history of whose downfall furnishes the material for the book, we will give a hasty sketch of the family group, as they are introduced to the reader by the author himself. . . . [Nearly all of Chapter II is given.]

We regret that our limited space prevents our giving, as still better specimens of the ability shown in the work, some scenes from among the gentry at the county races; or, still better, from the wild regions of Aughacashel, where the unfortunate Thady, flying from the police, hides among the illicit distillers. We have not often read anything more impressive than this part of the book. In conclusion, we advise our readers to get it into every circulating library in which they may have any voice; and by so doing they will oblige others as well as themselves.

245. Unsigned notice, *Douglas Jerrold's Shilling Magazine*

June 1847, v. 566

Essentially the same review, with only a few variants in phrasing, appears in *Douglas Jerrold's Weekly Newspaper*, 29 May 1847, p. 661. A column-long 'extract indicative of his colloquial writing' adds greatly to the size of the review, however. (No extract is printed in the *Magazine*; the notice is given here unabridged.)

'The Macdermots of Ballycloran,' by Mr. A. Trollope, is a story of Irish ignorance and wretchedness, a long-drawn-out narrative of the downfall of an ancient Irish family. It is strictly natural, as life-like and vigorous as could be desired; but the story might have been told in one volume. A tale, to bear the prolixity of three volumes, should abound in strong incidents, all tending towards the final disposition of the characters; and this requirement is much wanted in this work. The story is one of hard landlordism, poor tenantry, seduction, and the upshot—the gallows! The hero kills the seducer of his sister, and pays his life for so doing. We wish that the author had thought proper to modify his narrative, in some parts, for the roughness does not add one little to the full development of the story. His Irish dialogue is smartly and judiciously written, and is the evident result of residence. He is copious in his knowledge of Irishisms and local idioms, and this knowledge judiciously used adds to the vividness of his pictures. There are some stirring and life-like scenes in it, and we augur from it a successful career to the author. He evidently has inherited a keenness of observation and power of narrative.

246. Unsigned notice, *New Monthly Magazine*

June 1847, n.s. lxxx. 249

Such startling social anomalies as are presented to us in the history of the decline and fall of the M'Dermots of Ballycloran can only be met with in Irish life. . . . Setting aside the interest afforded by a wild heroine and a really good priest, there is an air of tarnished chivalry in the demeanour of Thady, the last representative of the M'Dermots, which is infinitely amusing. The ancestral pride and family pretensions ever struggling against a humiliating position, a vanishing estate, and a crumbling tenantry, is not only true to life, but makes of this account of the M'Dermots a most characteristic picture of Irish society.

THE KELLYS AND THE O'KELLYS

1848

For later reviews of *The Kellys and the O'Kellys*, see above, Nos. 118 and 139 (*b*).

247. Unsigned notice, *Athenaeum*

15 July 1848, p. 701

We like this novel better than Mr. Trollope's former one . . . because though not more powerful, it is less painful. . . . Humour pervades its scenes,—and it is the true 'emerald' humour, as incomparable after its kind as the genuine potato spirit battled with by the Apostle of Temperance. Widow Kelly is Irish to the backbone in her triumphant scolding and unselfish generosity. There is a touch of the unfeigned Hibernian *jont*leman in Lord Ballindine; and Dot Blake shows us that even so cosmopolite a science as gambling takes a local colour from the Curragh. . . . Then, though they are less national, Lord and Lady Cashel are a pair whom Miss Austen need not have disowned.

248. Unsigned notice, *Douglas Jerrold's Weekly Newspaper*

22 July 1848, p. 941

All readers who dislike to be wrought up to a pitch of strong sensation, and at the same time wish to be positively amused by a novel, will find the present work very much to their taste. It is an account of some remarkable passages in the history of two Connaught families; one plebeian, the other patrician. The great events upon which the tale is founded are the wooing and wedding of the two heroes, Frank O'Kelly, Lord Ballindine, and Martin Kelly, a young farmer, his tenant and far-off cousin. The book has one great virtue in our eyes. It is free from that outrageous exaggeration which is so common in sketches of Irish life and character. That the author knows well the subject on which he writes, is evident enough, even to those who have never been in Dublin or in Connaught; and that he has the power of putting his readers in possession of his own knowledge and experience will be quite as clear to all those who go through these three volumes. We may also say in their favour, that the style is even throughout; always clear, light, clever, and easy to read.

On the *per contra* side we may set down these items. There is no one character in the book who awakens an interest in the reader's mind except the poor half-despised old maid, 'Anty Lynch.' [No other *per contra* item is given; but nearly two columns of quotation and summary are supplied.]

249. Unsigned notice, *New Monthly Magazine*

August 1848, n.s. lxxxiii. 544

[A] well-told and an intensely Irish story. Truth to say, however, we cannot sympathize at the present moment with the whimsicalities of that strange, wild, imaginative people, herein so characteristically described, when these whims are exhausting themselves in disloyalty and rebellion, and threatening rapine and bloodshed. Mr. Trollope certainly does not spare the Irishmen of any rank or creed. . . . The humour of the Emerald Isle has too often that which is sensual and repugnant even in its very joyousness, and among a class with whom poverty, pathos, and passion, are ever alternating with fun, frolic, and folly,—what that is temperate, chaste, and ennobling, can be expected?

250. Unsigned notice, *Sharpe's London Magazine*

August 1848, vii. 118–21

The total review runs through more than four columns and nearly three thousand words, much of it quotation and synopsis.

It is, as far as we can see, a book written merely to amuse the reader; it is entertaining, and not instructive;—indeed, we will not pretend to say that we have discovered any moral in the book at all. . . . Moreover, there is a sad want of interesting characters. The reader has no admiration for, or sympathy with, any person in the book. They are all just as common-place as if you had sent for them *all haphazard* out of the street, and you do not much care if you never see them again. There is nothing elevated, nothing touching or tender throughout, except the character and conduct of a plain old maid, who is married by one of the heroes (?) for her money. Anty Lynch, *i.e.* Anastasia Lynch, whether intentionally or unintentionally it is not easy to say, is by far the most interesting person, although she is said to be half a simpleton. . . .

There is much amusing talk in these three volumes about the turf and the field. The jovial hilarity of a hunting-morning at Kelly's Court is well described. The hunt itself is well done: perhaps not as fully and scientifically as Tom Scott or Nimrod would have done it, but very well for a book not professedly sporting. . . .

In conclusion, let us inform our readers that 'The Kellys and the O'Kellys' is *remarkably easy to read*. The style is lively, clever, and uniformly amusing. It might be more polished, it might be more eloquent; but there is no wisdom in the criticism which finds fault with a plum because it is not a pine-apple.

251. Unsigned notice, *The Times*

7 September 1848, p. 6

This is the only review, Trollope tells us in *An Autobiography* (p. 65), that he ever read of any of his first three novels. A friend had induced a fellow club member, 'a man high in authority among the gods of *The Times*', to promise to write a notice. Trollope thought he had 'learned it by heart' and could provide 'if not the words, the exact purport', though nearly thirty years had passed since it was published. His version follows:

Of *The Kellys and the O'Kellys* we may say what the master said to his footman, when the man complained of the constant supply of legs of mutton on the kitchen table. 'Well, John, legs of mutton are good substantial food'; and we may say also what John replied: 'Substantial, sir;— yes, they are substantial, but a little coarse.' That was the review, and even that did not sell the book!

The actual review gave somewhat more credit to the novel.

In one of the recent numbers of *Punch* there is a woodcut representing a gentleman discussing a culinary question with his footmen. He contends that the leg of mutton he has provided for their dinner is substantial fare. This point is conceded by the spokesman of the flunkies, who, however, maintains his objection to the viand by declaring that it is '*corse*—very *corse*.' Mr. A. Trollope's novel of the '*Kelleys and the O'Kelleys*' may be likened to the leg of mutton according to the two estimates of the master and his servants. There is a native humour and a bold reality in the delineation of the characters, which honourably distinguish it from a host of abstract insipidities, and therefore it may be pronounced 'substantial,' while there is that [*sic*] predilection for the ruder manifestations of Irish life, taken rough as they come, that no great injustice will be done to the fare if we call it 'very *corse*.'

LA VENDÉE

1850

Contrary to the adage, Trollope's third trial seems to have brought even less response from the critics than either of his first two. Trollope received no information regarding sales (the *Kellys* had sold a total of 140 copies) and made no inquiry (*Autobiography*, pp. 65, 67).

252. Unsigned notice, *Examiner*

15 June 1850, pp. 373–4

La Vendée is rather a hackneyed subject for the romancist, and Mr. Trollope has hardly been successful in opening any new vein of interest in it, or in revivifying his version of this thrice-told tale with any special passion or imagination. His book has the fiction of a romance, but with a little too much of the phlegm of history. . . . Nevertheless, the book is not without merit. Apart from an ultra-royalist bias (real or affected), Mr. Trollope has good sense, candour, and some power of analysing character. His sketches of Robespierre and Santerre have truth and force. His defect is the want of energy and imagination to lend sufficient interest to a long story.

253. Unsigned notice, *Athenaeum*

6 July 1850, p. 708

A long quotation from the end of Chapter IV occupies well over a column.

This might almost be called 'a romantic history,' instead of a historical romance; so well known are the leaders in the war of La Vendée in England. The realities of the peasant life, of the simple loyalty and superstitious devotion which yielded to the Royalist cause such leaders as Cathelineau admit of little added colouring. They have been, more-over, shown to us in all their warmth and worth by Madame de Larochejacquelin and other eye-witnesses who have described the struggle. Mr. Trollope, however, has used the romancer's fair privilege fairly, in creating for heroine a Mademoiselle de Larochejaquelin, and in giving her as unsuccessful lover a worse sort of *Waverley*—Adolphe Denot, the renegade and repentant. That the author well understands the jealousies which, from the very first moment of popular success spring ready-armed into life among the successful,—and that he has a fair command of dialogue and feeling for humour,—one of the lighter scenes in his romance will prove. . . .

The above passage has been purposely preferred to one of the graver scenes of escape, onslaught, or massacre, which Mr. A. Trollope has also touched with spirit. Let it be treated ever so lightly, ever so philosophically, the Vendéan war is virtually a sad chronicle of noble blood poured like water, and of brave lives laid down with a but poor result of victory. We have dwelt on one of its lighter episodes from a natural wish to escape the painfulness of the main record.

Bibliography

Many additional books and shorter pieces are cited in the course of the Introduction and the headnotes and notes of this edition. The following list is confined to items of unusual value for background, for detailed information, or for especially significant criticism.

BAKER, JOSEPH, 'Trollope's Third Dimension', *College English* (1954), xvi. 222–32.

BEVINGTON, MERLE MOWBRAY, *The Saturday Review 1855–1868* (1941).

BOOTH, BRADFORD ALLEN, *Anthony Trollope: Aspects of His Life and Art* (1958). Judicious, full of helpful information.

BOWEN, ELIZABETH, Introduction to Trollope's *Doctor Thorne*, pp. v–xxv (1959).

COCKSHUT, A. O. J., *Anthony Trollope: A Critical Study* (1955).

HELLING, RAFAEL, *A Century of Trollope Criticism*, Helsingfors (1956). Not as extensive in its research as the dissertation of Iva Gwendolyn Jones (listed below), but an informed and judicious doctoral dissertation.

The History of The Times [Anonymous] (1939).

IRWIN, MARY LESLIE, *Anthony Trollope: A Bibliography* (1926). Though I have added many items to Miss Irwin's lists through 1883, they have proved very helpful (though sometimes overfull and indiscriminate). Still a reference tool of much value.

JONES, IVA GWENDOLYN, *A Study of the Literary Reputation of Anthony Trollope, 1847–1953*. Unpublished doctoral dissertation, Ohio State University (1953). An admirably ambitious study based almost exclusively for its materials through 1883 on the listings of Mary Leslie Irwin (see above). The manuscript runs to 434 pages.

JUMP, J. D., 'Weekly Reviewing in the Eighteen-Fifties', *Review of English Studies* (1948), xxiv. 42–57.

—— 'Weekly Reviewing in the Eighteen-Sixties', *Review of English Studies* (1952), n.s. iii. 244–62.

MIZENER, ARTHUR, 'Anthony Trollope: the Palliser Novels', *From Jane Austen to Joseph Conrad*, ed. Robert C. Rathburn and Martin Steinmann, Jr. (1958), pp. 160–76.

SADLEIR, MICHAEL, *Trollope: A Bibliography* (1928). A splendid book, a model for other author bibliographies, listing all first editions, dates of serial and part publication, etc.

—— *Trollope: A Commentary* (1928) (1947). Still the best of all studies of Trollope's life and writings.

SMALLEY, DONALD, 'Anthony Trollope', *Victorian Fiction: A Guide to Research*, ed. Lionel Stevenson (1964), pp. 188–213. A summary and evaluation of scholarship and criticism to 1962.

STEBBINS, LUCY POATE, and RICHARD POATE STEBBINS, *The Trollopes: The Chronicle of a Writing Family* (1945).

TENER, ROBERT H., 'The *Spectator* Records, 1874–1897', *The Victorian Newsletter* (Spring 1960), No. 17, 33–36. Valuable for identifying Richard Holt Hutton and Meredith White Townsend as authors of a few of the *Spectator*'s key reviews of Trollope, 1874–83.

THOMAS, WILLIAM BEACH, *The Story of the Spectator 1828–1928* (1928).

TINGAY, LANCE O., 'The Reception of Trollope's First Novel', *Nineteenth-Century Fiction* (1951), vi. 195–200. A helpful presentation of out-of-the-way reviews of *The Macdermots of Ballycloran*.

TROLLOPE, ANTHONY, *An Autobiography*, ed. Bradford Allen Booth (1947). This edition is cited by page throughout this book.

—— *The Letters of Anthony Trollope*, ed. Bradford Allen Booth (1951).

The Wellesley Index to Victorian Periodicals, 1824–1900, ed. Walter E. Houghton, Vol. I (1966). (Only Volume I has as yet been published.) A very useful reference work which identifies the anonymous authors in eight prominent Victorian periodicals, chiefly quarterlies, but including the *Cornhill Magazine*.

Select Index

II

Characters in Trollope's novels that
receive frequent or especially
interesting discussion:

III

Characteristics of Anthony Trollope
and aspects of his career receiving
frequent or especially significant
comment in the documents; also
relevant pages of the Introduction:

IV

Periodicals quoted or referred to:

73–4, 90–1, 115–16, 146–51,
197–201, 221–6, 245–8, 259–61,
268–9, 271–2, 275–6, 291–6,
309–13, 324–8, 341–4, 347–50,
357–8, 372–3, 378–81, 392,
397–400, 418, 419–23, 436–7, 444,
445–8, 452–3, 461, 470–1, 485,
488, 496, 500, 504–8, 509–11, 513,
518, 547

The Times, xviii, 2, 3, 4, 5; 15, 21,
25–6, 28, 29, 31, 32, 34–5, 45, 46,
50–2, 73, 101, 103–9, 120, 136,
160–3, 190–1, 215, 238, 329–32,
338, 339, 351, 374, 389, 407–9,
424–5, 431–2, 443, 455, 466, 478,
486, 490, 502, 523–4, 557
Trollopian, 13

Victorian Newsletter, 28

Westminster Review, 53–4, 133–4,
138–9, 192, 212, 231–2, 322, 390,
415–16, 474, 481, 517, 519

V

Authors, critics, scholars, artists, etc.,
quoted or referred to:

About, Edmond, 170
Apperley, Charles James ('Nimrod'),
556
Arnold, Matthew, 237
Austen, Jane, 14, 22, 28, 205, 377,
502, 503, 506, 509–11, 553

Bagehot, Walter, 4, 80
Baker, Ernest, 12
Baker, Joseph, 14, 27, 28, 560
Balzac, Honoré de, 183, 502, 503,
529, 536, 543, 544
Béranger, Jean-Pierre de, 175
Bevington, Merle, 29, 121, 560

Booth, Bradford Allen, 13, 28, 29,
80, 215, 467, 512, 560, 561
Booth, Wayne C., 536 note
Bowen, Elizabeth, 13, 27, 560
Braddon, Mary Elizabeth, 284, 329
Bright, John, 316–17
Brontë, Charlotte, 1, 146, 153, 171,
174, 502
Brown, Beatrice Curtis, 13
Brown, Charles Reynolds, 10
Browning, Elizabeth Barrett, 64, 140
Browning, Robert, 10, 20, 140, 548
Butler, Samuel, 488
Bryce, James, 25

Carlyle, Thomas, 32, 535
Cecil, David, 12
Chorley, H. F., 34, 45
Cockshut, A. O. J., 13, 475, 512, 560
Collins, Wilkie, 362, 371
Collins, W. L., 492
Crawley, T. W., 435
Cresswell, Sir Cresswell, 166, 167

Dallas, E. S., 15–16, 25, 26, 29,
103–9, 160–3
Daudet, Alphonse, 540
Dawkins, C. E., 520
Defoe, Daniel, 190
Dickens, Charles, 1, 5, 8, 16, 25, 29,
32, 104, 107, 124, 127, 132, 153,
156, 178, 183, 220, 233, 309, 351,
363, 364, 377, 431, 473, 477, 502,
525, 528, 535, 538
Disraeli, Benjamin, 314, 315, 380
Dumas, Alexandre, 167, 439, 503,
530

Edgeworth, Maria, 549
Edwards, Amelia, 25
Eliot, George, 1, 8–9, 13, 27, 110,
127, 134, 137, 171, 178, 190, 341,
361–2, 365, 387, 411, 502, 525,
528, 529

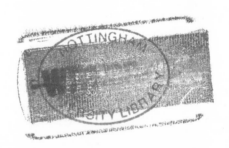